Luca Tonghini

Ligurian Sea
Northern Tyrrhenian Sea
Corsica
North Sardinia

ITALY & CORSICA 2

PILOT BOOK 2 NORTHERN ITALY & CORSICA

This username is associated with the book you purchased
and allows you to view it online.
Your username must be used during registration and
cannot be changed.

Scan this QRcode and follow the instructions.

il Frangente EDIZIONI

USERNAME: FR552432313875

Alternatively, type this URL address into your browser:
https://www.frangente-multimedia.com/d2ty8hj/

LUCA TONGHINI was born in Brescia, north Italy, in 1961. As a young boy, he went boating with his father, but he only became interested in sailing as an adult when he took a course on Lake Iseo. He was hooked; it was as though he had fulfilled a dream he never knew he had. His early sailing experiences were on Lake Garda on *Cristina*, a 21-ft sailing yacht, "alone or with friends, day and night, in good weather and bad. Getting out there was all that mattered!"

In 2000, Luca and three friends bought *Maladroxia*, a 34-ft cutter. A few years later, he left his job as a building designer so that he could devote more time to sailing. His travels took him around much of the Mediterranean. Luca and his partner Paola later decided to move to Lake Garda so that they could sail all year round, and in 2013 he became the sole owner of *Maladroxia*. After years of sailing the Tyrrhenian Sea, Luca has recently embarked on an extensive cruise around the Mediterranean in a bid to explore its myriad bays and anchorages, as well as to conduct surveys of all its ports. His love for cartography, offshore yachting and technical drawing has led him to combine his skills to write pilot guides.

By this author: *CHART-GUIDE ITALY 3 Central and Southern Tyrrhenian Sea, Sardinia,* published by Edizioni il Frangente.

CAUTION

This guide has been compiled with the utmost care. Please note, however, that neither the author nor the publisher are responsible for any errors or omissions, as it is designed for use as a navigation aid. In no way does it replace the official publications and charts that are part of mandatory onboard equipment.

All of the chart symbols are designed solely for use with this guide. They do not replace the official symbols used for nautical charts published in 5011 INT 1 by the UK Hydrographic Office.

UPDATES

This guide will be revised with updates that can be downloaded free-of-charge from the publisher's website: www.frangente.com.

Feel free to send us new information, amendments or corrections so that we can update the content of this pilot guide (aggiornamenti@frangente.com). We would be extremely grateful.

MEDITERRANEAN SEA CHART-GUIDE
ITALY & CORSICA 2
Ligurian Sea, Northern Tyrrhenian Sea, Corsica, North Sardinia

© 2019 Edizioni il Frangente S.a.s.
Via Gaetano Trezza 12 - 37129 Verona - Italy
Tel. +39 045-8012631 Fax +39 045-593881
frangente@frangente.com
www.frangente.com
www.frangente.it

ISBN 978-88-85719-70-5

© 2019 Texts and charts designed by Luca Tonghini

First English edition 2019

Translation in English by Andrew Bailey

Original title:
Portolano cartografico 2 Mar Ligure, Tirreno settentrionale, Corsica, Nord Sardegna
© 2019 Edizioni il Frangente S.a.s.

All rights reserved. No part of this publication may be reproduced, transmitted or used in any form by any means - graphic, electronic or mechanical, including photocopying, recording, taping or information storage and retrieval systems or otherwise - without the prior permission of the publisher.

Printed by ESPERIA Srl - Lavis (TN) - Italy

CONTENTS

MAIN ROUTES AND DISTANCES	4
PELAGOS SANCTUARY	5
NAUTICAL CHARTS	6
DIGITAL CHARTS	9
WEATHER	10
Weather on the internet	15
Weather Apps	15

AREA A	LIGURIA RIVIERA DI PONENTE (WEST COAST) CHARTS 1-15	16
AREA B	LIGURIA RIVIERA DI LEVANTE (EAST COAST) CHARTS 16-32	35
AREA C	FROM LERICI TO PROMONTORIO DELL' ARGENTARIO CHARTS 33-56	56
AREA D	ARCIPELAGO TOSCANO (TUSCAN ISLANDS) CHARTS 57-82	85
AREA E	NORTH SARDINIA AND LA MADDALENA ARCHIPELAGO CHARTS 83-104	116
AREA F	CORSICA CHARTS 105-162	145
INDEX		211

MAIN ROUTES AND DISTANCES

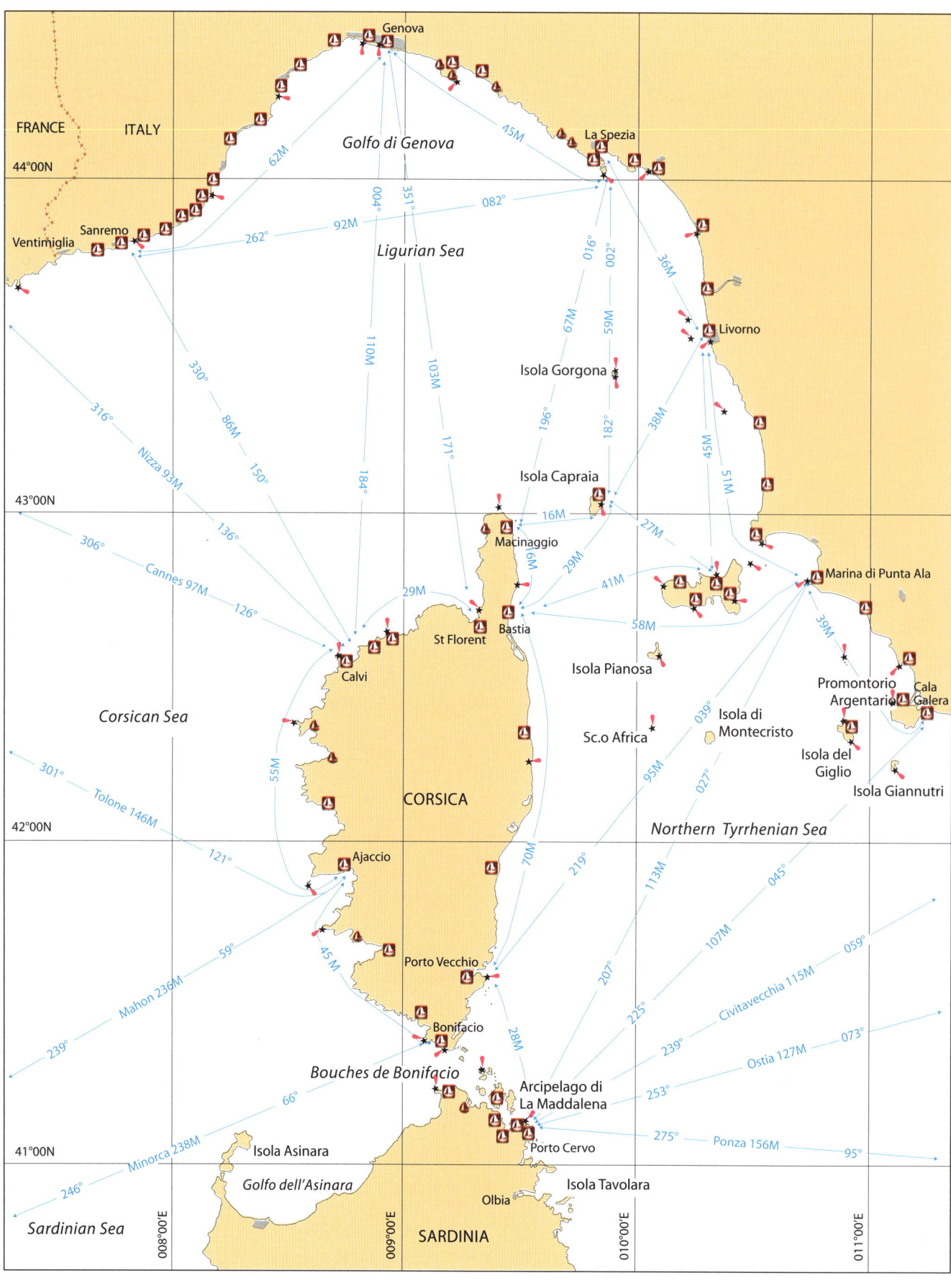

PELAGOS SANCTUARY

Pelagos Sanctuary for Mediterranean Marine Mammals

Sailing across this stretch of sea will most likely provide glimpses of dolphins and whales, especially when crossing from the mainland to the islands. This part of the Mediterranean teems with marine life and has the largest population of whales, dolphins and porpoises in the entire basin.

Since summer 1988, the Tethys Institute has been conducting research into Italy's wild cetaceans, mainly in the Corsica - Liguria - Provençal basin. Researchers have discovered that there are far more sightings in this region than in any of Italy's other seas. In 1992, Tethys commissioned Greenpeace and the University of Barcelona to conduct a census to estimate the number of stenella (32,800) and giant minke whales (830) in the region over the summer period.

This marine reserve, named "The Mammal Sanctuary", was set up by Italy's Environment ministry in 1991. The International Marine Protected Area, which covers 87,500km^2, stretches from Punta Escampobariou to Capo Falcone and from Capo Ferro in Sardinia up to Fosso Chiarone, which lies on border between Tuscany and Lazio. It was established in 1999 after an agreement between Italy, France and the Principality of Monaco.

A recent Greenpeace report, however, has revealed that unfortunately the cetacean population has slumped and that current protection measures are inadequate. Greenpeace data gathered in 2008 show that the number of whales has fallen to barely a quarter of the 1990s population and Stenella numbers have more than halved.

NAUTICAL CHARTS

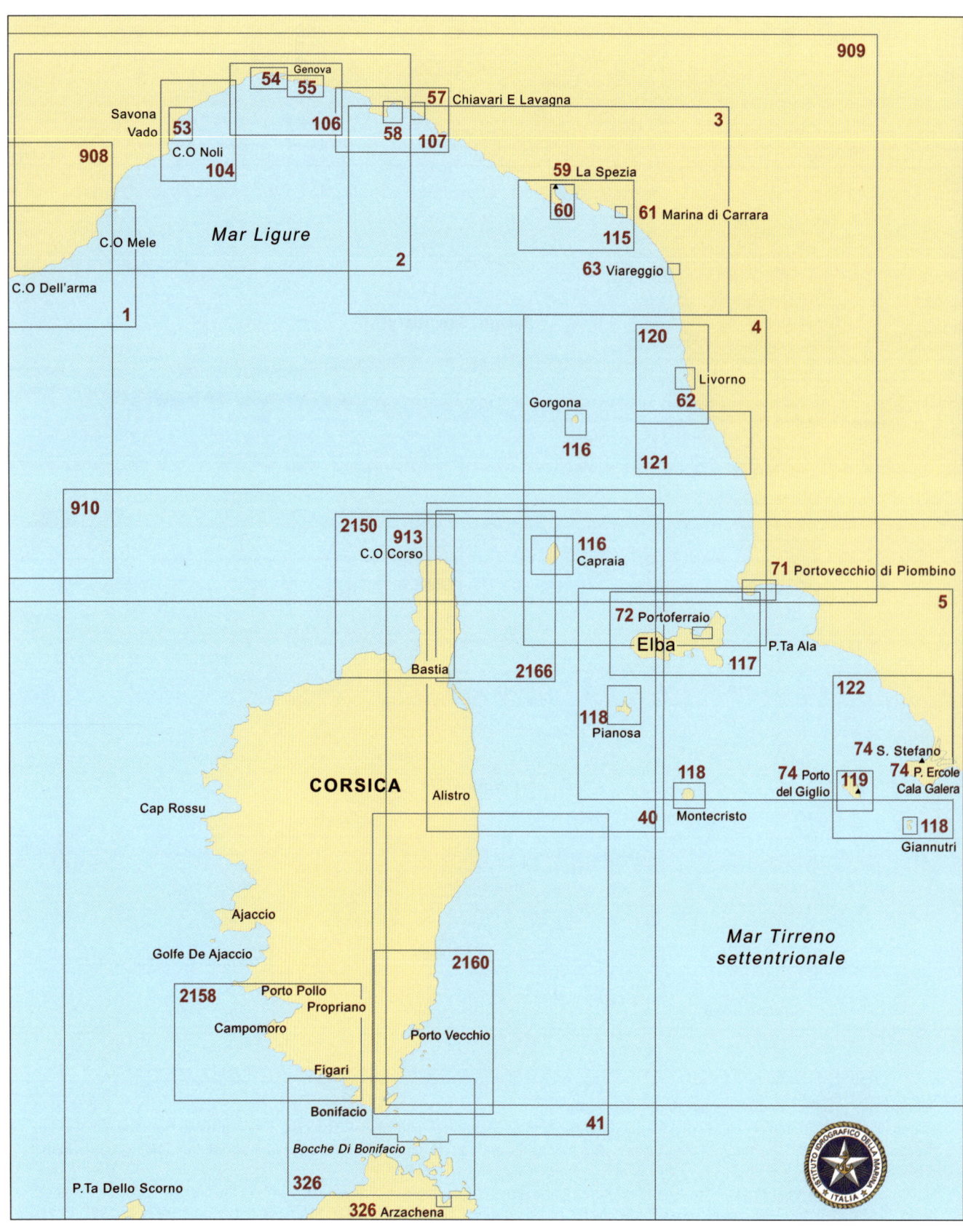

MAR LIGURE, MAR TIRRENO SETTENTRIONALE, CORSICA - Istituto Idrografico della Marina

CHART	DESCRIPTION	SCALE 1:
IIM 1	Da Cannes a Imperia	100.000
IIM 2	Da Imperia a Portofino	100.000
IIM 3	Da Portofino a San Rossore	100.000
IIM 4	Da S. Rossore al Canale di Piombino ed Isola d'Elba, Capraia e Gorgona	100.000

NAUTICAL CHARTS

CHART	DESCRIPTION	SCALE 1:
IIM 5	Dal Canale di Piombino al promontorio Argentario e Scoglio d'Africa	100.000
IIM 40	Da Cap Corse ad Alistro e all'Isola d'Elba	100.000
IIM 41	Da Alistro alle Bocche di Bonifacio	100.000
IIM 51	Porto di Sanremo	5.000
IIM 52	Porto di Imperia	5.000
IIM 53	Porto di Savona - Vado	10.000
IIM 54	Porto di Genova - Foglio Ovest	10.000
IIM 55	Porto di Genova - Foglio Est	10.000
IIM 57	Porto di Chiavari e Lavagna	5.000
IIM 58	Golfo Marconi (Golfo Tigullio)	10.000
IIM 59	Porto della Spezia	5.000
IIM 60	Rada della Spezia	10.000
IIM 61	Porto di Marina di Carrara	5.000
IIM 62	Porto di Livorno	10.000
IIM 63	Porto di Viareggio	5.000
IIM 71	Rada e porto di Piombino	10.000
IIM 72	Rada di Portoferraio	7.500
IIM 74	Porti dell'Argentario e dell'Isola del Giglio	5.000
IIM 101	Litorale di Imperia	30.000
IIM 104	Litorale di Savona	30.000
IIM 106	Litorale di Genova	30.000
IIM 107	Litorale da Nervi a Sestri Levante	30.000
IIM 115	Litorale della Spezia	30.000
IIM 116	Isole di Capraia e Gorgona	25.000
IIM 117	Isola d'Elba	40.000
IIM 118	Isole di Giannutri, Montecristo e Pianosa	25.000
IIM 119	Isola del Giglio	20.000
IIM 120	Litorale di Livorno	30.000
IIM 121	Litorale da Quercianella a Marina di Cecina e Secche di Vada	30.000
IIM 122	Dalla Foce dell'Ombrone al Promontorio Argentario	50.000
IIM 326	Bocche di Bonifacio - Golfo di Arzachena	50.000
IIM 908	Da Fos-Sur-Mer a Capo Mele	250.000
IIM 909	Da Nizza a Piombino	250.000
IIM 910	Isola di Corsica	250.000
IIM 913	Da Piombino a Fiumicino e costa orientale della Corsica	250.000
IIM 2150	Da Capo Corse a Punta di l'Acciolu - Golfo di Saint-Florent	50.300
IIM 2158	Da Capo Muro a Cap de Feno	50.000
IIM 2160	Litorale di Porto Vecchio, dall'Anse de Favone alle Iles Lavezzi	50.000
IIM 2166	Litorale a Nord di Bastia	50.300

LEISURE CHARTS colour paper charts (sheet size 50 x 35 cm) - Istituto Idrografico della Marina

KIT P1
Liguria - Da Capo Mortola a Cinquale
20 charts
scale 1: 100.000 / 30.000

KIT P2-A
Tirreno Settentrionale
Da Marina di Massa a Isola di Pianosa
25 charts
scale 1: 100.000 / 30.000

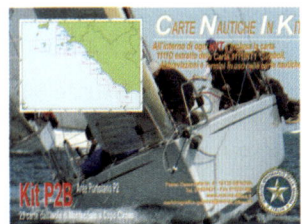

KIT P2-B
Toscana e Lazio - Da Isola Montecristo a Capo Circeo
23 charts
scale 1: 100.000 / 30.000

KIT P3-A
Sardegna Nord-Nordest
Da S. Pietro a Mare a Punta Sa Canna
18 charts
scale 1: 100.000 / 30.000

NAUTICAL CHARTS

PRINT & DIGITAL Atlas (size 35 x 45 cm), paper charts and digital download and App

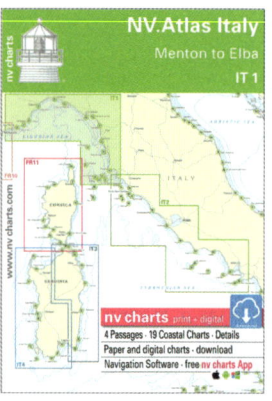

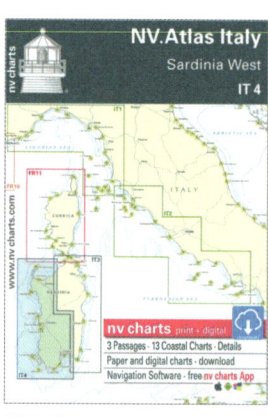

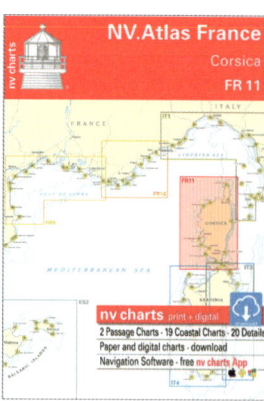

NV IT 1 - Atlas Italy
Menton to Elba
4 passage charts
19 coastal charts
37 details

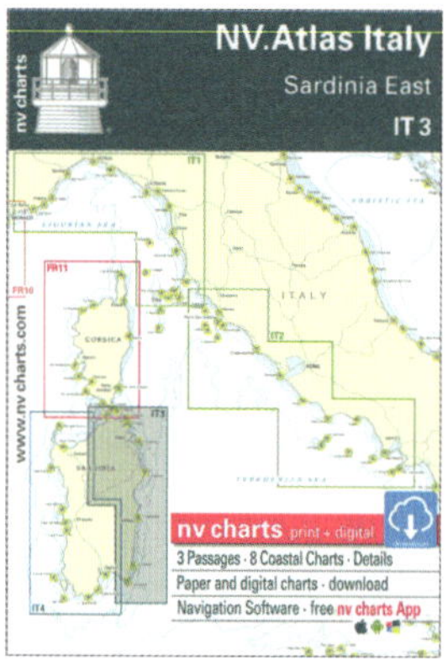

NV IT 3 - Atlas Italy
Sardinia East
4 passage charts
9 coastal charts
24 details

NV IT 4 - Atlas Italy
Sardinia West
5 passage charts
12 coastal charts
19 details

NV FR11 - Atlas France
Corsica
2 passage charts
19 coastal charts
21 details

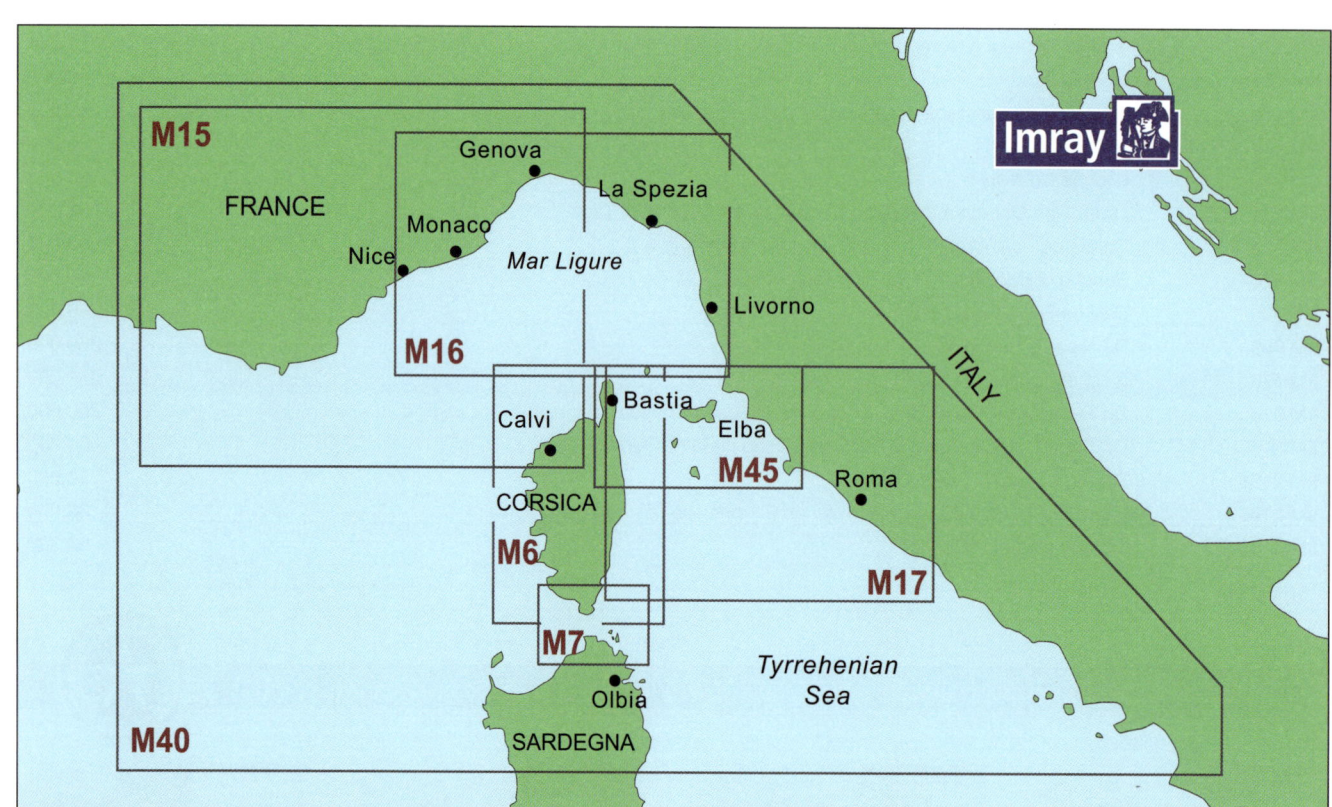

Imray charts: colour, waterproof leisure charts. Sheet size 64 x 90 cm. Folded in a plastic wallet.

CHART	DESCRIPTION	SCALE 1:
M6	Île de Corse	255.000
M7	Bonifacio Strait	65.000
M15	Marseille to San Remo	325.000
M16	Ligurian Sea	325.000
M17	North Tuscan Islands to Rome	325.000
M40	Ligurian and Tyrrhenian Seas	950.000
M45	Tuscan Archipelago	180.000

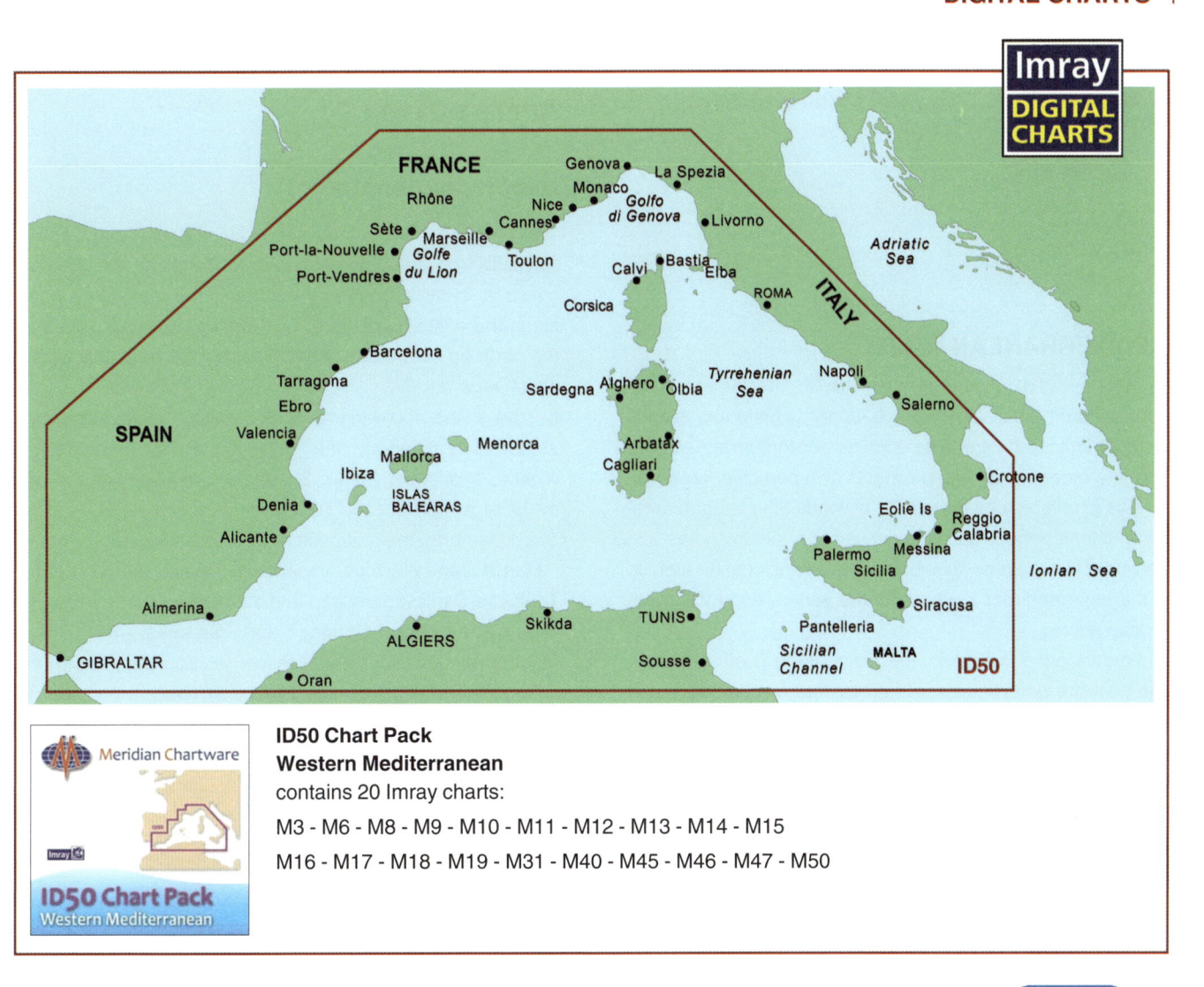

DIGITAL CHARTS

Imray DIGITAL CHARTS

ID50 Chart Pack
Western Mediterranean
contains 20 Imray charts:
M3 - M6 - M8 - M9 - M10 - M11 - M12 - M13 - M14 - M15
M16 - M17 - M18 - M19 - M31 - M40 - M45 - M46 - M47 - M50

NAVIONICS+

NAVIONICS+ LARGE	NAVIONICS+ SMALL	PLATINUM+ LARGE
☐ **43XG** Mediterranean & Black Sea	☐ **5G533S2** San Vincenzo - Salerno	☐ **32P+** Mediterranean West
☐ **46XG** Central & West Europe	☐ **5G534S2** Liguria - P. Ercole	**PLATINUM+ SMALL**
	☐ **5G535S2** Rapallo - Cavalaire	☐ **5P273XL** Thyrrenian Sea
	☐ **5G536S2** Corsica - Nord Sardegna	☐ **5P274XL** Mediterranean North West
	☐ **5G537S2** Sardegna	

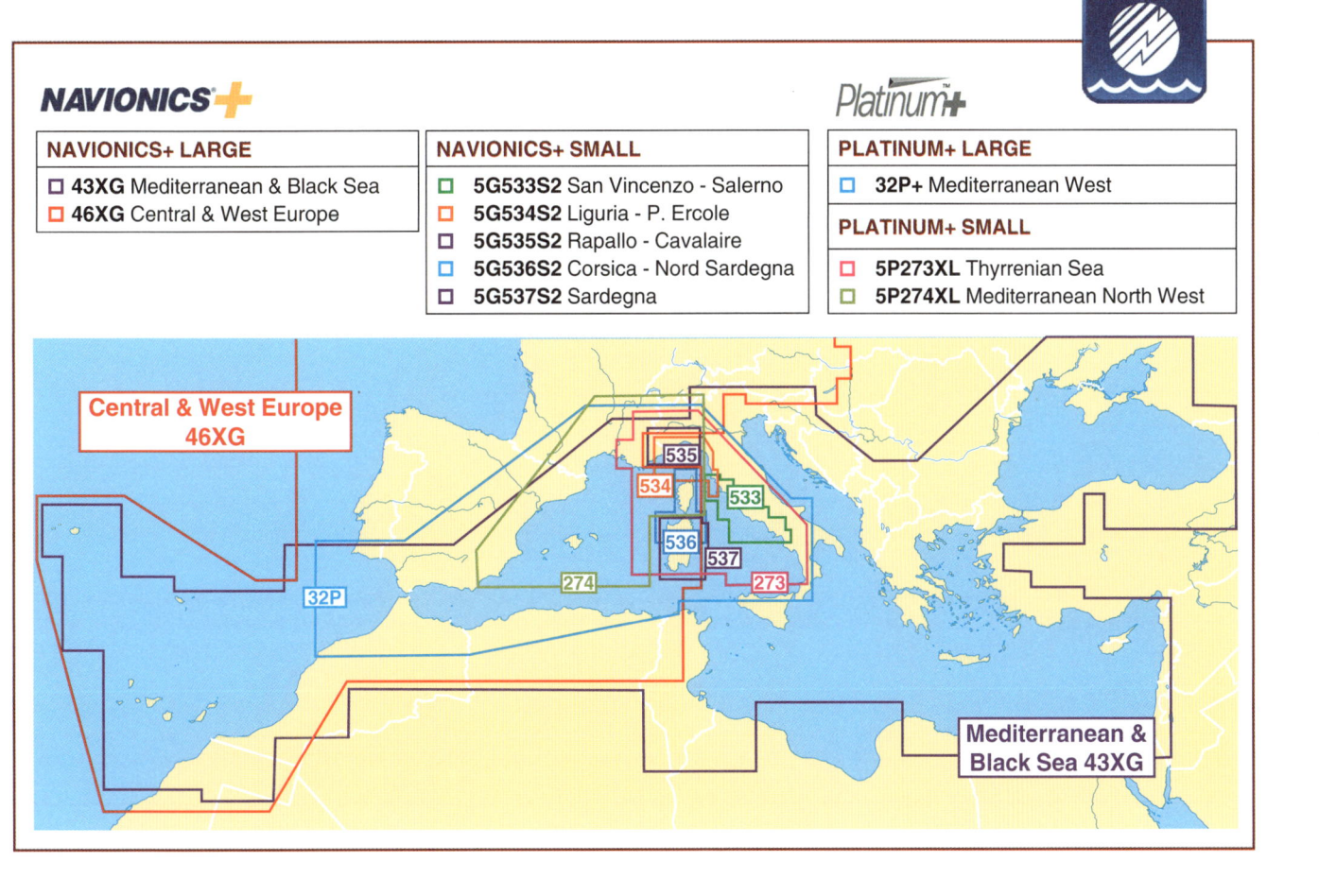

WEATHER

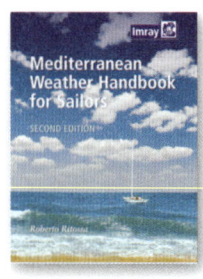

The text below is an excerpt from Imray's *Mediterranean Weather Handbook for Sailors*.

MEDITERRANEAN WINDS

As we have seen, weather-wise the Mediterranean is far from uniform: mountains, valleys, deserts, plateaux, islands etc contribute to differentiate each small Mediterranean area from the others, each one having its own particular features.

This is reflected by the variety of winds affecting the area. Many of these winds have a local name, and sometimes one particular wind can be known under different local names, as is the case of sirocco, whose name varies along the north African shore.

To add to the confusion, the same name is often used in two or more different areas, and related to different types of winds: for example, tramontane is the name given to a mistral-like northwesterly wind along the SW coast of France, but also to a NE katabatic wind along the western coast of Italy. Regardless of all local name variations, the most relevant winds are described in a hopefully organised way in order to make them clearly identifiable. However they may be locally labelled.

Figure 3.A.1. Depicts some of the most common names given to local winds.

WEST CENTRAL MEDITERRANEAN
GOLFE DU LION

Geographic features

This area is limited to the west by a line going from Cape St Sebastian on the Spanish coast, to Bejaia on the Algerian coast; its eastern boundary is roughly the meridian running along the eastern coasts of Corsica and Sardinia; and from the north tip of Corsica to the French / Italian border on the coast. *Figure 4.C.1.*

It covers the following GMDSS meteorological standard areas: Lion, Minorca, the eastern parts of Cabrera and Algeria, Provence, Corse, Bonifacio, Sardinia, Annaba and the western part of zone Tunisia.

To the north, the mountain range of the complex Pyrenees – Massif Central – Alps presents two major openings at the Toulouse/Carcassonne gap and at the river Rhone Valley.

To the east, Corsica and Sardinia, two major Mediterranean islands, represent a boundary from the different weather area of the Tyrrhenian Sea.

To the south, the Atlas mountains run almost uninterruptedly along the African coast. The western limit is represented by the weather boundary of mistral wind.

Seasonal weather overview

Winter

The Açores high having drifted south, the area is under the repeated influence of outbreaks of cold northerly air, and the passage/development of low pressure systems. These are responsible for extended periods of bad weather with winds from gale to violent storm force.

Mistral accounts for the majority of such events, and may

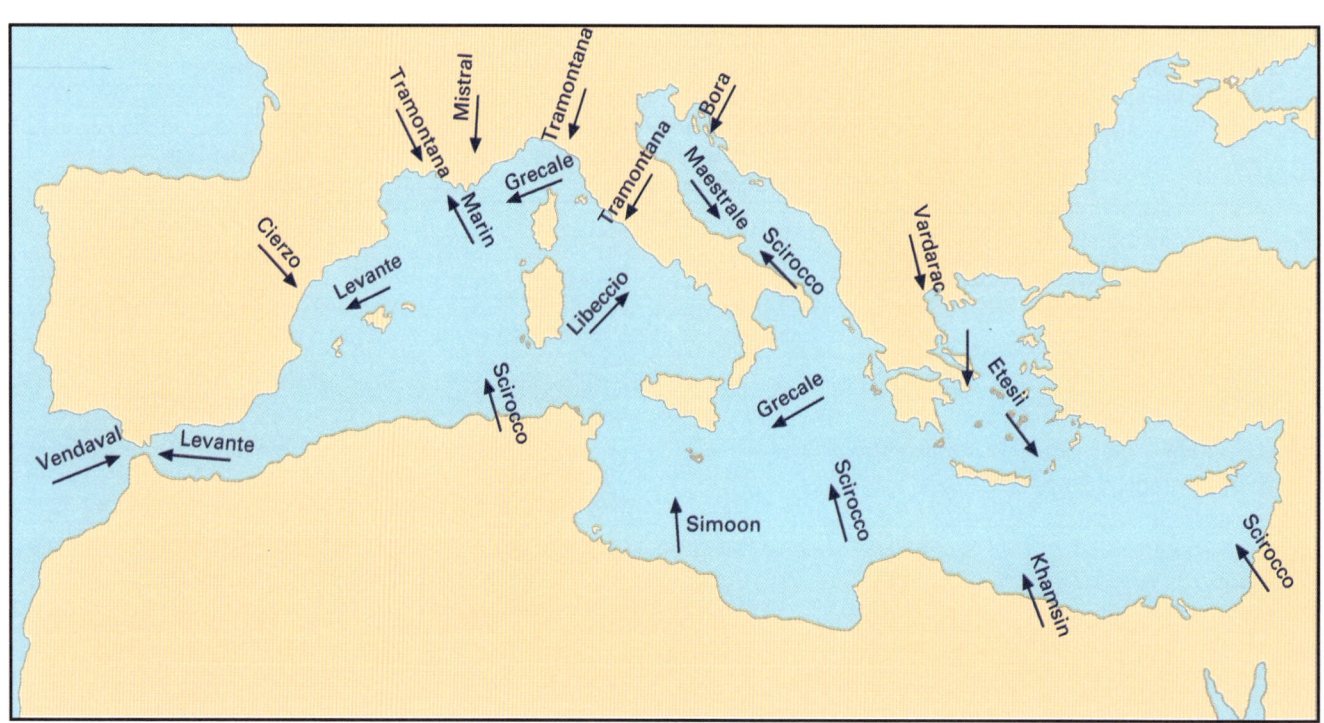

Figure 3.A.1 – Mediterranean winds.

WEATHER

Figure 4.C.1 - West central Mediterranean – Golfe du Lion sea area

occur as much as 20% of the time, especially in the northern half of the area.

Along the eastern portion of the south coast of France, long periods of calms are interrupted by easterly and southwesterly gale episodes (gregale and libeccio), or mistral tails which here tend to be oriented W–WSW.

The northern coast of Africa has a lower frequency of gales, roughly one third that of the north. Prevailing winds usually blow W to NW and can raise heavy seas along the coast, and although mistral does not reach the north Africa coast too often, its swell often does. Southwesterly gales occur along the western part of the coast when a secondary low pressure area develops south of the
Iberian peninsula. Thunderstorms are not rare along the eastern part of the north African coast.

Other bad weather occurrences are caused by low pressure systems and associated frontal features (Atlantic lows, Balearic lows, Genoa lows, etc).

Summer

An Açores high ridge usually extends northeast towards central Europe, and pushes the average path of depressions further north. The weather is usually nice and warm, sea-land breeze winds are the norm. Although rarer than during winter, mistral often makes its appearance, especially over the Golfe du Lion area.

Spring and autumn

These seasons generally show a succession of periods of winter and summer-type weather, until one of the two prevails. During spring, this transition lasts slightly longer, usually taking two or three months before mistral events get rarer and summer weather settles in. Autumn on the other hand is usually limited to the month of October, with summer weather lasting until the end of September, and well established winter-type phenomena from November onward.

Weather features and winds

Low pressure systems

Genoa lows

The main influence of Genoa depressions is related to mistral: when the Genoa low is well developed, mistral conditions tend to be stronger and affect a wider area. See the Mistral section for more details. At times, two or three of these different types of lows coexist in their early development stage. A wide area of low pressure but with very weak gradients may extend over the whole western Mediterranean, sometimes accompanied by frontal areas with weather features like isolated showers and thunderstorms.

In this case, some help about the likely evolution may be found in upper level charts. Whenever a 500 hPa trough approaches a weak surface low, this is more likely to develop into a more organized depression, which usually follows one of the typical evolutions described in the relevant sections.

Mistral

Mistral is by far the greatest concern for sailors in this area at any time of the year. Over the NE of the area, between the south coast of France and Corsica, mistral roughly blows to gale force one tenth of the time during the period from late autumn to early spring, while it is less likely during summer. Often, mistral over Corsica is of the black type, even if nearer the continent it is white. Sometimes along the SE coast of France/NW coast of Italy, a small scale cyclonic circulation develops on the lee of the mountains, *Figure 4.C.2*,
and NW to W winds near Toulon/Cap Sicié are often opposed to NE to E winds blowing from the Italian side.

A strong channelling effect occurs on the Bonifacio Strait,

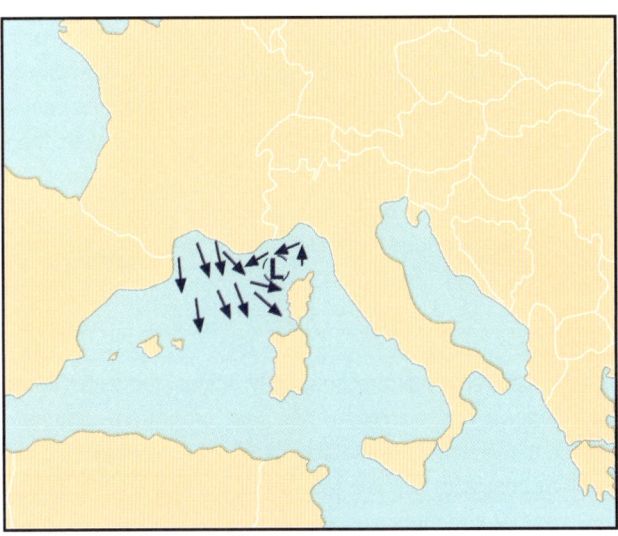

Figure 4.C.2 - Local lee depression leading to easterly winds along SE France/NW Italian coasts.

WEATHER

between Sardinia and Corsica: here mistral may blow with a westerly direction with speeds often in the range of 8/9Bft with gusts, creating high seas. It often extends several miles east of the Strait.

To the south, the coast of Africa is sometimes under the effect of a widespread mistral, especially with a well developed Genoa depression: conditions tend to worsen approaching the eastern third of the area, near the Strait of Sicily: waves of 4–6m and winds in the 8/9Bft range are not uncommon, especially during winter.

Its western boundary is usually well represented by a line from Perpignan to Bejaia in the Algerian coast, whose middle part crosses the Balearic archipelago somewhere between SW Mallorca and NW Minorca. While sailing in this area, shelter can usually be found on the lee of these islands, or by keeping a westward course.

Grecale

Over the central and southern parts of the area, gale force gregale is usually associated with sufficiently developed NWA depressions.

Over the northern part of the area, gregale is more related to Balearic depressions or Atlantic depressions drifting southeastward from the Gulf of Biscay. East of Toulon (where gregale is generally related to deep Genoa lows) it is likely to be E to NE, whereas to the west in the Golfe du Lion it tends to be southeasterly. Around Corsica, the wind is greatly accelerated at the Bonifacio Strait and around the northwestern coast, while relative shelter can be found along the southwestern coast.

On both cases, the rapid building of a high pressure area over northern Italy may contribute to greatly increase wind strength.

Scirocco

Gale episodes occur a few times a month during the transition seasons.

Along the northern coast of Africa, sirocco is mostly moderate though gusty. It is usually dry but desert dust can greatly affect visibility.

Along the southern coast of France sirocco is usually named Marin, and its direction may vary locally from SW to SE (when it usually takes the name of Autan). In some cases, sirocco over the open sea may be associated with local mistral along the coast.

During all sirocco occurrences in the northern half of the area, low level clouds, light rain and sometimes fog will be likely.

Libeccio

Gale force SW winds are frequently associated with Genoa cyclogenesis, especially in the sea area from southern France to Corsica. Libeccio may cause heavy seas along the western coasts of Corsica and Sardinia, and usually brings bad weather and precipitation.

Tramontana

Tramontana can blow to gale to strong gale force around Cap Corse on the northern tip of Corsica.

Winds around Corsica and Sardinia

To the north, NW to SW winds are prevalent all year long, more so during summer. They are usually strongly accelerated around the northern tip of Corsica.

The eastern Corsican and Sardinian coasts are more sheltered from westerlies, which are a concern to navigation at the mouth of the few valleys along the mountain range. Libeccio often blows with gusts, accelerated by foehn effects. Gales from the N to NE are not uncommon during winter.

The Bonifacio Strait with Sardinia strongly accelerates the prevalent easterly or westerly winds.

Along the western coasts breezes are the prevalent summer phenomenon, usually blowing no stronger than 4–5Bft. Gales are generally from WNW to SW, and more frequent during winter. Cirrus clouds often precede mistral onset by 12–24 hours.

The southern third of Sardinia is where sirocco is of some importance, especially during early spring; other gale force episodes are usually caused by gregale winds.

Useful signs of approaching bad weather are the absence of sea breezes around the two islands during summer, oncoming swells from the open sea while winds are still light, and the rise of the sea level inside port areas.

Fog

La Areas where fog is most likely include the Golfe du Lion, the coast around Corsica and Sardinia and the sea stretch between Sardinia and Tunisia. Along the African coast, visibility can be greatly reduced by sand and dust storms, which are usually short lived.

TYRRHENIAN SEA

Geographic features

The Tyrrhenian area is limited to the NE by the coast of the Italian peninsula, to the south by the northern coast of Sicily then to the northeastern tip of Tunisia. From there, northward to Cap Corse, then to the French/Italian border on the coast.

It includes GMDSS meteorological areas Ligure, Elba, Maddalena, Lipari, Carbonara and the eastern Tunisia area. (Denominations in use in the Italian Meteomar weather bulletins are Mar Ligure and Mar Tirreno – northern, central, southern, eastern and western).

The Alps to the north, the Apennines to the east, the three big islands Corsica, Sardinia and Sicily, are amongst many elements having a definite influence over local weather.

Channelling effects over the Bonifacio Strait (between Corsica and Sardinia), the Messina Strait (between Sicily and Italy), the Corsica Strait (between Corsica and Elba) and the Sicily Strait (between Sicily and Tunisia) are worth

WEATHER

Figure 4.D.1 - Tyhrrenian Sea area.

remembering, as with sustained winds these areas usually show a marked deterioration of weather conditions.

Seasonal weather overview

The most important weather producers in the area are Genoa depressions. Although they may form in any season, their intensity is somewhat different during the cold or warm seasons.

Winter

During winter, the Açores high usually drifts south over the Atlantic Ocean, giving free room for westerly flows over the area. Depressions develop in the Genoa Gulf area, and weather over the area is usually unsettled and often windy, with N–NE and SW winds accompanying the lows.

Gales and heavy seas are occasional, and can occur until early spring. They are relatively rarer in the southeastern Tyrrhenian, where southerly winds show a higher frequency than to the north.

NW and SE gales often occur in the channels between Sicily and Sardinia and Tunisia.

Summer

The northward migration of the Açores high ridge pushes the westerly flow to the north of Europe: fine, dry weather with light breeze is usually found throughout the area, sometimes coupled with low visibility.

Calm wind frequency is among the highest in the whole Mediterranean, especially over the southern half of the area.

The formation of Genoa depressions may occasionally deteriorate conditions for short periods of time.

Autumn and spring

As with other areas, autumn in the central Mediterranean usually lasts just the month of October, with a rather abrupt transition from summer-like weather to a winter type.

Again, spring characteristics are similar, although the transition from winter weather to summer weather usually takes a few months of unsettled weather of different types.

It is worth noting the high frequency of thunderstorms along the SW coast of the Italian peninsula (sometimes accompanied by waterspouts).

Weather features and winds

Low pressure systems

The Gulf of Genoa is an area where low systems develop with one of the highest frequencies in the entire world.

Various factors are responsible, the most important being the presence of the Alps: northerly flows over the mountain chain increase the likelihood of the development of lows along their concave southern edge; similarly, cold fronts are sometimes blocked by the Alps and help generate depressions to the south, etc.

The Alps, together with a temperature gradient between land and sea indicating thermal differences, the frequent interaction between polar and subtropical jet streams, and the channelling effects of the central Mediterranean mountain chains which tend to accumulate warm air over the area, make the Gulf of Genoa one of the most important weather areas in the Mediterranean.

Genoa low pressure minima are usually centred somewhere in the Gulf, but they may extend into the Po valley and the Gulf of Venice/northern Adriatic. The maximum gradient areas around these lows are not necessarily near the Gulf, but may happen in several different zones, synoptic charts can be useful in determining where the strongest winds are likely.

These depressions can develop all year round. During winter, especially if there is a cold air flow from the northeast into the Po valley, the highest frequency occurs in the relatively warmer Gulf of Genoa; whereas during summer (when cold northeasterly air flow is rarer) low centres develop more frequently in the Po valley–northern Adriatic; these lows often move SE along the eastern coast of Italy.

North West Africa (NWA) Depressions

Sometimes called Sahara lows, these depressions are generated in northwestern Africa, south of the Atlas mountain chain. They account for roughly 1/5 of Mediterranean depressions, and are more likely in autumn and spring (roughly one half of the total number of cyclones during each period); they are rare during summer. Related weather usually lasts three to four days.

Mistral

The northern part of the area is very rarely affected by mistral, except at the northern tip of Corsica.

Along the SE coast of France Ligurian coast of Italy, a

WEATHER

small scale cyclonic circulation sometimes develops on the lee of the mountains, *Figure 4.C.2.*, and NW to W winds near Toulon and Cap Sicié are often opposed to NE to E winds blowing from the Italian side.

Mistral may occasionally reach the central Tyrrhenian, where its direction is usually shifted to the SW.

A strong mistral can also be experienced for several miles eastward of the Bonifacio Strait.

It is not uncommon in the southwestern region, south of Sardinia and to the NW of Sicily. This usually occurs when an upper level trough extends south from central Europe, and a region of NW upper flow reaches the south of Sardinia.

Tramontana

Tramontana may blow with gale force all along the Italian coast, from the Gulf of Genoa to the northern and central Tyrrhenian.

Scirocco

As usual, sirocco is generally associated with the warm sector of depressions transiting over the area.

Over the Gulf of Genoa, it usually blows from the S or SE, generates a heavy swell, and visibility can be reduced by low level clouds and precipitation. Sometimes, local northeasterly breezes may affect an area extending several miles from the coast, but sirocco conditions will be experienced over the open sea.

Over the northern and central Tyrrhenian, when the wind blows from the SE light precipitation, fog and low level clouds may considerably reduce visibility, especially along the eastern coast of Sardinia. These effects are less important over the southern Tyrrhenian, as air is relatively less humid.

Over the Sicily Strait, gale force sirocco can raise heavy, breaking seas.

Along the northern coast of Sicily, sirocco is usually modified by a foehn effect, with dry, gusty winds with very limited precipitation.

Libeccio

Winds from the S or SW are generally caused by drifting depressions (see above). They generally cause heavy swells along the entire Italian coast, especially during the winter.

Winds around Corsica and Sardinia

To the north, NW to SW winds are prevalent all year long, more so during summer. They are usually strongly accelerated around the northern tip of Corsica.

The eastern Corsican and Sardinian coasts are more sheltered from westerlies, which are a concern to navigation at the mouth of the few valleys along the mountain range. Libeccio often blows with gusts, accelerated by foehn effects. Gales from the N to NE are not uncommon during winter.

The Bonifacio Strait with Sardinia strongly accelerates the prevalent easterly or westerly winds.

Along the western coasts breezes are the prevalent summer phenomenon, usually blowing no stronger than 4–5Bft. Gales are generally from WNW to SW, and more frequent during winter. Cirrus clouds often precede mistral onset by 12–24 hours.

The southern third of Sardinia is where sirocco is of some importance, especially during early spring; other gale force episodes are usually caused by gregale winds.

Useful signs of approaching bad weather are the absence of sea breezes around the two islands during summer, oncoming swells from the open sea while winds are still light, and the rise of the sea level inside port areas.

Fog

Fog (and reduced visibility) is usually associated with sirocco weather, especially in the area between Sardinia, Sicily and Tunisia, when it generally lasts one or two days.

Other areas prone to fog formations are the coasts of Corsica, Sardinia and northern Tyrrhenian.

Thunderstorms

Thunderstorms sometimes occur, in particular over the northern half of the area, but they usually have a limited duration.

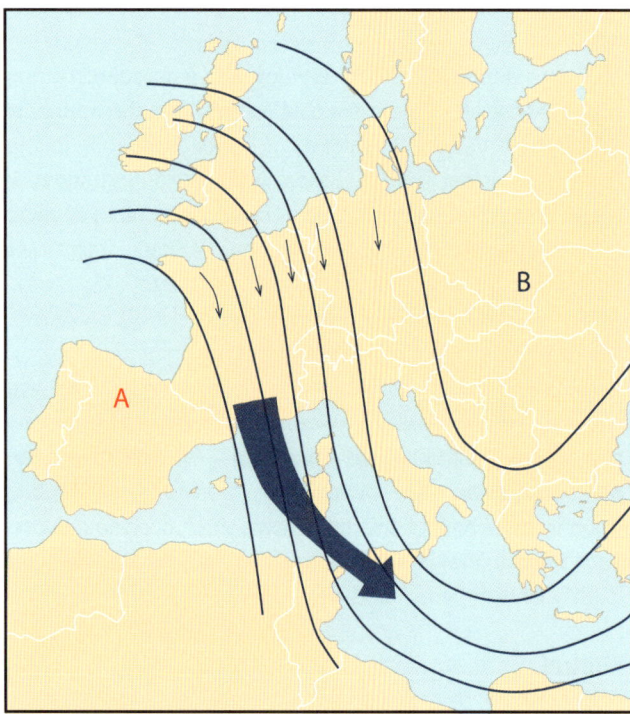

Figure 4.D.2 Deep upper level trough likely to bring mistral to south Sardinia and western Sicily.

WEATHER

WIND ROSES

The following diagrams report monthly wind roses for the whole Mediterranean.

They graphically show the average wind conditions for a one degree area (latitude by longitude) around their position on the map.

Every rose shows a set of arrows from eight directions (N, NE, E, SE, S, SW, W, NW), whose length is proportional to the frequency of wind blowing from that direction. If the frequency is above 30%, a number is indicated in place of a very long arrow.

The number of barbs at the end of the arrow indicates the average Beaufort force. The frequency of calms is indicated by the number inside the circle.

While wind roses can be interesting, cruisers are strongly advised not to overvalue their informative content.

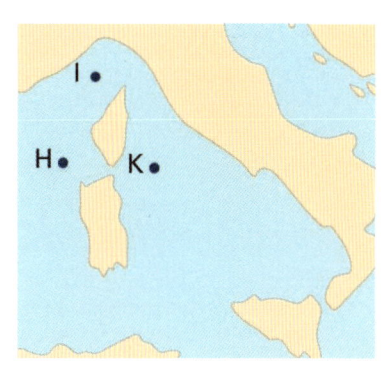

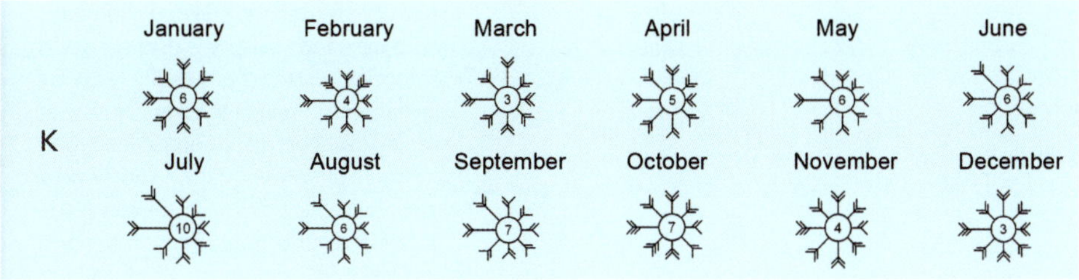

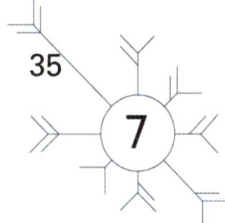

Wind rose

The length of each arrow is proportional to the frequency of the wind. The number of barbs indicates Beaufort force. The number in the centre indicates percentage of calms.

Weather on the internet

www.meteoam.it

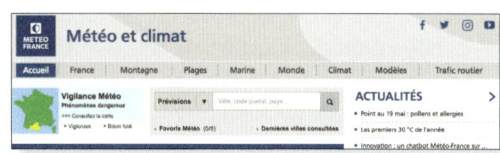

www.meteofrance.com

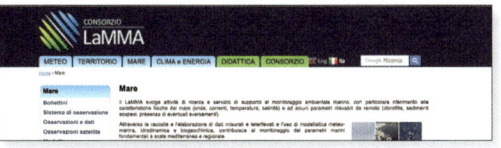

www.lamma.rete.toscana.it

www.eurometeo.com

Weather Apps

AREA A - LIGURIA RIVIERA DI PONENTE (WEST COAST)

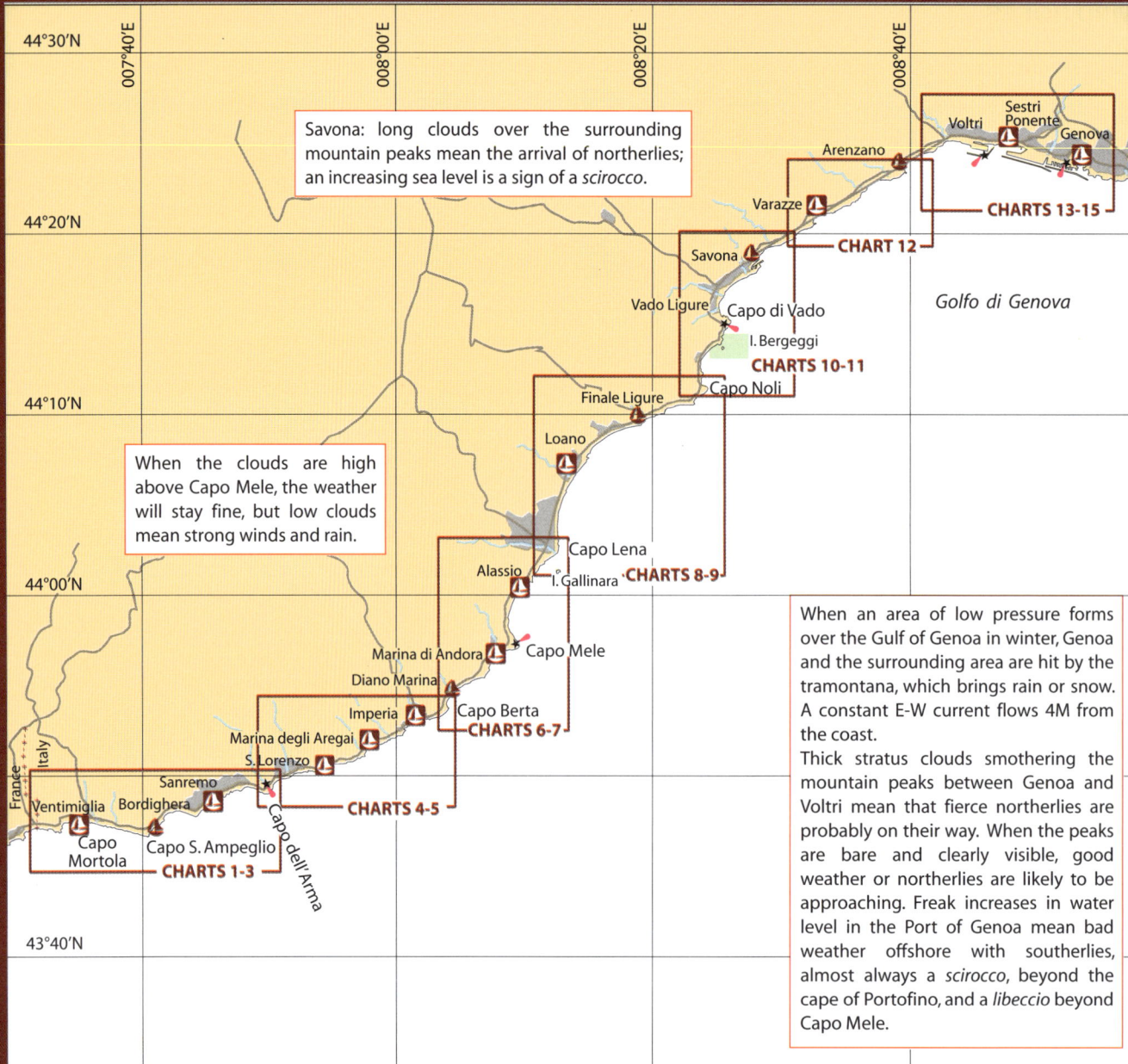

Savona: long clouds over the surrounding mountain peaks mean the arrival of northerlies; an increasing sea level is a sign of a *scirocco*.

When the clouds are high above Capo Mele, the weather will stay fine, but low clouds mean strong winds and rain.

When an area of low pressure forms over the Gulf of Genoa in winter, Genoa and the surrounding area are hit by the tramontana, which brings rain or snow. A constant E-W current flows 4M from the coast.

Thick stratus clouds smothering the mountain peaks between Genoa and Voltri mean that fierce northerlies are probably on their way. When the peaks are bare and clearly visible, good weather or northerlies are likely to be approaching. Freak increases in water level in the Port of Genoa mean bad weather offshore with southerlies, almost always a *scirocco*, beyond the cape of Portofino, and a *libeccio* beyond Capo Mele.

Riviera di Ponente

Riviera dei Fiori (*Rivea de Scioe* in local dialect) is the section of Ligurian coast that stretches from Marina di Andora as far as Ventimiglia. Its swathes of pebbly beaches become sandy as you head eastwards and they are frequently interspersed with rocky stretches. Its hilly inland stops just short of the sea. The coast from Varazze to Andora is called Riviera delle Palme and is similar to Riviera dei Fiori, but its beaches are wide and sandy.

The stretch from the Italian-French border to Genoa is more regular but, despite its promontories, provides very little shelter from prevailing winds or from its formidable and dangerous southerly gales. However, the area does boast a vast array of harbours, both large and small, for all pockets: some sheltered, others less so. Almost all of them have visitors berths on laid moorings tailed to the quay or mooring buoys (unless stated otherwise in the plan). Water and electricity are also available. The harbours are often very busy in high season, so it is advisable to call ahead to check availability and fees, which vary each year and according to season. Private and newly built marinas tend to charge higher fees, while municipal (Comunale) marinas, and those run by the port authority, or leased to cooperatives, sailing clubs and associations, are more affordable. Some municipal or HM (Capitaneria) harbours provide visitors berths free-of-charge (for 24 hours) or for a token fee, but they are not always available.

On summer days, a S-SE sea breeze gets up (as you move towards Riviera di Levante, it turns to the S-SW), but it is generally no stronger than Force 4 and dies down in the evening, making way for an offshore breeze at night. However, the swell, albeit very weak, continues into the night, making anchoring in the bay uncomfortable. From autumn to spring, the prevailing winds blow from the N-NE and gales are more frequent. Libeccio gales are the fiercest, with the wind's vast fetch blasting the Ligurian coast with some of the Mediterranean's largest waves. When this happens, navigation, and approaching harbours in particular, is often hazardous, if not impossible.

Recommended harbours and marinas: Sanremo Porto Comunale, Imperia Porto Maurizio, Marina di Alassio, Finale Ligure, Savona, and Sestri Ponente.

AREA A - LIGURIA RIVIERA DI PONENTE (WEST COAST)

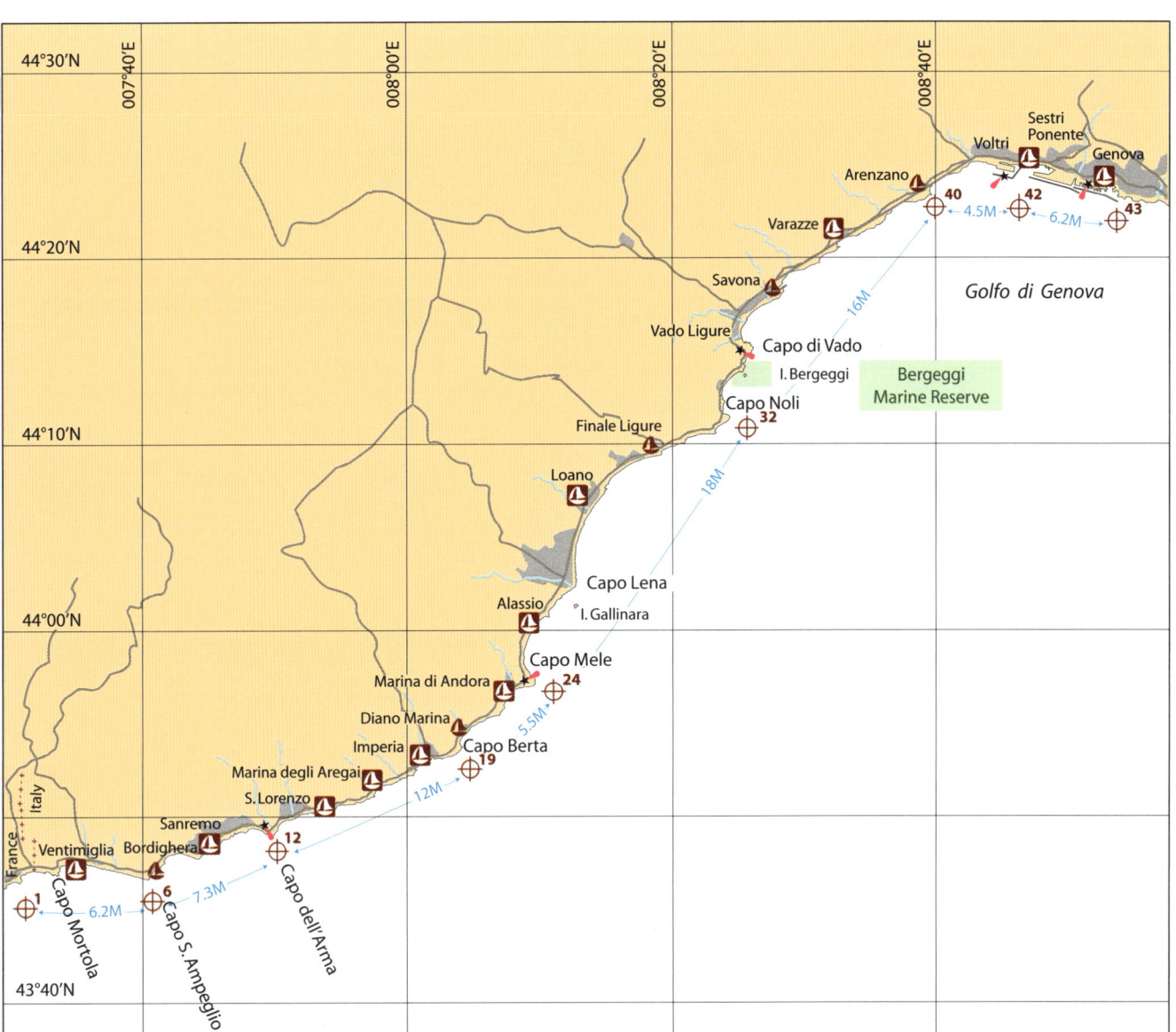

COASTAL NAVIGATION WAYPOINTS AND DISTANCES

⊕	DESCRIPTION	WGS 84 COORDINATES LATITUDE	LONGITUDE	CHART
1	0.5M off the Italian-French border	43°46'.25N	007°32'.02E	1
6	0.5M off Capo S. Ampeglio	43°46'.26N	007°40'.26E	1-2
12	0.5M off Capo dell'Arma	43°48'.49N	007°50'.03E	2-4
19	0.5M off Capo Berta	43°53'.26N	008°05'.21E	4-6
24	0.5M off Capo Mele	43°57'.30N	008°10'.59E	6-7
32	0.5M off Capo Noli	44°11'.70N	008°25'.53E	9-10
40	500m off Capo Arenzano	44°23'.37N	008°41'.22E	12
42	1M off Genova W approaches	44°23'.44N	008°47'.45E	13
43	1M off Genova E approaches	44°22'.27N	008°56'.12E	13-16

AREA A - LIGURIA RIVIERA DI PONENTE (WEST COAST)

HARBOURS AND MARINAS KEY FOR PLAN SYMBOLS

⊕	NAME	WGS 84 COORDINATES LATITUDE	WGS 84 COORDINATES LONGITUDE	CHART	⛵	⚓	🅿	LOA m	V	🛢	↕ m	⚡	🚿	WC	🚻	🏨	🍴	✂	🔧
5	Ventimiglia - Cala del Forte	43°47'.29N	007°35',80E	1				IU											
7	Bordighera	42°46'.80N	007°40',70E	1		•		250	19	•		6	•	•	•	•			
9	Ospedaletti / Marina di Baia Verde	43°47'.90N	007°42'.80E	2	•			IU				8							
10	Capo Pino	43°47'.81N	007°44'.61E	2		•		20	7			2	•	•	•				
11	Sanremo - Marina Portosole	43°48'.90N	007°47'.29E	3	•	•		850	90	•	•	10	•	•	•	•	•	•	•
13	Arma di Taggia	43°49'.48N	007°51'.37E	4		•		125	12			2		•		•	•		
14	Riva Ligure	43°50'.10N	007°53'.10E	4		•		IU	7			2		•					
15	Marina degli Aregai	43°50'.35N	007°55'.05E	4	•			980	40	•	•	7	•	•	•	•	•	•	•
16	Marina di S. Lorenzo	43°51'.58N	007°51'.34E	4	•			360	20	•	•	3.5	•	•	•	•	•	•	•
17	Imperia - Porto Maurizio	43°52'.50N	008°01'.80E	5	•	•		1200	90	•	•	7.7	•	•	•	•	•	•	•
18	Imperia - Oneglia	43°52'.95N	008°02'.40E	5		•		1278	90	•	•	9	•	•	•	•	•	•	•
21	Diano Marina	43°54'.44N	008°05'.19E	6		•		270	14	•		3	•	•	•	•	•	•	•
22	S. Bartolomeo al Mare	43°55'.00N	008°06'.48E	6		•		170	15			2.5	•	•		•			
23	Marina di Andora	43°57'.00N	008°09'.65E	7	•			856	18	•	•	5	•	•	•	•	•		
25	Marina di Alassio	44°01'.12N	008°11'.50E	7	•			550	35		•	5.8	•	•	•	•	•	•	•
28	Borghetto S. Spirito (Poseidon)	44°06'.80N	008°15'.00E	8		•		204	8		•	2	•	•	•	•			
29	Marina di Loano	44°08'.15N	008°16'.30E	9	•			855	77	•	•	5	•	•	•	•	•	•	•
30	Finale Ligure	44°10'.56N	008°22'.34E	9		•		550	17	•		3.5	•	•		•			
35	Vado Ligure	44°16'.00N	008°27'.02E	10		•		IU				10						•	
36	Savona	44°18'.90N	008°30'.30E	11	•			500	20	•	•	10	•	•	•	•	•		•
38	Cala Cravieu	44°20'.20N	008°36'.60E	12		•		80	8			3			•	•			
39	Marina di Varazze	44°21'.16N	008°34'.20E	12	•			707	35	•	•	4.5	•	•	•	•	•	•	•
41	Arenzano	44°23'.95N	008°41'.30E	12		•		185	20	•	•	2	•	•	•	•	•	•	•
44	Marina di Castelluccio	44°24'.43N	008°48'.46E	13	•			530	15	•	•	5	•	•	•	•	•		
46	Genova Sestri Ponente (Marina Genova Aeroporto e C.N. Sestri)	44°25'.05N	008°50'.50E	14	•			650	90	•	•	10	•	•	•				
47	Marina Fiera di Genova	44°23'.65N	008°56'.16E	14	•			305	25		•	10	•	•	•	•	•		
48	Porto Duca degli Abruzzi	44°23'.75N	008°55'.66E	14		•		380	25	•	•	10	•	•	•	•	•	•	•
49	Marina Molo Vecchio	44°24'.55N	008°55'.23E	15	•			160	90	•		8	•	•	•		•		
50	Marina Porto Antico	44°24'.62N	008°55'.25E	15		•		280	75	•		8	•	•	•				

IU= Information Unavailable

ANCHORAGES KEY FOR PLAN SYMBOLS

⊕	NAME	WGS 84 COORDINATES LATITUDE	WGS 84 COORDINATES LONGITUDE	CHART	Shelter	Seabed	Depth m	Landing	Facilities	Wind	Anchorage	Mooring buoy
2	Cala Balzi Rossi	43°46'.52N	007°32'.38E	1	P	s	5	•	B-R	E-W	•	
4	Baia del Latte	43°47'.11N	007°33'.58E	1	G	s	7	•		NE-SW	•	
8	Madonna della Ruota	43°47'.30N	007°41'.40E	2	G	s	5	•		N-S	•	
20	Capo Berta anchorage	43°54'.00N	008°04'.51E	6	G	s	5	•	B-R	NE-SW	•	
26	Isola Gallinara	44°01'.55N	008°13'.50E	8	P	s	10			W-E	•	
27	Albenga anchorage	44°03'.04N	008°13'.40E	8	P	s	6	•	B	N-SW	•	
31	Punta Crena	44°10'.53N	008°24'.33E	9	G	s	6	•	B-R-S	NW-SE	•	
33	Noli (Il Grugno)	44°12'.75N	008°25'.10E	10	G	s/w	7	•		N-SE	•	

Shelter: P = Poor G = Good E = Excellent   **Nature of seabed**: w = weed m = mud g = gravel p = pebbles/stones r = rock s = sand

Depths in metres   **Landing with dinghy**   **Facilities ashore**: B = Bar R = Restaurant S = Shop   **Anchorage**   **Mooring buoy**

Wind direction and exposure

AREA A - LIGURIA RIVIERA DI PONENTE (WEST COAST)

SAFETY AT SEA — AREA A

WEATHER BULLETINS

Mari d'Italia/Meteomar weather bulletin
(English and Italian)
VHF ch 68 frequency 156.425 MHz continuous

Coast radio station weather bulletin
0135 0735 1335 1935 UTC
Castellaccio (Genova) VHF ch 25
  frequency 161.850 MHz
Monte Bignone (Imperia) VHF ch 7
  frequency 160.950 MHz

Radiouno - Italian bulletin for the sea
0554 1408 2249 Monday-Friday

FRANCE AND CORSICA WEATHER FORECASTS
(French-English)

Monaco Radio 4363 kHz (ch 403)
0903 1403 1915 LT
Lyon, Provence, Corsican Sea, Sardinian Sea, Ligurian Sea, Northern Tyrrhenian Sea

Monaco Radio 8728, 8806 kHz (ch 804, 830) SSB
0715 1830 UTC West Mediterranean offshore seas

La Garde CROSS 1696, 2677 kHz SSB after the first call on the frequency 2182 kHz
0650 1433 1850 LT

HARBOURMASTERS

Genova ☎ +39 010 27771
genova@guardiacostiera.it
VHF ch 16 MF 2182, 2722 kHz

Imperia ☎ +39 0183 66061
cpimperia@mit.gov.it

Savona ☎ +39 019 856666
cpsavona@mit.gov.it

Guardia Costiera (Coast Guard)
☎ 1530 emergency - VHF ch 16

SAFETY AND RESCUE CENTRES

MRSC Genova ☎ +39 010 27771
genova@guardiacostiera.it

MRSC Livorno ☎ +39 0586 826011
cplivorno@guardiacostiera.gov.it

MRCC Roma MMSI 002 470 001
DSC VHF ch 70, 16 - DSC MF 2187.5 kHz, 2182 kHz
DSC HF 420.5, 6312, 8414.5 kHz
Direzione Marittima (Porth Authority) Roma Fiumicino
☎ +39 06 656171
cproma@mit.gov.it

CIRM International Medical Centre
☎ +39 06 559290263 - mobile +39 348 3984229
Fax +39 06 5923331/2
telesoccorso@cirm.it - www.cirm.it

CHART 1 — AREA A
LIGURIA WEST COAST — FROM THE ITALIAN-FRENCH BORDER TO BORDIGHERA

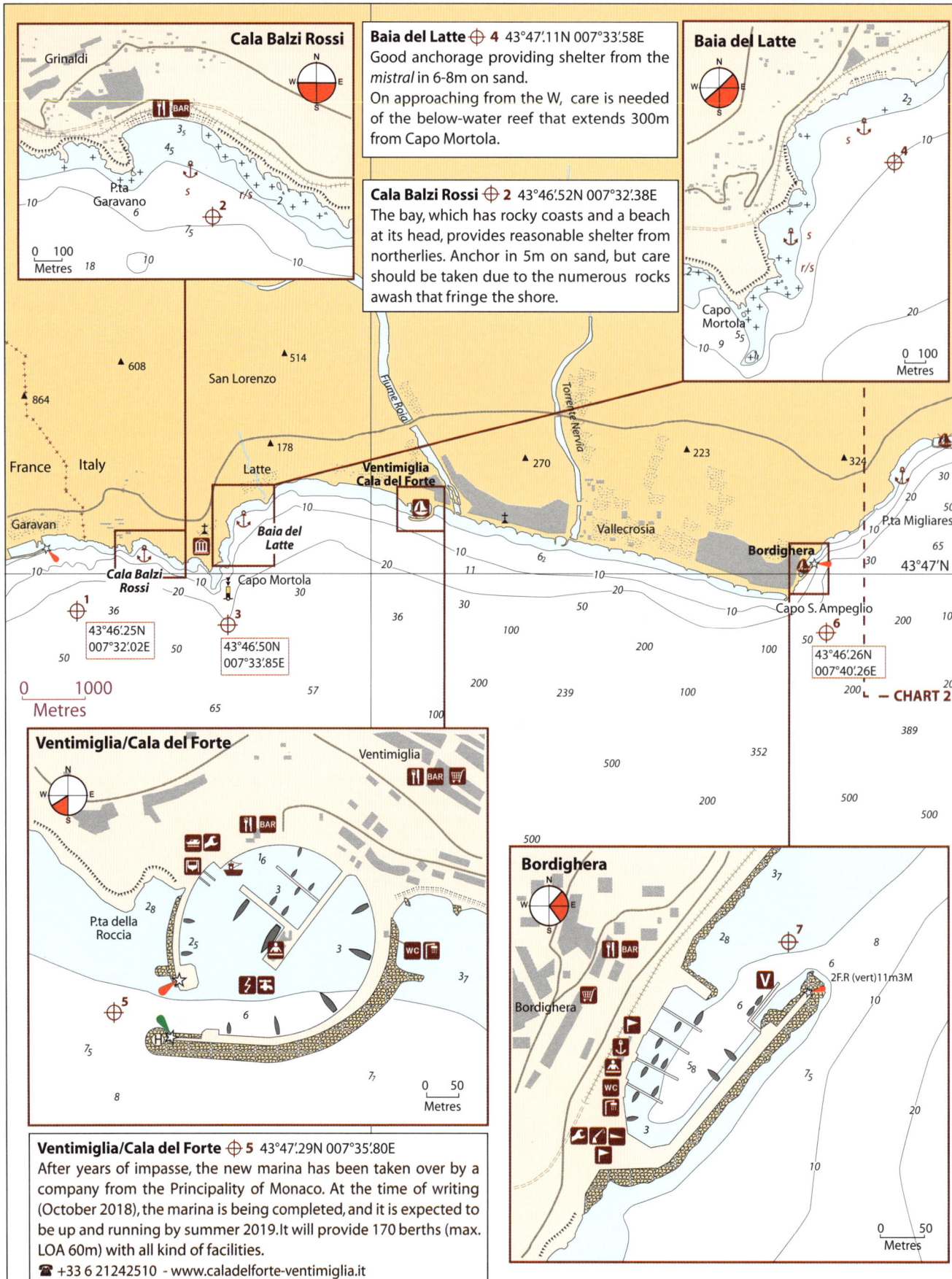

Baia del Latte ⊕ 4 43°47'.11N 007°33'.58E
Good anchorage providing shelter from the *mistral* in 6-8m on sand.
On approaching from the W, care is needed of the below-water reef that extends 300m from Capo Mortola.

Cala Balzi Rossi ⊕ 2 43°46'.52N 007°32'.38E
The bay, which has rocky coasts and a beach at its head, provides reasonable shelter from northerlies. Anchor in 5m on sand, but care should be taken due to the numerous rocks awash that fringe the shore.

Ventimiglia/Cala del Forte ⊕ 5 43°47'.29N 007°35'.80E
After years of impasse, the new marina has been taken over by a company from the Principality of Monaco. At the time of writing (October 2018), the marina is being completed, and it is expected to be up and running by summer 2019. It will provide 170 berths (max. LOA 60m) with all kind of facilities.
☎ +33 6 21242510 - www.caladelforte-ventimiglia.it

Bordighera ⊕ 7 42°46'.80N 007°40'.70E
Located NE of Capo S. Ampeglio, this small harbour is identified by its long outer breakwater which runs parallel to the coast for 260m. In strong winds, especially a *scirocco*, and E seas, entry can be hazardous. The harbour, which is invariably crowded, has 250 berths (max. LOA 19m) on four pontoons inside and on one pontoon at the end of its breakwater, which is allocated to visiting yachts (max. LOA 7m). Yachts should keep 100m off the breakwater. Entry to yachts over 20m length is prohibited. The harbour is administered by Bordighera Town Council.
Yacht harbour VHF ch 09 - ☎ +39 0184 263792 - Port authority ☎ +39 0184 265656

LIGURIA WEST COAST
FROM CAPO D'AMPEGLIO TO SANREMO — AREA A
CHART 2

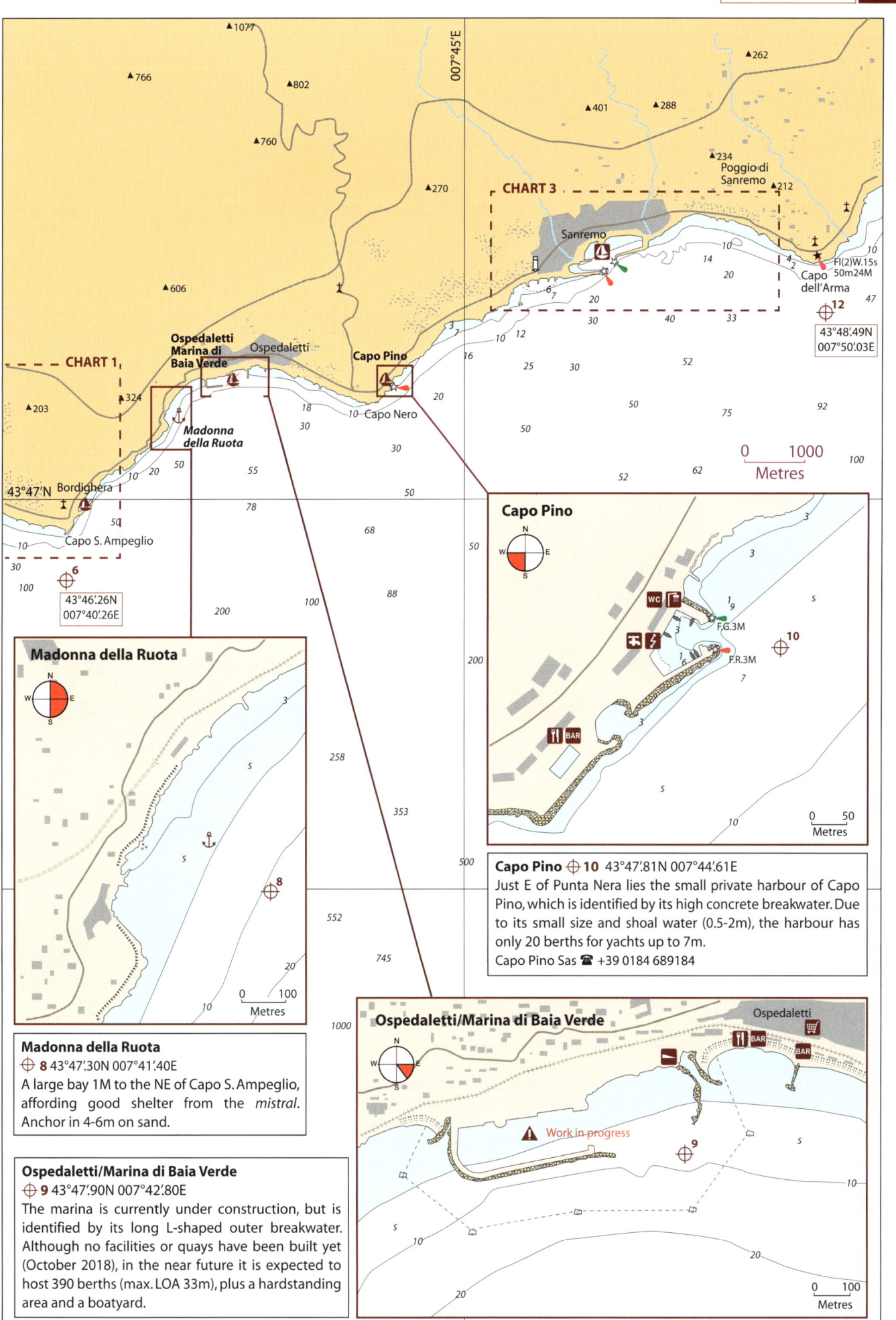

Capo Pino ⊕ 10 43°47'.81N 007°44'.61E
Just E of Punta Nera lies the small private harbour of Capo Pino, which is identified by its high concrete breakwater. Due to its small size and shoal water (0.5-2m), the harbour has only 20 berths for yachts up to 7m.
Capo Pino Sas ☎ +39 0184 689184

Madonna della Ruota
⊕ 8 43°47'.30N 007°41'.40E
A large bay 1M to the NE of Capo S. Ampeglio, affording good shelter from the *mistral*. Anchor in 4-6m on sand.

Ospedaletti/Marina di Baia Verde
⊕ 9 43°47'.90N 007°42'.80E
The marina is currently under construction, but is identified by its long L-shaped outer breakwater. Although no facilities or quays have been built yet (October 2018), in the near future it is expected to host 390 berths (max. LOA 33m), plus a hardstanding area and a boatyard.

CHART 3 — AREA A — LIGURIA WEST COAST — SANREMO

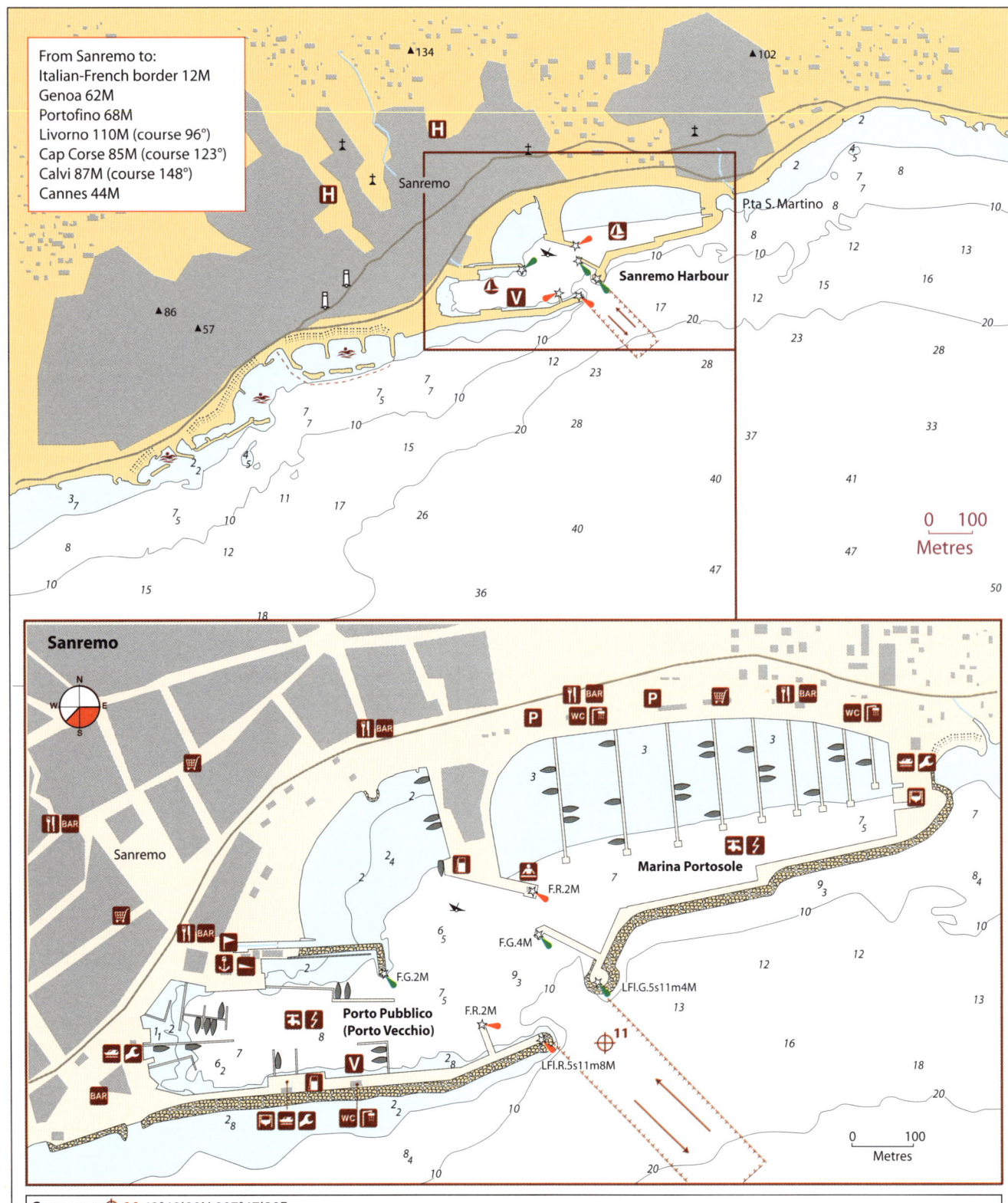

From Sanremo to:
- Italian-French border 12M
- Genoa 62M
- Portofino 68M
- Livorno 110M (course 96°)
- Cap Corse 85M (course 123°)
- Calvi 87M (course 148°)
- Cannes 44M

Sanremo ⊕ 11 43°48'.90N 007°47'.29E

The large harbour of Sanremo boasts two basins - one public, one private - both protected by its two long outer breakwaters. As the entrance faces SE, southerly gales make the approach dangerous and create an uncomfortable surge inside the basins. Also note that when the quay water-level rises considerably, a S-SW gale is probably on its way.

Porto Pubblico (Porto Vecchio - Old Harbour) The public harbour, in the W basin, hosts fishing boats, as well as 8 pontoons under private management with 450 berths. 15 visitors berths (max. LOA 16m) managed by Circomare Sanremo sit around the middle of the public quay on the W outer breakwater.
Port Authority VHF ch 16/14 - ☎ +39 0184 505531 - ucsanremo@mit.gov.it

Marina Portosole The city's large tourist harbour is extremely dear but has excellent facilities. Before approaching, radio the harbour authority (VHF ch 09). Approach and steer to the right into the basin, keeping to the starboard, then go alongside the "ormeggiatori" (marina staff) quay. The harbour provides 850 berths (max. LOA 90m) along the outer breakwater on 9 pontoons. All berths have moorings tailed to the quay in adequate depths.
Marina Portosole VHF ch 09 - CB ch 02 - ☎ +39 0184 500349 - info@portosolesanremo.it - www.portosolesanremo.it
Fuel: Molo Ponente Serafini ☎ +39 0184 503477 - Yacht Club Sanremo ☎ +39 0184 502023 - Emergencies ☎ +39 0184 524218/ 505050/ 505051

LIGURIA WEST COAST
FROM CAPO DELL'ARMA TO CAPO BERTA — AREA A

CHART 4

Arma di Taggia
⊕ 13 43°49'.48N 007°51'.37E

On the last stretch of the River Argentina is a small harbour for <2m draught-craft only. Keep to the middle of the river when entering the mouth. In moderate seas and strong SE-SW winds, the approach is hazardous if not impossible. The basin has 125 berths (max. LOA 12m).

Circolo Nautico Arma di Taggia
☎ +39 0184 41021 / 331 2381385
cna.arma@tiscali.it - www.cnarma.it

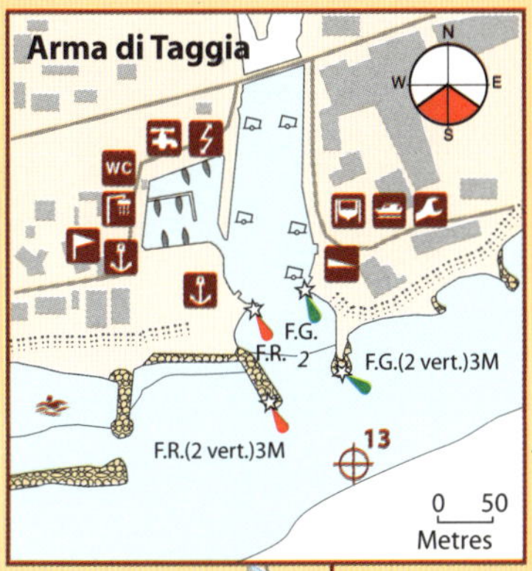

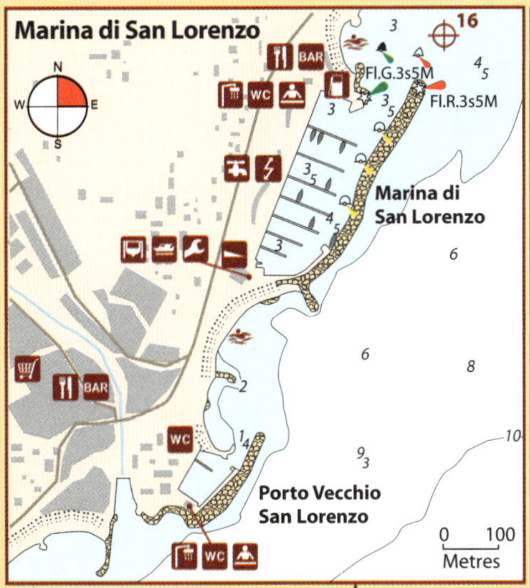

Marina di San Lorenzo
⊕ 16 43°51'.58N 007°51'.34E

The new marina provides 360 berths (max. LOA 20m), including 36 for visitors. At the time of writing (2018), it was operational but not yet completed. Although the marina enjoys good all-round shelter, entry and mooring may be troublesome in strong southerlies and easterlies.

Marina di San Lorenzo a Mare - VHF ch 09
☎ +39 0183 9352 - info@marinadisanlorenzo.it
www.marinadisanlorenzo.it

Porto Vecchio San Lorenzo

Just to the S of the marina lies the old small fishing harbour with 90 berths (LOA under 7.5m) for yachts drawing no more than 1m. Berths administered by:
Circolo Nautico I Delfini ☎ +39 335 6901909

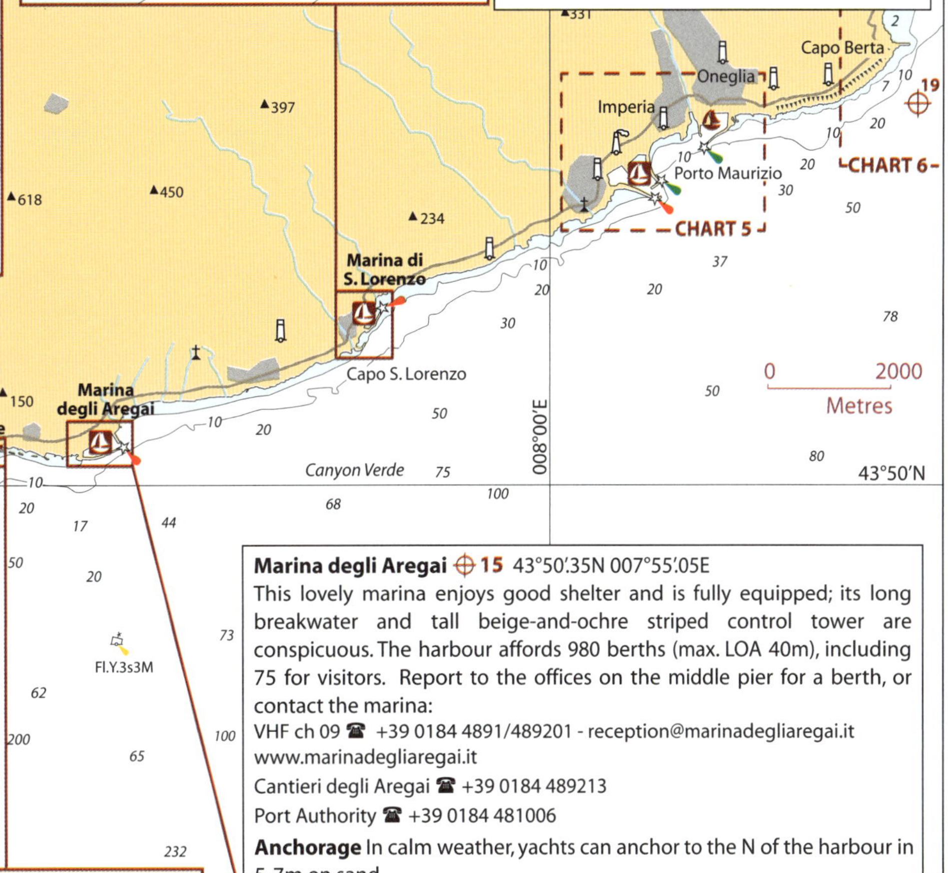

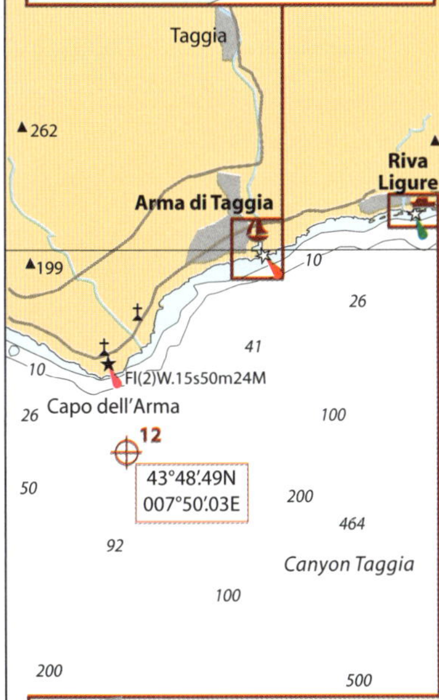

Marina degli Aregai ⊕ 15 43°50'.35N 007°55'.05E

This lovely marina enjoys good shelter and is fully equipped; its long breakwater and tall beige-and-ochre striped control tower are conspicuous. The harbour affords 980 berths (max. LOA 40m), including 75 for visitors. Report to the offices on the middle pier for a berth, or contact the marina:
VHF ch 09 ☎ +39 0184 4891/489201 - reception@marinadegliaregai.it
www.marinadegliaregai.it
Cantieri degli Aregai ☎ +39 0184 489213
Port Authority ☎ +39 0184 481006

Anchorage In calm weather, yachts can anchor to the N of the harbour in 5-7m on sand.

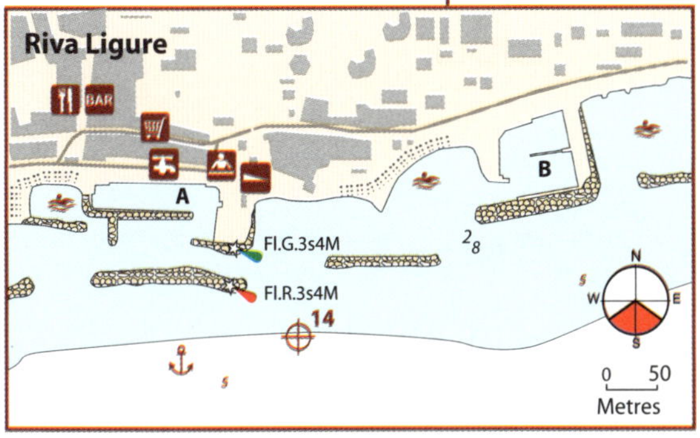

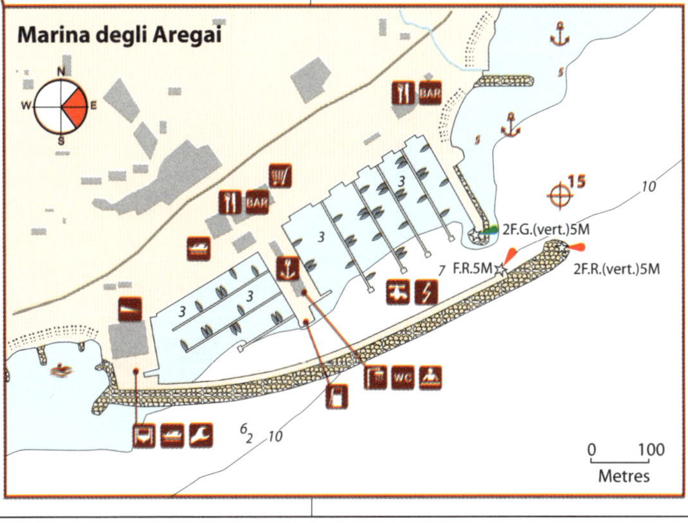

Riva Ligure ⊕ 14 43°50'.10N 007°53'.10E

This harbour has two small basins (A and B) for shallow-draught yachts max. length 7m.
Amatori del Mare ☎ +39 0184 485754

Anchorage In calm weather, yachts can anchor off the breakwaters in 4-6m on sand.

CHART 5 — AREA A — LIGURIA WEST COAST — IMPERIA

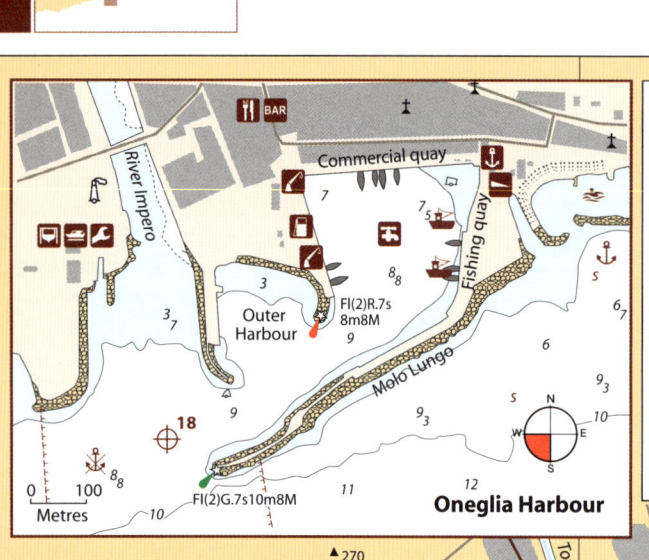

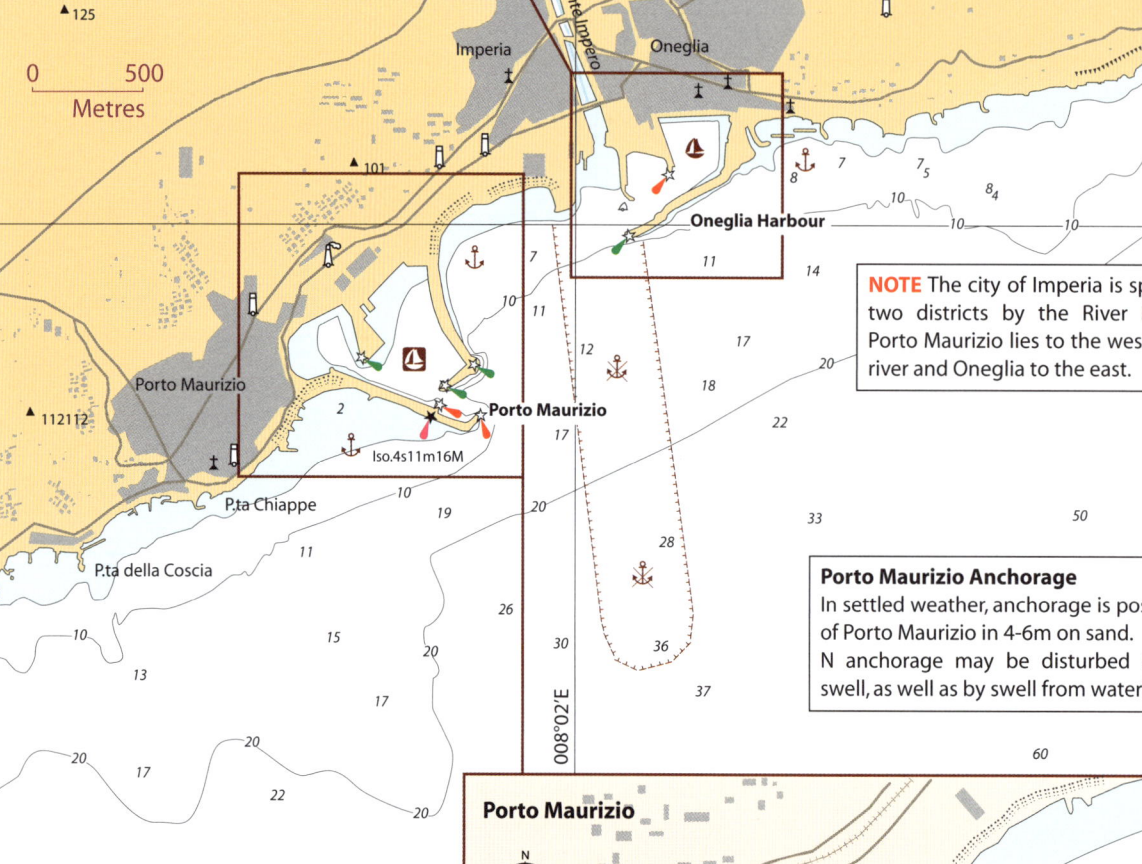

Imperia - Oneglia Harbour ⊕ 18 43°52'.95N 008°02'.40E

To the E of Porto Maurizio lies a large basin with a small outer harbour for commercial traffic and local fishing boats. If the marina is full, the harbourmaster can issue a permit for a yacht to moor inside Porto Oneglia. The size of this harbour makes it especially suited to larger yachts.

When entering and leaving, remember that commercial traffic always has right of way. In the approach, deep-draught yachts should keep to the middle to avoid the underwater ballastings that fringe both the outer breakwaters.

Porto di Imperia ☎ +39 0183 62679 - info@portodimperia.it
www.portodimperia.it
Harbourmaster VHF ch 16 - ☎ +39 0183 66061
cpimperia@mit.gov.it

NOTE The city of Imperia is split into two districts by the River Impero: Porto Maurizio lies to the west of the river and Oneglia to the east.

Porto Maurizio Anchorage

In settled weather, anchorage is possible N or S of Porto Maurizio in 4-6m on sand.
N anchorage may be disturbed by offshore swell, as well as by swell from waterborne traffic.

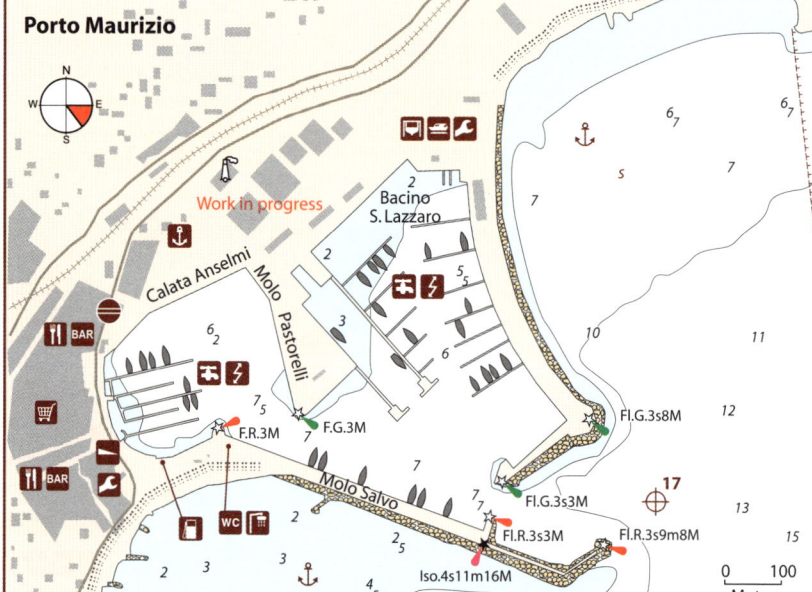

Imperia - Porto Maurizio

⊕ 17 43°52'.50N 008°01'.80E

Porto Maurizio is a large marina with a capacity of 1278 berths (max. LOA 90m), including 150 for visitors. The basin is protected by two breakwaters and is divided into two docks by a central concrete mole.

Despite there being plenty of room, the marina is always busy in summer, so it is advisable to contact the harbour authority in advance.

In moderate offshore seas and strong S winds, entry and berthing may be troublesome.

Go Imperia VHF ch 09 - ☎ +39 0183 62679
reception@goimperia.it - www.goimperia.it
Harbourmaster VHF ch16 - ☎ +39 0183 66061
cpimperia@mit.gov.it

Capo Berta ⊕ **20** 43°54'.00N 008°04'.51E
In settled weather, anchorage can be had to the N of the breakwater that stretches offshore. Anchor in 4-7m on sand with reasonable shelter from light westerlies.

San Bartolomeo al Mare
⊕ **22** 43°55'.00N 008°06'.48E
The small harbour accommodates 170 berths (max. LOA 15m) drawing no more than 2.5m. Yachts over 8m must go alongside the central pontoon and wait for instructions from marina staff. In strong southerlies and moderate seas, entering the harbour is very dangerous, if not impossible.
Sermar VHF ch 09 ☎ +39 0183 408089
www.sermar.it pna@sermarsm.it

NOTE A constant E-W current flows 4M from the coast.

CAUTION Approaching this stretch of coast and its small harbours is impossible in strong southern winds (*scirocco* and *libeccio*) and moderate seas.

Diano Marina ⊕ **21** 43°54'.44N 008°05'.19E
As this small harbour is difficult to spot offshore, look for the conspicuous tall belltower with its red dome rising from the town centre of Diano Marina.
It provides 270 berths (max. LOA 14m), including 12 for visitors. Depths at the quay range from 2.5-1.5m.
Diano Marina harbour office ☎ +39 0183 738134
Mooring +39 0183 753024
porto@gestionimunicipali.com
www.gestionimunicipali.com
Coast Guard VHF ch 16 - ☎ +39 0183 497458

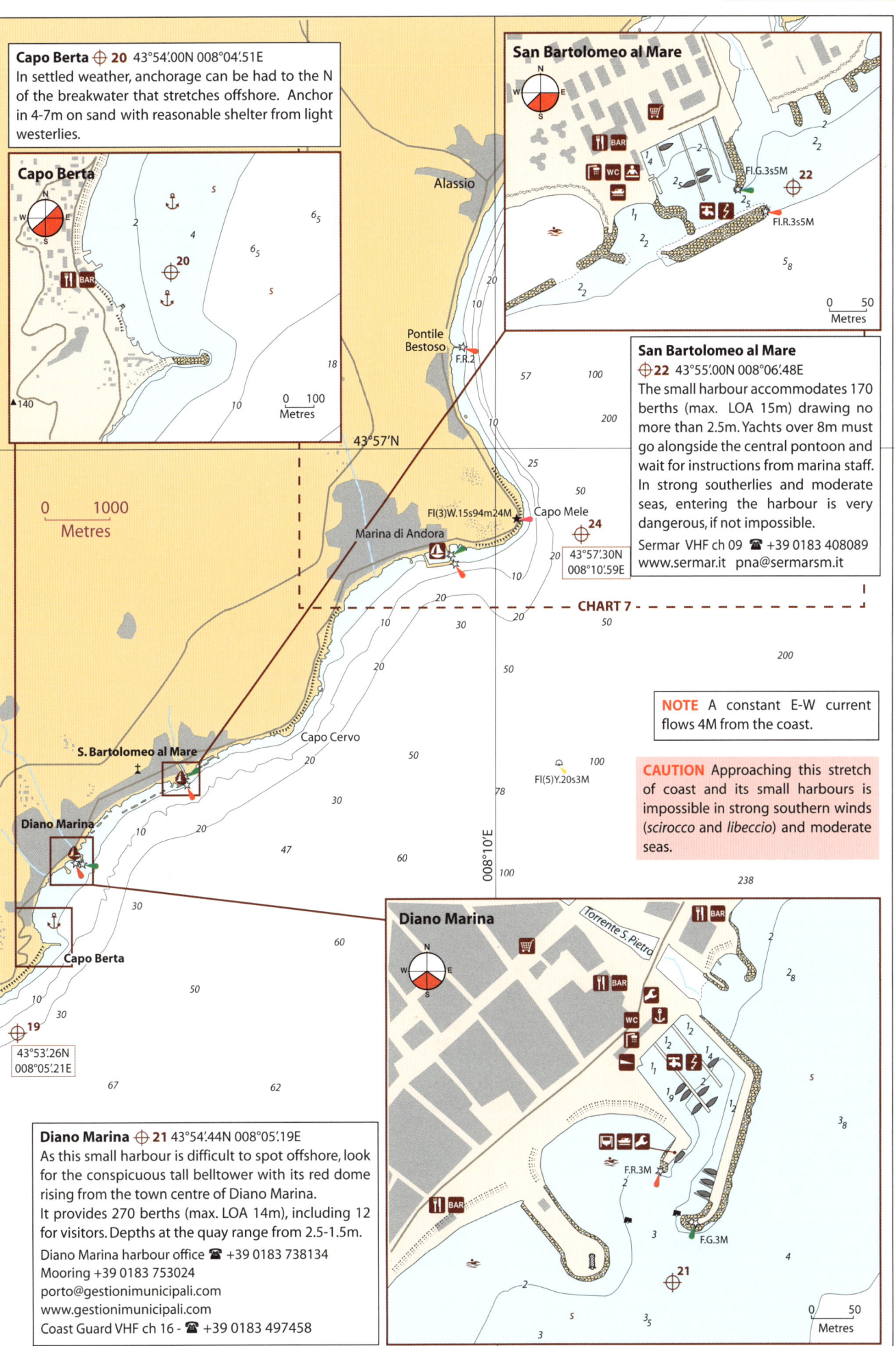

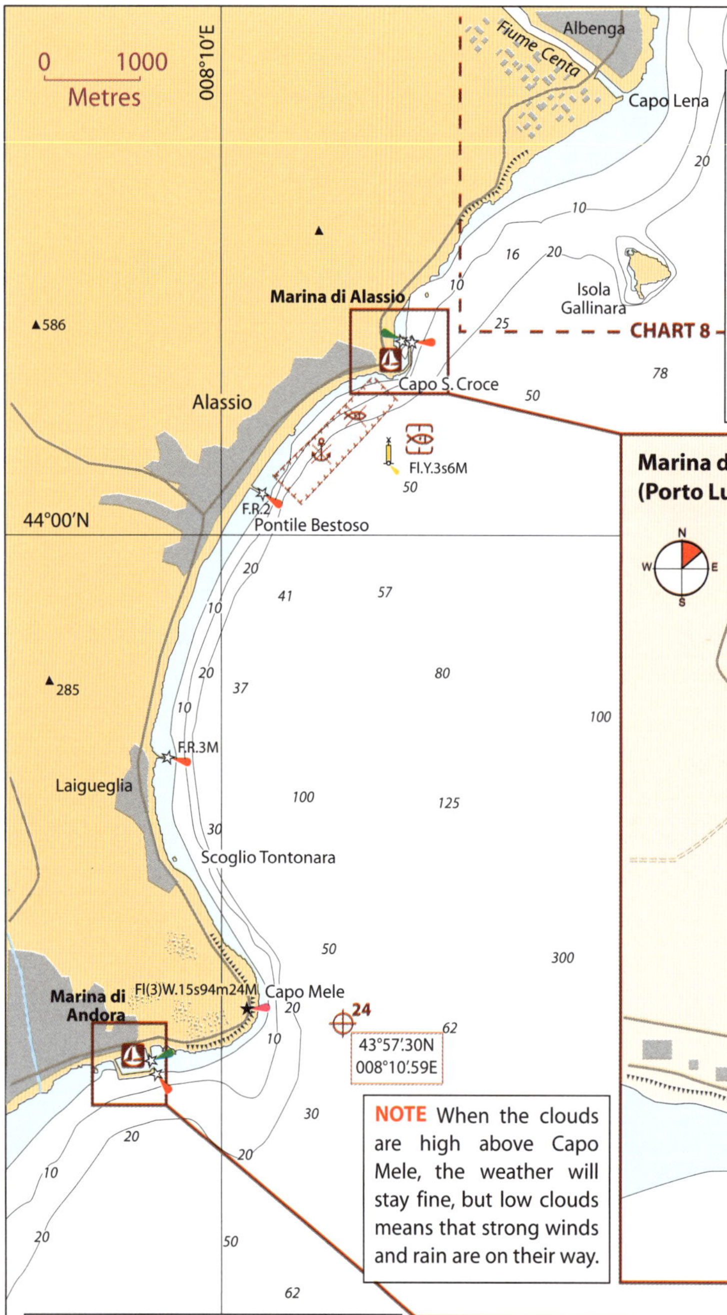

CHART 7 — AREA A

LIGURIA WEST COAST — FROM CAPO MELE TO CAPO LENA

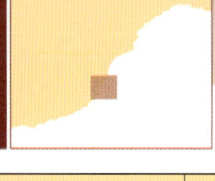

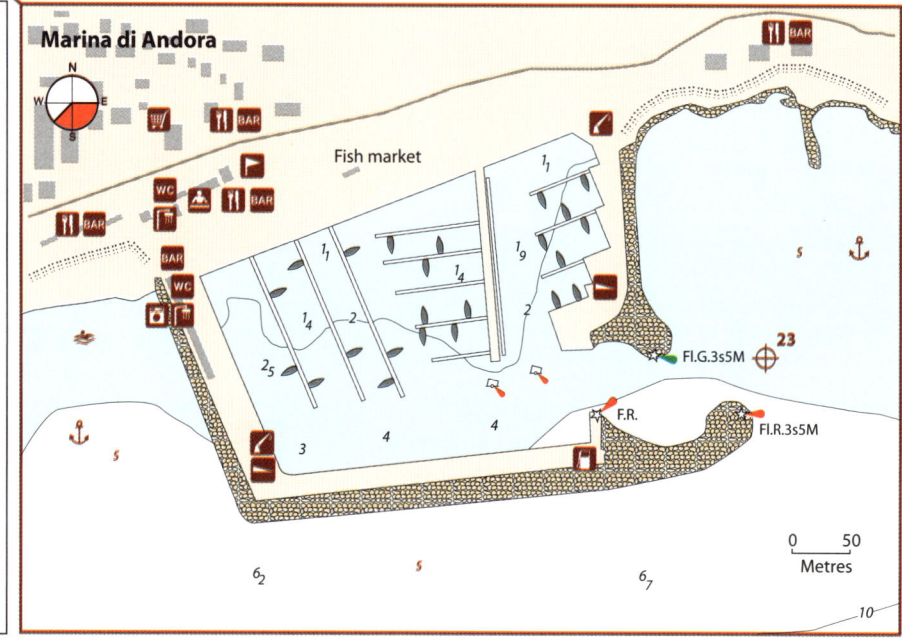

Marina di Alassio (Porto Luca Ferrari)
⊕ 25 44°01'.12N 008°11'.50E

The marina lies 1M from the town of Alassio on the N side of Capo di S. Croce and is protected by a long outer breakwater. It affords all-round shelter and has 550 berths (max. LOA 35m), including some for visitors. In E-SE wind and moderate seas, entry may be dangerous and mooring troublesome. Furthermore, the approach may be buffeted by strong gusts whipping down from the surrounding mountains.

Marina di Alassio VHF ch 09 ☎ +39 0182 645012
info@marinadialassio.net - www.marinadialassio.net
Harbourmaster ☎ 0182 640861

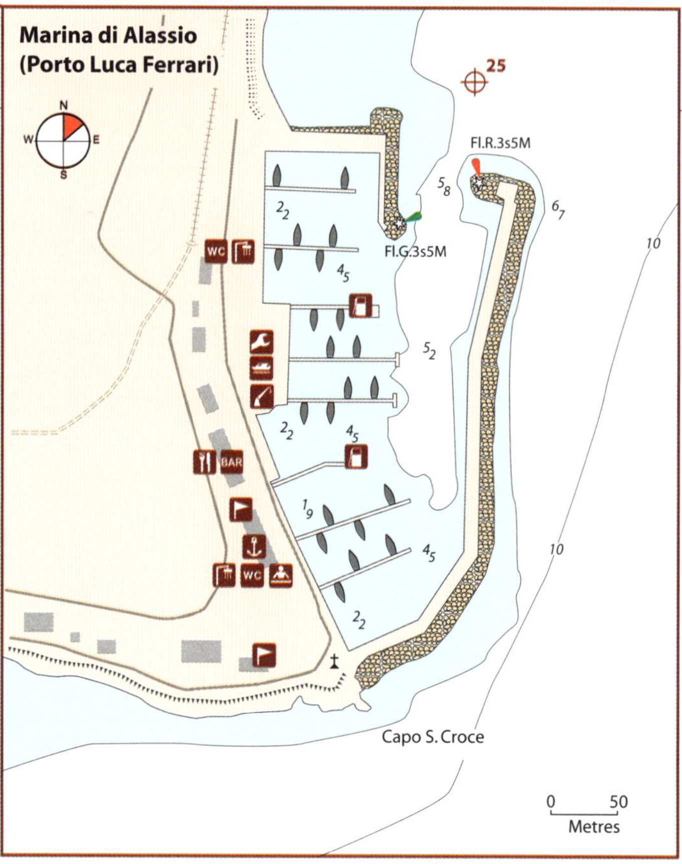

NOTE When the clouds are high above Capo Mele, the weather will stay fine, but low clouds means that strong winds and rain are on their way.

Marina di Andora
⊕ 23 43°57'.00N 008°09'.65E

Andora yacht harbour's breakwater lies S of Capo Mele and is easily identified. It is situated to the E of the town. The marina provides 856 berths (max. LOA 18m), including 56 for visitors, in 4-1m. Depths, however, may vary as the harbour is prone to silting. With strong *libeccio* entry may be dangerous. Also note that onshore winds and seas kick up a confused swell in the harbour mouth.

Azienda Comunale Multiservizi
VHF ch 09 - ☎ +39 0182 88313
info@portodiandora.it
www.portodiandora.it
Port Authority ☎/Fax +39 0182 88899

Anchorage Anchor where convenient off the town of Andora in 5-6m on sand. Anchorage provides shelter from northerlies and westerlies.

Borghetto Santo Spirito / Poseidon
⊕ **28** 44°06'.80N 008°15'.00E
A small harbour for yachts up to 8m with 2m max. draught. It hosts 204 berths, with 21 for visitors.
☎ +39 329 2421760
commerciale@portodiborghetto.it
www.portodiborghetto.it

Albenga Anchorage
⊕ **27** 44°03'.04N 008°13'.40E
The town does not have a harbour. Yachts wishing to stop can anchor off the beach in 4-6m on sand when settled weather is certain. The S breakwater provides better shelter.

Isola Gallinara ⊕ **26** 44°01'.55N 008°13'.50E
A private island where landing is prohibited. The small harbour on the N side may be used for emergency shelter, but you are not allowed to leave your boat. Diving is also forbidden here as sunken war relics lie on the seabed within a 500m radius.
In settled and calm weather it is possible to anchor N of the small island in about 10m on sand.

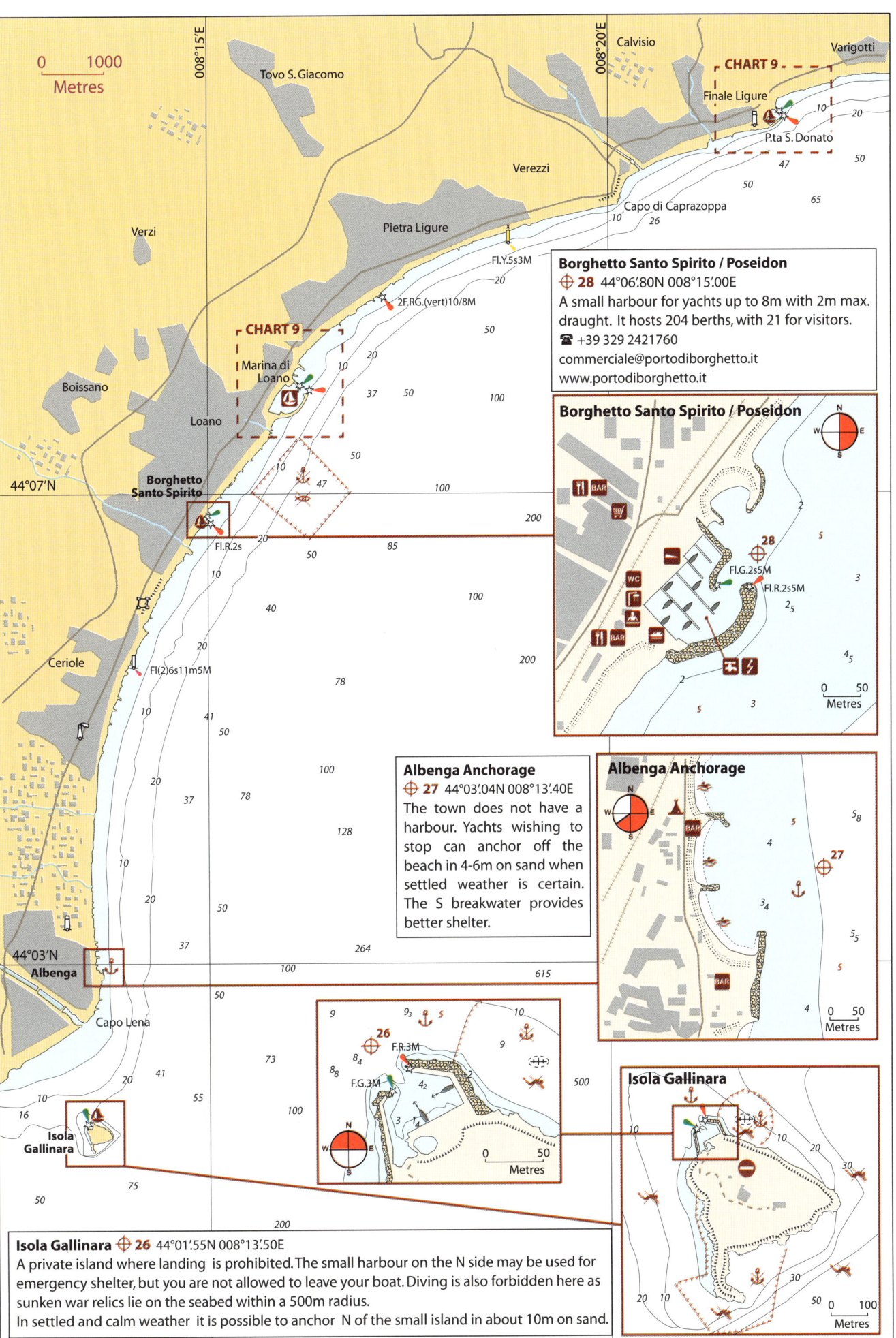

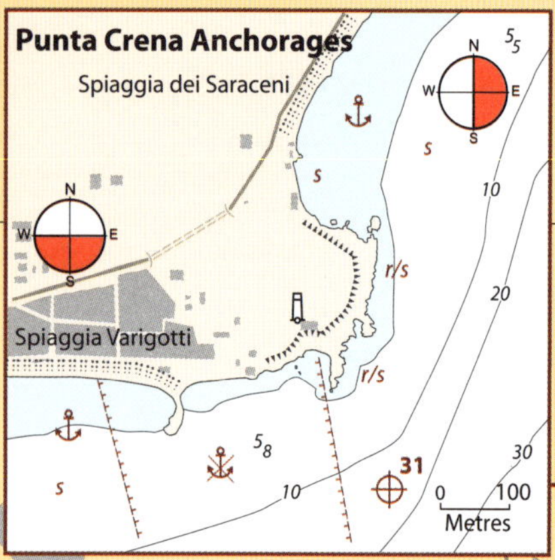

CHART 9 — AREA A — LIGURIA WEST COAST FROM LOANO TO CAPO NOLI

Punta Crena Anchorages ⊕ 31 44°10'.53N 008°24'.33E

Spiaggia Varigotti - S anchorages In settled and calm weather, anchor off the beach in 5-7m on sand. Although the anchorage is very open to the sea, it provides reasonable shelter from northerlies.

Spiaggia dei Saraceni - N anchorages In settled and calm weather, it is possible to anchor off the beach in 4-6m on sand. The beach is always packed.

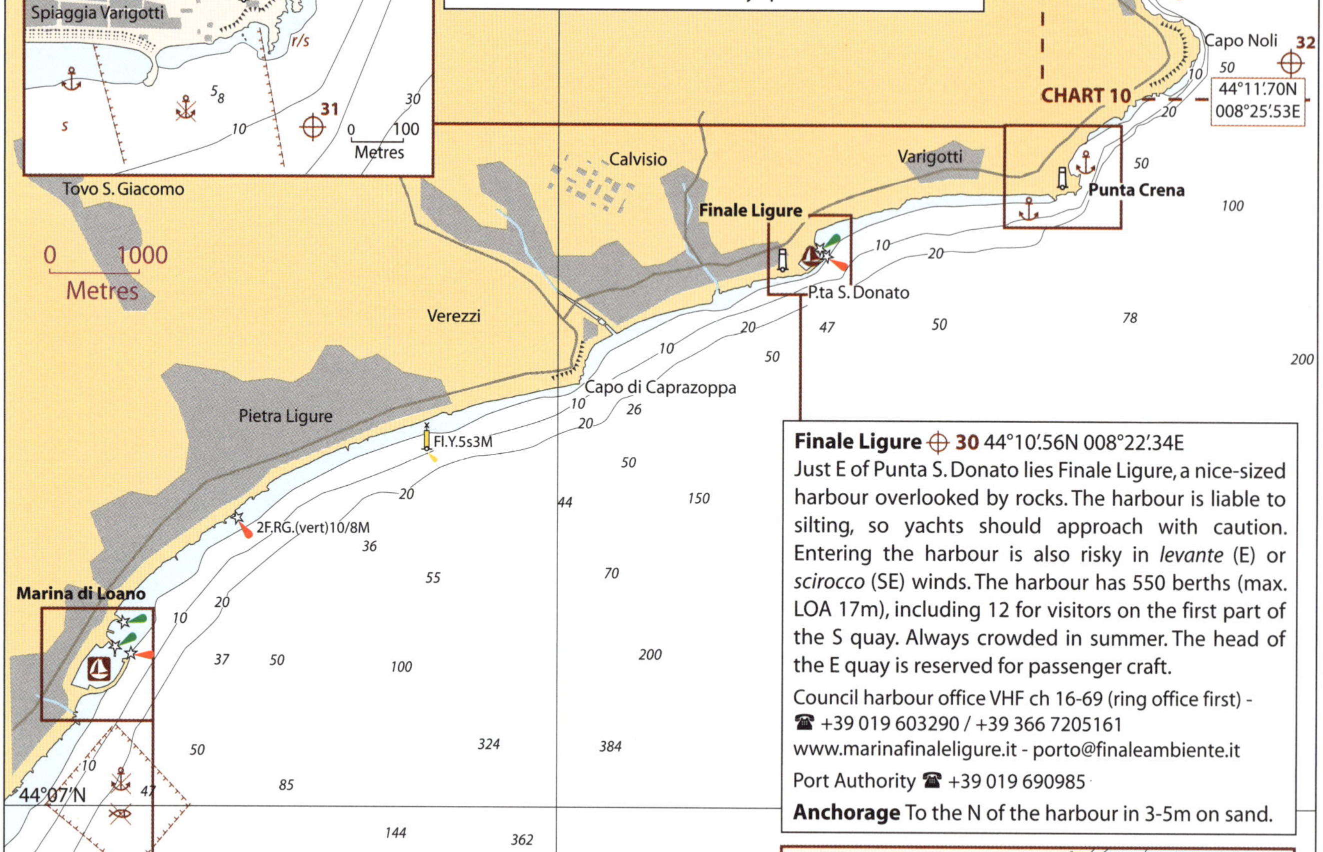

Finale Ligure ⊕ 30 44°10'.56N 008°22'.34E

Just E of Punta S. Donato lies Finale Ligure, a nice-sized harbour overlooked by rocks. The harbour is liable to silting, so yachts should approach with caution. Entering the harbour is also risky in *levante* (E) or *scirocco* (SE) winds. The harbour has 550 berths (max. LOA 17m), including 12 for visitors on the first part of the S quay. Always crowded in summer. The head of the E quay is reserved for passenger craft.

Council harbour office VHF ch 16-69 (ring office first) - ☎ +39 019 603290 / +39 366 7205161
www.marinafinaleligure.it - porto@finaleambiente.it
Port Authority ☎ +39 019 690985

Anchorage To the N of the harbour in 3-5m on sand.

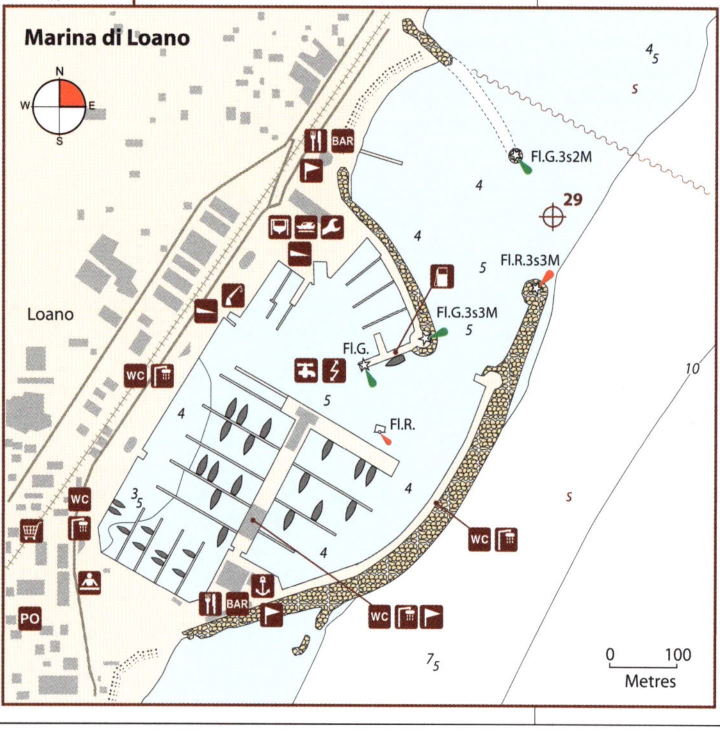

Marina di Loano ⊕ 29 44°08'.15N 008°16'.30E

As it stands just one hour away from Genoa airport, this large marina is invariably busy. Before mooring, contact the harbour authority and follow the staff's instructions. The harbour affords good all-round shelter and has 855 berths (max. LOA 77m), including 100 for visitors.

Marina di Loano VHF ch 09 - ☎ +39 019 675445
info@marinadiloano.it - www.marinadiloano.it
Port Authority VHF ch 16 - ☎ +39 019 666131

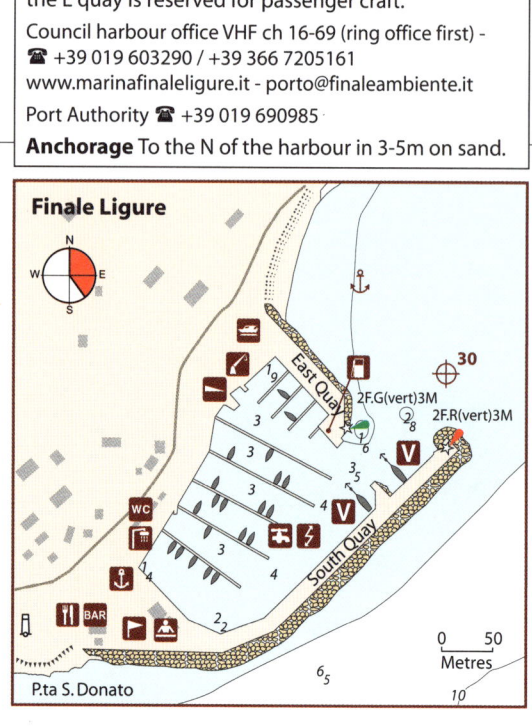

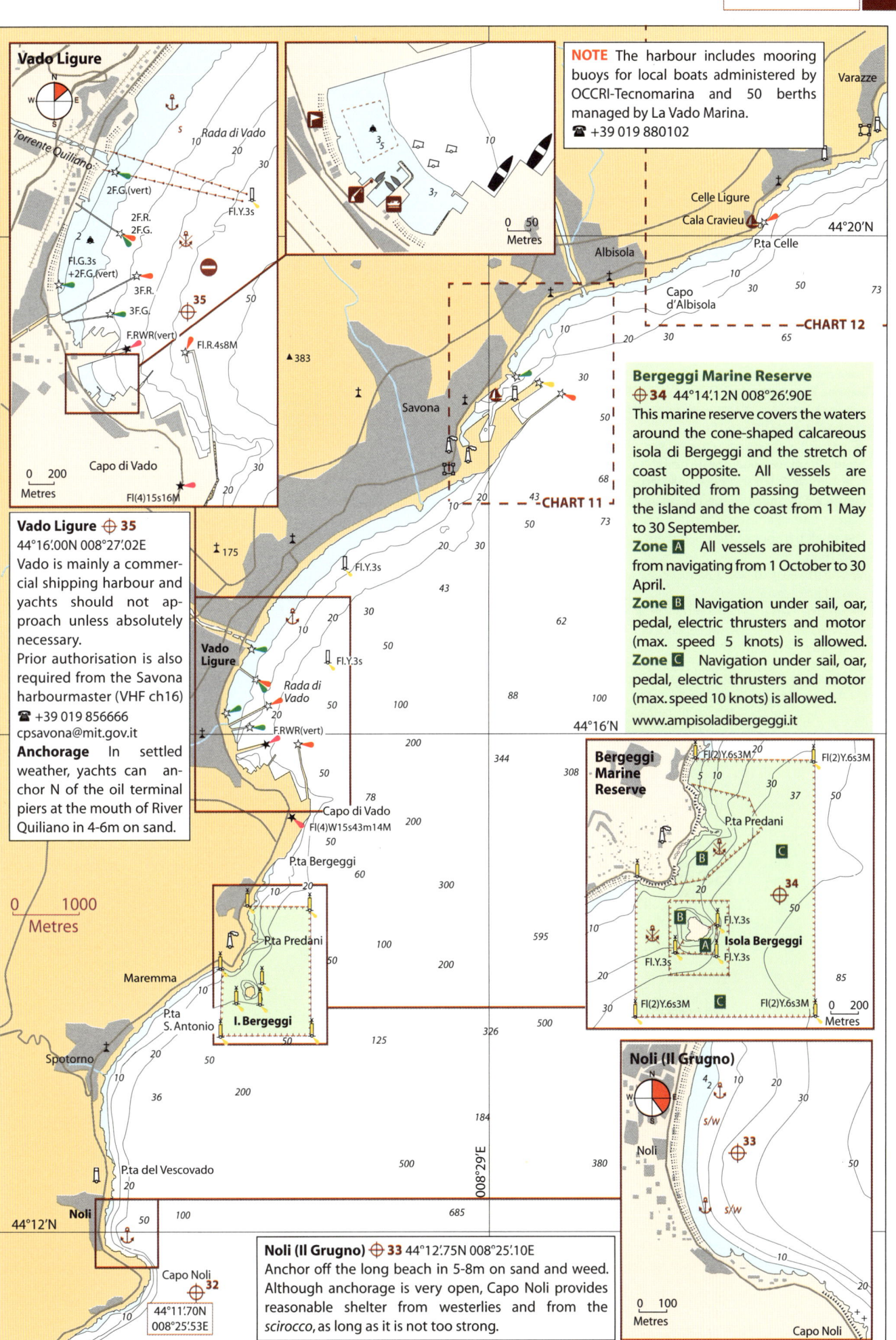

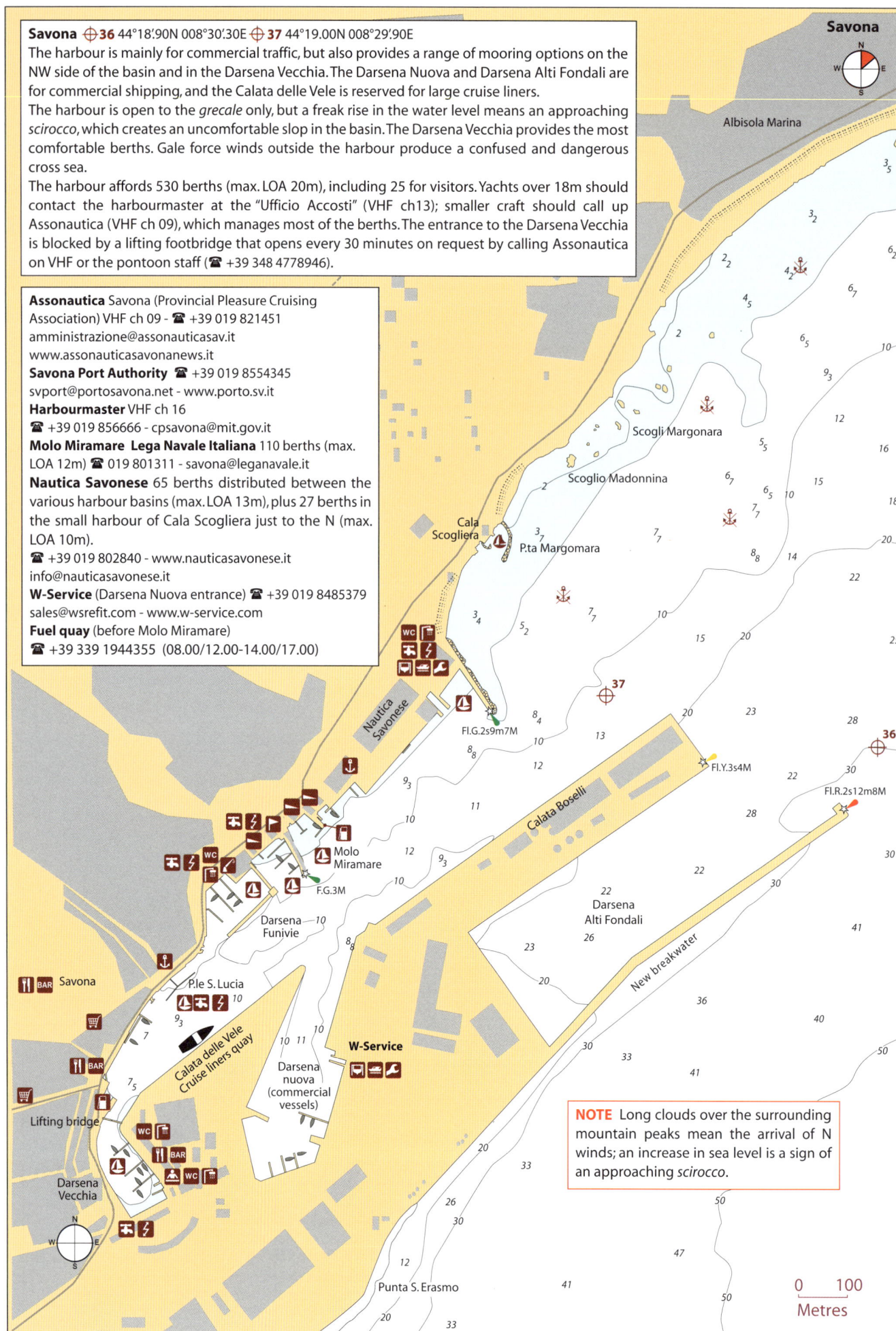

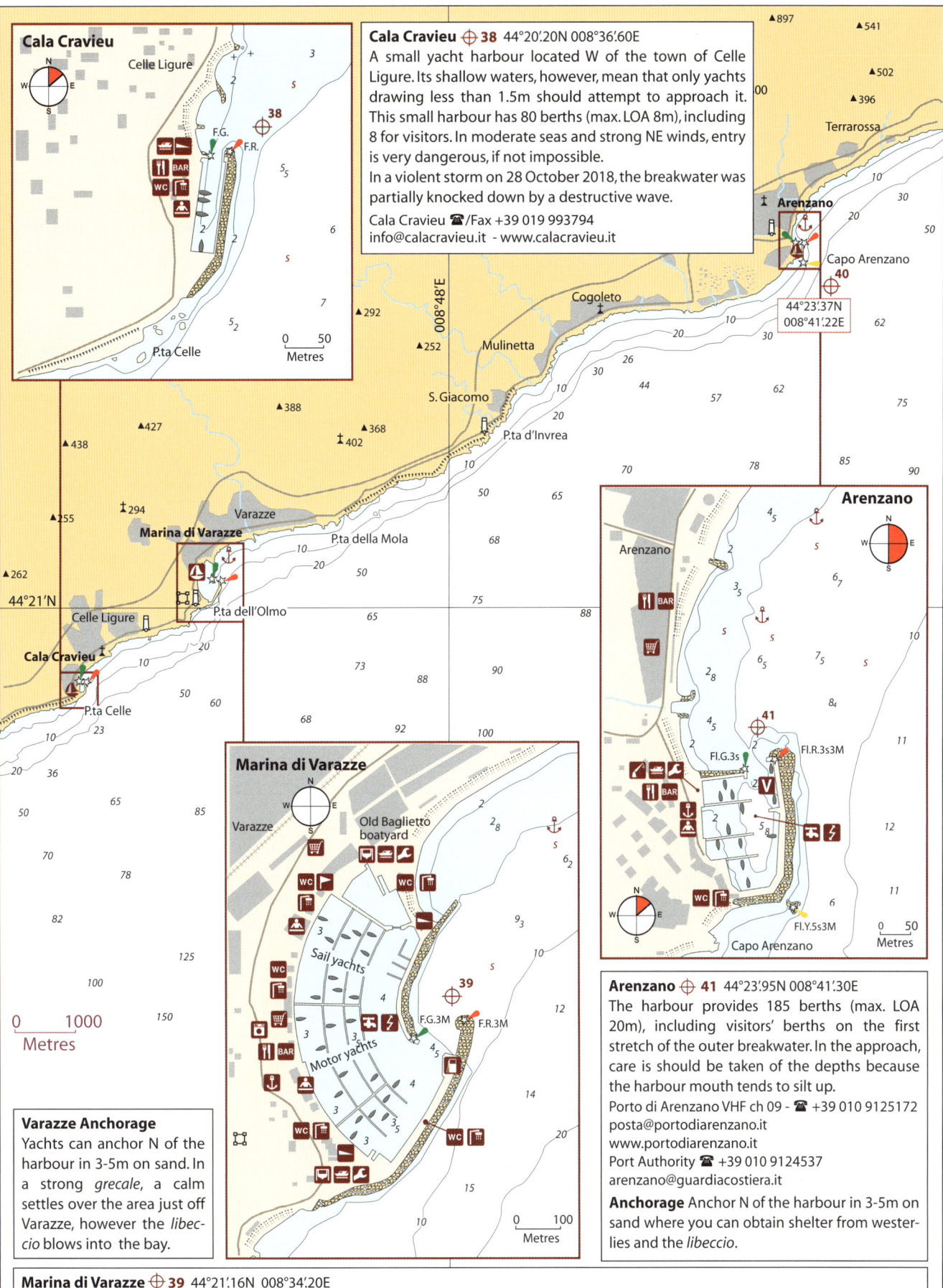

CHART 13 — AREA A — LIGURIA WEST COAST — GENOVA - VOLTRI

Genova ⊕ **44** 44°24'.43N 008°48'.46E ⊕ **45** 44°23'.19N 008°56'.34E

The city of Genoa is one of Italy's and Europe's main ports. This port stretches along 8M of coast, behind which lies Genoa itself. The city runs from Voltri to Nervi and is an uninterrupted expanse of tightly packed buildings. Its ports are split into two blocks: to the W lie the Voltri container terminal and the Sestri Ponente basin; while to the E is a commercial shipping area close to the city's lighthouse Faro della Lanterna, the Porto Antico (Old Port) and the Marina Fiera di Genova. The airport is easily identified when approaching from the W. From the SE, the pavilions of the Genoa Exhibition Centre (Fiera di Genova) and the Lanterna lighthouse will be seen.

Due to heavy commercial traffic, the port must be approached with caution and right of way given to ships entering or leaving. Moderate seas and strong winds at both entrances (⊕ 44 and 45) produce a high, confused reflected swell.

NOTE When the mountain peaks between Genoa and Voltri are shrouded in thick stratus clouds, strong northerly winds are probably on the way. Freak rises in port water-levels mean that bad weather with southerlies is brewing offshore; the wind is almost always a *scirocco*.

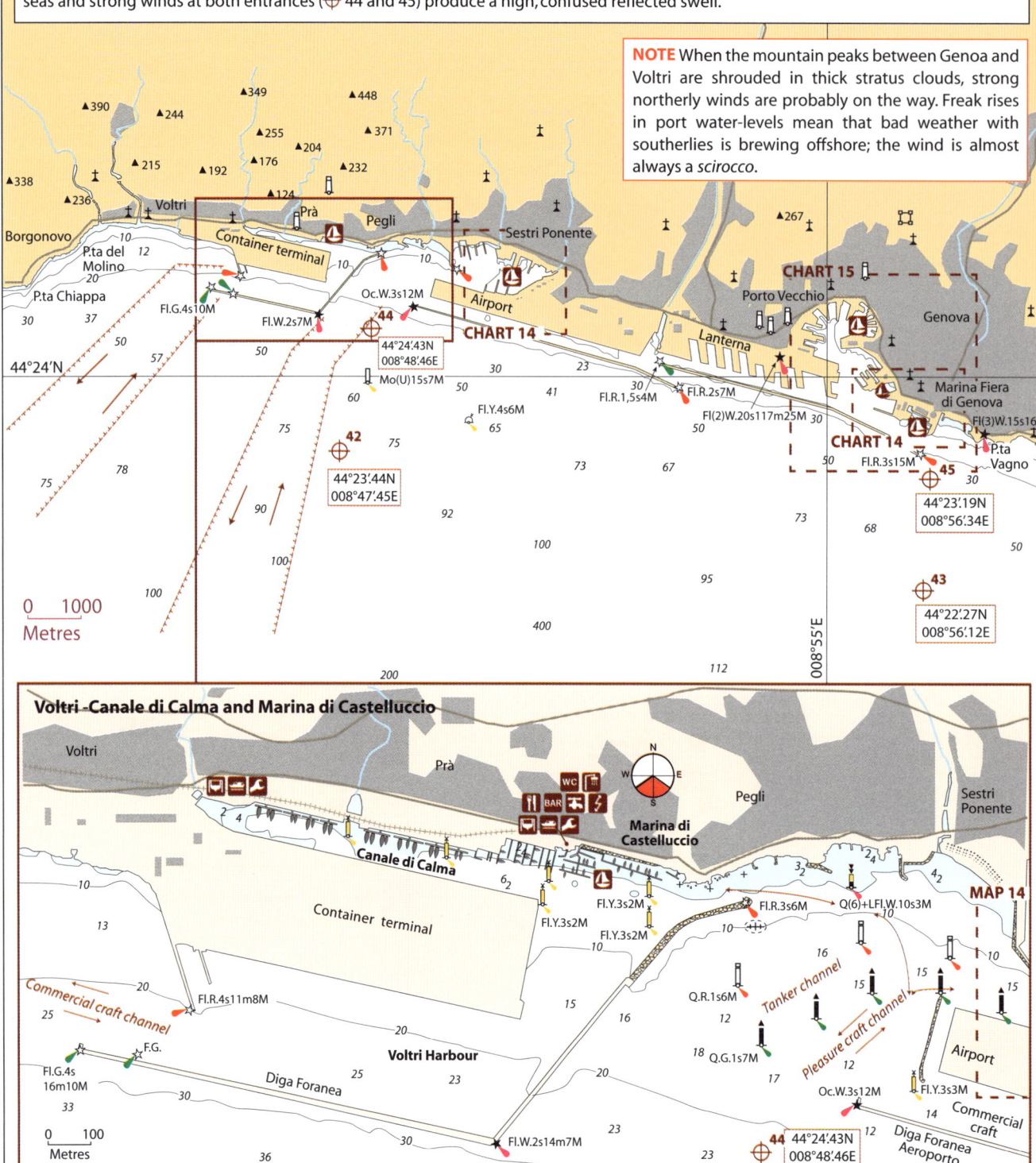

Voltri-Canale di Calma and Marina di Castelluccio ⊕ **44** 44°24'.43N 008°48'.46E

At the most westerly point of Genoa sits the city's new commercial port; consequently, the vast majority of traffic is commercial. The N side of Canale di Calma provides more than 1000 berths for local pleasure craft. They are administered by local clubs and associations. Castelluccio has a marina with a capacity of 530 berths (LOA 15m) on pontoons with some berths reserved for visitors. As pleasure craft are not allowed to use the commercial entrance, take the Sestri Ponente entrance (⊕ 44) to reach Canale di Calma. Proceed parallel to the breakwater that separates Sestri from Voltri, keeping to the starboard, and turn left to head towards the marina first and then Canale di Calma.

Marina di Castelluccio ☎ +39 010 6121111 - castelluccio@fastwebnet.it - www.bagnicastelluccio.com

LIGURIA WEST COAST GENOVA — AREA A — CHART 14

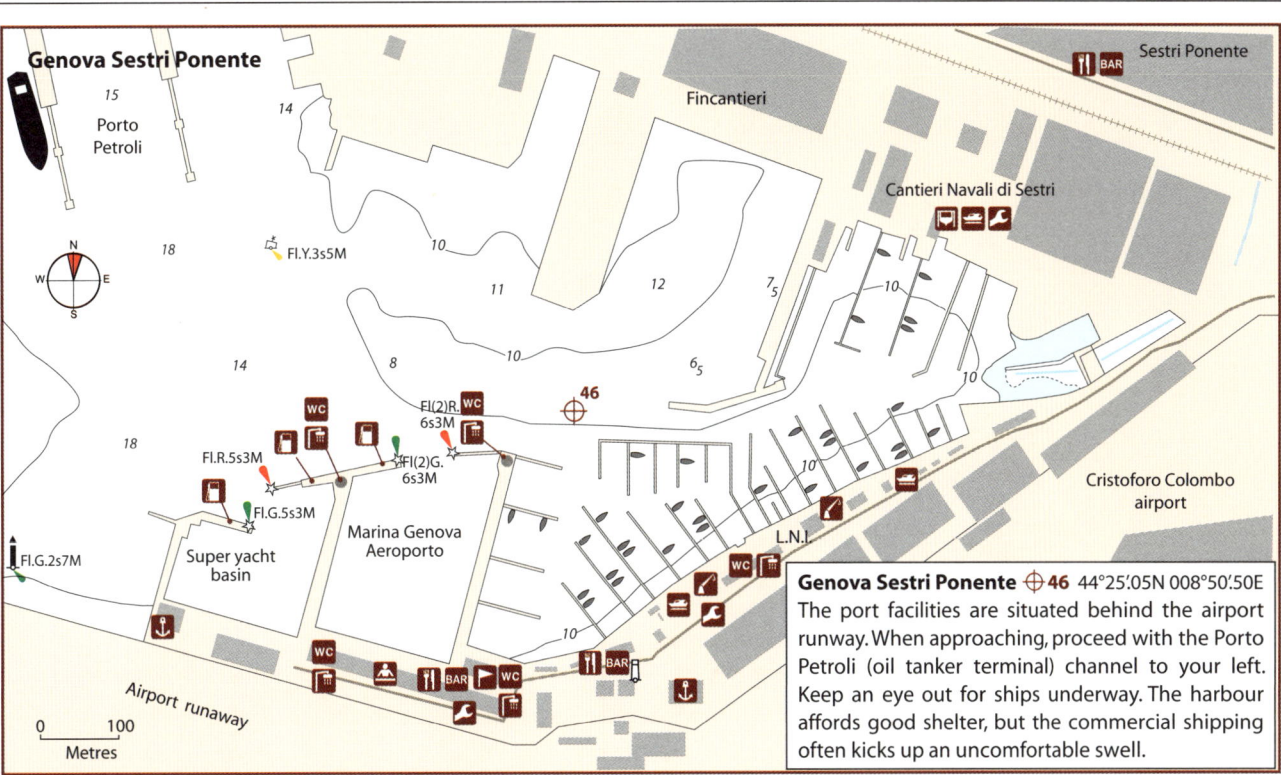

Genova Sestri Ponente ⊕ 46 44°25'.05N 008°50'.50E
The port facilities are situated behind the airport runway. When approaching, proceed with the Porto Petroli (oil tanker terminal) channel to your left. Keep an eye out for ships underway. The harbour affords good shelter, but the commercial shipping often kicks up an uncomfortable swell.

Marina Genova Aeroporto 500 berths (max. LOA 130m) - VHF ch 71 - ☎ +39 010 6143420 - info@marinagenova.it - www.marinagenova.it
Lega Navale Italiana Sez. Genova Sestri Ponente 476 berths (max. LOA 15m) - VHF ch 67 - ☎ +39 010 6512654 - genovasestri@leganavale.it - www.lni-genovasestri.it
Cantieri Navali di Sestri 150 berths (max. LOA 45m) - VHF ch 69 - ☎ +39 010 6512476 - info@cantierisestri.it - www.cantierisestri.it
Port Authority VHF ch16 - ☎ +39 010 27771 - genova@guardiacostiera.it

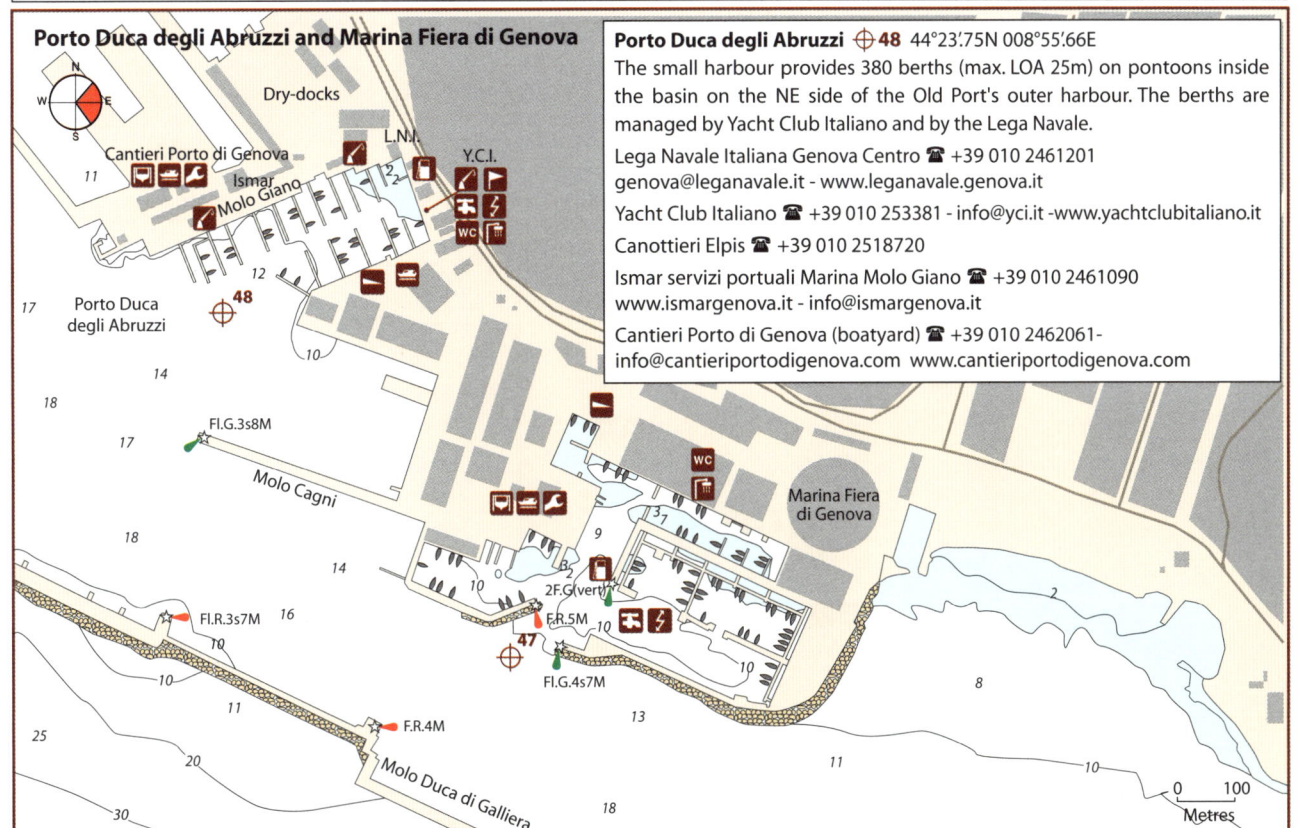

Porto Duca degli Abruzzi ⊕ 48 44°23'.75N 008°55'.66E
The small harbour provides 380 berths (max. LOA 25m) on pontoons inside the basin on the NE side of the Old Port's outer harbour. The berths are managed by Yacht Club Italiano and by the Lega Navale.
Lega Navale Italiana Genova Centro ☎ +39 010 2461201 genova@leganavale.it - www.leganavale.genova.it
Yacht Club Italiano ☎ +39 010 253381 - info@yci.it - www.yachtclubitaliano.it
Canottieri Elpis ☎ +39 010 2518720
Ismar servizi portuali Marina Molo Giano ☎ +39 010 2461090 www.ismargenova.it - info@ismargenova.it
Cantieri Porto di Genova (boatyard) ☎ +39 010 2462061- info@cantieriportodigenova.com www.cantieriportodigenova.com

Marina Fiera di Genova ⊕ 47 44°23'.65N 008°56'.16E
In September, the basin plays host to Genoa's annual international boat show, but provides 305 berths (max. LOA 25m) for the rest of the year. It takes one month to set up and take down the exhibition, and during this time craft are transferred to the commercial harbour.
VHF ch 74 - ☎ +39 010 594200 - www.fiera.ge.it - porto@marina-service.it - marina.service@libero.it Fuel ☎ +39 010 261252

AREA B - LIGURIA RIVIERA DI LEVANTE (EAST COAST)

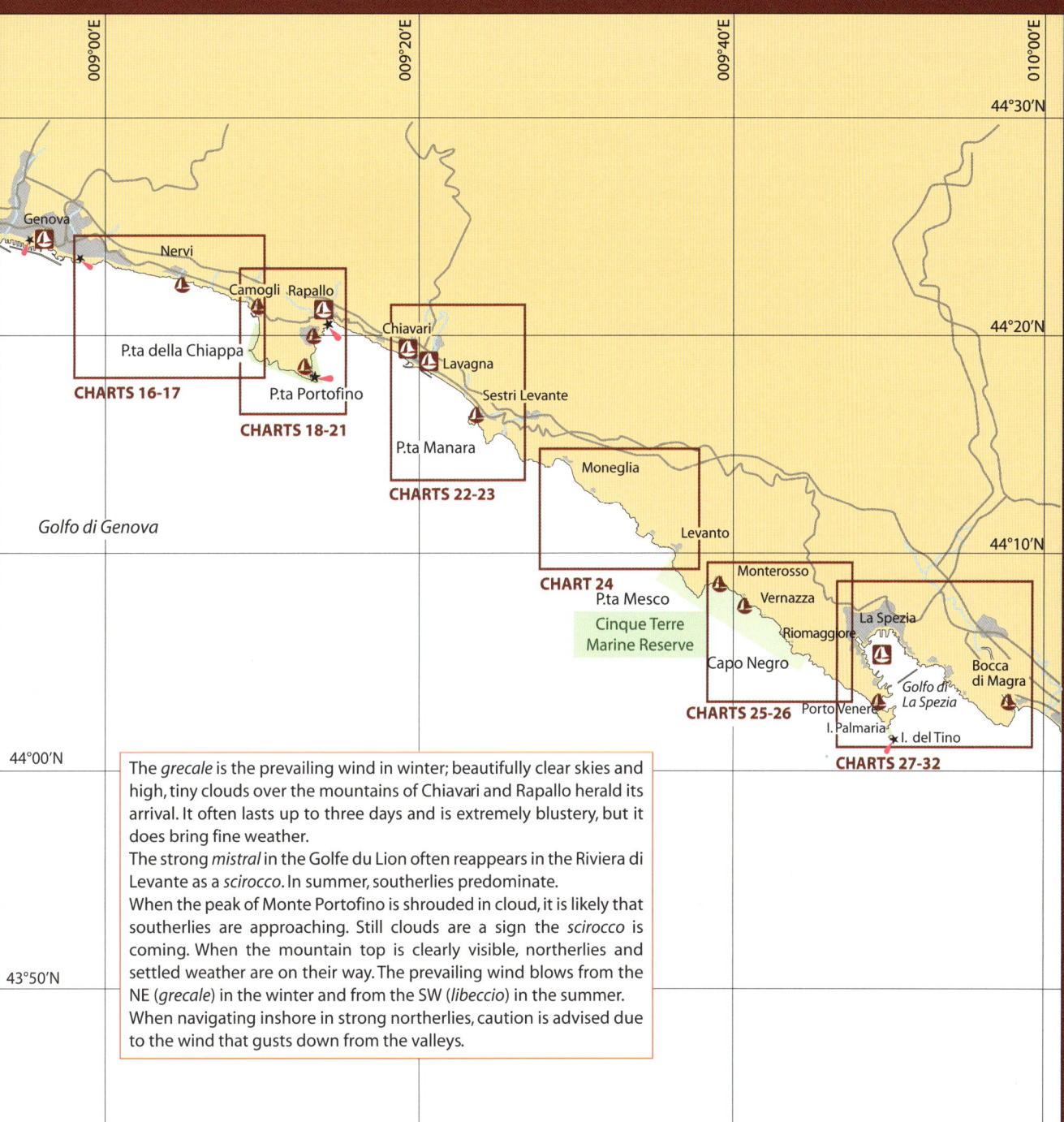

The *grecale* is the prevailing wind in winter; beautifully clear skies and high, tiny clouds over the mountains of Chiavari and Rapallo herald its arrival. It often lasts up to three days and is extremely blustery, but it does bring fine weather.
The strong *mistral* in the Golfe du Lion often reappears in the Riviera di Levante as a *scirocco*. In summer, southerlies predominate.
When the peak of Monte Portofino is shrouded in cloud, it is likely that southerlies are approaching. Still clouds are a sign the *scirocco* is coming. When the mountain top is clearly visible, northerlies and settled weather are on their way. The prevailing wind blows from the NE (*grecale*) in the winter and from the SW (*libeccio*) in the summer. When navigating inshore in strong northerlies, caution is advised due to the wind that gusts down from the valleys.

Riviera di Levante

The 130 km of coast between Genoa and La Spezia are rocky, tall and steep with small, deep inlets hemmed in by narrow promontories. The towns lie mainly at the foot of the valleys that descend towards the sea. Many of them are difficult to reach from the land due to the impenetrable nature of the local terrain. The coastline provides a good number of harbours and havens, but finding a spot is a tricky affair in summer as the area is packed with yachts. Most of the harbours have visitors berths on laid moorings tailed to the quay or mooring buoys (unless otherwise shown in the plan). Water and electricity are also available. In high season, they are frequently crowded, especially the ones in Golfo del Tigullio. It is therefore advisable to contact the harbour beforehand to check availability and mooring fees, as they vary each year and according to season. Private and new marinas tend to be the most expensive; municipal (comunale) marinas, those managed by the port authority, or leased to cooperatives, sailing clubs or associations are more affordable. Some municipal harbours or ones run by a harbourmaster, have visitors berths that are free or available for a token fee. However, they are often occupied by local craft or used for other purposes.
Calm days are frequent, although a S-SW breeze does blow in the summer. Usually it doesn't exceed Force 4 and dies down in the evening, making way for a gentle offshore breeze at night. The prevailing winds from autumn to spring are northerly and gales are more frequent. A gale-force *libeccio* is the most fearsome, as its vast fetch generates some of the Mediterranean's largest waves. They break on the Ligurian coast, making navigation and approaching harbours troublesome if not impossible. The most violent gusts occur around La Spezia and the Rapallo promontory. Low pressure in the Gulf of Genoa produces rain and a *tramontana*, which can turn violent; in winter it may even bring snow at low altitudes.

AREA B - LIGURIA RIVIERA DI LEVANTE (EAST COAST)

	COASTAL NAVIGATION WAYPOINTS AND DISTANCES			
⊕	DESCRIPTION	WGS 84 COORDINATES LATITUDE	LONGITUDE	CHART
43	1M off Genova E approaches	44°22'.27N	008°56'.12E	16
60	0.5M SW of Punta Chiappa	44°19'.04N	009°08'.10E	16-18
62	0.5M SE of Punta Portofino	44°17'.30N	009°13'.37E	18-19
74	0.5M S of Punta Manara	44°14'.59N	009°24'.11E	22-23-24
81	1500m S of Punta Mesco	44°07'.14N	009°37'.50E	25
98	500m S of Isolotto del Tinetto	44°01'.20N	009°51'.00E	26-27-29

AREA B - LIGURIA RIVIERA DI LEVANTE (EAST COAST)

HARBOURS AND MARINAS KEY FOR PLAN SYMBOLS

⊕	NOME	LATITUDE	LONGITUDE	CHART	⛵	⚓	⌐	LOA m	V	🅿	m	⚡	⛽	WC	🍴	⚓	🛒	🔧
52	Nervi	44°22'.65N	009°01'.50E	16	•		IU				2							
58	Camogli	44°21'.10N	009°09'.00E	17	•		200	10	•	•	5.5					•		•
63	Portofino	44°18'.05N	009°12'.07E	19	•		220	70	•		10				•	•	•	
66	Santa Margherita Ligure	41°19'.90N	009°13'.15E	20	•		355	60	•	•	8	•	•	•	•	•	•	
69	Rapallo	44°20'.65N	009°14'.15E	21	•	•	900	45	•	•	5.2							
70	Marina Chiavari	44°18'.75N	009°18'.92E	22	•		469	25	•		5	•	•		•	•	•	•
71	Lavagna	44°18'.20N	009°20'.60E	22	•		1400	50	•	•	5	•			•	•	•	•
72	Sestri Levante	44°16'.15N	009°23'.15E	23		•	150	20	•	•	14				•			
80	Levanto	44°10'.15N	009°36'.10E	24		•	60				3	•	•		•			
83	Vernazza	44°08'.16N	009°40'.84E	25		•	IU	12	•		3		•					
92	Portovenere	44°03'.03N	009°50'.24E	28		•	32	50	•		4	•	•					
93	Pontile Ignazio	44°03'.17N	009°50'.34E	28	•		45	25	•		10	•	•					
100	Seno delle Grazie	44°04'.20N	009°50'.60E	30		•	190	70	•		5	•	•		•	•	•	•
101	Marina del Fezzano	44°04'.09N	009°49'.10E	31	•		250	28	•		10	•	•		•	•	•	•
102	Seno di Cadimare	44°05'.05N	009°49'.55E	31	•		IU				4	•	•			•		
103	La Spezia - Porto Mirabello	44°05'.50N	009°49'.90E	31	•		470	100	•	•	6	•	•		•	•	•	•
104	La Spezia - Assonautica De B.	44°06'.15N	009°49'.85E	31	•		660	13	•		6	•	•		•	•	•	•
105	La Spezia - GS Olimpia	44°06'.50N	009°50'.95E	32	•		IU				3					•		
106	Porto Lotti	44°05'.80N	009°51'.45E	32	•		506	130	•	•	8.4	•	•		•	•	•	•
107	Cantieri Navali di La Spezia	44°05'.40N	009°51'.90E	32	•		120	25	•		10	•	•		•	•		•
108	Navalmare	44°05'.05N	009°52'.59E	32	•		160	40	•		8	•	•		•	•	•	•

IU= Information Unavailable

ANCHORAGES KEY FOR PLAN SYMBOLS

⊕	NAME	LATITUDE	LONGITUDE	CHART	🗺	🌿	m	🔲	🍸	🧭	⚓	🔔
51	Sturla	44°23'.25N	009°58'.50E	16	G	s	7	•	B-R-S	E-W	•	
53	S. Ilario	44°22'.25N	009°03'.40E	16	G	s	6	•		E-SW	•	
54	Bogliasco	44°22'.35N	009°03'.55E	16	G	s	5	•	B-R-S	E-W	•	
55	Pieve Ligure	44°22'.30N	009°04'.50E	17	G	s	7	•		SE-W	•	
56	Sori	44°22'.10N	009°08'.30E	17	P	s	5	•	B-R	SE-NW	•	
57	Recco	44°21'.40N	009°08'.50E	17	P	s	6	•	B-R	SE-NW	•	
59	Porto Pidocchio	44°19'.58N	009°08'.83E	18	G	s	10	•		NE-SW	•	
61	San Fruttuoso	44°18'.83N	009°10'.50E	18	E	s	7	•	B-R	S-SW	•	•
64	Golfo di Paraggi	44°18'.16N	009°12'.80E	19	G	s/w	10	•	B-R	E-SE	•	
65	Seno di Paraggi	44°19'.00N	009°12'.55E	19	G	s/w	8	•	B-R	NE-SE	•	
66	S. Margherita Ligure anchorage	44°19'.90N	009°13'.15E	20	G	s/w	5	•	B-R-S	NE-SE	•	
67	Seno di Pagana	44°20'.22N	009°13'.60E	21	G	s/w	6	•	B-R-S	NE-SE	•	
68	Porto San Michele	44°20'.38N	009°13'.65E	21	G	s/w	5	•	B-R-S	NE-SE	•	
51	Rapallo Golfo Marconi	44°20'.65N	009°14'.15E	21	E	m	4	•	B-R-S	SE-S	•	
72	Sestri Levante - Golfo di Ponente	44°16'.15N	009°23'.15E	23	G	s	7	•	B-R-S	W-N	•	•
73	Sestri Levante - Baia del Silenzio	44°15'.98N	009°23'.60E	23	G	s	5	•	B-R-S	S	•	
75	Riva Trigoso	44°15'.22N	009°25'.12E	23	G	s	5	•	B-R-S	SE-SW	•	
76	Moneglia	44°14'.00N	009°29'.10E	24	G	s	5	•	B-R-S	SE-SW	•	
77	Framura/Porto Pidocchio	44°12'.00N	009°33'.35E	24	P	s/r	7	•	B-R	SW-NW	•	
78	Bonassola	44°10'.45N	009°34'.45E	24	G	s	5	•	B-R-S	SE-SW	•	

AREA B - LIGURIA RIVIERA DI LEVANTE (EAST COAST)

	NAME	WGS 84 COORDINATES		CHART	🐟	🌊	⬇ m	🛥	🍷	🧭	⚓	🔔
		LATITUDE	LONGITUDE									
79	Levanto	44°10'.00N	009°36'.10E	24	G	s	5	•	B-R-S	SE-SW	•	
82	Monterosso	44°08'.27N	009°39'.00E	25	P	s	7	•	B-R-S	E-SW	•	
83	Vernazza	44°08'.16N	009°40'.84E	25	P	s/r	7	•	B-R-S	NW-S	•	•
84	Manarola	44°06'.41N	009°43'.50E	26	P	s/w	10	•	B-R-S	SE-NW	•	•
85	Rio Maggiore	44°05'.78N	009°44'.24E	26	P	s/r/w	10	•	B-R-S	SE-NW	•	•
87	Seno di Canneto	44°05'.15N	009°45'.15E	26	G	s	7	•		SE-W	•	•
88	Punta Pineda/Scoglio Ferale	44°04'.45N	009°46'.15E	26	G/P	s/r	7			SE-NW	•	
89	Rocce Rosse/Scoglio Galera	44°03'.75N	009°48'.33E	26	G	s/r	7			SE-NW	•	
94	Baia di Porto Venere	44°03'.25N	009°51'.10E	28	E	s	7	•	B-R-S	NE-SE	•	•
95	Palmaria Cala Fornace	44°02'.80N	009°51'.30E	29	G	s	7			NE-SE	•	
96	Palmaria Cala del Pozzale	44°02'.40N	009°51'.17E	29	G	s/g	7	•	B-R	N-S	•	
97	Isola del Tino	44°01'.45N	009°51'.20E	29	P	s	7			NE-NW		•
100	Seno delle Grazie	44°04'.20N	009°50'.60E	30	E	m	7	•	B-R-S	E	•	
111	Cala Chiappara	44°04'.83N	009°53'.14E	32	G	s	5	•		SE-SW	•	

🐟 **Shelter:** P = Poor G = Good E = Excellent   🌊 **Nature of seabed:** w = weed m = mud g = gravel p = pebbles/stones r = rock s = sand
⬇ **Depths in metres**   🛥 **Landing with dinghy**   🍷 **Facilities ashore:** B = Bar R = Restaurant S = Shop   ⚓ **Anchorage**   🔔 **Mooring buoy**
🧭 **Wind direction and exposure**

SAFETY AT SEA — AREA B

WEATHER BULLETINS

Mari d'Italia/Meteomar bulletin bulletin
(English and Italian)
VHF ch 68 frequency 156.425 MHz continuous

Coast radio station weather bulletin
0135 0735 1335 1935 UTC
Castellaccio (Genova) VHF ch 25
   frequency 161.850 MHz
Zoagli VHF ch 27 frequency 161.950 MHz

Radiouno - Italian bulletin for the sea
0554 1408 2249 Monday-Friday

FRANCE AND CORSICA WEATHER FORECASTS (French-English)

Monaco Radio 4363 kHz (ch 403) 0903 1403 1915 LT
Lyon, Provence, Corsican Sea, Sardinian Sea, Ligurian Sea, Northern Tyrrhenian Sea

Monaco Radio 8728, 8806 kHz (ch 804, 830) SSB
0715 1830 UTC West Mediterranean offshore seas

La Garde CROSS 1696, 2677 kHz SSB after the first call frequency 2182 kHz
0650 1433 1850 LT

HARBOURMASTERS

Genova ☎ +39 010 27771
genova@guardiacostiera.it
VHF ch 16 - MF 2182, 2722kHz

La Spezia ☎ +39 0187 258100
cplaspezia@mit.gov.it

Guardia Costiera (Coast Guard)
☎ 1530 emergency - VHF ch 16

SAFETY AND RESCUE CENTRES

MRSC Genova ☎ +39 010 27771
genova@guardiacostiera.it

MRSC Livorno ☎ +39 0586 826011
cplivorno@guardiacostiera.gov.it

MRCC Roma MMSI 002 470 001
DSC VHF ch 70, 16 - DSC MF 2187.5 kHz, 2182 kHz
DSC HF 420.5, 6312, 8414.5 kHz
Port Authority (Direzione Marittima) Roma Fiumicino
☎ +39 06 656171 - cproma@mit.gov.it

CIRM International Medical Centre
☎ +39 06 559290263 - mobile +39 348 3984229
Fax +39 06 5923331/2
telesoccorso@cirm.it - www.cirm.it

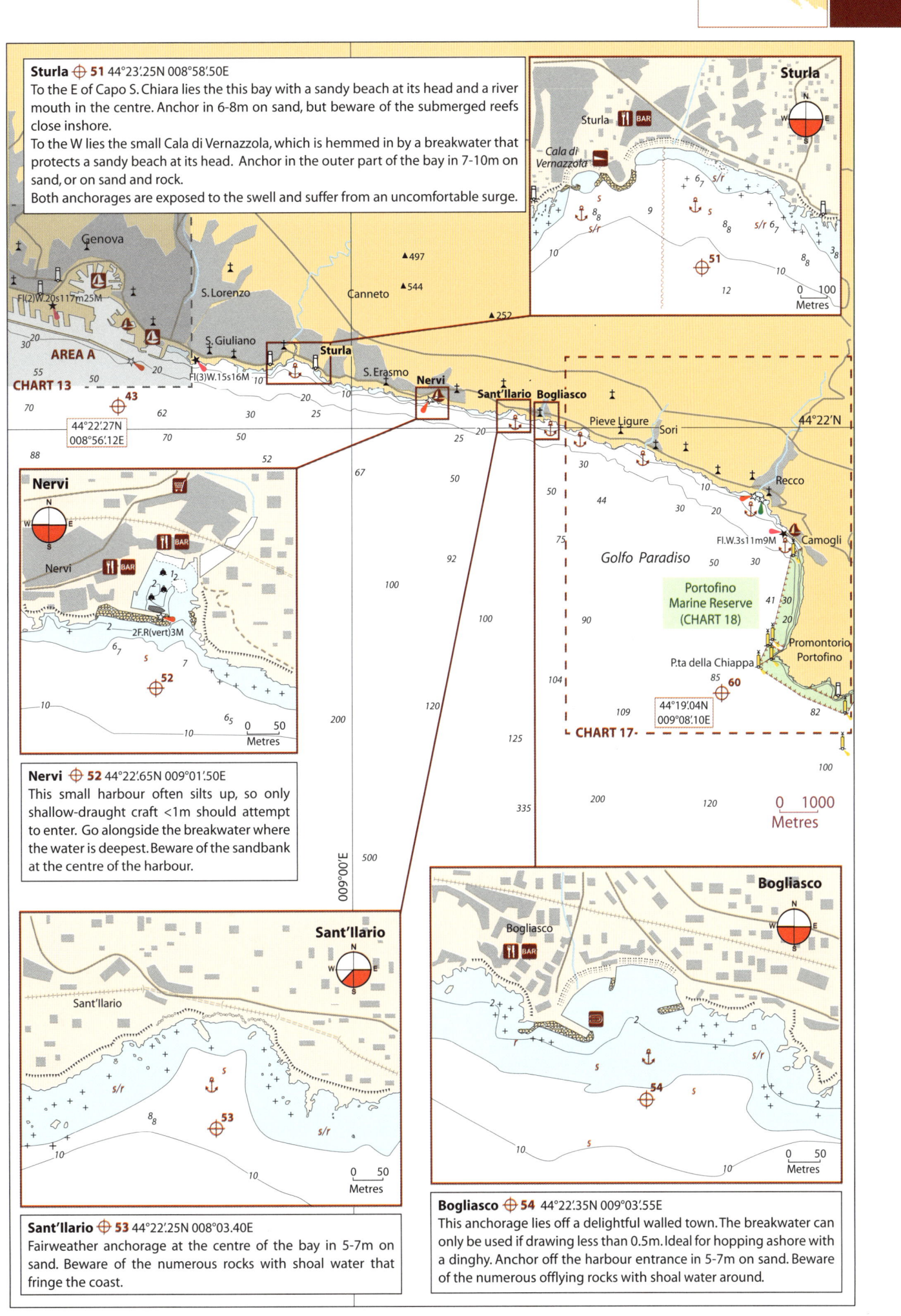

LIGURIA EAST COAST
FROM GENOVA TO BOGLIASCO — AREA B
CHART 16

Sturla ⊕ 51 44°23'.25N 008°58'.50E
To the E of Capo S. Chiara lies the this bay with a sandy beach at its head and a river mouth in the centre. Anchor in 6-8m on sand, but beware of the submerged reefs close inshore.
To the W lies the small Cala di Vernazzola, which is hemmed in by a breakwater that protects a sandy beach at its head. Anchor in the outer part of the bay in 7-10m on sand, or on sand and rock.
Both anchorages are exposed to the swell and suffer from an uncomfortable surge.

Nervi ⊕ 52 44°22'.65N 009°01'.50E
This small harbour often silts up, so only shallow-draught craft <1m should attempt to enter. Go alongside the breakwater where the water is deepest. Beware of the sandbank at the centre of the harbour.

Sant'Ilario ⊕ 53 44°22'.25N 008°03.40E
Fairweather anchorage at the centre of the bay in 5-7m on sand. Beware of the numerous rocks with shoal water that fringe the coast.

Bogliasco ⊕ 54 44°22'.35N 009°03'.55E
This anchorage lies off a delightful walled town. The breakwater can only be used if drawing less than 0.5m. Ideal for hopping ashore with a dinghy. Anchor off the harbour entrance in 5-7m on sand. Beware of the numerous offlying rocks with shoal water around.

39

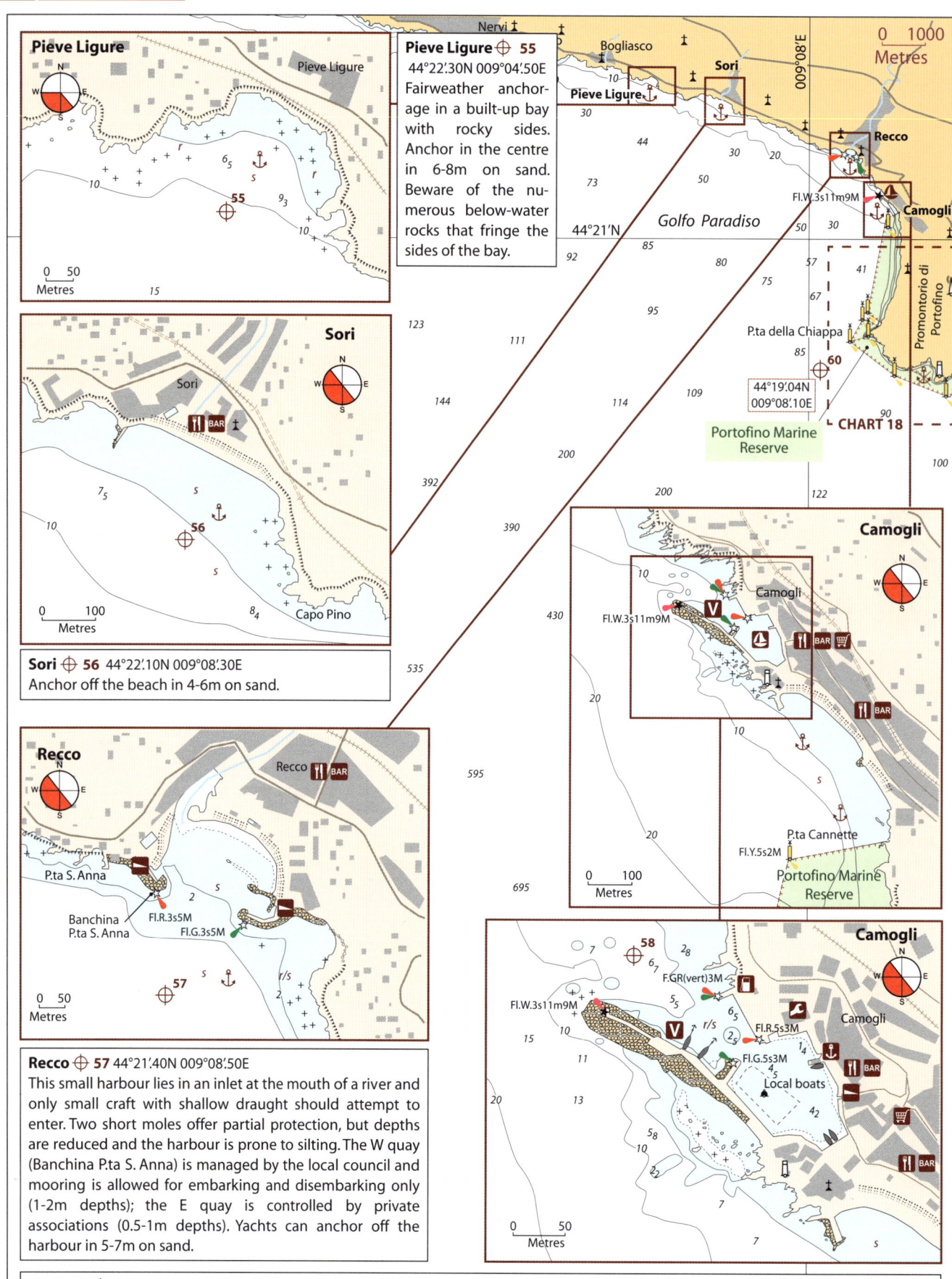

CHART 17 — AREA B
LIGURIA EAST COAST
FROM PIEVE LIGURE TO CAMOGLI

Pieve Ligure ⊕ 55 44°22'.30N 009°04'.50E
Fairweather anchorage in a built-up bay with rocky sides. Anchor in the centre in 6-8m on sand. Beware of the numerous below-water rocks that fringe the sides of the bay.

Sori ⊕ 56 44°22'.10N 009°08'.30E
Anchor off the beach in 4-6m on sand.

Recco ⊕ 57 44°21'.40N 009°08'.50E
This small harbour lies in an inlet at the mouth of a river and only small craft with shallow draught should attempt to enter. Two short moles offer partial protection, but depths are reduced and the harbour is prone to silting. The W quay (Banchina P.ta S. Anna) is managed by the local council and mooring is allowed for embarking and disembarking only (1-2m depths); the E quay is controlled by private associations (0.5-1m depths). Yachts can anchor off the harbour in 5-7m on sand.

Camogli ⊕ 58 44°21'.10N 009°09'.00E
The beautiful small harbour of Camogli has 200 berths (max. LOA 10m), including 5 for visitors in the outer harbour inside the breakwater. It is usually crowded with local and fishing boats, so it can be difficult to find a berth in summer. Contact the Port Authority that manages the berths in advance. Alternatively, anchor at the head of the bay to the S of the harbour in 7-10m on sand. When approaching, keep at least 100m off the end of the breakwater, which is fringed by rocks. With onshore gales, there is a dangerous surge inside the harbour, and in strong winds or southerly gales, entry is impossible.
Port Authority - Calata Porto - VHF ch 16 - ☎ +39 0185 770032 - camogli@guardiacostiera.it

LIGURIA EAST COAST
PROMONTORIO DI PORTOFINO — AREA B

CHART 18

Portofino Marine Reserve

Zone A *Riserva a tutela integrale* (Fully protected Reserve) In this area all activity, except for scientific research, is prohibited.

Zone B *Riserva Generale* (General Reserve) In this area navigation under sail, oar, pedal and electric thrusters is permitted, as is eco-compatible motor navigation (yachts with holding tank; engines must comply with Directive 2003/44/EC). Access is also permitted to craft using zero-emissions antifouling paints. Motor yachts not complying with these eco-requirements are allowed into the S. Fruttuoso mooring areas only ( ). Set a 90° course to the coast and navigate below 5 knots. Anchoring is prohibited, but mooring is allowed on the buoys set up by the reserve authorities. Diving is also permitted, but must be authorised by the reserve authority.

Zone C *Riserva Parziale* (Partial Reserve) In this area the rules for Zone B apply, but diving is allowed and anchoring is permitted at a minimum of 100m off the coast, except where marked off by buoys and no anchoring signs.

☎ +39 0185 289649 - info@portofinoamp.it - www.portofinoamp.it

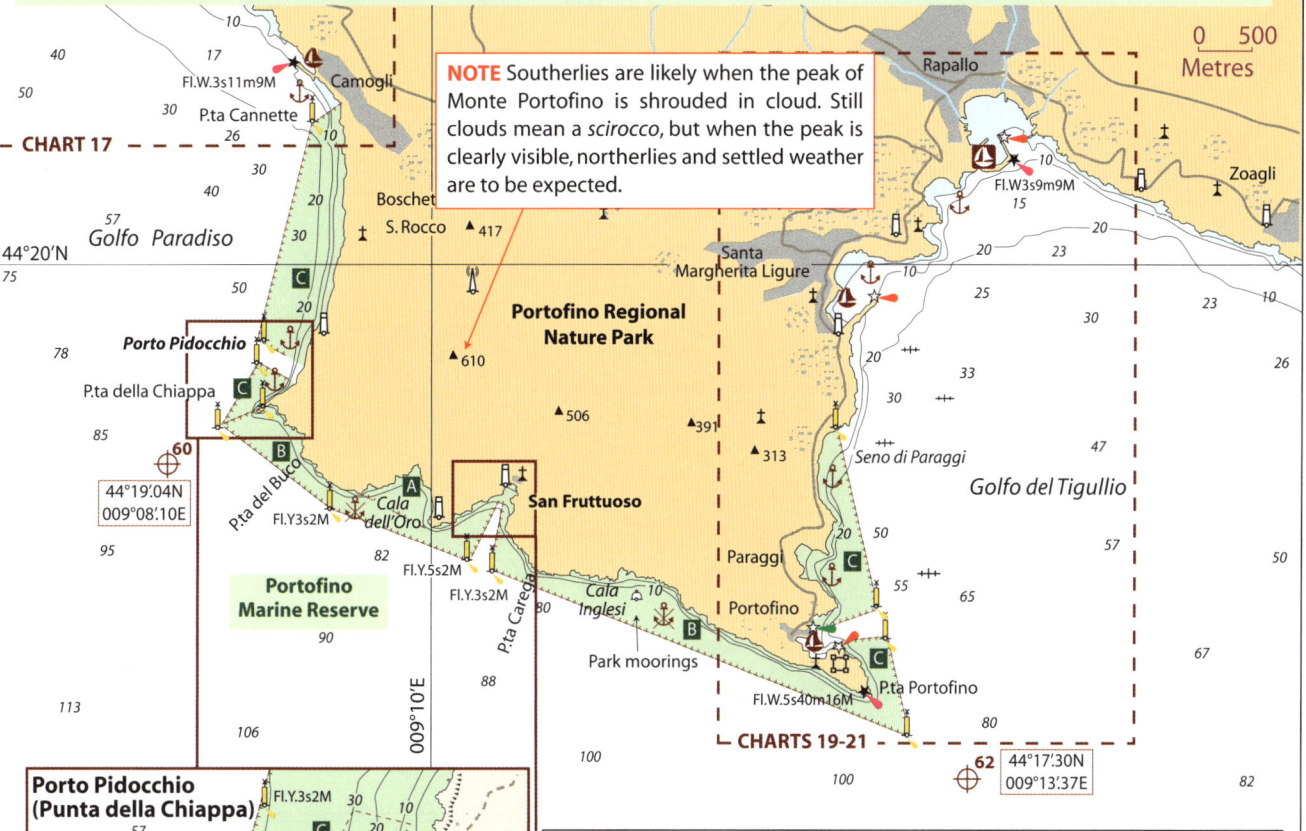

NOTE Southerlies are likely when the peak of Monte Portofino is shrouded in cloud. Still clouds mean a *scirocco*, but when the peak is clearly visible, northerlies and settled weather are to be expected.

Porto Pidocchio (Punta della Chiappa) ⊕ 59 44°19.58N 009°08.83E

Anchor N of Punta della Chiappa in Zone C of the Portofino AMP a minimum of 100m from the coast. Anchor in 7-15m on sand well off the moorings administered by Mar.Li.N.S (☎ +39 334 2549868). There is a small landing stage reserved for the authority's vessels. The only way to reach the harbour by land is through the Portofino Regional Nature Park.

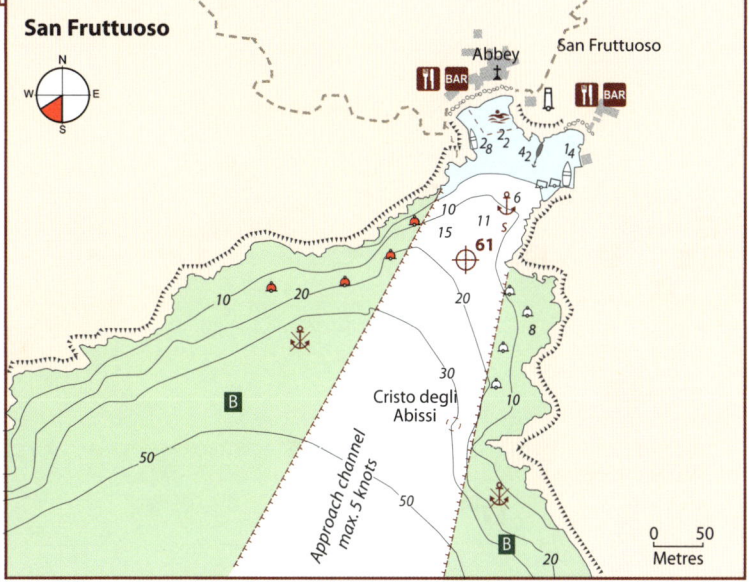

San Fruttuoso ⊕ 61 44°18.83N 009°10.50E

The inlet of San Fruttuoso provides good shelter, except from strong southerlies or a SW swell. Approach by the channel that cuts through the reserve. In season, 22 white moorings are laid on the E side (max. LOA 7.5m) and 15 red moorings on the W side (max. LOA 24m). Alternatively, anchor outside Zone B in 5-15m on sand. The quays are reserved for the tripper boats that drop off and collect day tourists who arrive by sea from the surrounding area. *Cristo degli Abissi* is a submerged statue of Christ.

Harbour attendants: Ormeggiatori Consorzio S. Fruttuoso
☎ +39 333 4352502 - www.consorziosanfruttuoso.it

41

CHART 19

AREA B — LIGURIA EAST COAST
PORTOFINO

Seno di Paraggi ⊕ 65
44°19'.00N 009°12'.55E
To the N of Punta della Cervara lies Seno di Paraggi, a large bay that affords protection from westerlies only. It is part of Zone C. Anchor where convenient in 8-15m on sand, or on sand and weed. The SW corner of the bay provides the best protection, despite the depths increasing more rapidly here.

Golfo di Paraggi ⊕ 64   44°18'.16N 009°12'.80E
In settled weather, it provides an alternative anchorage to Portofino, which is just a short dinghy-ride away. During summer, the swimming area takes up most of the bay, so yachts are obliged to anchor in 9-15m on sand, or on sand and weed.

Portofino ⊕ 63   44°18'.05N 009°12'.07E
The bay, which bites into the E side of the Portofino promontory, is open to the NE, and easterlies will push in an uncomfortable swell. The quayed area provides 220 berths, the vast majority on moorings. There are also 6 visitors berths, but these are almost always full. In summer, it is virtually impossible to find a place, and yachts over 16m should contact the harbour authority in advance. Baia Cannone, just N of the mouth of Baia di Portofino, has two berths for yachts up to 70m.
Port Authority VHF ch 16 - ☎ +39 0185 269040
portofino@guardiacostiera.it
Marina di Portofino 16 berths (max. LOA 70m) - VHF ch 12
☎ +39 0185 269580 - info@marinadiportofino.com
www.marinadiportofino.com
Ormeggiatori (Harbour attendants) ☎ +39 0185 269388
Anchorage In settled weather, anchor to the N of the harbour entrance as far as Seno Canne in 10-20m on sand and weed. Heavy yacht and tripper-boat traffic cause a disturbance.

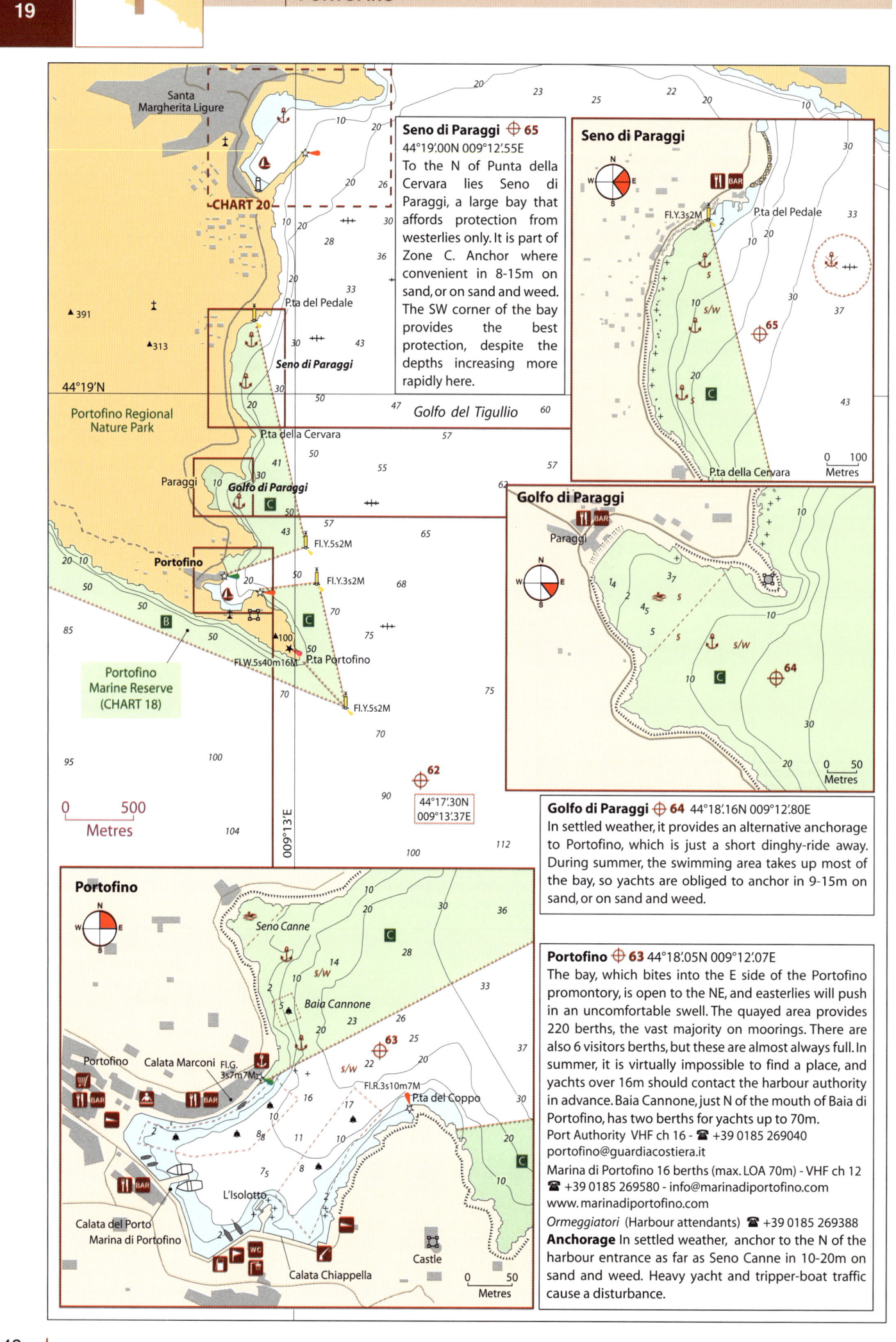

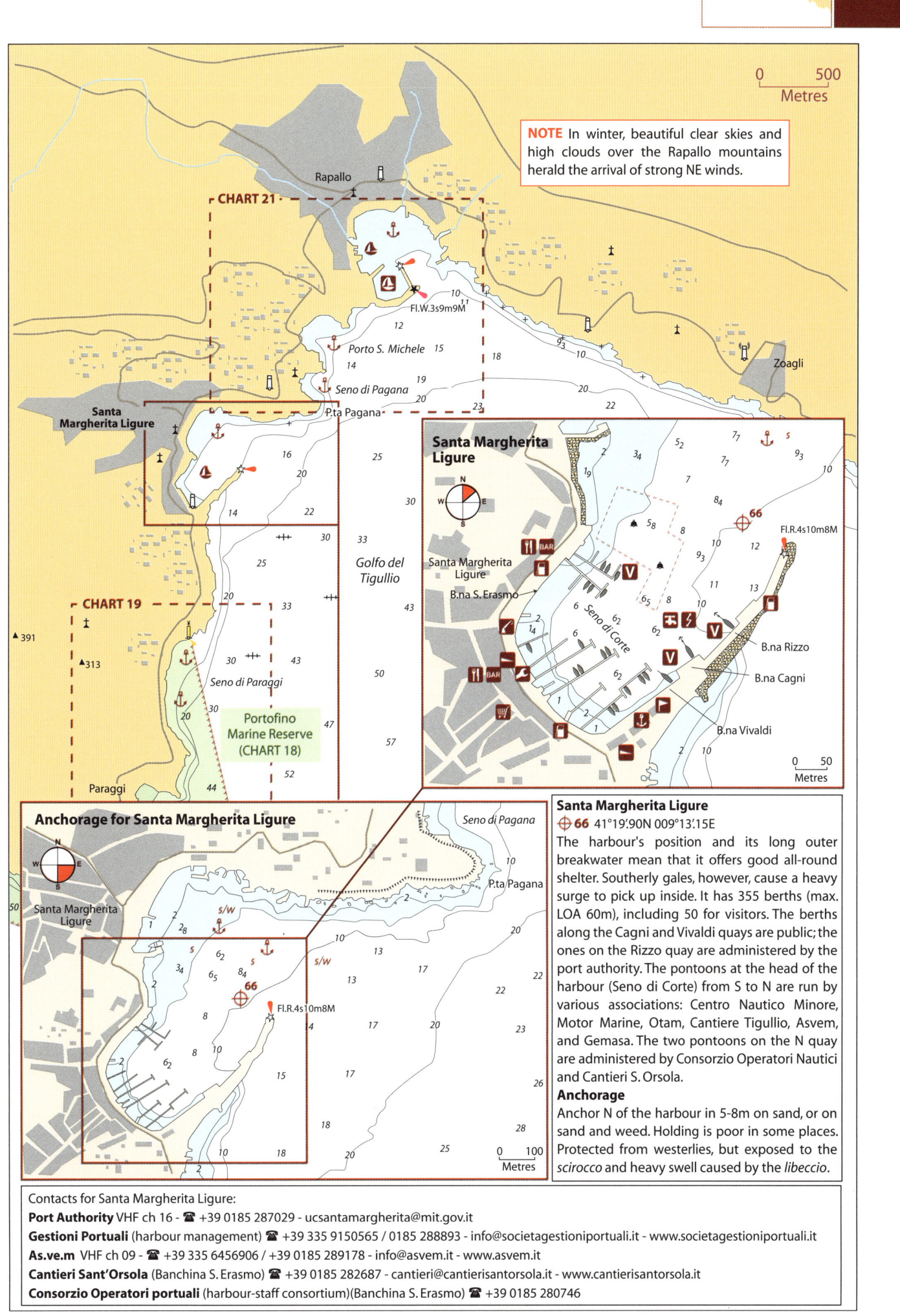

LIGURIA EAST COAST
SANTA MARGHERITA LIGURE — AREA B
CHART 20

NOTE In winter, beautiful clear skies and high clouds over the Rapallo mountains herald the arrival of strong NE winds.

Santa Margherita Ligure
⊕ **66** 41°19'.90N 009°13'.15E

The harbour's position and its long outer breakwater mean that it offers good all-round shelter. Southerly gales, however, cause a heavy surge to pick up inside. It has 355 berths (max. LOA 60m), including 50 for visitors. The berths along the Cagni and Vivaldi quays are public; the ones on the Rizzo quay are administered by the port authority. The pontoons at the head of the harbour (Seno di Corte) from S to N are run by various associations: Centro Nautico Minore, Motor Marine, Otam, Cantiere Tigullio, Asvem, and Gemasa. The two pontoons on the N quay are administered by Consorzio Operatori Nautici and Cantieri S. Orsola.

Anchorage
Anchor N of the harbour in 5-8m on sand, or on sand and weed. Holding is poor in some places. Protected from westerlies, but exposed to the *scirocco* and heavy swell caused by the *libeccio*.

Contacts for Santa Margherita Ligure:

Port Authority VHF ch 16 - ☎ +39 0185 287029 - ucsantamargherita@mit.gov.it
Gestioni Portuali (harbour management) ☎ +39 335 9150565 / 0185 288893 - info@societagestioniportuali.it - www.societagestioniportuali.it
As.ve.m VHF ch 09 - ☎ +39 335 6456906 / +39 0185 289178 - info@asvem.it - www.asvem.it
Cantieri Sant'Orsola (Banchina S. Erasmo) ☎ +39 0185 282687 - cantieri@cantierisantorsola.it - www.cantierisantorsola.it
Consorzio Operatori portuali (harbour-staff consortium)(Banchina S. Erasmo) ☎ +39 0185 280746

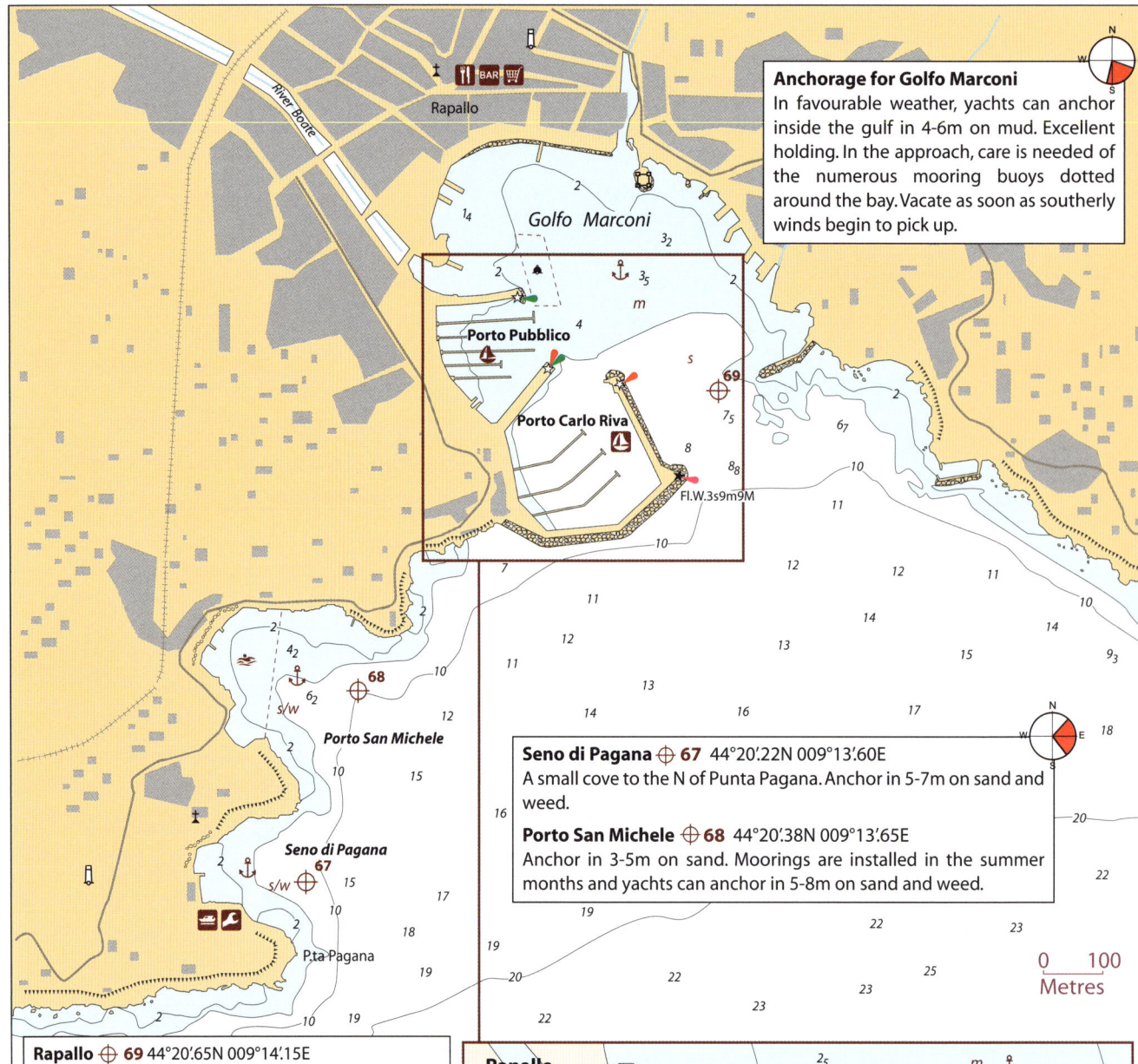

CHART 21

AREA B — LIGURIA EAST COAST
RAPALLO

Anchorage for Golfo Marconi
In favourable weather, yachts can anchor inside the gulf in 4-6m on mud. Excellent holding. In the approach, care is needed of the numerous mooring buoys dotted around the bay. Vacate as soon as southerly winds begin to pick up.

Seno di Pagana ⊕ 67 44°20'.22N 009°13'.60E
A small cove to the N of Punta Pagana. Anchor in 5-7m on sand and weed.

Porto San Michele ⊕ 68 44°20'.38N 009°13'.65E
Anchor in 3-5m on sand. Moorings are installed in the summer months and yachts can anchor in 5-8m on sand and weed.

Rapallo ⊕ 69 44°20'.65N 009°14'.15E
This harbour lies on the W shore of Golfo Marconi, just S of the mouth of the River Boate. It is divided into two by a long concrete inner breakwater (Molo Langano). To the N stands the Porto Pubblico with its 500 berths (max. LOA 25m), including 25 for visitors, and to the S is the Porto Carlo Riva marina with 400 berths (max. LOA 45m) and comprehensive facilities. From May to November, a small area with 6 mooring buoys (max. LOA 12m) for visitors is set up to the N of the Porto Pubblico entrance (free-of-charge for up to 48 hours).
Both harbours are crowded in summer and finding a berth is problematic.
During a violent storm on 28/10/2018, the Porto Carlo Riva outer breakwater was completely wiped out by a wave, causing enormous damage to the yachts berthed inside. At the moment (January 2019), the harbour is closed off.

Porto Pubblico
Harbourmaster VHF ch 16 - ☎ +39 0185 50583
Lega Navale Italiana ☎ +39 0185 55253
Circolo Nautico Rapallo ☎ +39 0185 51281
Consorzio Nautica da Diporto ☎ +39 0185 53345

Porto Carlo Riva
VHF ch 09 - ☎ +39 0185 6891- info@portocarloriva.it
www.portocarloriva.it

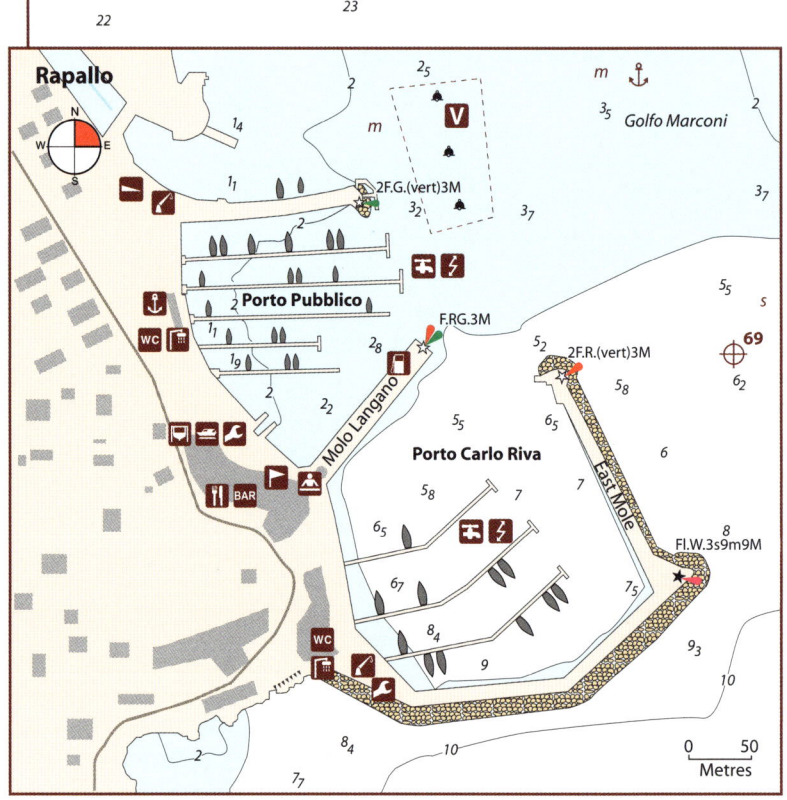

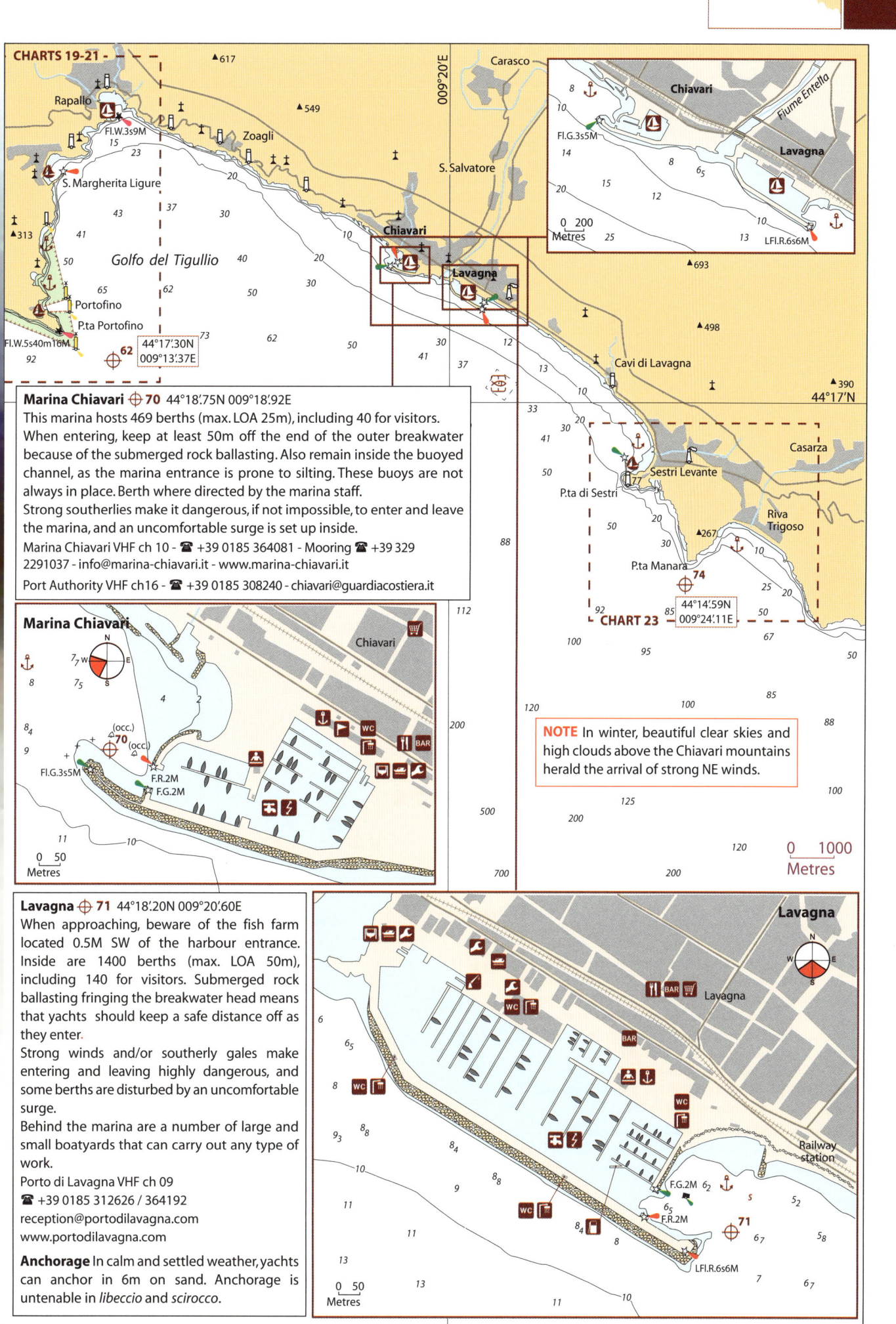

LIGURIA EAST COAST
CHIAVARI AND LAVAGNA
AREA B — **CHART 22**

Marina Chiavari ⊕ 70 44°18′.75N 009°18′.92E
This marina hosts 469 berths (max. LOA 25m), including 40 for visitors. When entering, keep at least 50m off the end of the outer breakwater because of the submerged rock ballasting. Also remain inside the buoyed channel, as the marina entrance is prone to silting. These buoys are not always in place. Berth where directed by the marina staff.
Strong southerlies make it dangerous, if not impossible, to enter and leave the marina, and an uncomfortable surge is set up inside.
Marina Chiavari VHF ch 10 - ☎ +39 0185 364081 - Mooring ☎ +39 329 2291037 - info@marina-chiavari.it - www.marina-chiavari.it
Port Authority VHF ch16 - ☎ +39 0185 308240 - chiavari@guardiacostiera.it

NOTE In winter, beautiful clear skies and high clouds above the Chiavari mountains herald the arrival of strong NE winds.

Lavagna ⊕ 71 44°18′.20N 009°20′.60E
When approaching, beware of the fish farm located 0.5M SW of the harbour entrance. Inside are 1400 berths (max. LOA 50m), including 140 for visitors. Submerged rock ballasting fringing the breakwater head means that yachts should keep a safe distance off as they enter.
Strong winds and/or southerly gales make entering and leaving highly dangerous, and some berths are disturbed by an uncomfortable surge.
Behind the marina are a number of large and small boatyards that can carry out any type of work.
Porto di Lavagna VHF ch 09
☎ +39 0185 312626 / 364192
reception@portodilavagna.com
www.portodilavagna.com

Anchorage In calm and settled weather, yachts can anchor in 6m on sand. Anchorage is untenable in *libeccio* and *scirocco*.

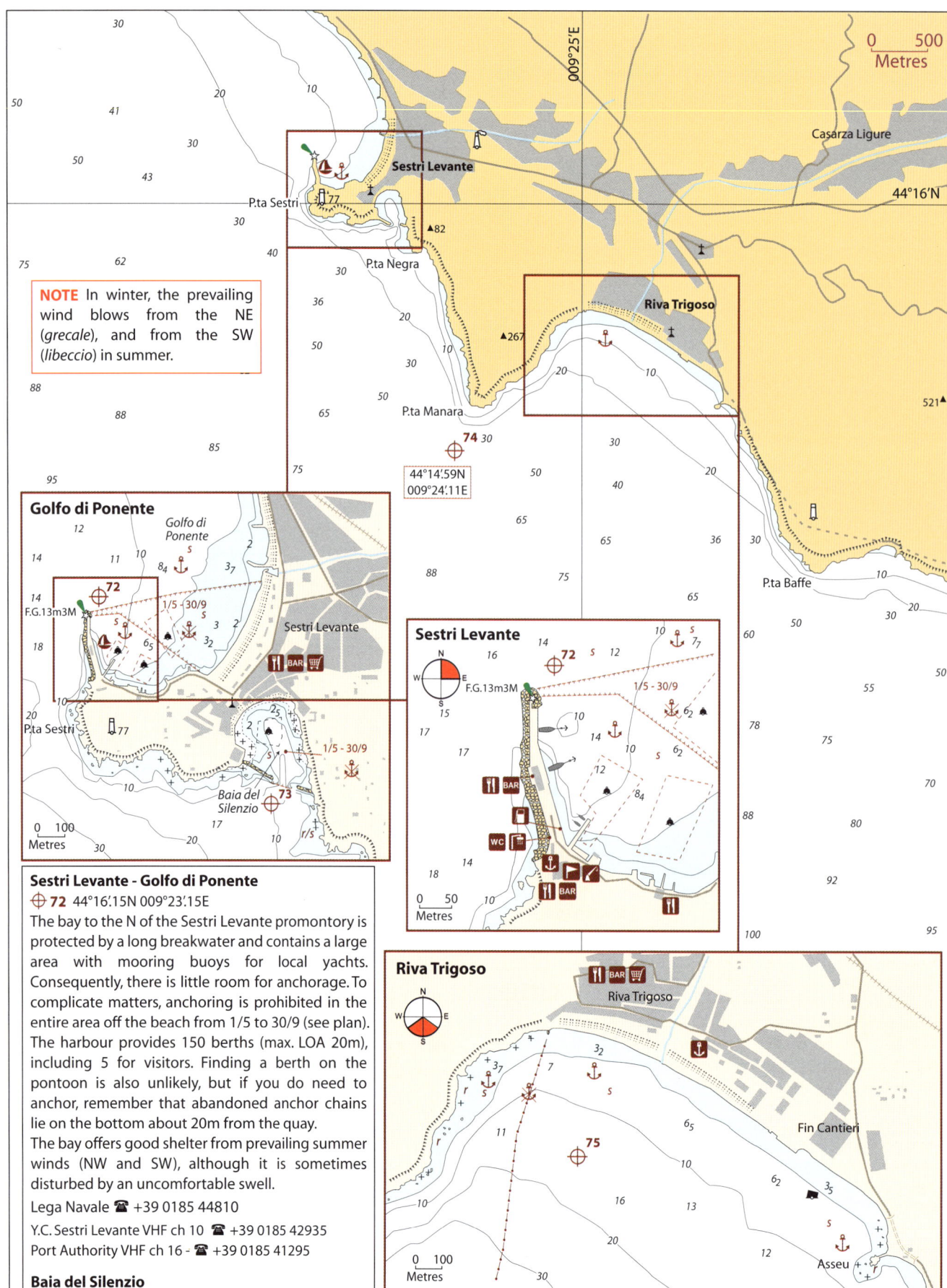

| CHART 23 | AREA B | **LIGURIA EAST COAST**
SESTRI LEVANTE AND RIVA TRIGOSO |

NOTE In winter, the prevailing wind blows from the NE (*grecale*), and from the SW (*libeccio*) in summer.

Sestri Levante - Golfo di Ponente
⊕ **72** 44°16'.15N 009°23'.15E

The bay to the N of the Sestri Levante promontory is protected by a long breakwater and contains a large area with mooring buoys for local yachts. Consequently, there is little room for anchorage. To complicate matters, anchoring is prohibited in the entire area off the beach from 1/5 to 30/9 (see plan). The harbour provides 150 berths (max. LOA 20m), including 5 for visitors. Finding a berth on the pontoon is also unlikely, but if you do need to anchor, remember that abandoned anchor chains lie on the bottom about 20m from the quay.
The bay offers good shelter from prevailing summer winds (NW and SW), although it is sometimes disturbed by an uncomfortable swell.

Lega Navale ☎ +39 0185 44810
Y.C. Sestri Levante VHF ch 10 ☎ +39 0185 42935
Port Authority VHF ch 16 - ☎ +39 0185 41295

Baia del Silenzio
⊕ **73** 44°15'.98N 09°23'.60E

The Sestri promontory is connected to the mainland by an isthmus, to the S of which lies this beautiful bay. However it is cluttered with numerous moorings for local boats and depths come up rapidly. Anchorage is prohibited here from 1/5 to 1/9.

Riva Trigoso
⊕ **75** 44°15'.22N 009°25'.12E

Just beyond Punta Manara lies the deep gulf of Riva Trigoso with its long beach. The Fin Cantieri shipyard stands at the head. Anchor in 5-10m on sand; the W corner of the bay is the most convenient and provides good shelter from westerlies.

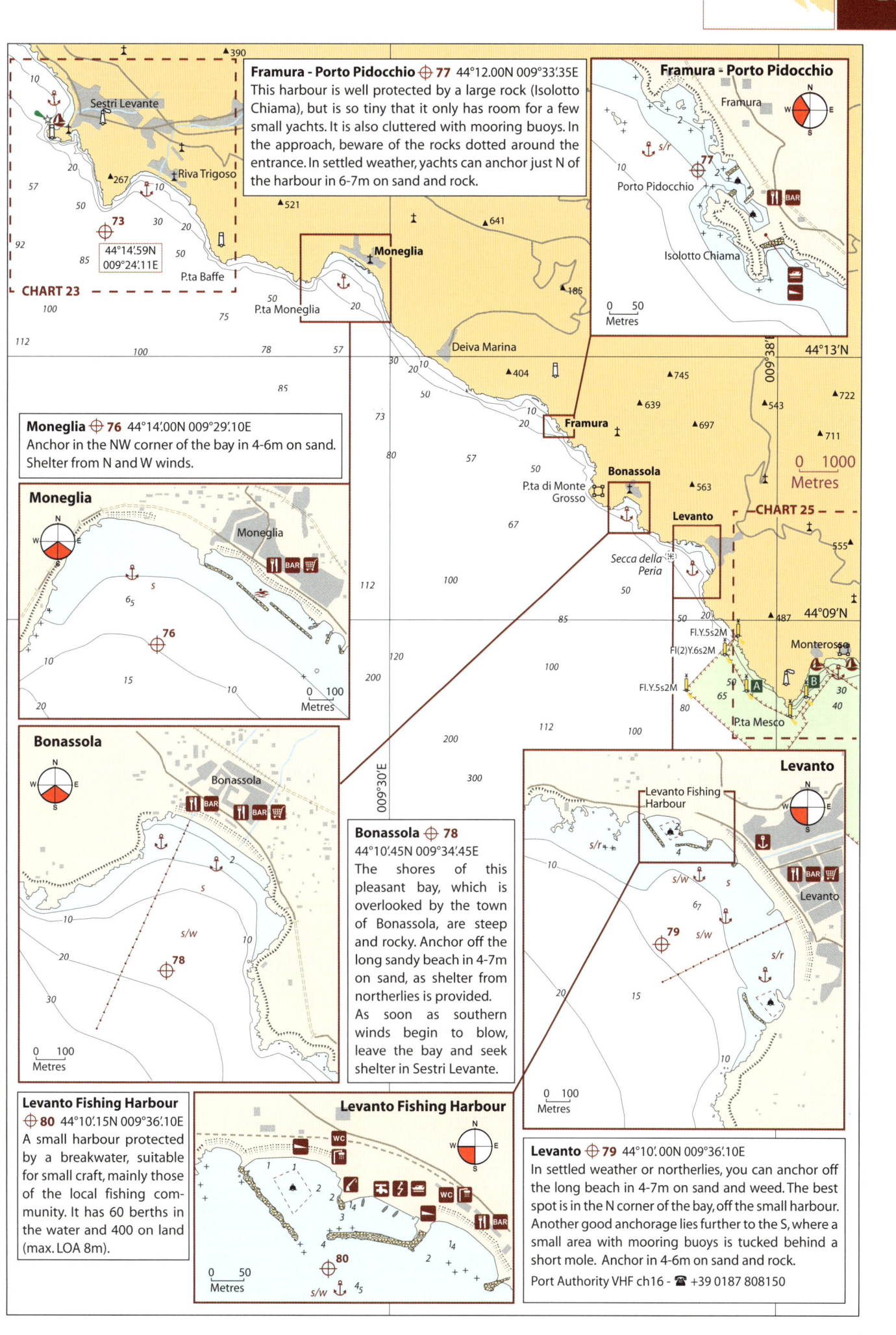

LIGURIA EAST COAST FROM MONEGLIA TO LEVANTO — AREA B — CHART 24

Framura - Porto Pidocchio ⊕ 77 44°12.00N 009°33.35E
This harbour is well protected by a large rock (Isolotto Chiama), but is so tiny that it only has room for a few small yachts. It is also cluttered with mooring buoys. In the approach, beware of the rocks dotted around the entrance. In settled weather, yachts can anchor just N of the harbour in 6-7m on sand and rock.

Moneglia ⊕ 76 44°14.00N 009°29.10E
Anchor in the NW corner of the bay in 4-6m on sand. Shelter from N and W winds.

Bonassola ⊕ 78
44°10.45N 009°34.45E
The shores of this pleasant bay, which is overlooked by the town of Bonassola, are steep and rocky. Anchor off the long sandy beach in 4-7m on sand, as shelter from northerlies is provided. As soon as southern winds begin to blow, leave the bay and seek shelter in Sestri Levante.

Levanto Fishing Harbour
⊕ 80 44°10.15N 009°36.10E
A small harbour protected by a breakwater, suitable for small craft, mainly those of the local fishing community. It has 60 berths in the water and 400 on land (max. LOA 8m).

Levanto ⊕ 79 44°10.00N 009°36.10E
In settled weather or northerlies, you can anchor off the long beach in 4-7m on sand and weed. The best spot is in the N corner of the bay, off the small harbour. Another good anchorage lies further to the S, where a small area with mooring buoys is tucked behind a short mole. Anchor in 4-6m on sand and rock.
Port Authority VHF ch16 - ☎ +39 0187 808150

47

CHART 25 — AREA B — LIGURIA EAST COAST — MONTEROSSO AND VERNAZZA

Cinque Terre Marine Reserve

Zone A *Riserva a tutela integrale* (Fully protected Reserve) In this area scientific research is permitted, as is swimming and diving on authorisation by the reserve authority. Navigation under sail, oar, pedal and electric thrusters is permitted at a speed of less than 5 knots.

Zone B *Riserva Generale* (General Reserve) In this area the following are permitted: swimming, navigation under sail and motor (except for jetskis and water-bikes) at a speed of less than 5 knots. Designated mooring buoys and diving are governed by reserve authority regulations.

Zona C *Riserva Parziale* (Partial Reserve) In this area the following are permitted: swimming, navigation under sail and motor (except for jetskis and water-bikes) at a speed of less than 10 knots, and sport fishing with static line and rod. The following are governed by reserve authority regulations: mooring in designated areas (⚓) and diving, both of which require prior authorisation, otherwise tough penalties apply.

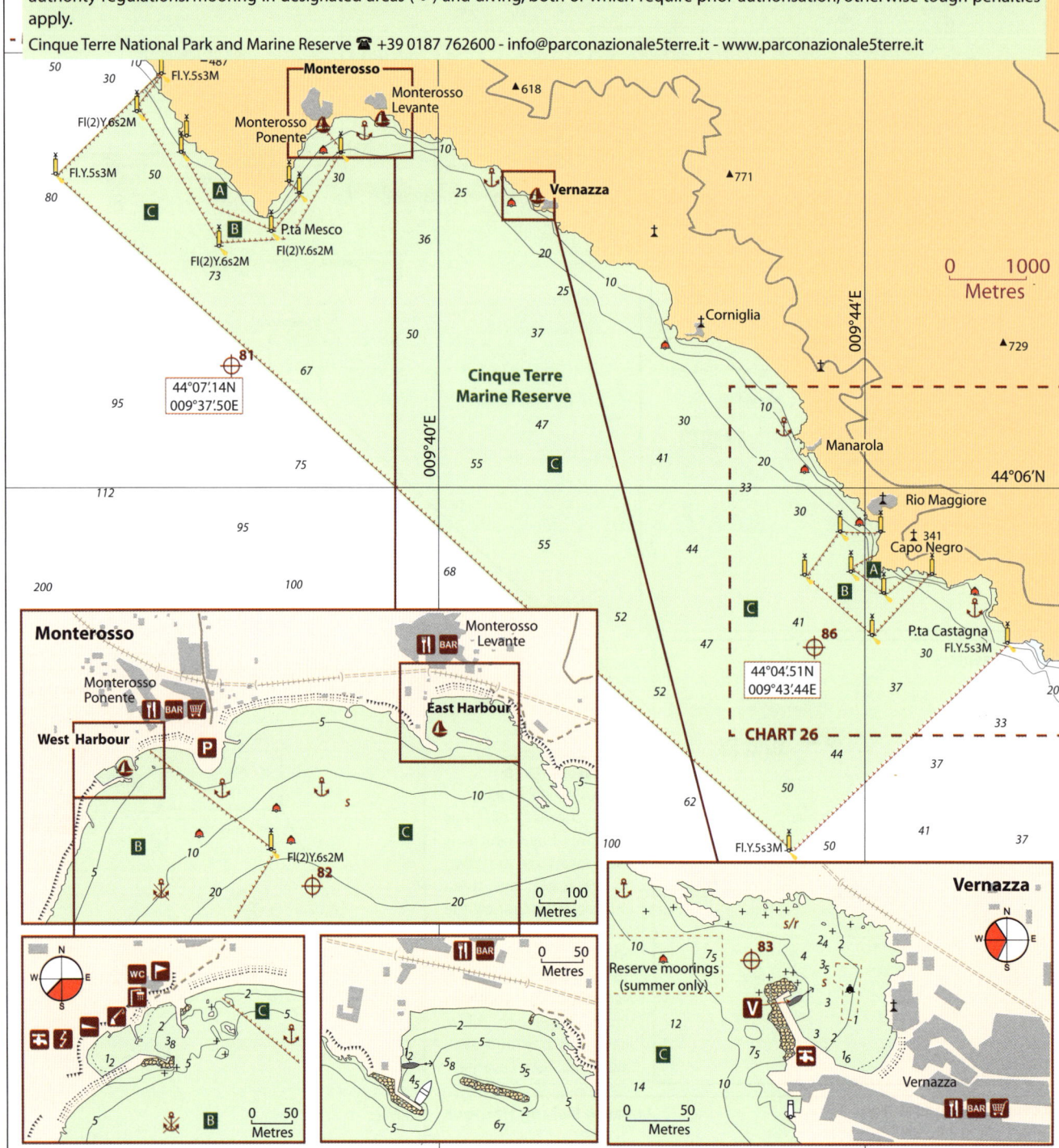

Cinque Terre National Park and Marine Reserve ☎ +39 0187 762600 - info@parconazionale5terre.it - www.parconazionale5terre.it

Monterosso ⊕ 82 44°08′.27N 009°39′.00E

In settled weather, yachts can anchor off the beach (Zone C), or pick up a reserve mooring buoy (Zones B/C). NW of the bay lies a small and shallow basin suitable for small craft (max. LOA 6m). In summer, the small harbour is administered by Circolo Velico Monterosso (☎ +39 0187 802571), and in winter it is used by local fishermen.

The mole in the E harbour is used by tripper boats during the day; mooring is available at night when there is space, but it needs to be vacated by 10 am. It is also liable to an uncomfortable slop.

Vernazza ⊕ 83 44°08′.16N 009°40′.84E

The harbour is small, shallow and occupied by local boats. Berths are available for 3-4 yachts (max. LOA 12m) using their own anchor on the outer end of the mole. There is, however, very little room for manoeuvre. In the approach care should be taken of the numerous rocks and shoal water fringing the shore. Entering the harbour is prohibited from May to September and mooring buoys are laid outside.

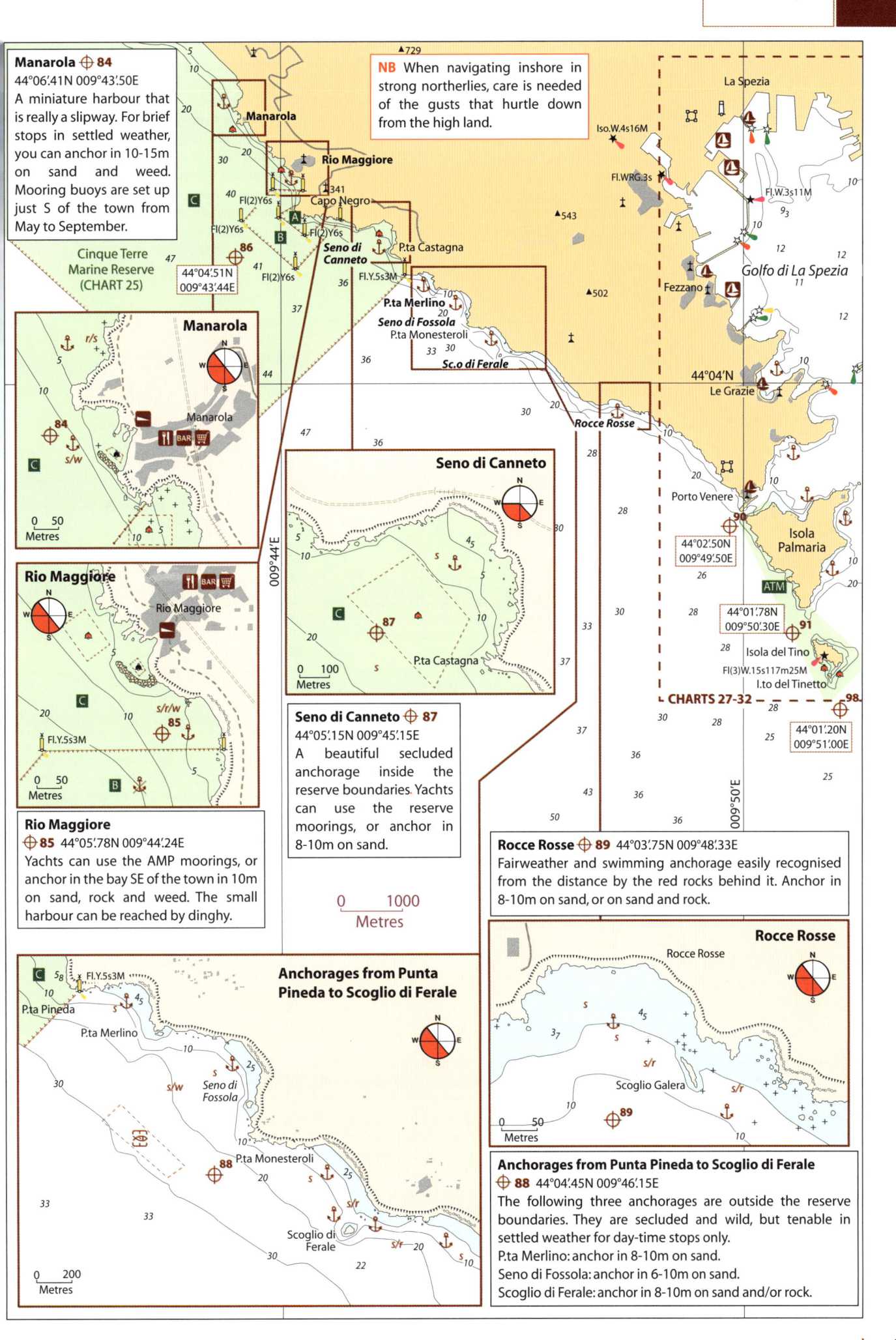

LIGURIA EAST COAST
FROM MANAROLA TO PORTO VENERE — AREA B
CHART 26

Manarola ⊕ 84
44°06'.41N 009°43'.50E
A miniature harbour that is really a slipway. For brief stops in settled weather, you can anchor in 10-15m on sand and weed. Mooring buoys are set up just S of the town from May to September.

NB When navigating inshore in strong northerlies, care is needed of the gusts that hurtle down from the high land.

Rio Maggiore
⊕ 85 44°05'.78N 009°44'.24E
Yachts can use the AMP moorings, or anchor in the bay SE of the town in 10m on sand, rock and weed. The small harbour can be reached by dinghy.

Seno di Canneto ⊕ 87
44°05'.15N 009°45'.15E
A beautiful secluded anchorage inside the reserve boundaries. Yachts can use the reserve moorings, or anchor in 8-10m on sand.

Rocce Rosse ⊕ 89 44°03'.75N 009°48'.33E
Fairweather and swimming anchorage easily recognised from the distance by the red rocks behind it. Anchor in 8-10m on sand, or on sand and rock.

Anchorages from Punta Pineda to Scoglio di Ferale
⊕ 88 44°04'.45N 009°46'.15E
The following three anchorages are outside the reserve boundaries. They are secluded and wild, but tenable in settled weather for day-time stops only.
P.ta Merlino: anchor in 8-10m on sand.
Seno di Fossola: anchor in 6-10m on sand.
Scoglio di Ferale: anchor in 8-10m on sand and/or rock.

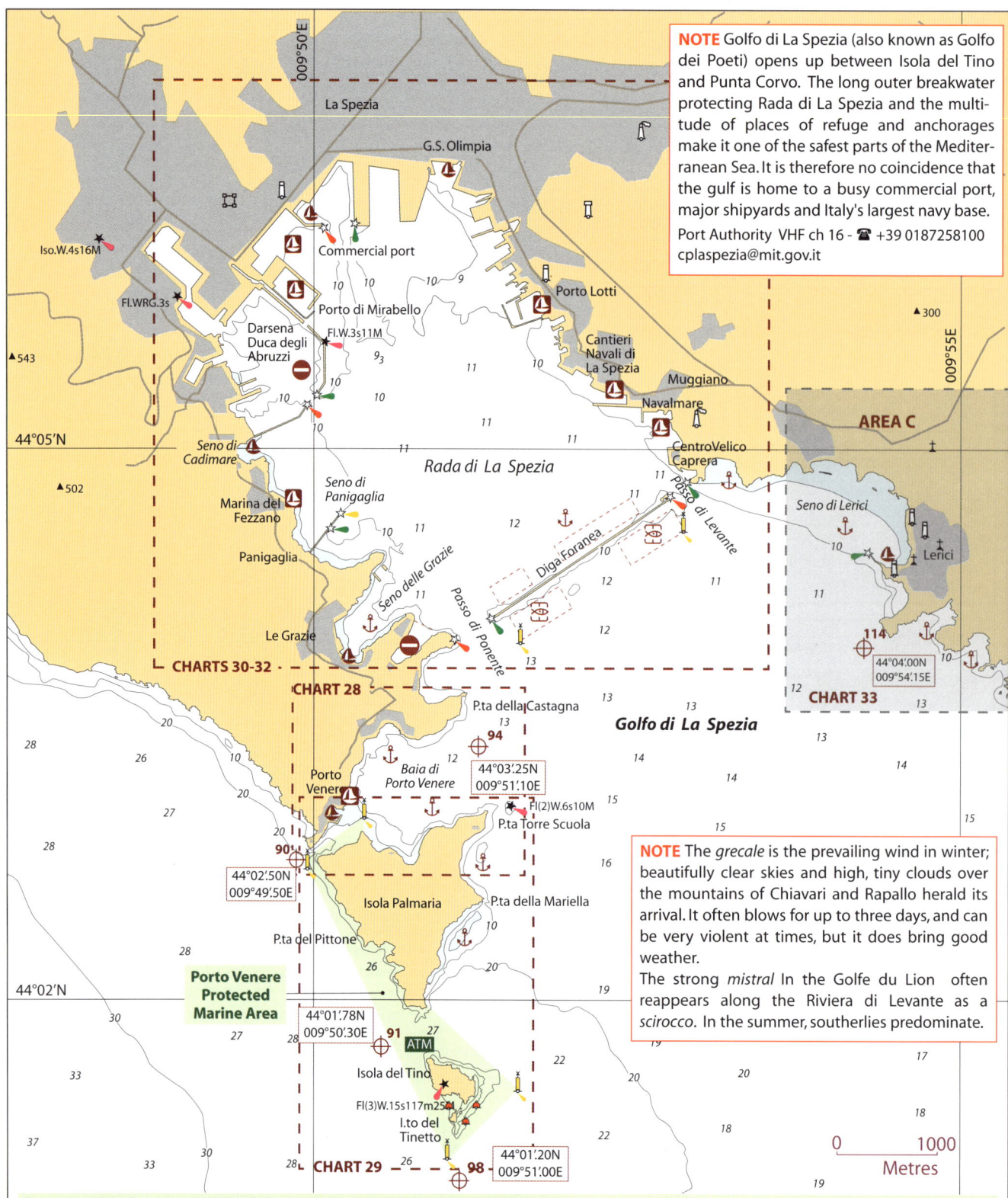

CHART 27 — AREA B
LIGURIA EAST COAST
GOLFO DI LA SPEZIA

NOTE Golfo di La Spezia (also known as Golfo dei Poeti) opens up between Isola del Tino and Punta Corvo. The long outer breakwater protecting Rada di La Spezia and the multitude of places of refuge and anchorages make it one of the safest parts of the Mediterranean Sea. It is therefore no coincidence that the gulf is home to a busy commercial port, major shipyards and Italy's largest navy base.
Port Authority VHF ch 16 - ☎ +39 0187258100
cplaspezia@mit.gov.it

NOTE The *grecale* is the prevailing wind in winter; beautifully clear skies and high, tiny clouds over the mountains of Chiavari and Rapallo herald its arrival. It often blows for up to three days, and can be very violent at times, but it does bring good weather.
The strong *mistral* In the Golfe du Lion often reappears along the Riviera di Levante as a *scirocco*. In the summer, southerlies predominate.

Protected Marine Area (ATM) of the Porto Venere Regional Natural Park
The ATM comprises the south-western area of Isola Palmaria, the islands of Tino and Tinetto, and the Prateria di Posidonia in the channel that separates Porto Venere from Isola Palmaria.
Permitted activities Navigation under sail and motor at a speed of less than 6 knots; moorings for craft in areas designated by the reserve authority; access and anchorage in the area between Isola del Tino and Isoletta del Tinetto (marked by red buoys) for pleasure craft <10m LOA; 10m/24m yachts can use the red mooring buoys; diving with breathing equipment authorised by the park authorities, with or without the support of diving schools or clubs.
Prohibited activities Craft are not allowed to stop or anchor in the sea area off Isola del Tino between Punta Bianca to Porticciolo, unless they have the navy's permission; anchorage is also prohibited between Punta Beffettuccio and Punta Secca (Isola Palmaria) and in the stretch between Capo dell'Isola and the southern boundary of the ATM. The park authorities, however, have marked off some areas for anchorage. Landing on Isola del Tino is prohibited unless you are on a park-organised tour and have prior permission from the navy. Landing on Isolotto del Tinetto, is prohibited unless you have the park authorities' permission. All activities that may damage or endanger the environment are also banned. See national, regional and local regulations.
Park Authorities ☎ 0187 794823/885 - atm@parconaturaleportovenere.it - www.parconaturaleportovenere.it

LIGURIA EAST COAST
BAIA DI PORTO VENERE — AREA B
CHART 28

Baia di Porto Venere ⊕ 94 44°03'.25N 009°51'.10E
Yachts navigating the Porto Venere channel must not exceed 6 knots and must keep to the starboard.
Seno dell'Olivo Yachts can anchor to the N of the Pontile Ignazio yacht harbour, off the extensive mussel beds and mooring buoys in about 10m on sand and mud. By day, anchorage is disturbed by the heavy maritime traffic crossing the channel as it causes an uncomfortable swell.
Seno di Terrizzo Yachts can anchor in 5-10m on mud, or on mud and weed just off Isola Palmaria. Excellent shelter. Care is needed of the mussel beds and the numerous moorings laid across the bay. The ferry channel that links Porto Venere with Isola Palmaria should be left clear.
Port Authority VHF ch 16 - ☎ +39 0187 790768

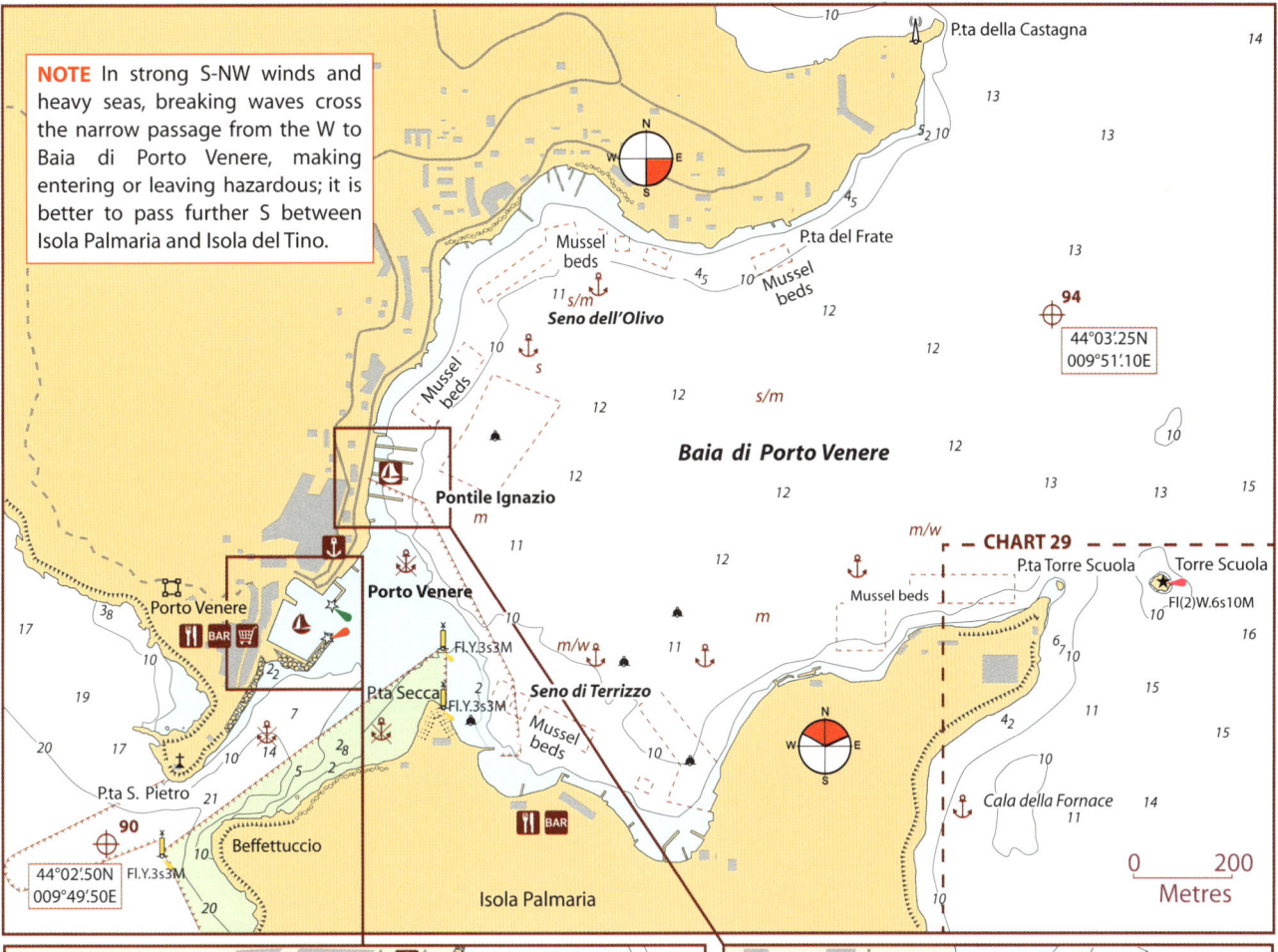

NOTE In strong S-NW winds and heavy seas, breaking waves cross the narrow passage from the W to Baia di Porto Venere, making entering or leaving hazardous; it is better to pass further S between Isola Palmaria and Isola del Tino.

Porto Venere ⊕ 92 44°03'.03N 009°50'.24E
This small harbour provides 32 berths (max. LOA 50m), including 6 for visitors. Finding a berth, however, is highly unlikely, so call up in advance to book or find out what berths are available. Molo Doria is reserved for passengers and goods. A strong *tramontana* or *grecale* makes berths slightly uncomfortable, otherwise the harbour is well protected.
Porto Venere Marina Misenti VHF ch 09 - ☎ +39 0187 793042
porto@portodiportovene.it - www.portodiportovenere.it

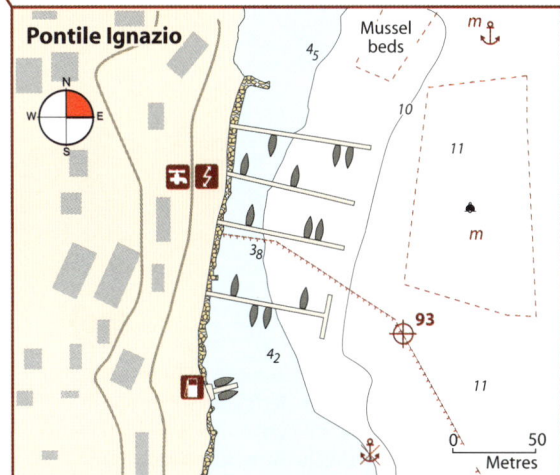

Pontile Ignazio ⊕ 93 44°03'.17N 009°50'.34E
Just N of the harbour are the Ignazio pontoons, which are well protected but disturbed by a constant flow of craft causing an uncomfortable wash. In the approach, care is needed of the numerous mooring buoys off the harbour. The pontoons have 45 berths (max. LOA 25m), but it is best to book or ring in advance to check availability.
☎ +39 0187 791364 / 366 4534446 / 339 7218248
info@pontileignazio.org - www.pontileignazio.org

51

CHART 29

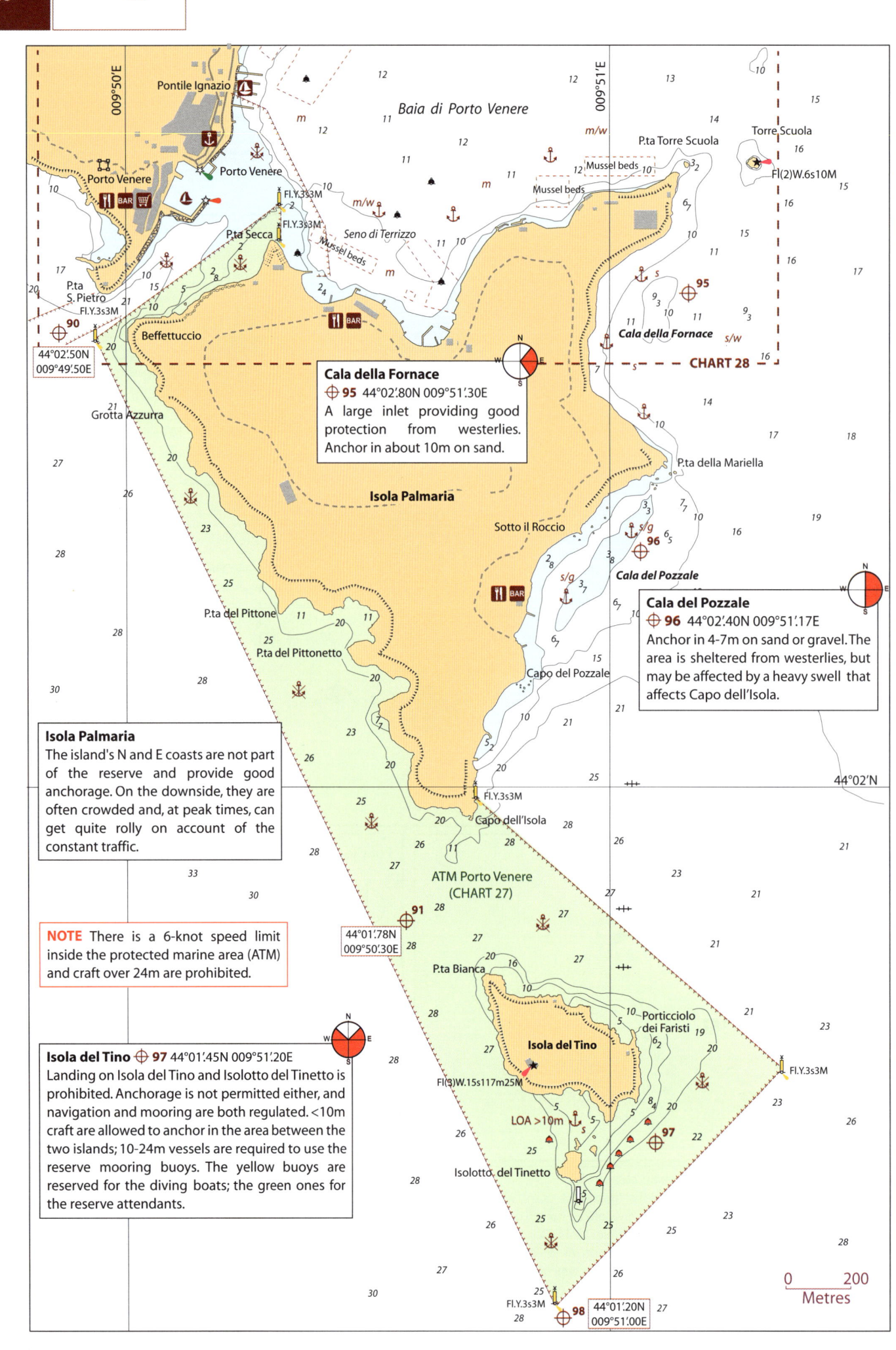

AREA B
LIGURIA EAST COAST
ISOLA PALMARIA AND ISOLA DEL TINO

Cala della Fornace
⊕ 95 44°02'.80N 009°51'.30E
A large inlet providing good protection from westerlies. Anchor in about 10m on sand.

Cala del Pozzale
⊕ 96 44°02'.40N 009°51'.17E
Anchor in 4-7m on sand or gravel. The area is sheltered from westerlies, but may be affected by a heavy swell that affects Capo dell'Isola.

Isola Palmaria
The island's N and E coasts are not part of the reserve and provide good anchorage. On the downside, they are often crowded and, at peak times, can get quite rolly on account of the constant traffic.

NOTE There is a 6-knot speed limit inside the protected marine area (ATM) and craft over 24m are prohibited.

Isola del Tino ⊕ 97 44°01'.45N 009°51'.20E
Landing on Isola del Tino and Isolotto del Tinetto is prohibited. Anchorage is not permitted either, and navigation and mooring are both regulated. <10m craft are allowed to anchor in the area between the two islands; 10-24m vessels are required to use the reserve mooring buoys. The yellow buoys are reserved for the diving boats; the green ones for the reserve attendants.

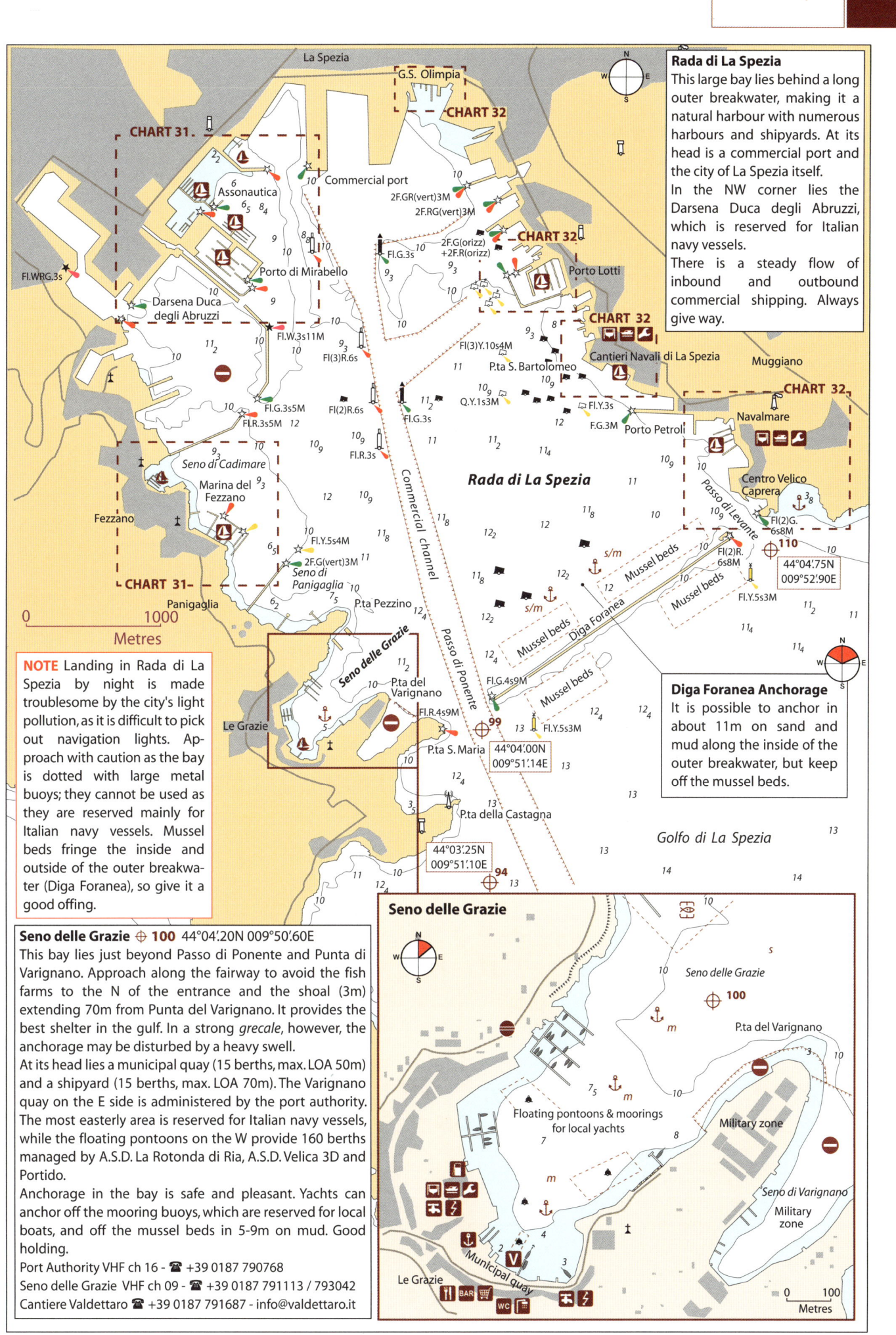

LIGURIA EAST COAST
RADA DI LA SPEZIA — AREA B
CHART 30

Rada di La Spezia
This large bay lies behind a long outer breakwater, making it a natural harbour with numerous harbours and shipyards. At its head is a commercial port and the city of La Spezia itself.
In the NW corner lies the Darsena Duca degli Abruzzi, which is reserved for Italian navy vessels.
There is a steady flow of inbound and outbound commercial shipping. Always give way.

Diga Foranea Anchorage
It is possible to anchor in about 11m on sand and mud along the inside of the outer breakwater, but keep off the mussel beds.

NOTE Landing in Rada di La Spezia by night is made troublesome by the city's light pollution, as it is difficult to pick out navigation lights. Approach with caution as the bay is dotted with large metal buoys; they cannot be used as they are reserved mainly for Italian navy vessels. Mussel beds fringe the inside and outside of the outer breakwater (Diga Foranea), so give it a good offing.

Seno delle Grazie ⊕ 100 44°04'.20N 009°50'.60E
This bay lies just beyond Passo di Ponente and Punta di Varignano. Approach along the fairway to avoid the fish farms to the N of the entrance and the shoal (3m) extending 70m from Punta del Varignano. It provides the best shelter in the gulf. In a strong *grecale*, however, the anchorage may be disturbed by a heavy swell.
At its head lies a municipal quay (15 berths, max. LOA 50m) and a shipyard (15 berths, max. LOA 70m). The Varignano quay on the E side is administered by the port authority. The most easterly area is reserved for Italian navy vessels, while the floating pontoons on the W provide 160 berths managed by A.S.D. La Rotonda di Ria, A.S.D. Velica 3D and Portido.
Anchorage in the bay is safe and pleasant. Yachts can anchor off the mooring buoys, which are reserved for local boats, and off the mussel beds in 5-9m on mud. Good holding.
Port Authority VHF ch 16 - ☎ +39 0187 790768
Seno delle Grazie VHF ch 09 - ☎ +39 0187 791113 / 793042
Cantiere Valdettaro ☎ +39 0187 791687 - info@valdettaro.it

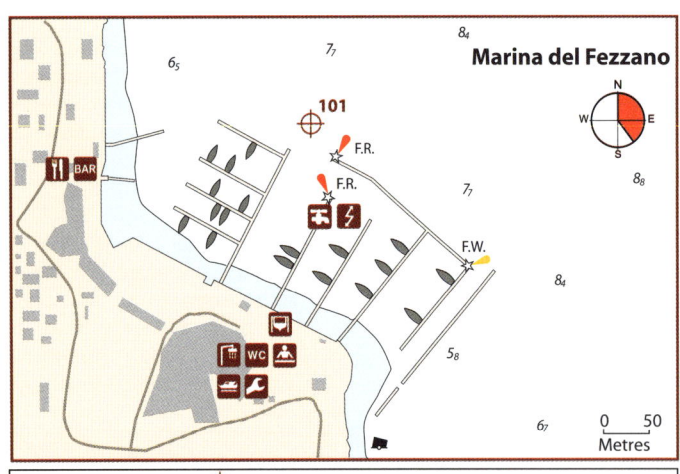

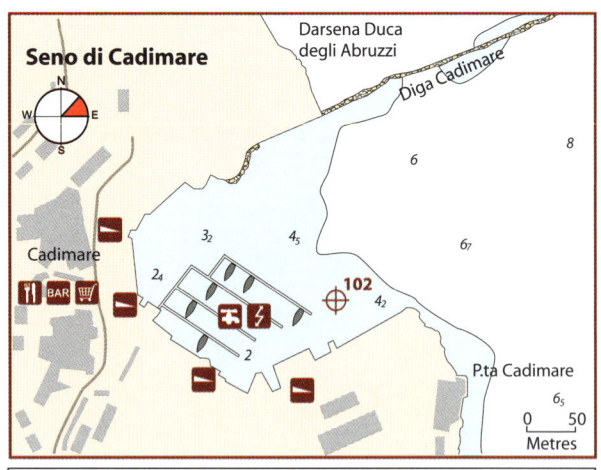

CHART 31

AREA B — **LIGURIA EAST COAST / RADA DI LA SPEZIA**

Marina del Fezzano ⊕ **101** 44°04′.09N 009°49′.10E
This marina has a host of facilities and a capacity of 250 berths (max. LOA 28m) on pontoons. The berths are well-sheltered, but a strong *grecale* and gale-force *scirocco* cause problems.
Call the harbour staff before entering: VHF ch 09 - ☎ +39 0187 790103 - info@marinadelfezzano.it - www.marinadelfezzano.it

Seno di Cadimare ⊕ **102** 44°05′.05N 009°49′.55E
This small harbour has some pontoons and a quay with berths for local boats and for Associazione Nautica Borgata.
Cadimare ☎ +39 0187 752602 - ac.cadimare2000@gmail.com
www.cadimare2000.it

La Spezia - Porto Mirabello ⊕ **103** 44°05′.50N 009°49′.90E
The large, modern Porto Mirabello marina just outside the centre provides 470 berths (max. LOA 100m). The berths are on large concrete piers and are well-protected. The position of the entrance and quays means that they are not affected by a strong *grecale* and a gale-force *scirocco*. The marina should be contacted beforehand: VHF ch 73 - ☎ +39 0187 778108 - info@portomirabello.it - www.portomirabello.it

Assonautica De Benedetti ⊕ **104** 44°06′.15N 009°49′.85E
The marina is situated along the quay (Banchina Morin) and is just a brisk stroll from the city centre. Its pontoons provide 660 berths (max. LOA 13m), including 66 for visitors. VHF ch 71 - ☎ +39 0187 770229 / +39 331 1827124 - www.assonauticasp.it - asso_sp@libero.it

Sardinia Cat 12 berths (max. LOA 18m) on a pontoon along the Banchina Morin. Catamarans have priority. ☎ +39 0187 75150 / 338 1454374

Harbourmaster VHF ch 16 - ☎ +39 0187 258100 - cplaspezia@mit.gov.it

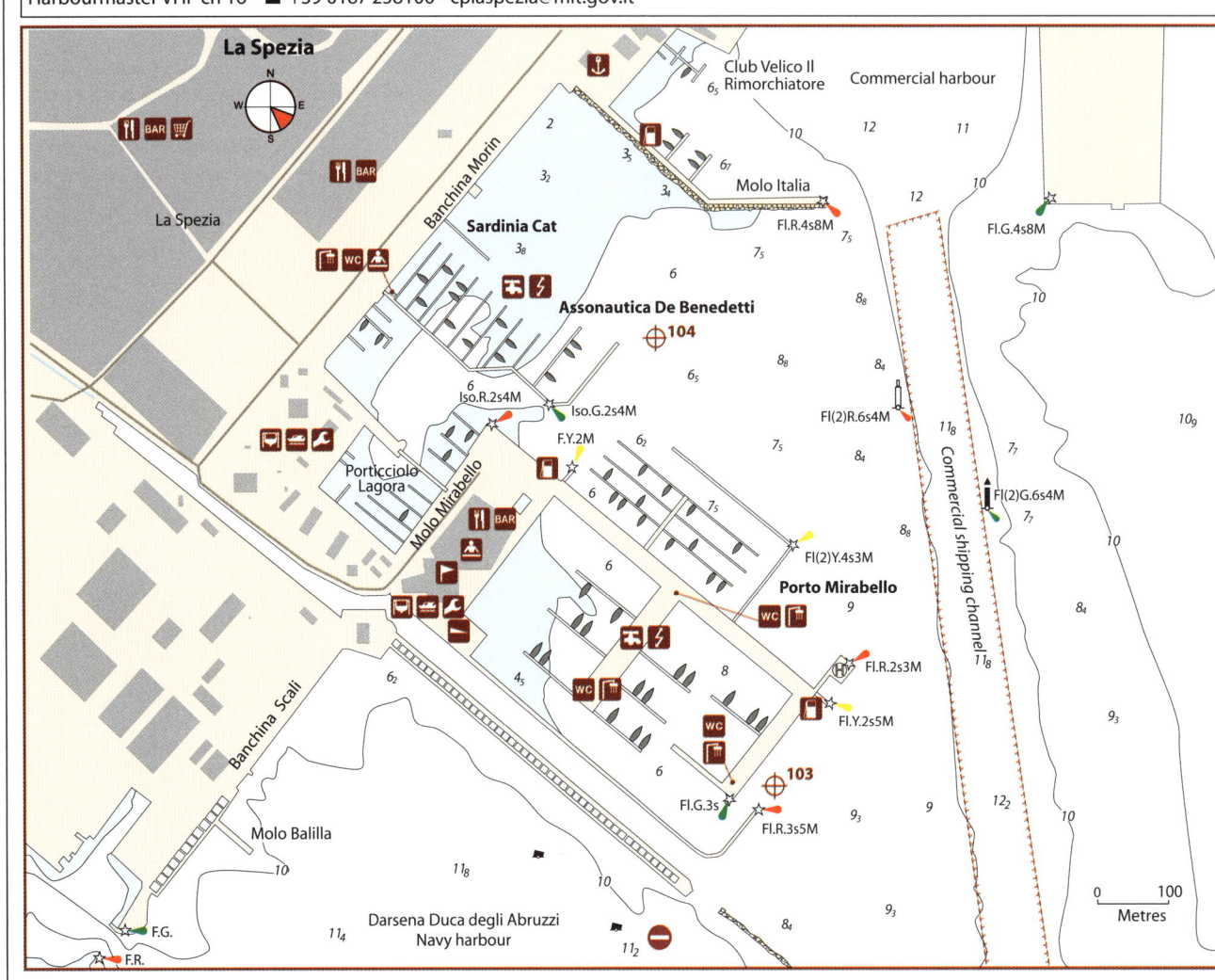

54

LIGURIA EAST COAST
RADA DI LA SPEZIA — AREA B

CHART 32

Port Authority
VHF ch16 - ☎ +39 0187 258100
cplaspezia@mit.gov.it

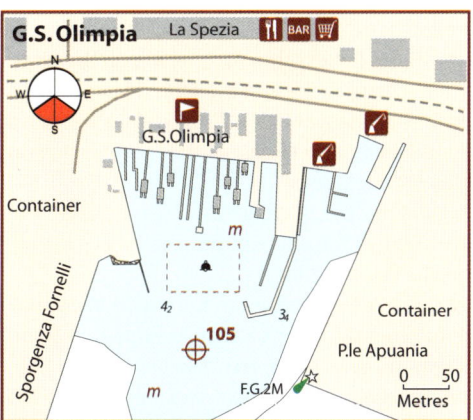

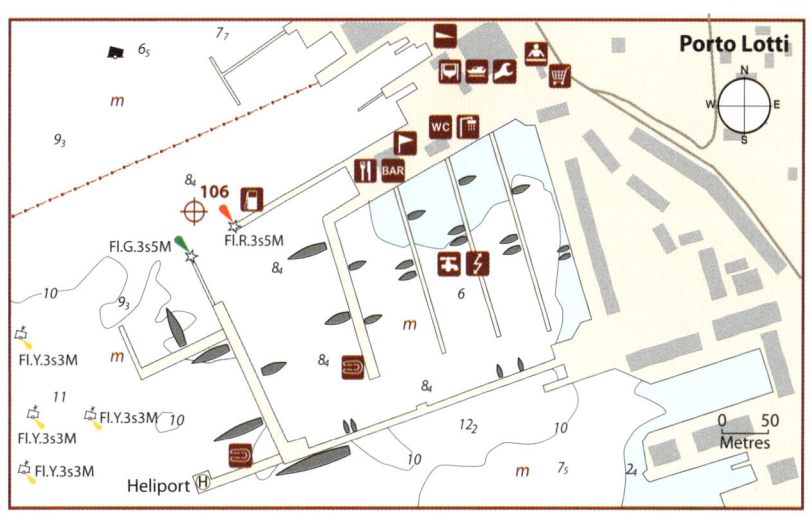

Porto Lotti ⊕ 106 44°05.80N 009°51.45E
This marina is expensive, but provides good shelter and is well-equipped. It lies on the E side of the bay and has 506 berths (max. LOA 80/130m). Once beyond Passo di Ponente and abeam of Punta Varignano, set a course of 009° towards the marina entrance. Before entering, contact the marina and follow the staff's instructions.
VHF ch 09 - ☎ +39 0187 5321/532203 - ufficio@portolotti.it - www.portolotti.it

G.S. Olimpia ⊕ 105 44°06.50N 009°50.95E
There are berths on long pontoons at the head of the commercial port just E of Sporgenza Fornelli, that are used by permanent berth-holders and the historical local sports club Fossamastra G. S. Olimpia.

Rada di La Spezia has a number of both large and small shipyards, mainly on the E side. Some of them have a number of berths, but they are reserved mainly for boatyard customers.

Cantieri Navali di La Spezia ⊕ 107 44°05.40N 009°51.90E
120 berths (max. LOA 25m) are available immediately S of Punta S. Bartolomeo. ☎ +39 0187 520937/523103 - info@cnlaspezia.com
www.cnlaspezia.com

Navalmare ⊕ 108 44°05.05N 009°52.59E
160 berths (max. LOA 40m) on pontoons inside Seno di Pertusola. ☎ +39 0187 560746 - nautica@navalmare.it - www.navalmare.it

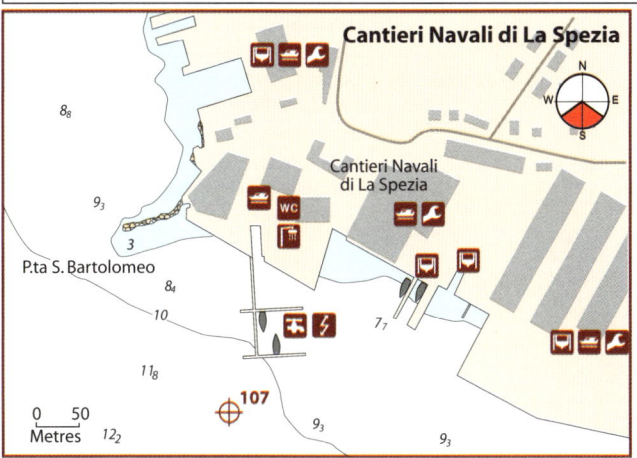

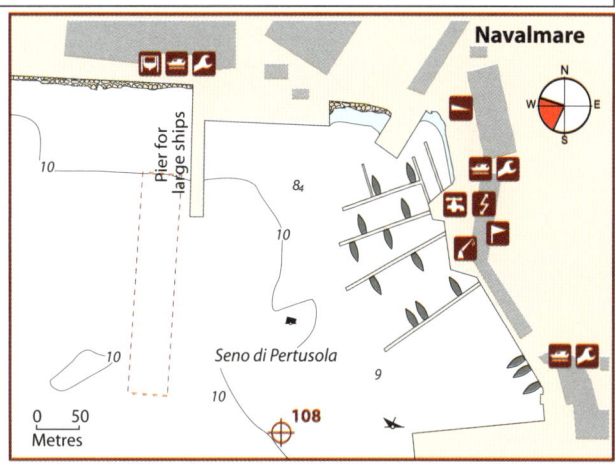

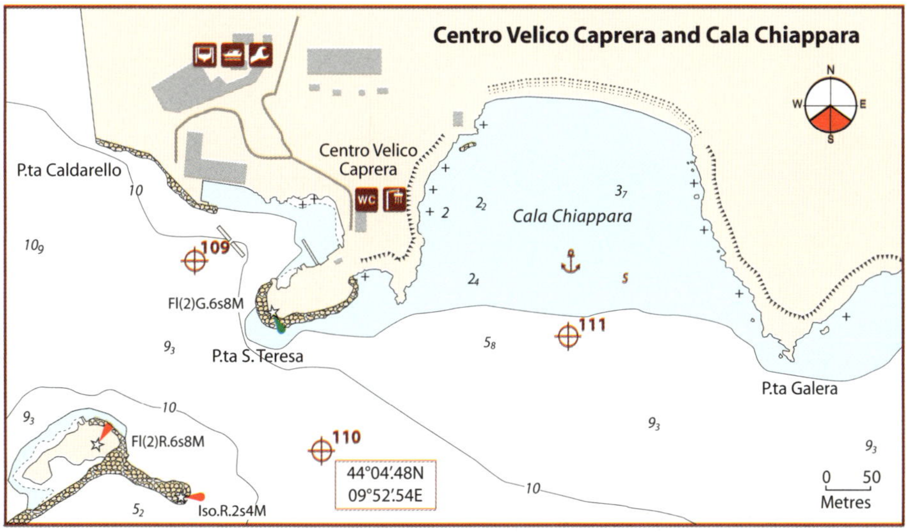

Centro Velico Caprera (CVC)
⊕ 109 44°04.90N 009°52.78E
A small bay lies at the entrance to Passo di Levante, between Punta S. Teresa and Punta Caldarello, and this is home to the headquarters of sailing club Centro Velico Caprera.
☎ +39 0187 971414
info@centrovelicocaprera.it
http//: centrovelicocaprera.it

Cala Chiappara
⊕ 111 44°04.83N 009°53.14E
A bay lying outside the outer breakwater, to the E of Punta S. Teresa. Anchorage (3-5m, sand) is reasonably protected from northerlies, but is disturbed by waterborne traffic converging on and leaving Rada di La Spezia.

55

AREA C - FROM LERICI TO PROMONTORIO DELL'ARGENTARIO

The shore between La Spezia and Argentario is mainly sandy punctuated by stretches of coast and rocky promontories. Harbours lie along the coast no more than 20M apart, but not all of them are easy to approach in a gale-force *libeccio*. Most of them have visitors berths on laid moorings tailed to the quay or mooring buoys (unless shown otherwise in the plan). Water and electricity are also available. They are often packed in high season, so call up before arrival to check availability and prices, as they vary each year and according to season.

The islands of the Arcipelago Toscano have few harbours, but a good range of protected bays, mainly on Elba, the largest island.

Days of calm are frequent in the summer. A W-SW day breeze may get up, but it rarely exceeds Force 4 and dies down in the evening to make way for a gentle offshore breeze at night. The prevailing winds from autumn to spring are northerly and gales are more frequent.

When the Apuan Alps and Magra Valley are shrouded in cloud and mist, E winds and rain are to be expected.

If the *mistral* has not died down by sunset and breezes are irregular, the weather is going to worsen.

When Isola Gorgona can be seen extremely clearly, strong westerlies are to be expected.

High sea levels in harbours and clouds over Isola Gorgona and Monte Nero herald the arrival of a *scirocco*. Consistently low waters and white clouds on the coast are a sign that a moderate *mistral* and settled weather are on their way. Streaks of cloud over Corsica and white cirrostratus in Canale di Piombino herald the arrival of the *libeccio* or southerly gales.

Low pressure over the Gulf of Genoa brings *tramontana* and rain.

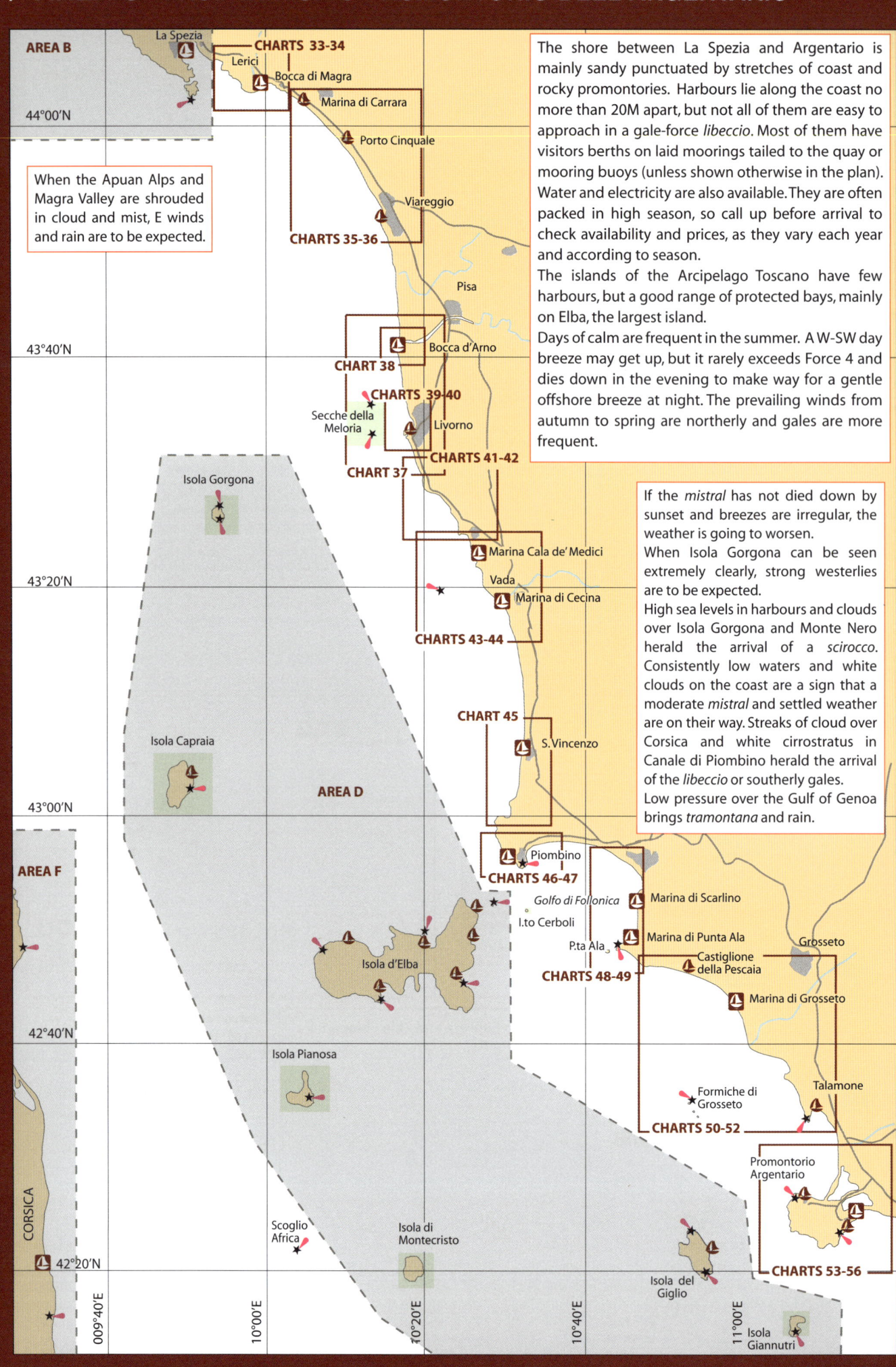

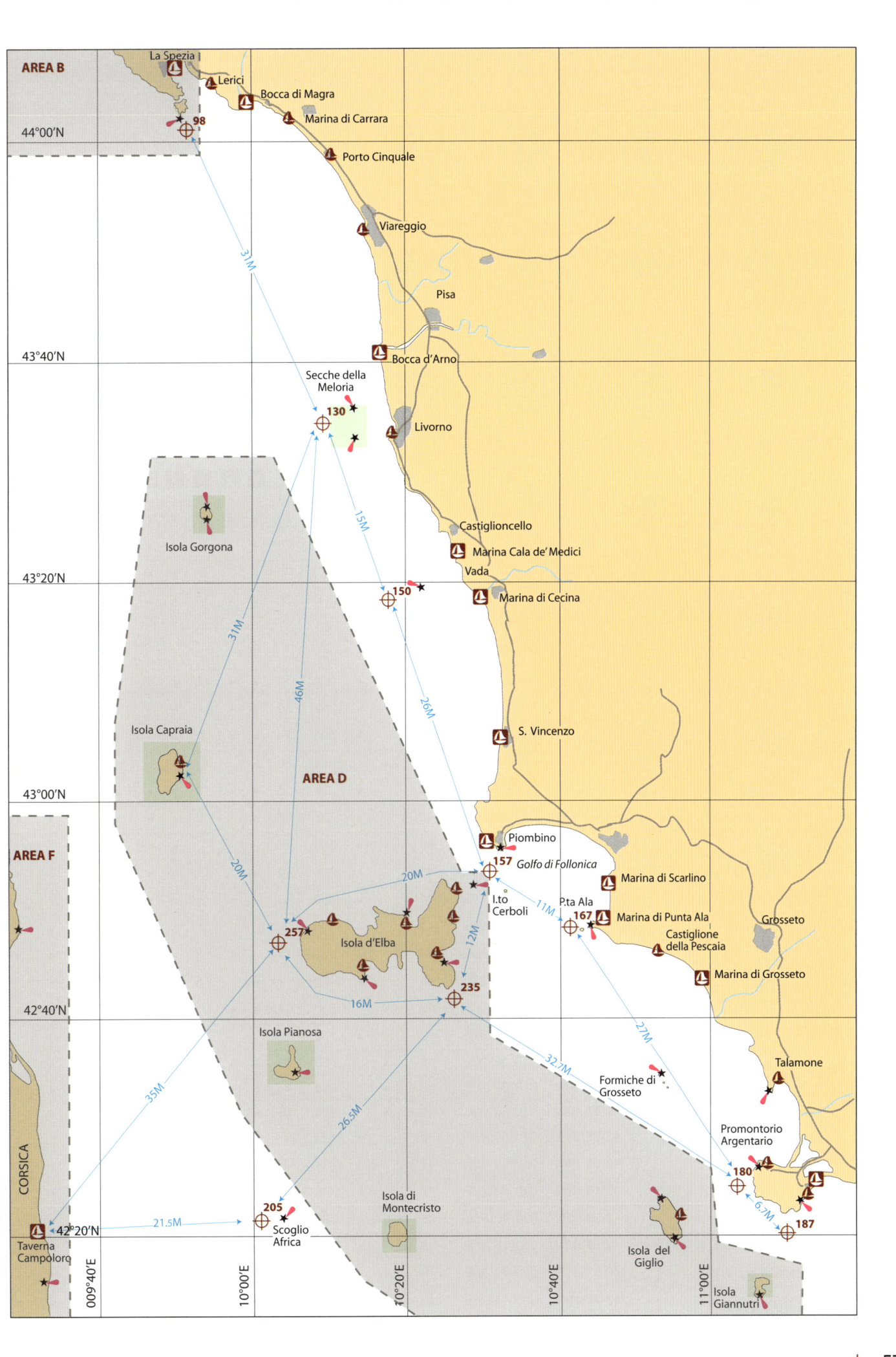

AREA C - FROM LERICI TO PROMONTORIO DELL' ARGENTARIO

AREA C - FROM LERICI TO PROMONTORIO DELL'ARGENTARIO

COASTAL NAVIGATION WAYPOINTS AND DISTANCES

⊕	DESCRIPTION	WGS 84 COORDINATES LATITUDE	LONGITUDE	CHART
98	500m S of isolotto del Tinetto	44°01'.20N	009°51'.00E	26-27-29
130	5M E of Secche della Meloria	43°32'.10N	010°06'.10E	37
150	6M W of Vada	43°19'.00N	010°18'.00E	44
157	Canale di Piombino	42°54'.00N	010°29'.20E	46
167	0.5M E of Scoglio dello Sparviero	42°47'.49N	010°42'.16E	50
180	1.5M W of Argentario	42°25'.00N	011°03'.00E	53
187	1M S of Argentario	42°20'.40N	011°10'.00E	55
205	2M W of Scoglio Africa	42°21'.50N	010°01'.50E	57
235	I. d'Elba - 500m S of Punta Ripalti	42°42'.09N	010°25'.16E	69
257	I. d'Elba - 0.5M W of Punta Nera	42°46'.10N	010°05'.21E	73

HARBOURS AND MARINAS KEY FOR PLAN SYMBOLS

⊕	NAME	LATITUDE	LONGITUDE	CHART	⛵	⚓	≡	LOA m	V	🛢	⚓ m	⚡	🚿	WC	🍽	—	🍴	🎣	🔧
113	Lerici	44°04'.50N	009°54'.26E	33		•	1300	15	•	•	9	•	•	•		•	•	•	•
121	Fiume Magra	44°02'.70N	009°59'.24E	34		•	2000	20	•	•	2	•	•	•		•	•	•	•
122	Bocca di Magra	44°02'.80N	009°59'.40E	34	•		230	30	•		2	•	•						
123	Marina di Carrara	44°01'.65N	010°02'.65E	35		•	190	30	•	•	10	•	•	•		•	•	•	•
124	Porto Lavello	44°01'.65N	010°03'.75E	35		•	60	7			1					•	•	•	•
125	Marina di Massa	44°00'.30N	010°05'.70E	35		•	60	7			2					•			
126	Porto Cinquale	43°58'.50N	010°08'.40E	36		•	300	14	•	•	1.6	•	•	•		•	•	•	•
127	Viareggio	43°51'.65N	010°14'.05E	36		•	2000	80	•	•	3.5	•	•	•		•	•	•	•
128	Moorings in Fiume Arno	43°40'.80N	010°16'.20E	38		•	500	20	•	•	3	•	•	•		•	•	•	•
129	Porto di Pisa	43°40'.80N	010°16'.20E	38	•		354	50	•		5	•	•	•		•	•	•	•
133	Livorno Porto Mediceo	43°33'.05N	010°17'.70E	40		•	84	15	•	•	10	•	•	•			•	•	
134	Darsena Morosini	43°32'.45N	010°17'.75E	40		•	70	65	•		5						•	•	
135	Porticciolo Nazario Sauro	43°32'.35N	010°18'.03E	40		•	200	9				•	•		•				
136	Ardenza	43°31'.00N	010°18'.95E	41		•	266	10	•		2	•					•	•	
137	Antignano	43°29'.75N	010°19'.24E	41		•	550	35		•	2	•	•	•		•	•	•	•
140	Quercianella	43°27'.50N	010°21'.83E	41		•	100	6			2		•			•	•		
141	Mouth of Fiume Chioma	43°26'.75N	010°22'.80E	42		•	40	14		•	1.5	•	•			•	•	•	
145	Castiglioncello	43°24'.00N	010°24'.83E	43		•	170	12	•		1.5					•	•		
146	Marina Cala de' Medici	43°23'.80N	010°25'.50E	43	•		650	40	•	•	7	•	•	•		•	•	•	•
147	Rosignano Solvay	43°23'.85N	010°25'.87E	43		•	130	9			2					•			
151	Cecina Marina	43°18'.16N	010°28'.90E	44	•		800	40	•	•	5	•	•	•		•			•
152	Marina di S. Vincenzo	43°05'.90N	010°32'.20E	45	•		283	18	•	•	4.5	•	•	•		•	•	•	•
155	Marina di Salivoli	42°55'.85N	010°30'.60E	46	•		488	18	•	•	4	•	•	•		•	•	•	•
156	Piombino Porto Antico	42°55'.24N	010°31'.43E	46		•	100	7			1					•			
158	Piombino Porto Vecchio	42°55'.85N	010°33'.15E	47				7	•							•			
159	Piombino Terre Rosse	42°56'.90N	010°33'.72E	47		•	1100	8.5	•	•	4.5	•	•	•		•	•	•	•
160	Carbonifera	42°56'.85N	010°40'.90E	48		•	320	8			1			•		•			
161	Scarlino Fiumara del Puntone	42°53'.30N	010°46'.95E	48		•	400	10	•		4	•	•	•		•	•	•	•
161	Marina di Scarlino	42°53'.30N	010°46'.95E	48	•		566	40	•	•	4.5	•	•	•		•	•	•	•
163	Marina di Punta Ala	42°48'.50N	010°44'.24E	49	•		893	32	•	•	5.2	•	•	•		•	•	•	•

AREA C - FROM LERICI TO PROMONTORIO DELL' ARGENTARIO

	NAME	WGS 84 COORDINATES LATITUDE	WGS 84 COORDINATES LONGITUDE	CHART	⛵	⚓	🅿	LOA m	V	🅿	⬇ m	⚡	🔌	WC	🍴	🛒	🔧
165	Castiglione della Pescaia	42°45'.70N	010°52'.70E	51		•	350	20	•	•	3	•	•	•	•	•	•
166	Marina di San Rocco	42°42'.80N	010°59'.11E	51	•		561	14	•	•	2.5	•	•	•		•	
171	Talamone	42°33'.35N	011°08'.25E	52		•	IU	24	•	•	5	•	•	•	•	•	
173	Fiume Albenga	42°30'.00N	011°11'.50E	52		•	150	8			1			•			
174	Santa Liberata	42°26'.05N	011°09'.35E	54		•	600	6			2.5	•	•	•	•	•	•
176	Santo Stefano/Porto del Valle	42°26'.32N	011°07'.55E	54		•	385	30	•	•	4.5	•	•	•	•	•	•
177	Santo Stefano/Porto Vecchio	42°26'.45N	011°07'.05E	54		•	105	40	•		5		•		•		
189	Porto Ercole	42°23'.60N	011°12'.70E	56		•	825	24	•	•	10	•	•	•	•	•	•
190	Marina di Cala Galera	42°24'.24N	011°12'.80E	56	•		700	50	•	•	6	•	•	•	•	•	•

IU= Information Unavailable

ANCHORAGES KEY FOR PLAN SYMBOLS

	NAME	WGS 84 COORDINATES LATITUDE	WGS 84 COORDINATES LONGITUDE	CHART	Shelter	Seabed	Depth m	Landing	Facilities	Wind	Anchorage	Mooring
112	San Terenzo	44°04'.10N	009°53'.00E	33	G	m	5	•	B-R-S	SE-W	•	
113	Baia di Lerici	44°04'.50N	009°54'.30E	33	G	s	7	•	B-R-S	S-NW	•	•
115	Cala di Maramozza	44°04'.15N	009°55'.66E	33	G	m	6	•		S-W	•	
116	Cala Eco del Mare	44°03'.91N	009°55'.00E	33	G	m	5	•		S-NW	•	
117	Cala Mezzana/Fiascherino	44°03'.75N	009°55'.17E	33	G	m	5			SW-NW	•	
118	Tellaro	44°03'.33N	009°55'.91E	33	P	s/r	7	•	B-R-S	SW-NW	•	
120	Bocca di Magra	44°02'.41N	009°59'.30E	34	G	s	5	•	B-R-S	E-SW	•	
138	Cala Leone	43°27'.75N	010°21'.16E	41	G	s/r	7	•		S-W	•	
139	Castelsonnino	43°27'.58N	010°21'.41E	41	G	s	5	•		SE-SW	•	
142	Porticciolo Rossana	43°26'.70N	010°22'.95E	42	G	s/r	5	•		S-W	•	
143	Fortulino	43°25'.58N	010°23'.75E	42	G	s/r	5	•		S-N	•	
144	Baia del Quercetano	43°24'.41N	010°24'.16E	42	G	s	10	•		S-W	•	
145	Castiglioncello	42°24'.00N	010°24'.83E	43	P	s/r	7	•	B-R-S	E-W	•	
149	Porto di Vada	43°21'.00N	010°26'.91E	44	P	s	2	•	B-R	SW-NW	•	
153	Porto Baratti - anchorage	42°59'.65N	010°30'.40E	45	G	s	4	•	B-R	W-N	•	
154	Porto Baratti - mooring	42°59'.55N	010°30'.24E	45	G	s	2	•	B-R	W-N	•	•
162	Cala Violina	42°51.50N	010°46'.00E	49	G	s	5	•		SW-NW	•	
164	Rocchette	42°46'.41N	010°47'.75E	50	G	s/r	4	•	B-R	E-SW	•	
168	Cala di Forno	42°37'.20N	011°05'.08E	50	G	s	4	•		W-N	•	
169	Uccellina	42°36'.16N	011°05'.83E	50	P	s	5			SW-NW	•	
170	Capo d'Uomo	42°33'.60N	011°07'.22E	50	P	s	6			S-N	•	
172	Foce dell'Osa	42°32'.90N	011°09'.83E	52	G	s	4	•		S-W	•	
175	Baia Pozzarello	42°26'.16N	011°08'.58E	53	G	s/w	5			NW-NE	•	
178	Cala Caciarella	45°26'.46N	011°05'.92E	53	G	s/r	10			W-N	•	
179	Cala Grande	42°25'.95N	011°05'.60E	53	G	s/w	5			SW-N	•	
181	Cala del Gesso	42°24'.90N	011°05'.35E	53	G	s	6	•		SW-NW	•	
182	Cala Piatti	42°24'.12N	011°05'.56E	53	G	s/w	12	•	B-R	SW-NW	•	
183	Isola Rossa	42°22'.50N	011°07'.83E	55	G	s/r	7	•		SE-SW	•	
184	Spiaggia Cannelle	42°22'.55N	011°08'.41E	55	G	s	4	•	B-R	SE-SW	•	
185	Cala Bocca d'Inferno	42°22'.14N	011°08'.83E	55	G	s	6	•		S-NW	•	
186	Cala Piazzoni	42°21'.83N	011°10'.48E	55	G	s	6	•		SE-SW	•	
188	L'Isolotto	42°22'.75N	011°12'.48E	55	G	s	5	•		E-SW	•	
191	Cala Galera - anchorage	42°24'.41N	011°12'.65E	56	G	s	5	•	B-R-S	E-S	•	

Shelter: P = Poor G = Good E = Excellent **Nature of seabed:** w = weed m = mud g = gravel p = pebbles/stones r = rock s = sand

Depths in metres **Landing with dinghy** **Facilities ashore:** B = Bar R = Restaurant S = Shop **Anchorage** **Mooring buoy**

Wind direction and exposure

AREA C - FROM LERICI TO PROMONTORIO DELL'ARGENTARIO

SAFETY AT SEA — AREA C

WEATHER BULLETIN

Mari d'Italia/Meteomar weather bulletin
(English and Italian)
VHF ch 68 frequency 156.425 MHz continuous

Coast radio station weather bulletin
0135 0735 1335 1935 UTC
Montenero (Livorno) VHF ch 61 frequency 160.675 MHz
Gorgona VHF ch 26 frequency 161.900 MHz
Monte Argentario VHF ch 01 frequency 160.650 MHz

Radiouno/Isoradio everyday weather bulletin
0554 1408 2249 Monday-Friday

FRANCE AND CORSICA WEATHER FORECASTS
(French-English)

Monaco Radio 4363 kHz (ch 403)
0903 1403 1915 LT
Lyon, Provence, Corsican Sea, Sardinian Sea, Ligurian Sea, Northern Tyrrhenian Sea

Monaco Radio 8728, 8806 kHz (ch 804, 830) SSB
0715 1830 UTC West Mediterranean offshore seas

La Garde CROSS 1696, 2677 kHz SSB after the first call
Frequency 2182 kHz
0650 1433 1850 LT

HARBOURMASTERS

La Spezia ☎ +39 0187 258100
cplaspezia@mit.gov.it

Marina di Carrara ☎ +39 0585 646701
cpcarrara@mit.gov.it

Livorno ☎ +39 0586 826011
cplivorno@guardiacostiera.gov.it

Viareggio ☎ +39 0584 43931
cpviareggio@mit.gov.it

Portoferraio ☎ 0565 914000
cpportoferraio@mit.gov.it

Guardia Costiera (Coast Guard)
☎ 1530 emergency - VHF ch 16

SAFETY AND RESCUE CENTRES

MRSC Genova ☎ +39 010 27771
genova@guardiacostiera.it

MRSC Livorno ☎ +39 0586 826011
cplivorno@guardiacostiera.gov.it

MRCC Roma MMSI 002 470 001
DSC VHF ch 70, 16 - DSC MF 2187.5 kHz, 2182 kHz
DSC HF 420.5, 6312, 8414.5 kHz
Direzione Marittima (Porth Authority) Roma Fiumicino
☎ +39 06 656171
cproma@mit.gov.it

MRSC Corsica VHF ch 16, 67
☎ +33 (0)495 201363
MMSI 002275420
(winter 0730-1900 - summer 0730-2300)

CIRM International Medical Centre
☎ +39 06 559290263 - mobile +39 348 3984229
Fax +39 06 5923331/2
telesoccorso@cirm.it - www.cirm.it

radio.guardiacostiera.it

FROM PUNTA GALERA TO TELLARO | AREA C | CHART 33

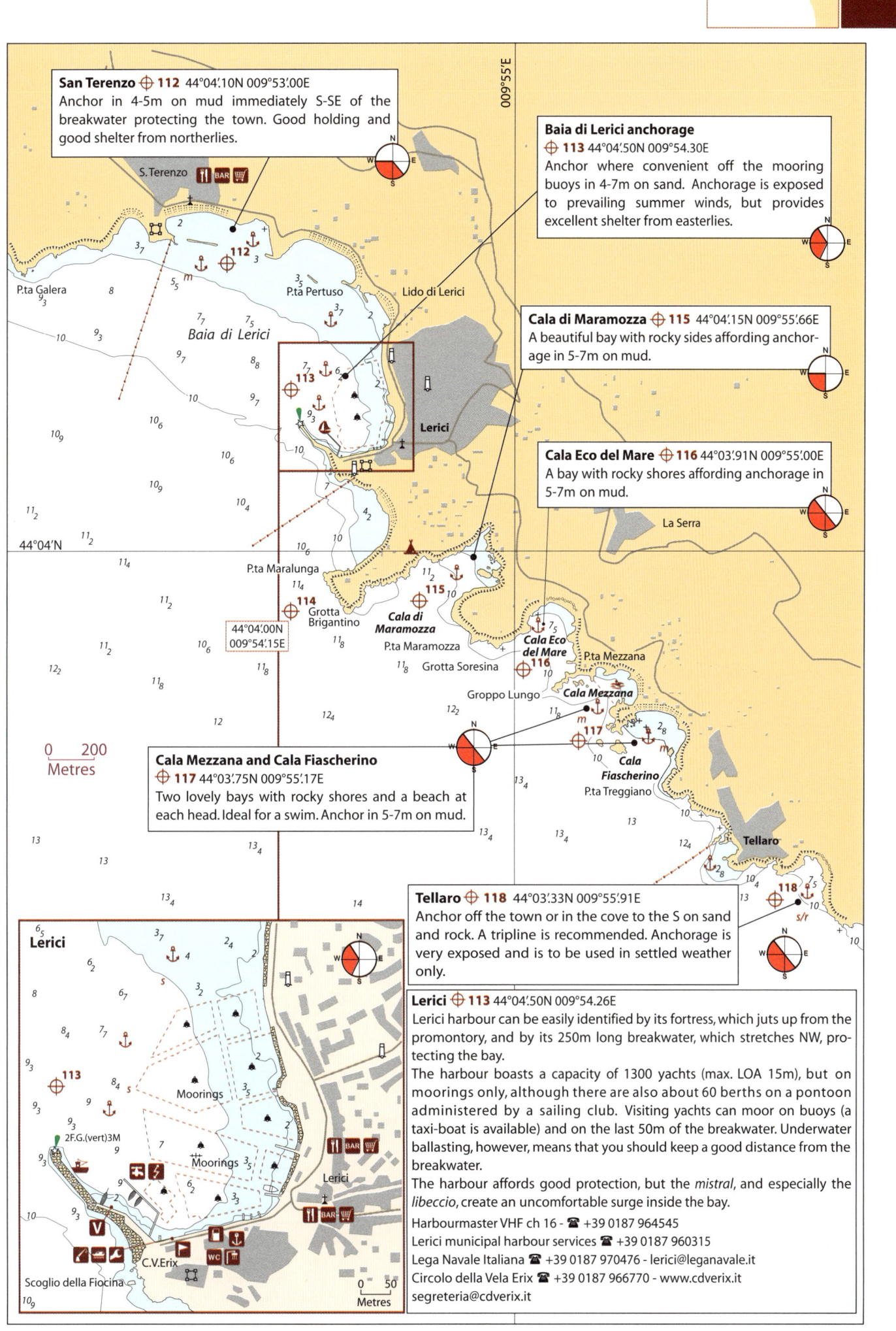

San Terenzo ⊕ 112 44°04'.10N 009°53'.00E
Anchor in 4-5m on mud immediately S-SE of the breakwater protecting the town. Good holding and good shelter from northerlies.

Baia di Lerici anchorage
⊕ 113 44°04'.50N 009°54.30E
Anchor where convenient off the mooring buoys in 4-7m on sand. Anchorage is exposed to prevailing summer winds, but provides excellent shelter from easterlies.

Cala di Maramozza ⊕ 115 44°04'.15N 009°55'.66E
A beautiful bay with rocky sides affording anchorage in 5-7m on mud.

Cala Eco del Mare ⊕ 116 44°03'.91N 009°55'.00E
A bay with rocky shores affording anchorage in 5-7m on mud.

Cala Mezzana and Cala Fiascherino
⊕ 117 44°03'.75N 009°55'.17E
Two lovely bays with rocky shores and a beach at each head. Ideal for a swim. Anchor in 5-7m on mud.

Tellaro ⊕ 118 44°03'.33N 009°55'.91E
Anchor off the town or in the cove to the S on sand and rock. A tripline is recommended. Anchorage is very exposed and is to be used in settled weather only.

Lerici ⊕ 113 44°04'.50N 009°54.26E
Lerici harbour can be easily identified by its fortress, which juts up from the promontory, and by its 250m long breakwater, which stretches NW, protecting the bay.
The harbour boasts a capacity of 1300 yachts (max. LOA 15m), but on moorings only, although there are also about 60 berths on a pontoon administered by a sailing club. Visiting yachts can moor on buoys (a taxi-boat is available) and on the last 50m of the breakwater. Underwater ballasting, however, means that you should keep a good distance from the breakwater.
The harbour affords good protection, but the *mistral*, and especially the *libeccio*, create an uncomfortable surge inside the bay.

Harbourmaster VHF ch 16 - ☎ +39 0187 964545
Lerici municipal harbour services ☎ +39 0187 960315
Lega Navale Italiana ☎ +39 0187 970476 - lerici@leganavale.it
Circolo della Vela Erix ☎ +39 0187 966770 - www.cdverix.it
segreteria@cdverix.it

CHART 34 | AREA C | FIUME MAGRA

Along the banks of the River Magra are numerous facilities with a total capacity of 2000 yachts. There is also a number of facilities for winter storage, as high water and occasional floods make it risky to leave boats on the water during winter.
When going upstream, keep about 50m from the W riverbank, as a sandbar runs down the middle of the riverbed. The E bank is reached by sailing upstream as far as the red buoy near the bridge. The buoy is in the centre of the river and marks where yachts can cross. The river level varies, so yachts drawing over 2m must proceed extremely carefully.

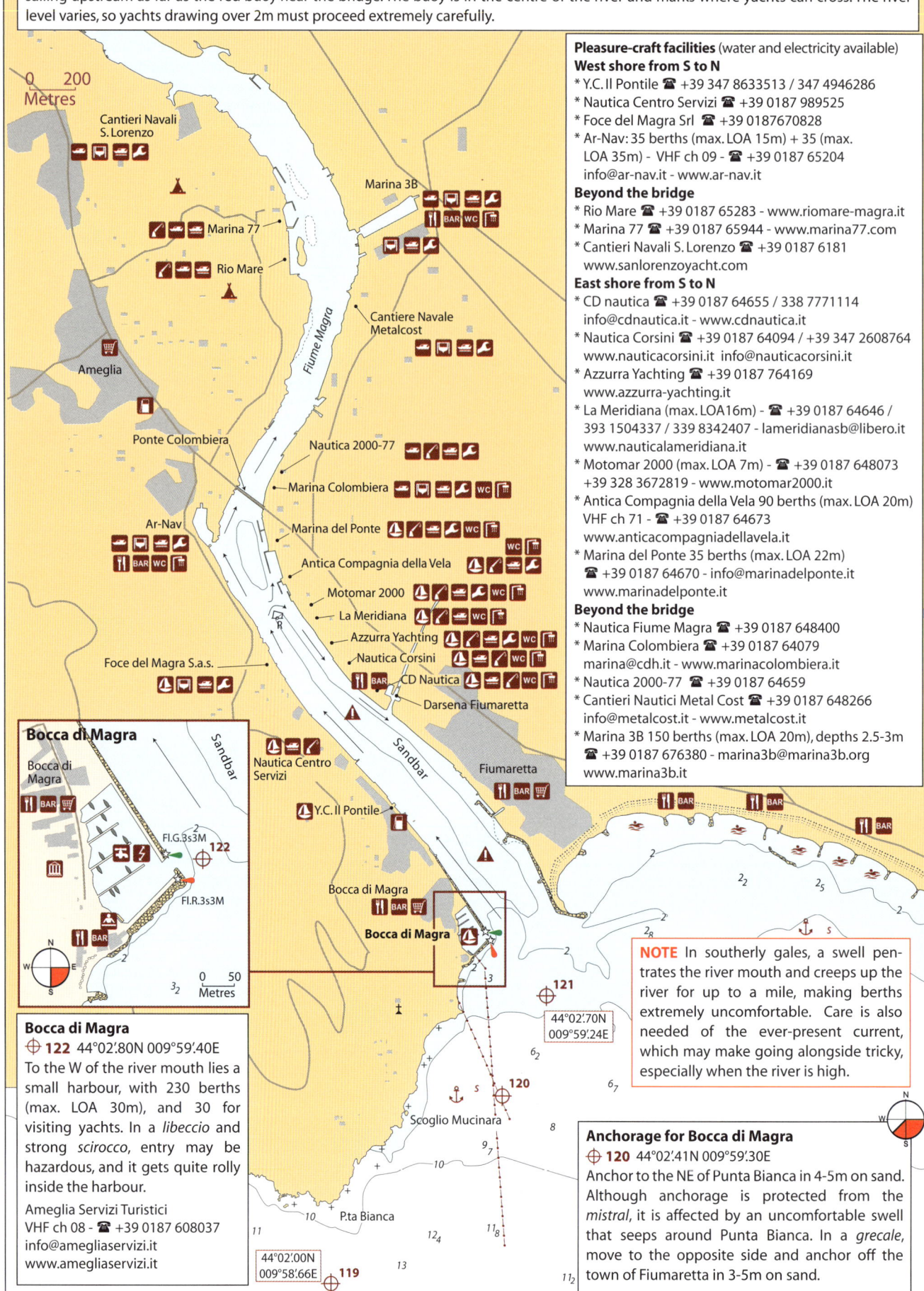

Pleasure-craft facilities (water and electricity available)
West shore from S to N
* Y.C. Il Pontile ☎ +39 347 8633513 / 347 4946286
* Nautica Centro Servizi ☎ +39 0187 989525
* Foce del Magra Srl ☎ +39 0187670828
* Ar-Nav: 35 berths (max. LOA 15m) + 35 (max. LOA 35m) - VHF ch 09 - ☎ +39 0187 65204 info@ar-nav.it - www.ar-nav.it

Beyond the bridge
* Rio Mare ☎ +39 0187 65283 - www.riomare-magra.it
* Marina 77 ☎ +39 0187 65944 - www.marina77.com
* Cantieri Navali S. Lorenzo ☎ +39 0187 6181 www.sanlorenzoyacht.com

East shore from S to N
* CD nautica ☎ +39 0187 64655 / 338 7771114 info@cdnautica.it - www.cdnautica.it
* Nautica Corsini ☎ +39 0187 64094 / +39 347 2608764 www.nauticacorsini.it info@nauticacorsini.it
* Azzurra Yachting ☎ +39 0187 764169 www.azzurra-yachting.it
* La Meridiana (max. LOA16m) - ☎ +39 0187 64646 / 393 1504337 / 339 8342407 - lameridianasb@libero.it www.nauticalameridiana.it
* Motomar 2000 (max. LOA 7m) - ☎ +39 0187 648073 +39 328 3672819 - www.motomar2000.it
* Antica Compagnia della Vela 90 berths (max. LOA 20m) VHF ch 71 - ☎ +39 0187 64673 www.anticacompagniadellavela.it
* Marina del Ponte 35 berths (max. LOA 22m) ☎ +39 0187 64670 - info@marinadelponte.it www.marinadelponte.it

Beyond the bridge
* Nautica Fiume Magra ☎ +39 0187 648400
* Marina Colombiera ☎ +39 0187 64079 marina@cdh.it - www.marinacolombiera.it
* Nautica 2000-77 ☎ +39 0187 64659
* Cantieri Nautici Metal Cost ☎ +39 0187 648266 info@metalcost.it - www.metalcost.it
* Marina 3B 150 berths (max. LOA 20m), depths 2.5-3m ☎ +39 0187 676380 - marina3b@marina3b.org www.marina3b.it

Bocca di Magra
⊕ 122 44°02'.80N 009°59'.40E
To the W of the river mouth lies a small harbour, with 230 berths (max. LOA 30m), and 30 for visiting yachts. In a *libeccio* and strong *scirocco*, entry may be hazardous, and it gets quite rolly inside the harbour.
Ameglia Servizi Turistici
VHF ch 08 - ☎ +39 0187 608037
info@amegliaservizi.it
www.amegliaservizi.it

NOTE In southerly gales, a swell penetrates the river mouth and creeps up the river for up to a mile, making berths extremely uncomfortable. Care is also needed of the ever-present current, which may make going alongside tricky, especially when the river is high.

Anchorage for Bocca di Magra
⊕ 120 44°02'.41N 009°59'.30E
Anchor to the NE of Punta Bianca in 4-5m on sand. Although anchorage is protected from the *mistral*, it is affected by an uncomfortable swell that seeps around Punta Bianca. In a *grecale*, move to the opposite side and anchor off the town of Fiumaretta in 3-5m on sand.

FROM PUNTA BIANCA TO VIAREGGIO | AREA C | CHART 35

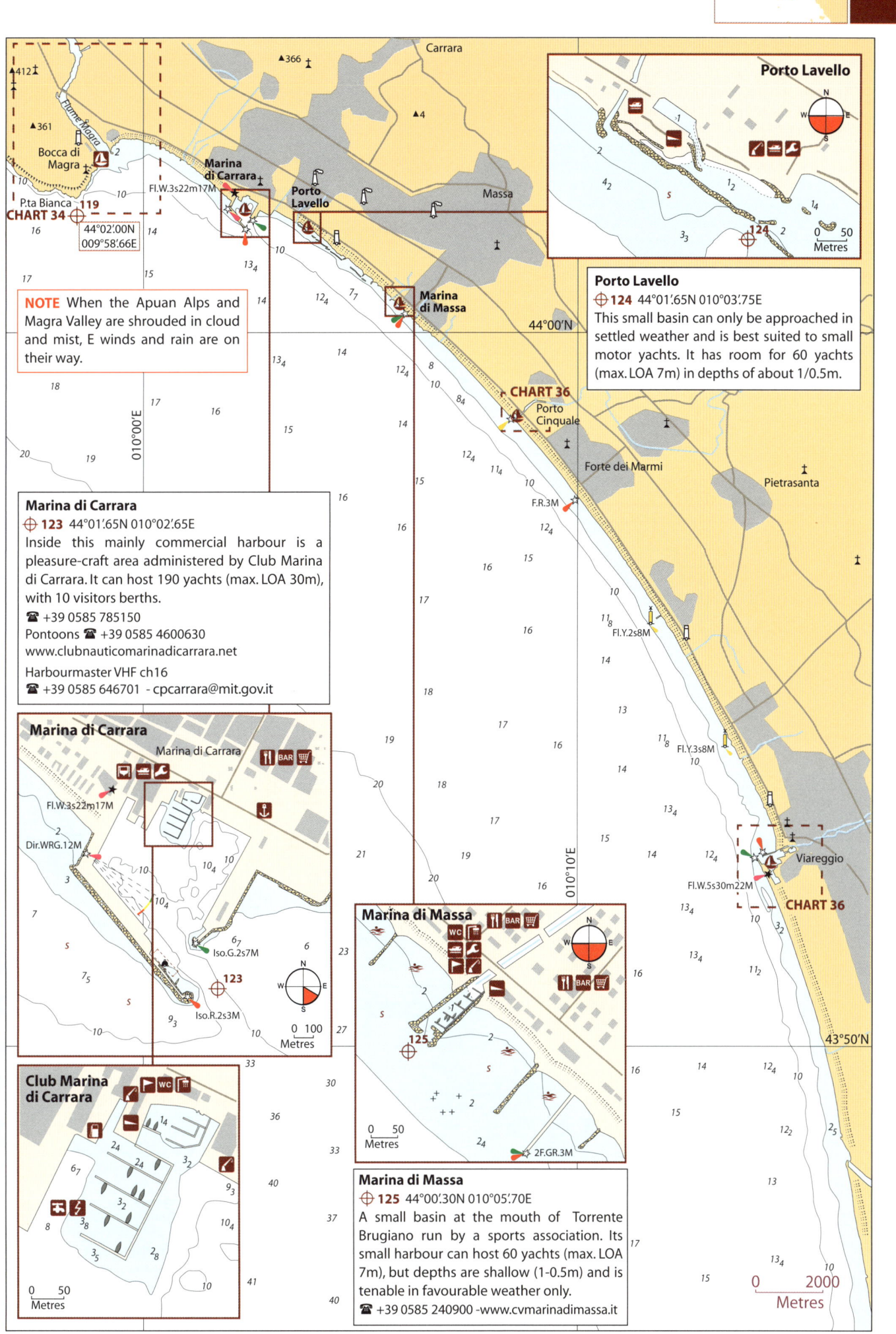

NOTE When the Apuan Alps and Magra Valley are shrouded in cloud and mist, E winds and rain are on their way.

Marina di Carrara
⊕ 123 44°01'.65N 010°02'.65E
Inside this mainly commercial harbour is a pleasure-craft area administered by Club Marina di Carrara. It can host 190 yachts (max. LOA 30m), with 10 visitors berths.
☎ +39 0585 785150
Pontoons ☎ +39 0585 4600630
www.clubnauticomarinadicarrara.net
Harbourmaster VHF ch16
☎ +39 0585 646701 - cpcarrara@mit.gov.it

Porto Lavello
⊕ 124 44°01'.65N 010°03'.75E
This small basin can only be approached in settled weather and is best suited to small motor yachts. It has room for 60 yachts (max. LOA 7m) in depths of about 1/0.5m.

Marina di Massa
⊕ 125 44°00'.30N 010°05'.70E
A small basin at the mouth of Torrente Brugiano run by a sports association. Its small harbour can host 60 yachts (max. LOA 7m), but depths are shallow (1-0.5m) and is tenable in favourable weather only.
☎ +39 0585 240900 - www.cvmarinadimassa.it

63

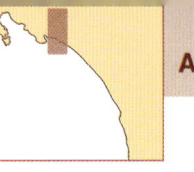

CHART 36

AREA C | HARBOURS OF CINQUALE AND VIAREGGIO

Porto Cinquale ⊕ **126** 43°58'.50N 010°08'.40E
Two harbours in the last stretch of the River Versilia, just before the mouth: Porto Cinquale, a small basin with 67 berths (max. LOA 14m), and 6 for visitors; and Approdo Turistico del Cinquale, which lies further upstream, with 240 berths (max. LOA 8.5m) and 18 for visitors. The river is shallow and can be approached by yachts drawing no more than 1m only. Approaching the canal in bad weather is very dangerous, if not impossible.
Porto Cinquale run by Automare 84 ☎ +39 0585 308032 www.portociquale.it
Approdo Turistico del Cinquale VHF ch 09 - ☎ +39 0585 309867
info@versilmarine.it - www.versilmarine.it

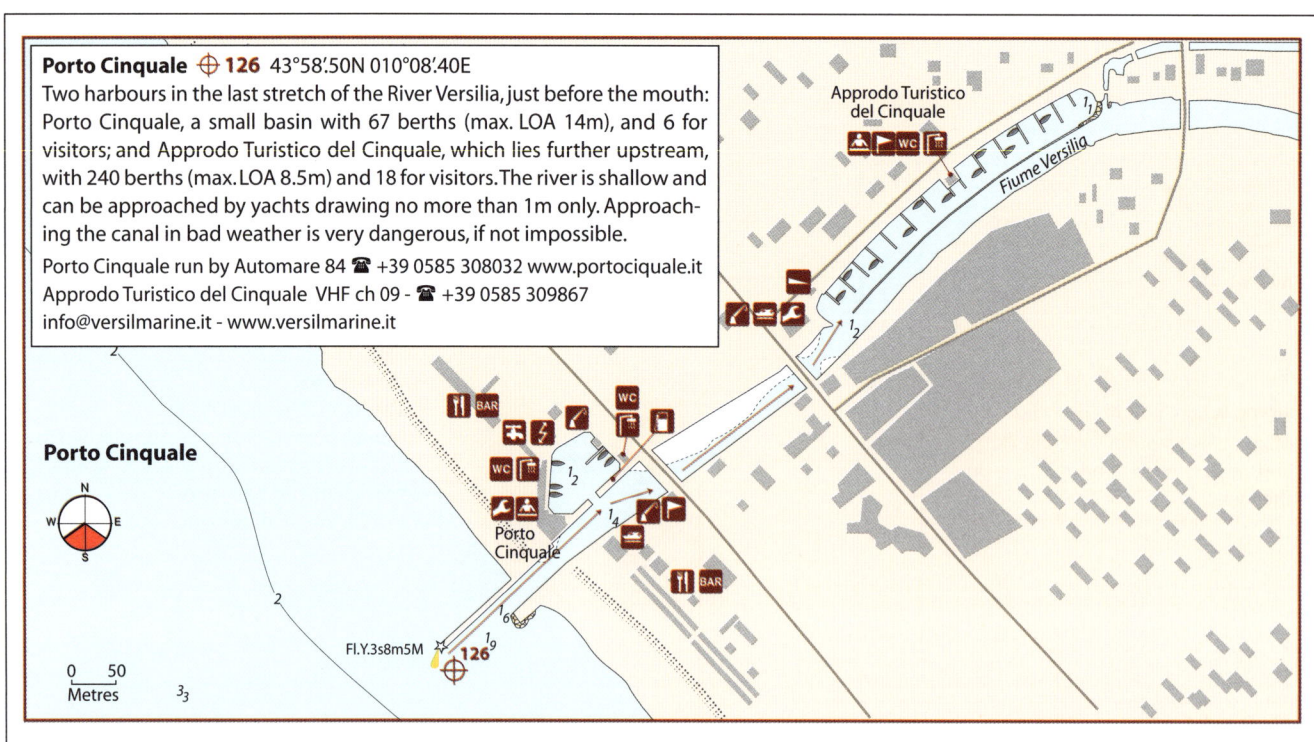

Viareggio ⊕ **127** 43°51'.65N 010°14'.05E
At the mouth of Canale Burlamacca stands the large harbour of Viareggio, which has six basins that can accommodate 2000 craft (max. LOA 80m), with 80 visitors berths. The harbour enjoys all-round shelter, but entry is very dangerous in W-SW gales. Also note that depths fluctuate considerably at the harbour entrance due to a sandbar (3m) which runs parallel to the shore for 600m off the outer end of the Diga Foranea (outer breakwater). A 150m section of the A. Antonini quay in Darsena Europa provides visitors berths free-of-charge. The Nuova Darsena is reserved for motor fishing vessels. There are other small basins in Canale Burlamacca that are suitable for motor yachts.

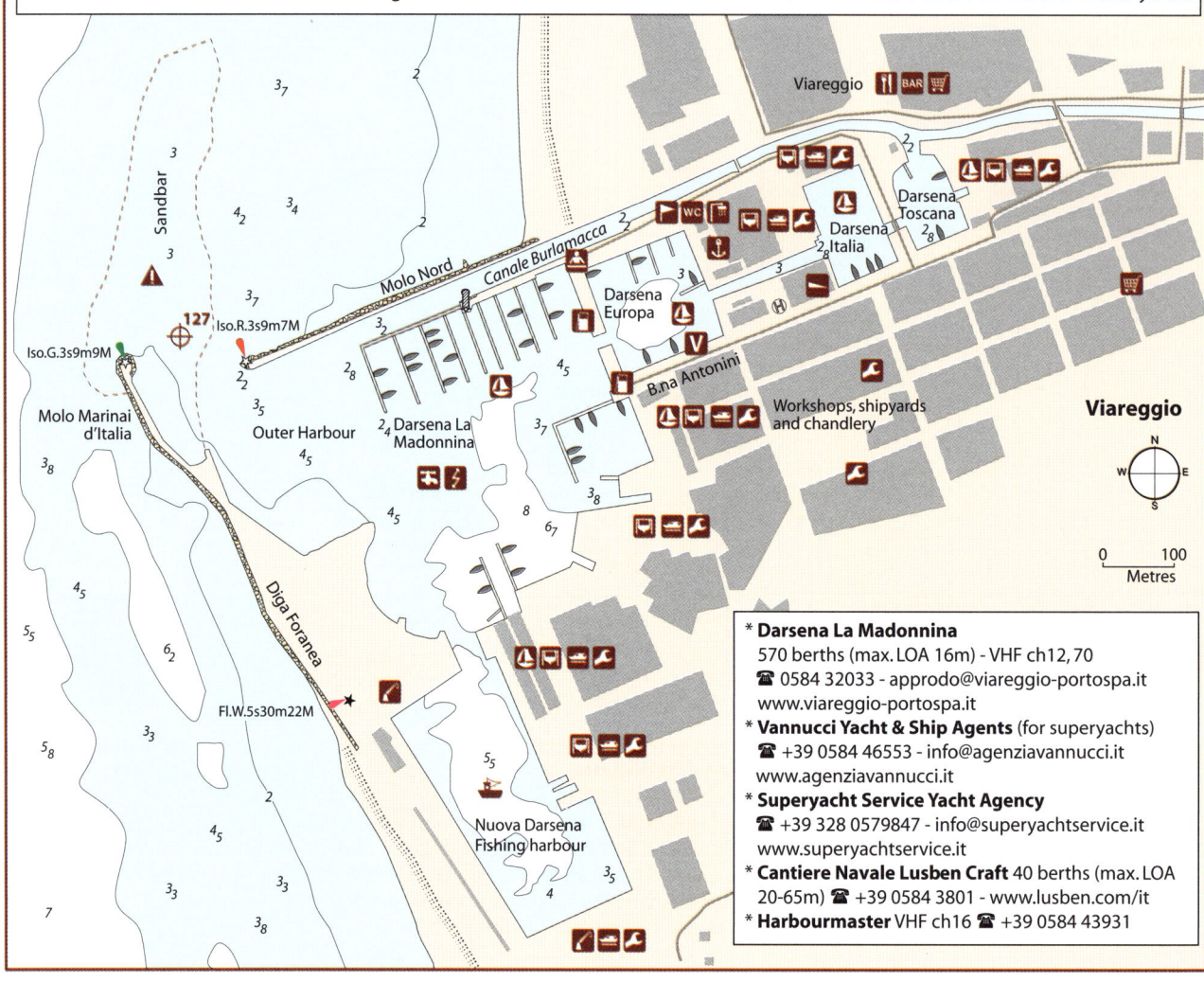

* **Darsena La Madonnina**
  570 berths (max. LOA 16m) - VHF ch12, 70
  ☎ 0584 32033 - approdo@viareggio-portospa.it
  www.viareggio-portospa.it
* **Vannucci Yacht & Ship Agents** (for superyachts)
  ☎ +39 0584 46553 - info@agenziavannucci.it
  www.agenziavannucci.it
* **Superyacht Service Yacht Agency**
  ☎ +39 328 0579847 - info@superyachtservice.it
  www.superyachtservice.it
* **Cantiere Navale Lusben Craft** 40 berths (max. LOA 20-65m) ☎ +39 0584 3801 - www.lusben.com/it
* **Harbourmaster** VHF ch16 ☎ +39 0584 43931

FROM VIAREGGIO TO LIVORNO | AREA C

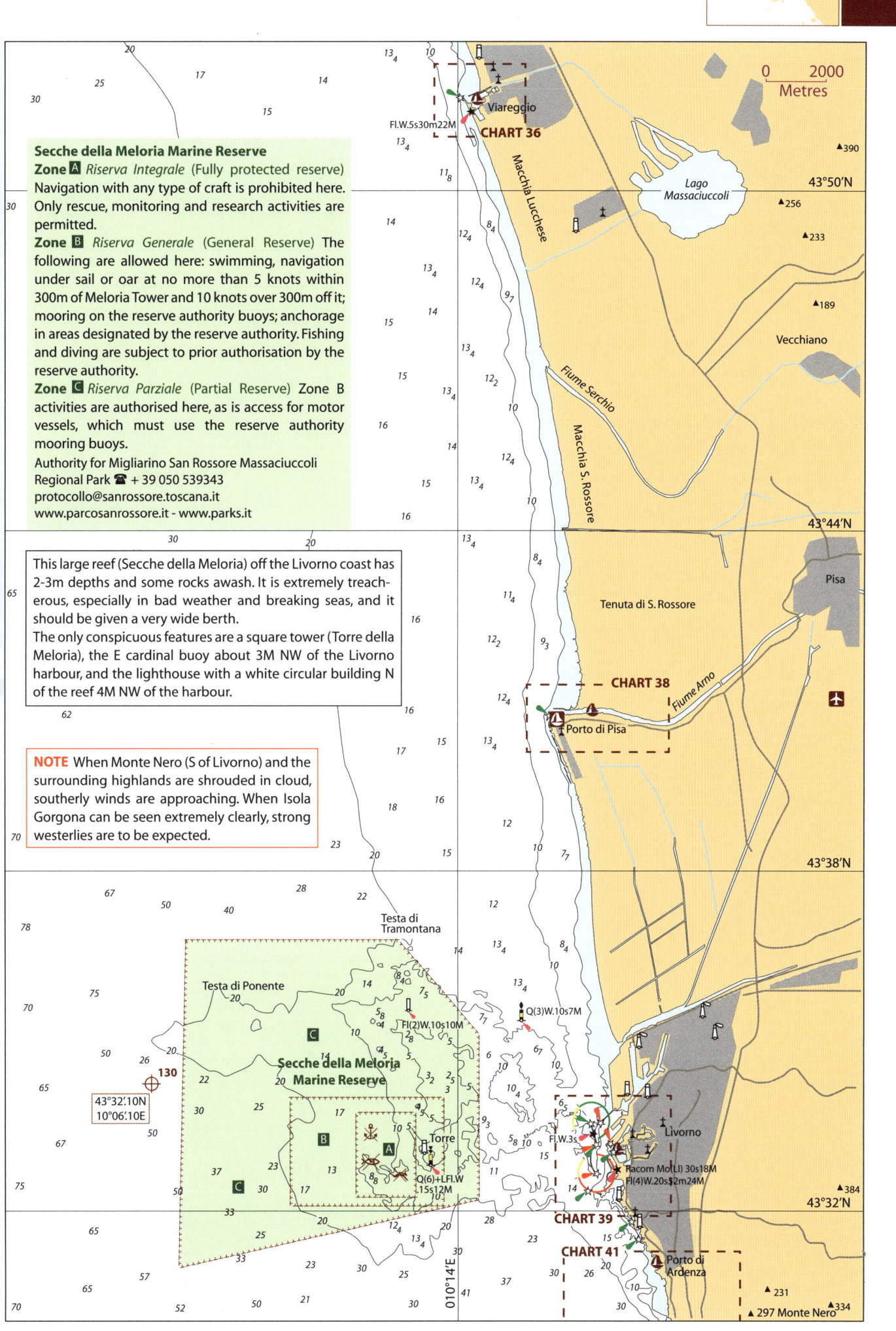

CHART 37

Secche della Meloria Marine Reserve

Zone A *Riserva Integrale* (Fully protected reserve) Navigation with any type of craft is prohibited here. Only rescue, monitoring and research activities are permitted.

Zone B *Riserva Generale* (General Reserve) The following are allowed here: swimming, navigation under sail or oar at no more than 5 knots within 300m of Meloria Tower and 10 knots over 300m off it; mooring on the reserve authority buoys; anchorage in areas designated by the reserve authority. Fishing and diving are subject to prior authorisation by the reserve authority.

Zone C *Riserva Parziale* (Partial Reserve) Zone B activities are authorised here, as is access for motor vessels, which must use the reserve authority mooring buoys.

Authority for Migliarino San Rossore Massaciuccoli Regional Park ☎ + 39 050 539343
protocollo@sanrossore.toscana.it
www.parcosanrossore.it - www.parks.it

This large reef (Secche della Meloria) off the Livorno coast has 2-3m depths and some rocks awash. It is extremely treacherous, especially in bad weather and breaking seas, and it should be given a very wide berth.

The only conspicuous features are a square tower (Torre della Meloria), the E cardinal buoy about 3M NW of the Livorno harbour, and the lighthouse with a white circular building N of the reef 4M NW of the harbour.

NOTE When Monte Nero (S of Livorno) and the surrounding highlands are shrouded in cloud, southerly winds are approaching. When Isola Gorgona can be seen extremely clearly, strong westerlies are to be expected.

65

CHART 38 | AREA C | FIUME ARNO

Moorings in Fiume Arno ⊕ 128 43°40'.80N 010°16'.20E

The last 2M of the S bank of the River Arno are home to facilities that can host up to 500 yachts (max. LOA 20m), plus toilet blocks and a hardstanding area. Water and electricity are available. Porto di Pisa stands at the mouth of river and has 354 berths (max. LOA 50m). The town of Marina di Pisa sits behind the harbour. Yachts can navigate the river up to the first bridge, which lies 3.5M further upstream. In normal conditions, depths average about 3-4m. Note that there is no red light at the river mouth, so in a night approach, set a course of 75° near to the green light in order to avoid the rock to the N.

Bear in mind the following when approaching the river: there is a strong descending current which can reach 3 knots. Cables are suspended about 500m from the river mouth about 18m above the water. They support drop nets attached to metal poles stationed along both riverbanks. There are sand banks at the river mouth, especially after W-SW gales. Entering and leaving the river in strong onshore winds and moderate seas is very dangerous, if not impossible.

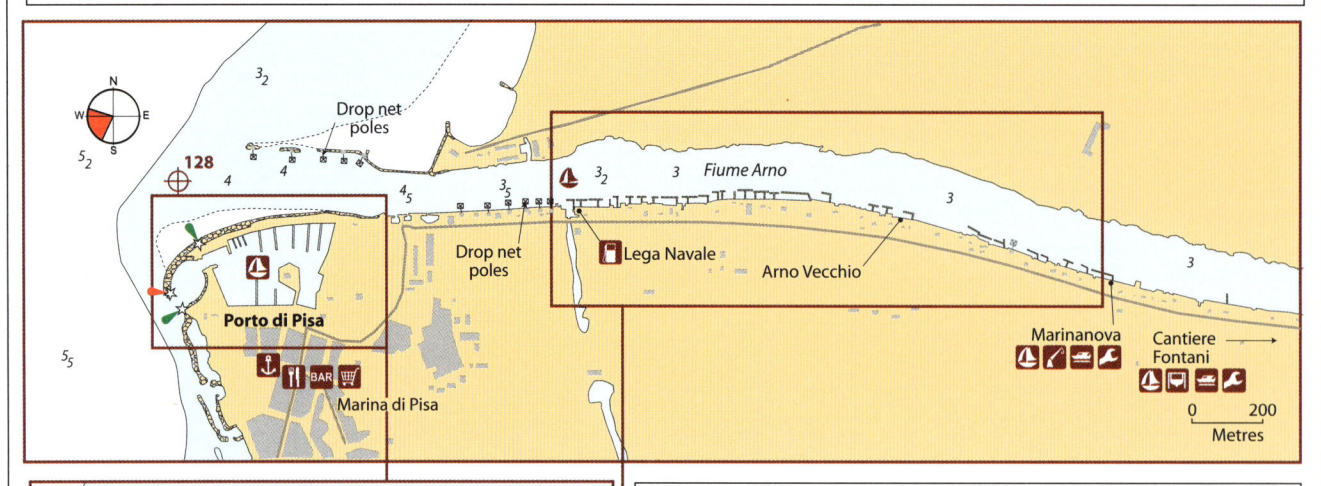

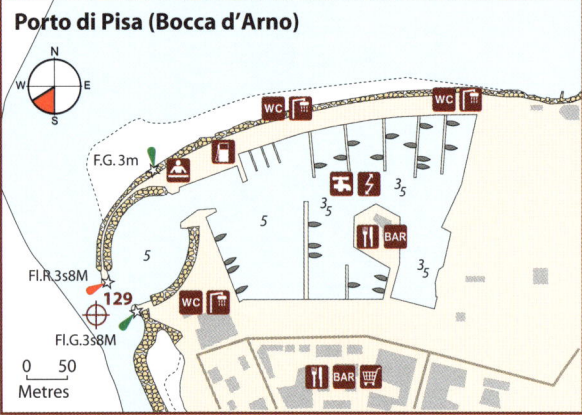

Porto di Pisa (Bocca d'Arno) ⊕ 129 43°40'.80N 010°16'.20E

This new marina can host 354 yachts (max. LOA 50m). Although it is protected by an outer harbour, approaching when a strong *libeccio* is blowing is hazardous, if not impossible.
VHF ch 74 - ☎ +39 050 36142 office / 347 5413372 *ormeggiatori* (marina attendants) - info@portodipisa.it - www.portodipisa.it

Contacts
* **Lega Navale** (max. LOA 10m) ☎ +39 050 36037 - www.leganavalepisa.it
* **Piccolo Cantiere Capocchi** ☎ +39 050 36391
* **Marine One Club** ☎ +39 335 6709919
* **Y. C. Repubblica Marinara Di Pisa** ☎ +39 050 310023 - info@ycrmp.com www.ycrmp.com
* **Sottocoperta 238** ☎ +39 347 0950866/339 3121983 sottocoperta238@gmail.com - www.sottocoperta238.it
* **Cantieri Navali del Serchio** ☎ +39 050 35384 www.cantieridelserchio.it info@cantieridelserchio.it - **Y.C. Serchio** ☎ +39 327 3747086
* **La Caletta** ☎ +39 050 311127
* **Marina Arnovecchio** 35 berths (max. LOA 20m) ☎ +39 050 34182 / 348 6197985 - arnovecchio@gmail.com - www.arnovecchio.com
* **Sandroni Base Nautica** 60 berths (max. LOA 11m) ☎ +39 050 310031
* **Asd Circolo Nautico Dlf** ☎ +39 050 35703
* **Del Cherico Maria Gabriella Club Nautico** ☎ +39 050 310007
* **Marina 204** ☎ +39 335 5413662 - marina204@arnomarine.it
* **Arno 206** ☎ +39 392 4635073 - info@arno206.it - www.arno206.it
* **Marinanova Punto Arno** 40 berths (max. LOA 15m) ☎ +39 050 310037 / 329 2451660 - info@marinanova.it - www.marinanova.it
* **Cantiere Fontani** 60 berths (max. LOA 14m) ☎ +39 050 960075 info@cantierefontani.it - www.cantierefontani.it

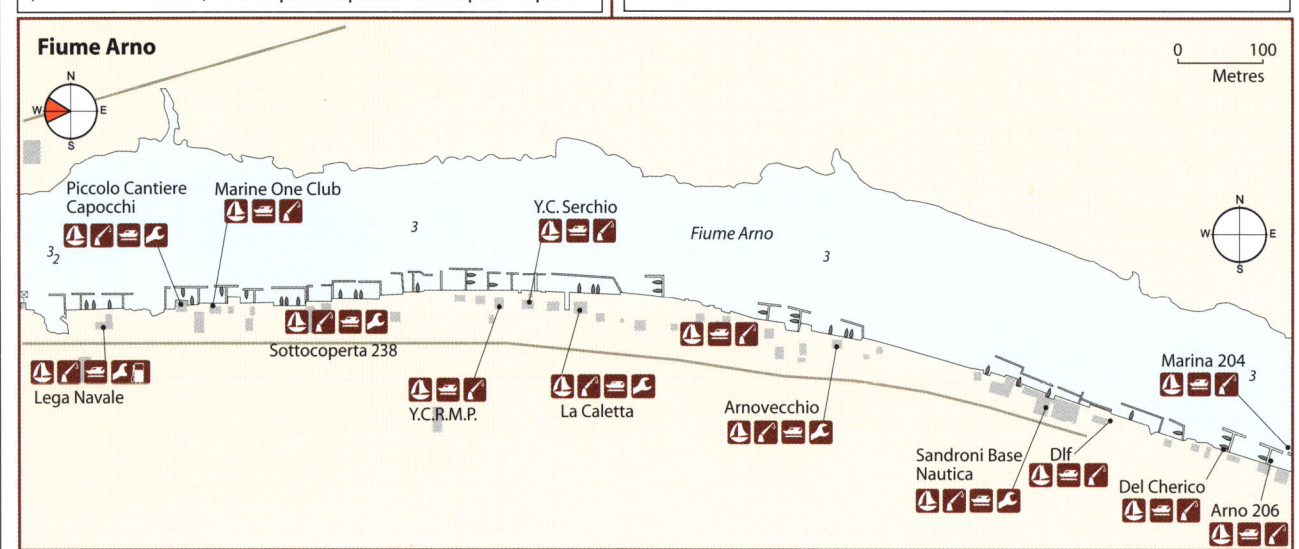

LIVORNO — AREA C — CHART 39

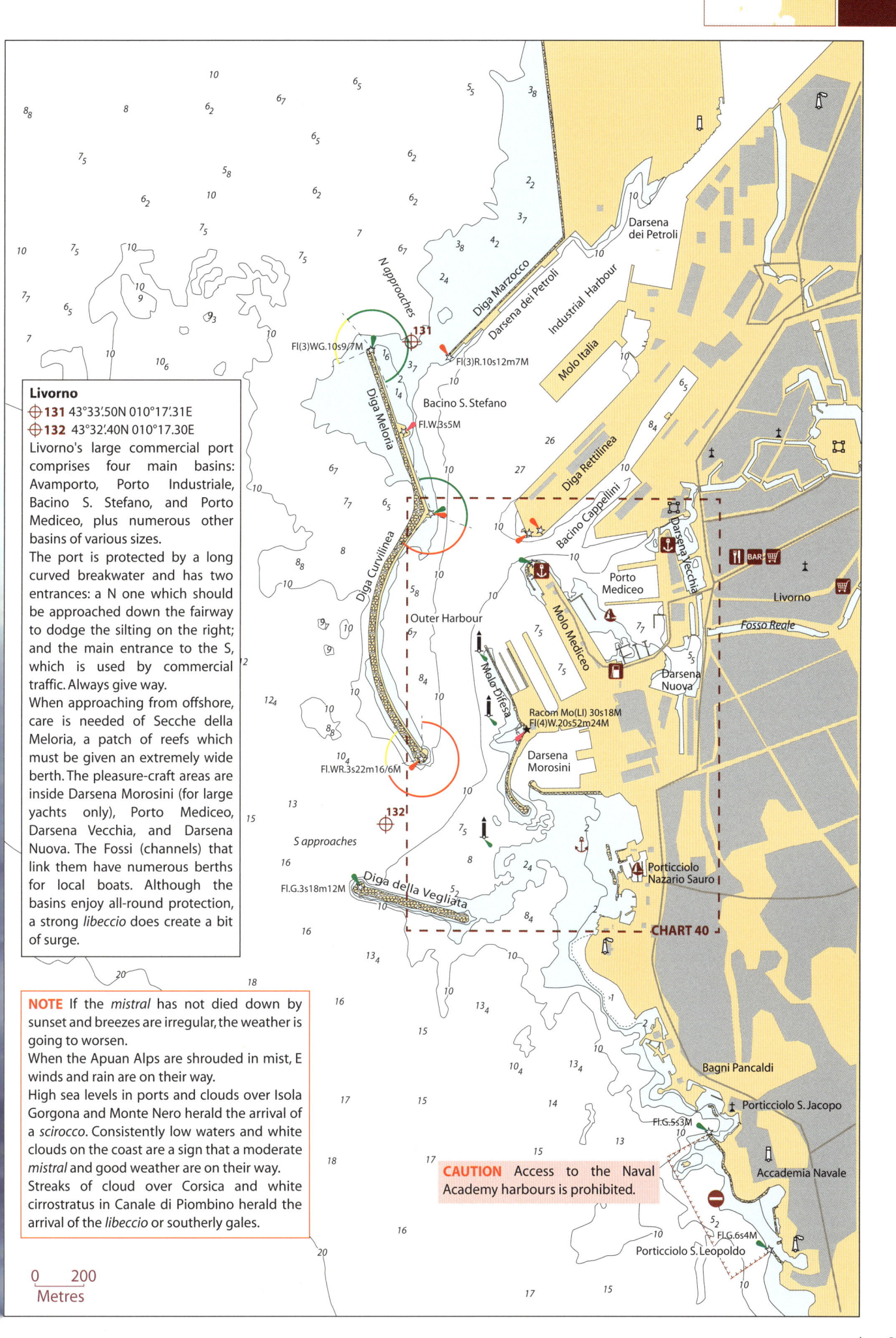

Livorno

⊕ **131** 43°33'.50N 010°17'.31E
⊕ **132** 43°32'.40N 010°17.30E

Livorno's large commercial port comprises four main basins: Avamporto, Porto Industriale, Bacino S. Stefano, and Porto Mediceo, plus numerous other basins of various sizes.

The port is protected by a long curved breakwater and has two entrances: a N one which should be approached down the fairway to dodge the silting on the right; and the main entrance to the S, which is used by commercial traffic. Always give way.

When approaching from offshore, care is needed of Secche della Meloria, a patch of reefs which must be given an extremely wide berth. The pleasure-craft areas are inside Darsena Morosini (for large yachts only), Porto Mediceo, Darsena Vecchia, and Darsena Nuova. The Fossi (channels) that link them have numerous berths for local boats. Although the basins enjoy all-round protection, a strong *libeccio* does create a bit of surge.

NOTE If the *mistral* has not died down by sunset and breezes are irregular, the weather is going to worsen.
When the Apuan Alps are shrouded in mist, E winds and rain are on their way.
High sea levels in ports and clouds over Isola Gorgona and Monte Nero herald the arrival of a *scirocco*. Consistently low waters and white clouds on the coast are a sign that a moderate *mistral* and good weather are on their way.
Streaks of cloud over Corsica and white cirrostratus in Canale di Piombino herald the arrival of the *libeccio* or southerly gales.

CAUTION Access to the Naval Academy harbours is prohibited.

0   200
Metres

CHART 40 | AREA C | LIVORNO

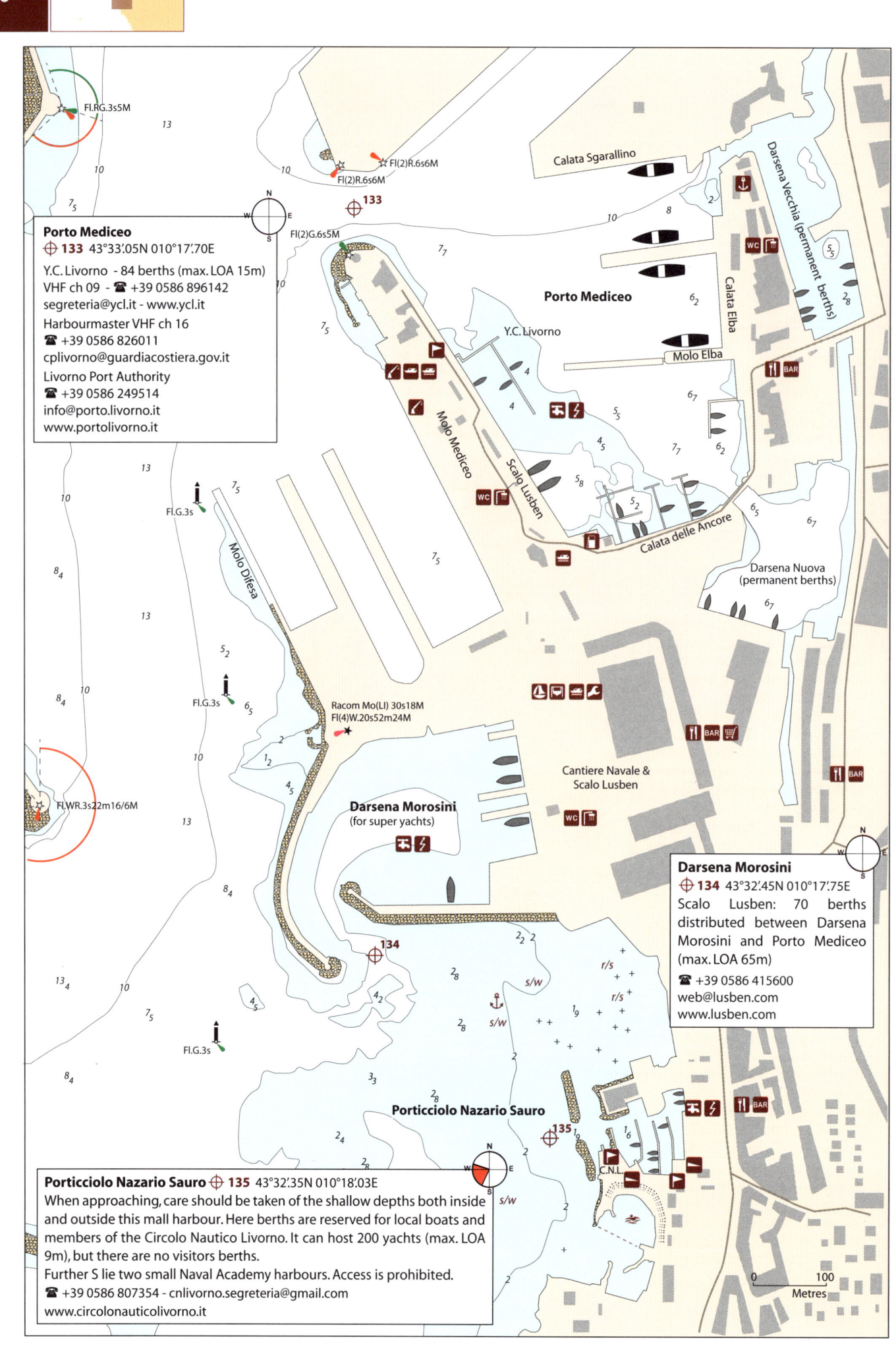

Porto Mediceo
⊕ **133** 43°33'.05N 010°17'.70E
Y.C. Livorno - 84 berths (max. LOA 15m)
VHF ch 09 - ☎ +39 0586 896142
segreteria@ycl.it - www.ycl.it
Harbourmaster VHF ch 16
☎ +39 0586 826011
cplivorno@guardiacostiera.gov.it
Livorno Port Authority
☎ +39 0586 249514
info@porto.livorno.it
www.portolivorno.it

Darsena Morosini
⊕ **134** 43°32'.45N 010°17'.75E
Scalo Lusben: 70 berths distributed between Darsena Morosini and Porto Mediceo (max. LOA 65m)
☎ +39 0586 415600
web@lusben.com
www.lusben.com

Porticciolo Nazario Sauro ⊕ **135** 43°32'.35N 010°18'.03E
When approaching, care should be taken of the shallow depths both inside and outside this mall harbour. Here berths are reserved for local boats and members of the Circolo Nautico Livorno. It can host 200 yachts (max. LOA 9m), but there are no visitors berths.
Further S lie two small Naval Academy harbours. Access is prohibited.
☎ +39 0586 807354 - cnlivorno.segreteria@gmail.com
www.circolonauticolivorno.it

FROM LIVORNO TO CASTEL SONNINO — AREA C

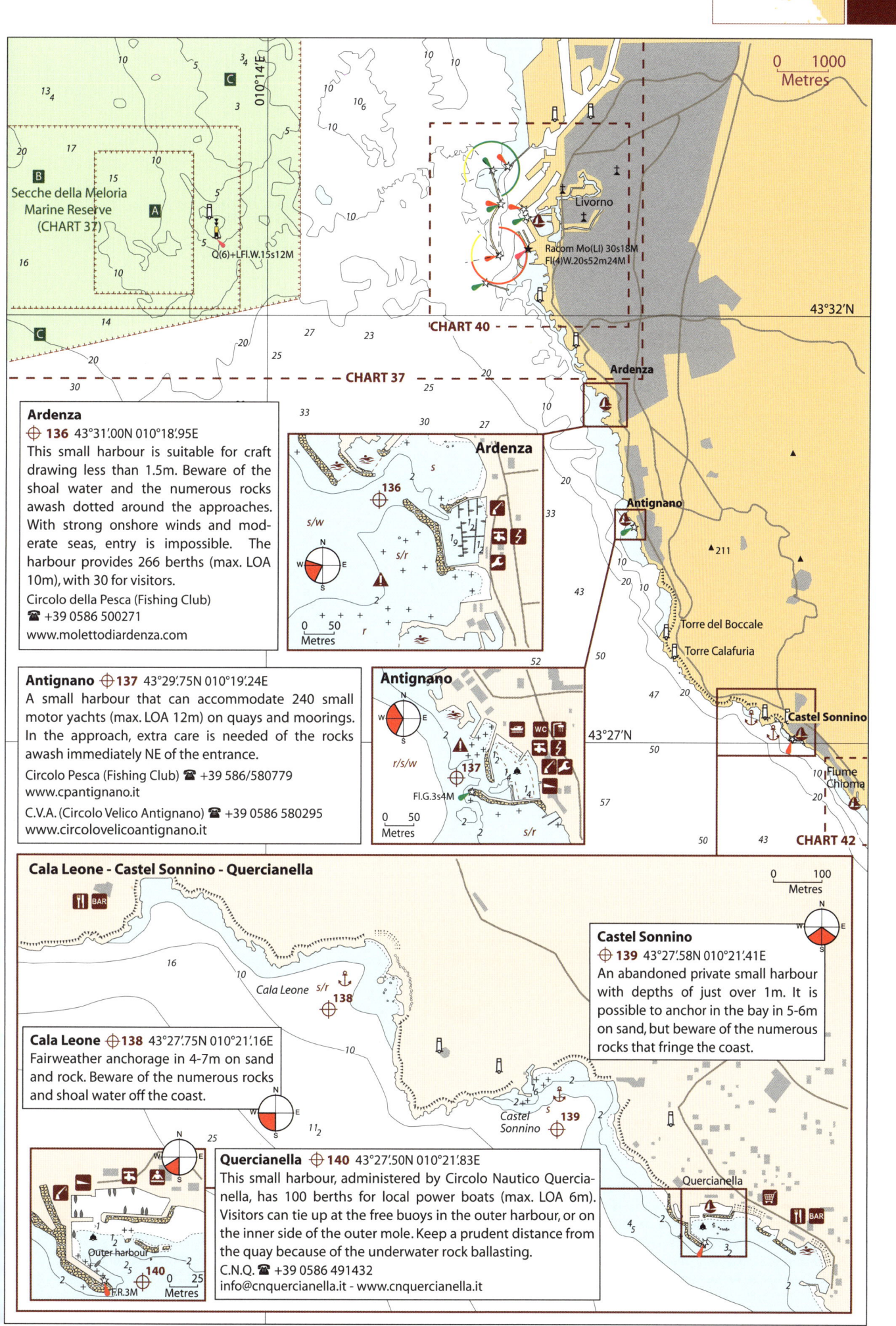

CHART 41

Ardenza
⊕ **136** 43°31′.00N 010°18′.95E
This small harbour is suitable for craft drawing less than 1.5m. Beware of the shoal water and the numerous rocks awash dotted around the approaches. With strong onshore winds and moderate seas, entry is impossible. The harbour provides 266 berths (max. LOA 10m), with 30 for visitors.
Circolo della Pesca (Fishing Club)
☎ +39 0586 500271
www.molettodiardenza.com

Antignano
⊕ **137** 43°29′.75N 010°19′.24E
A small harbour that can accommodate 240 small motor yachts (max. LOA 12m) on quays and moorings. In the approach, extra care is needed of the rocks awash immediately NE of the entrance.
Circolo Pesca (Fishing Club) ☎ +39 586/580779
www.cpantignano.it
C.V.A. (Circolo Velico Antignano) ☎ +39 0586 580295
www.circolovelicoantignano.it

Cala Leone - Castel Sonnino - Quercianella

Cala Leone
⊕ **138** 43°27′.75N 010°21′.16E
Fairweather anchorage in 4-7m on sand and rock. Beware of the numerous rocks and shoal water off the coast.

Castel Sonnino
⊕ **139** 43°27′.58N 010°21′.41E
An abandoned private small harbour with depths of just over 1m. It is possible to anchor in the bay in 5-6m on sand, but beware of the numerous rocks that fringe the coast.

Quercianella
⊕ **140** 43°27′.50N 010°21′.83E
This small harbour, administered by Circolo Nautico Quercianella, has 100 berths for local power boats (max. LOA 6m). Visitors can tie up at the free buoys in the outer harbour, or on the inner side of the outer mole. Keep a prudent distance from the quay because of the underwater rock ballasting.
C.N.Q. ☎ +39 0586 491432
info@cnquercianella.it - www.cnquercianella.it

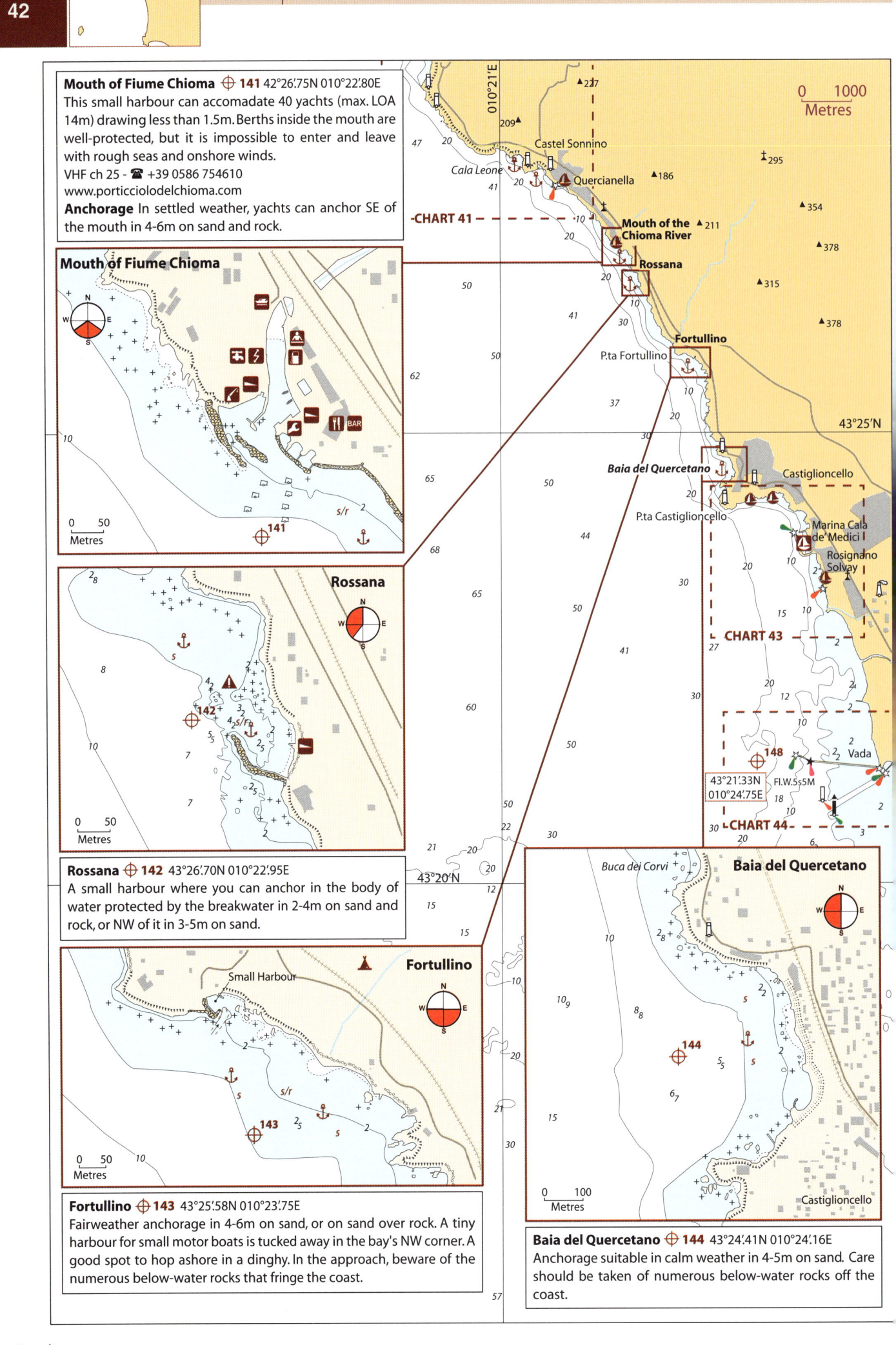

CHART 42 — AREA C — FROM QUERCIANELLA TO PUNTA CASTIGLIONCELLO

Mouth of Fiume Chioma ⊕ 141 42°26′.75N 010°22′.80E
This small harbour can accomadate 40 yachts (max. LOA 14m) drawing less than 1.5m. Berths inside the mouth are well-protected, but it is impossible to enter and leave with rough seas and onshore winds.
VHF ch 25 - ☎ +39 0586 754610
www.porticciolodelchioma.com
Anchorage In settled weather, yachts can anchor SE of the mouth in 4-6m on sand and rock.

Rossana ⊕ 142 43°26′.70N 010°22′.95E
A small harbour where you can anchor in the body of water protected by the breakwater in 2-4m on sand and rock, or NW of it in 3-5m on sand.

Fortullino ⊕ 143 43°25′.58N 010°23′.75E
Fairweather anchorage in 4-6m on sand, or on sand over rock. A tiny harbour for small motor boats is tucked away in the bay's NW corner. A good spot to hop ashore in a dinghy. In the approach, beware of the numerous below-water rocks that fringe the coast.

Baia del Quercetano ⊕ 144 43°24′.41N 010°24′.16E
Anchorage suitable in calm weather in 4-5m on sand. Care should be taken of numerous below-water rocks off the coast.

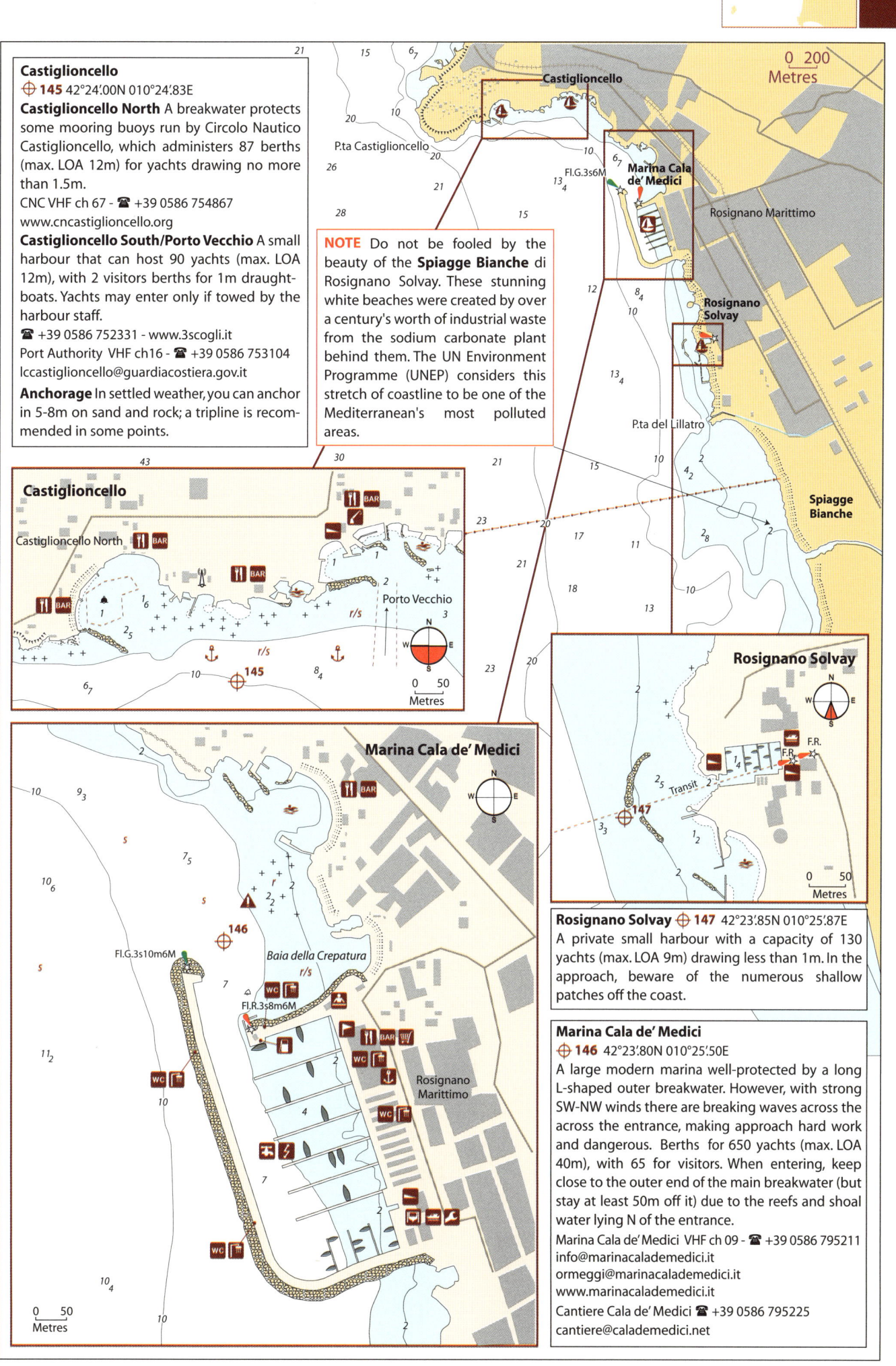

FROM PUNTA CASTIGLIONCELLO TO PUNTA LILLATRO | AREA C

CHART 43

Castiglioncello
⊕ **145** 42°24′.00N 010°24′.83E

Castiglioncello North A breakwater protects some mooring buoys run by Circolo Nautico Castiglioncello, which administers 87 berths (max. LOA 12m) for yachts drawing no more than 1.5m.
CNC VHF ch 67 - ☎ +39 0586 754867
www.cncastiglioncello.org

Castiglioncello South/Porto Vecchio A small harbour that can host 90 yachts (max. LOA 12m), with 2 visitors berths for 1m draught-boats. Yachts may enter only if towed by the harbour staff.
☎ +39 0586 752331 - www.3scogli.it
Port Authority VHF ch16 - ☎ +39 0586 753104
lccastiglioncello@guardiacostiera.gov.it

Anchorage In settled weather, you can anchor in 5-8m on sand and rock; a tripline is recommended in some points.

NOTE Do not be fooled by the beauty of the **Spiagge Bianche** di Rosignano Solvay. These stunning white beaches were created by over a century's worth of industrial waste from the sodium carbonate plant behind them. The UN Environment Programme (UNEP) considers this stretch of coastline to be one of the Mediterranean's most polluted areas.

Rosignano Solvay
⊕ **147** 42°23′.85N 010°25′.87E
A private small harbour with a capacity of 130 yachts (max. LOA 9m) drawing less than 1m. In the approach, beware of the numerous shallow patches off the coast.

Marina Cala de' Medici
⊕ **146** 42°23′.80N 010°25′.50E
A large modern marina well-protected by a long L-shaped outer breakwater. However, with strong SW-NW winds there are breaking waves across the across the entrance, making approach hard work and dangerous. Berths for 650 yachts (max. LOA 40m), with 65 for visitors. When entering, keep close to the outer end of the main breakwater (but stay at least 50m off it) due to the reefs and shoal water lying N of the entrance.
Marina Cala de' Medici VHF ch 09 - ☎ +39 0586 795211
info@marinacalademedici.it
ormeggi@marinacalademedici.it
www.marinacalademedici.it
Cantiere Cala de' Medici ☎ +39 0586 795225
cantiere@calademedici.net

CHART 44 — AREA C | VADA AND CECINA MARINA

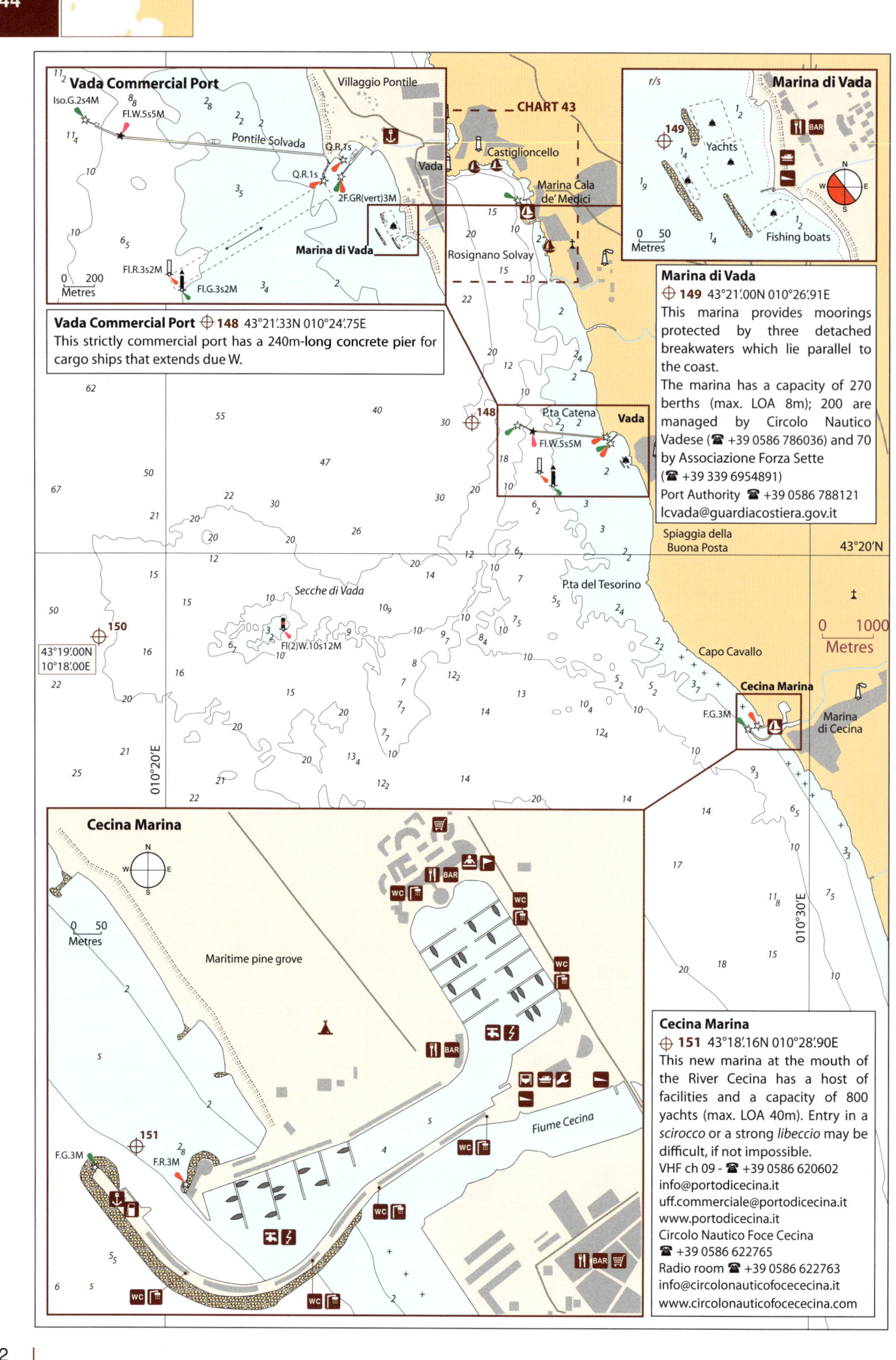

Vada Commercial Port ⊕ 148 43°21'.33N 010°24'.75E
This strictly commercial port has a 240m-long concrete pier for cargo ships that extends due W.

Marina di Vada
⊕ 149 43°21'.00N 010°26'.91E
This marina provides moorings protected by three detached breakwaters which lie parallel to the coast.
The marina has a capacity of 270 berths (max. LOA 8m); 200 are managed by Circolo Nautico Vadese (☎ +39 0586 786036) and 70 by Associazione Forza Sette (☎ +39 339 6954891)
Port Authority ☎ +39 0586 788121
lcvada@guardiacostiera.gov.it

Cecina Marina
⊕ 151 43°18'.16N 010°28'.90E
This new marina at the mouth of the River Cecina has a host of facilities and a capacity of 800 yachts (max. LOA 40m). Entry in a *scirocco* or a strong *libeccio* may be difficult, if not impossible.
VHF ch 09 - ☎ +39 0586 620602
info@portodicecina.it
uff.commerciale@portodicecina.it
www.portodicecina.it
Circolo Nautico Foce Cecina
☎ +39 0586 622765
Radio room ☎ +39 0586 622763
info@circolonauticofocececina.it
www.circolonauticofocececina.com

FROM CECINA MARINA TO PIOMBINO | AREA C | CHART 45

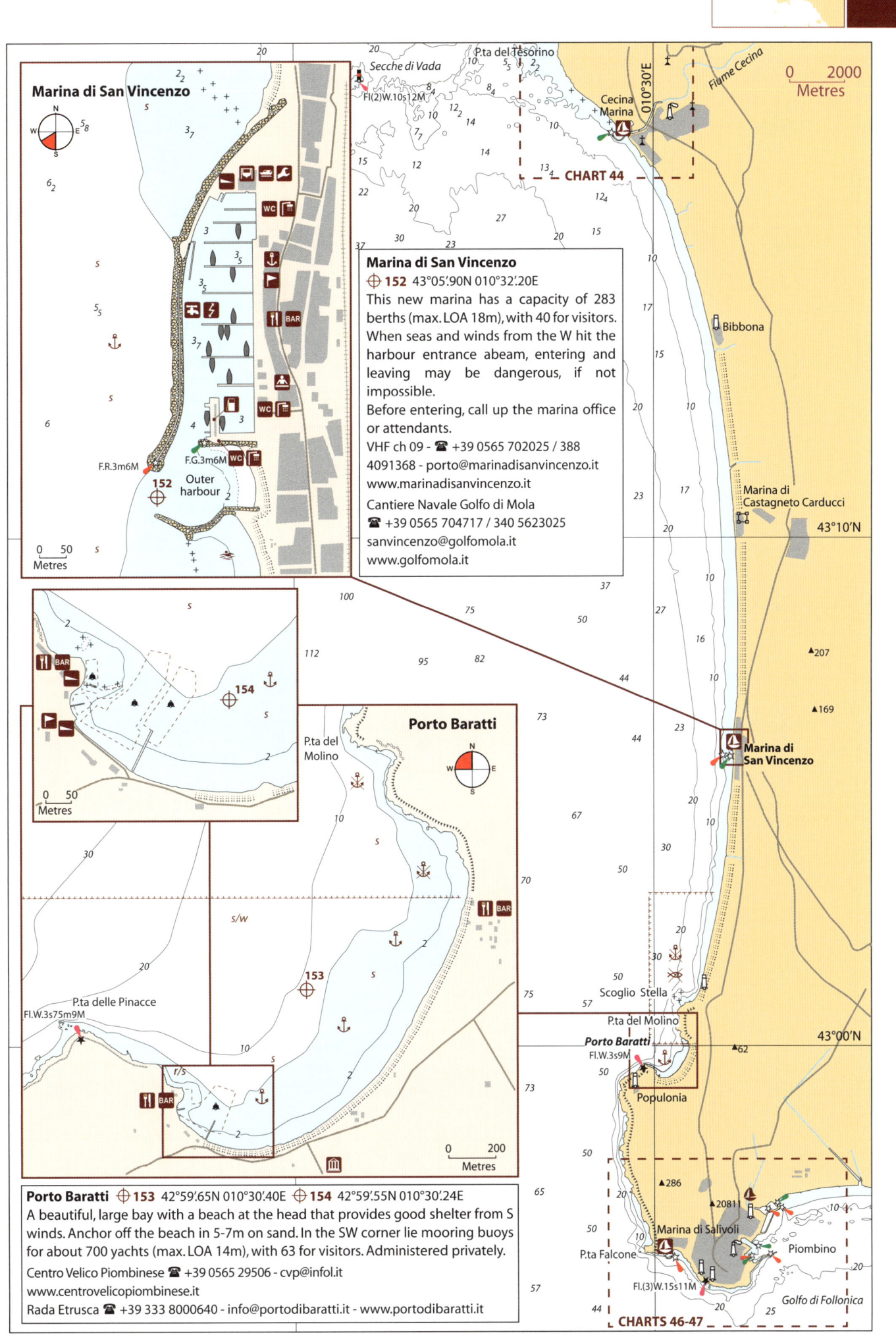

Marina di San Vincenzo
⊕ 152 43°05'.90N 010°32'.20E
This new marina has a capacity of 283 berths (max. LOA 18m), with 40 for visitors. When seas and winds from the W hit the harbour entrance abeam, entering and leaving may be dangerous, if not impossible.
Before entering, call up the marina office or attendants.
VHF ch 09 - ☎ +39 0565 702025 / 388 4091368 - porto@marinadisanvincenzo.it
www.marinadisanvincenzo.it
Cantiere Navale Golfo di Mola
☎ +39 0565 704717 / 340 5623025
sanvincenzo@golfomola.it
www.golfomola.it

Porto Baratti
⊕ 153 42°59'.65N 010°30'.40E   ⊕ 154 42°59'.55N 010°30'.24E
A beautiful, large bay with a beach at the head that provides good shelter from S winds. Anchor off the beach in 5-7m on sand. In the SW corner lie mooring buoys for about 700 yachts (max. LOA 14m), with 63 for visitors. Administered privately.
Centro Velico Piombinese ☎ +39 0565 29506 - cvp@infol.it
www.centrovelicopiombinese.it
Rada Etrusca ☎ +39 333 8000640 - info@portodibaratti.it - www.portodibaratti.it

CHART 46 | AREA C | SALIVOLI AND PIOMBINO

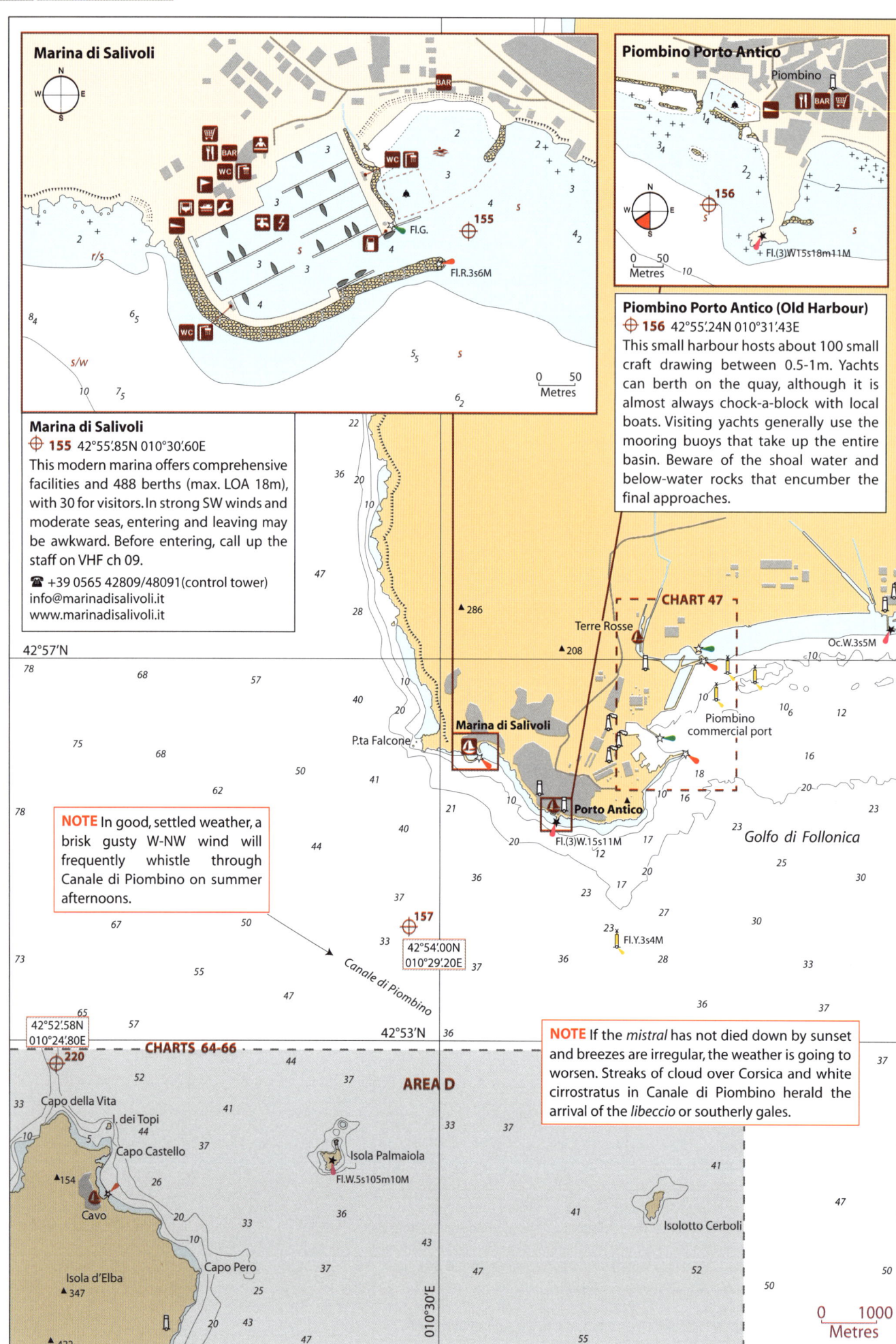

Marina di Salivoli

⊕ 155 42°55′.85N 010°30′.60E

This modern marina offers comprehensive facilities and 488 berths (max. LOA 18m), with 30 for visitors. In strong SW winds and moderate seas, entering and leaving may be awkward. Before entering, call up the staff on VHF ch 09.

☎ +39 0565 42809/48091(control tower)
info@marinadisalivoli.it
www.marinadisalivoli.it

Piombino Porto Antico (Old Harbour)

⊕ 156 42°55′.24N 010°31′.43E

This small harbour hosts about 100 small craft drawing between 0.5–1m. Yachts can berth on the quay, although it is almost always chock-a-block with local boats. Visiting yachts generally use the mooring buoys that take up the entire basin. Beware of the shoal water and below-water rocks that encumber the final approaches.

NOTE In good, settled weather, a brisk gusty W-NW wind will frequently whistle through Canale di Piombino on summer afternoons.

NOTE If the *mistral* has not died down by sunset and breezes are irregular, the weather is going to worsen. Streaks of cloud over Corsica and white cirrostratus in Canale di Piombino herald the arrival of the *libeccio* or southerly gales.

PIOMBINO | AREA C

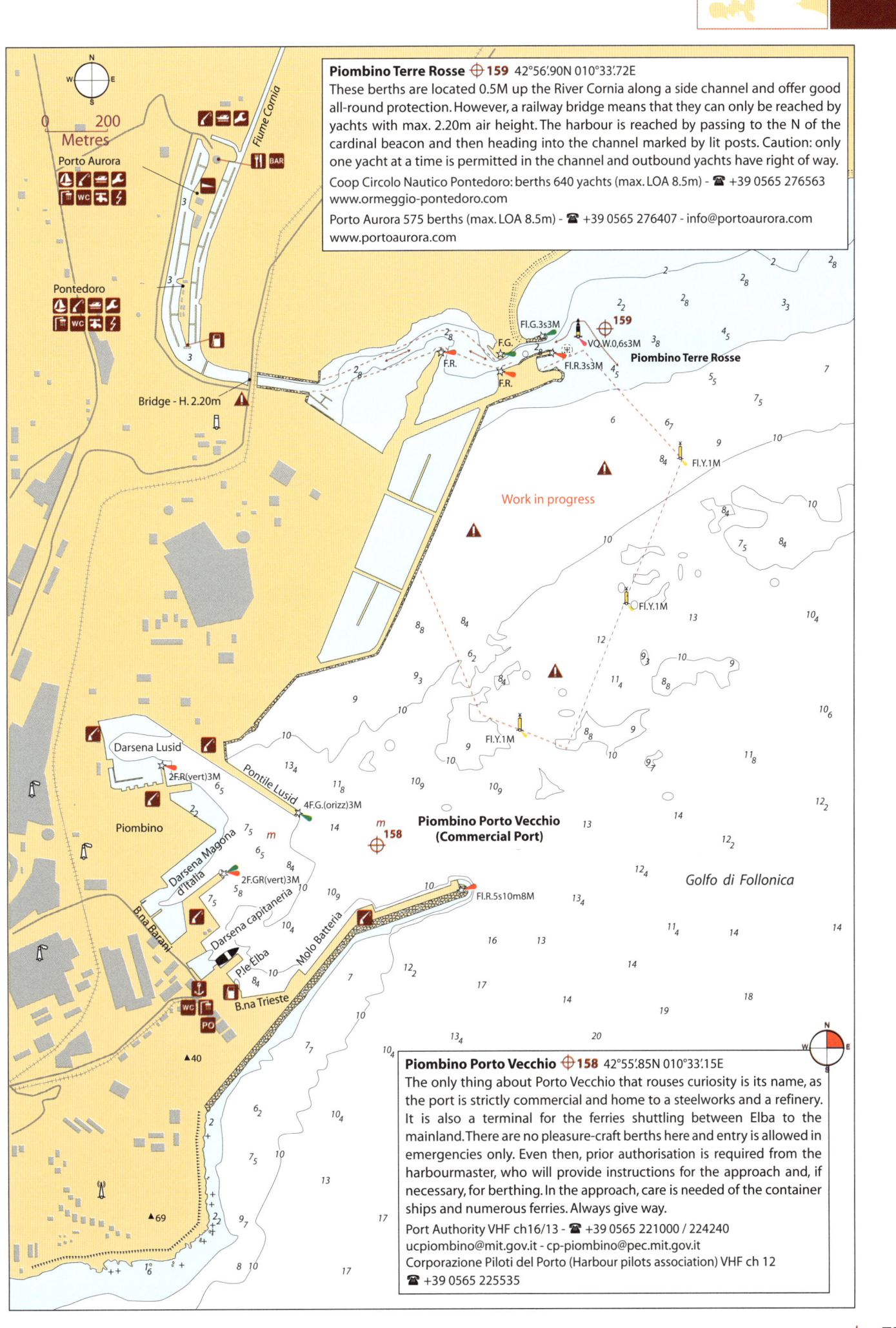

CHART 47

Piombino Terre Rosse ⊕ **159** 42°56.90N 010°33.72E
These berths are located 0.5M up the River Cornia along a side channel and offer good all-round protection. However, a railway bridge means that they can only be reached by yachts with max. 2.20m air height. The harbour is reached by passing to the N of the cardinal beacon and then heading into the channel marked by lit posts. Caution: only one yacht at a time is permitted in the channel and outbound yachts have right of way.
Coop Circolo Nautico Pontedoro: berths 640 yachts (max. LOA 8.5m) - ☎ +39 0565 276563
www.ormeggio-pontedoro.com
Porto Aurora 575 berths (max. LOA 8.5m) - ☎ +39 0565 276407 - info@portoaurora.com
www.portoaurora.com

Piombino Porto Vecchio ⊕ **158** 42°55.85N 010°33.15E
The only thing about Porto Vecchio that rouses curiosity is its name, as the port is strictly commercial and home to a steelworks and a refinery. It is also a terminal for the ferries shuttling between Elba to the mainland. There are no pleasure-craft berths here and entry is allowed in emergencies only. Even then, prior authorisation is required from the harbourmaster, who will provide instructions for the approach and, if necessary, for berthing. In the approach, care is needed of the container ships and numerous ferries. Always give way.
Port Authority VHF ch16/13 - ☎ +39 0565 221000 / 224240
ucpiombino@mit.gov.it - cp-piombino@pec.mit.gov.it
Corporazione Piloti del Porto (Harbour pilots association) VHF ch 12
☎ +39 0565 225535

75

CHART 48 — AREA C — FROM PIOMBINO TO PUNTA ALA

Carbonifera

⊕ **160** 42°56'.85N 010°40'.90E

The Carbonifera canal-harbour provides 320 berths for motor yachts (max. LOA 8m) with air height no more than, 2.90m. Entry to the basin involves negotiating a tight 9m buoyed channel. Care is needed of the 0.7m shoal patch in the fairway. Pass beneath the bridge (H. 2.97m) and head towards the harbour. With disturbed sea, entry is hazardous, if not impossible.

Circolo Nautico Carbonifera
☎ +39 0565 20238
www.circolonauticocarbonifera.it

Scarlino

⊕ **161** 42°53'.30N 010°46'.95E

Fiumara del Puntone

A canal-harbour with 3-2m depths along the fairway and 0.8-2m at the quay. Inside it can host 400 berths (max. LOA 10m), with 15 for visitors. Follow the beacons to reach the entrance. With strong W winds, there are treacherous breaking waves at the channel mouth, making entry dangerous and silting up the entrance.
Marina management VHF ch 72
☎ +39 0566 866302 - info@lamds.it

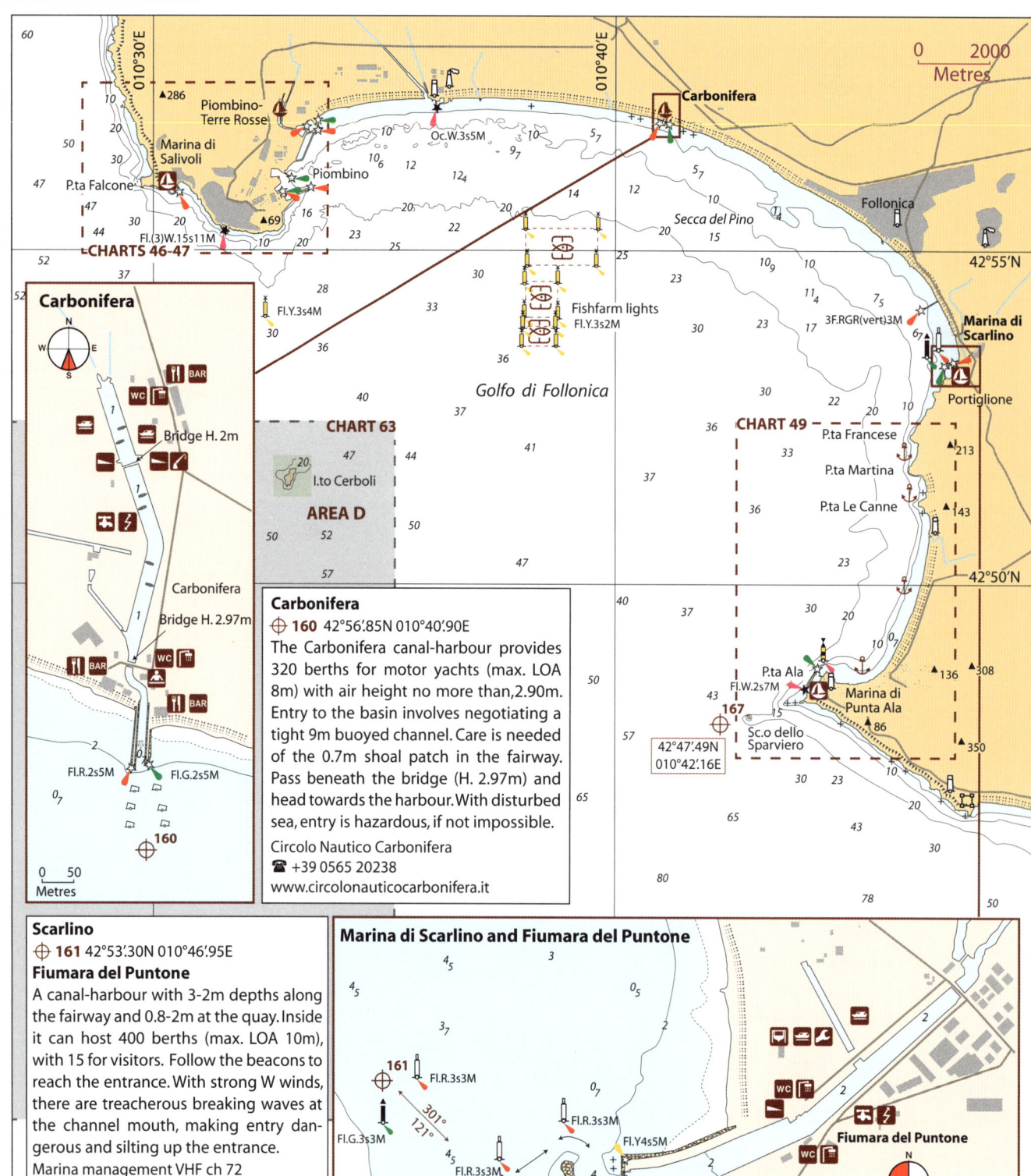

Marina di Scarlino

This well-equipped marina boasts 566 berths (max. LOA 40m), with 56 for visitors. Yachts should follow the beacons to reach the entrance and then contact the marina staff:

VHF ch 72 - ☎ +39 0566 866302
info@marinadiscarlino.com
www.marinadiscarlino.com

Club Nautico ☎ +39 0566 866302
info@clubnauticoscarlino.com

Scarlino Yacht Service ☎ +39 0566 867031
info@scarlino-ys.com
www.scarlino-ys.it

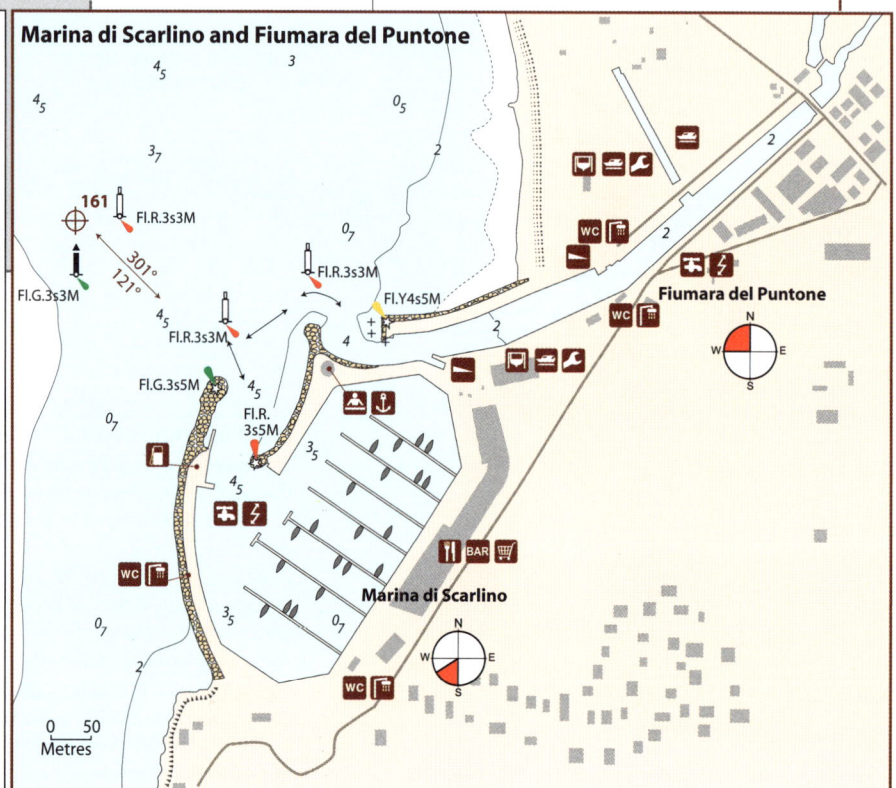

PUNTA ALA | AREA C | CHART 49

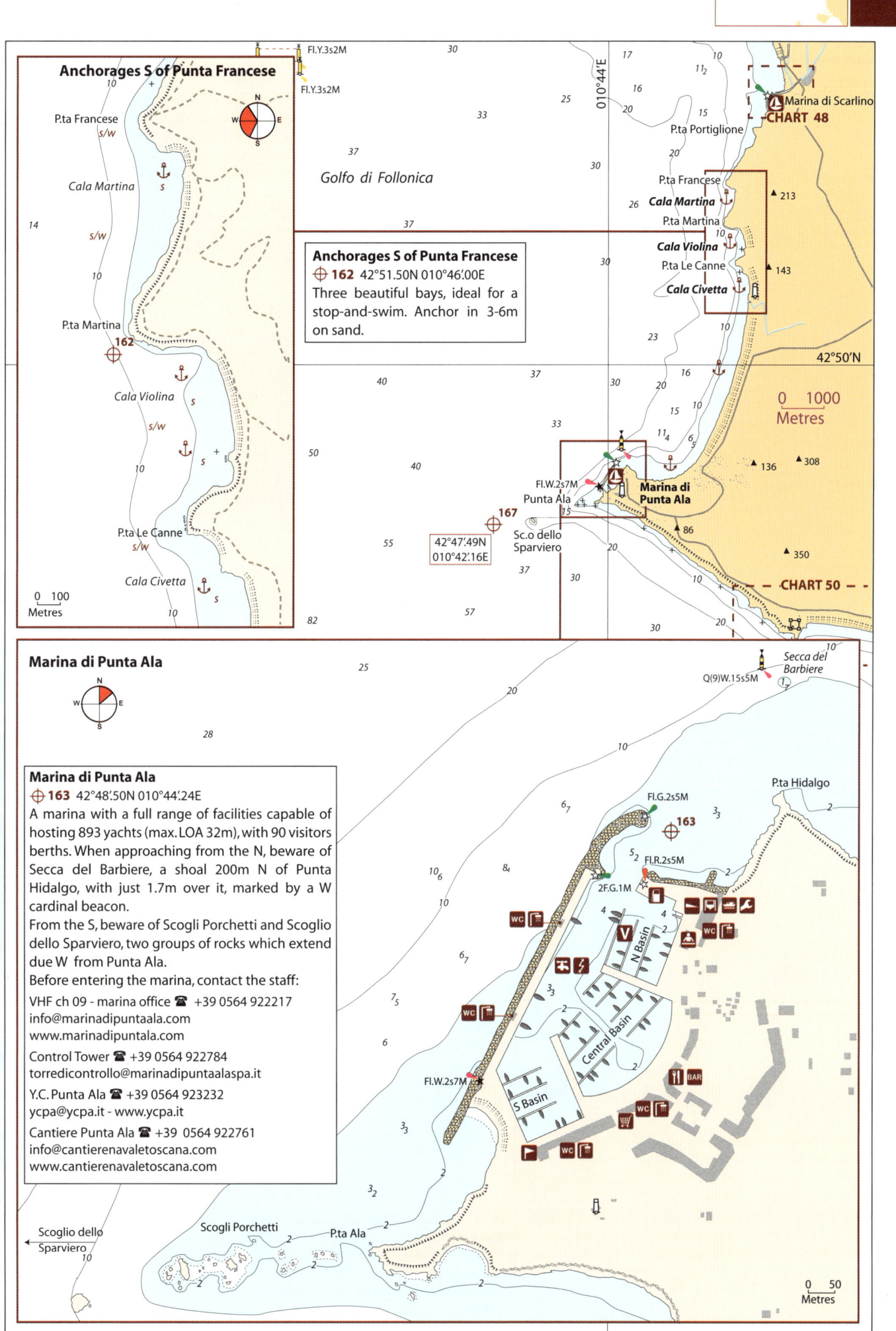

Anchorages S of Punta Francese

⊕ 162 42°51.50N 010°46.00E
Three beautiful bays, ideal for a stop-and-swim. Anchor in 3-6m on sand.

Marina di Punta Ala

⊕ 163 42°48.50N 010°44.24E
A marina with a full range of facilities capable of hosting 893 yachts (max. LOA 32m), with 90 visitors berths. When approaching from the N, beware of Secca del Barbiere, a shoal 200m N of Punta Hidalgo, with just 1.7m over it, marked by a W cardinal beacon.
From the S, beware of Scogli Porchetti and Scoglio dello Sparviero, two groups of rocks which extend due W from Punta Ala.
Before entering the marina, contact the staff:
VHF ch 09 - marina office ☎ +39 0564 922217
info@marinadipuntaala.com
www.marinadipuntala.com

Control Tower ☎ +39 0564 922784
torredicontrollo@marinadipuntaalaspa.it

Y.C. Punta Ala ☎ +39 0564 923232
ycpa@ycpa.it - www.ycpa.it

Cantiere Punta Ala ☎ +39 0564 922761
info@cantierenavaletoscana.com
www.cantierenavaletoscana.com

77

CHART 50

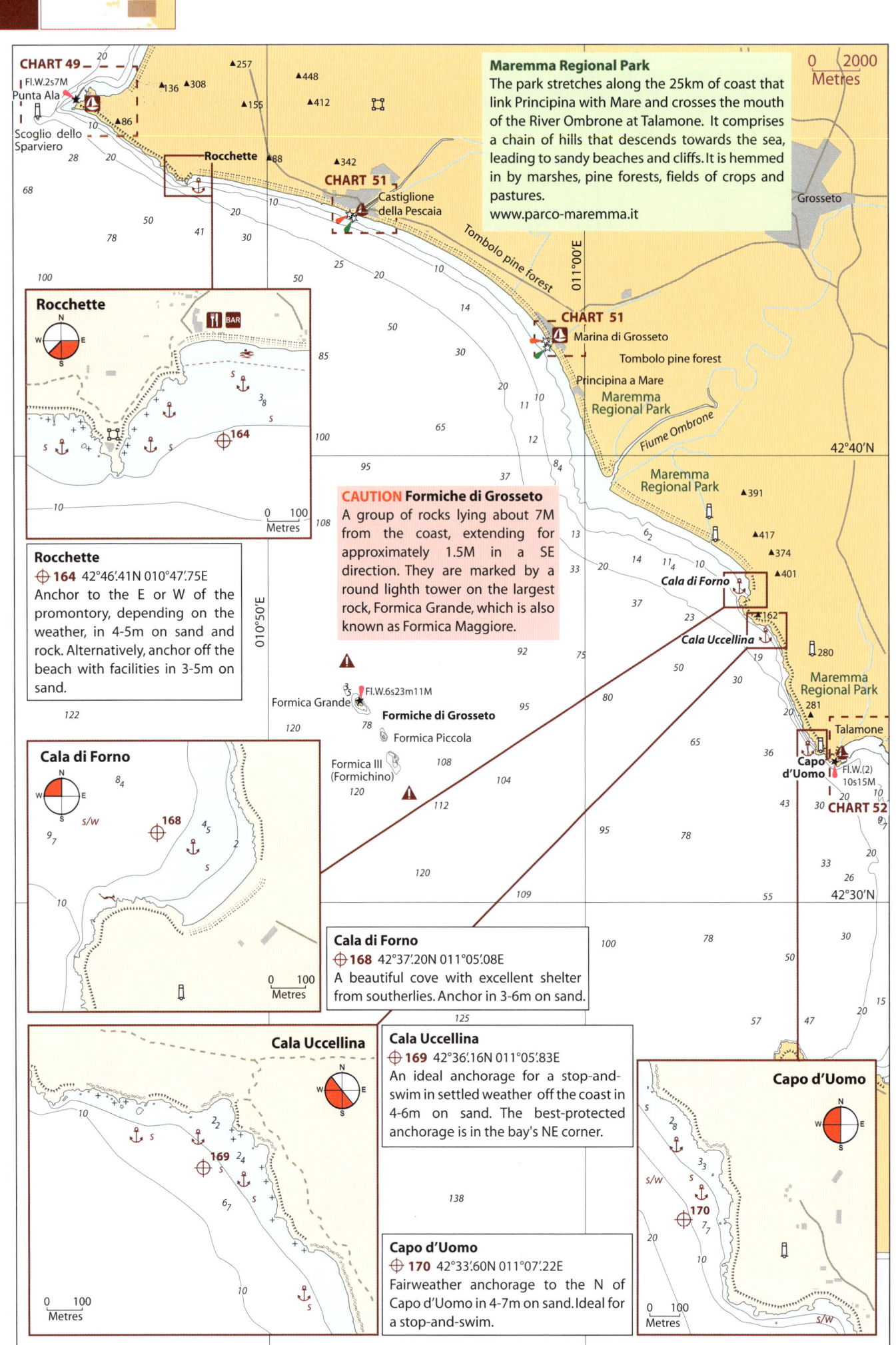

AREA C — FROM PUNTA ALA TO TALAMONE

Maremma Regional Park
The park stretches along the 25km of coast that link Principina with Mare and crosses the mouth of the River Ombrone at Talamone. It comprises a chain of hills that descends towards the sea, leading to sandy beaches and cliffs. It is hemmed in by marshes, pine forests, fields of crops and pastures.
www.parco-maremma.it

CAUTION Formiche di Grosseto
A group of rocks lying about 7M from the coast, extending for approximately 1.5M in a SE direction. They are marked by a round light tower on the largest rock, Formica Grande, which is also known as Formica Maggiore.

Rocchette
⊕ 164 42°46´.41N 010°47´.75E
Anchor to the E or W of the promontory, depending on the weather, in 4-5m on sand and rock. Alternatively, anchor off the beach with facilities in 3-5m on sand.

Cala di Forno
⊕ 168 42°37´.20N 011°05´.08E
A beautiful cove with excellent shelter from southerlies. Anchor in 3-6m on sand.

Cala Uccellina
⊕ 169 42°36´.16N 011°05´.83E
An ideal anchorage for a stop-and-swim in settled weather off the coast in 4-6m on sand. The best-protected anchorage is in the bay's NE corner.

Capo d'Uomo
⊕ 170 42°33´.60N 011°07´.22E
Fairweather anchorage to the N of Capo d'Uomo in 4-7m on sand. Ideal for a stop-and-swim.

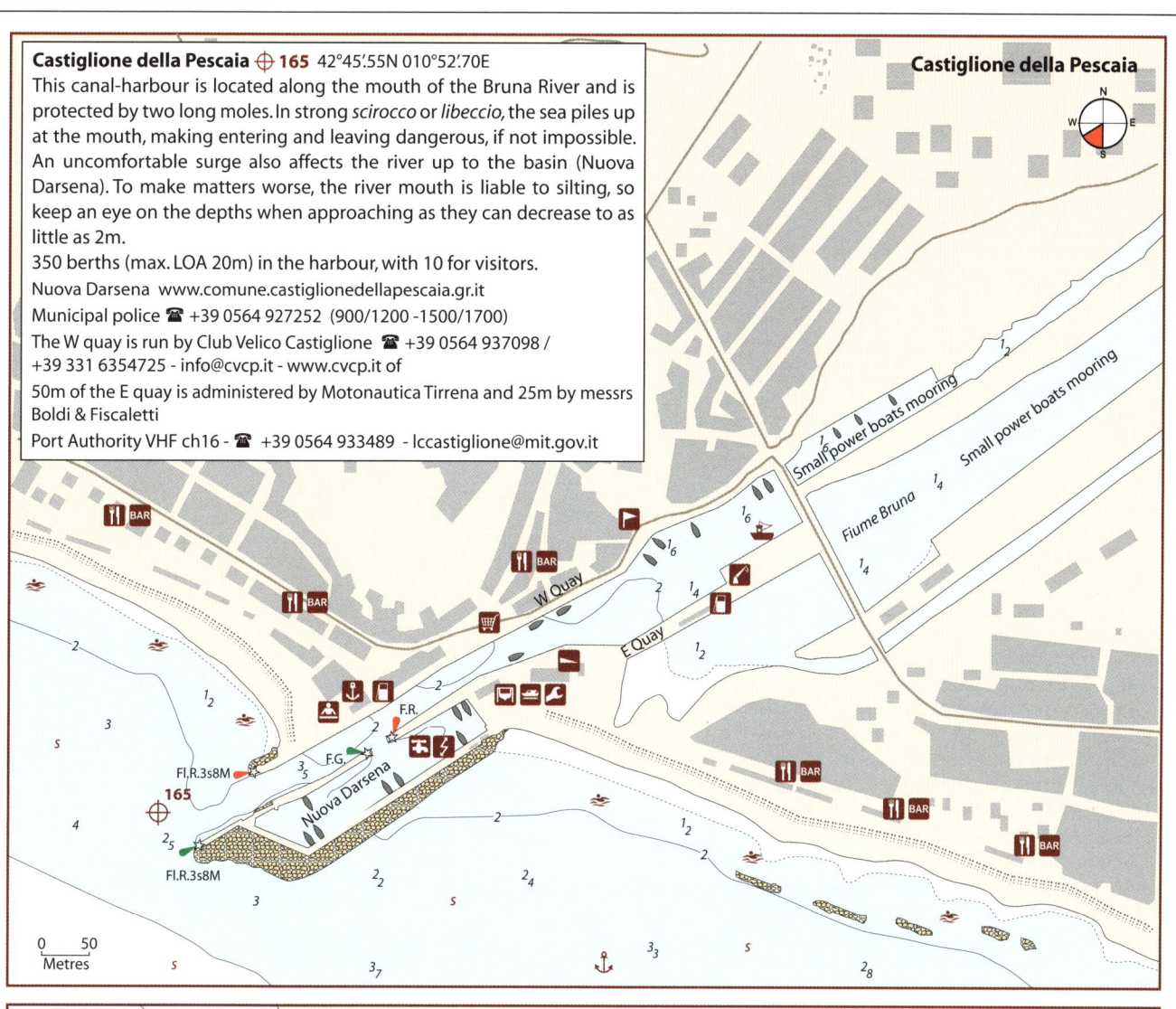

CASTIGLIONE DELLA PESCAIA AND MARINA DI S. ROCCO/GROSSETO | AREA C | CHART 51

Castiglione della Pescaia ⊕ **165** 42°45'.55N 010°52'.70E

This canal-harbour is located along the mouth of the Bruna River and is protected by two long moles. In strong *scirocco* or *libeccio*, the sea piles up at the mouth, making entering and leaving dangerous, if not impossible. An uncomfortable surge also affects the river up to the basin (Nuova Darsena). To make matters worse, the river mouth is liable to silting, so keep an eye on the depths when approaching as they can decrease to as little as 2m.
350 berths (max. LOA 20m) in the harbour, with 10 for visitors.
Nuova Darsena www.comune.castiglionedellapescaia.gr.it
Municipal police ☎ +39 0564 927252 (900/1200 -1500/1700)
The W quay is run by Club Velico Castiglione ☎ +39 0564 937098 / +39 331 6354725 - info@cvcp.it - www.cvcp.it of
50m of the E quay is administered by Motonautica Tirrena and 25m by messrs Boldi & Fiscaletti
Port Authority VHF ch16 - ☎ +39 0564 933489 - lccastiglione@mit.gov.it

Marina di San Rocco (Porto della Maremma) (Marina di Grosseto) ⊕ **166** 42°42'.80N 010°59'.11E

This marina is situated at the mouth of Canale San Rocco and comprises three yacht basins and a stretch of quayed canal. Depths range between 3-1m. It can accommodate 561 yachts (max. LOA 14m), with 56 visitors berths. In strong onshore winds and moderate seas, entering and leaving are dangerous and there is some surge inside. Before berthing, contact the marina and follow the staff's instructions.
VHF ch 09 - ☎ +39 0564 330075 - info@portodellamaremma.it - www.portodellamaremma.it
Porth Authority Marina di Grosseto ☎ +39 0564 34434 - dlmarinadigrosseto@mit.gov.it

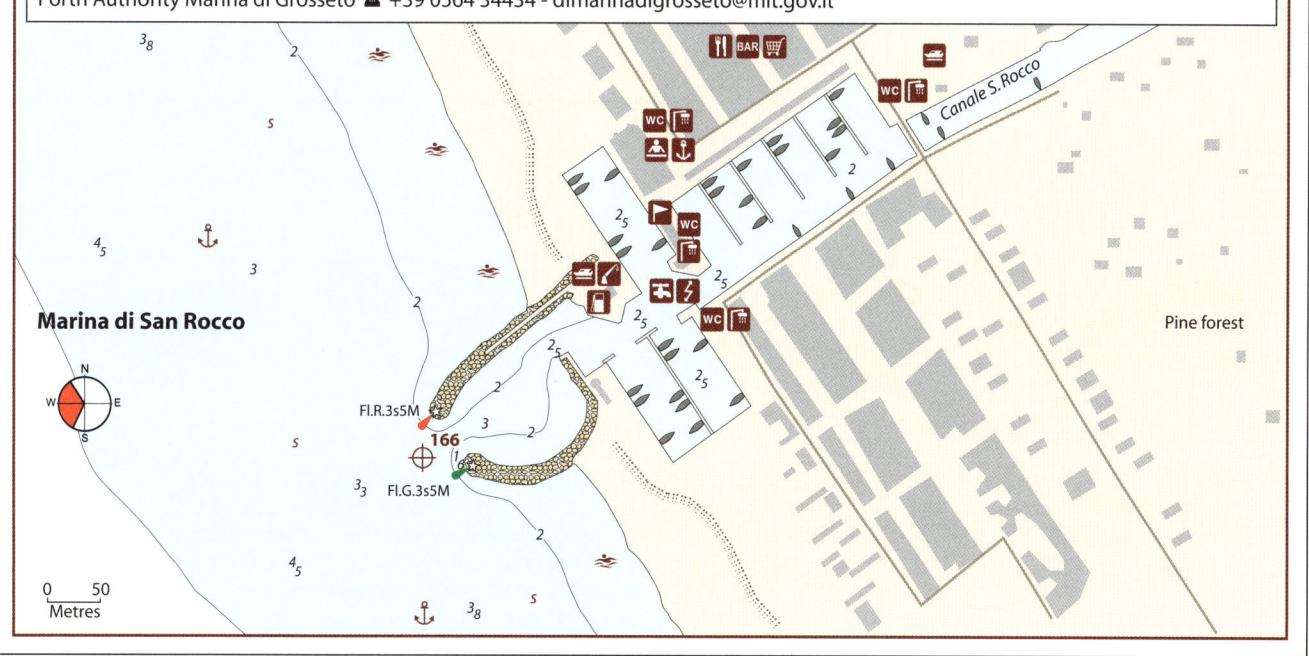

CHART 52

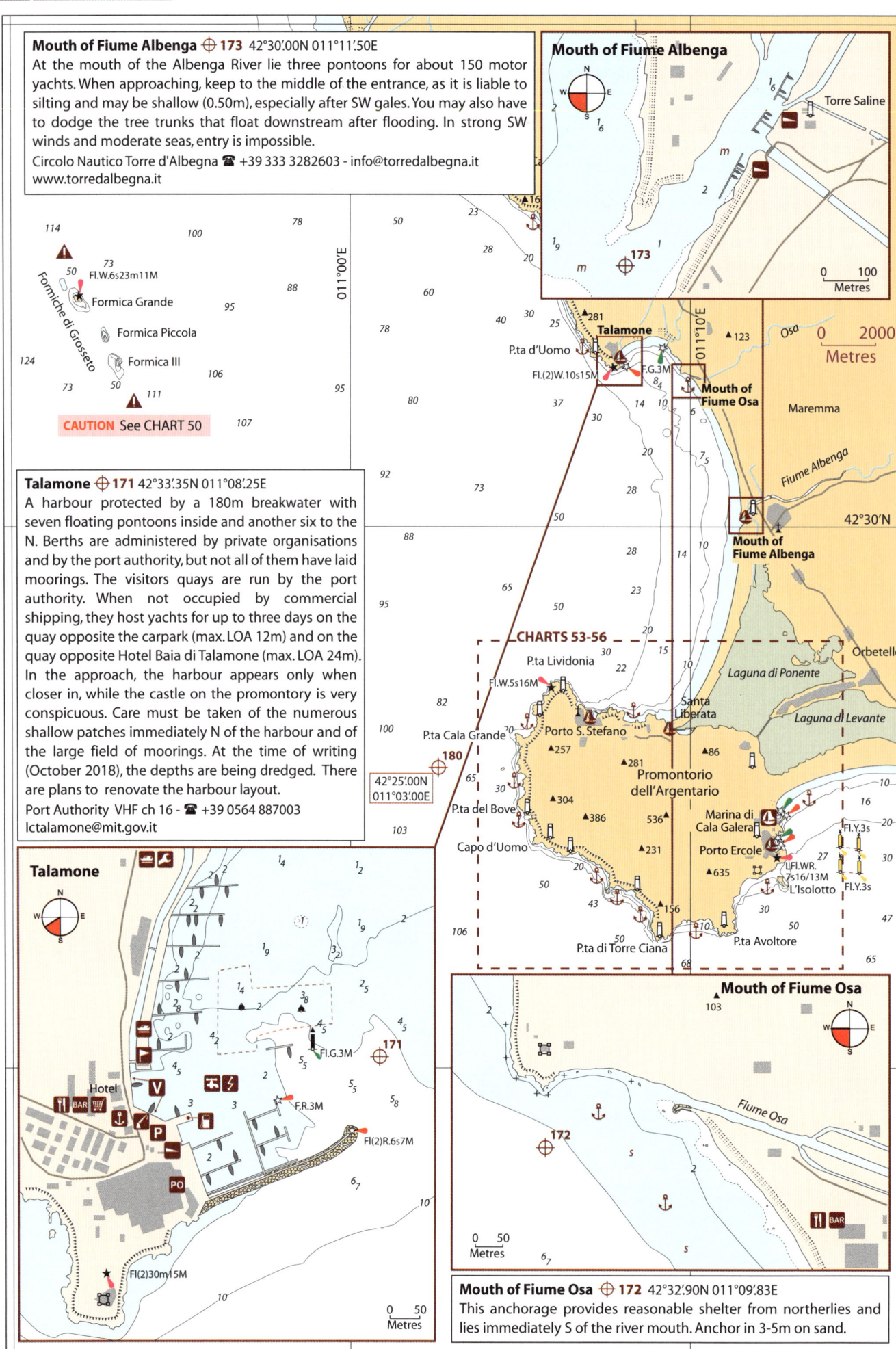

AREA C — FROM TALAMONE TO PROMONTORIO DELL' ARGENTARIO

Mouth of Fiume Albenga ⊕ **173** 42°30′.00N 011°11′.50E
At the mouth of the Albenga River lie three pontoons for about 150 motor yachts. When approaching, keep to the middle of the entrance, as it is liable to silting and may be shallow (0.50m), especially after SW gales. You may also have to dodge the tree trunks that float downstream after flooding. In strong SW winds and moderate seas, entry is impossible.
Circolo Nautico Torre d'Albegna ☎ +39 333 3282603 - info@torredalbegna.it
www.torredalbegna.it

CAUTION See CHART 50

Talamone ⊕ **171** 42°33′.35N 011°08′.25E
A harbour protected by a 180m breakwater with seven floating pontoons inside and another six to the N. Berths are administered by private organisations and by the port authority, but not all of them have laid moorings. The visitors quays are run by the port authority. When not occupied by commercial shipping, they host yachts for up to three days on the quay opposite the carpark (max. LOA 12m) and on the quay opposite Hotel Baia di Talamone (max. LOA 24m). In the approach, the harbour appears only when closer in, while the castle on the promontory is very conspicuous. Care must be taken of the numerous shallow patches immediately N of the harbour and of the large field of moorings. At the time of writing (October 2018), the depths are being dredged. There are plans to renovate the harbour layout.
Port Authority VHF ch 16 - ☎ +39 0564 887003
lctalamone@mit.gov.it

Mouth of Fiume Osa ⊕ **172** 42°32′.90N 011°09′.83E
This anchorage provides reasonable shelter from northerlies and lies immediately S of the river mouth. Anchor in 3-5m on sand.

80

PROMONTORIO DELL'ARGENTARIO NW COAST | AREA C

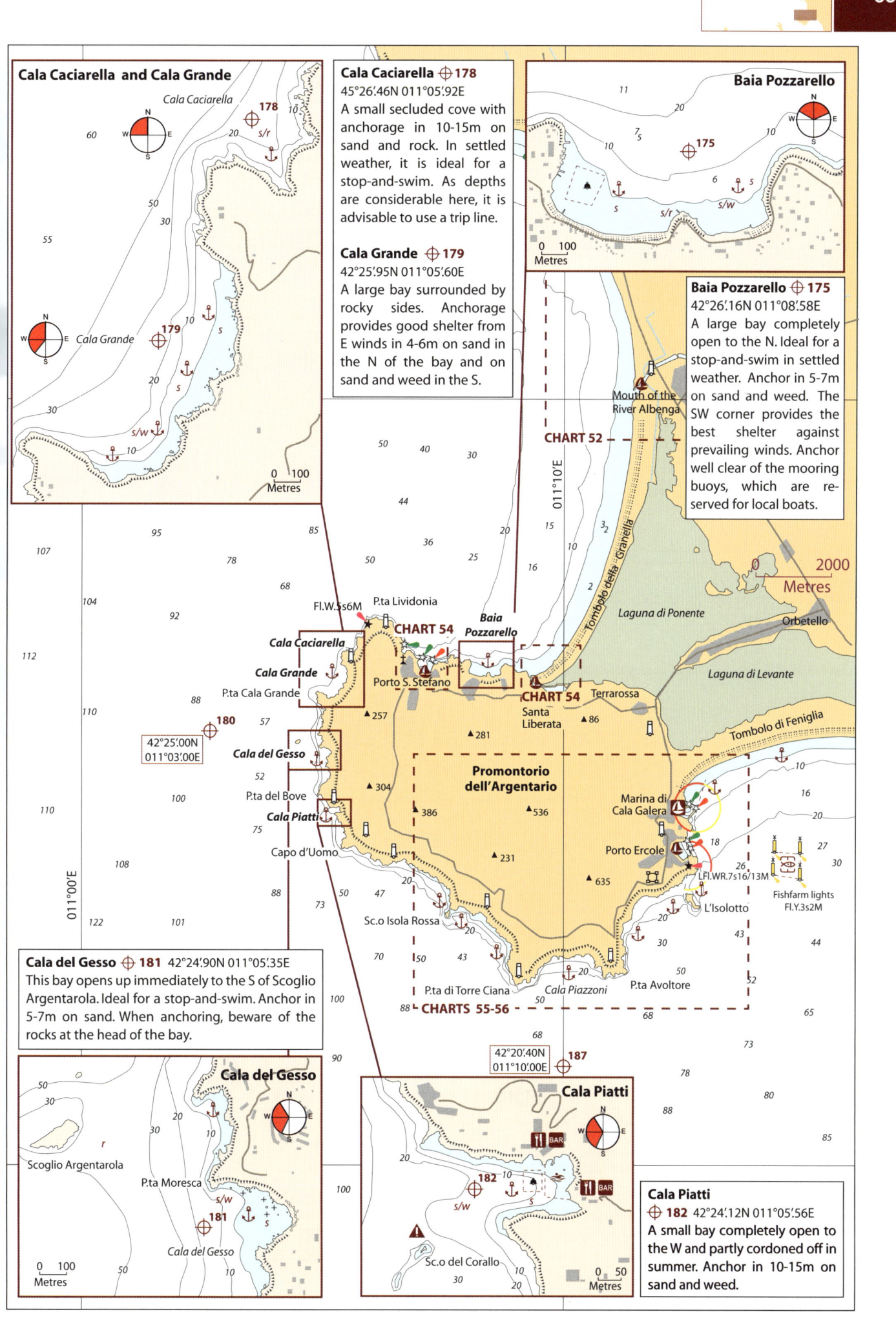

CHART 53

Cala Caciarella and Cala Grande

Cala Caciarella ⊕ 178
45°26.46N 011°05.92E
A small secluded cove with anchorage in 10-15m on sand and rock. In settled weather, it is ideal for a stop-and-swim. As depths are considerable here, it is advisable to use a trip line.

Cala Grande ⊕ 179
42°25.95N 011°05.60E
A large bay surrounded by rocky sides. Anchorage provides good shelter from E winds in 4-6m on sand in the N of the bay and on sand and weed in the S.

Baia Pozzarello

Baia Pozzarello ⊕ 175
42°26.16N 011°08.58E
A large bay completely open to the N. Ideal for a stop-and-swim in settled weather. Anchor in 5-7m on sand and weed. The SW corner provides the best shelter against prevailing winds. Anchor well clear of the mooring buoys, which are reserved for local boats.

Cala del Gesso ⊕ 181   42°24.90N 011°05.35E
This bay opens up immediately to the S of Scoglio Argentarola. Ideal for a stop-and-swim. Anchor in 5-7m on sand. When anchoring, beware of the rocks at the head of the bay.

Cala del Gesso

Cala Piatti

Cala Piatti
⊕ 182 42°24.12N 011°05.56E
A small bay completely open to the W and partly cordoned off in summer. Anchor in 10-15m on sand and weed.

81

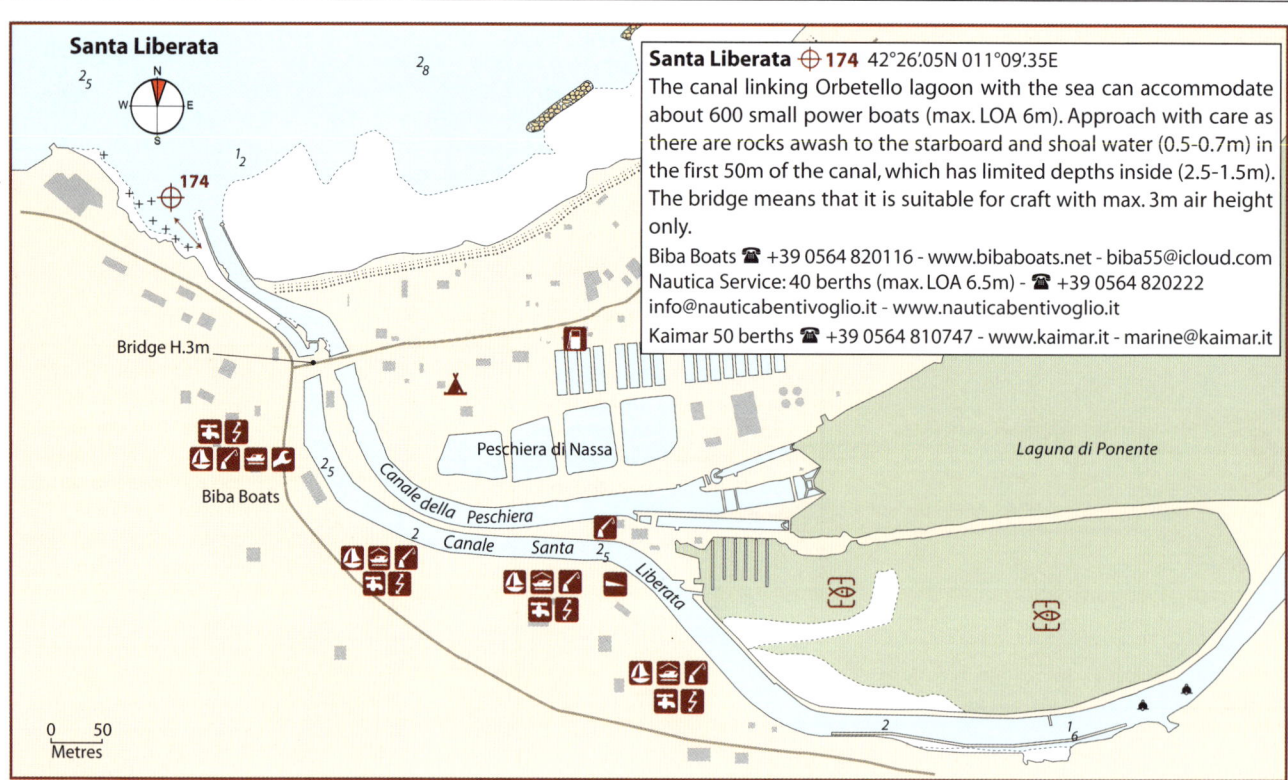

CHART 54

AREA C — SANTA LIBERATA AND SANTO STEFANO

Santa Liberata

Santa Liberata ⊕ 174 42°26'.05N 011°09'.35E

The canal linking Orbetello lagoon with the sea can accommodate about 600 small power boats (max. LOA 6m). Approach with care as there are rocks awash to the starboard and shoal water (0.5-0.7m) in the first 50m of the canal, which has limited depths inside (2.5-1.5m). The bridge means that it is suitable for craft with max. 3m air height only.

Biba Boats ☎ +39 0564 820116 - www.bibaboats.net - biba55@icloud.com
Nautica Service: 40 berths (max. LOA 6.5m) - ☎ +39 0564 820222
info@nauticabentivoglio.it - www.nauticabentivoglio.it
Kaimar 50 berths ☎ +39 0564 810747 - www.kaimar.it - marine@kaimar.it

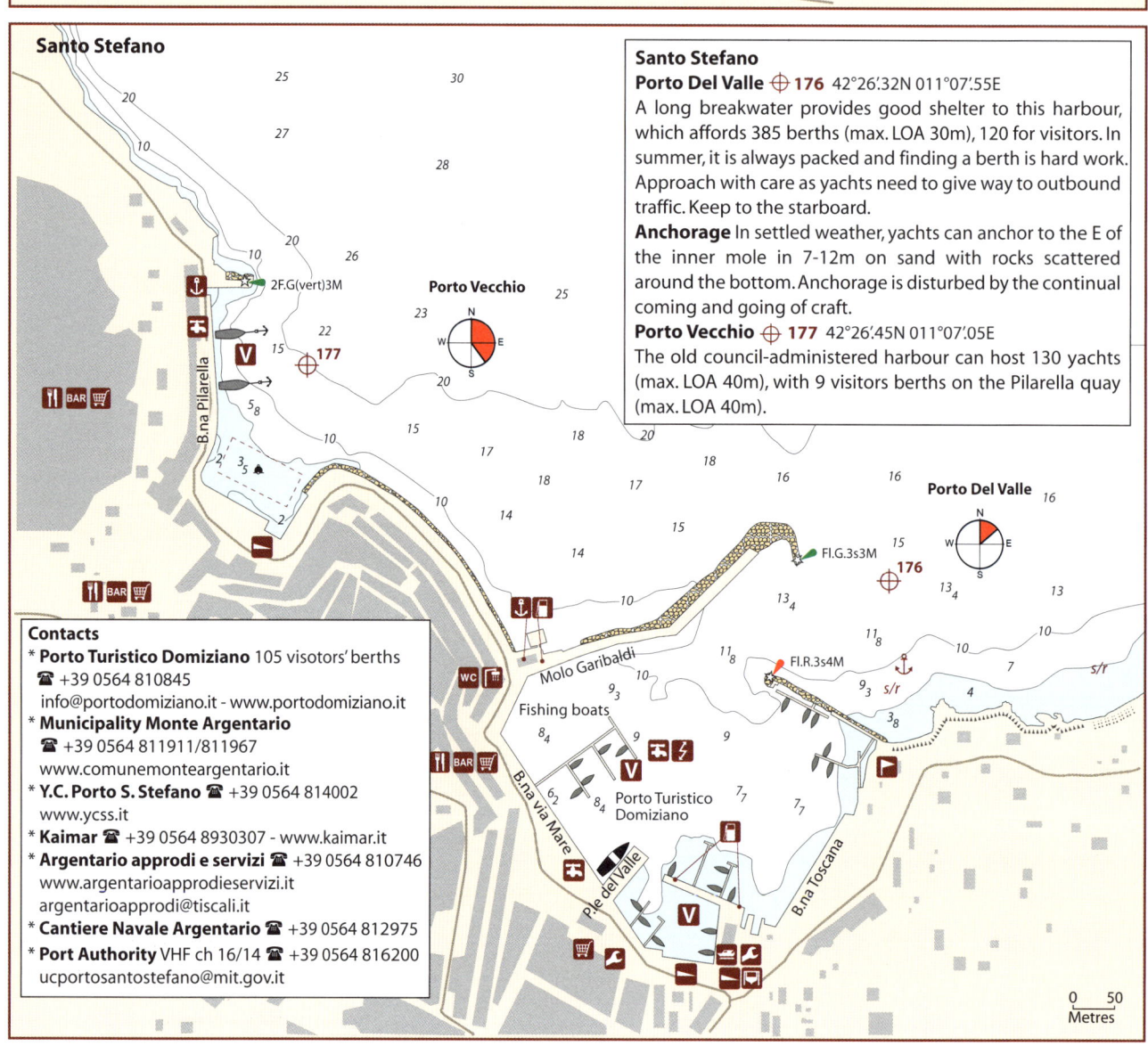

Bridge H.3m
Biba Boats
Peschiera di Nassa
Canale della Peschiera
Canale Santa Liberata
Laguna di Ponente

Santo Stefano

Santo Stefano
Porto Del Valle ⊕ 176 42°26'.32N 011°07'.55E

A long breakwater provides good shelter to this harbour, which affords 385 berths (max. LOA 30m), 120 for visitors. In summer, it is always packed and finding a berth is hard work. Approach with care as yachts need to give way to outbound traffic. Keep to the starboard.

Anchorage In settled weather, yachts can anchor to the E of the inner mole in 7-12m on sand with rocks scattered around the bottom. Anchorage is disturbed by the continual coming and going of craft.

Porto Vecchio ⊕ 177 42°26'.45N 011°07'.05E
The old council-administered harbour can host 130 yachts (max. LOA 40m), with 9 visitors berths on the Pilarella quay (max. LOA 40m).

Porto Vecchio
2F.G(vert)3M
B.na Pilarella
Fl.G.3s3M
Fl.R.3s4M
Molo Garibaldi
Fishing boats
B.na via Mare
Porto Turistico Domiziano
P.le del Valle
B.na Toscana

Contacts

* **Porto Turistico Domiziano** 105 visotors' berths
  ☎ +39 0564 810845
  info@portodomiziano.it - www.portodomiziano.it
* **Municipality Monte Argentario**
  ☎ +39 0564 811911/811967
  www.comunemonteargentario.it
* **Y.C. Porto S. Stefano** ☎ +39 0564 814002
  www.ycss.it
* **Kaimar** ☎ +39 0564 8930307 - www.kaimar.it
* **Argentario approdi e servizi** ☎ +39 0564 810746
  www.argentarioapprodieservizi.it
  argentarioapprodi@tiscali.it
* **Cantiere Navale Argentario** ☎ +39 0564 812975
* **Port Authority** VHF ch 16/14 ☎ +39 0564 816200
  ucportosantostefano@mit.gov.it

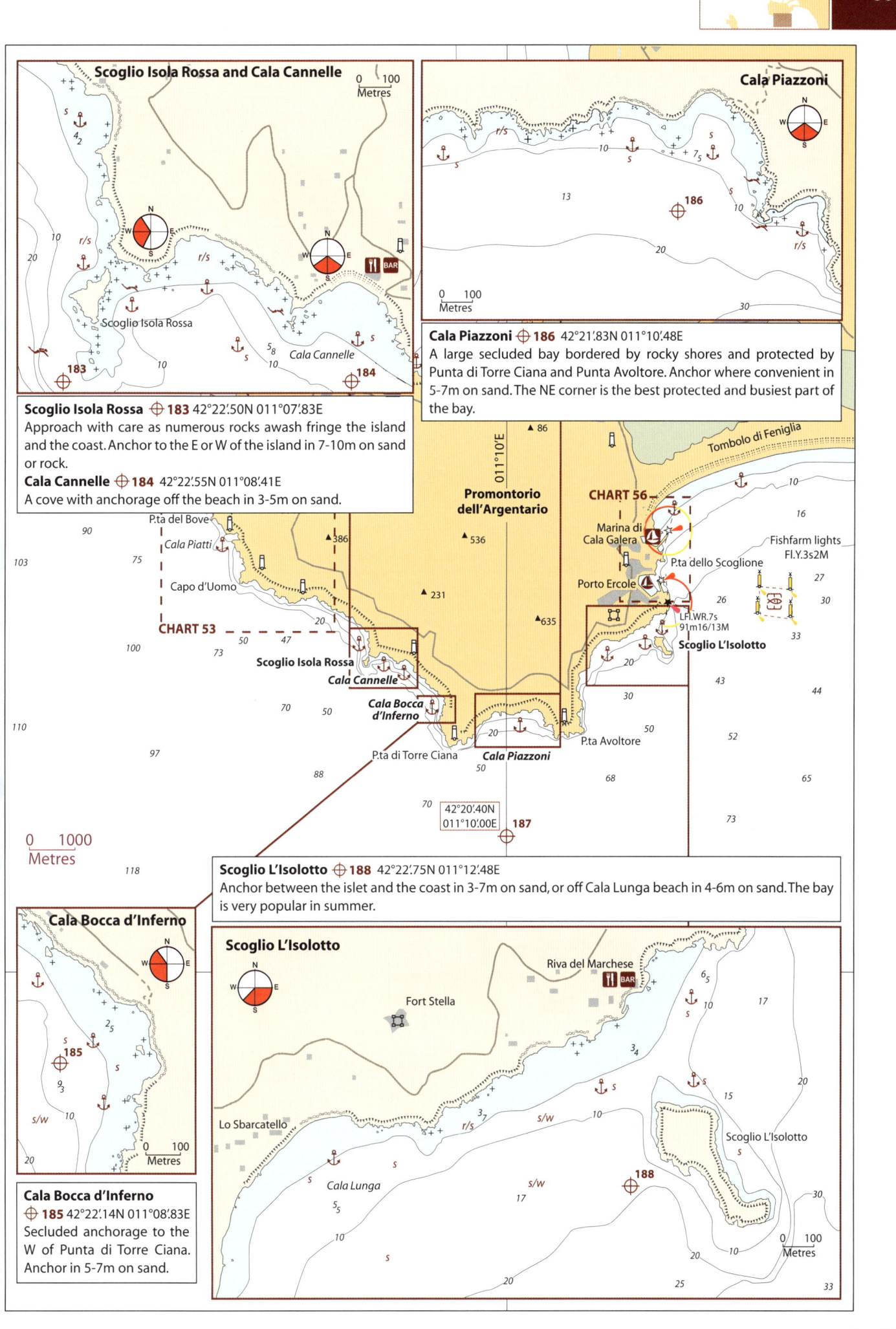

PROMONTORIO DELL' ARGENTARIO SOUTH COAST | AREA C | CHART 55

Scoglio Isola Rossa and Cala Cannelle

Scoglio Isola Rossa ⊕ 183 42°22'.50N 011°07'.83E
Approach with care as numerous rocks awash fringe the island and the coast. Anchor to the E or W of the island in 7-10m on sand or rock.

Cala Cannelle ⊕ 184 42°22'.55N 011°08'.41E
A cove with anchorage off the beach in 3-5m on sand.

Cala Piazzoni

Cala Piazzoni ⊕ 186 42°21'.83N 011°10'.48E
A large secluded bay bordered by rocky shores and protected by Punta di Torre Ciana and Punta Avoltore. Anchor where convenient in 5-7m on sand. The NE corner is the best protected and busiest part of the bay.

Scoglio L'Isolotto ⊕ 188 42°22'.75N 011°12'.48E
Anchor between the islet and the coast in 3-7m on sand, or off Cala Lunga beach in 4-6m on sand. The bay is very popular in summer.

Cala Bocca d'Inferno

Scoglio L'Isolotto

Cala Bocca d'Inferno
⊕ 185 42°22'.14N 011°08'.83E
Secluded anchorage to the W of Punta di Torre Ciana. Anchor in 5-7m on sand.

83

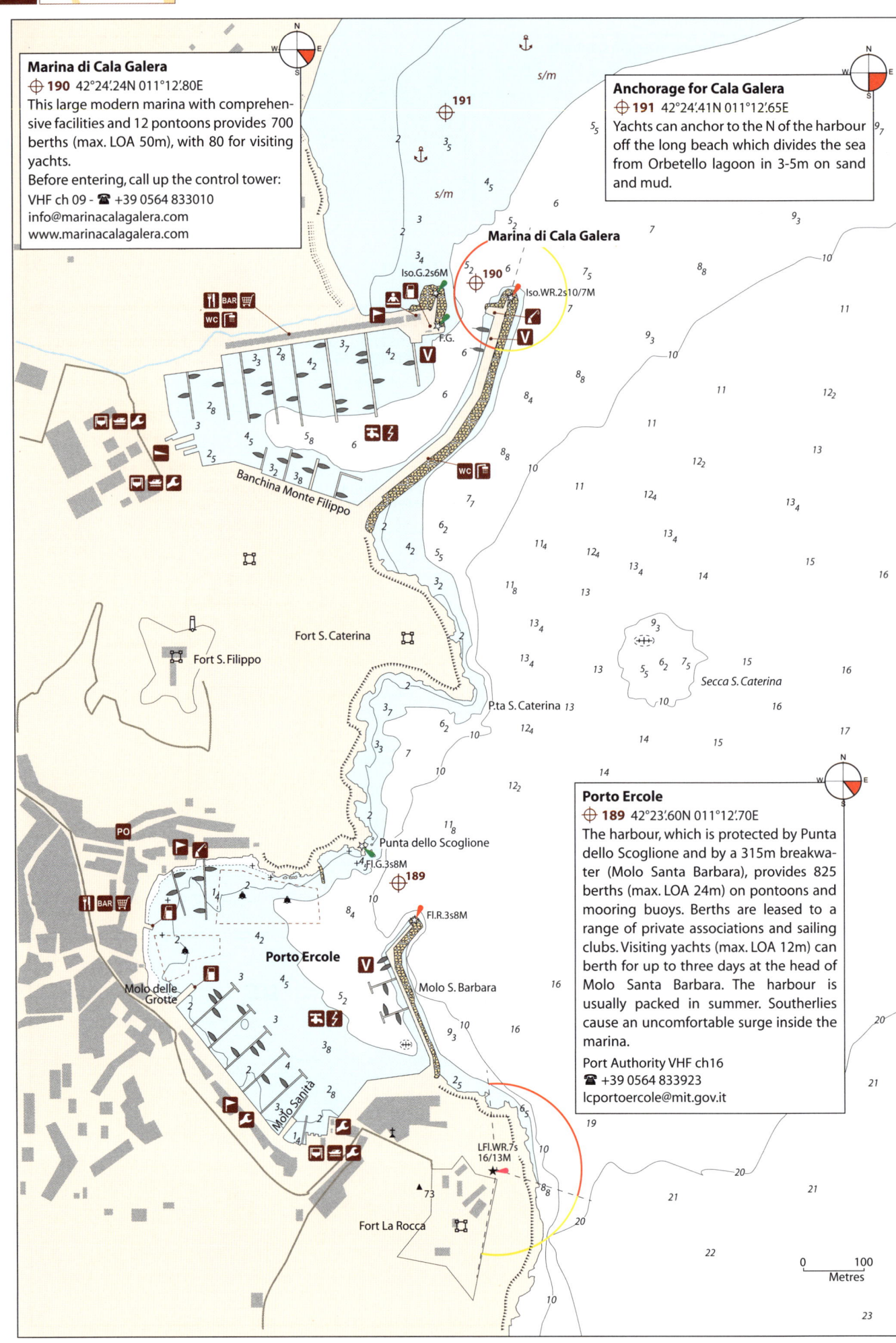

CHART 56 — AREA C | PORTO ERCOLE AND MARINA DI CALA GALERA

Marina di Cala Galera
⊕ 190 42°24′.24N 011°12′.80E
This large modern marina with comprehensive facilities and 12 pontoons provides 700 berths (max. LOA 50m), with 80 for visiting yachts.
Before entering, call up the control tower:
VHF ch 09 - ☎ +39 0564 833010
info@marinacalagalera.com
www.marinacalagalera.com

Anchorage for Cala Galera
⊕ 191 42°24′.41N 011°12′.65E
Yachts can anchor to the N of the harbour off the long beach which divides the sea from Orbetello lagoon in 3-5m on sand and mud.

Porto Ercole
⊕ 189 42°23′.60N 011°12′.70E
The harbour, which is protected by Punta dello Scoglione and by a 315m breakwater (Molo Santa Barbara), provides 825 berths (max. LOA 24m) on pontoons and mooring buoys. Berths are leased to a range of private associations and sailing clubs. Visiting yachts (max. LOA 12m) can berth for up to three days at the head of Molo Santa Barbara. The harbour is usually packed in summer. Southerlies cause an uncomfortable surge inside the marina.

Port Authority VHF ch16
☎ +39 0564 833923
lcportoercole@mit.gov.it

AREA D - ARCIPELAGO TOSCANO (TUSCAN ISLANDS)

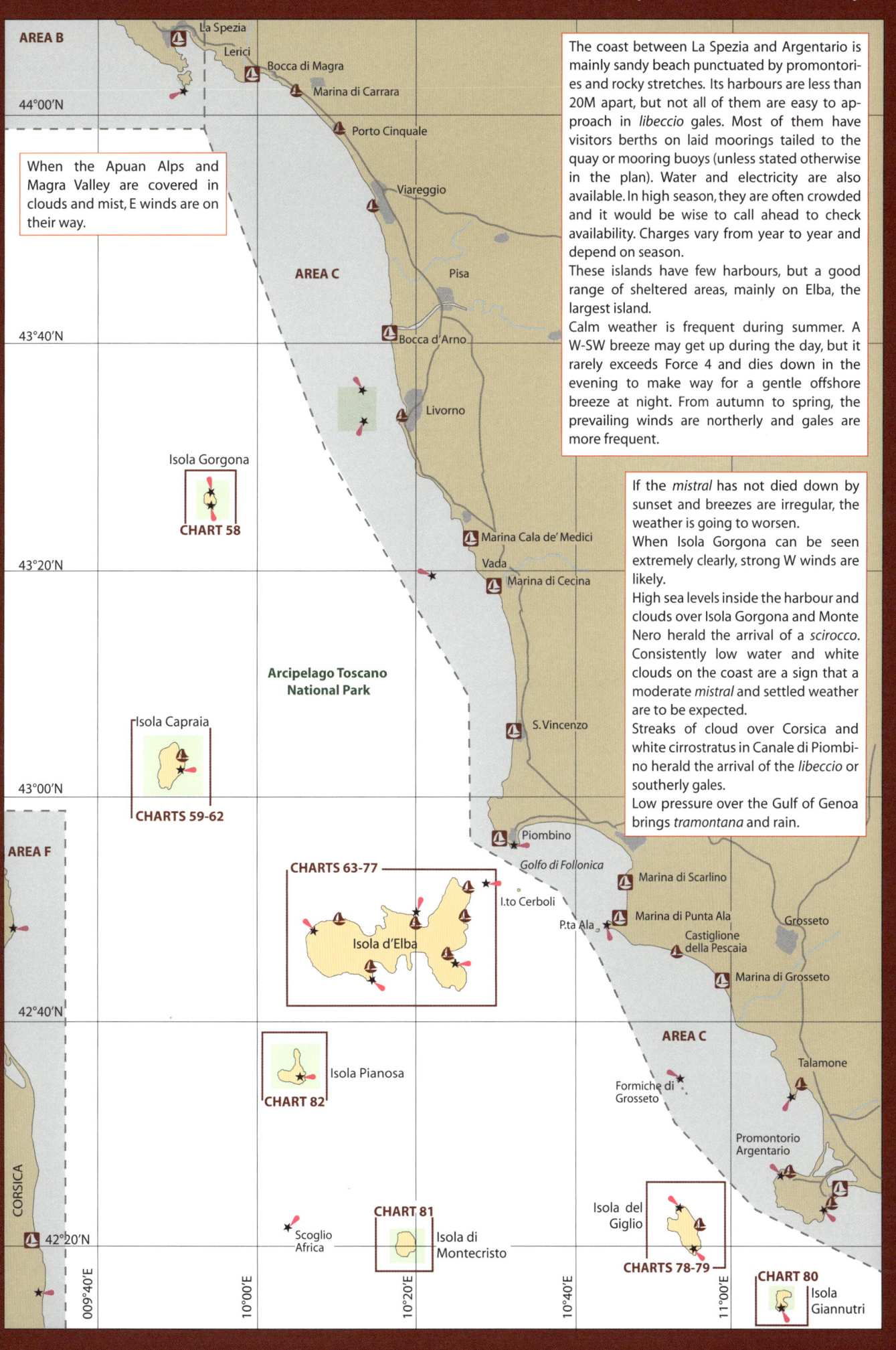

The coast between La Spezia and Argentario is mainly sandy beach punctuated by promontories and rocky stretches. Its harbours are less than 20M apart, but not all of them are easy to approach in *libeccio* gales. Most of them have visitors berths on laid moorings tailed to the quay or mooring buoys (unless stated otherwise in the plan). Water and electricity are also available. In high season, they are often crowded and it would be wise to call ahead to check availability. Charges vary from year to year and depend on season.

These islands have few harbours, but a good range of sheltered areas, mainly on Elba, the largest island.

Calm weather is frequent during summer. A W-SW breeze may get up during the day, but it rarely exceeds Force 4 and dies down in the evening to make way for a gentle offshore breeze at night. From autumn to spring, the prevailing winds are northerly and gales are more frequent.

> When the Apuan Alps and Magra Valley are covered in clouds and mist, E winds are on their way.

If the *mistral* has not died down by sunset and breezes are irregular, the weather is going to worsen.

When Isola Gorgona can be seen extremely clearly, strong W winds are likely.

High sea levels inside the harbour and clouds over Isola Gorgona and Monte Nero herald the arrival of a *scirocco*. Consistently low water and white clouds on the coast are a sign that a moderate *mistral* and settled weather are to be expected.

Streaks of cloud over Corsica and white cirrostratus in Canale di Piombino herald the arrival of the *libeccio* or southerly gales.

Low pressure over the Gulf of Genoa brings *tramontana* and rain.

AREA D - ARCIPELAGO TOSCANO (TUSCAN ISLANDS)

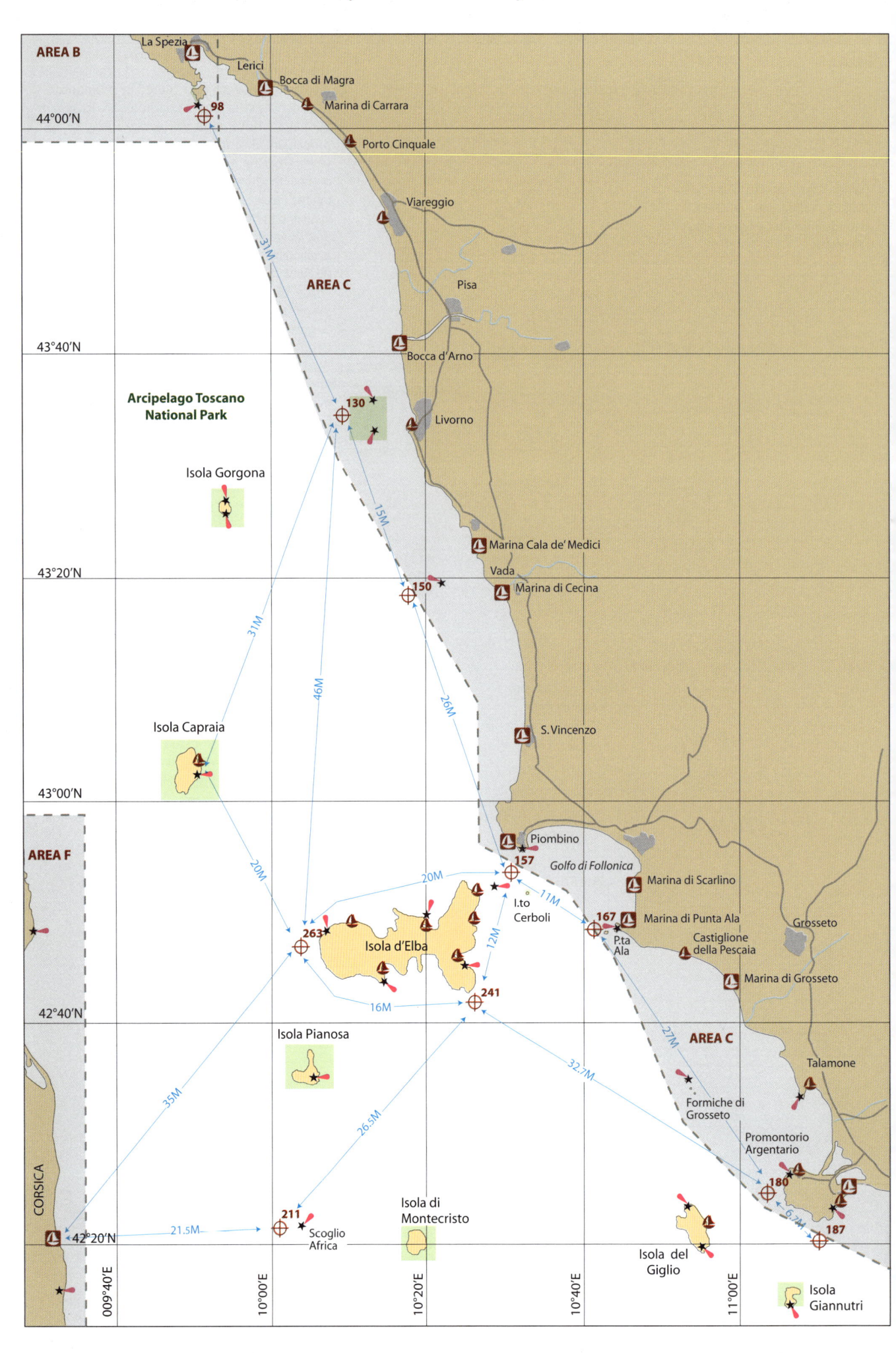

AREA D - ARCIPELAGO TOSCANO (TUSCAN ISLANDS)

COASTAL NAVIGATION WAYPOINTS AND DISTANCES

#	DESCRIPTION	LATITUDE	LONGITUDE	CHART
98	500m S of isolotto del Tinetto	44°01'.20N	009°51'.00E	26-27-29
130	5M E of Secca della Meloria	43°32'.10N	010°06'.10E	37
150	6M W of Vada	43°19'.00N	010°18'.00E	44
157	Canale di Piombino	42°54'.00N	010°29'.20E	46
167	0.5M E of Scoglio Dello Sparviero	42°47'.49N	010°42'.16E	50
180	1.5M W of Argentario	42°25'.00N	011°03'.00E	53
187	1M S of Argentario	42°20'.40N	011°10'.00E	55
211	2M W of Scoglio Africa	42°21'.50N	010°01'.50E	57
241	I. d'Elba - 500m S of Punta Ripalti	42°42'.09N	010°25'.16E	71
263	I. d'Elba - 0.5M W of Punta Nera	42°46'.10N	010°05'.21E	75

HARBOURS AND MARINAS KEY FOR PLAN SYMBOLS

#	NAME	LATITUDE	LONGITUDE	CHART	⛵	⚓	≡	LOA m	V	⛽	↓ m	⚡	🚿	WC	🍽	🛒	🔧
192	I. Gorgona - Cala dello Scalo	43°25'.90N	009°54'.50E	58			IU				2						
197	I. Capraia - Harbour	43°03'.05N	009°50'.25E	61		•	240	30	•	•	4.5	•	•	•	•	•	•
215	I. d'Elba - S. Giovanni	42°48'.24N	010°19'.41E	64		•	30				2	•	•				
216	I. d'Elba - Magazzini	42°48'.05N	010°21'.40E	64		•	70	8			2	•	•				
217	I. d'Elba - Portoferraio Mediceo	42°48'.72N	010°19'.77E	65		•	150	70	•	•	10	•	•	•			
218	I. d'Elba - Marina Esaom Cesa	42°48'.51N	010°19'.00E	65	•		175	40	•	•	4.5	•	•	•	•	•	•
219	I. d'Elba - Edilnautica Marina	42°48'.45N	010°18'.98E	65	•		100	35	•		3	•	•	•		•	
229	I. d'Elba - Cavo	42°51'.66N	010°25'.50E	67		•	270	12	•	•	2.5	•	•	•	•	•	
231	I. d'Elba - Rio Marina	42°49'.00N	010°25'.84E	68		•	130	16		•	5.8	•	•	•	•		•
236	I. d'Elba - Porto Azzurro	42°45'.66N	010°23'.66E	70		•	190	20	•	•	10	•	•	•	•		
237	I. d'Elba - Cantiere N. Golfo di Mola	42°45'.58N	010°23'.58E	70	•		200	40	•		5	•	•	•	•	•	•
254	I. d'Elba - Marina di Campo	42°44'.60N	010°14'.38E	74		•	IU	IU	•	•	6.5	•	•	•	•	•	
269	I. d'Elba - Marciana Marina	42°48'.47N	010°11'.95E	76		•	500	35	•	•	6	•	•	•	•	•	
278	I. del Giglio - Giglio Porto	42°21'.66N	010°55'.23E	79		•	196	20	•	•	8	•	•	•	•	•	
290	Isola di Montecristo	42°20'.30N	010°17'.52E	81		•	IU				2.5						
291	I. Pianosa - Harbour	42°35'.38N	010°06'.00E	82			IU				2.5						

IU= Information Unavailable

ANCHORAGES KEY FOR PLAN SYMBOLS

#	NAME	LATITUDE	LONGITUDE	CHART	🗺	🐟	↓ m	🔆	🔻	🧭	⚓	🔔
194	I. Capraia - Cala della Mortola	43°03'.98N	009°49'.97E	60	G	s/w	5	•		NW-E	•	
195	I. Capraia - Cala Porto Vecchio	43°03'.49N	009°50'.00'E	60	G	s	7			N-S	•	
196	I. Capraia - Rada di Capraia	43°03'.05N	009°50'.40E	61	E	s/w	7	•	B-R-S	NE-E	•	•
198	I. Capraia - Cala dello Zurletto	43°02'.65N	009°50'.77'E	61	G	s/w/r	8			NE-S	•	
199	I. Capraia - Cala Ceppo	43°01'.55N	009°50'.78E	61	G	s	5			E-S	•	
200	I. Capraia - Cala Carbicina	43°01'.22N	009°49'.75E	60	G	s	7			NE-S	•	
201	I. Capraia - Io Scoglione	43°00'.90N	009°49'.40E	60	P	s/r	8			N-SW	•	
202	I. Capraia - Cala Rossa	43°00'.15N	009°45'.75E	60	G	s	7			E-SW	•	
203	I. Capraia - Cala del Moreto	43°00'.32N	009°48'.42E	60	G	s/r	7			SE-W	•	
204	I. Capraia - Le Cote	43°01'.08N	009°47'.59E	62	P	s/w/r	10			S/N	•	
205	I. Capraia -Cala del Vetriolo	43°01'.63N	009°47'.55E	62	P	s/r	6			S/N	•	
206	I. Capraia - Seno della Peruccia e Cala del Reciso	43°02'.58N	009°47'.80E	62	P	s/w/r	10			S/N	•	
207	I. Capraia -Scogli del Mosè	43°03'.03N	009°48'.00E	62	P	s/w/r	11			S/N	•	
208	I. Capraia -Punta della Seccatoia	43°03'.55N	009°48'.40E	62	P	s/w/r	8			SW/NE	•	
209	I. Capraia - Punta dell'Acquissucola	43°03'.78N	009°48'.66E	62	P	s/w/p	9			S/NE	•	
210	Isolotto di Cerboli	42°51'.43N	010°33'.08E	63	P	s/r	10			N-N	•	

AREA D - ARCIPELAGO TOSCANO (TUSCAN ISLANDS)

#	NAME	LATITUDE	LONGITUDE	CHART	🗺	⚓type	m	💡	🍷	Winds	⚓	🔔
214	I. d'Elba - Rada di Portoferraio	42°48'.22N	010°20'.75E	64	G	s	8	•		SW-NE	•	
215	I. d'Elba - S. Giovanni	42°48'.24N	010°19'.41E	64	E	s/m	4	•	B-R-S	SW-NE	•	
216	I. d'Elba - Magazzini	42°48'.05N	010°21'.40E	64	E	m/w	7	•	B-R	SW-N	•	•
220	I. d'Elba - Cala Bagnaia	42°48'.66N	010°21'.45E	66	G	s	5	•	B-R	SW-NW		•
221	I. d'Elba - Cala Zupignano	42°49'.15N	010°21'.94E	66	G	s/w/r	5	•		SW-NW	•	
222	I. d'Elba - Cala Nisporto	42°49'.66N	010°22'.66E	66	G	s/w	6	•	BR	W-N	•	
223	I. d'Elba - Cala Nisportino	42°50'.05N	010°22'.92E	66	G	s/g	7	•		W-N	•	
224	I. d'Elba - Cala Piscatoio	42°50'.43N	010°23'.23E	66	G	s/g	6			W-N	•	
225	I. d'Elba - Cala Mandriola	42°51'.73N	010°24'.07E	66	G	s	5	•		SW-NW	•	
227	I. d'Elba - Capo della Vita	42°52'.16N	010°25'.14E	67	G	s/w	5	•		NW-SE	•	
228	I. d'Elba - Capo Castello	42°51'.90N	010°25'.41E	67	G	s/w	5	•		N-S	•	
230	Isola Palmaiola	42°51'.75N	010°28'.34E	68	P	s/r	7			W-E	•	
232	I. d'Elba - Seno d'Ortano	42°47'.55N	010°26'.05E	69	G	s/r	6	•		NE-SE	•	
233	I. d'Elba - Cala Terranera	42°46'.16N	010°25'.24E	69	P	s/r	7		B-R	NE-SW	•	
234	I. d'Elba - Cala Barbarossa	42°46'.03N	010°24'.50E	70	G	s/w	7	•	B-R	SE-S	•	
237	I. d'Elba - Golfo di Mola	42°45'.58N	010°23'.58E	70	G	s/w	7	•	B-R-S	E-SE	•	•
238	I. d'Elba - Cala Naregno	42°45'.35N	010°24'.24E	70	P	s	5	•		N-E	•	
239	I. d'Elba - Capo Bandi/Punta Lestia	42°44'.82N	010°24'.78E	69	G	s	5	•	B-R	NE-SE	•	
240	I. d'Elba - Cala dello Stagnone	42°43'.75N	010°25'.91E	69	P	s/r	7	•		N-S	•	
242	I. d'Elba - Cala del Remaiolo	42°42'.82N	010°24'.65E	71	G	s	5	•		SE-W	•	
243	I. d'Elba - Punta Calamita	42°42'.74N	010°23'.48E	71	P	s/p	5	•		SE-NW	•	
244	I. d'Elba - Isolotti Gemini	42°42'.85N	010°22'.16E	71	P	s/r	4	•		S-NW	•	
245	I. d'Elba - Cala Innamorata	42°43'.35N	010°22'.49E	71	P	s	5	•	B-R	S-NW	•	
246	I. d'Elba - Cala Morcone	42°43'.80N	010°22'.30E	71	G	s	5	•	B-R	S-NW	•	
247	I. d'Elba - Cala Barabarca	42°44'.91N	010°21'.33E	72	P	s	4	•	B-R	S-N	•	
248	I. d'Elba - Golfo Stella	42°45'.41N	010°20'.41E	72	G	s	4	•		SE-SW	•	
249	I. d'Elba - Margidore	42°45'.55N	010°19'.23E	72	G	s	5	•	B-R-S	E-S	•	•
250	I. d'Elba - Golfo della Lacona	42°45'.33N	010°18'.32E	72	G	s	5	•	B-R	SE-SW	•	
251	I. d'Elba - Punta della Contessa	42°45'.24N	010°17'.70E	72	G	s	7	•		SE-SW	•	
252	I. d'Elba - Cala Fonza	42°44'.51N	010°15'.74E	74	G	s	5	•		SE-NW	•	
253	I. d'Elba - Marina di Campo	42°44'.78N	010°14'.53E	74	G	s	5	•	B-R-S	SE-SW	•	•
255	I. d'Elba - Cala Galenzana	42°44'.32N	010°14'.40E	74	P	s/w	4	•		NE-SE	•	
257	I. d'Elba - Cala Cavoli	42°43'.98N	010°11'.05E	73	G	s	8	•	B-R	SE-SW	•	
258	I. d'Elba - Fetovaia	42°43'.75N	010°09'.76E	73	G	s/w	5	•	B-R	NE-SW	•	
260	I. d'Elba - Cala Le Tombe	42°43'.84N	010°08'.42E	73	G	s/r	5	•		E-W	•	
261	I. d'Elba - Relitto *Elviscot*	42°44'.58N	010°07'.10E	73	P	s	8			SE-N	•	
262	I. d'Elba - Cala Punta Nera	42°45'.86N	010°06'.23E	75	P	s	5			SE-NW	•	
264	I. d'Elba - Cala le Buche	42°47'.25N	010°06'.16E	75	P	s	4	•		S-NE	•	
265	I. d'Elba - Punta Polveraia	42°47'.59N	010°06'.50E	75	P	s	8	•	B-R	S-NE	•	
266	I. d'Elba - Cala la Cotaccia	42°48'.07N	010°07'.21E	75	G	s	6	•		S-N	•	
267	I. d'Elba - S.Andrea	42°48'.58N	010°08'.65E	76	G	s	7	•	B-R-S	W-E	•	
268	I. d'Elba - Cala Ripa Barata	42°48'.55N	010°10'.63E	76	G	s	5	•		SW-N	•	
269	I. d'Elba - Marciana Marina	42°48'.47N	010°11'.95E	76	P	s	6	•	B-R-S	W-SE	•	•
270	I. d'Elba - Golfo di Procchio	42°47'.55N	010°14'.63E	77	G	s	5	•	B-R	W-NE	•	
271	I. d'Elba - Golfo della Biodola	42°48'.21N	010°15'.84E	77	G	s	4	•	B-R	W-N	•	
272	I. d'Elba - Golfo di Viticcio	42°49'.10N	010°16'.21E	77	G	s/w	5	•	BR	SW-NW	•	
274	I. d'Elba - Cala Sansone	42°49'.48N	010°16'.72E	77	P	s	5	•		W-S	•	
275	I. del Giglio - Cala Calbugina	42°23'.17N	010°53'.92E	78	P	s/w	5	•		W-SE	•	
276	I. del Giglio - Cala Arenella	42°22'.17N	010°54'.84E	79	P	s	7	•		W-SE	•	
277	I. del Giglio - Cala del Lazzaretto	42°21'.75N	010°55'.42E	79	G	s	6	•	B-R-S	NE-S	•	

AREA D - ARCIPELAGO TOSCANO (TUSCAN ISLANDS)

⊕	NAME	WGS 84 COORDINATES		CHART	🐚	🐟	📏 m	⛴	🍽	✣	⚓	🔔
		LATITUDE	LONGITUDE									
279	I. del Giglio - Cala Cannelle	42°21'.11N	010°55'.55E	79	G	s	7	•	B-R	N-S	•	
280	I. del Giglio - Cala Caldane	42°20'.65N	010°55'.59E	79	G	s/w	7	•		N-S	•	
281	I. del Giglio - Cala del Corvo	42°20'.23N	010°53'.51E	78	G	s	7	•		SE-W	•	
282	I. del Giglio - Cala dell'Allume	42°21'.03N	010°52'.80E	78	G	s	7	•		SE-W	•	
283	I. del Giglio - Seno di Campese	42°22'.13N	010°52'.64E	78	G	s	6	•	B-R-S	W-NE	•	
284	I. di Giannutri - Cala Maestra	42°15'.33N	011°05'.66E	80	G	s	10	•		SW-N	•	
286	I. di Giannutri - Golfo Spalmatoi	42°15'.20N	011°06'.55E	80	G	s	8			SE-SW	•	
287	I. di Giannutri - Cala Spalmatoi	42°15'.21N	011°06'.39E	80	G	s/r	7	•	B-R-S	E-SE	•	•
288	I. di Giannutri - Cala Schiavone	42°14'.93N	011°06'.24E	80	G	s	10	•		NE-SE	•	
290	I. di Montecristo - Cala Maestra	42°20'.30N	010°17'.52E	81	G	s	5	•		SW-NW		•

Shelter: P = Poor G = Good E = Excellent   **Nature of seabed:** w = weed m = mud g = gravel p = pebbles/stones r = rock s = sand
Depths in metres   **Landing with dinghy**   **Facilities ashore:** B = Bar R = Restaurant S = Shop   **Anchorage**   **Mooring buoy**
Wind direction and exposure

SAFETY AT SEA — AREA D

WEATHER BULLETINS

Mari d'Italia/Meteomar weather bulletin
(English and Italian)
VHF ch 68 frequency 156.425 MHz continuous

Coast radio station weather bulletin
Monte Moro (North Sardinia and Strait of Bonifacio)
VHF ch 28 frequency 162.000 MHz
Porto Torres VHF ch 26 frequency 161.900 MHz
0510 0810 1210 1610 2010 UTC
Radio Porto Cervo local bulletin VHF ch 26, 28, 85
(English and Italian) with advance call on ch 16
0150 0750 1350 1950 UTC

Radiouno - Italian bulletin for the sea
0554 1408 2249 Monday-Friday

FRANCE AND CORSICA WEATHER FORECASTS (French-English)

Monaco Radio 4363 kHz (ch 403)
0903 1403 1915 LT Lyon, Provence, Corsican Sea, Sardinian Sea, Ligurian Sea, Northern Tyrrhenian Sea

Monaco Radio 8728, 8806 kHz (ch 804, 830) SSB
0715 1830 UTC West Mediterranean offshore seas

La Garde CROSS 1696, 2677 kHz SSB after the first call
frequency 2182 kHz
0650 1433 1850 LT

HARBOURMASTERS

La Spezia ☎ +39 0187 258100
cplaspezia@mit.gov.it

Marina di Carrara ☎ +39 0585 646701
cpcarrara@mit.gov.it

Livorno ☎ +39 0586 826011
cplivorno@guardiacostiera.gov.it

Viareggio ☎ +39 0584 43931
cpviareggio@mit.gov.it

Portoferraio ☎ +39 0565 914000
cpportoferraio@mit.gov.it

Guardia Costiera (Coast Guard)
☎ 1530 emergency - VHF ch 16

SAFETY AND RESCUE CENTRES

MRSC Genova ☎ +39 010 27771
genova@guardiacostiera.it

MRSC Livorno ☎ +39 0586 826011
cplivorno@guardiacostiera.gov.it

MRCC Roma MMSI 002 470 001
DSC VHF ch 70, 16 - DSC MF 2187.5 kHz, 2182 kHz
DSC HF 420.5, 6312, 8414.5 kHz
Direzione Marittima (Port Authority) Roma Fiumicino
☎ +39 06 656171
cproma@mit.gov.it

MRSC Corsica VHF ch 16, 67
☎ +33 (0)495 201363
MMSI 002275420
(winter 0730-1900 - summer 0730-2300)

CIRM International Medical Centre
☎ +39 06 559290263 / mobile +39 348 3984229
Fax +39 06 5923331/2
telesoccorso@cirm.it - www.cirm.it

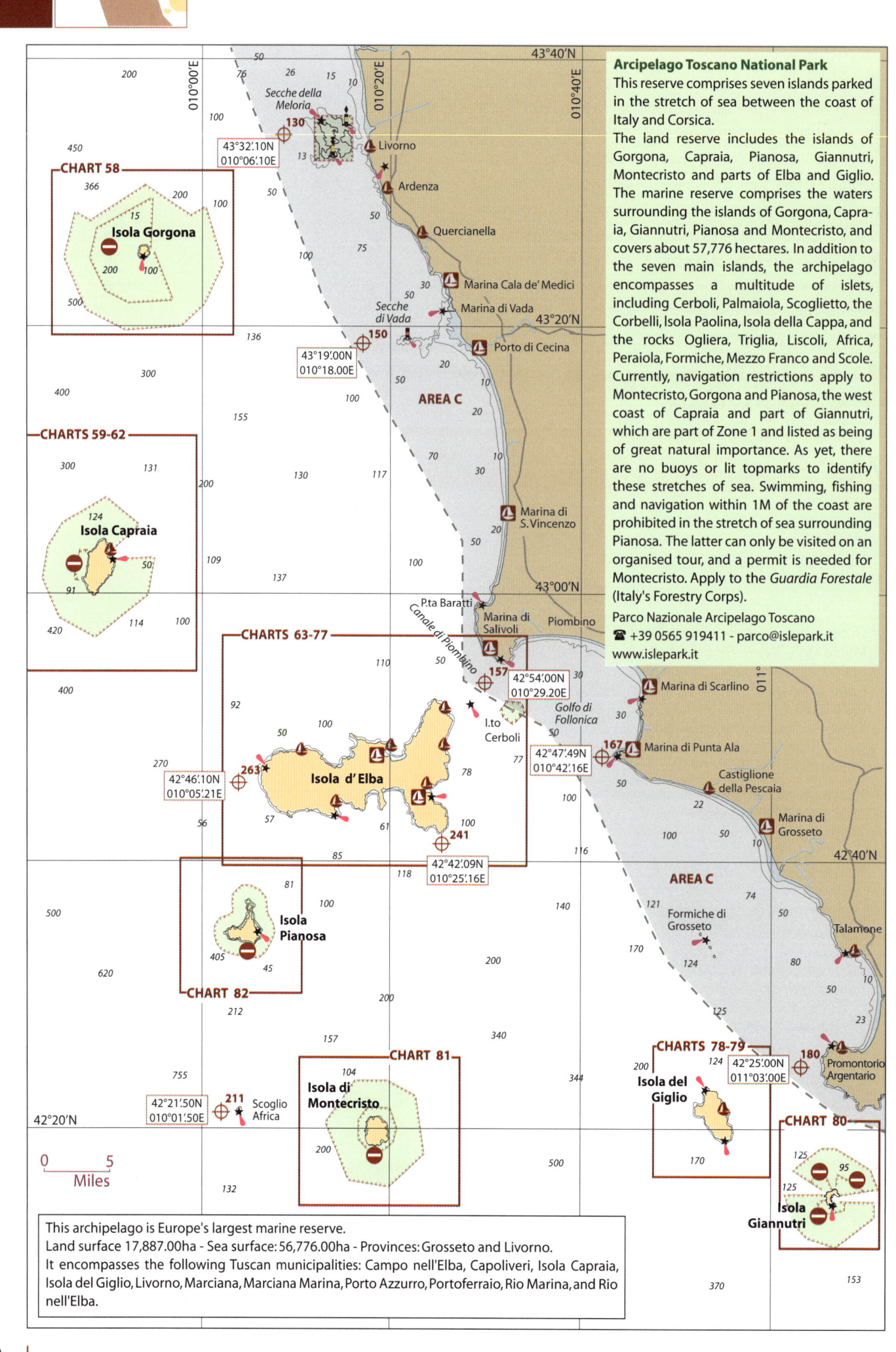

CHART 57 — AREA D — ARCIPELAGO TOSCANO (TUSCAN ISLANDS)

Arcipelago Toscano National Park

This reserve comprises seven islands parked in the stretch of sea between the coast of Italy and Corsica.

The land reserve includes the islands of Gorgona, Capraia, Pianosa, Giannutri, Montecristo and parts of Elba and Giglio. The marine reserve comprises the waters surrounding the islands of Gorgona, Capraia, Giannutri, Pianosa and Montecristo, and covers about 57,776 hectares. In addition to the seven main islands, the archipelago encompasses a multitude of islets, including Cerboli, Palmaiola, Scoglietto, the Corbelli, Isola Paolina, Isola della Cappa, and the rocks Ogliera, Triglia, Liscoli, Africa, Peraiola, Formiche, Mezzo Franco and Scole. Currently, navigation restrictions apply to Montecristo, Gorgona and Pianosa, the west coast of Capraia and part of Giannutri, which are part of Zone 1 and listed as being of great natural importance. As yet, there are no buoys or lit topmarks to identify these stretches of sea. Swimming, fishing and navigation within 1M of the coast are prohibited in the stretch of sea surrounding Pianosa. The latter can only be visited on an organised tour, and a permit is needed for Montecristo. Apply to the *Guardia Forestale* (Italy's Forestry Corps).

Parco Nazionale Arcipelago Toscano
☎ +39 0565 919411 - parco@islepark.it
www.islepark.it

This archipelago is Europe's largest marine reserve.
Land surface 17,887.00ha - Sea surface: 56,776.00ha - Provinces: Grosseto and Livorno.
It encompasses the following Tuscan municipalities: Campo nell'Elba, Capoliveri, Isola Capraia, Isola del Giglio, Livorno, Marciana, Marciana Marina, Porto Azzurro, Portoferraio, Rio Marina, and Rio nell'Elba.

ISOLA GORGONA — AREA D

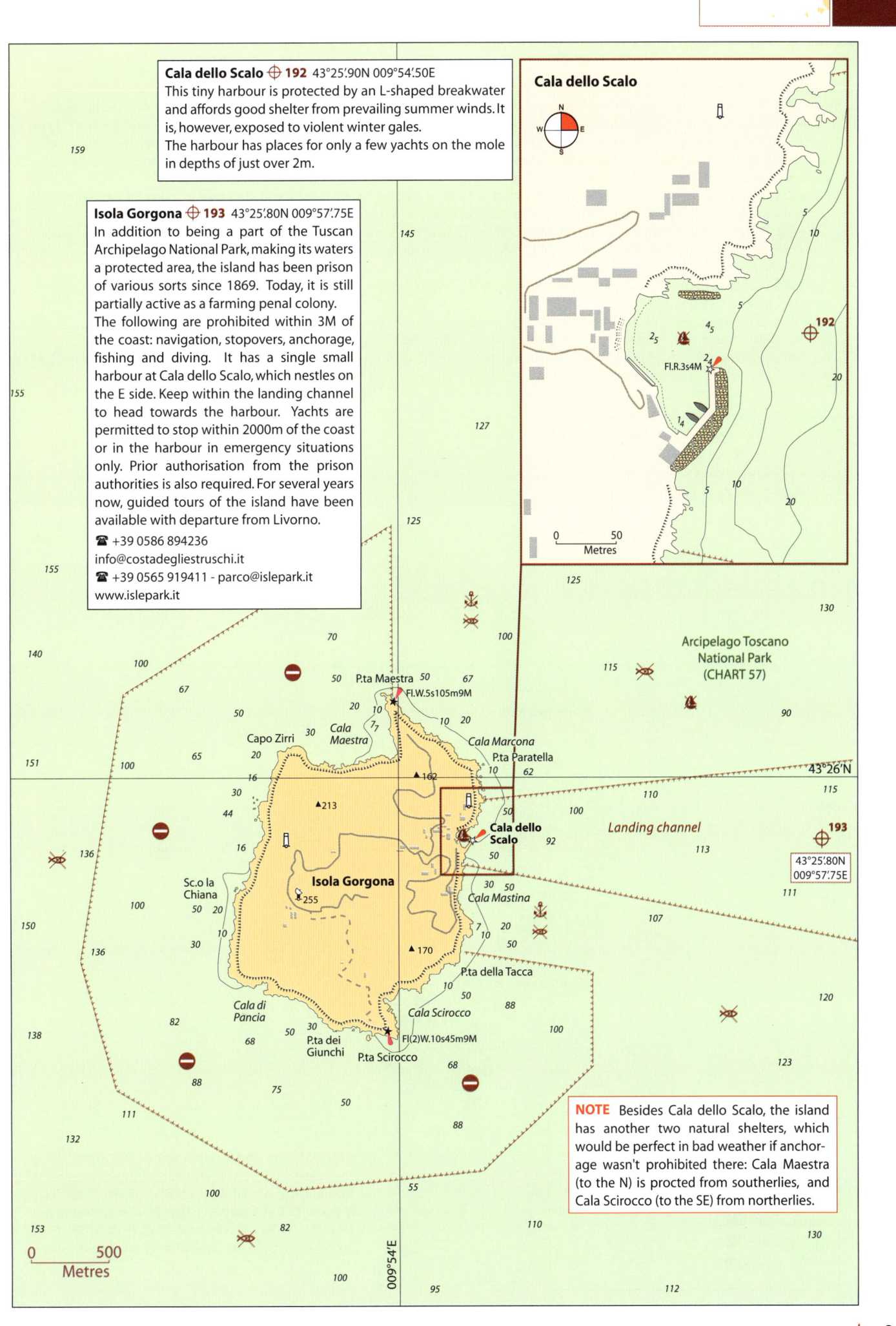

CHART 58

Cala dello Scalo ⊕ **192** 43°25'.90N 009°54'.50E
This tiny harbour is protected by an L-shaped breakwater and affords good shelter from prevailing summer winds. It is, however, exposed to violent winter gales.
The harbour has places for only a few yachts on the mole in depths of just over 2m.

Isola Gorgona ⊕ **193** 43°25'.80N 009°57'.75E
In addition to being a part of the Tuscan Archipelago National Park, making its waters a protected area, the island has been prison of various sorts since 1869. Today, it is still partially active as a farming penal colony.
The following are prohibited within 3M of the coast: navigation, stopovers, anchorage, fishing and diving. It has a single small harbour at Cala dello Scalo, which nestles on the E side. Keep within the landing channel to head towards the harbour. Yachts are permitted to stop within 2000m of the coast or in the harbour in emergency situations only. Prior authorisation from the prison authorities is also required. For several years now, guided tours of the island have been available with departure from Livorno.
☎ +39 0586 894236
info@costadegliestruschi.it
☎ +39 0565 919411 - parco@islepark.it
www.islepark.it

NOTE Besides Cala dello Scalo, the island has another two natural shelters, which would be perfect in bad weather if anchorage wasn't prohibited there: Cala Maestra (to the N) is procted from southerlies, and Cala Scirocco (to the SE) from northerlies.

| CHART 59 | | AREA D | ISOLA CAPRAIA MARINE RESRVE |

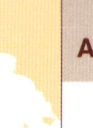

Isola Capraia Marine Reserve
On 22/9/2017 the new sea zoning for Isola Capraia was officialy introduced.
Zone MA *Riserva Integrale* (Fully protected reserve) Rescue, monitoring and scientific research are the only activities allowed in this area.
Zone MB *Regolamentazione ristretta Riserva Generale* (Partly regulated General Reserve) The following are allowed here: swimming/snorkelling, navigation under sail, oar, pedal or electric thrusters; navigation and anchorage by motorboats and motor yachts (max. LOA 10m) meeting eco-compatibility requirements*; mooring in designated marine-reserve areas; fishing by residents; and organised underwater-diving tours on marine-reserve authorisation.
Zone MB *Riserva Generale* (General Reserve) Yachts with LOA 10m+ are allowed to navigate and anchor here, as long as they comply with eco-compatibility requirements. The activities permitted in Zone MB (partly regulated reserve) are also permitted here.
Zone MC *Di Protezione* (Protected Reserve) Restriction-free navigation for motor yachts is allowed here, as are sport fishing by non-residents (regulations apply) and restriction-free individual and group diving during the day. The activities permitted in Zone MB are also permitted here.
Zone MD Free anchorage, individual and group diving both day and night, water-skiing and spearfishing (regulations apply) are allowed here, as are the activities in Zone MC.
* The marine reserves classify pleasure craft both by size and by their environmental impact.
A1) "Minimum impact" craft meet the following requirements: craft navigating under sail, oar, pedal, or electric motor only.
A2) "Eco-compatible" craft meet the following requirements: they comply with Directive 2003/44/EC, are equipped with holding tank, and are equipped with in- or outboard motor powered by biodiesel, ethanol, gas or other "ecological" fuels.

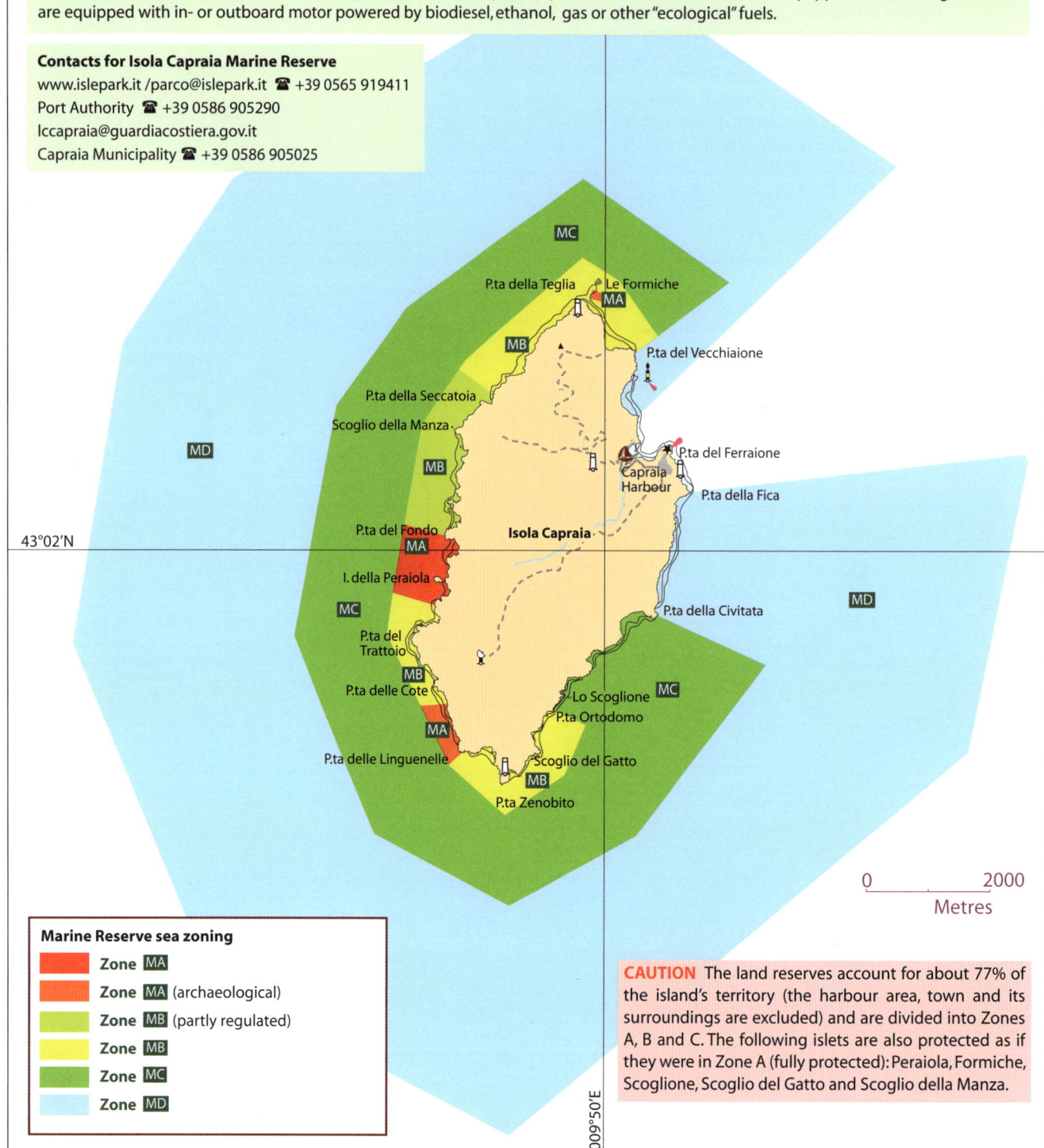

Contacts for Isola Capraia Marine Reserve
www.islepark.it /parco@islepark.it ☎ +39 0565 919411
Port Authority ☎ +39 0586 905290
lccapraia@guardiacostiera.gov.it
Capraia Municipality ☎ +39 0586 905025

Marine Reserve sea zoning
- Zone MA
- Zone MA (archaeological)
- Zone MB (partly regulated)
- Zone MB
- Zone MC
- Zone MD

CAUTION The land reserves account for about 77% of the island's territory (the harbour area, town and its surroundings are excluded) and are divided into Zones A, B and C. The following islets are also protected as if they were in Zone A (fully protected): Peraiola, Formiche, Scoglione, Scoglio del Gatto and Scoglio della Manza.

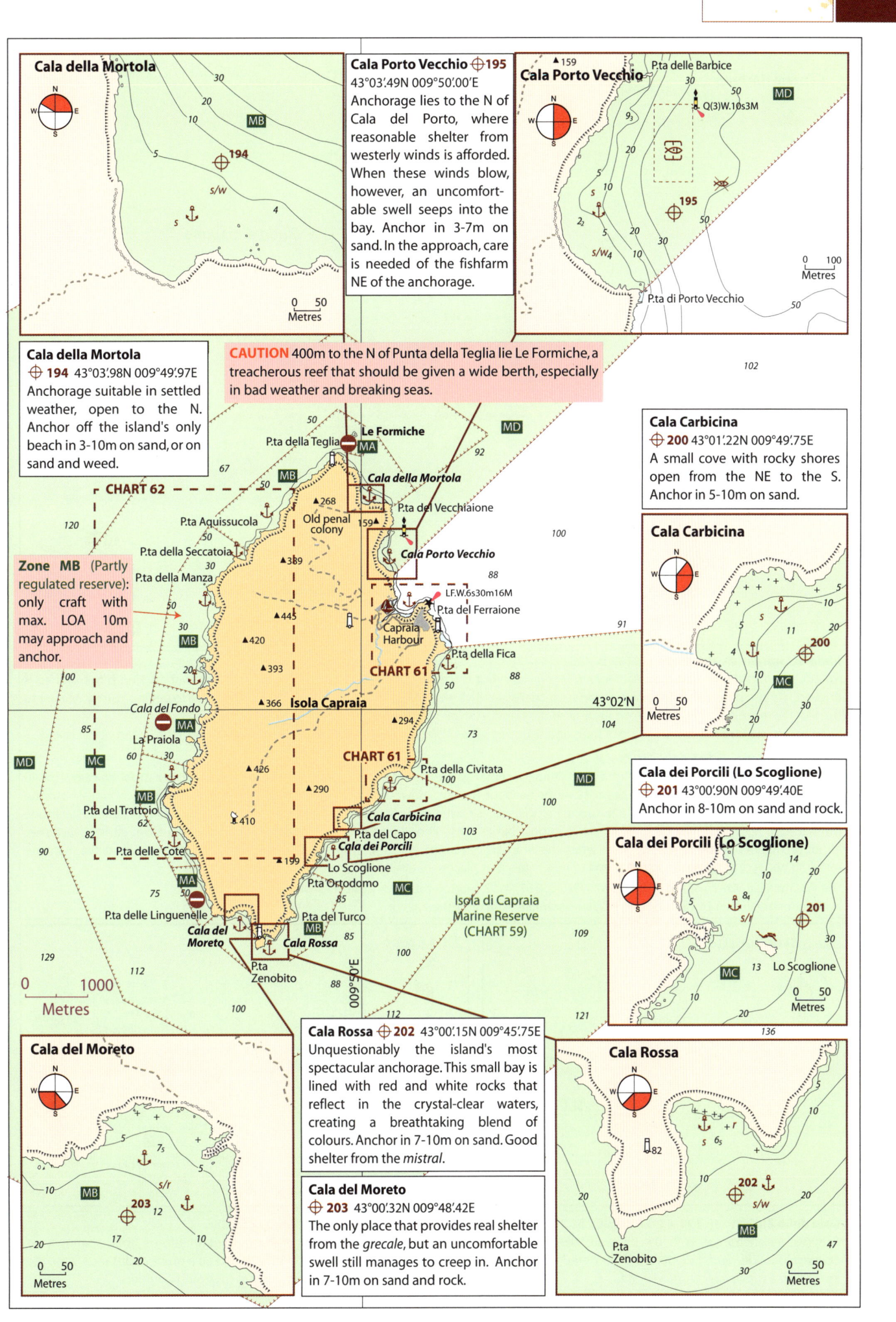

ISOLA CAPRAIA - EAST COAST | AREA D | CHART 60

Cala della Mortola

Cala Porto Vecchio ⊕ 195
43°03'.49N 009°50'.00'E
Anchorage lies to the N of Cala del Porto, where reasonable shelter from westerly winds is afforded. When these winds blow, however, an uncomfortable swell seeps into the bay. Anchor in 3-7m on sand. In the approach, care is needed of the fishfarm NE of the anchorage.

Cala Porto Vecchio

Cala della Mortola
⊕ 194 43°03'.98N 009°49'.97E
Anchorage suitable in settled weather, open to the N. Anchor off the island's only beach in 3-10m on sand, or on sand and weed.

CAUTION 400m to the N of Punta della Teglia lie Le Formiche, a treacherous reef that should be given a wide berth, especially in bad weather and breaking seas.

Cala Carbicina
⊕ 200 43°01'.22N 009°49'.75E
A small cove with rocky shores open from the NE to the S. Anchor in 5-10m on sand.

Zone MB (Partly regulated reserve): only craft with max. LOA 10m may approach and anchor.

Cala Carbicina

Cala dei Porcili (Lo Scoglione)
⊕ 201 43°00'.90N 009°49'.40E
Anchor in 8-10m on sand and rock.

Cala dei Porcili (Lo Scoglione)

Cala Rossa ⊕ 202 43°00'.15N 009°45'.75E
Unquestionably the island's most spectacular anchorage. This small bay is lined with red and white rocks that reflect in the crystal-clear waters, creating a breathtaking blend of colours. Anchor in 7-10m on sand. Good shelter from the *mistral*.

Cala del Moreto
⊕ 203 43°00'.32N 009°48'.42E
The only place that provides real shelter from the *grecale*, but an uncomfortable swell still manages to creep in. Anchor in 7-10m on sand and rock.

Cala del Moreto

Cala Rossa

93

AREA D ISOLA CAPRAIA - EAST COAST

Capraia Harbour

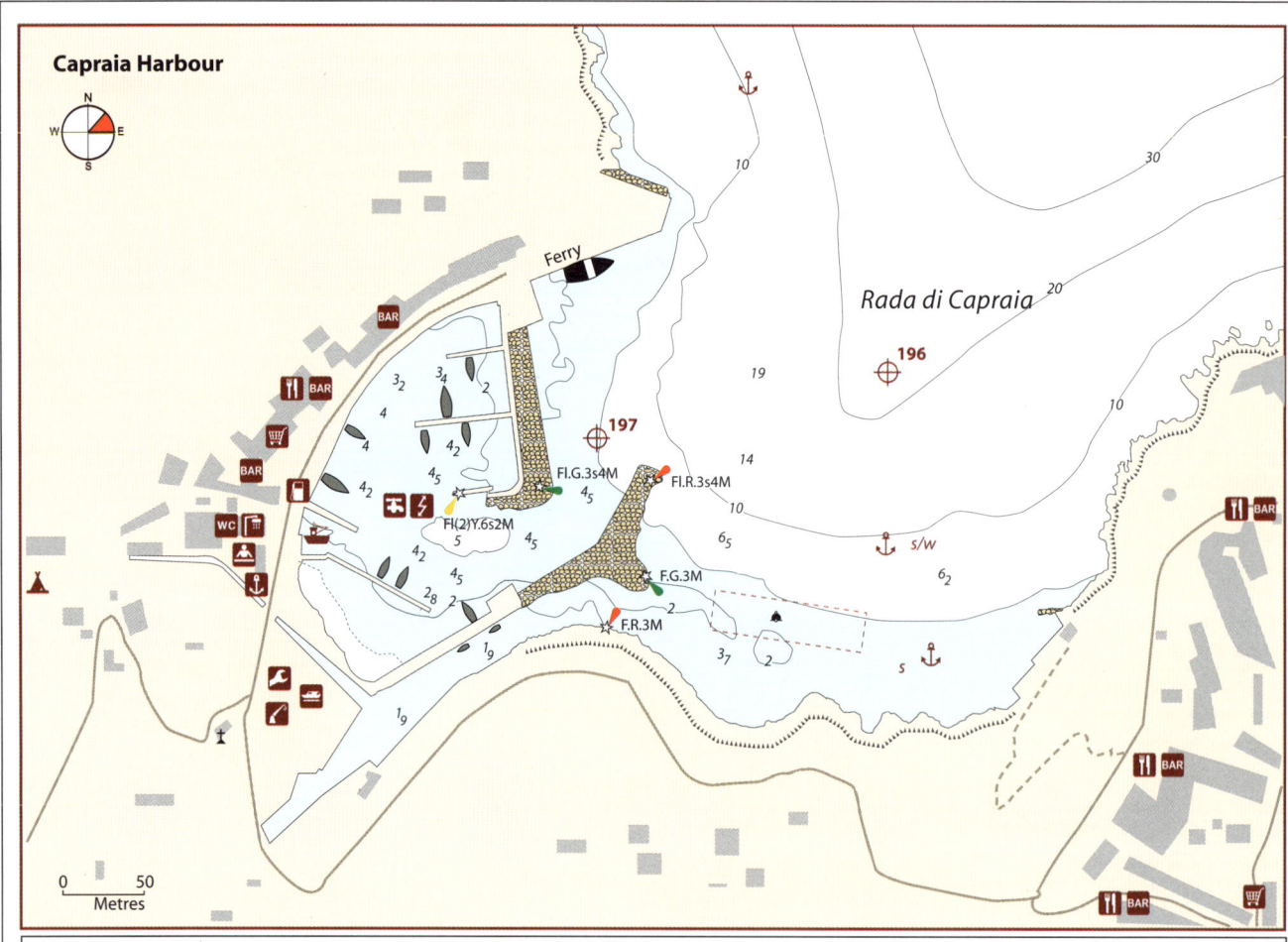

Rada di Capraia ⊕ 196 43°03'.05N 009°50'.40E
Anchorage outside the harbour is untenable in a *grecale*, but is well-protected from westerly winds. Check your anchor as the seabed is uneven; it is also pitted with deep depressions and coated in thick weed, which means that the anchor struggles to get in securely. Anchor to the E of the mooring buoys in 3-5m on sand, or to the N in 5-10m on sand and weed.
Keen hikers will love the island's maze of trails and stunning views. You can also ask to visit the ex penal colony in the N part of the island.

Capraia Harbour ⊕ 197 43°03'.05N 009°50'.25E
Capraia harbour can host 200 yachts (max. LOA 30m for motor yachts, 26m for sailing yachts). From April to October, mooring buoys for 40 yachts (max. LOA 20m) are laid in the bay outside the harbour. The area, however, is completely open to the *grecale*, and anchorage should be vacated at the slightest hint of wind. In a strong *grecale*, waves crash viciously onto the breakwater, creating an uncomfortable surge inside the harbour. Approach may be difficult, if not impossible in these conditions. The harbour affords good shelter from strong westerlies, although manoeuvering can be awkward when the wind gusts into the harbour. In summer, the harbour is invariably packed; the management do not accept bookings, so call ahead to make sure that places are available.
Soc. Pro. Tur. S.p.a. VHF ch 69 - ☎ +39 0586 905307 / 338 3744102 - portodicapraia@virgilio.it - www.portodicapraia.it
Harbourmaster VHF ch 16 - ☎ +39 0586 905290 - lccapraia@guardiacostiera.gov.it

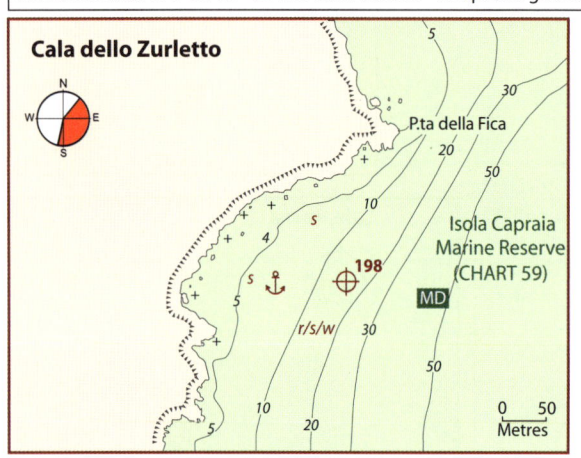

Cala dello Zurletto

Cala dello Zurletto ⊕ 198 43°02'.65N 009°50.77'E
Fairweather anchorage in 8-10m on sand, weed and rock. Numerous rocks and boulders are scattered across the seabed, so a trip line is recommended.

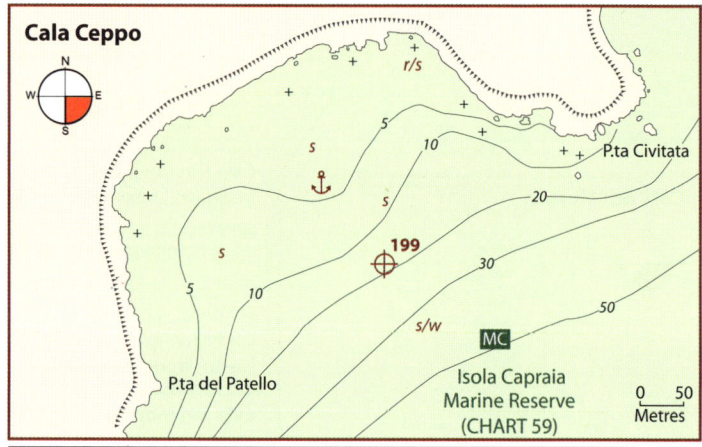

Cala Ceppo

Cala Ceppo ⊕ 199 43°01'.55N 009°50'.78E
This anchorage to the SW of Punta Civitata affords good shelter from westerlies. Anchor in 5-8m on sand, but keep a prudent distance from the coast as it is littered with below-water rocks and boulders.

ISOLA CAPRAIA - WEST COAST | AREA D | CHART 62

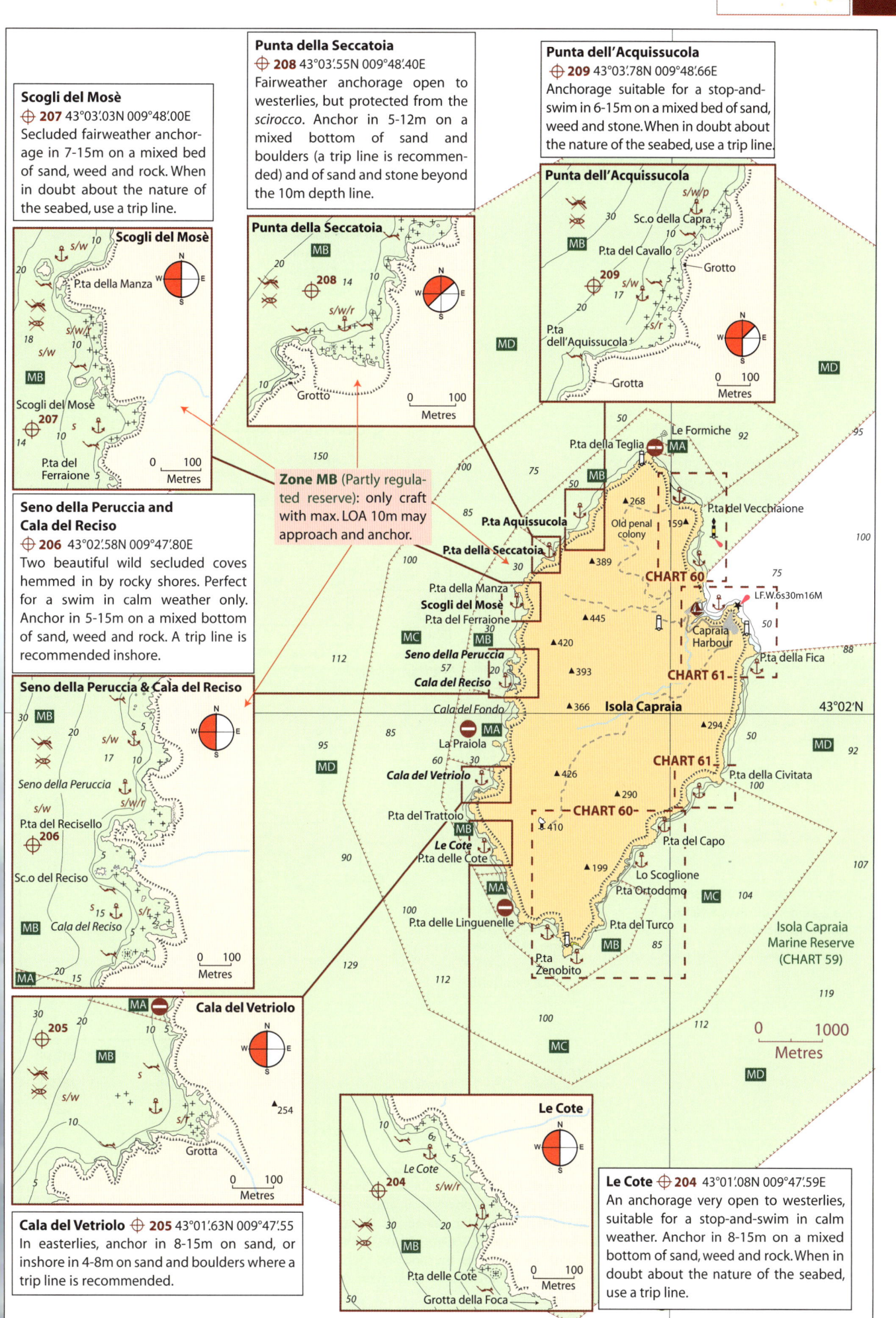

Scogli del Mosè
⊕ **207** 43°03'.03N 009°48'.00E
Secluded fairweather anchorage in 7-15m on a mixed bed of sand, weed and rock. When in doubt about the nature of the seabed, use a trip line.

Punta della Seccatoia
⊕ **208** 43°03'.55N 009°48'.40E
Fairweather anchorage open to westerlies, but protected from the *scirocco*. Anchor in 5-12m on a mixed bottom of sand and boulders (a trip line is recommended) and of sand and stone beyond the 10m depth line.

Punta dell'Acquisucola
⊕ **209** 43°03'.78N 009°48'.66E
Anchorage suitable for a stop-and-swim in 6-15m on a mixed bed of sand, weed and stone. When in doubt about the nature of the seabed, use a trip line.

Zone MB (Partly regulated reserve): only craft with max. LOA 10m may approach and anchor.

Seno della Peruccia and Cala del Reciso
⊕ **206** 43°02'.58N 009°47'.80E
Two beautiful wild secluded coves hemmed in by rocky shores. Perfect for a swim in calm weather only. Anchor in 5-15m on a mixed bottom of sand, weed and rock. A trip line is recommended inshore.

Cala del Vetriolo ⊕ **205** 43°01'.63N 009°47'.55
In easterlies, anchor in 8-15m on sand, or inshore in 4-8m on sand and boulders where a trip line is recommended.

Le Cote ⊕ **204** 43°01'.08N 009°47'.59E
An anchorage very open to westerlies, suitable for a stop-and-swim in calm weather. Anchor in 8-15m on a mixed bottom of sand, weed and rock. When in doubt about the nature of the seabed, use a trip line.

CHART 63 | AREA D | ISOLA D'ELBA

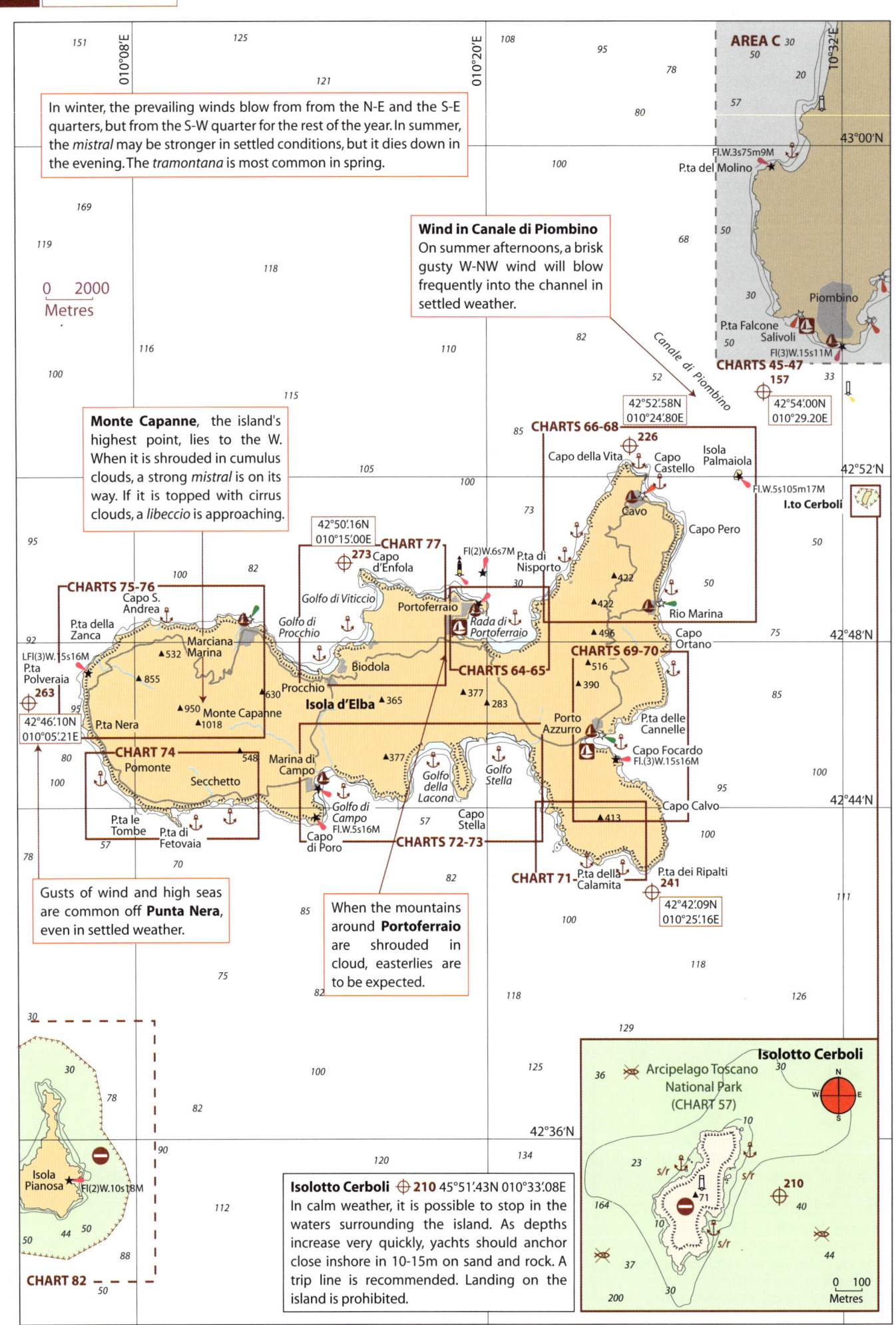

In winter, the prevailing winds blow from from the N-E and the S-E quarters, but from the S-W quarter for the rest of the year. In summer, the *mistral* may be stronger in settled conditions, but it dies down in the evening. The *tramontana* is most common in spring.

Wind in Canale di Piombino
On summer afternoons, a brisk gusty W-NW wind will blow frequently into the channel in settled weather.

Monte Capanne, the island's highest point, lies to the W. When it is shrouded in cumulus clouds, a strong *mistral* is on its way. If it is topped with cirrus clouds, a *libeccio* is approaching.

Gusts of wind and high seas are common off **Punta Nera**, even in settled weather.

When the mountains around **Portoferraio** are shrouded in cloud, easterlies are to be expected.

Isolotto Cerboli ⊕ 210 45°51'.43N 010°33'.08E
In calm weather, it is possible to stop in the waters surrounding the island. As depths increase very quickly, yachts should anchor close inshore in 10-15m on sand and rock. A trip line is recommended. Landing on the island is prohibited.

Isolotto Cerboli
Arcipelago Toscano National Park (CHART 57)

ISOLA D'ELBA - RADA DI PORTOFERRAIO | AREA D

CHART 64

Rada di Portoferraio ⊕ **212** 42°49'.83N 010°20'.08E ⊕ **213** 42°49'.08N 010°20'.91E ⊕ **214** 42°48'.22N 010°20'.75E

The approach to Rada di Portoferraio is straightforward and dangers will only be encountered when arriving from the W, i.e. Secca di Capo Bianco, a shoal marked by a lit N cardinal beacon, and Scoglietto, an islet marked by a lighthouse. Care is needed of the heavy ferry traffic that links Elba with the mainland. The ferries travel along the access channel bordered by Punta Falcone and have right of way. Anchorage is prohibited in part of Rada di Portoferrario.

This large bay provides a range of mooring and anchorage options: Darsena Medicea, in the centre of Portoferraio, plus the Esacom Cesa and Edilnautica marinas, which are outside the town. Further S lie the Circolo Nautico S. Giovanni or Magazzini pontoons, but they are available to small craft with shallow draught only.

Anchorage in the bay is tightly regulated and any yachts not observing the "no anchoring" signs will be towed away and tough penalties applied. Anchorage in the SW corner (3-5m on mud) is the best protected and closest to the town centre, but is somewhat rolly due to the constant vessel traffic. The anchorages in the S and SE part up to Cala della Concia (3-8m on mud and weed) are much more peaceful, but more exposed, and are thus suitable in settled weather only. Strong southerlies blow into the bay and violent gusts fall down from the surrounding highlands. The best shelter lies in the lee of the S coast.

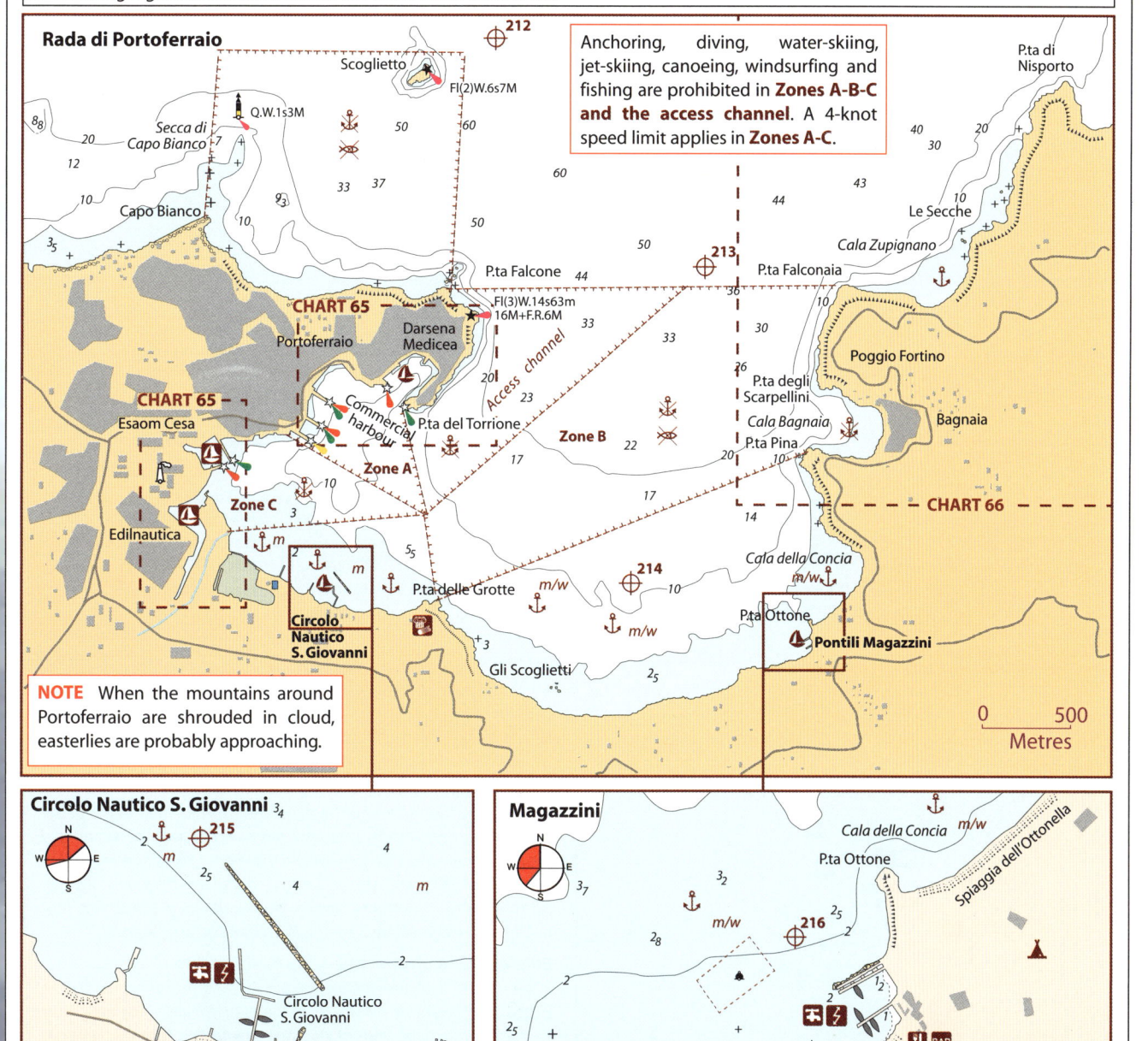

Anchoring, diving, water-skiing, jet-skiing, canoeing, windsurfing and fishing are prohibited in **Zones A-B-C and the access channel**. A 4-knot speed limit applies in **Zones A-C**.

NOTE When the mountains around Portoferraio are shrouded in cloud, easterlies are probably approaching.

Circolo Nautico S. Giovanni
⊕ **215** 42°48'.24N 010°19'.41E
A floating pontoon with about 30 berths administered by the sailing club looks onto the beautiful town of S. Giovanni, but it is difficult to find a place. Alternatively, anchor NW of the pontoon in 3m on mud.
Circolo Nautico S. Giovanni ☎ +39 0565 917165
info@circolonauticosangiovanni.it

Magazzini
⊕ **216** 42°48'.05N 010°21'.40E
A small yacht harbour with 70 berths on floating pontoons (max. LOA 7.5m), 7 for visitors. All berths are suited to craft with shallow draught (max. 1.5m) as depths come up quickly here. Alternatively, anchor off the small harbour in 3-5m on mud and weed, or to the NE in nearby Cala della Concia in 3-5m on mud and weed.
Circolo Nautico Magazzini ☎ +39 0565 933288
Corsi Andrea ☎ +39 0565 933396

CHART 65 — AREA D — ISOLA D'ELBA - PORTOFERRAIO

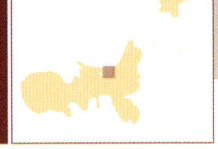

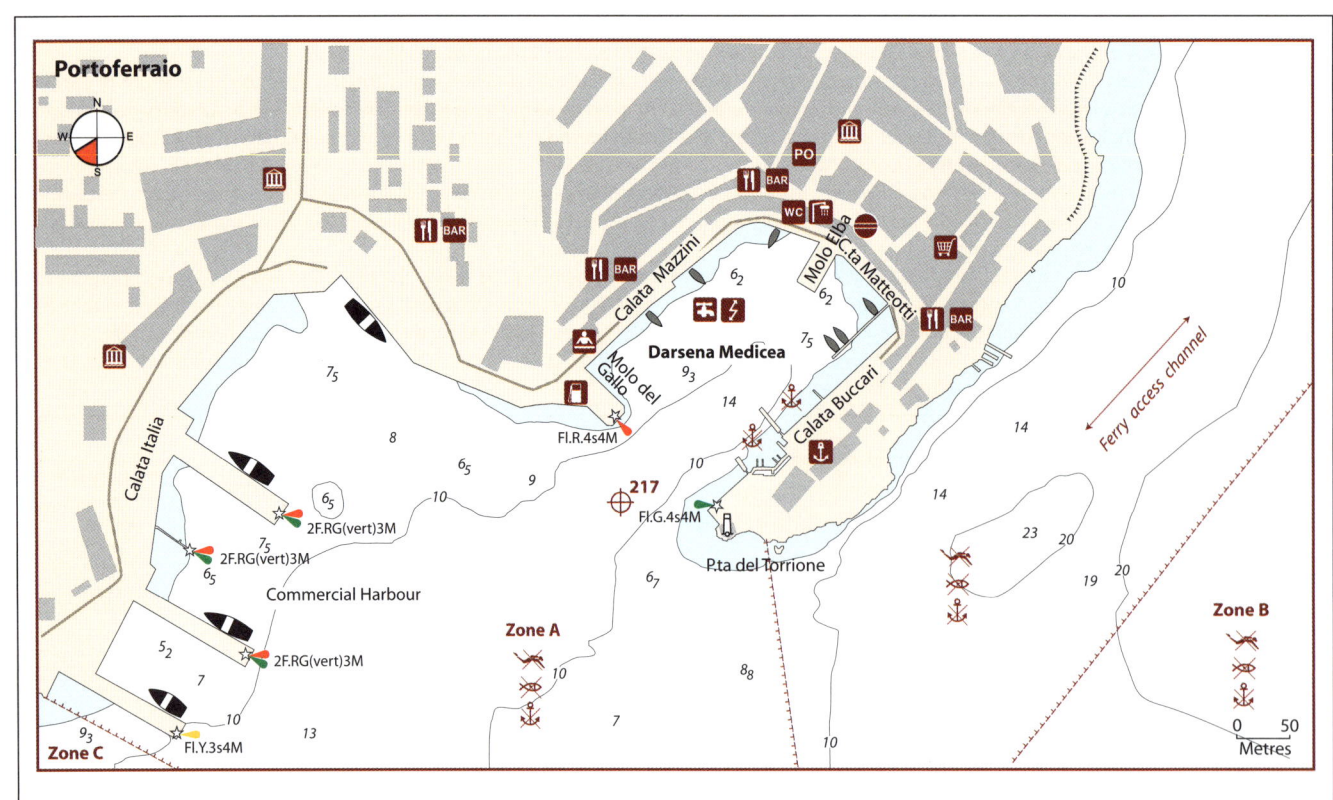

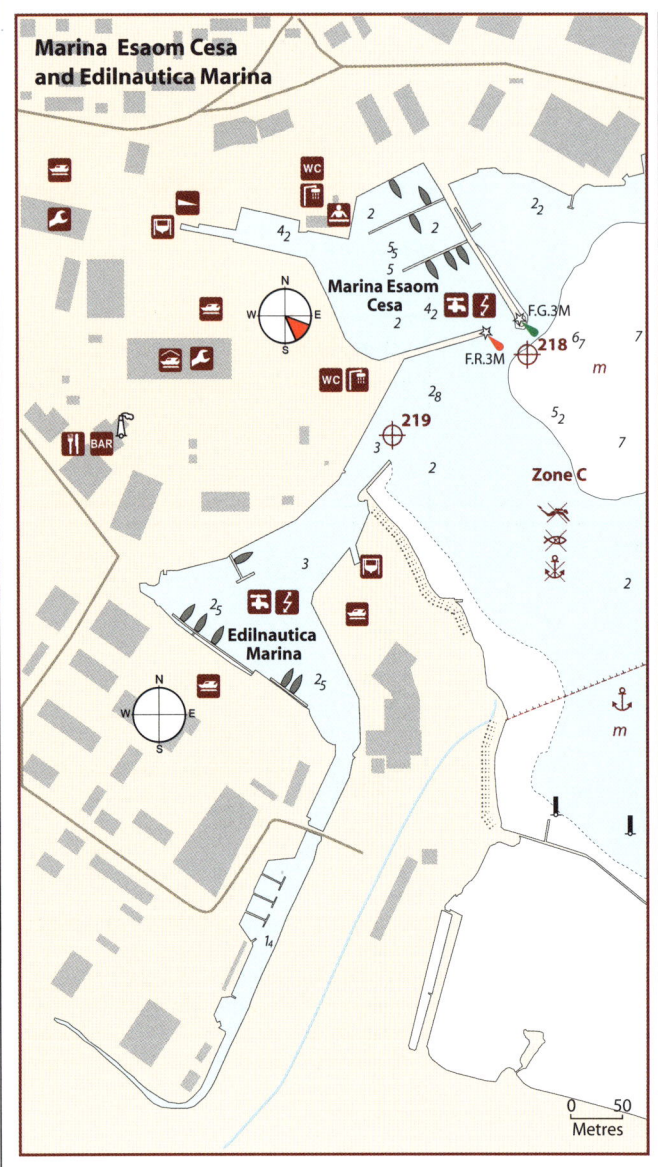

Darsena Medicea ⊕ 217 42°48'.72N 010°19'.77E
Mooring in high season at Darsena Medicea is as atmospheric as it is noisy, especially in Calata Matteotti where passing cars brush past the sterns of the boats moored there. Despite this, a stopover at Portoferraio is a must. Not only is it the island's main harbour, but the town is a delightful, lively place to explore.
Darsena Medicea has a capacity of 150 yachts, with room for 70 in the yacht harbour (max. LOA 70m) divided between Calata Matteotti and Calata Mazzini. There are 7 visitors berths. Yachts can berth for a maximum of one night in high season. In summer, the marina is always extremely busy, so booking well in advance is advisable. Marina staff will assign a berth and help with mooring manoeuvres. In strong SW winds, the basin is battered by strong gusts and disturbed by an uncomfortable swell.
Darsena Medicea Cosimo de' Medici Srl   VHF ch 09
☎ +39 0565 944024 / 914121 - porto@marinadiportoferraio.it
www.marinadiportoferraio.it - info@marinadiportoferraio.it

Marina Esaom Cesa ⊕ 218 42°48'.51N 010°19'.00E
Just under a half mile W of Darsena Medicea lies the marina of the Esaom Cesa shipyard. It is equipped with finger pontoons and laid moorings tailed to the quay. Inside there are 175 berths (max. LOA 40m), with 20 for visitors. Depths fluctuate between 2.5-5m. Although good all-round shelter is provided, the *scirocco* is funnelled into the harbour, causing an uncomfortable slop.

Edilnautica Marina ⊕ 219 42°48'.45N 010°18'.98E
Immediately S of the Marina Esaom Cesa is the entrance to the Edilnautica basin, which is part of the eponymous shipyard group. In the approach, beware of the shallows to the E of the harbour mouth. The marina offers good all-round shelter and has 100 berths (max. LOA 35m) on laid moorings tailed to the quay or on floating pontoons. It has the same contact details as Marina Esaom Cesa.
Esaom Cesa Spa VHF ch 09 (call sign Esaom) - ☎ +39 0565 919311
www.esaom.it info@esaom.it (shipyard)
marina ☎ +39 0565 919309 - marina@esaom.it

Anchorage As an alternative to the marinas, anchor in the SW corner of Rada di Portoferraio, a safe distance from the ferry manoeuvre area in 2-5m on mud.

Harbourmaster ☎ +39 0565 914000 - cpportoferraio@mit.gov.it
Croce Verde Calata Buccari 1 - ☎ +39 0565 916650

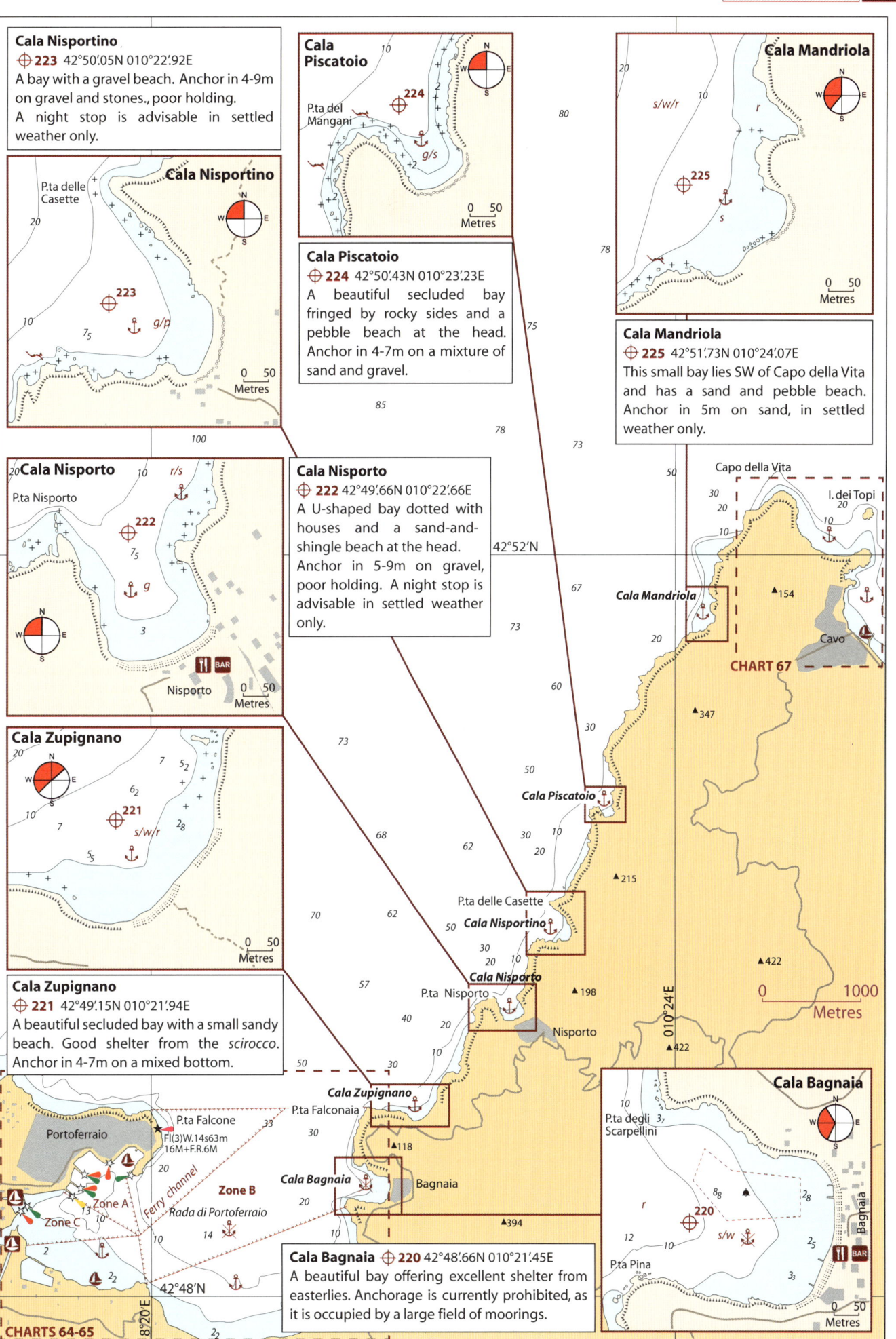

ISOLA D'ELBA - FROM PUNTA FALCONAIA TO CAPO DELLA VITA — AREA D

CHART 66

Cala Nisportino
⊕ **223** 42°50'.05N 010°22'.92E
A bay with a gravel beach. Anchor in 4-9m on gravel and stones., poor holding. A night stop is advisable in settled weather only.

Cala Piscatoio
⊕ **224** 42°50'.43N 010°23'.23E
A beautiful secluded bay fringed by rocky sides and a pebble beach at the head. Anchor in 4-7m on a mixture of sand and gravel.

Cala Mandriola
⊕ **225** 42°51'.73N 010°24'.07E
This small bay lies SW of Capo della Vita and has a sand and pebble beach. Anchor in 5m on sand, in settled weather only.

Cala Nisporto
⊕ **222** 42°49'.66N 010°22'.66E
A U-shaped bay dotted with houses and a sand-and-shingle beach at the head. Anchor in 5-9m on gravel, poor holding. A night stop is advisable in settled weather only.

Cala Zupignano
⊕ **221** 42°49'.15N 010°21'.94E
A beautiful secluded bay with a small sandy beach. Good shelter from the *scirocco*. Anchor in 4-7m on a mixed bottom.

Cala Bagnaia
⊕ **220** 42°48'.66N 010°21'.45E
A beautiful bay offering excellent shelter from easterlies. Anchorage is currently prohibited, as it is occupied by a large field of moorings.

99

CHART 67

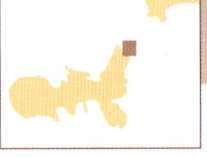

AREA D | **ISOLA D'ELBA - FROM CAPO DELLA VITA TO CAVO**

Capo della Vita ⊕ **227** 41°52'.16N 010°25'.14E
This is the most northerly of Elba's promontories. Immediately E of it and SW of Isola dei Topi lies a pleasant anchorage. Suitable in calm weather only, as it is open towards Canale di Piombino. Anchor off the pebble beach in 3-7m on sand and weed.

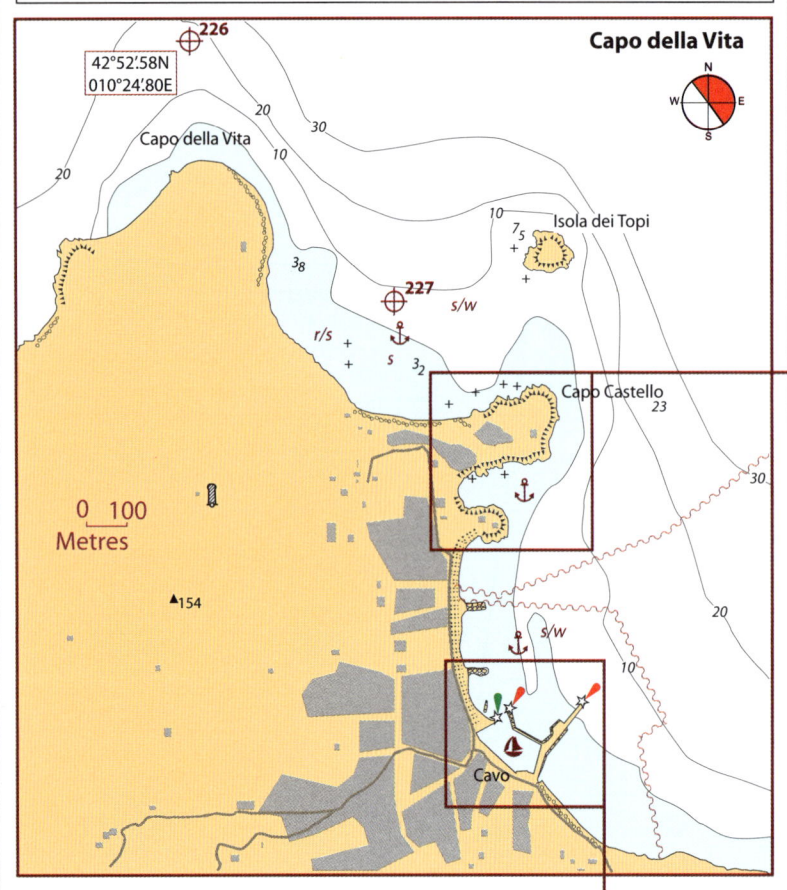

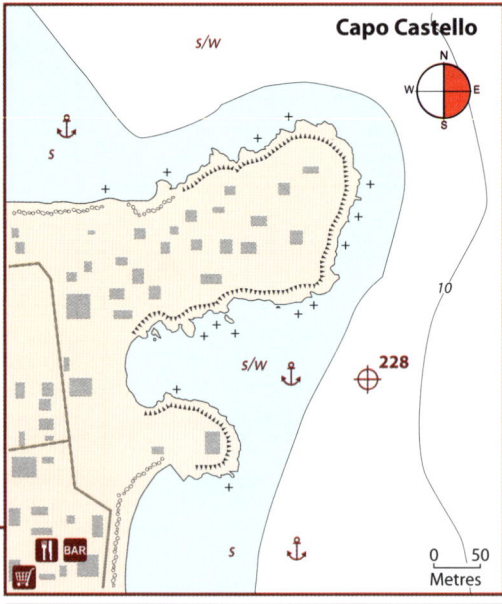

Capo Castello ⊕ **228** 41°51'.90N 010°25'.41E
A small bay with reasonable shelter from the *mistral* opens up to the S of Capo Castello. Anchorage, however, may be disturbed by an uncomfortable slop.
Anchor in 3-7m on sand and weed. Make sure the anchor has a good grip.

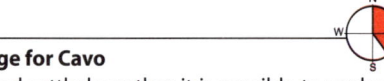

Anchorage for Cavo
In calm and settled weather, it is possible to anchor off the beach to the N of the harbour. Night anchorage may be disturbed by an uncomfortable tidal wave. Anchor in 3-5m on sand and weed.

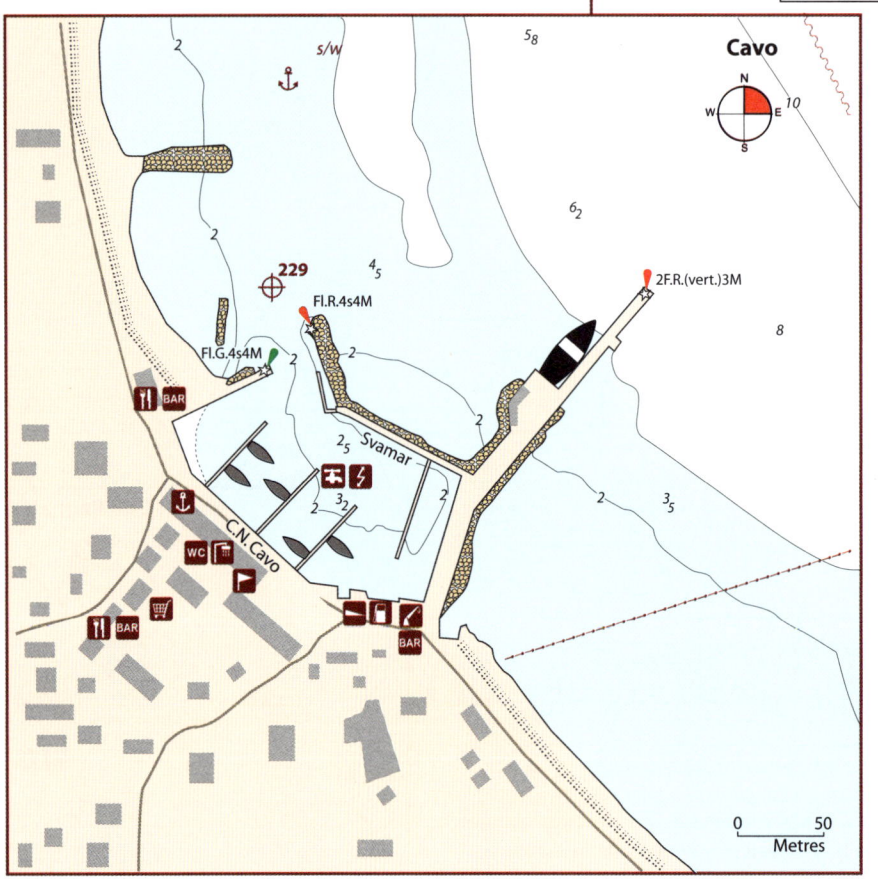

Cavo ⊕ **229** 41°51'.66N 010°25'.50E
Once round Capo della Vita, proceed down the island's E side towards the small yacht harbour of Cavo. The harbour is protected by an L-shaped breakwater, the E outer end of which is used by the ferry and hydrofoil that link it with Portoferraio. The harbour accommodates about 270 craft (max. LOA 12m) and has 40 visitors berths. The 2m-or-so depths at the entrance shallow up to 1m inside. The limited depths, plus a lack of manoeuvring room, makes the harbour suitable for small- and medium-sized craft only. In strong NE winds, mooring manoeuvres may be difficult due to the swell that affects the harbour.

Circolo Nautico Cavo - 130 berths on 3 floating pontoons with respective quays on the S-SW side.
VHF ch 09 - ☎ +39 0565 931023 / 389 8394242 info@circolonauticocavo.it
www.circolonauticocavo.it

Svamar - 130 berths (max. LOA 10m) on a N-side pontoon and a quay.
☎ +39 0565 962011 / +39 338 5097341
info@portoturisticoriocavo.it
www.portoturisticoriocavo.it

Port Authority ☎ +39 0565 949910
Ormeggiatori (harbour attendants)
☎ +39 0565 931056

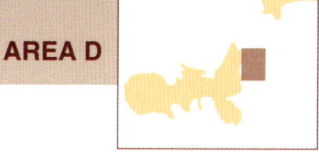

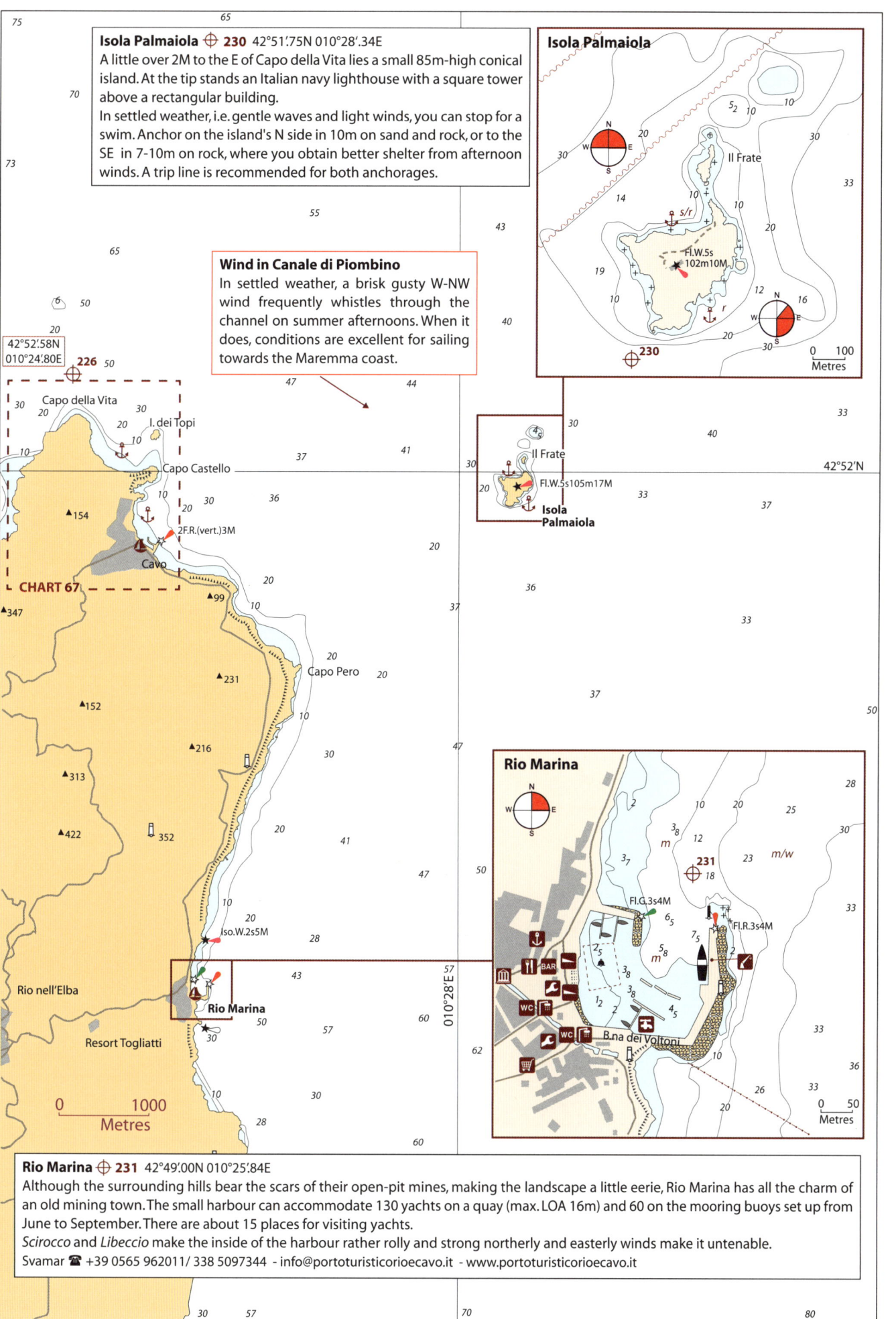

ISOLA D'ELBA - ISOLA PALMAIOLA AND RIO MARINA — AREA D

CHART 68

Isola Palmaiola ⊕ 230 42°51'.75N 010°28'.34E

A little over 2M to the E of Capo della Vita lies a small 85m-high conical island. At the tip stands an Italian navy lighthouse with a square tower above a rectangular building.

In settled weather, i.e. gentle waves and light winds, you can stop for a swim. Anchor on the island's N side in 10m on sand and rock, or to the SE in 7-10m on rock, where you obtain better shelter from afternoon winds. A trip line is recommended for both anchorages.

Wind in Canale di Piombino

In settled weather, a brisk gusty W-NW wind frequently whistles through the channel on summer afternoons. When it does, conditions are excellent for sailing towards the Maremma coast.

Rio Marina ⊕ 231 42°49'.00N 010°25'.84E

Although the surrounding hills bear the scars of their open-pit mines, making the landscape a little eerie, Rio Marina has all the charm of an old mining town. The small harbour can accommodate 130 yachts on a quay (max. LOA 16m) and 60 on the mooring buoys set up from June to September. There are about 15 places for visiting yachts.

Scirocco and *Libeccio* make the inside of the harbour rather rolly and strong northerly and easterly winds make it untenable.

Svamar ☎ +39 0565 962011/ 338 5097344 - info@portoturisticorioecavo.it - www.portoturisticorioecavo.it

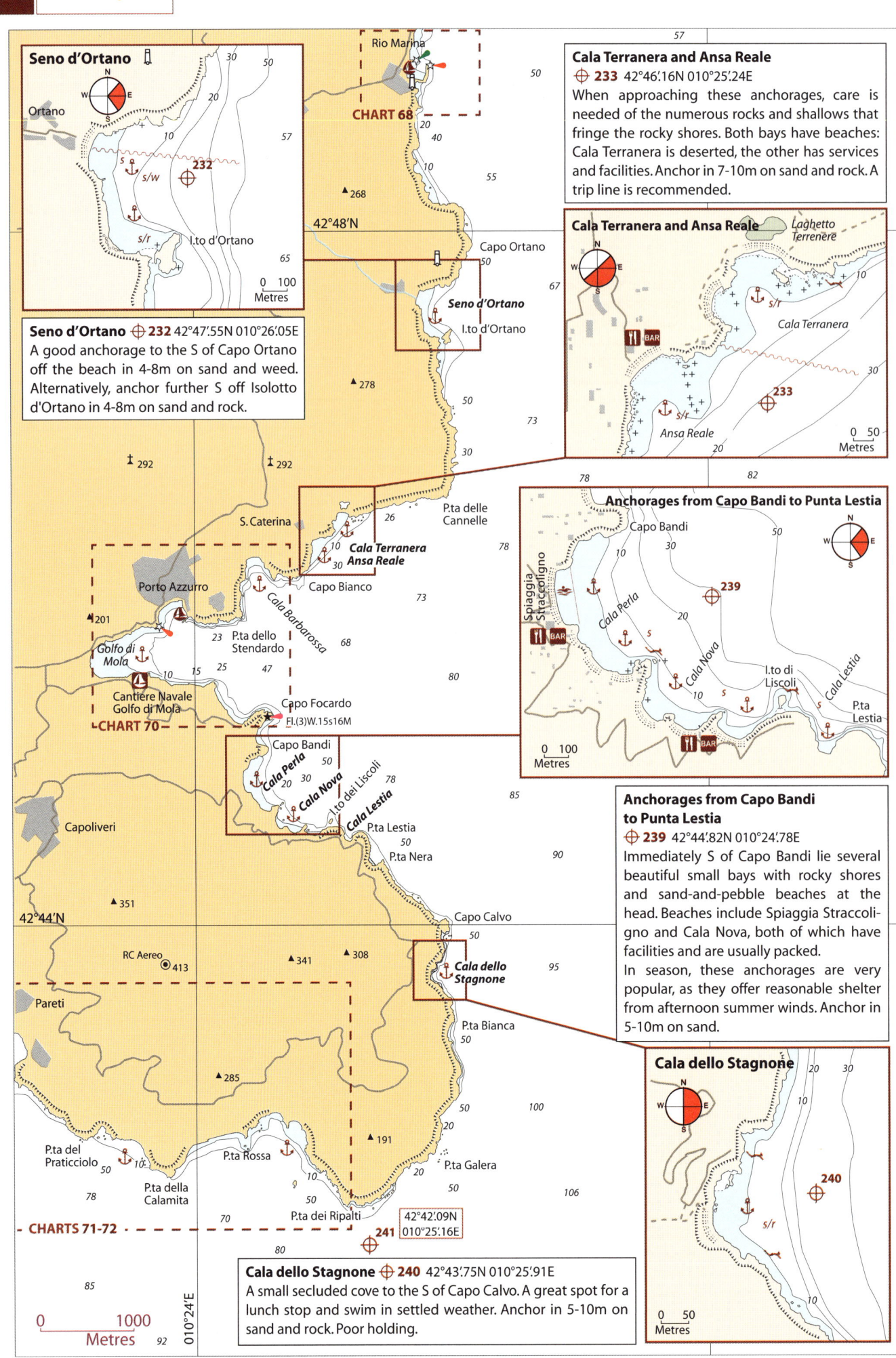

CHART 69 — AREA D — ISOLA D'ELBA - FROM CAPO ORTANO TO PUNTA DEI RIPALTI

Seno d'Ortano
⊕ **232** 42°47'.55N 010°26'.05E
A good anchorage to the S of Capo Ortano off the beach in 4-8m on sand and weed. Alternatively, anchor further S off Isolotto d'Ortano in 4-8m on sand and rock.

Cala Terranera and Ansa Reale
⊕ **233** 42°46'.16N 010°25'.24E
When approaching these anchorages, care is needed of the numerous rocks and shallows that fringe the rocky shores. Both bays have beaches: Cala Terranera is deserted, the other has services and facilities. Anchor in 7-10m on sand and rock. A trip line is recommended.

Anchorages from Capo Bandi to Punta Lestia
⊕ **239** 42°44'.82N 010°24'.78E
Immediately S of Capo Bandi lie several beautiful small bays with rocky shores and sand-and-pebble beaches at the head. Beaches include Spiaggia Straccoligno and Cala Nova, both of which have facilities and are usually packed.
In season, these anchorages are very popular, as they offer reasonable shelter from afternoon summer winds. Anchor in 5-10m on sand.

Cala dello Stagnone
⊕ **240** 42°43'.75N 010°25'.91E
A small secluded cove to the S of Capo Calvo. A great spot for a lunch stop and swim in settled weather. Anchor in 5-10m on sand and rock. Poor holding.

241 42°42'.09N 010°25'.16E

ISOLA D'ELBA - PORTO AZZURRO — AREA D

CHART 70

Porto Azzurro
⊕ **236** 42°45'.66N 010°23'.66E

Approach is straightforward. Forte Focardo, at the far southern end of the gulf, plus the citadel on the promontory that hides Porto Azzurro, are conspicuous. The small harbour has 190 berths (max. LOA 20m), with 25 for visitors. It provides good all-round protection, although the *scirocco* produces an uncomfortable slop inside. The administration of the berths along the outer mole, on Banchina IV Novembre, and on the pontoons is shared between the local municipality and private associations.

Port Authority ☎ +39 0565 95195

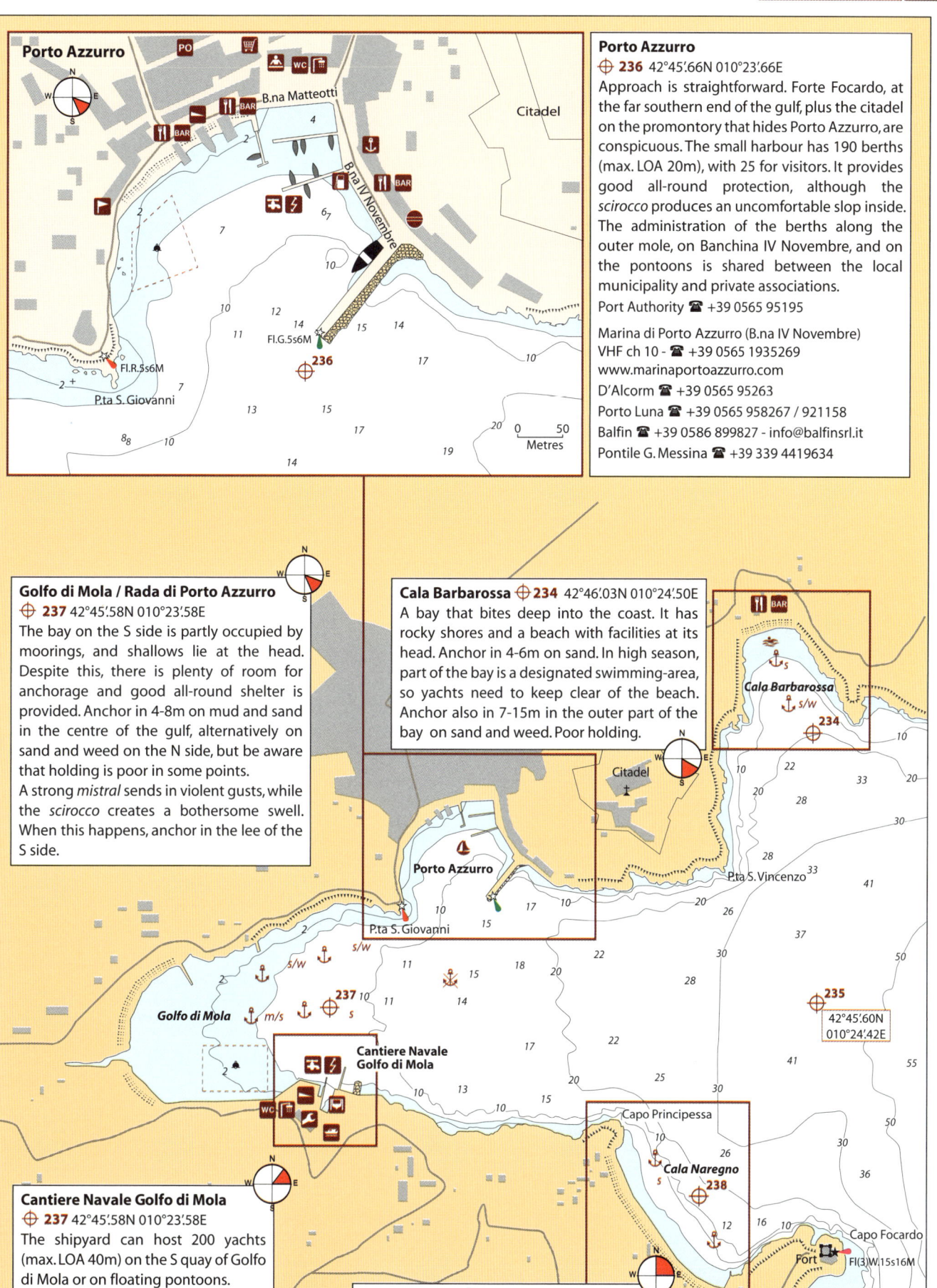

Marina di Porto Azzurro (B.na IV Novembre)
VHF ch 10 - ☎ +39 0565 1935269
www.marinaportoazzurro.com
D'Alcorm ☎ +39 0565 95263
Porto Luna ☎ +39 0565 958267 / 921158
Balfin ☎ +39 0586 899827 - info@balfinsrl.it
Pontile G. Messina ☎ +39 339 4419634

Golfo di Mola / Rada di Porto Azzurro
⊕ **237** 42°45'.58N 010°23'.58E

The bay on the S side is partly occupied by moorings, and shallows lie at the head. Despite this, there is plenty of room for anchorage and good all-round shelter is provided. Anchor in 4-8m on mud and sand in the centre of the gulf, alternatively on sand and weed on the N side, but be aware that holding is poor in some points.

A strong *mistral* sends in violent gusts, while the *scirocco* creates a bothersome swell. When this happens, anchor in the lee of the S side.

Cala Barbarossa ⊕ **234** 42°46'.03N 010°24'.50E

A bay that bites deep into the coast. It has rocky shores and a beach with facilities at its head. Anchor in 4-6m on sand. In high season, part of the bay is a designated swimming-area, so yachts need to keep clear of the beach. Anchor also in 7-15m in the outer part of the bay on sand and weed. Poor holding.

Cantiere Navale Golfo di Mola
⊕ **237** 42°45'.58N 010°23'.58E

The shipyard can host 200 yachts (max. LOA 40m) on the S quay of Golfo di Mola or on floating pontoons.
VHF ch 09 - ☎ +39 0565 968692
www.golfomola.it - info@golfomola.it

Cala Naregno ⊕ **238** 42°45'.35N 010°24'.24E

Anchor off the beach in 5-10m on sand. Although the bay is very open, Capo Focardo provides reasonable shelter from southerlies.

103

CHART 71

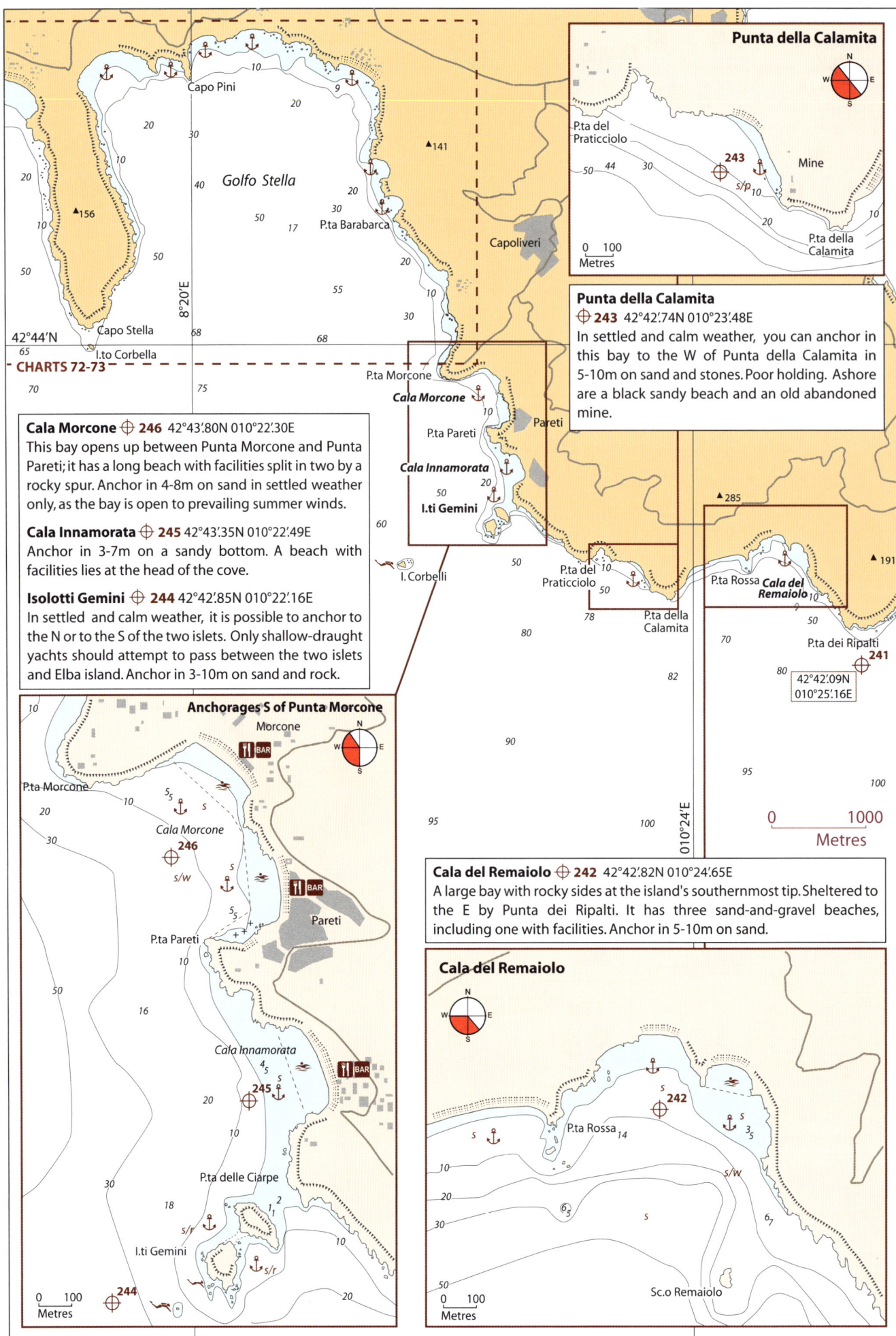

AREA D — ISOLA D'ELBA - FROM PUNTA DEI RIPALTI TO PUNTA MORCONE

Punta della Calamita
⊕ 243 42°42'.74N 010°23'.48E
In settled and calm weather, you can anchor in this bay to the W of Punta della Calamita in 5-10m on sand and stones. Poor holding. Ashore are a black sandy beach and an old abandoned mine.

Cala Morcone ⊕ 246 42°43'.80N 010°22'.30E
This bay opens up between Punta Morcone and Punta Pareti; it has a long beach with facilities split in two by a rocky spur. Anchor in 4-8m on sand in settled weather only, as the bay is open to prevailing summer winds.

Cala Innamorata ⊕ 245 42°43'.35N 010°22'.49E
Anchor in 3-7m on a sandy bottom. A beach with facilities lies at the head of the cove.

Isolotti Gemini ⊕ 244 42°42'.85N 010°22'.16E
In settled and calm weather, it is possible to anchor to the N or to the S of the two islets. Only shallow-draught yachts should attempt to pass between the two islets and Elba island. Anchor in 3-10m on sand and rock.

Cala del Remaiolo ⊕ 242 42°42'.82N 010°24'.65E
A large bay with rocky sides at the island's southernmost tip. Sheltered to the E by Punta dei Ripalti. It has three sand-and-gravel beaches, including one with facilities. Anchor in 5-10m on sand.

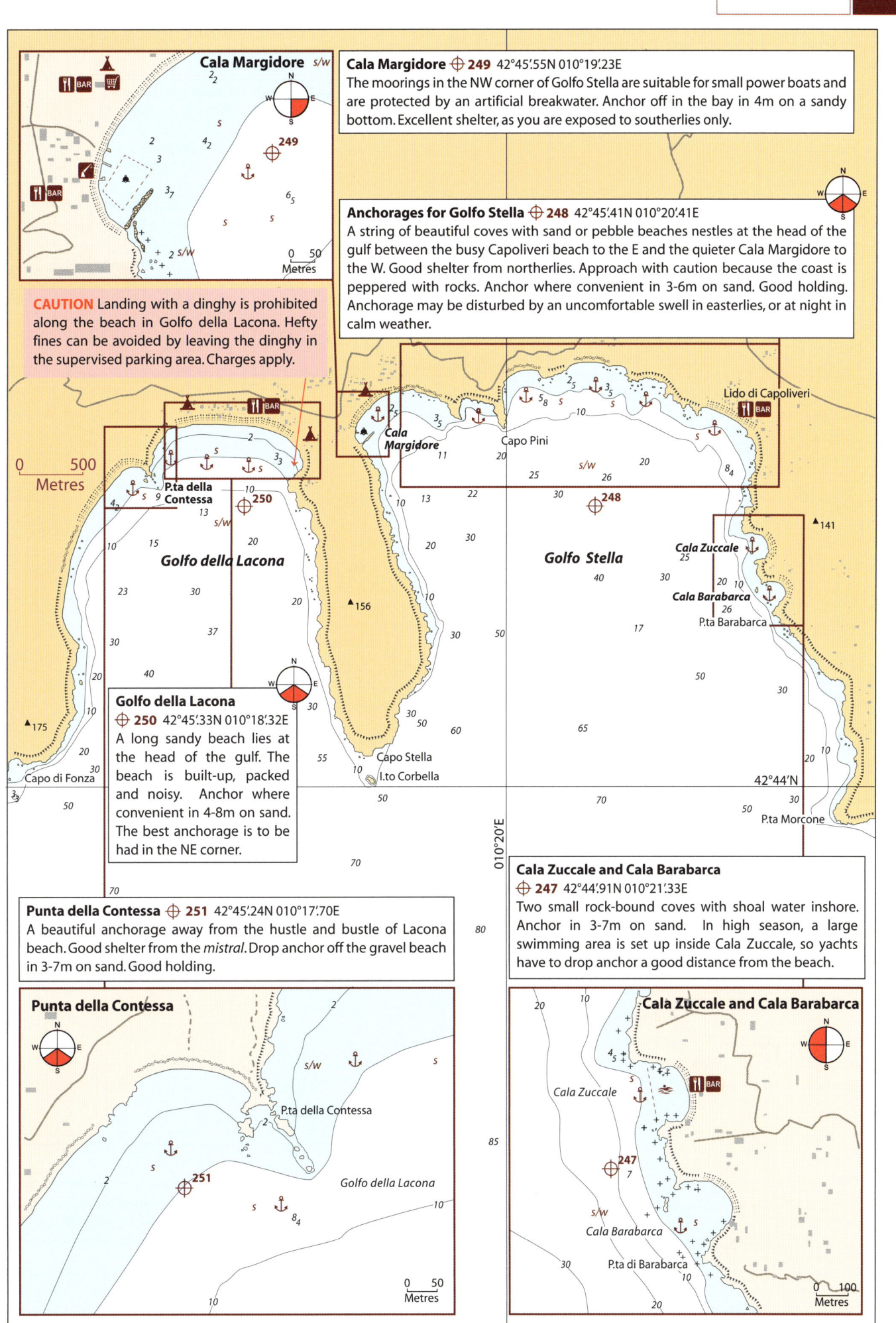

ISOLA D'ELBA - GOLFO STELLA AND GOLFO DELLA LACONA — AREA D

CHART 72

Cala Margidore ⊕ 249 42°45´.55N 010°19´.23E
The moorings in the NW corner of Golfo Stella are suitable for small power boats and are protected by an artificial breakwater. Anchor off in the bay in 4m on a sandy bottom. Excellent shelter, as you are exposed to southerlies only.

Anchorages for Golfo Stella ⊕ 248 42°45´.41N 010°20´.41E
A string of beautiful coves with sand or pebble beaches nestles at the head of the gulf between the busy Capoliveri beach to the E and the quieter Cala Margidore to the W. Good shelter from northerlies. Approach with caution because the coast is peppered with rocks. Anchor where convenient in 3-6m on sand. Good holding. Anchorage may be disturbed by an uncomfortable swell in easterlies, or at night in calm weather.

CAUTION Landing with a dinghy is prohibited along the beach in Golfo della Lacona. Hefty fines can be avoided by leaving the dinghy in the supervised parking area. Charges apply.

Golfo della Lacona
⊕ 250 42°45´.33N 010°18´.32E
A long sandy beach lies at the head of the gulf. The beach is built-up, packed and noisy. Anchor where convenient in 4-8m on sand. The best anchorage is to be had in the NE corner.

Punta della Contessa ⊕ 251 42°45´.24N 010°17´.70E
A beautiful anchorage away from the hustle and bustle of Lacona beach. Good shelter from the *mistral*. Drop anchor off the gravel beach in 3-7m on sand. Good holding.

Cala Zuccale and Cala Barabarca
⊕ 247 42°44´.91N 010°21´.33E
Two small rock-bound coves with shoal water inshore. Anchor in 3-7m on sand. In high season, a large swimming area is set up inside Cala Zuccale, so yachts have to drop anchor a good distance from the beach.

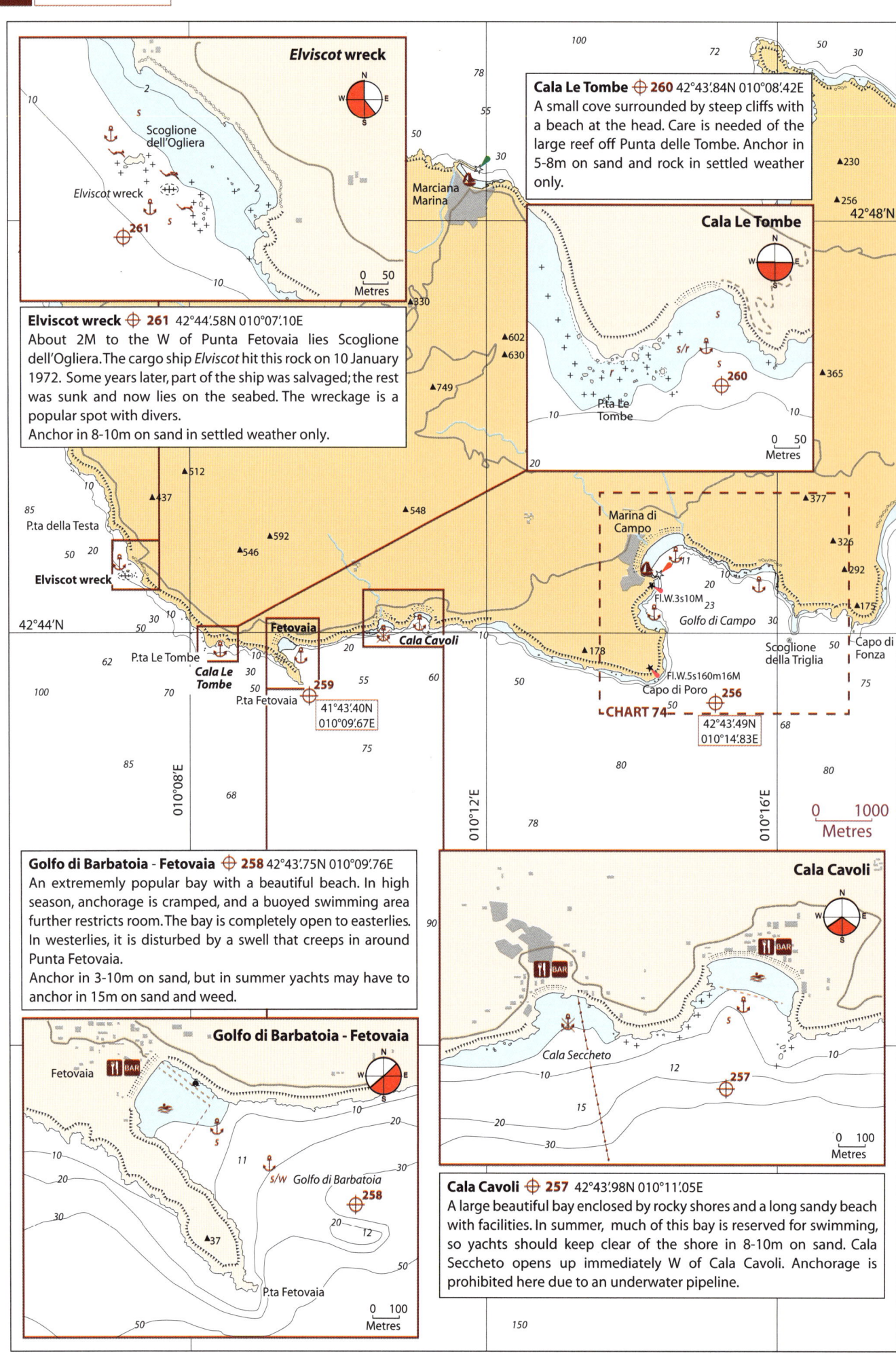

CHART 73 — AREA D — ISOLA D'ELBA - FROM CAPO DI FONZA TO PUNTA DELLA TESTA

Cala Le Tombe ⊕ **260** 42°43'.84N 010°08'.42E
A small cove surrounded by steep cliffs with a beach at the head. Care is needed of the large reef off Punta delle Tombe. Anchor in 5-8m on sand and rock in settled weather only.

Elviscot wreck ⊕ **261** 42°44'.58N 010°07'.10E
About 2M to the W of Punta Fetovaia lies Scoglione dell'Ogliera. The cargo ship *Elviscot* hit this rock on 10 January 1972. Some years later, part of the ship was salvaged; the rest was sunk and now lies on the seabed. The wreckage is a popular spot with divers.
Anchor in 8-10m on sand in settled weather only.

Golfo di Barbatoia - Fetovaia ⊕ **258** 42°43'.75N 010°09'.76E
An extrememly popular bay with a beautiful beach. In high season, anchorage is cramped, and a buoyed swimming area further restricts room. The bay is completely open to easterlies. In westerlies, it is disturbed by a swell that creeps in around Punta Fetovaia.
Anchor in 3-10m on sand, but in summer yachts may have to anchor in 15m on sand and weed.

Cala Cavoli ⊕ **257** 42°43'.98N 010°11'.05E
A large beautiful bay enclosed by rocky shores and a long sandy beach with facilities. In summer, much of this bay is reserved for swimming, so yachts should keep clear of the shore in 8-10m on sand. Cala Seccheto opens up immediately W of Cala Cavoli. Anchorage is prohibited here due to an underwater pipeline.

ISOLA D'ELBA - GOLFO DI CAMPO | AREA D

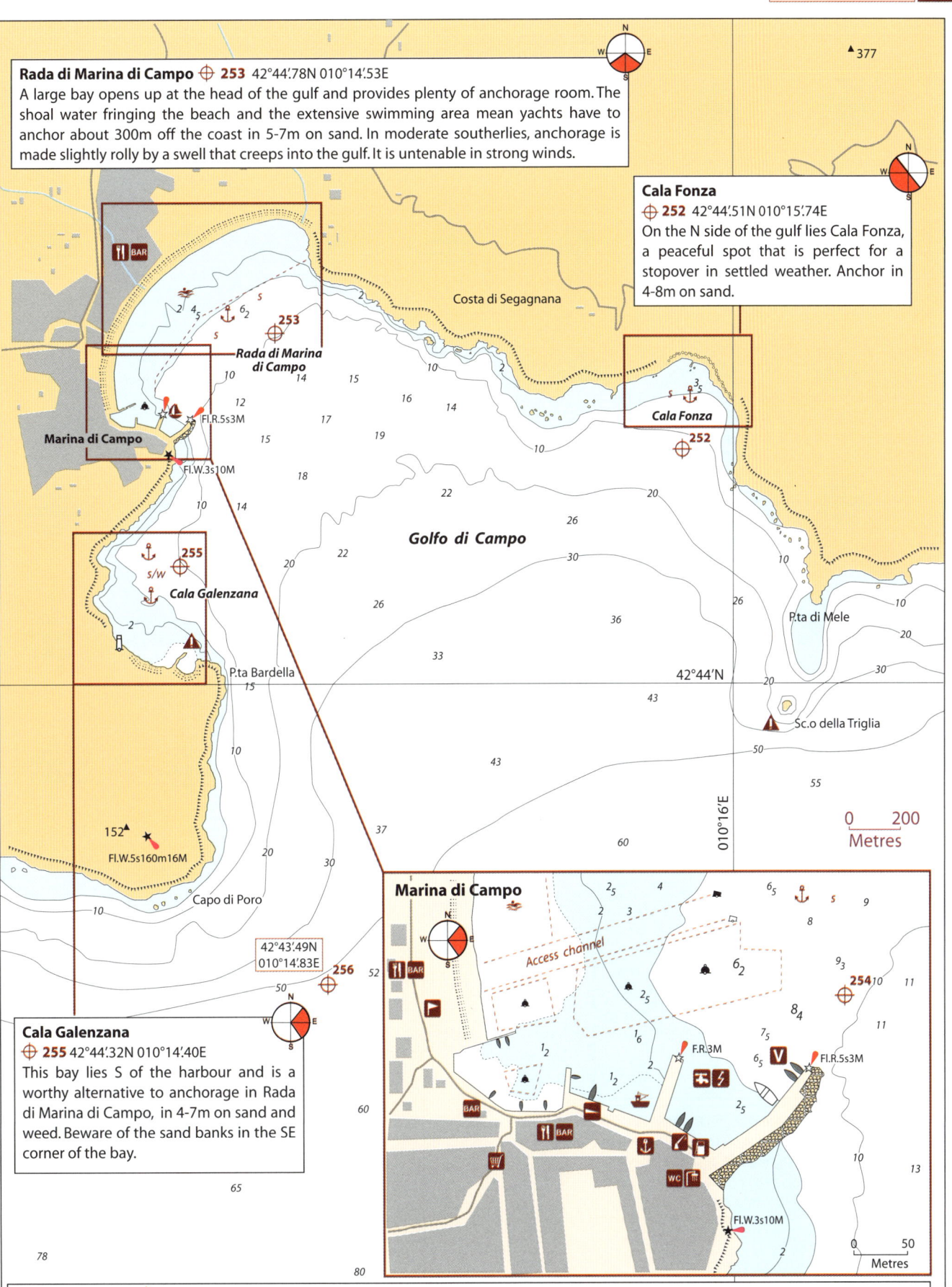

CHART 74

Rada di Marina di Campo ⊕ **253** 42°44'.78N 010°14'.53E
A large bay opens up at the head of the gulf and provides plenty of anchorage room. The shoal water fringing the beach and the extensive swimming area mean yachts have to anchor about 300m off the coast in 5-7m on sand. In moderate southerlies, anchorage is made slightly rolly by a swell that creeps into the gulf. It is untenable in strong winds.

Cala Fonza
⊕ **252** 42°44'.51N 010°15'.74E
On the N side of the gulf lies Cala Fonza, a peaceful spot that is perfect for a stopover in settled weather. Anchor in 4-8m on sand.

Cala Galenzana
⊕ **255** 42°44'.32N 010°14'.40E
This bay lies S of the harbour and is a worthy alternative to anchorage in Rada di Marina di Campo, in 4-7m on sand and weed. Beware of the sand banks in the SE corner of the bay.

Marina di Campo ⊕ **254** 42°44'.60N 010°14'.38E
A small harbour providing good all-round shelter, except from a strong *grecale* or *scirocco*, which make the harbour very rolly to the extent that it may become untenable. The last 25m of the outer breakwater are administered by the port authority and they are reserved for visiting yachts. These berths are free of charge and can be used for up to three days (VHF Ch 16 - ☎ 0565 977080). The rest of the harbour is occupied by local boats, while the three fields of moorings off the harbour are administered by private individuals.
Port Authority VHF ch 16 - ☎ +39 0565 976263 - dlmarinadicampo@mit.gov.it - Harbour attendants ☎ +39 333 8475728 - VHF ch 09.
Moorings: Cottone A. ☎ +39 340 4697569 - Pappalardo C. ☎ +39 339 6163471 - Ricci V. ☎ +39 339 4294544

107

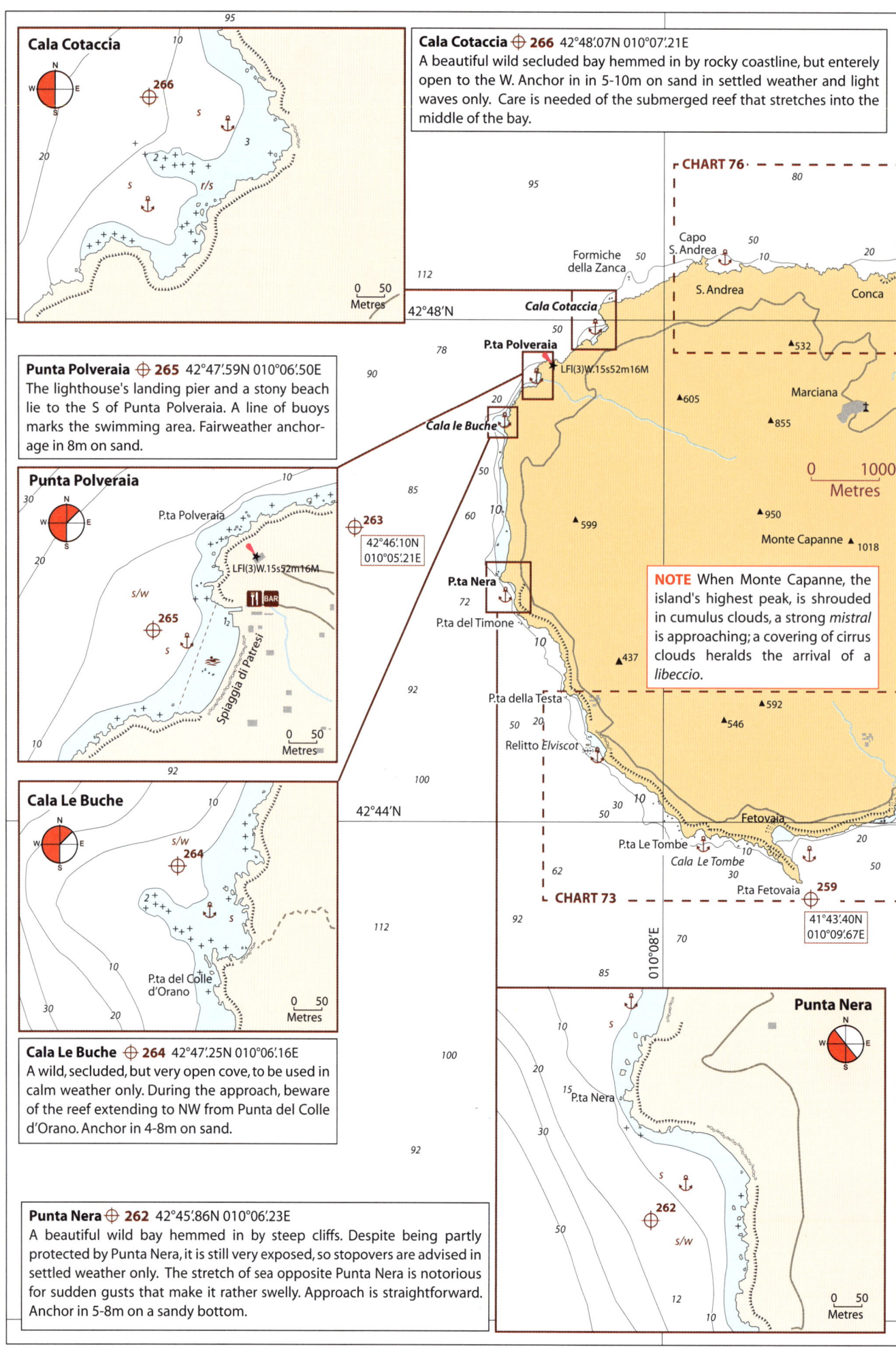

CHART 75 — AREA D — ISOLA D'ELBA - FROM PUNTA DELLA TESTA TO CAPO S. ANDREA

Cala Cotaccia ⊕ **266** 42°48'.07N 010°07'.21E
A beautiful wild secluded bay hemmed in by rocky coastline, but enterely open to the W. Anchor in in 5-10m on sand in settled weather and light waves only. Care is needed of the submerged reef that stretches into the middle of the bay.

Punta Polveraia ⊕ **265** 42°47'.59N 010°06'.50E
The lighthouse's landing pier and a stony beach lie to the S of Punta Polveraia. A line of buoys marks the swimming area. Fairweather anchorage in 8m on sand.

NOTE When Monte Capanne, the island's highest peak, is shrouded in cumulus clouds, a strong *mistral* is approaching; a covering of cirrus clouds heralds the arrival of a *libeccio*.

Cala Le Buche ⊕ **264** 42°47'.25N 010°06'.16E
A wild, secluded, but very open cove, to be used in calm weather only. During the approach, beware of the reef extending to NW from Punta del Colle d'Orano. Anchor in 4-8m on sand.

Punta Nera ⊕ **262** 42°45'.86N 010°06'.23E
A beautiful wild bay hemmed in by steep cliffs. Despite being partly protected by Punta Nera, it is still very exposed, so stopovers are advised in settled weather only. The stretch of sea opposite Punta Nera is notorious for sudden gusts that make it rather swelly. Approach is straightforward. Anchor in 5-8m on a sandy bottom.

ISOLA D'ELBA - FROM CAPO S. ANDREA TO MARCIANA MARINA — AREA D — CHART 76

Marciana Marina

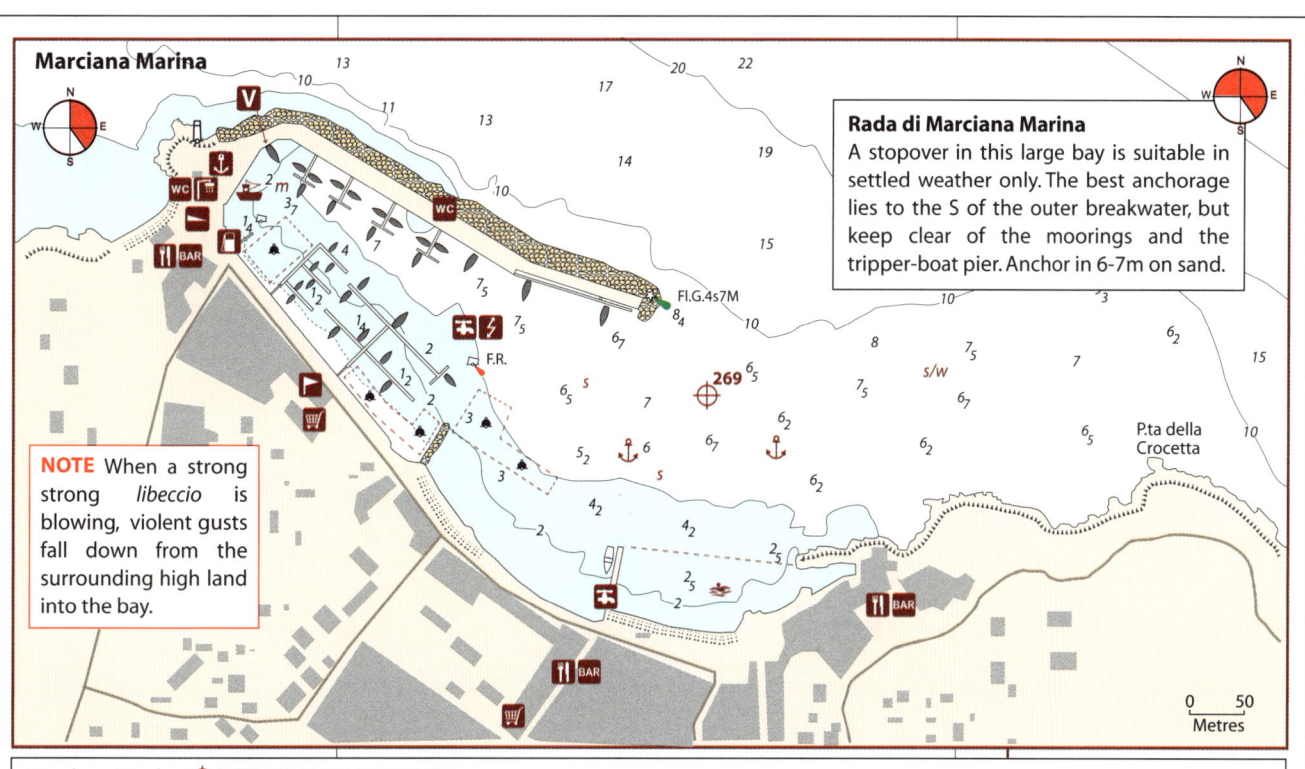

Rada di Marciana Marina
A stopover in this large bay is suitable in settled weather only. The best anchorage lies to the S of the outer breakwater, but keep clear of the moorings and the tripper-boat pier. Anchor in 6-7m on sand.

NOTE When a strong strong *libeccio* is blowing, violent gusts fall down from the surrounding high land into the bay.

Marciana Marina ⊕ 269 42°48'.47N 010°11'.95E
A beautiful harbour protected by a long outer breakwater and overlooked by a pretty town. The approach is straightforward. In moderate N-NE winds, a surge makes berths uncomfortable, while in N-SE gales, the harbour becomes untenable.
The harbour has a capacity of 500 berths (max. LOA 35m) divided between the quay and the pontoons. The berths are administered by Circolo della Vela and by Società Porto di Marciana Marina. In high season, there are three fields of moorings with an extra 45 places (max. LOA 12m).
Porto di Marciana Marina (Gruppo Golfo di Mola - hosts up to 115 yachts (max. LOA 30m) - VHF ch 09 - ☎ +39 340 7960008 info@portodimarcianamarina.it - www.portodimarcianamarina.it
Circolo della Vela with 280 berths (max. LOA 30m) - VHF ch 09 - ☎ +39 0565 99027 - segreteria@cvmm.it - www.cvmm.it
Moorings: Elba Yacht Assistance ☎ +39 338 7433696 / +39 329 4171385 - Giuntini Marcello ☎ +39 335 5326015 / 349 7830222
Harbourmaster VHF ch16 - ☎ +39 0565 99169 - marcianamarina@guardiacostiera.it

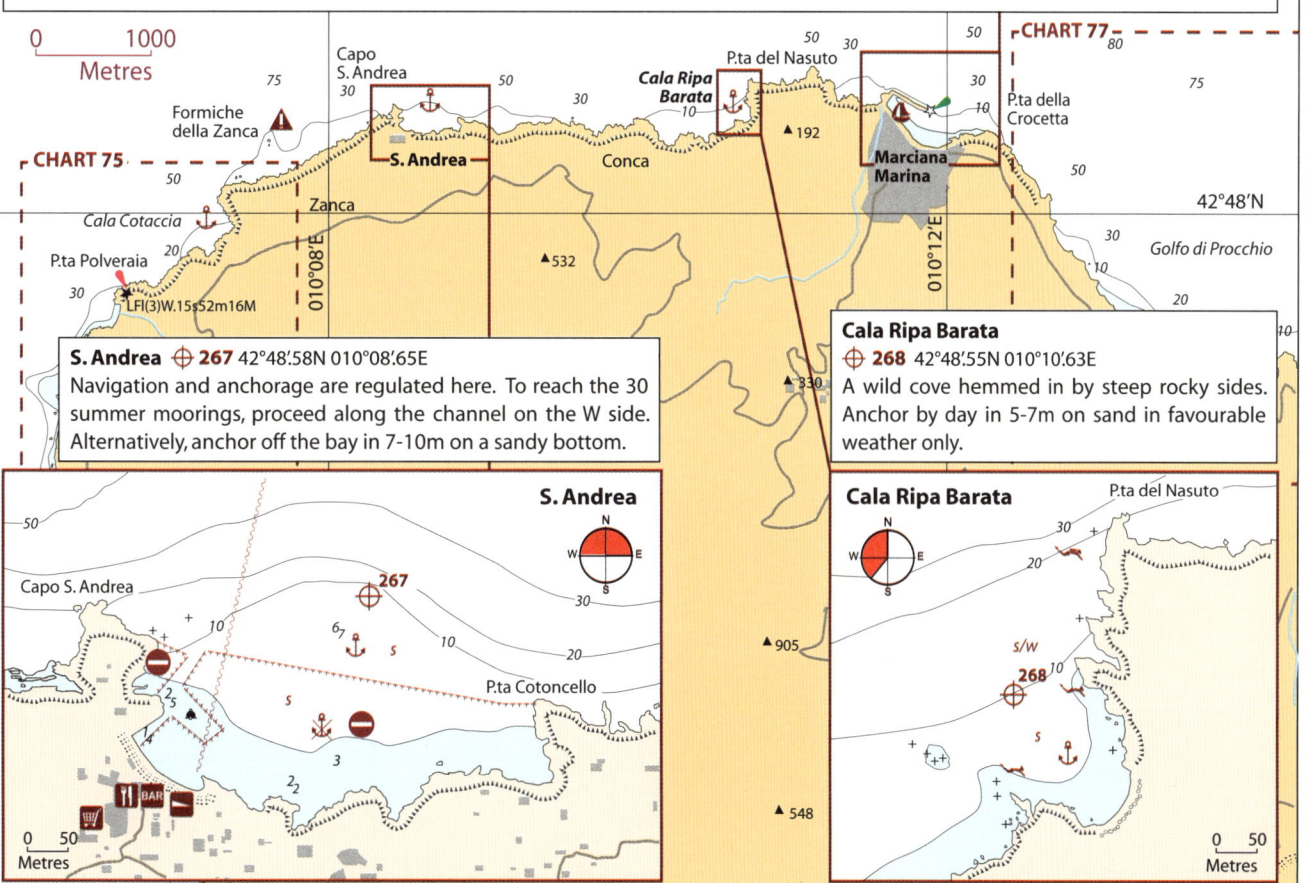

S. Andrea ⊕ 267 42°48'.58N 010°08'.65E
Navigation and anchorage are regulated here. To reach the 30 summer moorings, proceed along the channel on the W side. Alternatively, anchor off the bay in 7-10m on a sandy bottom.

Cala Ripa Barata
⊕ 268 42°48'.55N 010°10'.63E
A wild cove hemmed in by steep rocky sides. Anchor by day in 5-7m on sand in favourable weather only.

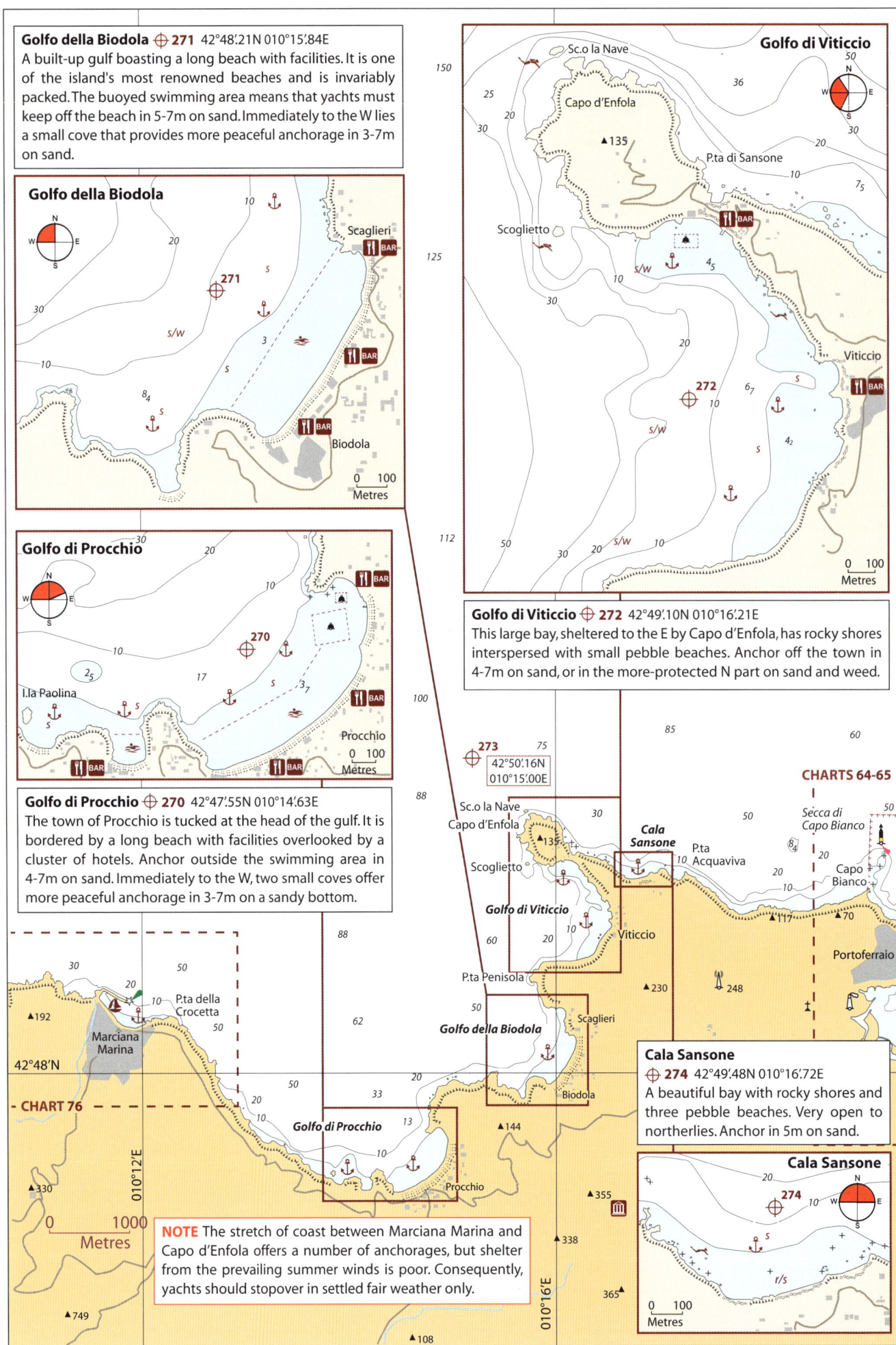

CHART 77 — AREA D — ISOLA D'ELBA - FROM GOLFO DI PROCCHIO TO CAPO BIANCO

Golfo della Biodola ⊕ **271** 42°48'.21N 010°15'.84E
A built-up gulf boasting a long beach with facilities. It is one of the island's most renowned beaches and is invariably packed. The buoyed swimming area means that yachts must keep off the beach in 5-7m on sand. Immediately to the W lies a small cove that provides more peaceful anchorage in 3-7m on sand.

Golfo di Viticcio ⊕ **272** 42°49'.10N 010°16'.21E
This large bay, sheltered to the E by Capo d'Enfola, has rocky shores interspersed with small pebble beaches. Anchor off the town in 4-7m on sand, or in the more-protected N part on sand and weed.

Golfo di Procchio ⊕ **270** 42°47'.55N 010°14'.63E
The town of Procchio is tucked at the head of the gulf. It is bordered by a long beach with facilities overlooked by a cluster of hotels. Anchor outside the swimming area in 4-7m on sand. Immediately to the W, two small coves offer more peaceful anchorage in 3-7m on a sandy bottom.

Cala Sansone
⊕ **274** 42°49'.48N 010°16'.72E
A beautiful bay with rocky shores and three pebble beaches. Very open to northerlies. Anchor in 5m on sand.

NOTE The stretch of coast between Marciana Marina and Capo d'Enfola offers a number of anchorages, but shelter from the prevailing summer winds is poor. Consequently, yachts should stopover in settled fair weather only.

ISOLA DEL GIGLIO NW COAST — AREA D — CHART 78

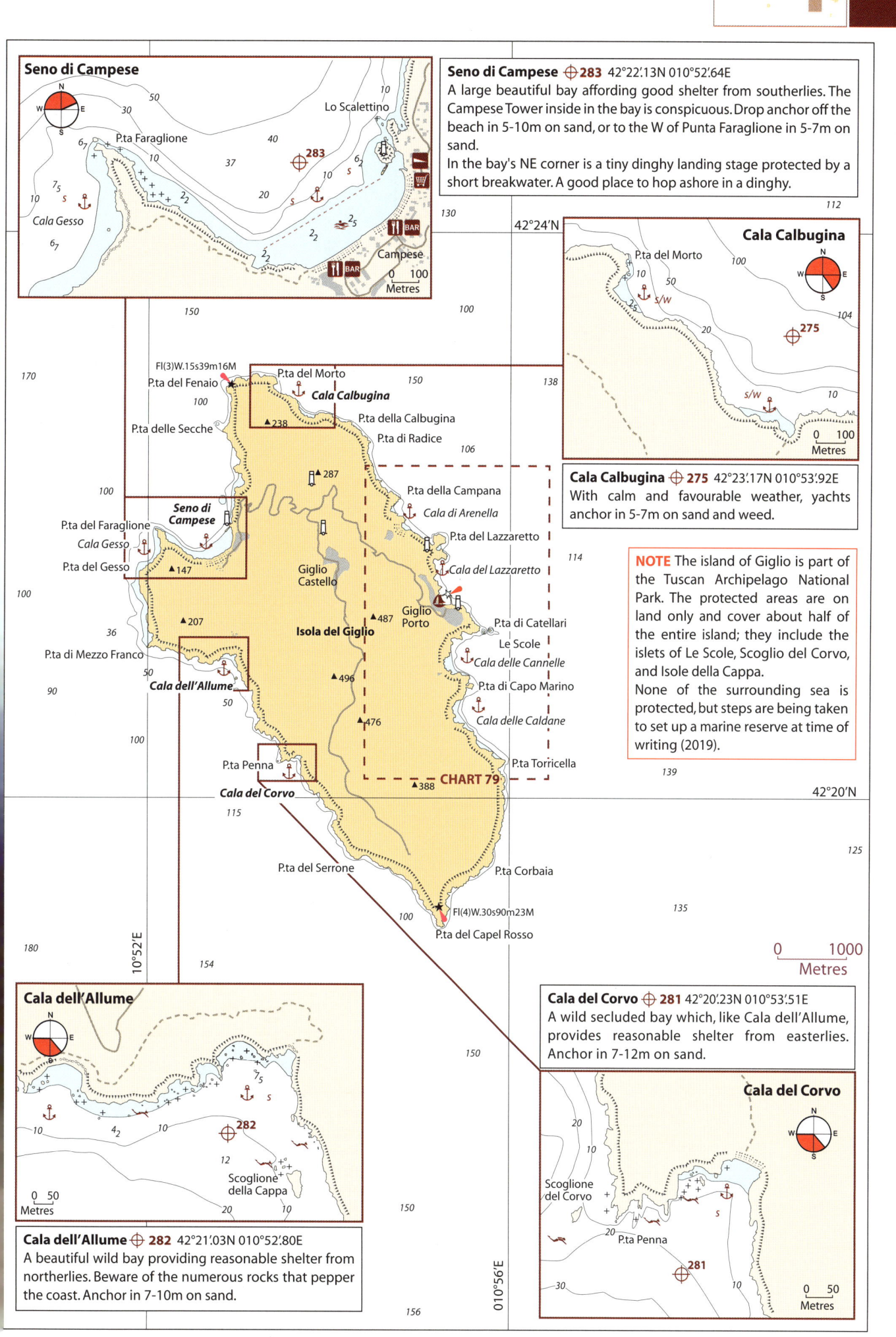

Seno di Campese

Seno di Campese ⊕ **283** 42°22′.13N 010°52′.64E
A large beautiful bay affording good shelter from southerlies. The Campese Tower inside in the bay is conspicuous. Drop anchor off the beach in 5-10m on sand, or to the W of Punta Faraglione in 5-7m on sand.
In the bay's NE corner is a tiny dinghy landing stage protected by a short breakwater. A good place to hop ashore in a dinghy.

Cala Calbugina

Cala Calbugina ⊕ **275** 42°23′.17N 010°53′.92E
With calm and favourable weather, yachts anchor in 5-7m on sand and weed.

NOTE The island of Giglio is part of the Tuscan Archipelago National Park. The protected areas are on land only and cover about half of the entire island; they include the islets of Le Scole, Scoglio del Corvo, and Isole della Cappa.
None of the surrounding sea is protected, but steps are being taken to set up a marine reserve at time of writing (2019).

Cala dell'Allume

Cala dell'Allume ⊕ **282** 42°21′.03N 010°52′.80E
A beautiful wild bay providing reasonable shelter from northerlies. Beware of the numerous rocks that pepper the coast. Anchor in 7-10m on sand.

Cala del Corvo

Cala del Corvo ⊕ **281** 42°20′.23N 010°53′.51E
A wild secluded bay which, like Cala dell'Allume, provides reasonable shelter from easterlies. Anchor in 7-12m on sand.

111

AREA D — ISOLA DEL GIGLIO - EAST COAST

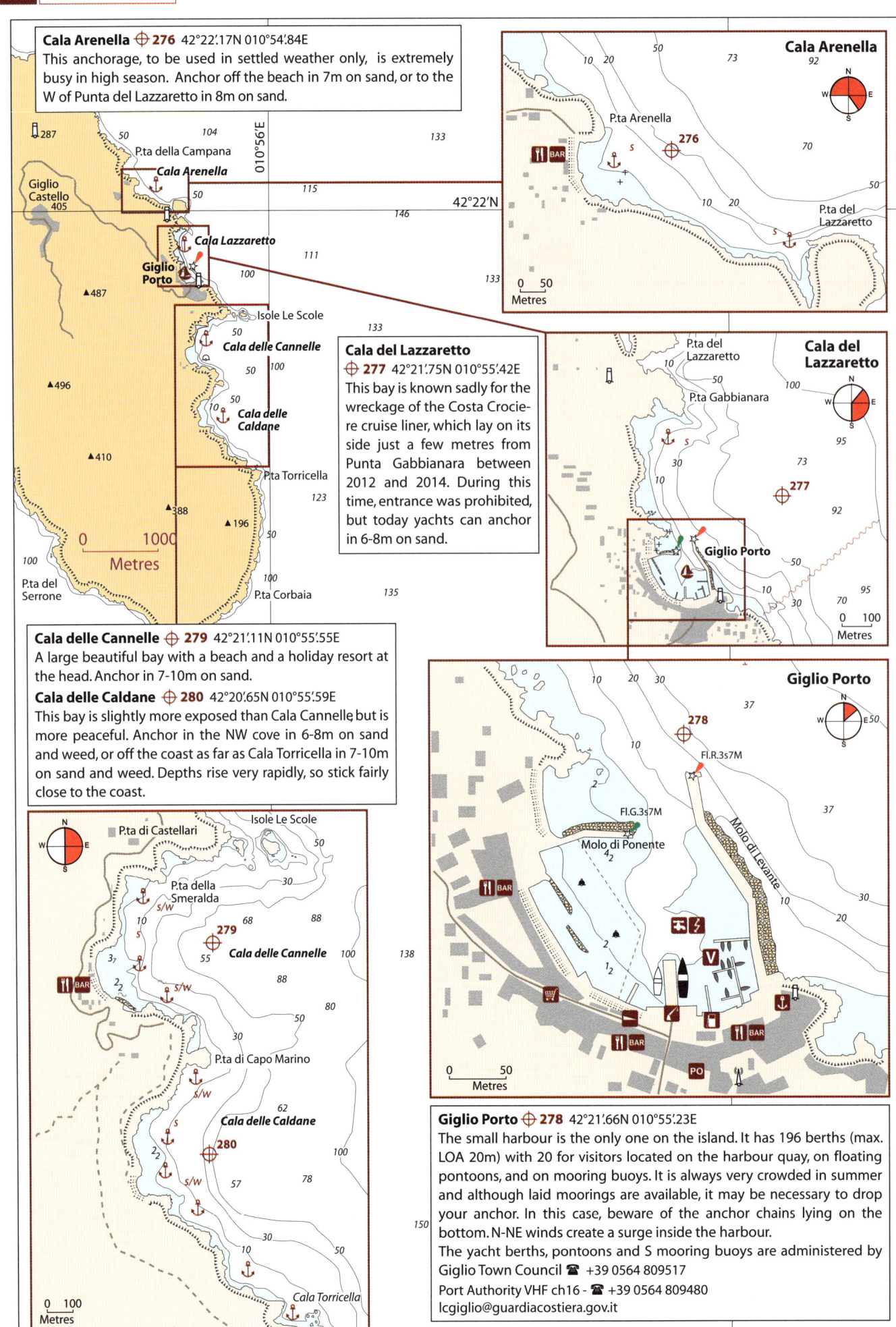

CHART 79

Cala Arenella ⊕ **276** 42°22'.17N 010°54'.84E
This anchorage, to be used in settled weather only, is extremely busy in high season. Anchor off the beach in 7m on sand, or to the W of Punta del Lazzaretto in 8m on sand.

Cala del Lazzaretto ⊕ **277** 42°21'.75N 010°55'.42E
This bay is known sadly for the wreckage of the Costa Crociere cruise liner, which lay on its side just a few metres from Punta Gabbianara between 2012 and 2014. During this time, entrance was prohibited, but today yachts can anchor in 6-8m on sand.

Cala delle Cannelle ⊕ **279** 42°21'.11N 010°55'.55E
A large beautiful bay with a beach and a holiday resort at the head. Anchor in 7-10m on sand.

Cala delle Caldane ⊕ **280** 42°20'.65N 010°55'.59E
This bay is slightly more exposed than Cala Cannelle, but is more peaceful. Anchor in the NW cove in 6-8m on sand and weed, or off the coast as far as Cala Torricella in 7-10m on sand and weed. Depths rise very rapidly, so stick fairly close to the coast.

Giglio Porto ⊕ **278** 42°21'.66N 010°55'.23E
The small harbour is the only one on the island. It has 196 berths (max. LOA 20m) with 20 for visitors located on the harbour quay, on floating pontoons, and on mooring buoys. It is always very crowded in summer and although laid moorings are available, it may be necessary to drop your anchor. In this case, beware of the anchor chains lying on the bottom. N-NE winds create a surge inside the harbour.
The yacht berths, pontoons and S mooring buoys are administered by Giglio Town Council ☎ +39 0564 809517
Port Authority VHF ch16 - ☎ +39 0564 809480
lcgiglio@guardiacostiera.gov.it

ISOLA GIANNUTRI | AREA D | CHART 80

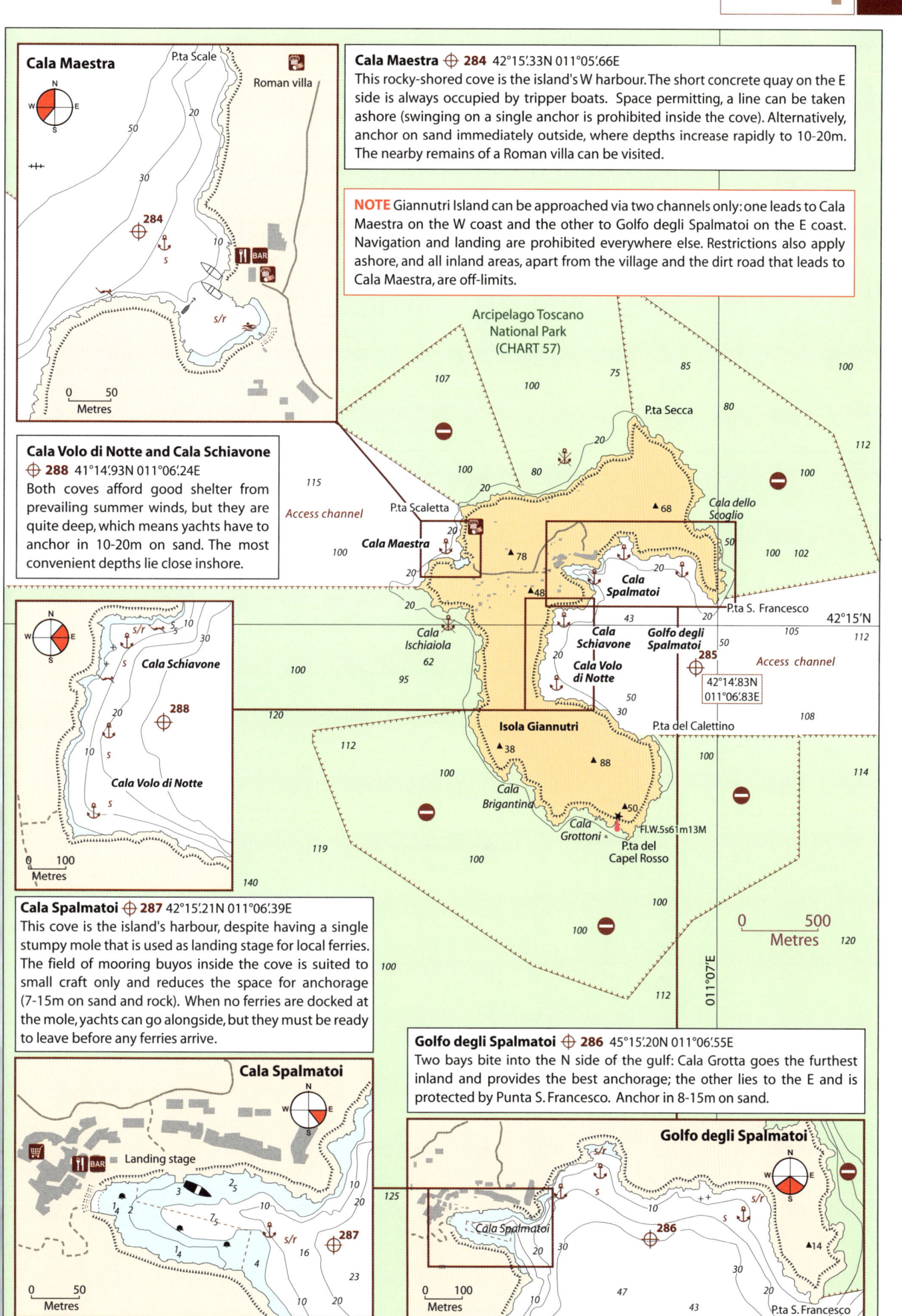

Cala Maestra

Cala Maestra ⊕ **284** 42°15'.33N 011°05'.66E
This rocky-shored cove is the island's W harbour. The short concrete quay on the E side is always occupied by tripper boats. Space permitting, a line can be taken ashore (swinging on a single anchor is prohibited inside the cove). Alternatively, anchor on sand immediately outside, where depths increase rapidly to 10-20m. The nearby remains of a Roman villa can be visited.

> **NOTE** Giannutri Island can be approached via two channels only: one leads to Cala Maestra on the W coast and the other to Golfo degli Spalmatoi on the E coast. Navigation and landing are prohibited everywhere else. Restrictions also apply ashore, and all inland areas, apart from the village and the dirt road that leads to Cala Maestra, are off-limits.

Cala Volo di Notte and Cala Schiavone
⊕ **288** 41°14'.93N 011°06'.24E
Both coves afford good shelter from prevailing summer winds, but they are quite deep, which means yachts have to anchor in 10-20m on sand. The most convenient depths lie close inshore.

Cala Spalmatoi ⊕ **287** 42°15'.21N 011°06'.39E
This cove is the island's harbour, despite having a single stumpy mole that is used as landing stage for local ferries. The field of mooring buoys inside the cove is suited to small craft only and reduces the space for anchorage (7-15m on sand and rock). When no ferries are docked at the mole, yachts can go alongside, but they must be ready to leave before any ferries arrive.

Golfo degli Spalmatoi ⊕ **286** 45°15'.20N 011°06'.55E
Two bays bite into the N side of the gulf: Cala Grotta goes the furthest inland and provides the best anchorage; the other lies to the E and is protected by Punta S. Francesco. Anchor in 8-15m on sand.

113

CHART 81 | AREA D | ISOLA DI MONTECRISTO

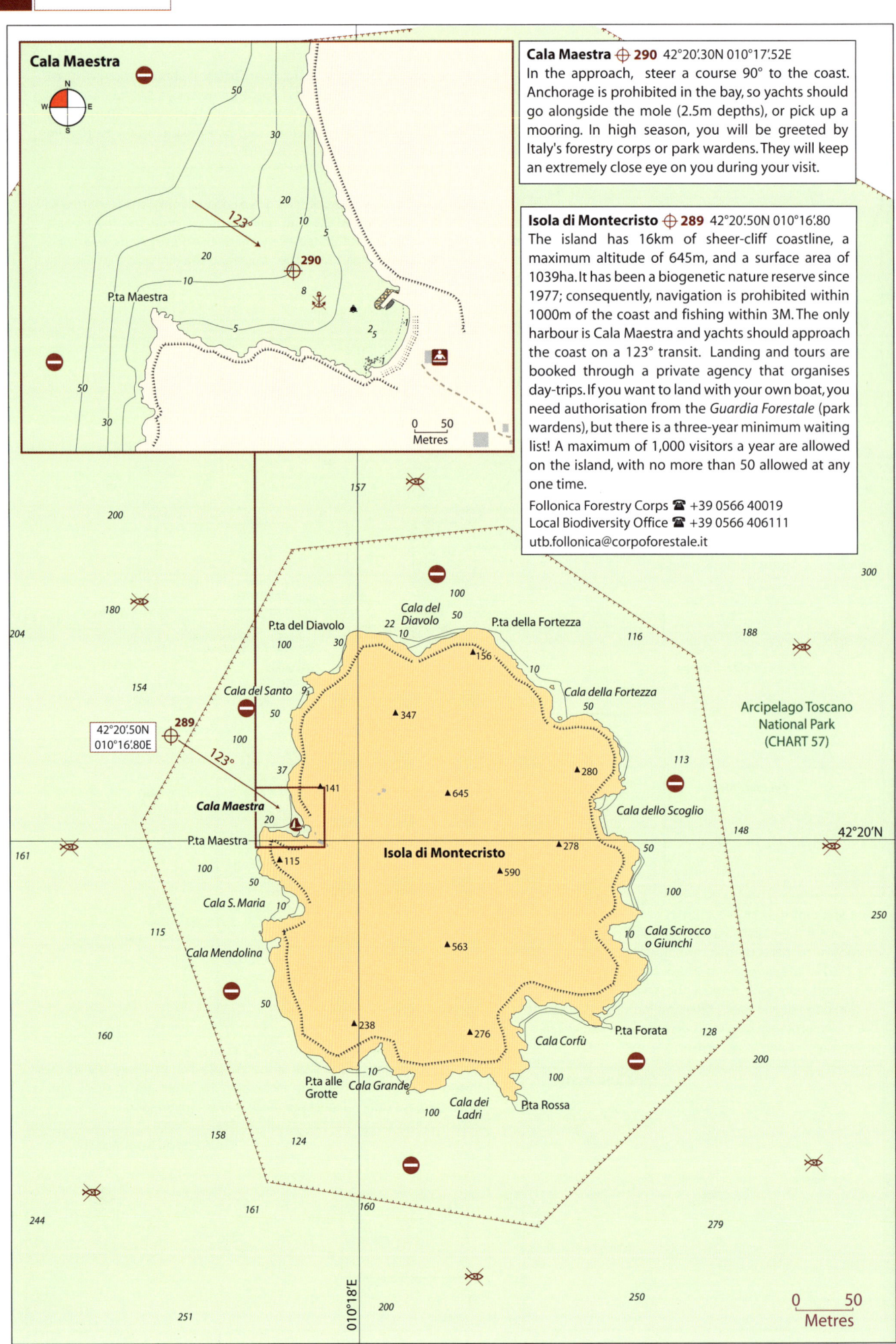

Cala Maestra ⊕ **290** 42°20′.30N 010°17′.52E
In the approach, steer a course 90° to the coast. Anchorage is prohibited in the bay, so yachts should go alongside the mole (2.5m depths), or pick up a mooring. In high season, you will be greeted by Italy's forestry corps or park wardens. They will keep an extremely close eye on you during your visit.

Isola di Montecristo ⊕ **289** 42°20′.50N 010°16′.80
The island has 16km of sheer-cliff coastline, a maximum altitude of 645m, and a surface area of 1039ha. It has been a biogenetic nature reserve since 1977; consequently, navigation is prohibited within 1000m of the coast and fishing within 3M. The only harbour is Cala Maestra and yachts should approach the coast on a 123° transit. Landing and tours are booked through a private agency that organises day-trips. If you want to land with your own boat, you need authorisation from the *Guardia Forestale* (park wardens), but there is a three-year minimum waiting list! A maximum of 1,000 visitors a year are allowed on the island, with no more than 50 allowed at any one time.

Follonica Forestry Corps ☎ +39 0566 40019
Local Biodiversity Office ☎ +39 0566 406111
utb.follonica@corpoforestale.it

ISOLA PIANOSA | AREA D | CHART 82

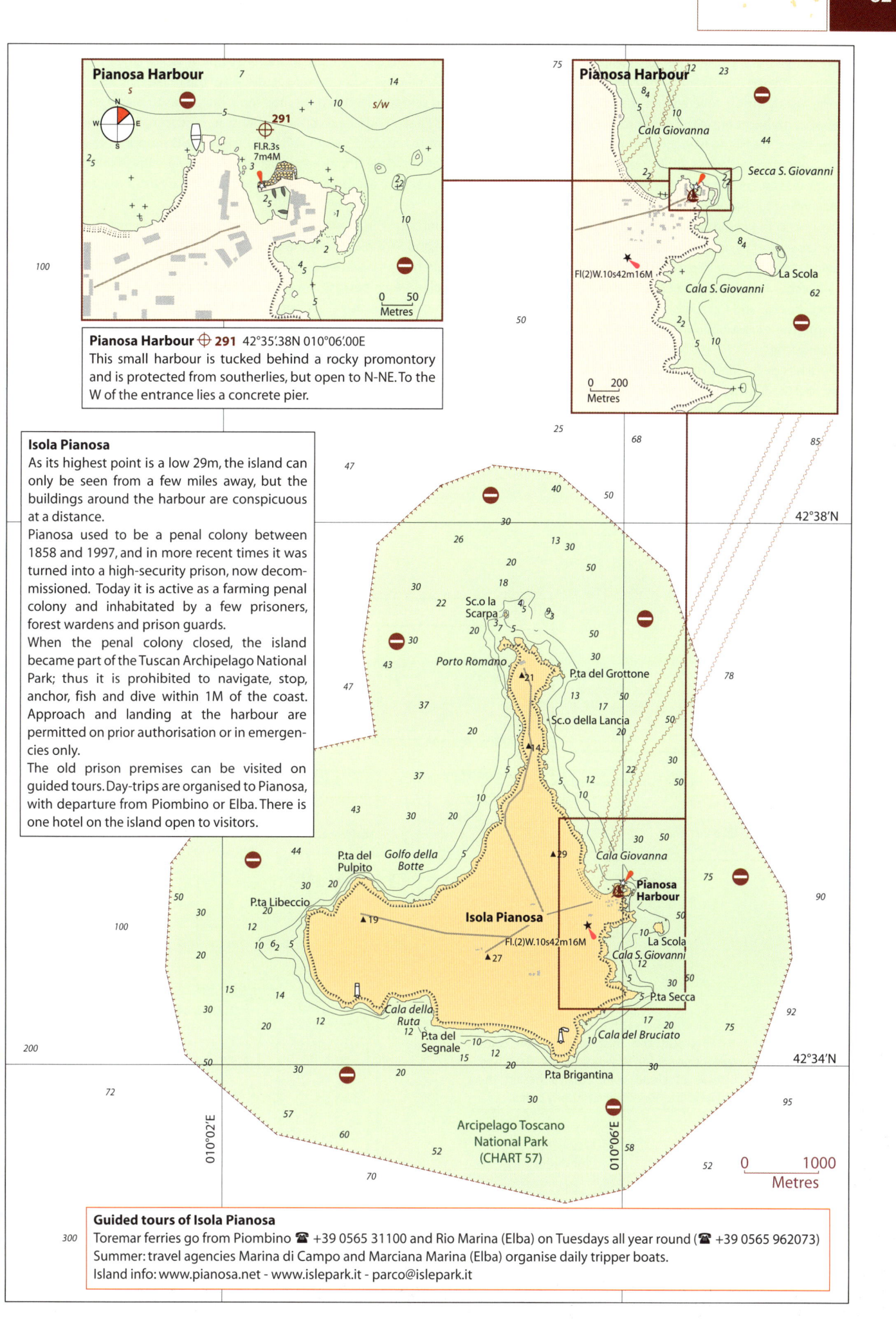

Pianosa Harbour

Pianosa Harbour ⊕ 291 42°35'.38N 010°06'.00E
This small harbour is tucked behind a rocky promontory and is protected from southerlies, but open to N-NE. To the W of the entrance lies a concrete pier.

Isola Pianosa

As its highest point is a low 29m, the island can only be seen from a few miles away, but the buildings around the harbour are conspicuous at a distance.

Pianosa used to be a penal colony between 1858 and 1997, and in more recent times it was turned into a high-security prison, now decommissioned. Today it is active as a farming penal colony and inhabitated by a few prisoners, forest wardens and prison guards.

When the penal colony closed, the island became part of the Tuscan Archipelago National Park; thus it is prohibited to navigate, stop, anchor, fish and dive within 1M of the coast. Approach and landing at the harbour are permitted on prior authorisation or in emergencies only.

The old prison premises can be visited on guided tours. Day-trips are organised to Pianosa, with departure from Piombino or Elba. There is one hotel on the island open to visitors.

Guided tours of Isola Pianosa

Toremar ferries go from Piombino ☎ +39 0565 31100 and Rio Marina (Elba) on Tuesdays all year round (☎ +39 0565 962073)
Summer: travel agencies Marina di Campo and Marciana Marina (Elba) organise daily tripper boats.
Island info: www.pianosa.net - www.islepark.it - parco@islepark.it

115

AREA E - NORTH SARDINIA AND LA MADDALENA ARCHIPELAGO

North Sardinia and La Maddalena Archipelago

NE Sardinia is a cruiser's paradise with its jagged coasts, granite rocks, breathtaking panoramas, tropical sandy coves, crystal-clear waters, myriad islands and islets, capricious regular breezes, plus numerous harbours and havens. All of this makes the Emerald Coast one of Italy's most coveted tourist and sailing destinations. Having said that, its much-merited fame has prices to match, so be aware that its harbours are in the top bracket for charges. Fortunately, its coasts and islands offer countless havens, including some far from the island's bustling luxury hotels and jet-set guests. Almost all of the harbours have visitors berths on laid moorings tailed to the quay or mooring buoys (unless otherwise shown in the plan). Water and electricity are also available. They are invariably packed in high season, and it is essential that you contact the facilities beforehand for availability and charges, which vary from year to year and according to season.

You need to keep a close eye on the weather in Bouches de Bonifacio. The prevailing winter winds are easterly and the summer winds westerly. They are funnelled into the strait between Corsica and Sardinia, where the Venturi effect increases their ferocity. The winds have a major impact on both sea and weather, and consequently on navigation. Navigation is hard work in this stretch of sea on account of the jagged coastline and the islands of La Maddalena Archipelago. Life is further complicated by Corsica's Lavezzi Archipelago and Cavallo island, plus a multitude of shoals and rocks just awash. Last but by no means least, care is needed of the cargo ships crossing from the Sea of Sardinia to the Tyrrhenian Sea (and back again) via the international waters of La Grande Passe de Bouches.

Bouches de Bonifacio are split into two distinct marine and land reserves: La Maddalena Archipelago National Park in Italian territory, and the Bouches de Bonifacio marine reserve, which belongs to France. In 2012, Italy and France signed an agreement that set up a European Grouping of Territorial Cooperation (EGTC), which led to the Bouches de Bonifacio International Marine Reserve. The aim was to introduce joint management of the two reserves.

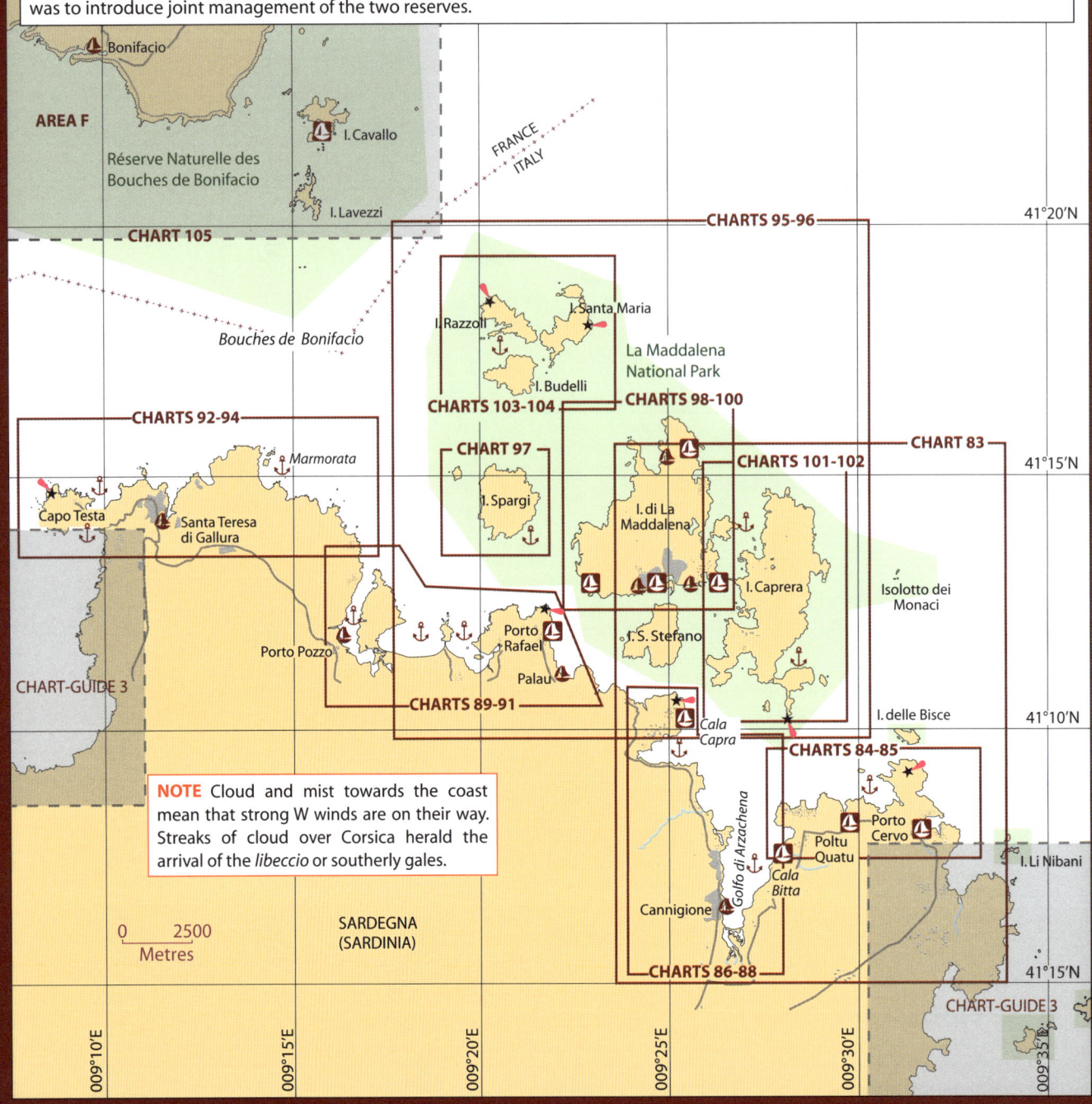

NOTE Cloud and mist towards the coast mean that strong W winds are on their way. Streaks of cloud over Corsica herald the arrival of the *libeccio* or southerly gales.

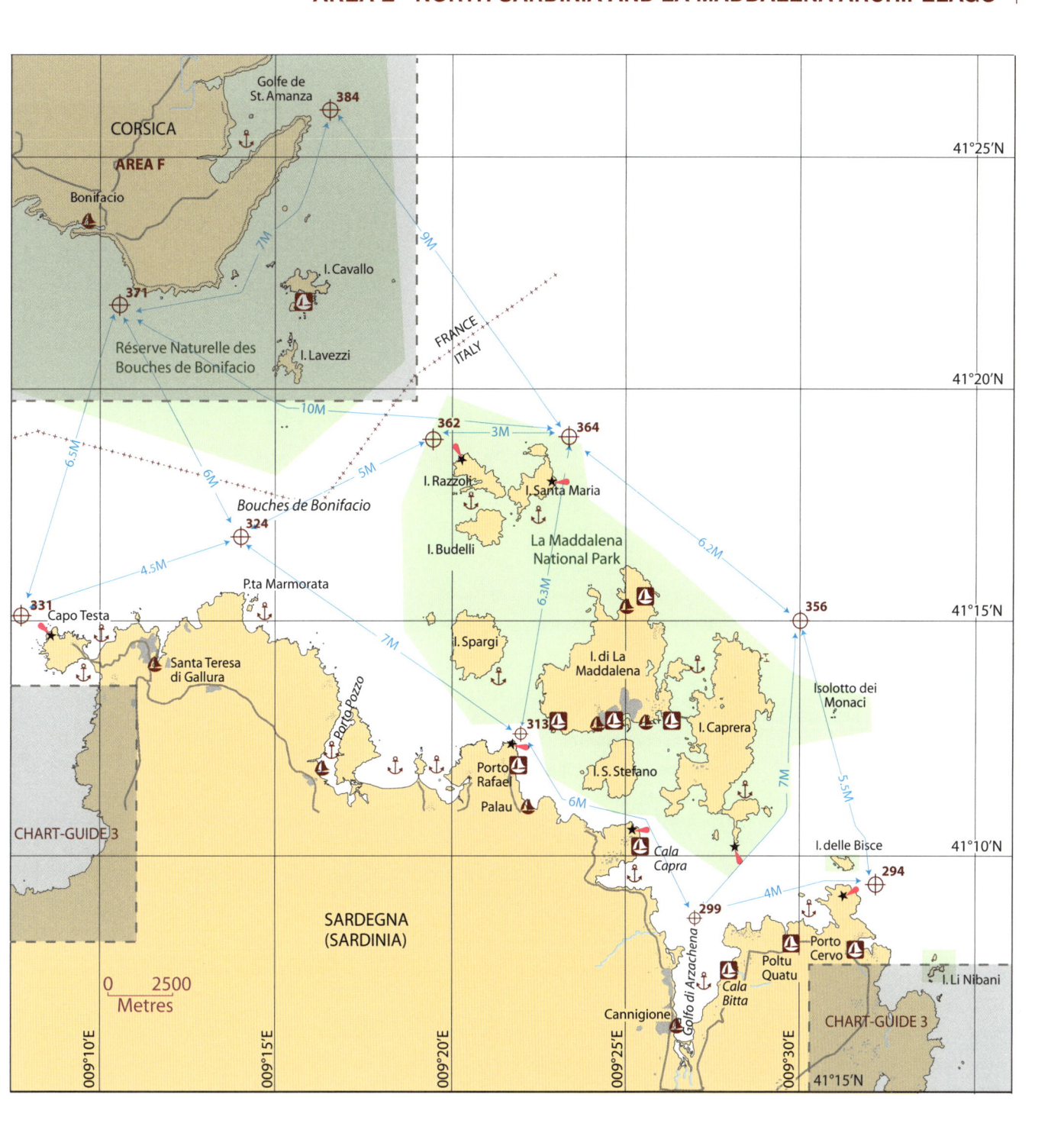

AREA E - NORTH SARDINIA AND LA MADDALENA ARCHIPELAGO

COASTAL NAVIGATION WAYPOINTS AND DISTANCES

⊕	DESCRIPTION	WGS 84 COORDINATES		CHART
		LATITUDE	LONGITUDE	
294	Passo delle Bisce E	41°09'.50N	009°31'.83E	83 84
299	Golfo di Arzachena	41°08'.31N	009°27'.09E	83 86
313	I. Sardegna - 500m N of Punta Sardegna	41°12'.50N	009°21'.95E	88-89-90
324	I. Sardegna - 0.5M N of Punta Marmorata	41°16'.09N	009°13'.45E	90
331	I. Sardegna - 1M NW of Capo Testa	41°15'.30N	009°08'.00E	90
356	I. Caprera - 1M NE of Caprera	41°15'.00N	009°30'.00E	83
362	I. Razzoli - 0.5M NW of Razzoli	41°18'.66N	009°19'.64E	103
364	I. S. Maria - 0.5M NE of Isola S. Maria	41°18'.83N	009°23'.50E	103
371	I. Corsica - 500m SW of Capo Pertusato	41°21'.66N	009°10'.54E	105
384	I. Corsica - 500m NE of Punta Capicciolo	41°25'.82N	009°16'.15E	106

117

AREA E - NORTH SARDINIA AND LA MADDALENA ARCHIPELAGO

HARBOURS AND MARINAS KEY FOR PLAN SYMBOLS

⊕	NAME	WGS 84 COORDINATES LATITUDE	WGS 84 COORDINATES LONGITUDE	CHART	⚓	⛵	🏠	LOA m	V	🔲	🔽 m	⚡	🚿	WC	🍴	🛒	📞	🔧
292	Porto Cervo	41°08'.22N	009°32'.33E	85	•		720	100	•	•	13	•	•	•	•	•	•	•
297	Poltu Quatu (Marina dell'Orso)	41°08'.48N	009°29'.70E	84	•		400	35	•	•	4	•	•	•	•	•	•	•
301	Cala Bitta	41°07'.72N	009°27'.95E	86	•		180	27	•		3.5	•	•	•	•	•	•	•
303	Cannigione	41°06'.41N	009°26'.60E	87		•	400	25	•	•	3.5	•	•	•	•	•	•	•
305	Cala Porteddu	41°07'.08N	009°26'.65E	86		•	IU				2	•	•					
307	Marina di Cala Capra	41°10'.08N	009°25'.32E	88	•		50		•		3	•	•	•				•
310	Palau	41°10'.93N	009°23'.30E	89		•	380	18	•	•	3.8	•	•	•	•	•	•	•
312	Marina di Porto Rafael	41°11'.75N	009°22'.00E	89	•		70	50	•		5	•	•	•	•			
319	Porto Pozzo	41°12'.10N	009°16'.65E	91		•	80	7			2.5	•			•	•	•	
326	Porto Longosardo	41°14'.75N	009°11'.90E	93		•	760	35	•	•	6	•	•	•	•	•	•	•
338	I. Maddalena - Cala Capo Ferrari	41°15'.40N	009°24'.80E	98		•	IU				2							
341	I. Maddalena - Cala Nido d'Aquila	41°12'.80N	009°22'.85E	98	•		90	18			3.5	•	•	•				
342	I. Maddalena - Cala Gavetta	41°12'.58N	009°24'.35E	99		•	120	12	•	•	10						•	
343	I. Maddalena - Cala Mangiavolpe	41°12'.72N	009°24'.59E	99	•		120	18	•		5							
344	I. Maddalena - Cala Camiciotto	41°12'.81N	009°25'.63E	99		•	160	20	•		5							
345	I. Maddalena - Marina del Ponte	41°13'.00N	009°26'.40E	99	•		160	30	•	•	3	•	•	•				•
347	I. Maddalena - Porto Massimo	41°15'.40N	009°25'.58E	100	•		140	50	•		6	•	•	•	•			

IU= Information Unavailable

ANCHORAGES KEY FOR PLAN SYMBOLS

⊕	NAME	WGS 84 COORDINATES LATITUDE	WGS 84 COORDINATES LONGITUDE	CHART	🏝	🐟	🔽 m	D	🍸	🧭	⚓	🔔
293	Cala Granu	41°08'.75N	009°31'.82E	85	G	s	4	•	B-R	N-E	•	
296	Liscia di Vacca	41°08'.74N	009°32'.35E	85	G	s/w	4	•		W-N	•	
298	Cala Battistone	41°08'.66N	009°28'.12E	84	G	s	7	•	B-R	NW-NE	•	
300	Cala Tre Monti	41°07'.96N	009°28'.04E	86	G	s/w	4	•		SW-W	•	
302	Rada di Cannigione	41°06'.57N	009°26'.82E	87	E	s/m	5	•	B-R-S	N-NE	•	•
304	Cala Laconia	41°07'.50N	009°26'.58E	86	P	s	3	•	B	N-S	•	
306	Golfo Saline	41°09'.58N	009°24'.95E	88	E	s	5	•	B-R-S	NE-E	•	
307	Cala Capra	41°10'.08N	009°25'.32E	88	P	s	5	•	B-R-S	N-S	•	•
308	Cala P.ta Cardinalino	41°10'.33N	009°25'.41E	88	P	s	3	•		N-S	•	
310	Palau	41°10'.93N	009°23'.30E	89	P	s/w	4	•	B-R-S	NW-NE	•	•
311	Rada di Mezzo Schifo	41°11'.19N	009°22'.33E	89	P	s	5	•		NW-NE	•	
314	Cala Trana	41°12'.33N	009°21'.24E	90	G	s	5	•		NW-NE	•	
315	Porto Puddu	41°11'.85N	009°19'.59E	90	G	s/r	6	•	B-R-S	N-NE	•	
316	Porto Liscia	41°12'.00N	009°18'.50E	90	G	s	4	•	B-R-S	N-NE	•	
317	Cala Fico	41°12'.51N	009°17'.84E	91	P	s	4	•		N-S	•	
319	Porto Pozzo	41°12'.10N	009°16'.65E	91	E	s/w	5	•	B-R-S	N	•	•
320	Cala Licciola	41°14'.08N	009°16'.58E	92	P	s	4	•		NW-SE	•	
321	Cala Barcaccia	41°14'.40N	009°15'.83E	92	P	s	4	•		NW-NE	•	
322	Cala Sambuco	41°14'.68N	009°15'.10E	92	P	s	4	•		N-/E	•	
323	Cala Marmorata	41°15'.00N	009°14'.40E	92	G	s	5	•	B	N-E	•	
325	Porto Quadro	41°15'.04N	009°12'.10E	93	P	s	5	•		NW-NE	•	
327	Cala Rena Bianca	41°14'.83N	009°11'.33E	93	G	s	4	•	B	NW-NE	•	
328	Isola Municca	41°14'.98N	009°10'.90E	93	P	s/r	4	•		S-NE	•	
329	Baia Santa Reparata	41°14'.40N	009°09'.95E	94	G	s	5	•		N-E	•	
330	Cala Spinosa	41°14'.75N	009°08'.90E	94	G	s	7	•		NW-SE	•	

AREA E - NORTH SARDINIA AND LA MADDALENA ARCHIPELAGO

	NAME	WGS 84 COORDINATES		CHART	Shelter	Seabed	Depth m	Landing	Facilities	Wind	Anchor	Buoy
		LATITUDE	LONGITUDE									
332	Baia La Colba	41°13'.80N	009°09'.50E	94	G	s	5	•		SE-SW	•	
333	I. S. Stefano - Cala Villamarina	41°11'.33N	009°24'.40E	96	G	s/r	5			SE-SW	•	
334	I. Spargi - Cala Corsara	41°13'.66N	009°20'.55E	97	G	s	5			SW-W	•	
335	I. Spargi - Cala Granara	41°14'.00N	009°21'.33E	97	P	s/r	4			NE-SW	•	•
336	I. Spargi - Cala Connari	41°14'.40N	009°21'.66E	97	P	s	4			N-S	•	•
337	I. Spargi - Cala Ferrigno	41°14'.68N	009°21'.50E	97	P	s/r	4	•		NW-SE	•	
339	I. Maddalena - Stagno Torto	41°15'.45N	009°24'.58E	98	G	s	6	•		NW/N	•	
340	I. Maddalena - Cala Francese	41°13'.42N	009°22'.42E	98	E	s	5	•	B-R	S-W	•	
346	I. Maddalena - Porto Lungo	41°15'.50N	009°25'.80E	100	G	s/r	6	•	B-R-S	E-SW	•	•
348	I. Maddalena - Cala Spalmatore	41°15'.00N	009°25'.95E	100	G	s	4	•	B	N-E		•
349	I. Maddalena - Punta Rossa	41°14'.45N	009°26'.33E	100	G	s	4			N-SE	•	
350	I. Maddalena - Cala Peticchia	41°14'.13N	009°26'.17E	100	G	s	4	•		N	•	
351	I. Maddalena - Isolotto Giardinelli	41°13'.58N	009°26'.74E	100	G	s	3			N-SE	•	
352	I. Caprera - Porto Garibaldi	41°13'.65N	009°27'.26E	101	G	s	5	•	B-R	W-N	•	
353	I. Caprera - Cala Napoletana	41°14'.50N	009°27'.57E	101	G	s/w	4			SW-NW	•	
354	I. Caprera - Cala Coticcio	41°12'.78N	009°29'.16E	101	G	s/r	5			SE-S	•	
355	I. Caprera - Cala Brigantino	41°12'.35N	009°28'.66E	101	G	s	4			NE-E	•	
357	I. Caprera - Cala Portese	41°11'.23N	009°28'.05E	102	E	s	5	•		N-E	•	•
358	I. Caprera - Isolotto Porco	41°10'.42N	009°27'.80E	102	P	s/w/r	3			N-S	•	
359	I. Caprera - Porto Palma	41°11'.02N	009°27'.00E	102	E	s w	5	•		S	•	
360	I. Caprera - Cala Stagnali	41°12'.34N	009°26'.60E	102	G	s/r	3	•		N-W	•	
361	I. Razzoli - Cala Lunga	41°17'.90N	009°20'.34E	103	E	s/w	5	•		W	•	•
363	I. S. Maria - Cala Muro	41°18'.33N	009°22'.25E	103	G	s	7			W-N		•
365	I. S. Maria - Cala Santa Maria	41°17'.48N	009°22'.65E	104	E	s	5	•		E-S	•	•
366	Passo Cecca Morto	41°16'.85N	009°21'.73E	104	E	s/w	7	•		NE-S	•	•
367	I. Budelli - Cala Punta Sud	41°16'.60N	009°20'.61E	104	G	s	5			SE-SW	•	
368	I. Razzoli - S side anchorages	41°17'.66N	009°20'.85E	104	G	s/r	5	•		W-SW	•	
369	Porto Madonna - G. Marino	41°17'.50N	009°21'.25E	104	E	s	5			W	•	•

Shelter: P = Poor G = Good E = Excellent **Nature of seabed:** w = weed m = mud g = gravel p = pebbles/stones r = rock s = sand

Depths in metres **Landing with dinghy** **Facilities ashore:** B = Bar R = Restaurant S = Shop **Anchorage** **Mooring buoy**

Wind direction and exposure

AREA E - NORTH SARDINIA AND LA MADDALENA ARCHIPELAGO

SAFETY AT SEA — AREA E

WEATHER BULLETINS

Mari d'Italia/Meteomar weather bulletin
(English and Italian)
VHF ch 68 frequency 156.425 MHz continuous

Coast radio station weather bulletin
Monte Moro (North Sardinia and Strait of Bonifacio)
VHF ch 28 frequency 162.000 MHz
Porto Torres VHF ch 26 frequency 161.900 MHz
0510 0810 1210 1610 2010 UTC
Radio Porto Cervo local bulletin VHF ch 26, 28, 85
(English and Italian) advance call on ch 16
0150 0750 1350 1950 UTC

Radiouno - Italian bulletin for the sea
0554 1408 2249 Monday-Friday

FRANCE AND CORSICA WEATHER FORECASTS
(French-English)

Monaco Radio 4363 kHz (ch 403) 0903 1403 1915 LT
Lyon, Provence, Corsican Sea, Sardinian Sea, Ligurian Sea, Northern Tyrrhenian Sea

Monaco Radio 8728, 8806 kHz (ch 804, 830) SSB
0715 1830 UTC West Mediterranean offshore seas

La Garde CROSS 1696, 2677 kHz SSB after the first call
Frequency 2182 kHz
0650 1433 1850 LT

HARBOURMASTERS

Olbia ☎ +39 0789 56360
cpolbia@mit.gov.it

La Maddalena
Offices ☎ +39 00789 730632 / 799351
Operations room ☎ +39 0789 736709
cplamaddalena@mit.gov.it

Porto Torres ☎ +39 0789 563670 (switchboard)
+39 079 515151 (emergency)
cpportotorres@mit.gov.it

Guardia Costiera (Coast Guard)
☎ 1530 emergency - VHF ch 16

SAFETY AND RESCUE CENTRES

MRSC Olbia ☎ +39 0789 56360
cpolbia@mit.gov.it

MRSC Cagliari ☎ +39 070 678861
cpcagliari@mit.gov.it

MRSC Livorno ☎ +39 0586 826011
cplivorno@guardiacostiera.gov.it

Porto Cervo Heliport VHF ch 26 - Man & Auto ch 88

MRCC Roma MMSI 002 470 001
DSC VHF ch 70, 16 - DSC MF 2187.5 kHz, 2182 kHz
DSC HF 420.5, 6312, 8414.5 kHz
Port Authority Roma Fiumicino
☎ +39 06 656171
cproma@mit.gov.it

MRSC Corsica VHF ch 16, 67
☎ +33 (0)495 201363
MMSI 002275420
(winter 0730-1900 - summer 0730-2300)

CIRM International Medical Centre
☎ +39 06 559290263 - mobile + 39 348 3984229
Fax +39 06 5923331/2
telesoccorso@cirm.it - www.cirm.it

radio.guardiacostiera.it

FROM PORTO CERVO TO CAPO D'ORSO — AREA E

CHART 83

CHART 84

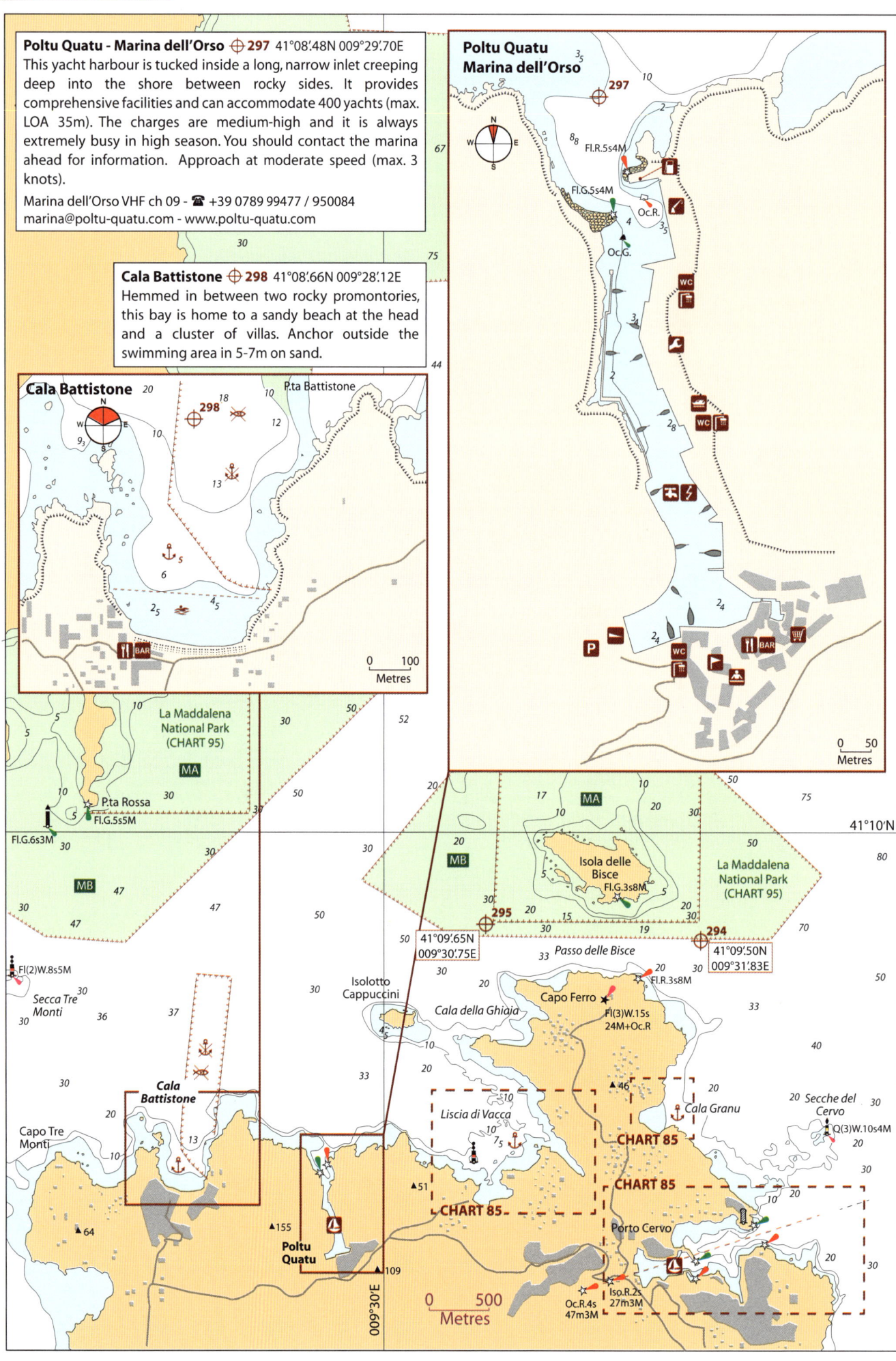

AREA E — CALA BATTISTONE AND POLTU QUATU

Poltu Quatu - Marina dell'Orso ⊕ **297** 41°08'.48N 009°29'.70E
This yacht harbour is tucked inside a long, narrow inlet creeping deep into the shore between rocky sides. It provides comprehensive facilities and can accommodate 400 yachts (max. LOA 35m). The charges are medium-high and it is always extremely busy in high season. You should contact the marina ahead for information. Approach at moderate speed (max. 3 knots).
Marina dell'Orso VHF ch 09 - ☎ +39 0789 99477 / 950084
marina@poltu-quatu.com - www.poltu-quatu.com

Cala Battistone ⊕ **298** 41°08'.66N 009°28'.12E
Hemmed in between two rocky promontories, this bay is home to a sandy beach at the head and a cluster of villas. Anchor outside the swimming area in 5-7m on sand.

FROM LISCIA DI VACCA TO PORTO CERVO — AREA E — CHART 85

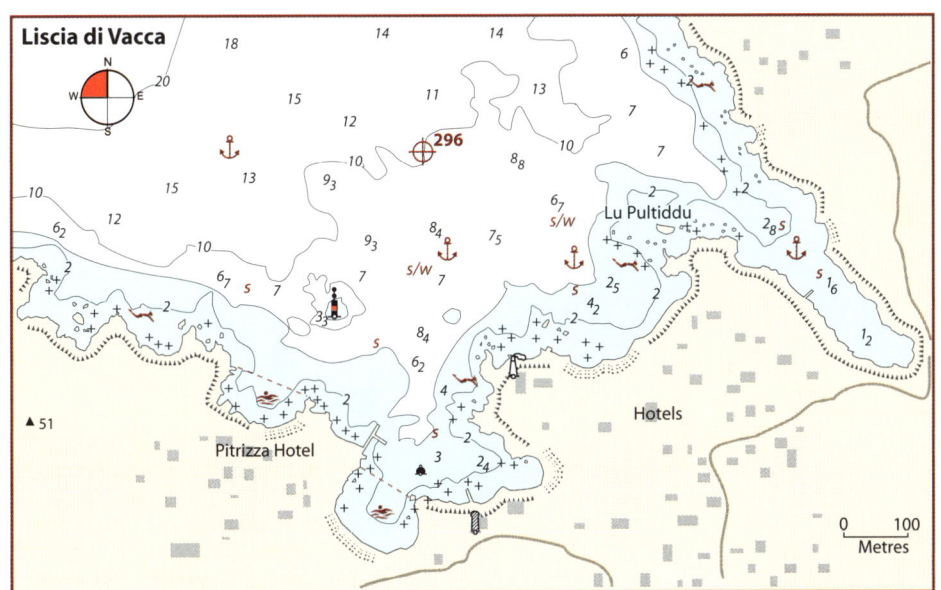

Liscia di Vacca

⊕ 296 41°08'.74N 009°32'.35E

A large bay with jagged rocky coasts, but open to the NW. It is extremely built-up and touristy, with the exclusive Pitrizza Hotel facing onto the sea. In the approach, care is needed of the numerous rocks and shoal water that fringe the entire bay. Anchor in 4-7m on sand, or on sand and weed. Yachts drawing less than 1.5m can slip into the inlet to the SE of the bay.

Cala Granu

⊕ 293 41°08'.75N 009°31'.82E

A small bay to the SE of Capo Ferro with rocky shores and a sandy beach at the head. Anchor in 3-5m on sand.

Porto Cervo ⊕ 292 41°08'.22N 009°32'.33E

In addition to being Sardinia's, if not the Mediterranean's most famous harbour, it is also one of the most expensive. In summer, it plays host to mega-yachts and their famous owners, who pour into the luxury restaurants and bars in the evening.

The harbour enjoys excellent shelter and can accommodate 720 yachts, with 80 visitors berths (max. LOA 100m). A dozen or so mooring buoys (max. LOA 15m) are also available. A taxi-boat service is provided. The E quay of the Porto Vecchio is set aside for large yachts, but it is reported to be free-of-charge in low season.

In a N approach, care is needed of a rock (Secche del Cervo). Once closer to the harbour entrance, contact the marina and await instructions.

Port Authority VHF ch16 - ☎ +39 0789 563648 - lcportocervo@mit.gov.it
Porto Cervo Marina VHF ch 09 (24h) - ☎ +39 0789 905111
www.marinadiportocervo.com - info@marinadiportocervo.com

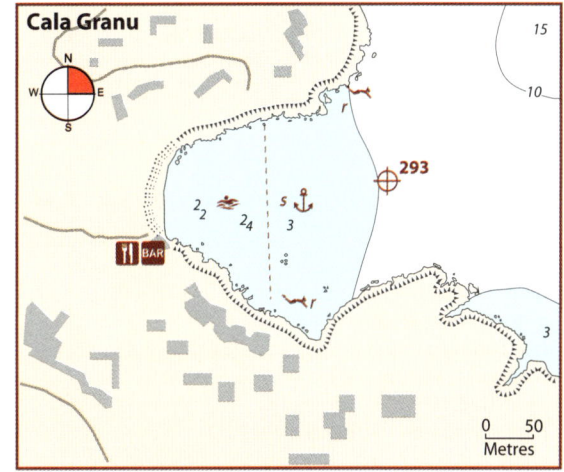

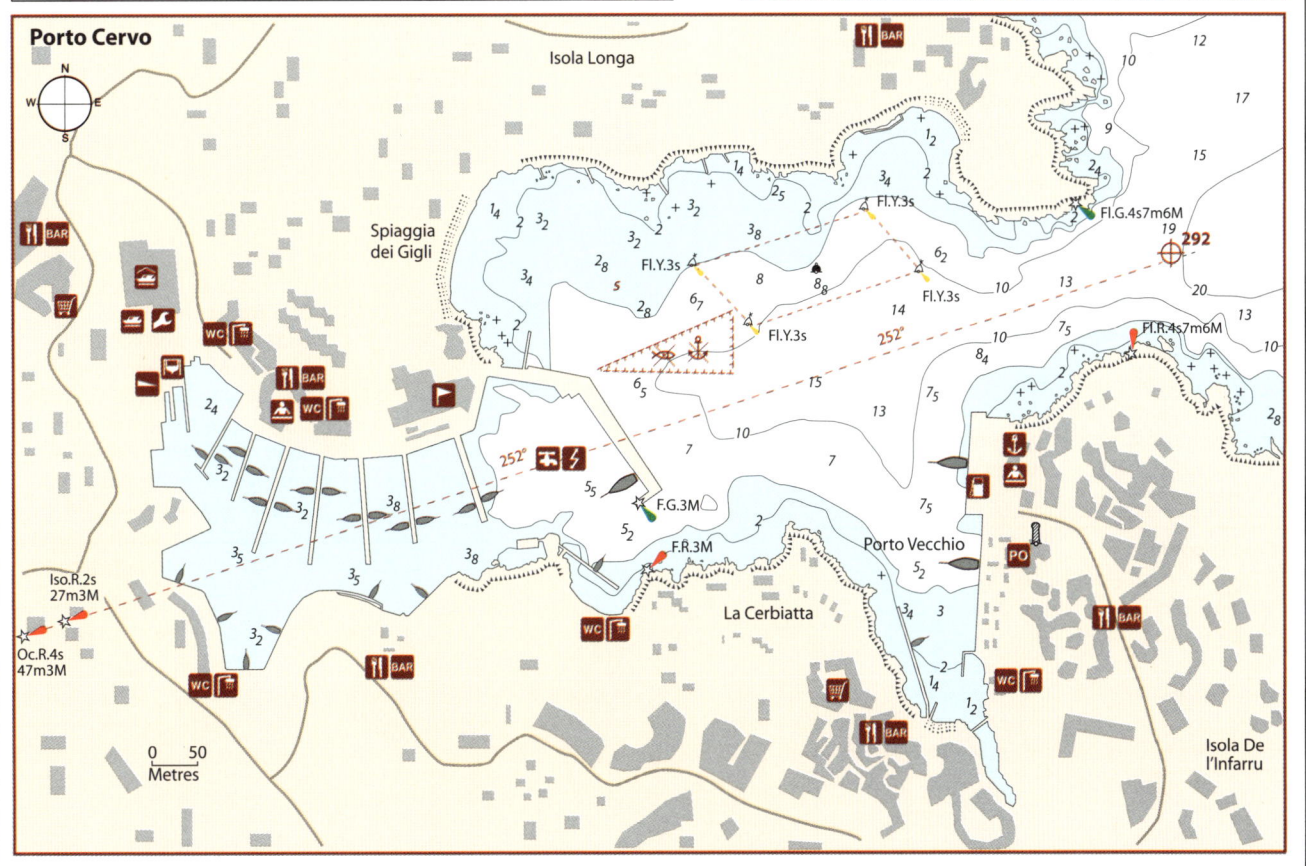

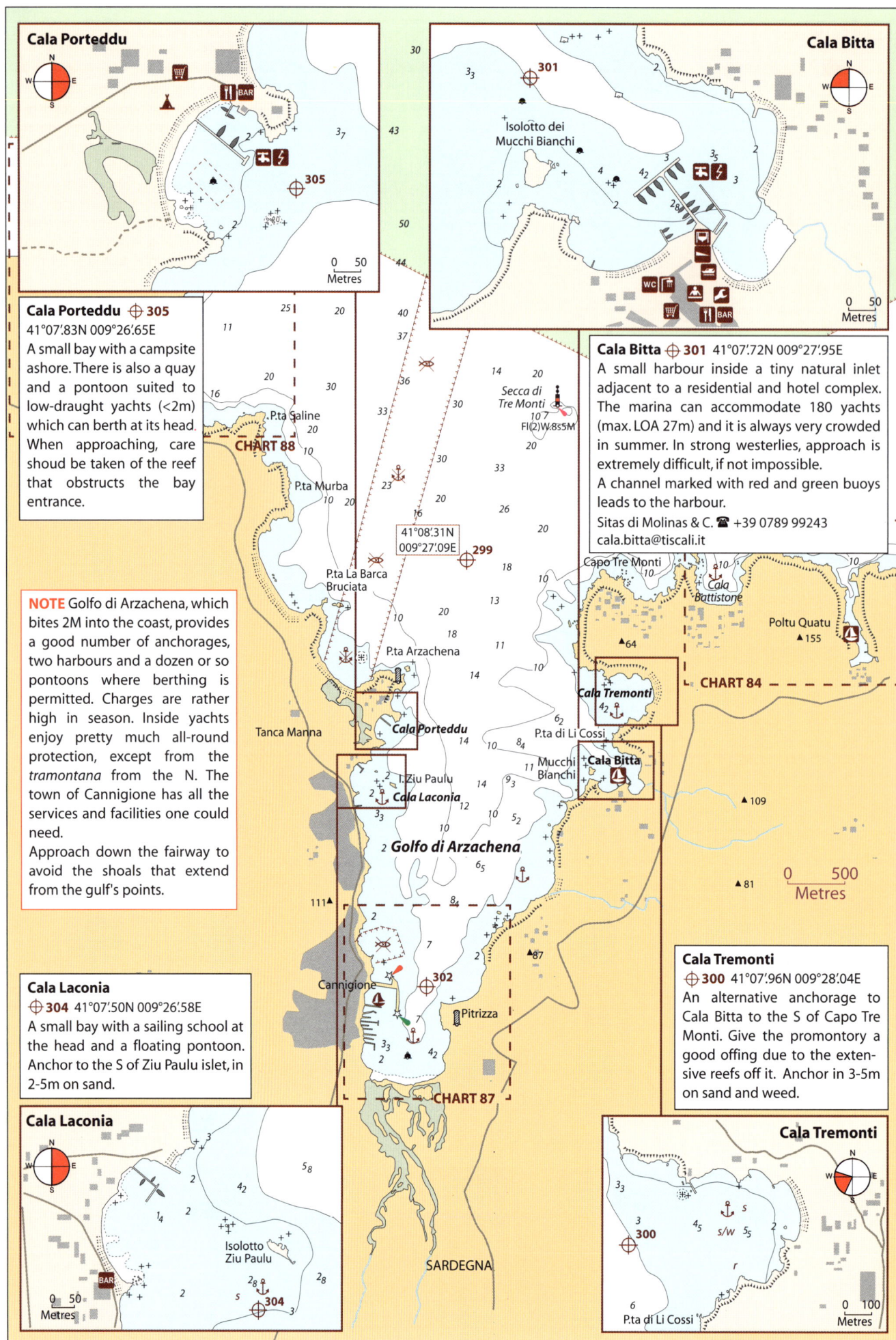

CHART 86 — AREA E — GOLFO DI ARZACHENA

Cala Porteddu ⊕ 305
41°07'.83N 009°26'.65E
A small bay with a campsite ashore. There is also a quay and a pontoon suited to low-draught yachts (<2m) which can berth at its head. When approaching, care shoud be taken of the reef that obstructs the bay entrance.

NOTE Golfo di Arzachena, which bites 2M into the coast, provides a good number of anchorages, two harbours and a dozen or so pontoons where berthing is permitted. Charges are rather high in season. Inside yachts enjoy pretty much all-round protection, except from the *tramontana* from the N. The town of Cannigione has all the services and facilities one could need.
Approach down the fairway to avoid the shoals that extend from the gulf's points.

Cala Bitta ⊕ 301   41°07'.72N 009°27'.95E
A small harbour inside a tiny natural inlet adjacent to a residential and hotel complex. The marina can accommodate 180 yachts (max. LOA 27m) and it is always very crowded in summer. In strong westerlies, approach is extremely difficult, if not impossible.
A channel marked with red and green buoys leads to the harbour.
Sitas di Molinas & C. ☎ +39 0789 99243
cala.bitta@tiscali.it

Cala Laconia
⊕ 304   41°07'.50N 009°26'.58E
A small bay with a sailing school at the head and a floating pontoon. Anchor to the S of Ziu Paulu islet, in 2-5m on sand.

Cala Tremonti
⊕ 300   41°07'.96N 009°28'.04E
An alternative anchorage to Cala Bitta to the S of Capo Tre Monti. Give the promontory a good offing due to the extensive reefs off it. Anchor in 3-5m on sand and weed.

| CANNIGIONE | AREA E | | CHART 87 |

Cannigione ⊕ **303** 41°06'.41N 009°26'.60E
The harbour breakwater has been recently extended by about 200m so that it now shelters the basin from easterlies as well. It has a capacity of about 400 berths (max. LOA 25m), with 50 for visitors, in the harbour and on pontoons. As it is close to La Maddalena, the harbour is always extremely busy in summer, so it is best to book in advance. The harbour charges are medium-high.
Consorzio Marina di Cannigione ☎ +39 346 806 5848 consorziomc@tiscali.it www.marinacannigione.it
Pontile Albatros (LOA 24m) ☎ +39 339 4337030 www.albatrosmarinacannigione.it aldoalbatros@gmail.com
Nautilus s.n.c. Pontile del Fico (max. LOA 8m) ☎ +39 336 814182 www.nautilussardegna.it nautilussardegna@tiscali.it
Sardamar (harbour office) ☎ +39 0789 88422 - VHF ch 11 (07.00/19.00) info@coop.sardamar.it
Pontile Destriero 90 berths (max. LOA 30m) ☎ +39 0789 88485 - www.pontiledestriero.com- pontiledestriero@tiscali.it
Pontile Golfo di Arzachena ☎ +39 0789 892010 160 ormeggi (max. LOA 30m) pontilelasciumara@tiscali.it - noleggiopostibarcacannigione.com
Boat Service ☎ +39 0789 892212 / Carburanti Medusa Service (Fuel) ☎ +39 0789 88472

Anchorage ⊕ **302** 41°06'.57N 009°26'.82E
Alternatively, anchor in the bay as it is comfortable and protected from prevailing summer winds. Anchor where convenient, but keep a safe distance from the harbour entrance, the pontoons and the large field of moorings at the head of the gulf. Anchor in 3-10m on sand, mud or sand and weed. Good holding almost everywhere.

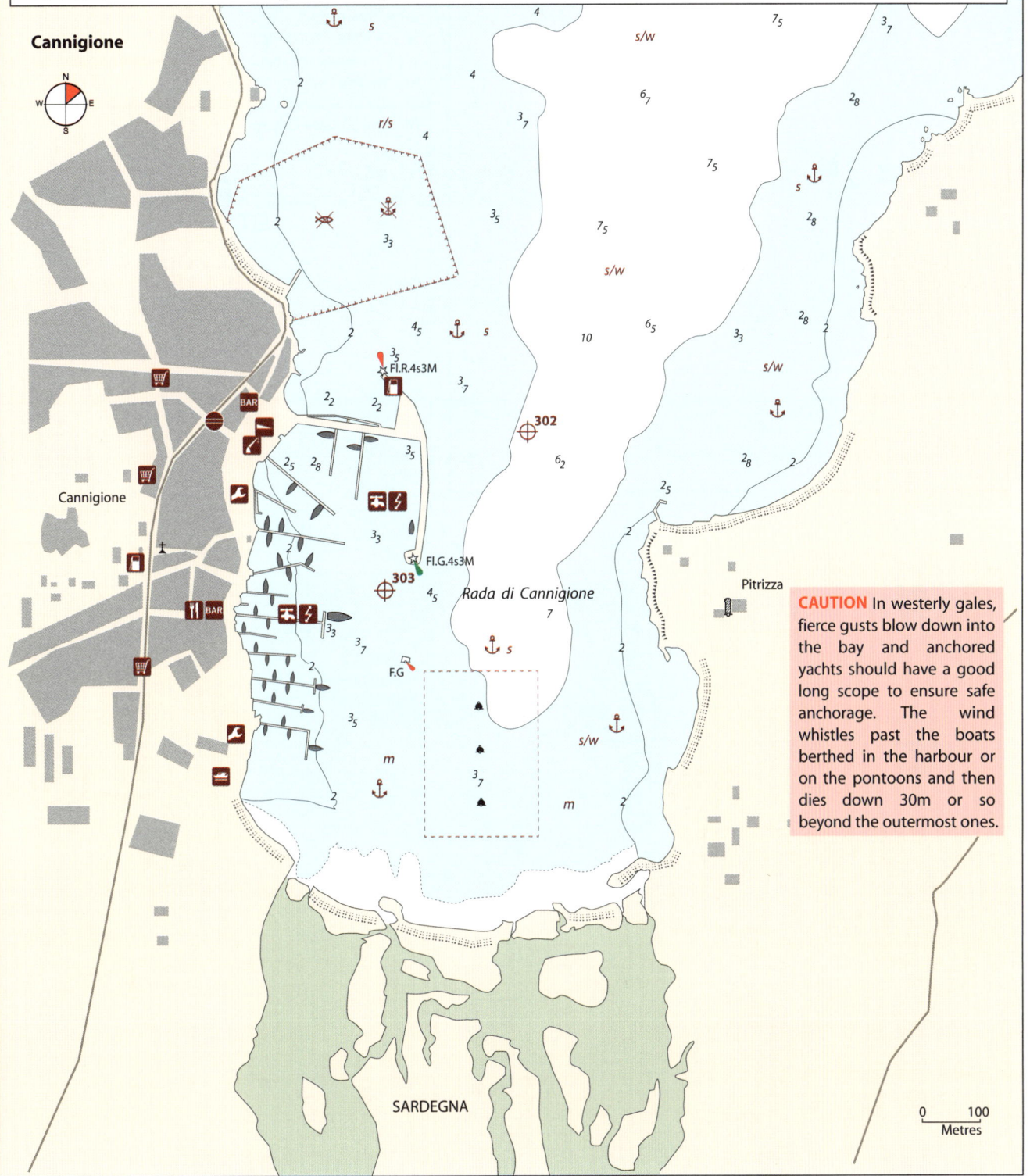

CAUTION In westerly gales, fierce gusts blow down into the bay and anchored yachts should have a good long scope to ensure safe anchorage. The wind whistles past the boats berthed in the harbour or on the pontoons and then dies down 30m or so beyond the outermost ones.

CHART 88 — AREA E — FROM PUNTA SALINE TO CAPO D'ORSO

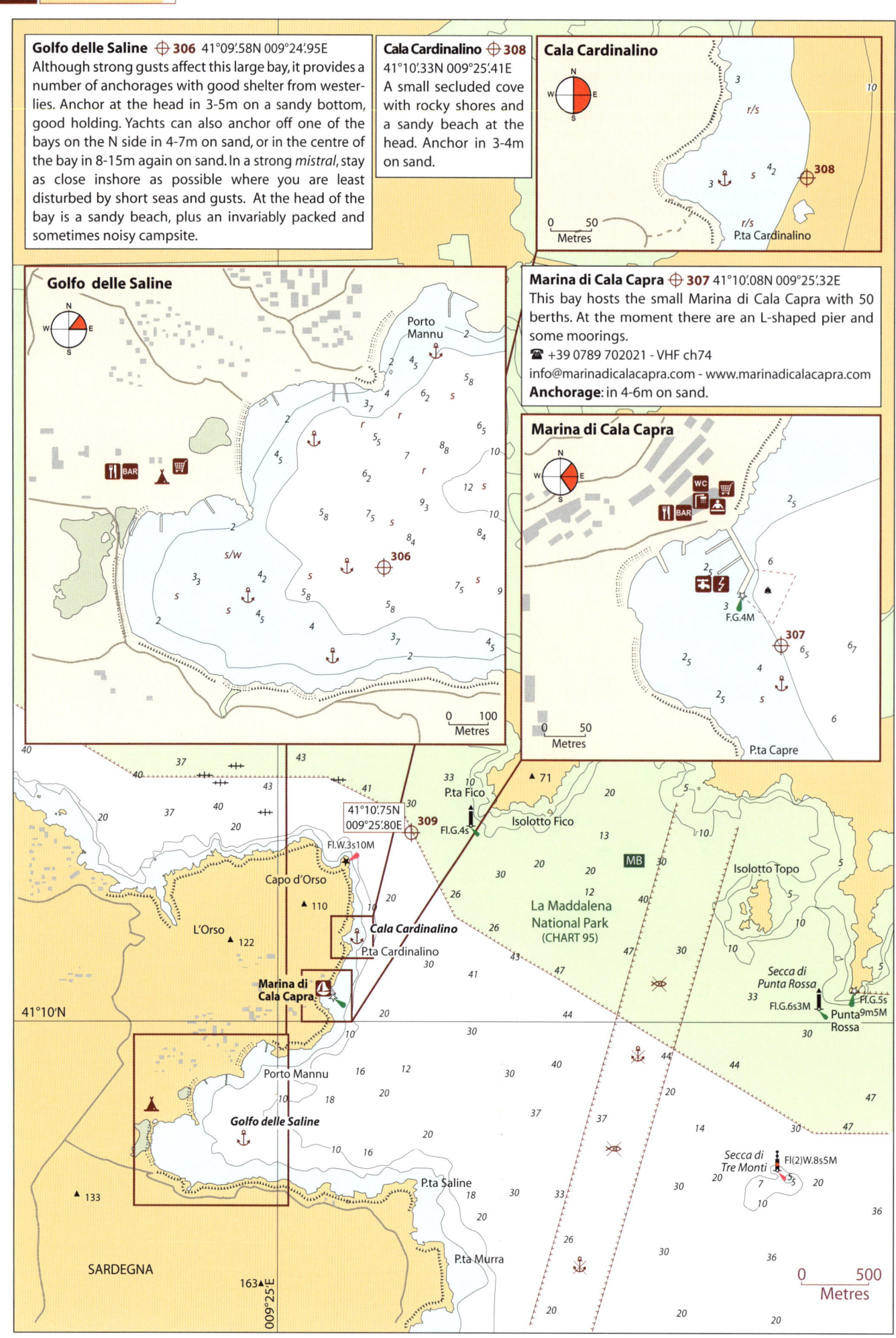

Golfo delle Saline ⊕ **306** 41°09'.58N 009°24'.95E
Although strong gusts affect this large bay, it provides a number of anchorages with good shelter from westerlies. Anchor at the head in 3-5m on a sandy bottom, good holding. Yachts can also anchor off one of the bays on the N side in 4-7m on sand, or in the centre of the bay in 8-15m again on sand. In a strong *mistral*, stay as close inshore as possible where you are least disturbed by short seas and gusts. At the head of the bay is a sandy beach, plus an invariably packed and sometimes noisy campsite.

Cala Cardinalino ⊕ **308** 41°10'.33N 009°25'.41E
A small secluded cove with rocky shores and a sandy beach at the head. Anchor in 3-4m on sand.

Marina di Cala Capra ⊕ **307** 41°10'.08N 009°25'.32E
This bay hosts the small Marina di Cala Capra with 50 berths. At the moment there are an L-shaped pier and some moorings.
☎ +39 0789 702021 - VHF ch74
info@marinadicalacapra.com - www.marinadicalacapra.com
Anchorage: in 4-6m on sand.

126

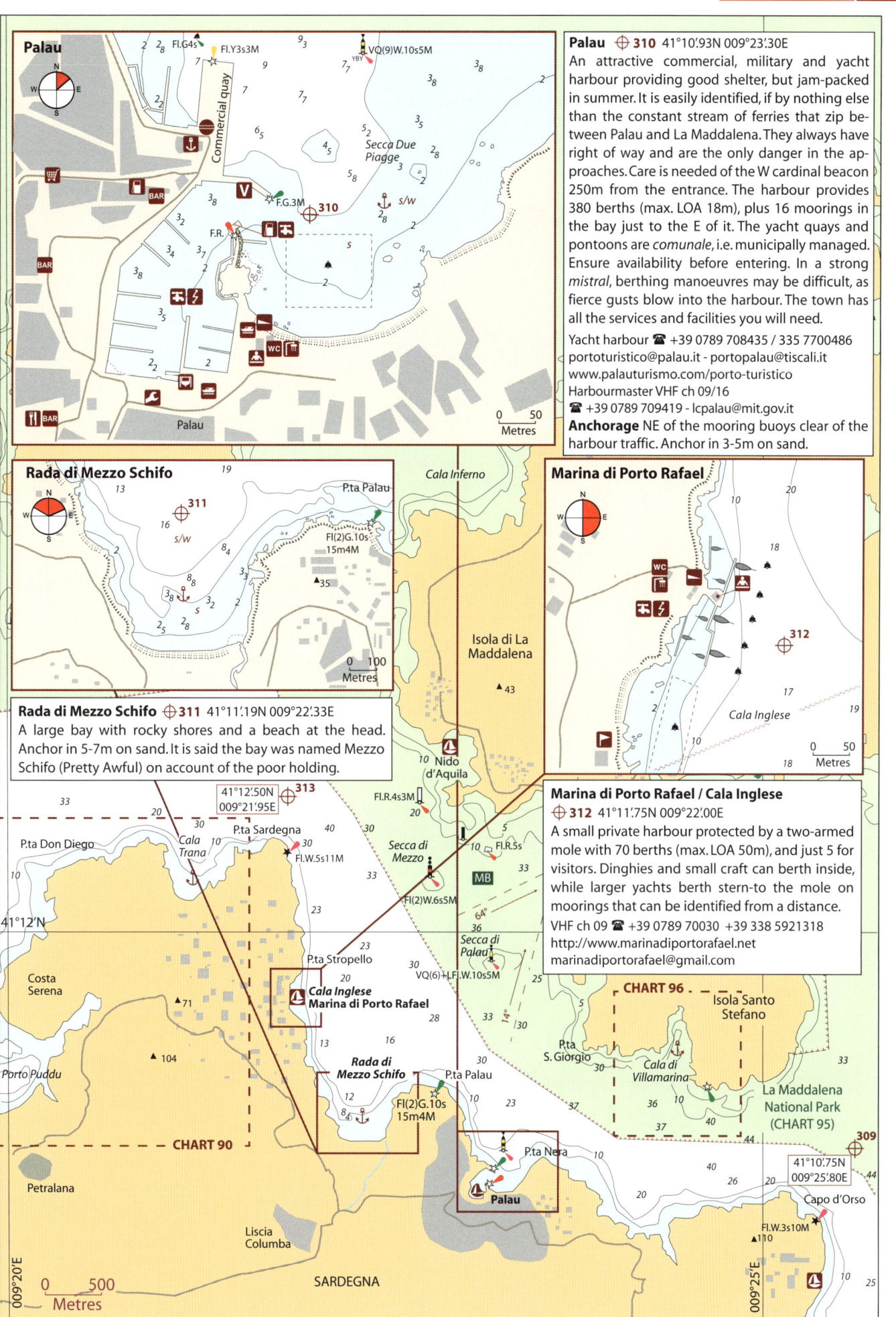

FROM CAPO D'ORSO TO PUNTA SARDEGNA — AREA E — CHART 89

Palau ⊕ 310   41°10'.93N 009°23'.30E

An attractive commercial, military and yacht harbour providing good shelter, but jam-packed in summer. It is easily identified, if by nothing else than the constant stream of ferries that zip between Palau and La Maddalena. They always have right of way and are the only danger in the approaches. Care is needed of the W cardinal beacon 250m from the entrance. The harbour provides 380 berths (max. LOA 18m), plus 16 moorings in the bay just to the E of it. The yacht quays and pontoons are *comunale*, i.e. municipally managed. Ensure availability before entering. In a strong *mistral*, berthing manoeuvres may be difficult, as fierce gusts blow into the harbour. The town has all the services and facilities you will need.

Yacht harbour ☎ +39 0789 708435 / 335 7700486
portoturistico@palau.it - portopalau@tiscali.it
www.palauturismo.com/porto-turistico
Harbourmaster VHF ch 09/16
☎ +39 0789 709419 - lcpalau@mit.gov.it

Anchorage NE of the mooring buoys clear of the harbour traffic. Anchor in 3-5m on sand.

Rada di Mezzo Schifo ⊕ 311   41°11'.19N 009°22'.33E

A large bay with rocky shores and a beach at the head. Anchor in 5-7m on sand. It is said the bay was named Mezzo Schifo (Pretty Awful) on account of the poor holding.

Marina di Porto Rafael / Cala Inglese
⊕ 312   41°11'.75N 009°22'.00E

A small private harbour protected by a two-armed mole with 70 berths (max. LOA 50m), and just 5 for visitors. Dinghies and small craft can berth inside, while larger yachts berth stern-to the mole on moorings that can be identified from a distance.
VHF ch 09 ☎ +39 0789 70030 +39 338 5921318
http://www.marinadiportorafael.net
marinadiportorafael@gmail.com

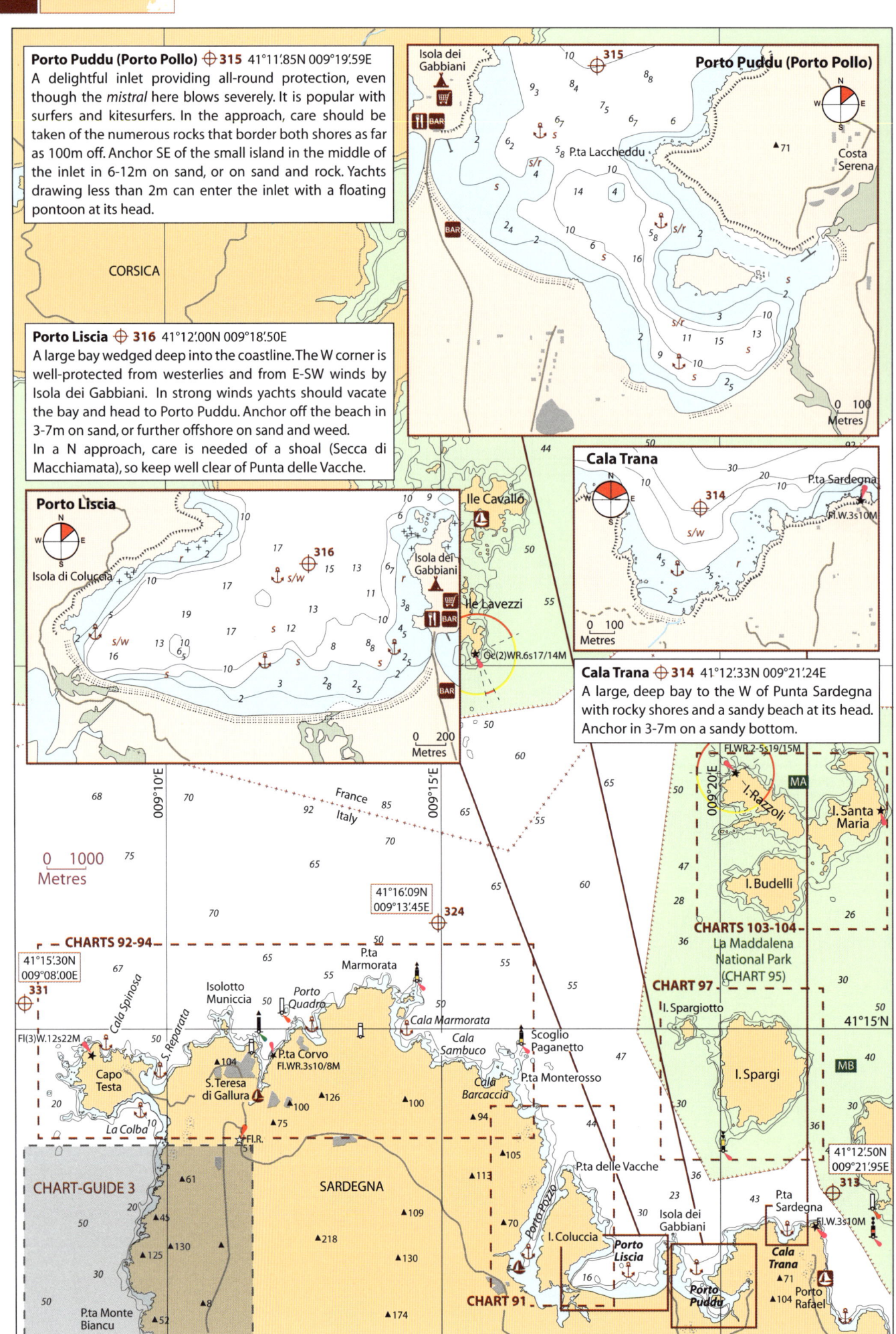

CHART 90 — AREA E — FROM PUNTA SARDEGNA TO CAPO TESTA

Porto Puddu (Porto Pollo) ⊕ 315 41°11′.85N 009°19′.59E
A delightful inlet providing all-round protection, even though the *mistral* here blows severely. It is popular with surfers and kitesurfers. In the approach, care should be taken of the numerous rocks that border both shores as far as 100m off. Anchor SE of the small island in the middle of the inlet in 6-12m on sand, or on sand and rock. Yachts drawing less than 2m can enter the inlet with a floating pontoon at its head.

Porto Liscia ⊕ 316 41°12′.00N 009°18′.50E
A large bay wedged deep into the coastline. The W corner is well-protected from westerlies and from E-SW winds by Isola dei Gabbiani. In strong winds yachts should vacate the bay and head to Porto Puddu. Anchor off the beach in 3-7m on sand, or further offshore on sand and weed.
In a N approach, care is needed of a shoal (Secca di Macchiamata), so keep well clear of Punta delle Vacche.

Cala Trana ⊕ 314 41°12′.33N 009°21′.24E
A large, deep bay to the W of Punta Sardegna with rocky shores and a sandy beach at its head. Anchor in 3-7m on a sandy bottom.

PORTO POZZO | AREA E | CHART 91

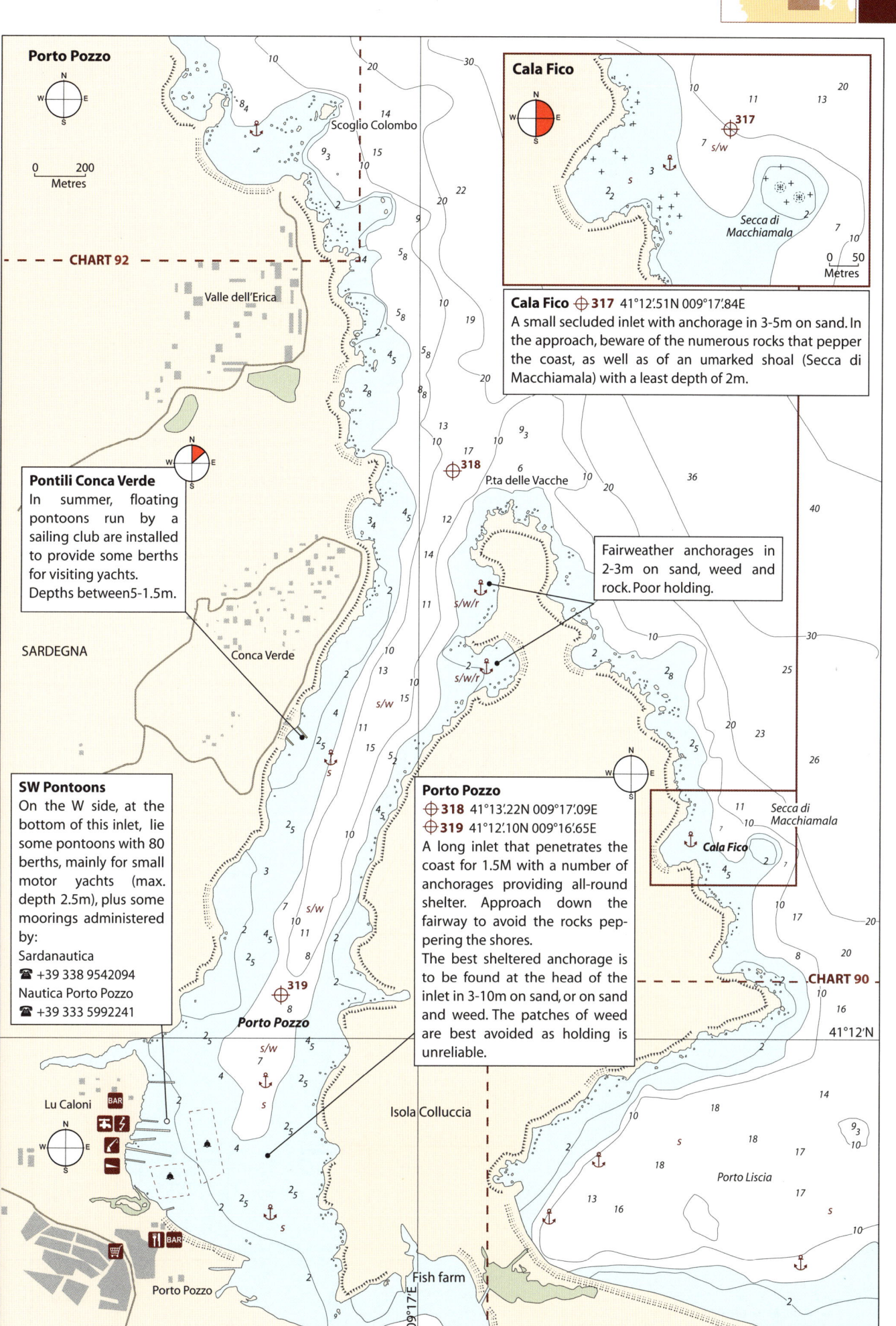

Porto Pozzo

Scoglio Colombo

Valle dell'Erica

CHART 92

Pontili Conca Verde
In summer, floating pontoons run by a sailing club are installed to provide some berths for visiting yachts. Depths between 5-1.5m.

SARDEGNA

Conca Verde

Cala Fico

Secca di Macchiamala

Cala Fico ⊕ 317 41°12'.51N 009°17'.84E
A small secluded inlet with anchorage in 3-5m on sand. In the approach, beware of the numerous rocks that pepper the coast, as well as of an umarked shoal (Secca di Macchiamala) with a least depth of 2m.

P.ta delle Vacche

Fairweather anchorages in 2-3m on sand, weed and rock. Poor holding.

SW Pontoons
On the W side, at the bottom of this inlet, lie some pontoons with 80 berths, mainly for small motor yachts (max. depth 2.5m), plus some moorings administered by:
Sardanautica
☎ +39 338 9542094
Nautica Porto Pozzo
☎ +39 333 5992241

Porto Pozzo
⊕ 318 41°13'.22N 009°17'.09E
⊕ 319 41°12'.10N 009°16'.65E
A long inlet that penetrates the coast for 1.5M with a number of anchorages providing all-round shelter. Approach down the fairway to avoid the rocks peppering the shores.
The best sheltered anchorage is to be found at the head of the inlet in 3-10m on sand, or on sand and weed. The patches of weed are best avoided as holding is unreliable.

Secca di Macchiamala

Cala Fico

CHART 90

Lu Caloni

Porto Pozzo

Isola Coluccia

Porto Liscia

Fish farm

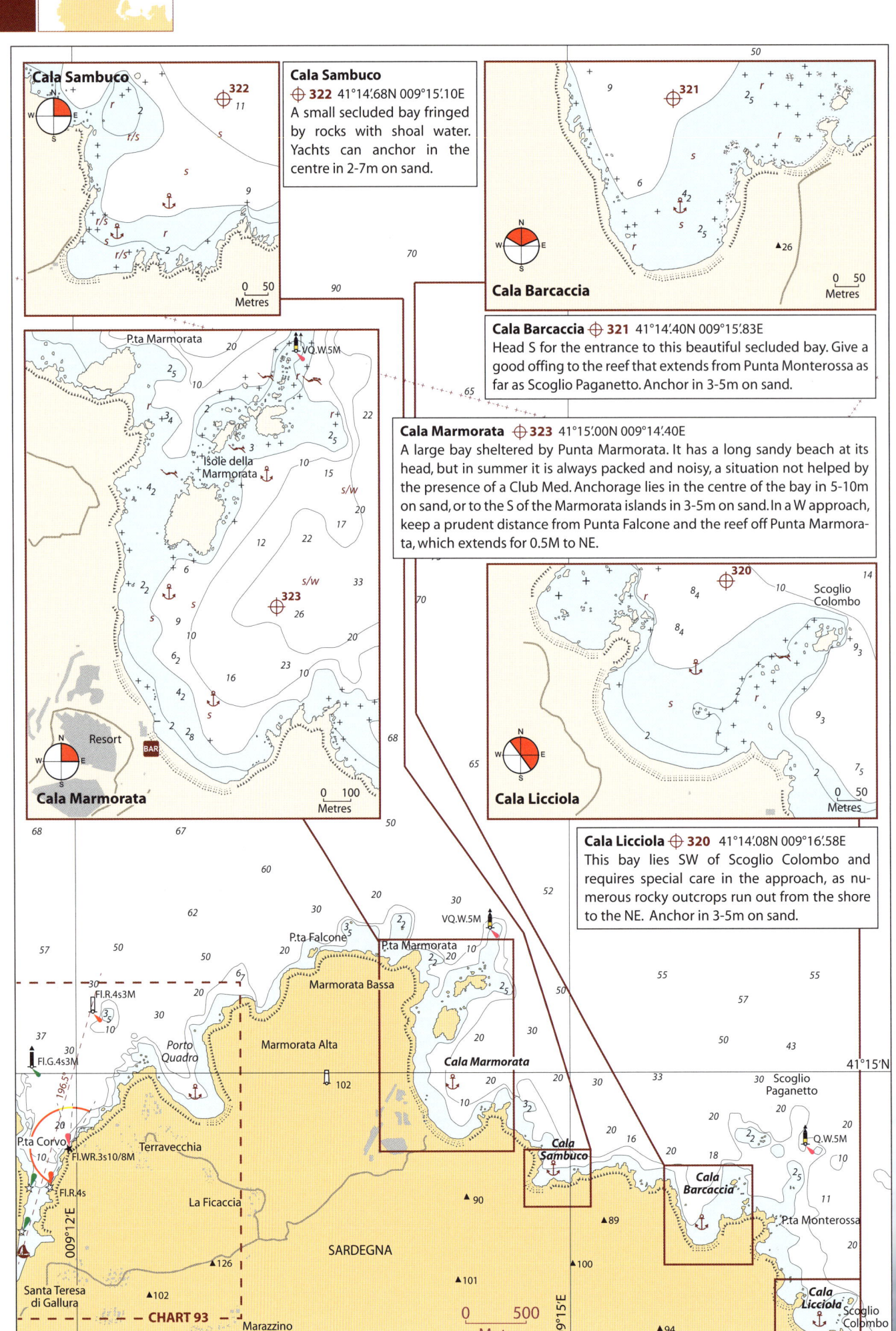

CHART 92 — AREA E — FROM CALA LICCIOLA TO PUNTA MARMORATA

Cala Sambuco ⊕ 322 41°14'.68N 009°15'.10E
A small secluded bay fringed by rocks with shoal water. Yachts can anchor in the centre in 2-7m on sand.

Cala Barcaccia ⊕ 321 41°14'.40N 009°15'.83E
Head S for the entrance to this beautiful secluded bay. Give a good offing to the reef that extends from Punta Monterossa as far as Scoglio Paganetto. Anchor in 3-5m on sand.

Cala Marmorata ⊕ 323 41°15'.00N 009°14'.40E
A large bay sheltered by Punta Marmorata. It has a long sandy beach at its head, but in summer it is always packed and noisy, a situation not helped by the presence of a Club Med. Anchorage lies in the centre of the bay in 5-10m on sand, or to the S of the Marmorata islands in 3-5m on sand. In a W approach, keep a prudent distance from Punta Falcone and the reef off Punta Marmorata, which extends for 0.5M to NE.

Cala Licciola ⊕ 320 41°14'.08N 009°16'.58E
This bay lies SW of Scoglio Colombo and requires special care in the approach, as numerous rocky outcrops run out from the shore to the NE. Anchor in 3-5m on sand.

PORTO LONGOSARDO (SANTA TERESA DI GALLURA) | AREA E

CHART 93

Cala Rena Bianca ⊕ 327 41°14'.83N 009°11'.33E
A large bay surrounded by rocky shores completely open to the N. A beautiful sandy beach lies at the head, but it is always very crowded in summer. A tower, Torre Longosardo, is conspicuous on the E promontory. Anchor in 3-7m on sand.

Isola Municca
⊕ 328 41°14'.98N 009°10'.90E
Fairweather anchorage at the far SW tip of the island in 3-7m on sand with scattered rock.

NOTE The long inlet that leads to Porto Longosardo is a slender 75m wide and is straightforward. Care, however, is needed of the commercial shipping. Always give way.

Porto Quadro
⊕ 325 41°15'.04N 009°12'.10E
A large inlet that bites deep into the coast. It is eclosed by cliffs with a sandy beach at its head. Anchor in the centre in 3-5m on sand.

Porto Longosardo (Santa Teresa di Gallura) ⊕ 326 41°14'.75N 009°11'.90E
The Longosardo commercial/yacht harbour lies at the end of a fjord. It is hemmed in by high land covered in vegetation, which heads inland for 0.75M. The harbour is overlooked by the town of Santa Teresa di Gallura to the W and provides excellent all-round shelter, but a strong *mistral* makes entry very dangerous, if not impossible. In these conditions, berthing is disturbed by a swell that creeps into the harbour. It accommodates 760 yachts (max. LOA 35m), but contacting the harbour beforehand to check availability is recommended.
Santa Teresa di Gallura Harbour VHF ch12 ☎ +39 0789 751936
customercare@portosantateresa.com - www.portosantateresa.com
Port Authority VHF ch 16/09 - ☎ +39 0789 754602
santateresagallura@guardiacostiera.it

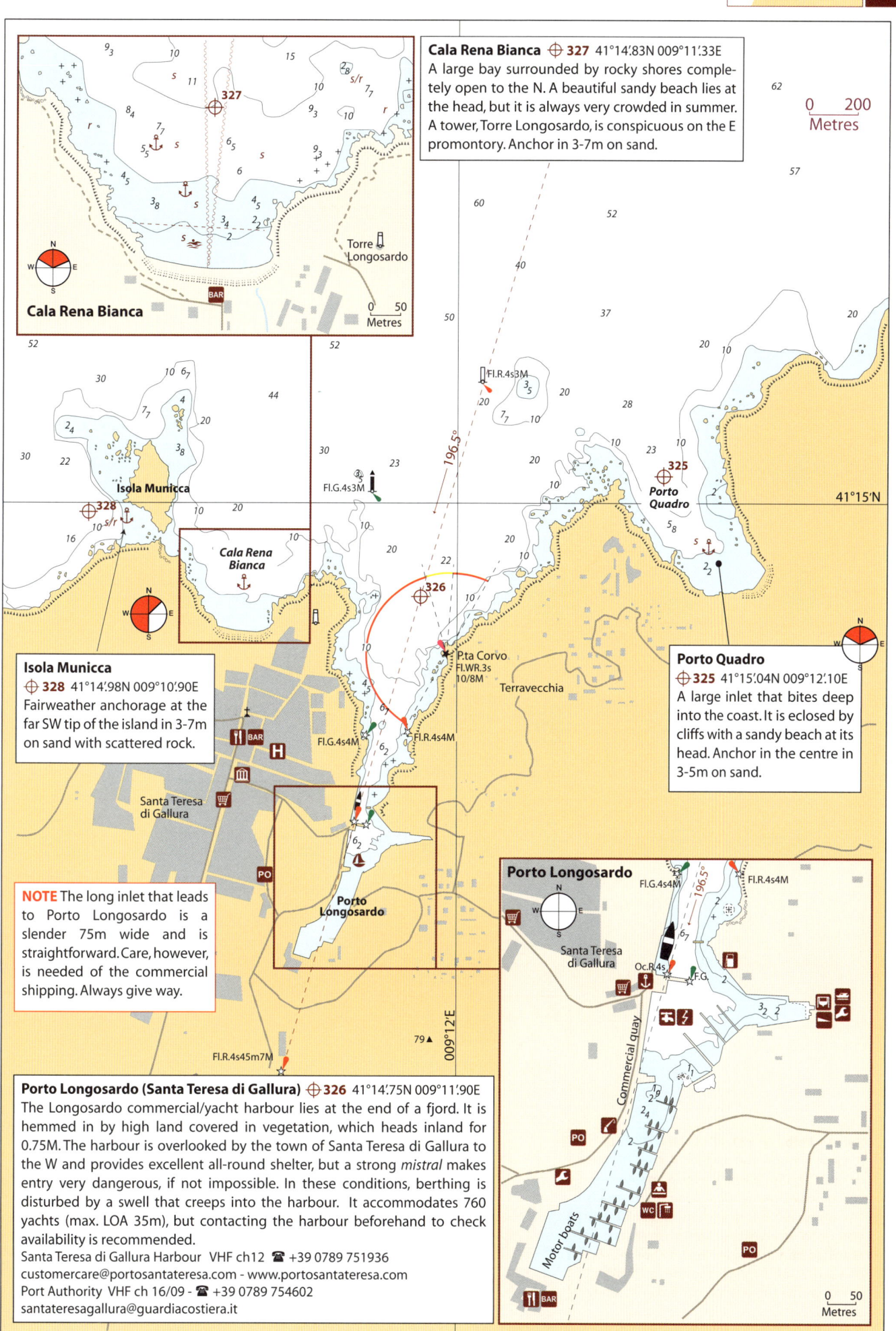

AREA E — CAPO TESTA

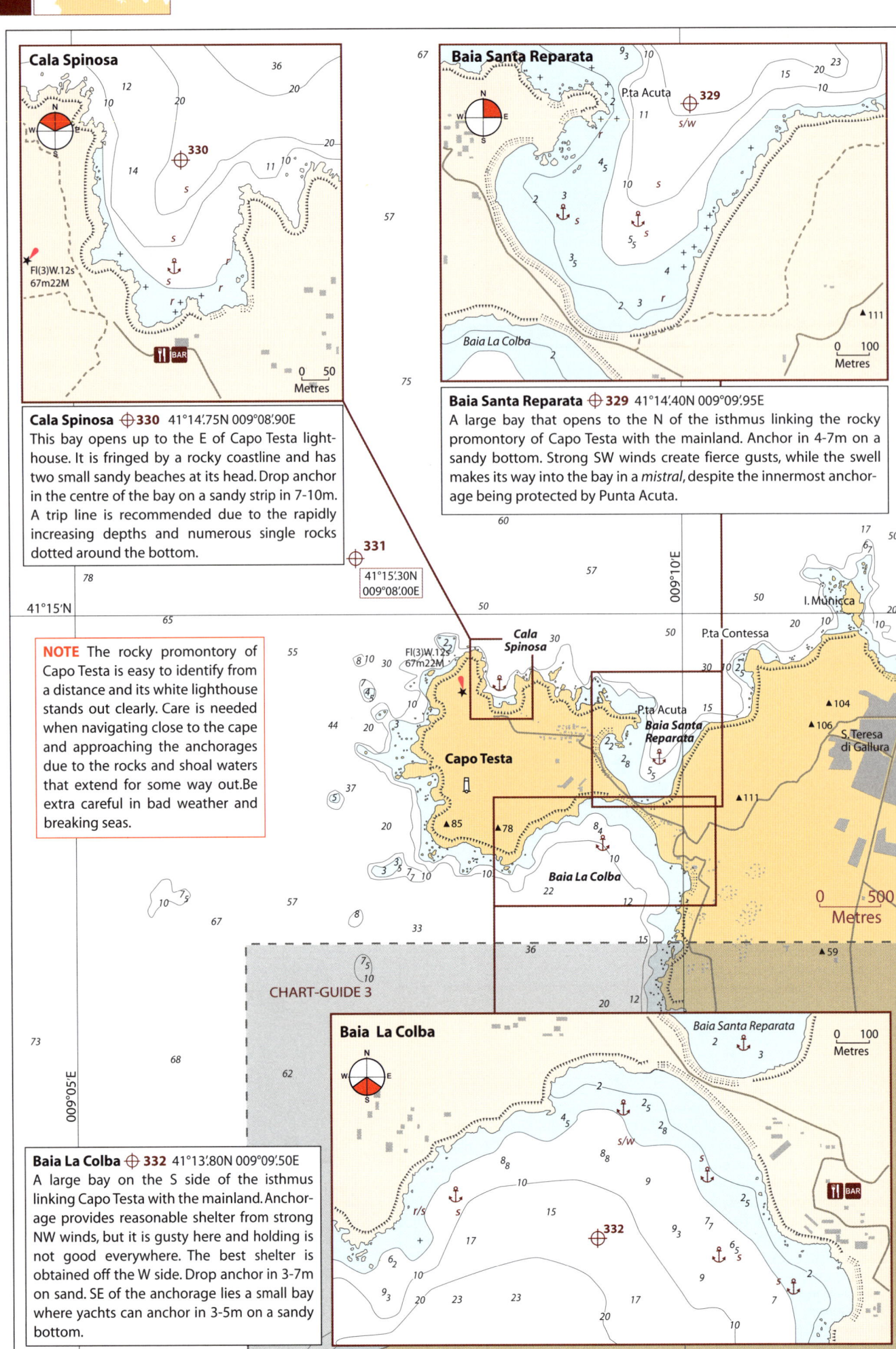

Cala Spinosa ⊕ 330 41°14'.75N 009°08'.90E
This bay opens up to the E of Capo Testa lighthouse. It is fringed by a rocky coastline and has two small sandy beaches at its head. Drop anchor in the centre of the bay on a sandy strip in 7-10m. A trip line is recommended due to the rapidly increasing depths and numerous single rocks dotted around the bottom.

Baia Santa Reparata ⊕ 329 41°14'.40N 009°09'.95E
A large bay that opens to the N of the isthmus linking the rocky promontory of Capo Testa with the mainland. Anchor in 4-7m on a sandy bottom. Strong SW winds create fierce gusts, while the swell makes its way into the bay in a *mistral*, despite the innermost anchorage being protected by Punta Acuta.

NOTE The rocky promontory of Capo Testa is easy to identify from a distance and its white lighthouse stands out clearly. Care is needed when navigating close to the cape and approaching the anchorages due to the rocks and shoal waters that extend for some way out. Be extra careful in bad weather and breaking seas.

⊕ 331 41°15'.30N 009°08'.00E

Baia La Colba ⊕ 332 41°13'.80N 009°09'.50E
A large bay on the S side of the isthmus linking Capo Testa with the mainland. Anchorage provides reasonable shelter from strong NW winds, but it is gusty here and holding is not good everywhere. The best shelter is obtained off the W side. Drop anchor in 3-7m on sand. SE of the anchorage lies a small bay where yachts can anchor in 3-5m on a sandy bottom.

LA MADDALENA NATIONAL PARK — AREA E

CHART 95

La Maddalena National Park
Zone **TA** *Riserva integrale* (Fully protected reserve) Areas of major natural importance with limited or no human interference.
Zone **TB** *Riserva generale* (General reserve) Land of major natural or historical importance, outstanding beauty, or with a higher level of human interference.
Zone **TC** *Riserva parziale* (Partial reserve) Land with a high level of human interference.

La Maddalena National Park (AMP)
Zone **MA** *Zona marina di riserva integrale* (Fully protected marine reserve) All activity not covered by its regulations is prohibited. When MA zones are not covered by the Reserve Plan and its regulations, unauthorised navigation, entry and stopovers are prohibited unless for rescues or scientific research. Small mooring buoys may be set up throughout the area on the prior authorisation of the reserve authority. Reserve regulations apply.
Zone **MB** *Riserva generale* (General Reserve) (within/beyond 300m of the coast) After yachts have bought an entrance ticket, they may navigate freely, moor at the reserve's buoys, and anchor in sand and mud only. Note that anchorage is prohibited in particularly sensitive areas designated by the authority. From 1/6 to 30/10, anchorage is permitted from dawn to dusk only; from 1/6 to 30/10, mooring is allowed from dawn to dusk only unless you are equipped with a holding tank. A speed limit of 7 knots applies in the strip of sea within 300m from the coast. A 15-knot limit is in force beyond that. Jet-skiing and water-skiing are allowed 300m or more from the coast. Fishing is regulated.
Zone **PIP** *Immersione protetta* (Protected dive sites) Navigation, stopping, mooring, fishing and free-diving are prohibited.

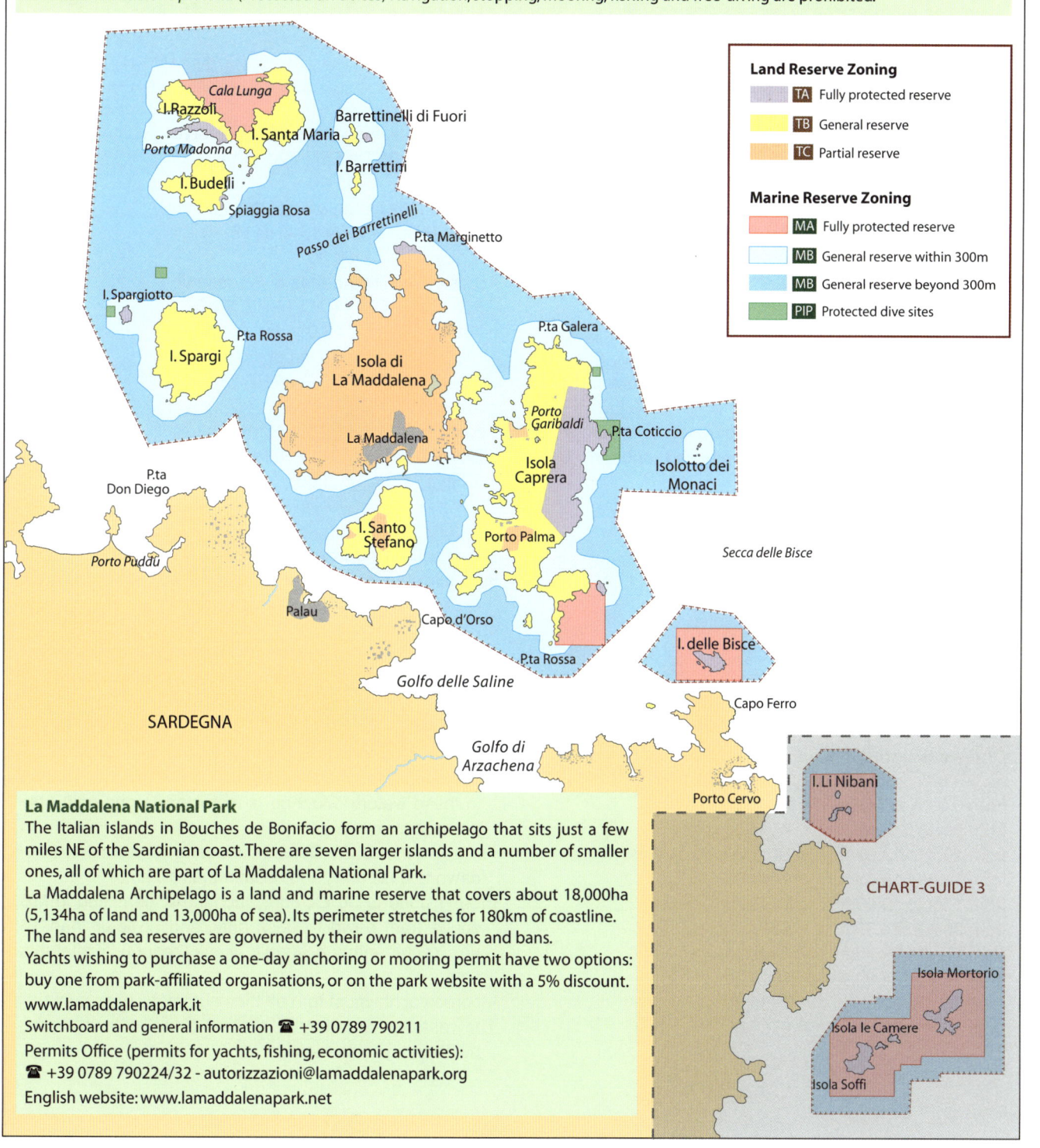

Land Reserve Zoning
- **TA** Fully protected reserve
- **TB** General reserve
- **TC** Partial reserve

Marine Reserve Zoning
- **MA** Fully protected reserve
- **MB** General reserve within 300m
- **MB** General reserve beyond 300m
- **PIP** Protected dive sites

La Maddalena National Park
The Italian islands in Bouches de Bonifacio form an archipelago that sits just a few miles NE of the Sardinian coast. There are seven larger islands and a number of smaller ones, all of which are part of La Maddalena National Park.
La Maddalena Archipelago is a land and marine reserve that covers about 18,000ha (5,134ha of land and 13,000ha of sea). Its perimeter stretches for 180km of coastline. The land and sea reserves are governed by their own regulations and bans.
Yachts wishing to purchase a one-day anchoring or mooring permit have two options: buy one from park-affiliated organisations, or on the park website with a 5% discount.
www.lamaddalenapark.it
Switchboard and general information ☎ +39 0789 790211
Permits Office (permits for yachts, fishing, economic activities):
☎ +39 0789 790224/32 - autorizzazioni@lamaddalenapark.org
English website: www.lamaddalenapark.net

CHART-GUIDE 3

133

LA MADDALENA NATIONAL PARK - EXCERPT FROM REGULATIONS

Note This is a vast a marine reserve and frequent changes are made to the regulations governing both the land and sea areas. It is therefore crucial that visitors check information with the authorities as soon as they arrive, or visit the reserve website (see contacts on the next page).

PERMITS

Pleasure yachting, sport fishing, diving and money-making sea activities require a permit. Two types of permit are available: "free" and "for a charge".

PERMITS ARE FREE FOR: fishing, pleasure yachting (residents and the equivalent) and diving with breathing apparatus (residents only).

A CHARGE APPLIES TO PERMITS FOR: pleasure yachting (non-residents), money-making activities, and diving with breathing aparatus (non-residents).

NB: yachts which do not have a permit before they enter the marine reserve will be in breach of reserve regulations. Anyone unable to provide reserve staff with a valid permit will be required to purchase one on-the-spot with a 40% surcharge. It is therefore strongly advisable to obtain a permit in advance (see above).

Permits for pleasure-cruising and diving can be purchased as follows:

- Payment online by CREDIT CARD.
- At AFFILIATED ORGANISATIONS (e.g. harbours and agencies) in the municipalities of La Maddalena, Palau, Arzachena and Santa Teresa Gallura. A list is available at www.lamaddalenapark.it/ente-parco/rilascio-permessi
- One-day permits can be purchased onboard from authorized park staff.

2019 PRICE LIST

One-day permit fee
from 0m to 10.00m	€2.00
from 10.01m to 24m	€3.00
from 24.01m to 35m	€4.50
from 35.01m to 200m	€5.00

One-week permit fee
from 0m to 6m	€34.00
from 6.01m to 7.99m	€39.00
from 8m to 9.99m	€50.00
from 10m to 13.99m	€101.00
from 14m to 16.99m	€144.00
from 17m to 19.99m	€173.00
from 20m to 24.99m	€211.00
from 25m to 29.99m	€437.00
from 30m to 34.99m	€518.00
from 35m to 39.99m	€666.00
from 40m to 200m	€760.00

15 days fee
from 0m to 6m	€58.00
from 6.01m to 7.99m	€67.00
from 8m to 9.99m	€86.00
from 10m to 13.99m	€173.00
from 14m to 16.99m	€252.00
from 17m to 19.99m	€302.00
from 20m to 24.99m	€370.00
from 25m to 29.99m	€778.00
from 30m to 34.99m	€922.00
from 35m to 39.99m	€1184.00
from 40m to 200m	€1440.00

SCUBA DIVING

Individual diving permit: One-day fee	€5.00
Individual diving permit: solar year fee	€75.00

PERMITS

Access to the inland area of the reserve
CHILDREN BETWEEN 8 AND 14
7 days   €2.00

Access to the inland area of the reserve
PEOPLE BETWEEN 15 AND 65
7 days   €5.00

Access to the inland area of the reserve
GROUPS FROM 11 TO 15 PEOPLE
7 days   €45.00

Access to the inland area of the reserve
GROUPS FROM 16 TO 20 PEOPLE
7 days   €75.00

Access to the inland area of the reserve
GROUPS FROM 21 TO 25 PEOPLE
7 days   €95.00

DISCOUNTS

5% discount for online purchases
50% discount for residents in the municipalities of Palau, Arzachena and Santa Teresa Gallura
40% discount for sailing yachts
Pleasure yachting fees are to be paid between 1 May and 31 October.

MOORING

Mooring is prohibited in the MA zones except in designated mooring areas. NB: anchoring is prohibited in these waters. Mooring is restricted to one craft only per reserve buoy.

From 1 June to 30 October, mooring is permitted from dawn to dusk only, and no later than 10 pm.

From 1 June to 30 October, mooring is permitted in MB zones from dawn to dusk only, and no later than 10 pm. Yachts with a holding tank may moor until after this time.

Moored yachts must turn off their automatic bilge pumps.

The reserve authorithy is entitled to set a limit on the number of yachts moored.

LA MADDALENA NATIONAL PARK - EXCERPT FROM REGULATIONS

ANCHORAGE

Anchorage is prohibited in the MA zones.

Anchorage is permitted in the MB zones, but on the prior authorisation by the eserve authorithy only. Yachts must anchor on sand or mud only off the sea grass (*Prateria di Poseidonia oceanica*(, but not in the particularly sensitive areas. These areas are marked by reserve authority signs.

From 1 June to 30 October, anchorage is permitted from dusk to dawn only, and no later than 10 pm. This regulation does not apply to yachts with a holding tank that are owned by La Maddalena residents, who are allowed to remain after this time.

Anchored yachts must turn off their automatic bilge pumps.

The reserve authorities are entitled to set a limit on the number of yachts moored.

SPECIFIC BANS FOR SEA AREAS OUTSIDE THE MA ZONE

Isola Budelli - Spiaggia Rosa

In the part of Cala di Roto, marked "Spiaggia Rosa", in the sea area marked by the following coordinates:
A: (Lat.= 41°16'.4 N; Long.=009°21'.5 E)
B: (Lat.= 41°16'.7 N; Long.=009°21'.7 E)
C: (Lat.= 41°16'.8 N; Long.=009°21'.5 E)
D: (Lat.= 41°16'.7 N; Long.=009°21'.2 E),
The following are also prohibited in the State-owned area and in the sandy land between the beach and the path: navigation, stopovers, anchorage, swimming in the area between the beach and the round yellow buoys about 70m from it; walking on the sand is prohibited.

Isola Budelli - Porto Madonna

In the sea area between the islands of Budelli, Razzoli and Santa Maria, known locally as Porto Madonna, in the area marked by the following coordinates:
A: (Lat.= 41°17'.3 N; Long.=009°21'.4 E)
B: (Lat.= 41°17'.5 N; Long.=009°21'.6 E)
C: (Lat.= 41°17'.12 N; Long.=009°21'.6 E)
D: (Lat.= 41°17'.2 N; Long.=009°21'.8 E),
swimming and access under oar only are permitted. Yachts are allowed to navigate, stop and anchor in the rest of the bay, but are not permitted to approach it from Passo Cecca Morto, Passo del Topo and Passo degli Asinelli.

GENERAL GUIDELINES FOR SPORT FISHING

Sport fishing is prohibited in MA zones.

Sport fishing from a boat

Sport fishing aboard in MB zones is restricted to: people born and residing in La Maddalena and Palau municipalities, who must have a personal free-of-charge permit issued by the Park Authority (children under the age of 16 do not need permit). The Park Authority also issues free-of-charge fishing permits to: residential owners located in La Maddalena; workers or military officials with one-year assignment; berth owners in authorised harbours of La Maddalena municipality for a miminum period of 4 months.

Underwater sport fishing

Underwater sport fishing is prohibited in MA zones.

Underwater sport fishing in the MB zones is permitted to adult residents in La Maddalena who must have a personal and free-of-charge permit issued by the Park Authority. They are allowed to fish between 1 June and 30 September, from Friday to Sunday, including national holidays.

The removal of corals, crustaceans and shellfish (excluding cephalopods) is prohibited.

Fishing is prohibited in the protected dive sites (PIP).

Possession of underwater fishing equipment must be authorized by the Park Authority. The equipment must be kept disassembled in designated containers.

Scuba diving

Authorised societies, clubs and associations are allowed to go on accompanied scuba diving excursions for recreational purposes using designated tenders. Prior authorisation by the Park Authority is required.

Head Office

Via Giulio Cesare, 7 - 07024 La Maddalena (OT)

Switchboard and General Information: ☎ +39 0789 790211

Public Relations Office: ☎ +39 0789 790233

Permits Office (permits for yachts, fishing, economic activities): ☎ +39 0789 790224/32
autorizzazioni@lamaddalenapark.org

Records Office: ☎ +39 0789 790212
protocollo@lamaddalenapark.org

Pec: lamaddalenapark@pec.it
(receives certified emails only)

Website: www.lamaddalenapark.it

English website: www.lamaddalenapark.net

CHART 96 | AREA E | ARCIPELAGO DI LA MADDALENA

Cala Villamarina ⊕ 333
41°11.33'N 009°24.40'E
The only bay on the island open to yachts. Until a few years ago, it was home to a NATO base, so anchorage and landing are prohibited almost everywhere. Cala Villamarina provides excellent shelter from the prevailing winds. When approaching, care should be taken of the rocks and shoal water fringing the shores. Anchor in 5-10m on sand, or on sand and rock.

ISOLA SPARGI | AREA E | CHART 97

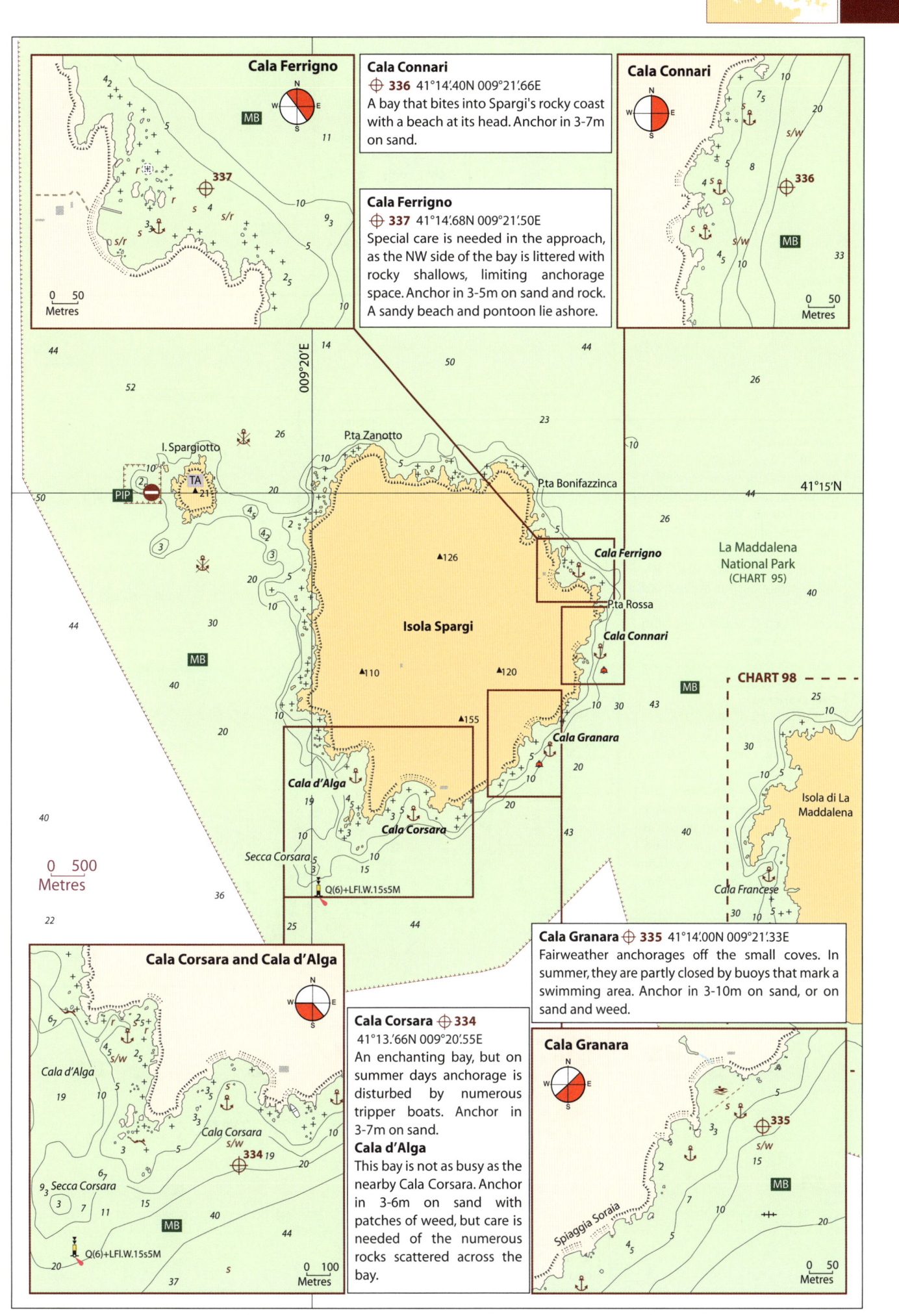

Cala Ferrigno

Cala Connari
⊕ **336** 41°14′.40N 009°21′.66E
A bay that bites into Spargi's rocky coast with a beach at its head. Anchor in 3-7m on sand.

Cala Connari

Cala Ferrigno
⊕ **337** 41°14′.68N 009°21′.50E
Special care is needed in the approach, as the NW side of the bay is littered with rocky shallows, limiting anchorage space. Anchor in 3-5m on sand and rock. A sandy beach and pontoon lie ashore.

La Maddalena National Park (CHART 95)

CHART 98

Cala Corsara and Cala d'Alga

Cala Corsara ⊕ 334
41°13′.66N 009°20′.55E
An enchanting bay, but on summer days anchorage is disturbed by numerous tripper boats. Anchor in 3-7m on sand.

Cala d'Alga
This bay is not as busy as the nearby Cala Corsara. Anchor in 3-6m on sand with patches of weed, but care is needed of the numerous rocks scattered across the bay.

Cala Granara ⊕ 335 41°14′.00N 009°21′.33E
Fairweather anchorages off the small coves. In summer, they are partly closed by buoys that mark a swimming area. Anchor in 3-10m on sand, or on sand and weed.

Cala Granara

137

CHART 98 — AREA E — ISOLA DI LA MADDALENA - WEST COAST

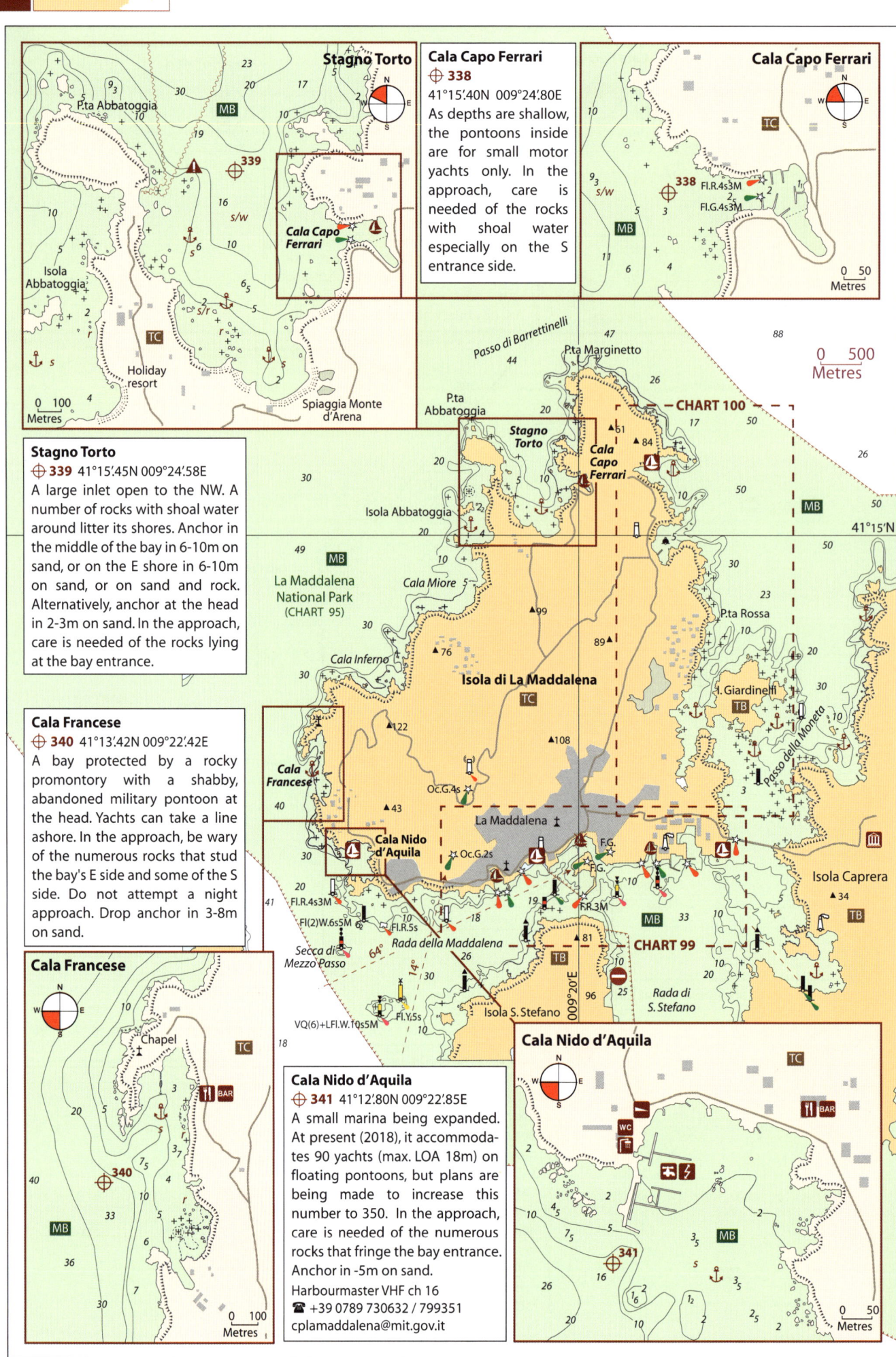

Stagno Torto
⊕ 339 41°15'.45N 009°24'.58E
A large inlet open to the NW. A number of rocks with shoal water around litter its shores. Anchor in the middle of the bay in 6-10m on sand, or on the E shore in 6-10m on sand, or on sand and rock. Alternatively, anchor at the head in 2-3m on sand. In the approach, care is needed of the rocks lying at the bay entrance.

Cala Capo Ferrari
⊕ 338 41°15'.40N 009°24'.80E
As depths are shallow, the pontoons inside are for small motor yachts only. In the approach, care is needed of the rocks with shoal water especially on the S entrance side.

Cala Francese
⊕ 340 41°13'.42N 009°22'.42E
A bay protected by a rocky promontory with a shabby, abandoned military pontoon at the head. Yachts can take a line ashore. In the approach, be wary of the numerous rocks that stud the bay's E side and some of the S side. Do not attempt a night approach. Drop anchor in 3-8m on sand.

Cala Nido d'Aquila
⊕ 341 41°12'.80N 009°22'.85E
A small marina being expanded. At present (2018), it accommodates 90 yachts (max. LOA 18m) on floating pontoons, but plans are being made to increase this number to 350. In the approach, care is needed of the numerous rocks that fringe the bay entrance. Anchor in -5m on sand.
Harbourmaster VHF ch 16
☎ +39 0789 730632 / 799351
cplamaddalena@mit.gov.it

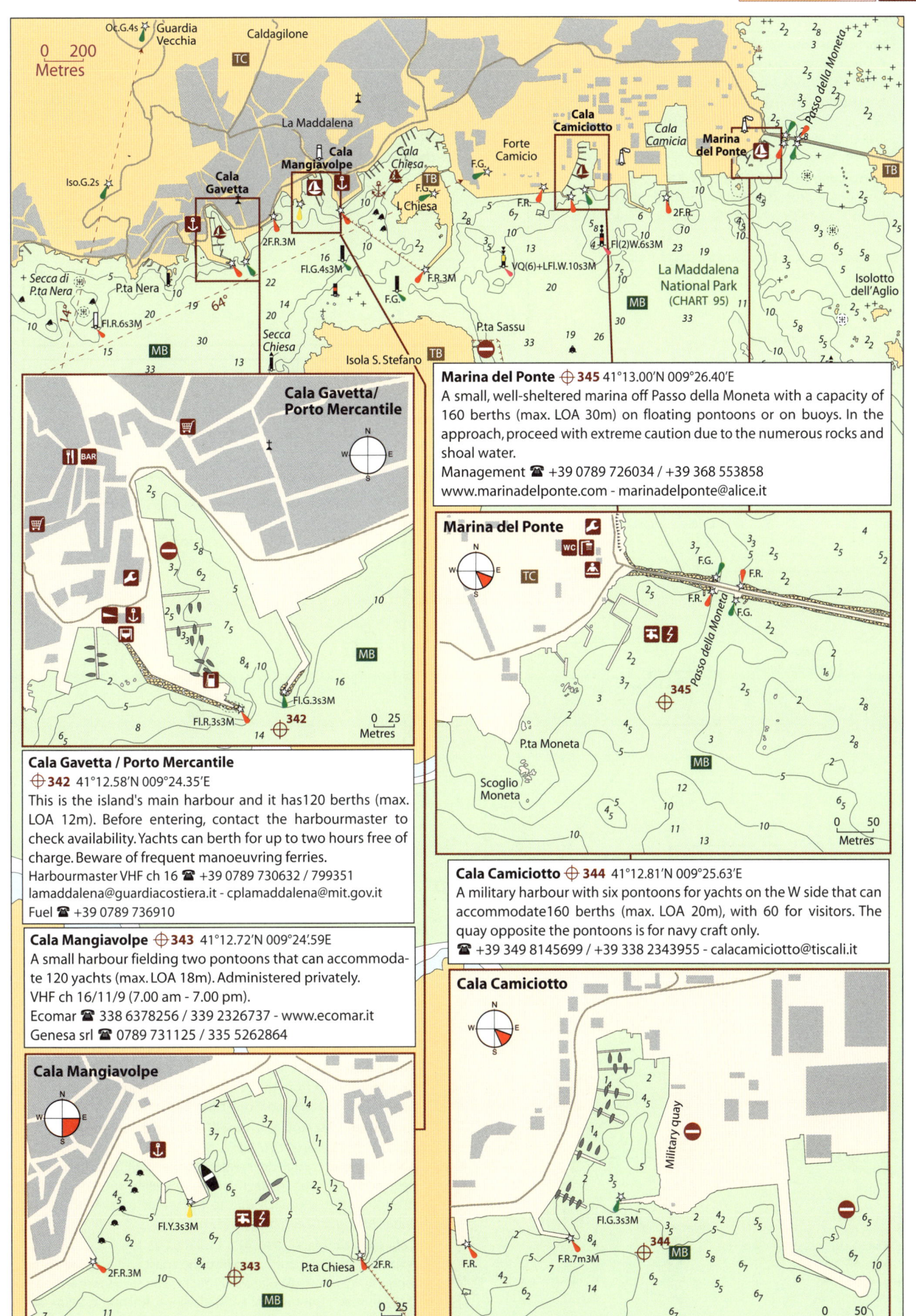

ISOLA DI LA MADDALENA - SOUTH COAST | AREA E

CHART 99

Cala Gavetta / Porto Mercantile
⊕ **342** 41°12.58'N 009°24.35'E
This is the island's main harbour and it has 120 berths (max. LOA 12m). Before entering, contact the harbourmaster to check availability. Yachts can berth for up to two hours free of charge. Beware of frequent manoeuvring ferries.
Harbourmaster VHF ch 16 ☎ +39 0789 730632 / 799351
lamaddalena@guardiacostiera.it - cplamaddalena@mit.gov.it
Fuel ☎ +39 0789 736910

Cala Mangiavolpe ⊕ 343 41°12.72'N 009°24'.59E
A small harbour fielding two pontoons that can accommodate 120 yachts (max. LOA 18m). Administered privately.
VHF ch 16/11/9 (7.00 am - 7.00 pm).
Ecomar ☎ 338 6378256 / 339 2326737 - www.ecomar.it
Genesa srl ☎ 0789 731125 / 335 5262864

Marina del Ponte ⊕ 345 41°13.00'N 009°26.40'E
A small, well-sheltered marina off Passo della Moneta with a capacity of 160 berths (max. LOA 30m) on floating pontoons or on buoys. In the approach, proceed with extreme caution due to the numerous rocks and shoal water.
Management ☎ +39 0789 726034 / +39 368 553858
www.marinadelponte.com - marinadelponte@alice.it

Cala Camiciotto ⊕ 344 41°12.81'N 009°25.63'E
A military harbour with six pontoons for yachts on the W side that can accommodate 160 berths (max. LOA 20m), with 60 for visitors. The quay opposite the pontoons is for navy craft only.
☎ +39 349 8145699 / +39 338 2343955 - calacamiciotto@tiscali.it

139

AREA E — ISOLA DI LA MADDALENA - EAST COAST

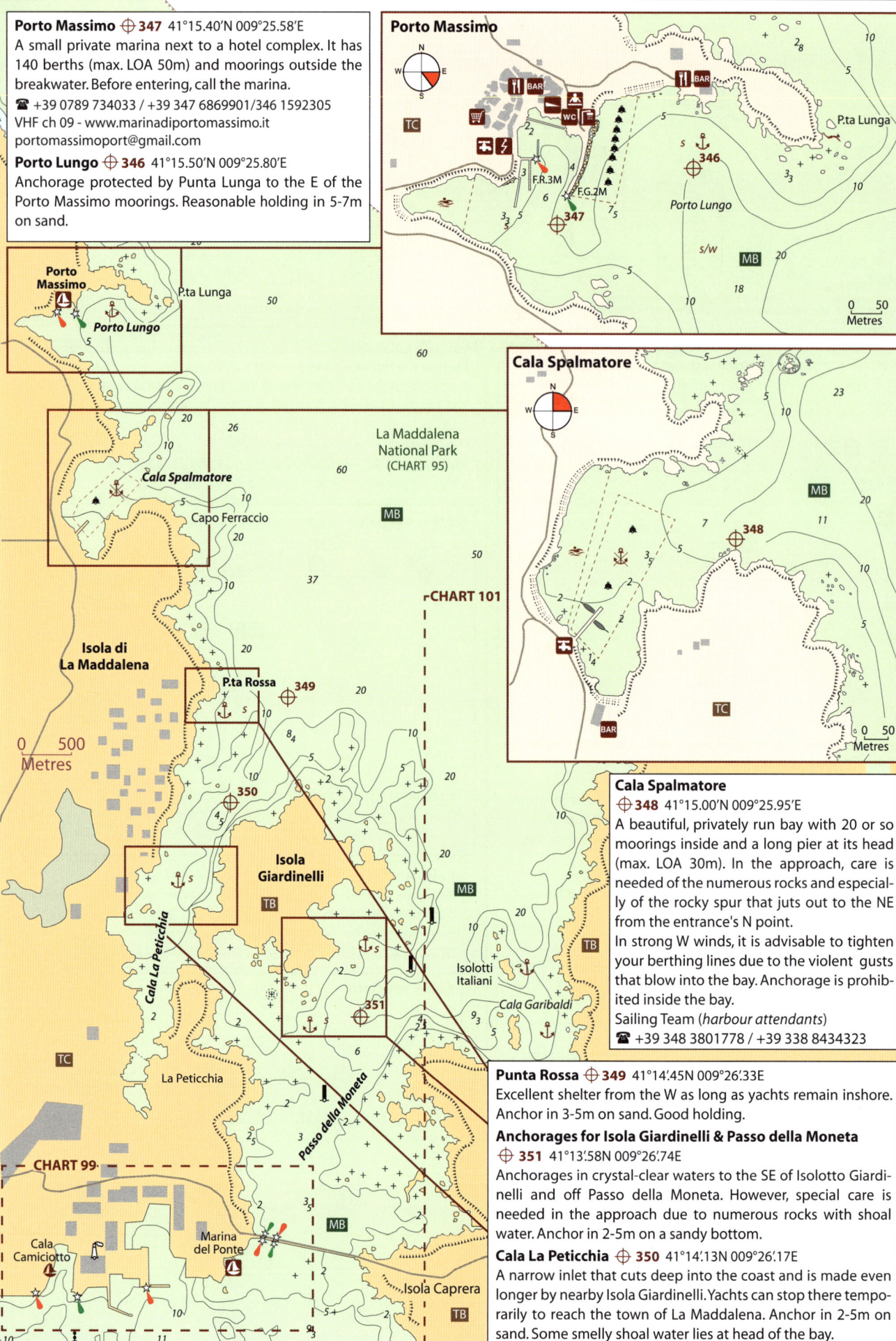

CHART 100

Porto Massimo ⊕ 347 41°15.40'N 009°25.58'E
A small private marina next to a hotel complex. It has 140 berths (max. LOA 50m) and moorings outside the breakwater. Before entering, call the marina.
☎ +39 0789 734033 / +39 347 6869901/346 1592305
VHF ch 09 - www.marinadiportomassimo.it
portomassimoport@gmail.com

Porto Lungo ⊕ 346 41°15.50'N 009°25.80'E
Anchorage protected by Punta Lunga to the E of the Porto Massimo moorings. Reasonable holding in 5-7m on sand.

Cala Spalmatore
⊕ 348 41°15.00'N 009°25.95'E
A beautiful, privately run bay with 20 or so moorings inside and a long pier at its head (max. LOA 30m). In the approach, care is needed of the numerous rocks and especially of the rocky spur that juts out to the NE from the entrance's N point.
In strong W winds, it is advisable to tighten your berthing lines due to the violent gusts that blow into the bay. Anchorage is prohibited inside the bay.
Sailing Team (*harbour attendants*)
☎ +39 348 3801778 / +39 338 8434323

Punta Rossa ⊕ 349 41°14.45N 009°26.33E
Excellent shelter from the W as long as yachts remain inshore. Anchor in 3-5m on sand. Good holding.

Anchorages for Isola Giardinelli & Passo della Moneta
⊕ 351 41°13.58N 009°26.74E
Anchorages in crystal-clear waters to the SE of Isolotto Giardinelli and off Passo della Moneta. However, special care is needed in the approach due to numerous rocks with shoal water. Anchor in 2-5m on a sandy bottom.

Cala La Peticchia ⊕ 350 41°14.13N 009°26.17E
A narrow inlet that cuts deep into the coast and is made even longer by nearby Isola Giardinelli. Yachts can stop there temporarily to reach the town of La Maddalena. Anchor in 2-5m on sand. Some smelly shoal water lies at head of the bay.

ISOLA CAPRERA | AREA E

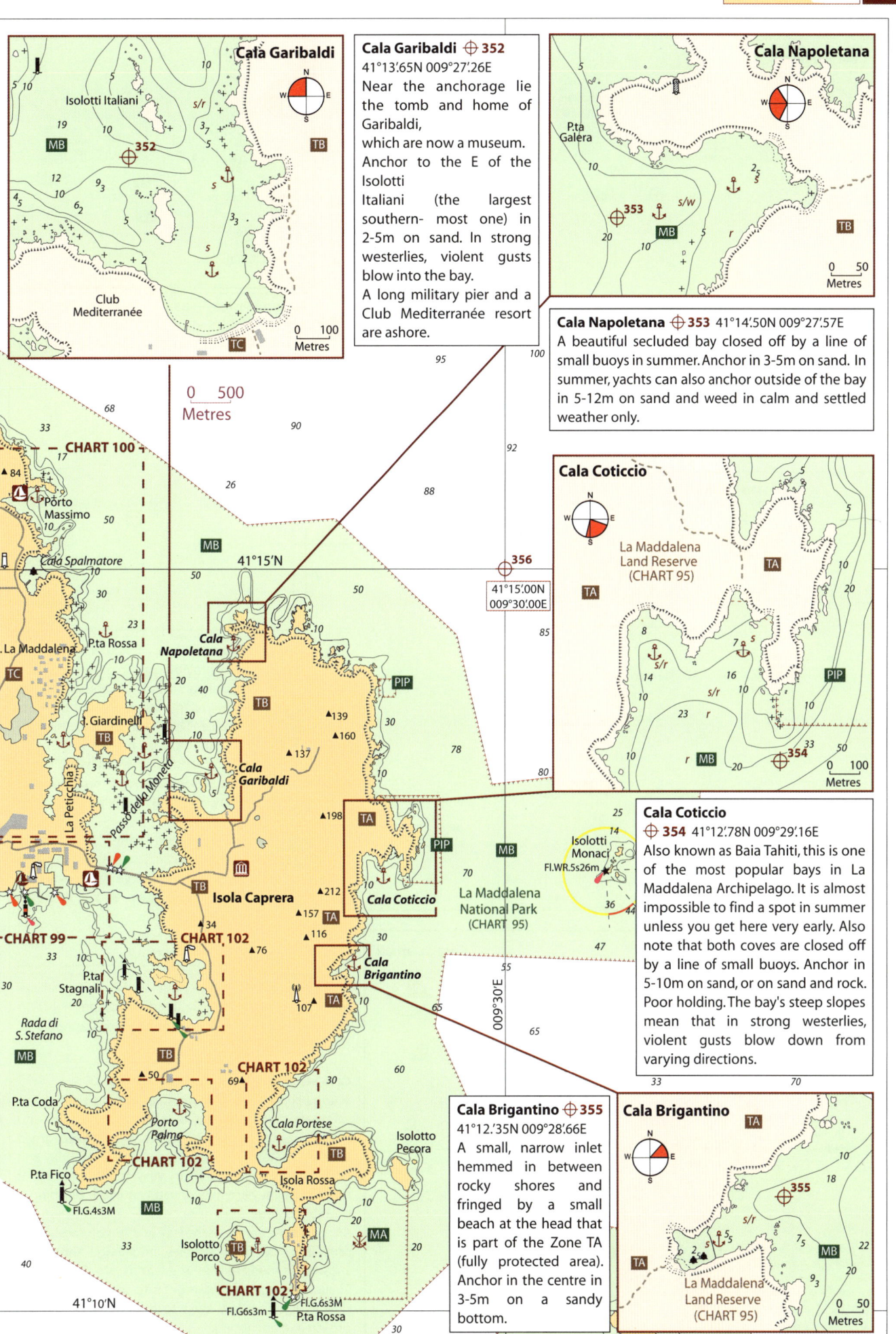

CHART 101

Cala Garibaldi ⊕ 352
41°13´.65N 009°27´.26E
Near the anchorage lie the tomb and home of Garibaldi, which are now a museum. Anchor to the E of the Isolotti Italiani (the largest southern-most one) in 2-5m on sand. In strong westerlies, violent gusts blow into the bay.
A long military pier and a Club Méditerranée resort are ashore.

Cala Napoletana ⊕ 353 41°14´.50N 009°27´.57E
A beautiful secluded bay closed off by a line of small buoys in summer. Anchor in 3-5m on sand. In summer, yachts can also anchor outside of the bay in 5-12m on sand and weed in calm and settled weather only.

Cala Coticcio
⊕ 354 41°12´.78N 009°29´.16E
Also known as Baia Tahiti, this is one of the most popular bays in La Maddalena Archipelago. It is almost impossible to find a spot in summer unless you get here very early. Also note that both coves are closed off by a line of small buoys. Anchor in 5-10m on sand, or on sand and rock. Poor holding. The bay's steep slopes mean that in strong westerlies, violent gusts blow down from varying directions.

Cala Brigantino ⊕ 355
41°12´.35N 009°28´.66E
A small, narrow inlet hemmed in between rocky shores and fringed by a small beach at the head that is part of the Zone TA (fully protected area). Anchor in the centre in 3-5m on a sandy bottom.

141

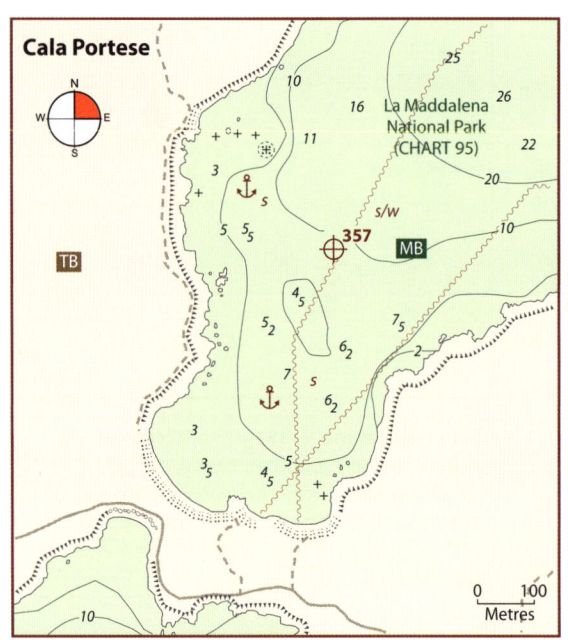

AREA E | ISOLA CAPRERA

CHART 102

Cala Portese ⊕ 357
41°11'.23N 009°28'.05E
A large bay that bites deep into the coast. It is enclosed between rocky shores, with a sandy beach at its head. Anchor in 3-7m on sand. Good holding. In summer, park moorings are laid in the centre, but there is still ample anchorage. The bay affords good protection from strong westerlies, especially close inshore on the NW side where you should be safe from the violent gusts into the bay.

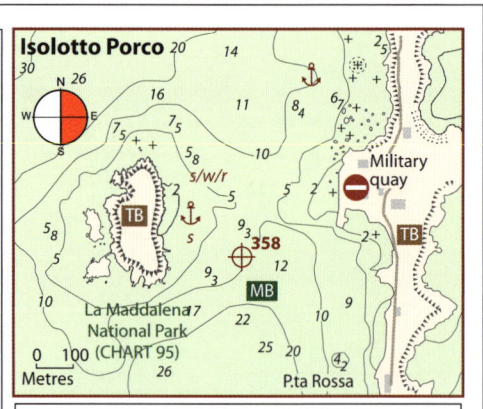

Isolotto Porco ⊕ 358 41°10'.42N 009°27'.80E
Anchor in settled weather only to the E of Isolotto Porco in 2-5m on sand, or on a bottom of sand and rock and weed.

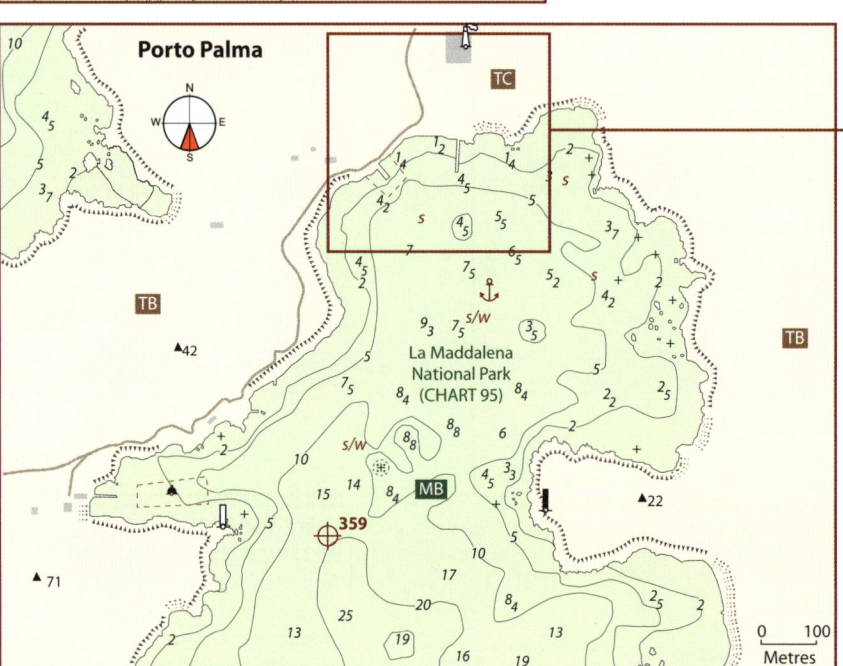

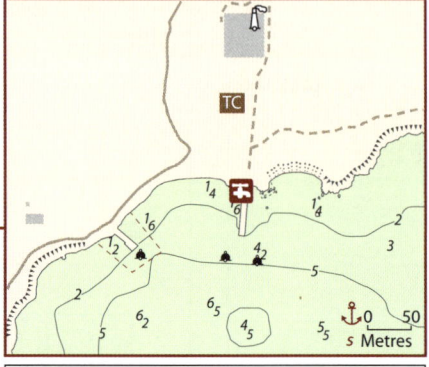

Porto Palma ⊕ 359 41°11'.02N 009°27'.00E
A large bay providing good protection from the prevailing winds. Approach with caution due to the two reefs that obstruct the entrance. They are marked by two pyramid-shaped pillars. Anchor in 3-7m on sand, or on sand and weed with better holding. In a strong *mistral*, strong gusts get into the bay, so it is advisable to seek shelter on the W side.
The bay is the headquarters of the Caprera Sailing School, so care is needed in this area from May to September when regattas are held. Inside the bay are a pier and two mooring buoys.
www.centrovelicocaprera.it
info@centrovelicocaprera.it

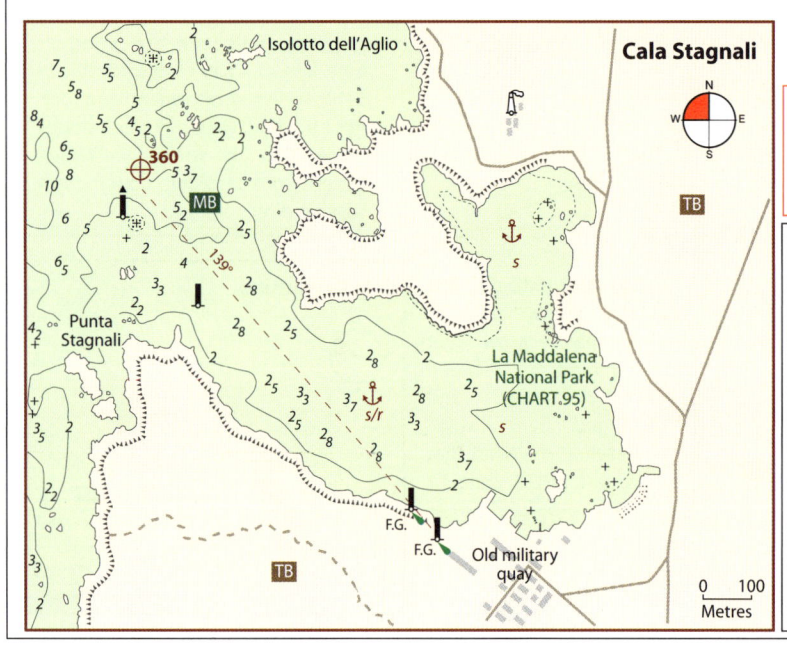

NOTE Cala Portese, Porto Palma and Cala Stagnali are a 45-minute walk from Garibaldi's museum home. In summer, a shuttle service is run between Caprera and the island of La Maddalena.

Cala Stagnali ⊕ 360 41°12'.34N 009°26'.60E
A large shallow, rock-bound inlet with low cliffs. The safest approach is marked by a buoy on the S side and by two leading marks (beacons with a fixed green light). At its head, on the SW side, there are a quay and two concrete piers for military vessels, although recent reports say they are now privately owned. Berthing is prohibited here.
Anchor in the centre of the bay in 2-4m on sand, or on sand and rock. In westerlies, anchorage should be vacated immediately as the winds are fierce here. Shallow-draught craft can get into the cove on the N side, as long as they keep to the centre during approach and anchoring.

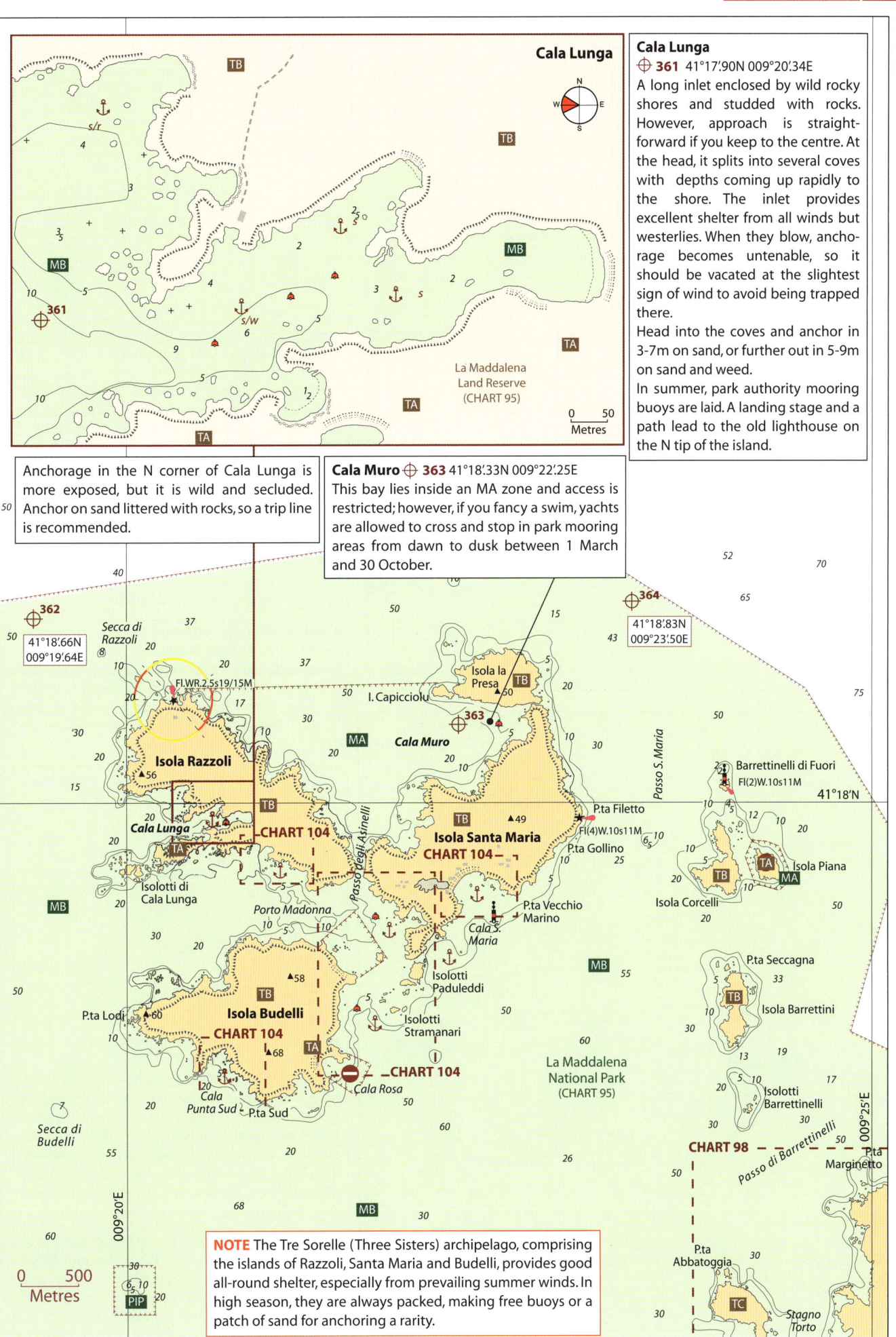

ISOLE RAZZOLI, SANTA MARIA AND BUDELLI — AREA E — CHART 103

Cala Lunga
⊕ **361** 41°17'.90N 009°20'.34E

A long inlet enclosed by wild rocky shores and studded with rocks. However, approach is straightforward if you keep to the centre. At the head, it splits into several coves with depths coming up rapidly to the shore. The inlet provides excellent shelter from all winds but westerlies. When they blow, anchorage becomes untenable, so it should be vacated at the slightest sign of wind to avoid being trapped there.

Head into the coves and anchor in 3-7m on sand, or further out in 5-9m on sand and weed.

In summer, park authority mooring buoys are laid. A landing stage and a path lead to the old lighthouse on the N tip of the island.

Anchorage in the N corner of Cala Lunga is more exposed, but it is wild and secluded. Anchor on sand littered with rocks, so a trip line is recommended.

Cala Muro
⊕ **363** 41°18'.33N 009°22'.25E

This bay lies inside an MA zone and access is restricted; however, if you fancy a swim, yachts are allowed to cross and stop in park mooring areas from dawn to dusk between 1 March and 30 October.

362 41°18'.66N 009°19'.64E

364 41°18'.83N 009°23'.50E

NOTE The Tre Sorelle (Three Sisters) archipelago, comprising the islands of Razzoli, Santa Maria and Budelli, provides good all-round shelter, especially from prevailing summer winds. In high season, they are always packed, making free buoys or a patch of sand for anchoring a rarity.

CHART 104 — AREA E — ISOLE RAZZOLI, SANTA MARIA AND BUDELLI

NOTE Although the Tre Sorelle (Three Sisters) archipelago offers all-round protection, don't get stuck here in bad weather, especially in westerly summer gales. Remember that a W wind funnelled into Bouches de Bonifacio grows increasingly stronger until it reaches full power around La Maddalena archipelago.

Isola Razzoli - South anchorages
⊕ **368** 41°17'.66N 009°20'.85E

At first glance, the S coast of Razzoli is inhospitable and open to the wind, yet it provides a number of anchorages. The coast, however, is peppered with rocks and shoal water, so extreme caution is needed when approaching. Anchor in 4-10m on sand, or on sand and rock.

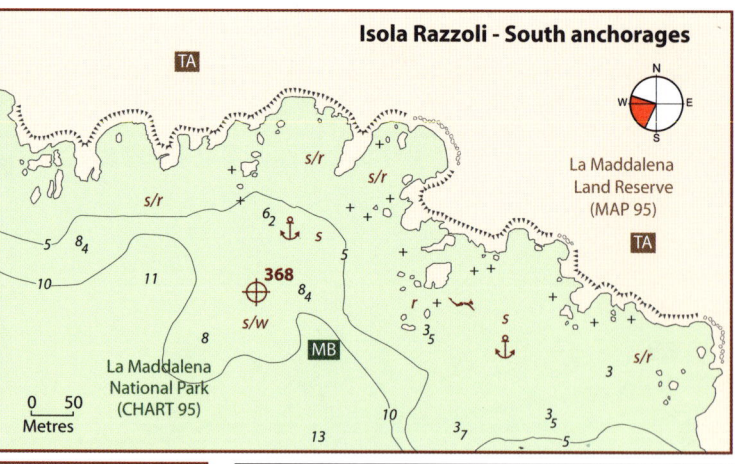

Isola Santa Maria - Cala Santa Maria
⊕ **365** 41°17'.48N 009°22'.65E

A breathtaking semi-circular gulf SE of Isola Santa Maria with a sandy beach at its head. When approaching care is needed of the two reefs lying SW of the entrance, which should be kept to the left. Anchor in 3-6m on a sandy bottom. The bay fields some moorings, including a couple occupied by tripper boats. Consequently, they can only be used at night. In summer, the bay is always packed with yachts and local boats touring the islands, so anchorage may be disturbed and noisy during the day. Come late afternoon, however, the bay empties, making it an excellent sheltered place to spend the night.

Isola Budelli - Cala Punta Sud
⊕ **367** 41°16'.60N 009°20'.61E

A wild, secluded cove overlooked by a sheer cliff and with a pebble-and-stone beach at its head. Anchor in 4-7m on a central patch of sand. A trip line is recommended. Beware of the reefs off the E side of the cove.

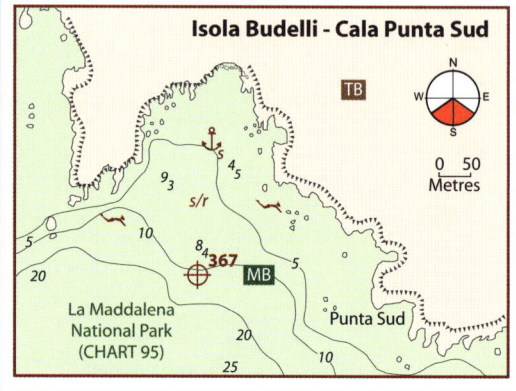

Porto Madonna / Golfo Giorgio Marino
⊕ **369** 41°17'.50N 009°21'.25E

An anchorage protected by three islands off the W side of Isola S. Maria. Yachts drawing less than 0.80m can also approach from the S via Passo Cecca di Morto. Alternatively, approach from the W and use the passage between Isola Razzoli and Isola Budelli. In summer, the reserve authority sets up some red mooring buoys. Anchorage is prohibited inside the mooring-buoy areas. Anchor in 3-5m on sand.

Passo Cecca di Morto
⊕ **366** 41°16'.85N 009°21'.73E

Between Spiaggia Rosa and Passo Cecca di Morto lies another anchorage that is partly occupied by a large field of moorings which is laid in summer by the reserve authority. Anchor in 5-10m on sand.

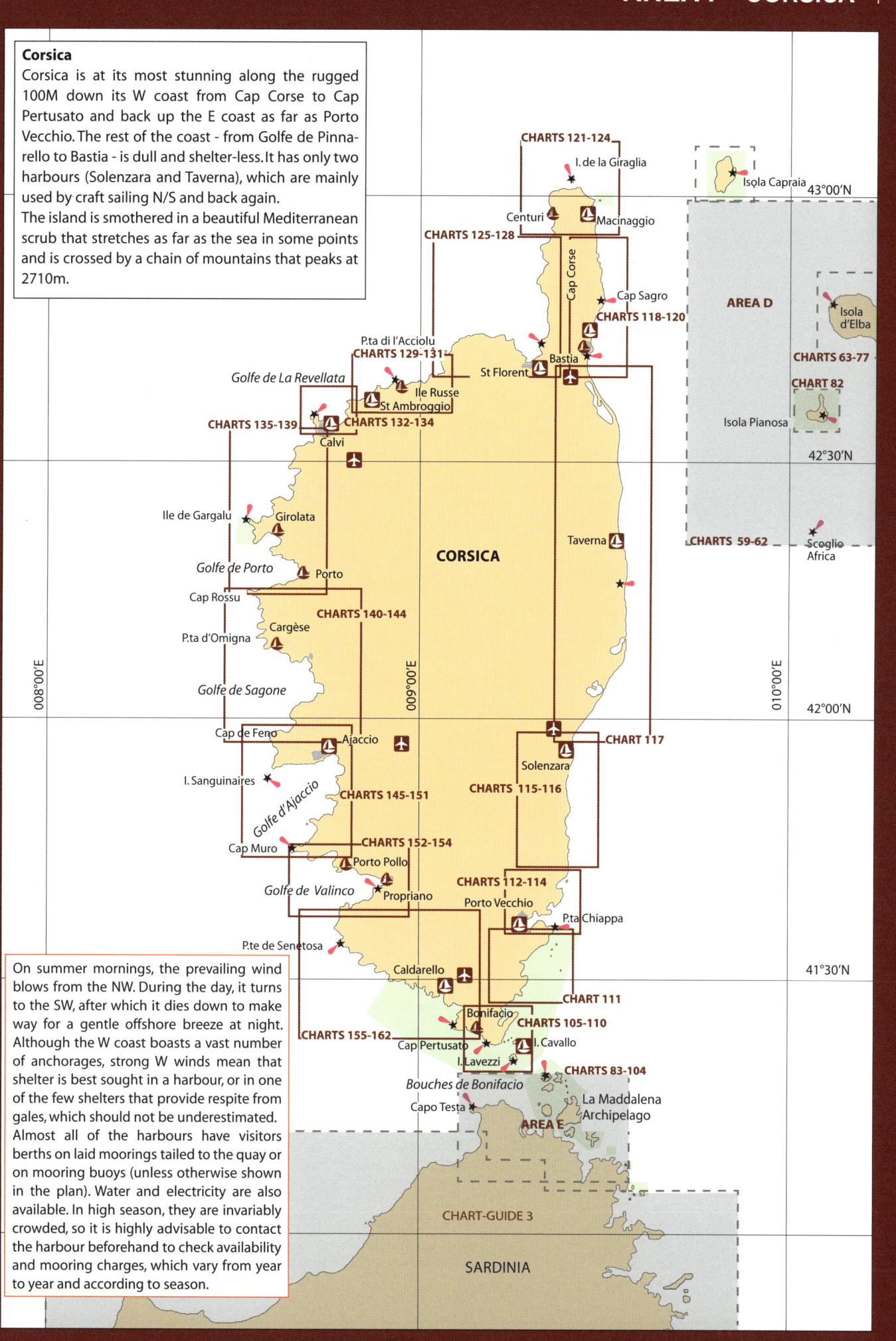

AREA F - CORSICA

Corsica

Corsica is at its most stunning along the rugged 100M down its W coast from Cap Corse to Cap Pertusato and back up the E coast as far as Porto Vecchio. The rest of the coast - from Golfe de Pinnarello to Bastia - is dull and shelter-less. It has only two harbours (Solenzara and Taverna), which are mainly used by craft sailing N/S and back again.

The island is smothered in a beautiful Mediterranean scrub that stretches as far as the sea in some points and is crossed by a chain of mountains that peaks at 2710m.

On summer mornings, the prevailing wind blows from the NW. During the day, it turns to the SW, after which it dies down to make way for a gentle offshore breeze at night. Although the W coast boasts a vast number of anchorages, strong W winds mean that shelter is best sought in a harbour, or in one of the few shelters that provide respite from gales, which should not be underestimated. Almost all of the harbours have visitors berths on laid moorings tailed to the quay or on mooring buoys (unless otherwise shown in the plan). Water and electricity are also available. In high season, they are invariably crowded, so it is highly advisable to contact the harbour beforehand to check availability and mooring charges, which vary from year to year and according to season.

Locations and Charts

- CHARTS 121-124 — I. de la Giraglia
- Isola Capraia — 43°00'N
- Centuri, Macinaggio
- CHARTS 125-128 — Cap Corse
- Cap Sagro
- CHARTS 118-120
- AREA D — Isola d'Elba
- CHARTS 63-77
- CHART 82
- Isola Pianosa — 42°30'N
- P.ta di l'Acciolu
- CHARTS 129-131
- Golfe de La Revellata
- Ile Rousse, St Ambroggio
- St Florent, Bastia
- CHARTS 132-134
- CHARTS 135-139 — Calvi
- Ile de Gargalu, Girolata
- Golfe de Porto — Porto
- Cap Rossu
- CORSICA
- Taverna
- CHARTS 59-62 — Scoglio Africa
- P.ta d'Omigna, Cargèse
- CHARTS 140-144
- Golfe de Sagone
- 008°00'E / 009°00'E / 010°00'E — 42°00'N
- Cap de Feno, Ajaccio
- CHART 117
- I. Sanguinaires
- Solenzara
- CHARTS 145-151
- CHARTS 115-116
- Golfe d'Ajaccio
- Cap Muro
- CHARTS 152-154 — Porto Pollo
- Golfe de Valinco — Propriano
- CHARTS 112-114 — Porto Vecchio, P.ta Chiappa
- P.te de Senetosa
- Caldarello
- 41°30'N
- CHART 111
- Bonifacio, CHARTS 105-110
- CHARTS 155-162 — Cap Pertusato, I. Cavallo
- I. Lavezzi — CHARTS 83-104
- Bouches de Bonifacio
- Capo Testa — AREA E — La Maddalena Archipelago
- CHART-GUIDE 3 — SARDINIA

145

AREA F - CORSICA

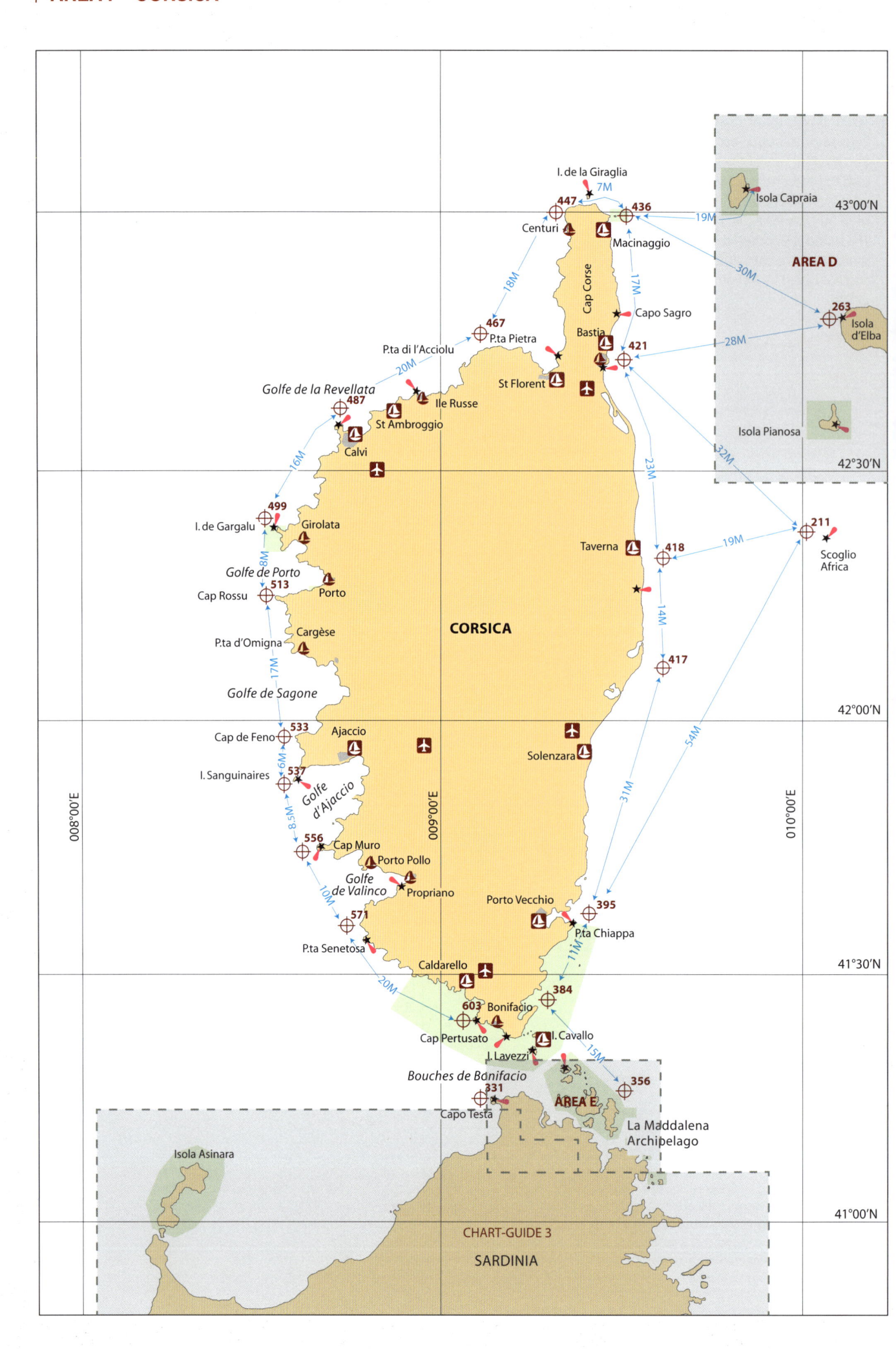

AREA F - CORSICA

COASTAL NAVIGATION WAYPOINTS AND DISTANCES

⊕	DESCRIPTION	WGS 84 COORDINATES LATITUDE	LONGITUDE	CHART
211	2M W of Scoglio Africa	42°21'.50N	010°01'.50E	117
263	I. d'Elba - 0.5M W of Punta Nera	42°46'.10N	010°05'.21E	75
331	I. Sardegna - 1M NW of Capo Testa	41°15'.30N	009°08'.00E	90
356	I. Caprera - 1M NE of Caprera	41°15'.00N	009°30'.00E	83
384	I. Corsica - 500m NE of Punta Capicciolu	41°25'.82N	009°16'.15E	106
395	I. Corsica - 0.5M NE of Punta di a Chiappa	41°36'.10N	009°22'.66E	112
417	I. Corsica - 2M off stagno di Diane	42°06'.00N	009°36'.00E	117
418	I. Corsica - 2M off Port de Taverna	42°20'.00N	009°36'.00E	117
421	I. Corsica - 0.5M off Bastia	42°42'.09N	009°27'.74E	117-118
436	I. Corsica - 300m NE of I. Finocchiarola	42°59'.00N	009°28'.64E	121
447	I. Corsica - 0.5M W of Punta di Corno di Becco	43°00'.00N	009°20'.00E	121-124
467	I. Corsica - 1M off Punta Pietra Alta	42°44'.83N	009°07'.47E	128
487	I. Corsica - 500m off P.te de la Revellata	42°35'.39N	008°43'.58E	132 134 135
499	I. Corsica - 500m W of Punta Palazzu	42°22'.82N	008°31'.70E	135-136-137
513	I. Corsica - 500m W of Cap Rossu	42°14'.23N	008°31'.86E	137-140
533	I. Corsica - 0.5M W of Cap de Feno	41°57'.67N	008°34'.93E	145
537	I. Corsica - 1M W of Grande Sanguinaire	41°52'.00N	008°34'.00E	145
556	I. Corsica - 0.5M W of Cap Muro	41°44'.33N	008°38'.91E	147-152
571	I. Corsica - 1000m off I. d'Eccica	41°35'.00N	008°45'.00E	152-154-155
603	I. Corsica - 1000m W of Cap de Feno	41°23'.16N	009°05'.00E	161-162

HARBOURS AND MARINAS KEY FOR PLAN SYMBOLS

⊕	NAME	WGS 84 COORDINATES LATITUDE	LONGITUDE	CHART	⛵	⚓	🅿	LOA m	V	🚽	m	⚡	🚻	WC	🛒	🛏	🔧	🔨
377	I. Cavallo/Port de Cavallo	41°21'.60N	009°15'.80E	109	•		230	30	•	•	3	•	•	•				
381	Port de Bonifacio	41°23'.10N	009°08'.75E	107		•	450	55	•	•	10	•	•	•	•	•	•	•
401	Port de Porto-Vecchio	41°35'.50N	009°17'.05E	113	•		540	40	•	•	3.5	•	•	•	•	•	•	•
416	Port de Solenzara	41°51'.34N	009°24'.18E	116	•		450	30	•	•	3	•	•	•	•	•	•	•
419	Port de Taverna	42°20'.50N	009°32'.55E	117	•		500	25	•	•	3	•	•	•	•	•	•	•
422	Bastia - Vieux Port	42°41'.67N	009°27'.22E	119		•	270	35	•	•	8.5	•	•	•	•			•
423	Bastia - Port de Toga	42°42'.60N	009°27'.35E	119	•		360	30	•	•	4.5	•	•	•	•	•	•	•
430	Marine de Luri	42°53'.23N	009°28'.51E	120		•	130	12	•	•	3	•	•		•			
433	Port de Macinaggio	42°57'.65N	009°27'.25E	121	•		585	40	•	•	3.5	•	•	•	•	•	•	•
442	Port de Barcaggio	43°00'.40N	009°24'.16E	123		•	IU				2				•			
449	Port de Centuri	42°58'.05N	009°20'.94E	124		•	60	10			3				•			
459	Port de St-Florent	42°40'.80N	009°17'.83E	127	•		800	40	•	•	5	•	•	•	•	•	•	•
473	L'Ile Rousse	42°38'.34N	008°56'.16E	130		•	215	12	•	•	2.5	•	•	•	•			
476	Port d'Algajola	42°36'.64N	008°51'.39E	131		•	IU											•
480	Marine de St Ambroggio	42°36'.16N	008°49'.75E	132	•		150	15	•	•	2.5	•	•	•	•	•	•	•
484	Port de Calvì	42°34'.00N	008°45'.60E	133	•		500	65	•	•	4	•	•	•	•			
510	Porto Marina	42°16'.00N	008°41'.41E	137		•	120	40	•	•	2				•			
523	Port de Cargèse	42°07'.85N	008°35'.86E	142	•		235	18	•	•	4	•	•	•	•	•		
543	Ajaccio/Port Tino Rossi	41°55'.17N	008°44'.66E	148		•	300	50	•	•	10	•	•	•	•			
544	Ajaccio/Port Charles Ornano	41°55'.80N	008°44'.82E	148	•		800	35	•	•	10	•	•	•	•	•	•	•
561	Port de Porto Pollo	41°42'.48N	008°47'.74E	152		•	IU	12	•		2				•			
565	Port de Propriano	41°40'.70N	008°54'.35E	153	•		500	70	•	•	6	•	•	•	•	•	•	•
578	Port de Tizzano	42°32'.51N	008°51'.00E	156		•	IU				1.5							
596	Port de Pianottoli - Caldarello	41°28'.44N	009°04'.33E	160	•		160	18	•		1.7	•	•	•	•			

IU= Information Unavailable

AREA F - CORSICA

ANCHORAGES KEY FOR PLAN SYMBOLS

⊕	NAME	WGS 84 COORDINATES LATITUDE	WGS 84 COORDINATES LONGITUDE	CHART	🗺	🐟	m	🚻	🍷	🧭	⚓	🔔
From Bonifacio to Bastia												
373	I. Lavezzi/Cala di Ghiuncu	41°20'.17N	009°15'.33E	108	G	s	4	•		S-SW	•	
374	I. Lavezzi/Cala Lazarina	41°20'.20N	009°15'.10E	108	G	s	3	•		S-SW	•	
375	I. Lavezzi/Cala della Chiesa	41°20'.80N	009°15'.15E	108	P	s	4	•		W-N	•	
376	I. Lavezzi/Cala di U Grecu	41°20'.57N	009°15'.58E	108	G	s	5	•		N-E	•	
378	I. Cavallo/Cala di u Ghiuncu	41°21'.98N	009°15'.24E	109	G	s	4			SE-W	•	
379	I. Cavallo/Cala di Zeri	41°22'.30N	009°16'.31E	109	G	s	5			N-E	•	
380	I. Cavallo/Cala di Palma	41°21'.77N	009°16'.25E	109	G	s	4			E-S	•	
382	Ile Piana	41°22'.50N	009°13'.58E	106	G	s	3	•		N-S	•	
383	Cala Longa	41°23'.66N	009°14'.41E	106	P	s	4	•		NE-SW	•	
386	Golfe de St Amanza	41°24'.50N	009°13'.24E	110	E	s/w	4	•	B-R	N-NE	•	
387	Cala di Stentinu	41°24'.75N	009°13'.32E	110	G	s	1.2	•			•	
388	Capu Biancu	41°25'.40N	009°13'.76E	110	G	s	4	•		N-E	•	
389	Anse de Balistra	41°26'.38N	009°13'.56E	110	G	s/w	5	•		NE-SE	•	
390	Golfe de Rondinara	41°28'.10N	009°16'.48E	111	E	s	5	•		NE-SE	•	
391	Golfe de Porto Novo	41°30'.15N	009°16'.68E	111	G	s	4	•		N-E	•	
392	Golfe de Santa Giulia	41°31'.51N	009°17'.08E	111	E	s	4	•	B-R	NE-SE	•	
393	Baie de Palombaggia	41°33'.17N	009°19'.73E	111	G	s	4	•	B-R	E-SW	•	
394	Anse de Carataggio	41°34'.48N	009°21'.05E	111	G	s	4	•		NE-S	•	
396	Marina d'Arje	41°35'.80N	009°20'.58E	112	G	s	4	•		N-E	•	
397	Marina Vizza	41°36'.25N	009°19'.75E	112	G	s	4	•		NW-NE	•	
399	Ilot Ziglione	41°35'.70N	009°18'.33E	113	G	s	4	•		NW-N	•	
402	Baie de Stagnolu	41°37'.00N	009°18'.67E	112	G	s	3	•			•	
403	Anse de Tramulimacchia	41°37'.05N	009°20'.14E	112	G	s	3	•		SE-SW	•	
404	Anse Punta San Cipriànu	41°37'.00N	009°21'.05E	112	G	s	4	•		S-SW	•	
405	Baie de San Cipriànu	41°37'.67N	009°21'.75E	114	E	s	5	•	B-R	E-S	•	
406	Punta Capicciola	41°38'.50N	009°22'.66E	114	G	s/w	4	•		E-S	•	
407	Golfe de Pinarellu	41°40'.73N	009°23'.42E	114	E	s/w	5	•	B-R-S	NE-SE	•	
408	Anse de Fautea (S)	41°42'.50N	009°24'.33E	115	G	s/w	5	•		E-/S	•	
409	Anse de Fautea (N)	41°43'.08N	009°24'.33E	115	G	s	4	•	B-R	NE-SE	•	
410	Anse de Tarcu	41°45'.00N	009°24'.33E	115	P	s	4	•	B-R	NE-SE	•	
411	Anse de Favone	41°46'.50N	009°24'.05E	115	G	s	4	•	B-R-S	N-E	•	
412	Anse de Tanone	41°47'.00N	009°24'.03E	115	P	s/w	4			NE-SE	•	
413	Anse de Cannella	41°47'.85N	009°23'.86E	116	P	s	4	•	B-R	NE-S	•	
414	Cala D'Oru	41°49'.48N	009°24'.35E	116	G	s	3	•		NE-SE	•	
415	Marine de Manichino	41°50'.42N	009°24'.24E	116	P	s	4	•		NE-S	•	
From Bastia to St-Florent												
424	Marine de La Vasina	42°45'.48N	009°28'.07E	118	P	s/g	5	•		N-S	•	
425	Marine de Erbalunga	42°46'.21N	009°28'.33E	118	G	s/g	4	•	B-R-S	N-SW	•	
427	Marine de Sisco	42°48'.59N	009°29'.65E	120	G	s	4	•	B-R-S	N-S	•	
428	Marine de Pietracorbara	42°50'.33N	009°29'.10E	120	G	s	4	•	B-R	NE-SE	•	
429	Marine de Porticciolo	42°52'.52N	009°28'.67E	120	G	s	5	•		NE-SE	•	
430	Marine de Luri	42°53'.23N	009°28'.51E	120	P	s/g	4	•	B-R	NE-SE	•	
431	Marine de Meria	42°55'.93N	009°28'.07E	120	P	s/g	4	•	B-R	NE-SE	•	
432	Baie de Macinaggio	42°57'.82N	009°27'.35E	121	E	s	4	•	B-R-S	NE-SE	•	
434	Baie de Tamarone	42°58'.42N	009°27'.48E	122	G	s	5	•		N-S	•	
435	Rade de Finocchiarola	42°58'.83N	009°28'.08E	122	G	s	4	•		NW-S	•	
437	Rade de Santa Maria	42°59'.55N	009°27'.40E	122	G	s/w	5	•		NW-SE	•	
438	Baie de Capandola	43°00'.25N	009°26'.16E	123	P	s	5			NW-SE	•	

AREA F - CORSICA

	NAME	WGS 84 COORDINATES		CHART	🗺	🐟	⬇ m	🔋	🍷	🧭	⚓	🔔
		LATITUDE	LONGITUDE									
440	Anse d'Agnello	43°00'.67N	009°25'.55E	123	G	s	4			NW-E	•	
441	Marine de Barcaggio	43°00'.55N	009°24'.73E	123	G	s	4	•	B-R-S	W-E	•	
444	Marine de Tollare	43°00'.50N	009°23'.35E	123	P	s/w	4	•		E-W	•	
445	Anse de l'Arinella	43°00'.39N	009°22'.48E	124	P	s/w	5			W-E	•	
448	Baie de Centuri	42°57'.91N	009°20'.66E	124	G	s/w	6	•	B-R-S	W-N	•	
450	Marine de Morsiglia	42°57'.65N	009°20'.65E	124	P	s/r	4	•		SW-NW	•	
451	Golfe de Morsiglia	42°56'.74N	009°21'.23E	124	P	s/r	8			S-N	•	
452	Golfu Alisu	42°55'.51N	009°21'.43E	125	P	s/r	4	•		NW-SW	•	
453	Marina de Giottani	42°52'.00N	009°20'.26E	125	G	s	5	•	B-R	NW-SW	•	
455	Marina d'Albo	42°48'.54N	009°19'.83E	125	P	s/p	4		B-R	NW-S	•	
456	Cala Farinole	42°43'.49N	009°19'.85E	125	P	s	4		B-R	SW-N	•	
458	Baie de St-Florent	42°40'.78N	009°17'.53E	127	G	s	5	•	B-R-S	NW-NE	•	
From St-Florent to Golfe de Porto												
460	Anse de Fornali	42°41'.32N	009°16'.75E	126	G	s	4	•		N-SW	•	
461	Anse de Fiume Santu	42°42'.41N	009°15'.58E	126	G	s	3	•		N-SW	•	
463	Plage du Loto	42°43'.42N	009°14'.54E	128	G	s	4	•		NE-E	•	
464	Plage de Saleccia	42°43'.84N	009°12'.14E	128	G	s	4	•		NW-NE	•	
465	Punta Negra	42°44'.25N	009°08'.87E	128	G	s	4	•		W-NE	•	
466	Marina di Molfalcu	42°43'.75N	009°06'.83E	128	G	s	4	•		NW-NE	•	
468	Baie de l'Acciolu	42°41'.83N	009°03'.95E	128	G	s	5	•		NW-NE	•	
469	Anse de Peraiola	42°39'.83N	009°03'.50E	129	G	s	4	•		SW-N	•	
470	Anse de Lozari	42°38'.76N	009°01'.00E	129	G	s	4	•	B-R	W-E	•	
471	Cala d'Olivu	42°38'.30N	008°57'.77E	129	P	s	5	•		W-E	•	
472	Baie de L'Ile Rousse	42°38'.22N	008°56'55E	130	G	s	7	•	B-R-S	NW-SE	•	
475	Anse d'Algajola	42°36'.80N	008°52'.09E	131	G	s	5	•	B-R-S	W-NE	•	
479	Baie de St Ambrogio	42°36'.24N	008°49'.91E	131	G	s	5	•	B-R-S	NW-NE	•	
481	Cala Stella	42°36'.25N	008°49'.14E	132	P	s/w/r	6	•		W-E	•	
482	Baia Agajo	42°35'.50N	008°48'.52E	132	G	s	4			S-NW	•	
483	Golfe de Calvi	42°33'.73N	008°46'.23E	133	G	s/w	7	•	B-R-S	NW-E	•	•
485	Golfe de la Revellata	42°33'.80N	008°43'.70E	134	G	s/w	5			N-E	•	
486	Anse de l'Oscelluccia	42°34'.50N	008°43'.52E	134	G	s/w	5	•		N-SE	•	
488	Portu Vecchiu	42°34'.08N	008°42'.83E	134	G	s	6	•		SE-NW	•	
489	Porto d'Agro	42°32'.75N	008°43'.05E	134	P	s/r	7	•		S-N	•	
490	Baia di Nichiareto	42°31'.74N	008°42'.45E	135	G	s/r	7	•		SW-N	•	
491	Anse d'Alusi	42°31'.05N	008°41'.05E	135	P	s/r	7	•		SW-SE	•	
492	Baia de Crovani	42°28'.05N	008°40'.00E	135	G	s	6	•	B-R	S-NW	•	
493	Golfe de Galéria	42°25'.33N	008°39'.00E	136	G	s	5	•		W-NE	•	
495	Baia de Focolara	42°23'.40N	008°36'.15E	136	G	s/r	6	•		W-N	•	
496	Anse Porri	42°23'.15N	008°34'.60E	136	G	s/w/r	4			W-NW	•	
497	Baia d'Elbo	42°22'.50N	008°33'.84E	136	G	s/r	4			NW-NE	•	
498	Marina d'Elbo	42°22'.32N	008°34'.26E	136	E	s	4	•		NW-N	•	
501	Cala Muretta & Cala Scandola	42°20'.23N	008°34'.52E	138	G	s	8			NE-SW	•	
502	Cala Vecchia	42°20'.89N	008°35'.03E	138	G	s/w/r	5			SW-E	•	
503	Girolata	42°20'.77N	008°36'.90E	138	E	m/s	4	•	B-R-S	S	•	•
504	Cala Tuara	42°20'.35N	008°37'.58E	138	G	s	4	•		SE-NW	•	
506	Cala di Lignaghia	42°18'.58N	008°37'.58E	139	G	s	5			SE-SW	•	
507	Cala Gradelle & Cala Caspiu	42°18'.00N	008°39'.10E	139	G	s	5	•	B-R	SE-SW	•	
508	Marine de Bussagghia	42°16'.85N	08°41'.10E	139	G	s	6	•	B-R	SE-SW	•	
509	Baie de Porto	42°15'.97N	008°41'.40E	137	G	s/g	6	•	B-R-S	SW-N	•	
511	Anse de Ficajola	42°15'.10N	08°37'.58E	139	P	s	9	•	B-R	W-E	•	

AREA F - CORSICA

⊕	NAME	WGS 84 COORDINATES		CHART	🗺	🐟	⬇ m	🅿	🍷	🧭	⚓	🔔
		LATITUDE	LONGITUDE									
From Golfe de Porto to Ajaccio												
512	Cala Sbiro	42°14'.48N	008°32'.84E	140	G	s/r	5			W-E		
514	Cala Genovese	42°14'.08N	008°32'.33E	140	P	s/r	6			S-W	•	
515	Cala di Palu	42°13'.60N	008°34'.00E	140	G	s/r	6			S-W	•	
516	Portu Leccia	42°12'.90N	008°34'.27E	140	G	s/w/r	7			SW-NW	•	
517	Porto d'Arone	42°12'.10N	008°34'.58E	141	G	s	5	•	B-R	S-W	•	
518	Golfe de Topidi	42°10'.83N	008°34'.75E	141	G	s/r	5	•		W-N	•	
519	Anse de Chiuni	42°10'.03N	008°35'.15E	141	G	s	5	•		SW-NW	•	
521	Golfe de Peru	42°08'.75N	008°35'.24E	141	G	s	5	•		S-W	•	
522	Baie de Cargèse	42°07'.88N	008°36'.00E	142	P	s/w/r	5	•	B-R-S	SE-W	•	
524	Baie de Menasina	42°07'.83N	008°36'.75E	142	G	s	5	•		SE-W	•	
525	Porto Monaghi/Baia de Stagnoli	42°07'.07N	008°37'.97E	143	P	s	5	•		SE-NW	•	
526	Baie de Sagone	42°06'.58N	008°41'.61E	144	G	s	5	•	B-R-S	SE-SW	•	
527	Baie de St-Joseph	42°04'.97N	008°42'.42E	143	G	s	5	•		SE-NW	•	
528	Baie de Liscia	42°03'.76N	008°44'.09E	144	G	s/w	6	•	B-R-S	SE-/W	•	
529	Anse Stagnonu	42°02'.55N	008°44'.40E	144	P	s/w	6	•		SW-N	•	
530	Anse d'Ancone	42°02'.09N	008°43'.24E	144	P	s/r	6	•		SW-N	•	
531	Anse de Portu Provençale	41°59'.41N	008°39'.83E	144	G	s	6	•	B-R-S	SW-NW	•	
532	Cigntra	41°58'.16N	008°36'.40E	145	P	s	6	•		SW-/NE	•	
534	Anse de Fica	41°57'.00N	008°36'.35E	145	G	s/w	6	•		SE-W	•	
535	Anse de Minaccia	41°56'.10N	008°36'.76E	145	G	s	5	•	B	SW-NW	•	
538	Grande Sanguinaire/Anchorage SW	41°52'.39N	008°35'.27E	146	P	s/r	5			E-SW	•	
539	Grande Sanguinaire/Anchorage E	41°52'.51N	008°35'.80E	146	P	s/w/r	4	•		NE-S	•	
540	Grande Sanguinaire/Cala d'Alga	41°52°.84N	008°35'.95E	146	P	s/w/r	5			NE-SW	•	
From Ajaccio to Bonifacio												
545	Porticcio	41°52'.59N	008°46'.74E	149	P	s	5	•		S-NW	•	
546	Anse de Stagnola and Anse de Ste Barbe	41°51'.16N	008°46'.16E	149	P	s/w	5	•		W-E	•	
547	Anse Medea	41°50'.43N	008°45'.75E	149	G	s/w	6	•		SE-W	•	
548	Anse Ottioni	41°49'.90N	008°46'.88E	149	G	s	5	•	B-R	SW-NW	•	
549	Portu de Chiavari	41°48'.85N	008°46'.16E	150	G	s	5	•	B	W-/N	•	
550	Ile Piana	41°48'.84N	008°44'.93E	150	P	s/w	7	•		NE-E	•	
551	Anse de Portigliolo	41°48'.00N	008°44'.32E	150	G	s	6	•		W-N	•	
552	Cala U Vecchiu	41°48'.05N	008°43'.40E	150	G	s/r	6	•		NW-NE	•	
553	Cala di a Castagna	41°47'.59N	008°42'.91E	150	G	s/r	6	•		S-W	•	
554	Cala Rossa	41°46'.76N	008°43'.65E	151	G	s	6	•		SW-NW	•	
555	Anse de Cacalau	41°45'.08N	008°41'.00E	151	G	s/r	6	•		NW-E	•	
557	Cala di Muru	41°44'.24N	008°41'.21E	151	G	s/r	4	•		SE-SW	•	
558	Cala d'Orzu	41°44'.22N	008°42'.16E	151	P	s	5	•	B-R	S-/NW	•	
559	Baie de Cupabia	41°44'.16N	008°46'.58E	151	G	s	5	•	B-R	S-W	•	
560	Baie de Porto Pollo	41°42'.50N	008°47'.91E	152	G	s/w	6	•	B-R-S	SW-/E	•	
564	Propriano/Slage de Baraci	41°41'.10N	008°54'.58E	153	G	s	5	•	B-R-S	SW-NW	•	
566	Portigliolo	41°38'.94N	008°52'.22E	154	G	s	4	•		W-N	•	
567	Baie de Campomoro	41°38'.05N	008°49'.05E	154	G	s/w	7	•	B-R	NW-NE	•	
568	Cala d'Agulia	41°35'.90N	008°47'.08E	154	G	s/w	4	•		W/N	•	
569	Anse de Ferru	41°35'.30N	008°46'.65E	155	G	s/w	4	•		S-W	•	
570	Anse d'Arana	41°35'.03N	008°47'.22E	155	G	s/w/r	6	•		S-W	•	
572	Cala di Conca	41°34'.40N	008°47'.85E	155	G	s	5	•		SW-NW	•	
573	Scoliu Biancu	41°34'.02N	008°47'.20E	155	P	s r	5	•		W-/E	•	
574	Anse de Tivella	41°33'.30N	008°48'.48E	155	P	s r	6	•		S-W	•	
575	Cala Longa	41°33'.10N	008°48'.80E	155	G	s	4	•		S-SW	•	

AREA F - CORSICA

	NAME	WGS 84 COORDINATES		CHART	Shelter	Seabed	Depth m	Dinghy	Facilities	Wind	Anchor	Buoy
		LATITUDE	LONGITUDE									
576	Anse de Portu	41°32'.80N	008°49'.92E	155	G	s	4	•		SE-SW	•	
577	Cala di Tizzano	41°32'.34N	008°50'.85E	156	G	s	5	•	B-R-S	S-SW	•	
580	Cala di Brija	41°31'.12N	008°51'.55E	156	G	s/w	4	•		SE-SW	•	
581	Plage de Tralicetu	41°31'.16N	008°52'.58E	157	G	s	4	•		SE-W	•	
582	Plage d'Argent	41°30'.88N	008°53'.04E	157	G	s	4	•		S-W	•	
583	Murtoli	41°30'.41N	008°54'.22E	157	P	s	3	•		SE-W	•	
584	Plage d'Erbaju	41°30'.17N	008°54'.76E	157	P	s/w	4	•		SE-/W	•	
585	Cala di Roccapina	41°29'.25N	008°56'.04E	157	G	s	4	•		SE-/SW	•	
588	Cala d'I Pastori	41°29'.48N	008°57'.58E	157	P	s	4	•		SE-/W	•	
589	Anse delli Balconi	41°29'.16N	008°57'.73E	158	P	s	4	•		S-NW	•	
590	Anse du Prêtre	41°28'.90N	008°58'.30E	158	P	s	4	•		S-NW	•	
591	Cala di Fornellu	41°28'.57N	008°59'.57E	158	G	s	4	•		SE-/SW	•	
592	Anse d'Arbitru	41°28'.35N	009°00'.66E	159	G	s/r	4	•		S-SW	•	
593	Anse de Chevanau	41°28'.00N	009°02'.07E	159	G	s	5	•		SE-SW	•	
595	Anchorage in Baie de Figari	41°27'.55N	009°03'.41E	160	G	s/w	5	•		S-SW	•	•
597	Anse de Porticciu	41°26'.59N	009°05'.52E	161	G	s/w/r	5	•		SE-SW	•	
598	Anse de Pesciucane	41°26'.43N	009°06'.30E	161	G	s/r	4	•		SE-SW	•	
599	Golfe de Ventilegne E	41°26'.30N	009°06'.85E	161	P	s/r	4	•		S-W	•	
600	Iles de la Tonnara	41°25'.77N	009°06'.16E	162	P	s/w/r	4	•	B-R	S-NE	•	
601	Cala di Stagnolu	41°25'.16N	009°06'.16E	162	G	s	4	•		S-NW	•	
602	Cala Grande	41°23'.50N	009°05'.47E	162	G	s/r	4	•		S-SW	•	
604	Cala di Paragnanu	41°23'.66N	009°07'.50E	162	G	s/r	4	•		S-SW	•	
605	Anse de Fazziuolu	41°23'.50N	009°07'.83E	162	G	s	4	•		S-SW	•	

Shelter: P = Poor G = Good E = Excellent **Nature of seabed:** w = weed m = mud g = gravel p = pebbles/stones r = rock s = sand

Depths in metres **Landing with dinghy** **Facilities ashore:** B = Bar R = Restaurant S = Shop **Anchorage** **Mooring buoy**

Wind direction and exposure

AREA F - CORSICA

SAFETY AT SEA — AREA F

WEATHER BULLETINS

Corsica weather bulletins
VHF ch 79 frequency 161.575 MHz
(French-English)
Ersa 07333, 1233 1933 LT
Serra di Pigno 0745 1245 1945 LT
Conca 0803 1303 2003 LT
Serragia 0815 1315 2003 LT
La Punta 0833 1333 2033 LT
Piana 0845 1345 2045 LT

Mari d'Italia/Meteomar weather bulletin
(English-Italian)
VHF ch 68 frequency 156.425 MHz continuous

Coast radio station weather bulletin
Monte Moro (North Sardina Strait of Bonifacio)
VHF ch 28 frequency 162.000 MHz

Porto Torres VHF ch 26 frequency 161.900 MHz
0510 0810 1210 1610 2010 UTC
Radio Porto Cervo local bulletin VHF ch 26, 28, 85
(English and Italian) at 0150 0750 1350 1950
call ahead on ch 16

FRANCE AND CORSICA WEATHER FORECASTS
(French-English)

Monaco Radio 4363 kHz (ch 403) 09031403 1915 LT Lyon, Provence, Corsican Sea, Sardinian Sea, Ligurian Sea, Northern Tyrrhenian Sea

Monaco Radio 8728, 8806 kHz (ch 804, 830) SSB
0715 1830 UTC West Mediterranean offshore seas

La Garde CROSS 1696, 2677 kHz SSB after the first call frequency 2182 kHz 0650 1433 1850 LT

HARBOURMASTERS

Bonifacio VHF Ch 09 ☎ +33 (0)495 731007
(summer 07.00-21.30, other seasons 08.00-12.00/
14.00-18.00)
Fax +33 (0)495 731873
info@bonifaciomarina.com

Porto Vecchio VHF Ch 09 ☎ +33 (0)495 701793
Fax +33 (0)495 702768 (summer 08.00-21.00
winter 08.30-12.00 /14.00-17.30)
port@porto-vecchio.fr.

Solenzara VHF ch 09 ☎ +33 (0)495 574642
Fax +33 (0)495 574466
capitainerie@mairie-sari-solenzara.fr.

Bastia VHF Ch 09 ☎ +33 (0)495 313110
Fax +33 (0)495 559655
www.port-de-bastia.net

St-Florent VHF Ch 09 ☎ +33 (0)495 370079
Fax +33 (0)495 371137 (summer 07.00-21.00
winter 08.00-12.00/15.00-18.00)
contact@portsaintflorent.com

Calvi VHF Ch 09 ☎ +33 (0)495 650171
Fax +33 (0)495 651513
portplaisance@ville-calvi.fr

Ajaccio VHF Ch 09 ☎ +33 495 223198 / 512272
Fax +33 (0)495 209808 (summer 07.00-22.00
winter 08.00-12.00 /14.00-18.00)
capitainerie.ajaccio@sudcorse.cci.fr

SAFETY AND RESCUE CENTRES

MRSC Corsica VHF ch 16, 67
☎ +33 (0)495 201363
MMSI 002275420
(winter 07.30-19.00 summer 0730-2300)

MRSC Olbia ☎ +39 0789 56360
cpolbia@mit.gov.it

MRSC Livorno ☎ +39 0586 826011
cplivorno@guardiacostiera.gov.it

Porto Cervo Heliport VHF ch 26 - Man & Auto ch 88
MRCC Roma MMSI 002 470 001
DSC VHF ch 70, 16 - DSC MF 2187.5 kHz, 2182 kHz
DSC HF 420.5, 6312, 8414.5 kHz
Direzione Marittima (Port Authority) Roma Fiumicino
☎ +39 06 656171
cproma@mit.gov.it

CIRM International Medical Centre
☎ +39 06 559290263 - mobile +39 348 3984229
Fax +39 06 5923331/2
telesoccorso@cirm.it - www.cirm.it

CORSICA SW COAST | AREA F | CHART 105

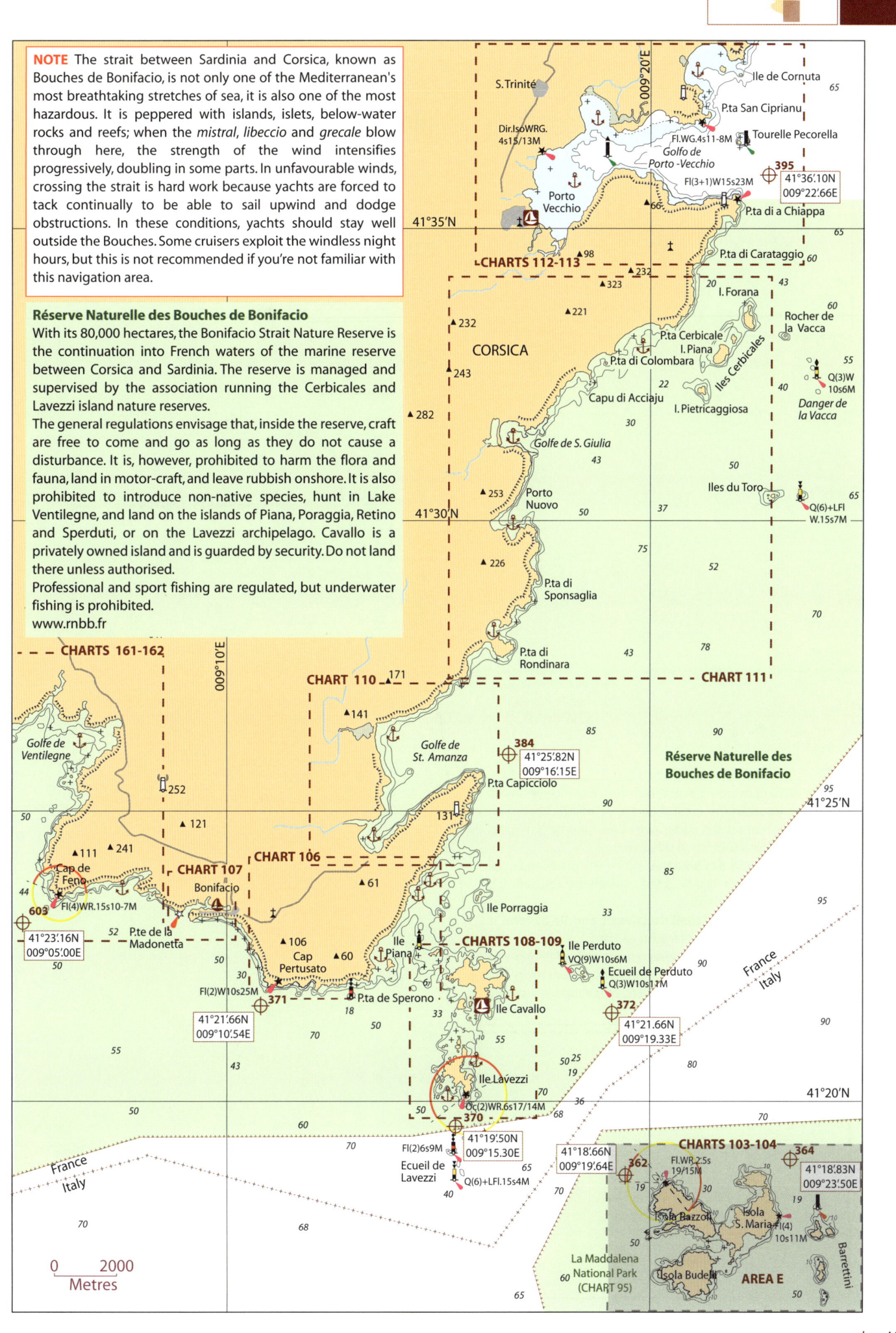

NOTE The strait between Sardinia and Corsica, known as Bouches de Bonifacio, is not only one of the Mediterranean's most breathtaking stretches of sea, it is also one of the most hazardous. It is peppered with islands, islets, below-water rocks and reefs; when the *mistral*, *libeccio* and *grecale* blow through here, the strength of the wind intensifies progressively, doubling in some parts. In unfavourable winds, crossing the strait is hard work because yachts are forced to tack continually to be able to sail upwind and dodge obstructions. In these conditions, yachts should stay well outside the Bouches. Some cruisers exploit the windless night hours, but this is not recommended if you're not familiar with this navigation area.

Réserve Naturelle des Bouches de Bonifacio

With its 80,000 hectares, the Bonifacio Strait Nature Reserve is the continuation into French waters of the marine reserve between Corsica and Sardinia. The reserve is managed and supervised by the association running the Cerbicales and Lavezzi island nature reserves.

The general regulations envisage that, inside the reserve, craft are free to come and go as long as they do not cause a disturbance. It is, however, prohibited to harm the flora and fauna, land in motor-craft, and leave rubbish onshore. It is also prohibited to introduce non-native species, hunt in Lake Ventilegne, and land on the islands of Piana, Poraggia, Retino and Sperduti, or on the Lavezzi archipelago. Cavallo is a privately owned island and is guarded by security. Do not land there unless authorised.

Professional and sport fishing are regulated, but underwater fishing is prohibited.
www.rnbb.fr

AREA F — FROM BONIFACIO TO PUNTA DI U CAPICCIOLU

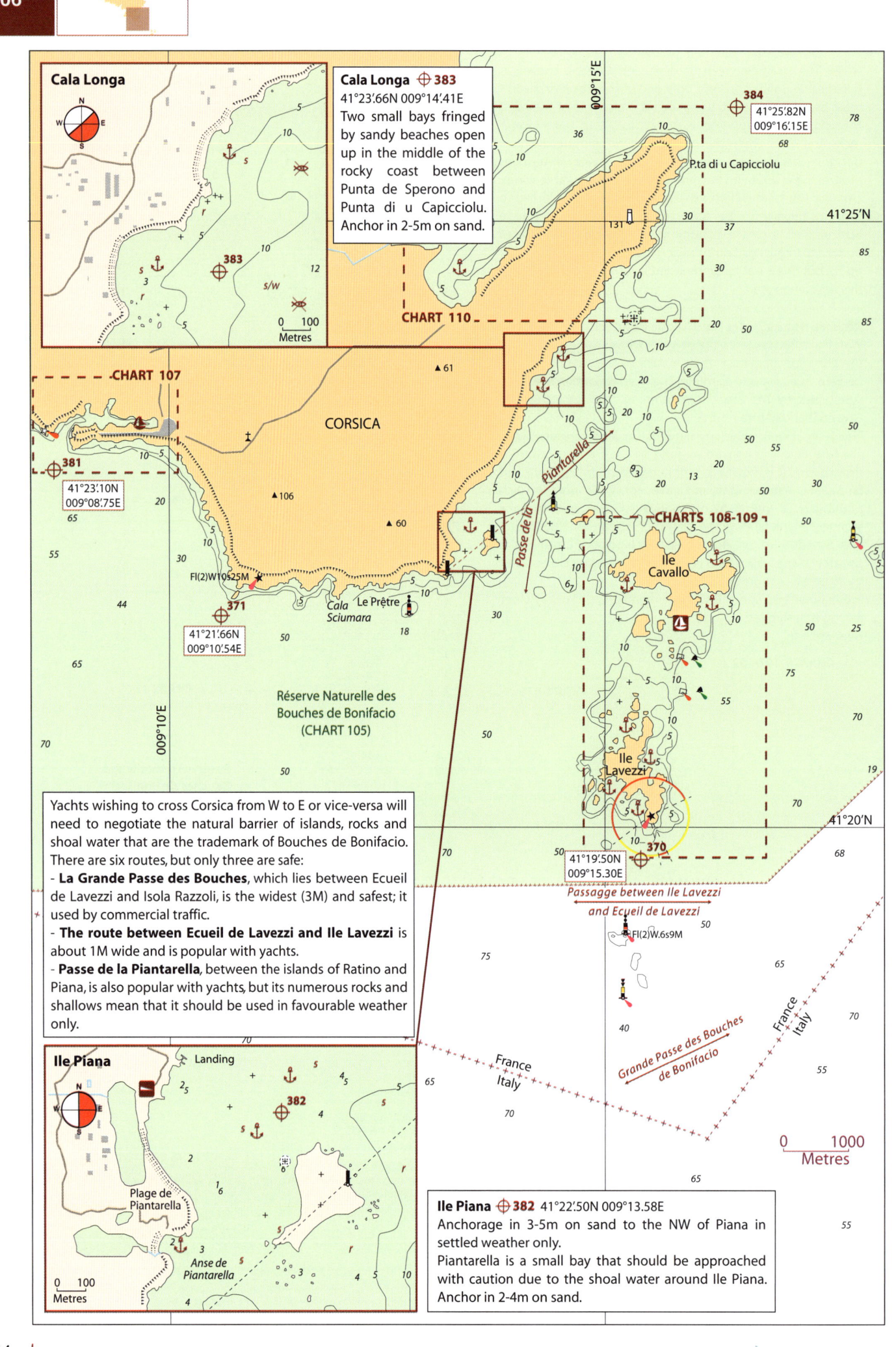

CHART 106

Cala Longa ⊕ 383
41°23.66N 009°14.41E
Two small bays fringed by sandy beaches open up in the middle of the rocky coast between Punta de Sperono and Punta di u Capicciolu. Anchor in 2-5m on sand.

384 — 41°25.82N 009°16.15E

381 — 41°23.10N 009°08.75E

371 — 41°21.66N 009°10.54E

Réserve Naturelle des Bouches de Bonifacio (CHART 105)

Yachts wishing to cross Corsica from W to E or vice-versa will need to negotiate the natural barrier of islands, rocks and shoal water that are the trademark of Bouches de Bonifacio. There are six routes, but only three are safe:

- **La Grande Passe des Bouches**, which lies between Ecueil de Lavezzi and Isola Razzoli, is the widest (3M) and safest; it used by commercial traffic.
- **The route between Ecueil de Lavezzi and Ile Lavezzi** is about 1M wide and is popular with yachts.
- **Passe de la Piantarella**, between the islands of Ratino and Piana, is also popular with yachts, but its numerous rocks and shallows mean that it should be used in favourable weather only.

370 — 41°19.50N 009°15.30E

Passage between Ile Lavezzi and Ecueil de Lavezzi

Grande Passe des Bouches de Bonifacio

Ile Piana ⊕ 382 41°22.50N 009°13.58E
Anchorage in 3-5m on sand to the NW of Piana in settled weather only.
Piantarella is a small bay that should be approached with caution due to the shoal water around Ile Piana. Anchor in 2-4m on sand.

BONIFACIO | AREA F | CHART 107

The scenery that greets yachts landing at Bonifacio is considered to be some of the Mediterranean's most spectacular. In good visibility, its tall, white limestone cliffs with a sheer drop into the sea can be glimpsed from Sardinia. The entrance to the calanque leading to Bonifacio harbour is difficult to spot from the sea and, even closer in, is hidden and confusing. Cap Pertusato and Cap de Feno are good landmarks and easily recognised. Between them lies Punta de la Madonetta, which is the W side of the calanque entrance. Atop stands the square red tower of the lighthouse. Another good landmark is the citadel of Bonifacio, which is conspicuous atop the rock on the E side of the entrance.

Port de Bonifacio

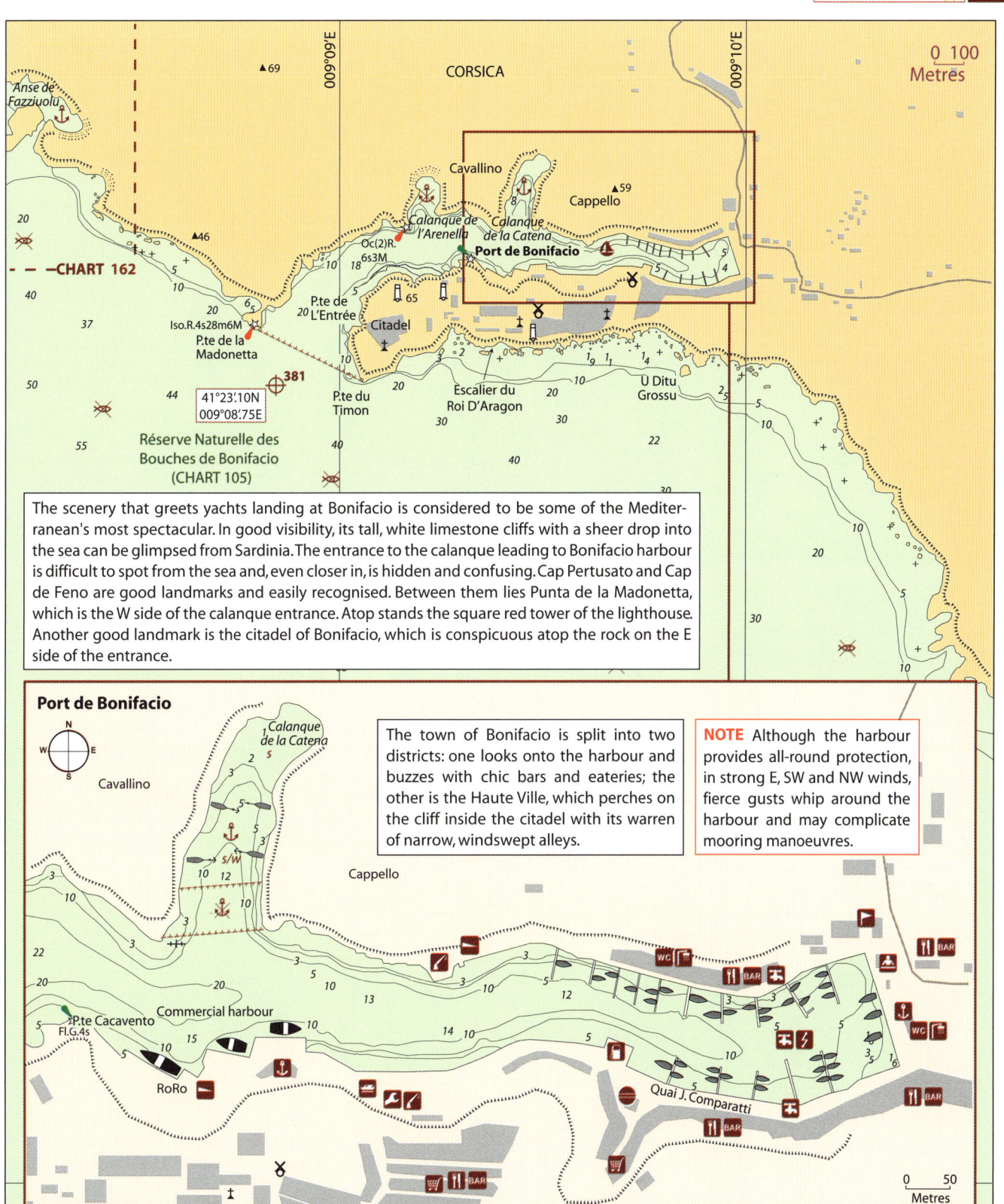

The town of Bonifacio is split into two districts: one looks onto the harbour and buzzes with chic bars and eateries; the other is the Haute Ville, which perches on the cliff inside the citadel with its warren of narrow, windswept alleys.

NOTE Although the harbour provides all-round protection, in strong E, SW and NW winds, fierce gusts whip around the harbour and may complicate mooring manoeuvres.

Port de Bonifacio ⊕ 381 41°23'.10N 009°08'.75E
Bonifacio is mainly a commercial and fishing harbour, but it does have two areas set aside for pleasure craft. The harbour offers all-round shelter and accommodates 450 yachts, with 220 visitors berths (max. LOA 55m). The harbour approach is straightforward, but care is needed of the cargo ships and ferry traffic. Always give way inside the harbour. In high season, it is always jam-packed and finding a place is a mammoth task. Late morning is the best time to enter, as most of the yachts vacate the harbour for other anchorages. All the berths are administered by the local council, so before approaching call up the harbour authorities (VHF Ch 09) and await instructions. Alternatively, speak with marine staff, who will point you towards a berth.
Capitainerie de Bonifacio: VHF Ch 09 - ☎ +33 (0)4 95 731007 (08.30 am-12.15 pm/01:00 pm-05.00 pm) - info@bonifaciomarina.com
www.port-bonifacio.corsica
Online reservations: www.resaportcorse.com - Fuel quay ☎ +33 495 730641 (winter 8.00 am -12.00 pm, summer 8.00 am/6.00 pm)
Anchorage Instead of berthing at the quay, yachts may anchor inside the inlet on the N side of the harbour. Calanque de la Catena offers 90 berths and is equipped with floating pontoons onto which you can tail a line.

155

CHART 108

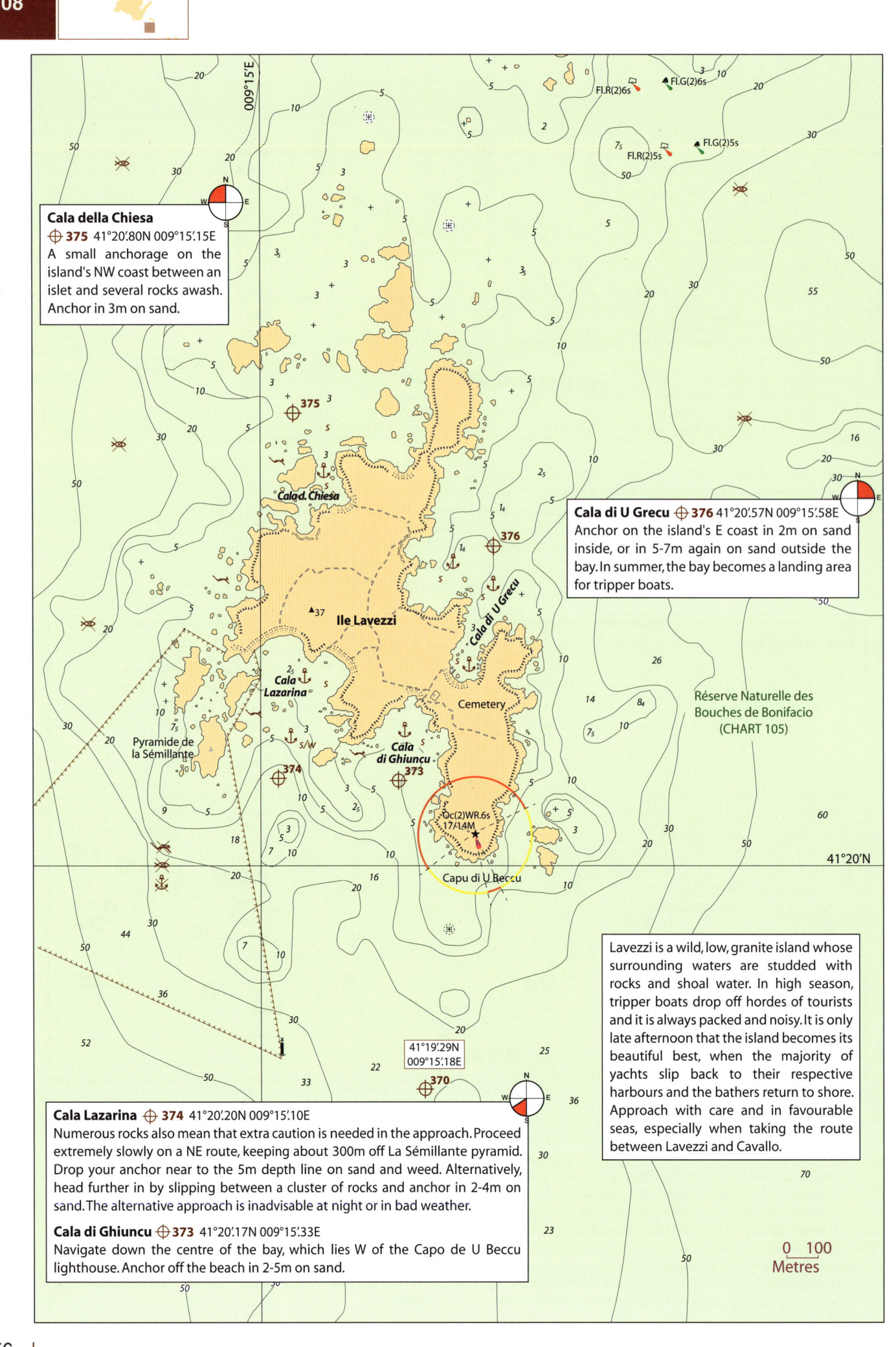

AREA F — ILE LAVEZZI

Cala della Chiesa
⊕ **375** 41°20'.80N 009°15'.15E
A small anchorage on the island's NW coast between an islet and several rocks awash. Anchor in 3m on sand.

Cala di U Grecu ⊕ 376 41°20'.57N 009°15'.58E
Anchor on the island's E coast in 2m on sand inside, or in 5-7m again on sand outside the bay. In summer, the bay becomes a landing area for tripper boats.

Cala Lazarina ⊕ 374 41°20'.20N 009°15'.10E
Numerous rocks also mean that extra caution is needed in the approach. Proceed extremely slowly on a NE route, keeping about 300m off La Sémillante pyramid. Drop your anchor near to the 5m depth line on sand and weed. Alternatively, head further in by slipping between a cluster of rocks and anchor in 2-4m on sand. The alternative approach is inadvisable at night or in bad weather.

Cala di Ghiuncu ⊕ 373 41°20'.17N 009°15'.33E
Navigate down the centre of the bay, which lies W of the Capo de U Beccu lighthouse. Anchor off the beach in 2-5m on sand.

Lavezzi is a wild, low, granite island whose surrounding waters are studded with rocks and shoal water. In high season, tripper boats drop off hordes of tourists and it is always packed and noisy. It is only late afternoon that the island becomes its beautiful best, when the majority of yachts slip back to their respective harbours and the bathers return to shore. Approach with care and in favourable seas, especially when taking the route between Lavezzi and Cavallo.

Réserve Naturelle des Bouches de Bonifacio (CHART 105)

ILE CAVALLO | AREA F | CHART 109

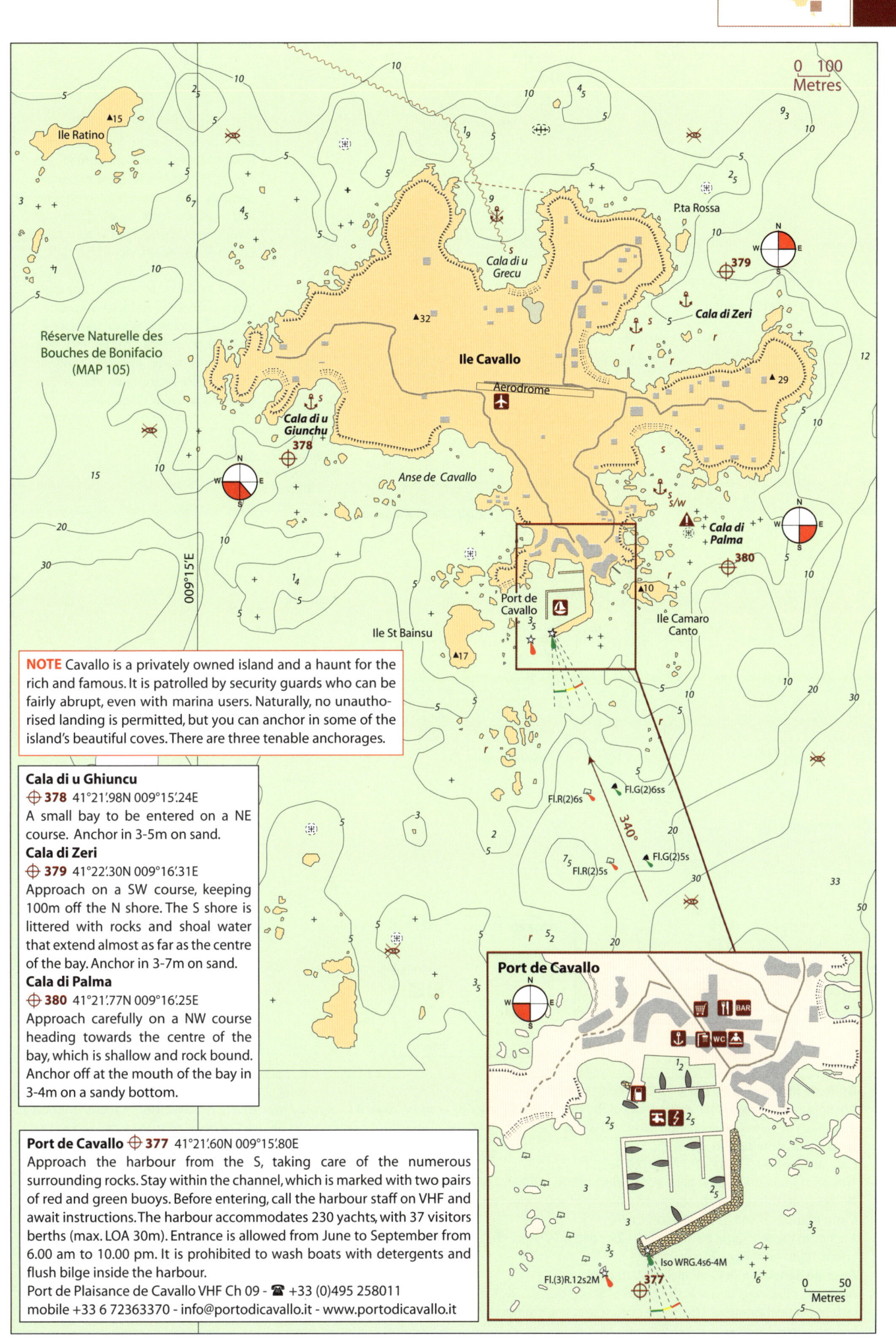

NOTE Cavallo is a privately owned island and a haunt for the rich and famous. It is patrolled by security guards who can be fairly abrupt, even with marina users. Naturally, no unauthorised landing is permitted, but you can anchor in some of the island's beautiful coves. There are three tenable anchorages.

Cala di u Ghiuncu
⊕ **378** 41°21'.98N 009°15'.24E
A small bay to be entered on a NE course. Anchor in 3-5m on sand.

Cala di Zeri
⊕ **379** 41°22'.30N 009°16'.31E
Approach on a SW course, keeping 100m off the N shore. The S shore is littered with rocks and shoal water that extend almost as far as the centre of the bay. Anchor in 3-7m on sand.

Cala di Palma
⊕ **380** 41°21'.77N 009°16'.25E
Approach carefully on a NW course heading towards the centre of the bay, which is shallow and rock bound. Anchor off at the mouth of the bay in 3-4m on a sandy bottom.

Port de Cavallo ⊕ **377** 41°21'.60N 009°15'.80E
Approach the harbour from the S, taking care of the numerous surrounding rocks. Stay within the channel, which is marked with two pairs of red and green buoys. Before entering, call the harbour staff on VHF and await instructions. The harbour accommodates 230 yachts, with 37 visitors berths (max. LOA 30m). Entrance is allowed from June to September from 6.00 am to 10.00 pm. It is prohibited to wash boats with detergents and flush bilge inside the harbour.
Port de Plaisance de Cavallo VHF Ch 09 - ☎ +33 (0)495 258011
mobile +33 6 72363370 - info@portodicavallo.it - www.portodicavallo.it

AREA F | GOLFE DE ST AMANZA

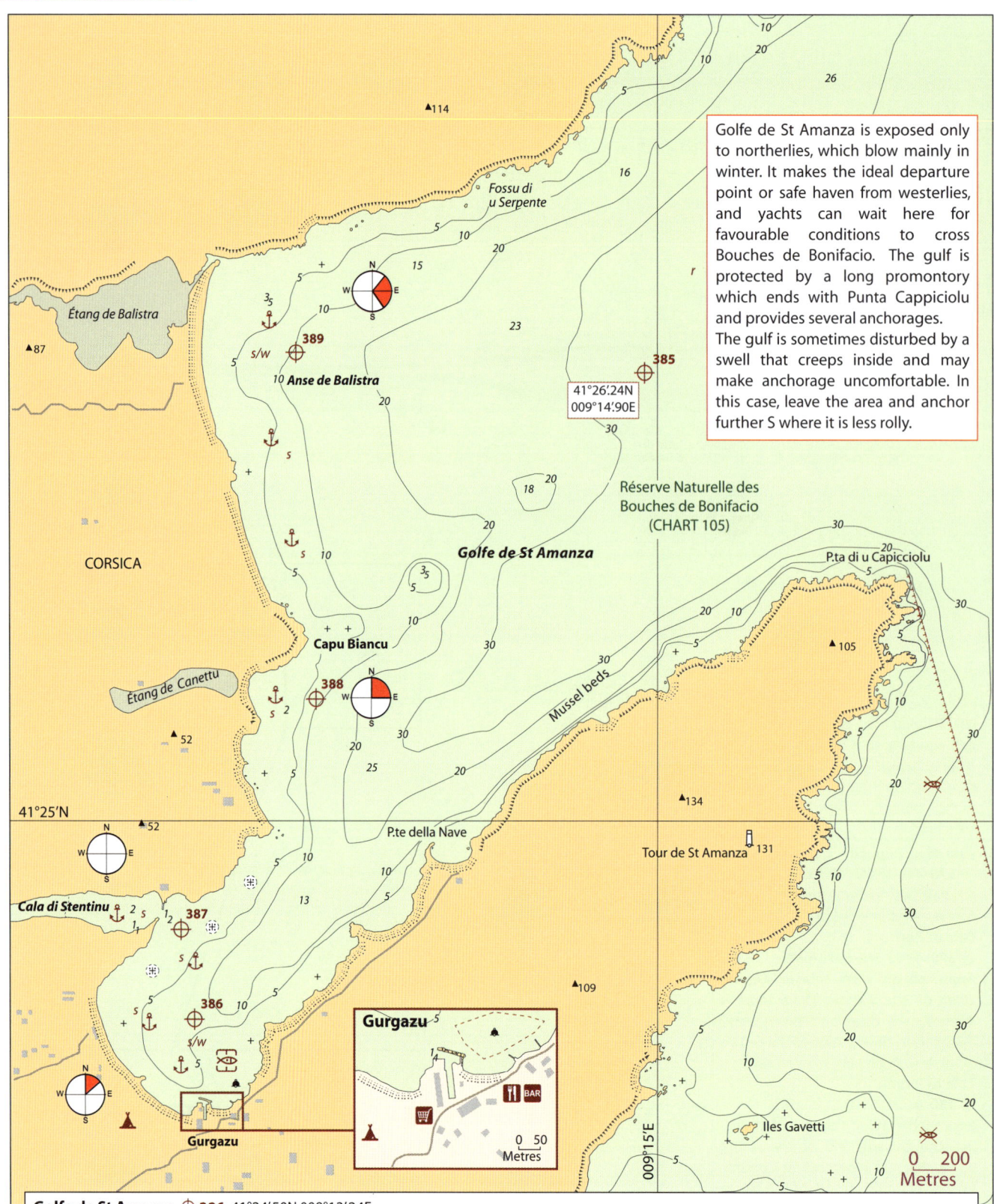

CHART 110

Golfe de St Amanza is exposed only to northerlies, which blow mainly in winter. It makes the ideal departure point or safe haven from westerlies, and yachts can wait here for favourable conditions to cross Bouches de Bonifacio. The gulf is protected by a long promontory which ends with Punta Cappiciolu and provides several anchorages.
The gulf is sometimes disturbed by a swell that creeps inside and may make anchorage uncomfortable. In this case, leave the area and anchor further S where it is less rolly.

Golfe de St Amanza ⊕ 386 41°24'.50N 009°13'.24E
Anchorage is also available at the head of the gulf in the S corner near the village of Gurgazu. Alternatively, head further W and anchor off the beach in 3-7m on sand, or on sand and weed. The village of Gargazu hosts a basin that can be used by small motor yachts. Yachts can stock up on provisions here.

Cala di Stentinu ⊕ 387 41°24'.75N 009°13'.32E
This anchorage offers all-round protection, but is suitable for yachts drawing 1.2m max. The entrance is a river mouth and liable to silting. Silting aside, this area is absolutely stunning and you should take a dinghy as far as the head of the bay to explore.

Capu Biancu ⊕ 388 41°25'.40N 009°13'.76E
Anchor to the S of Capu Biancu in 3-5m on sand off Canettu beach (Étang de Canettu). Care is needed of the submerged reef extending for about 100m from Capu Biancu.

Anse de Balistra ⊕ 389 41°26'.38N 009°13'.56E
Anchor off the long beach at the E end of Étang de Balistra. The best point is in the NW corner in 3-5m on a sand and weed. As this is the outermost anchorage and the most open to the sea, it suffers from a swell that creeps into the gulf.

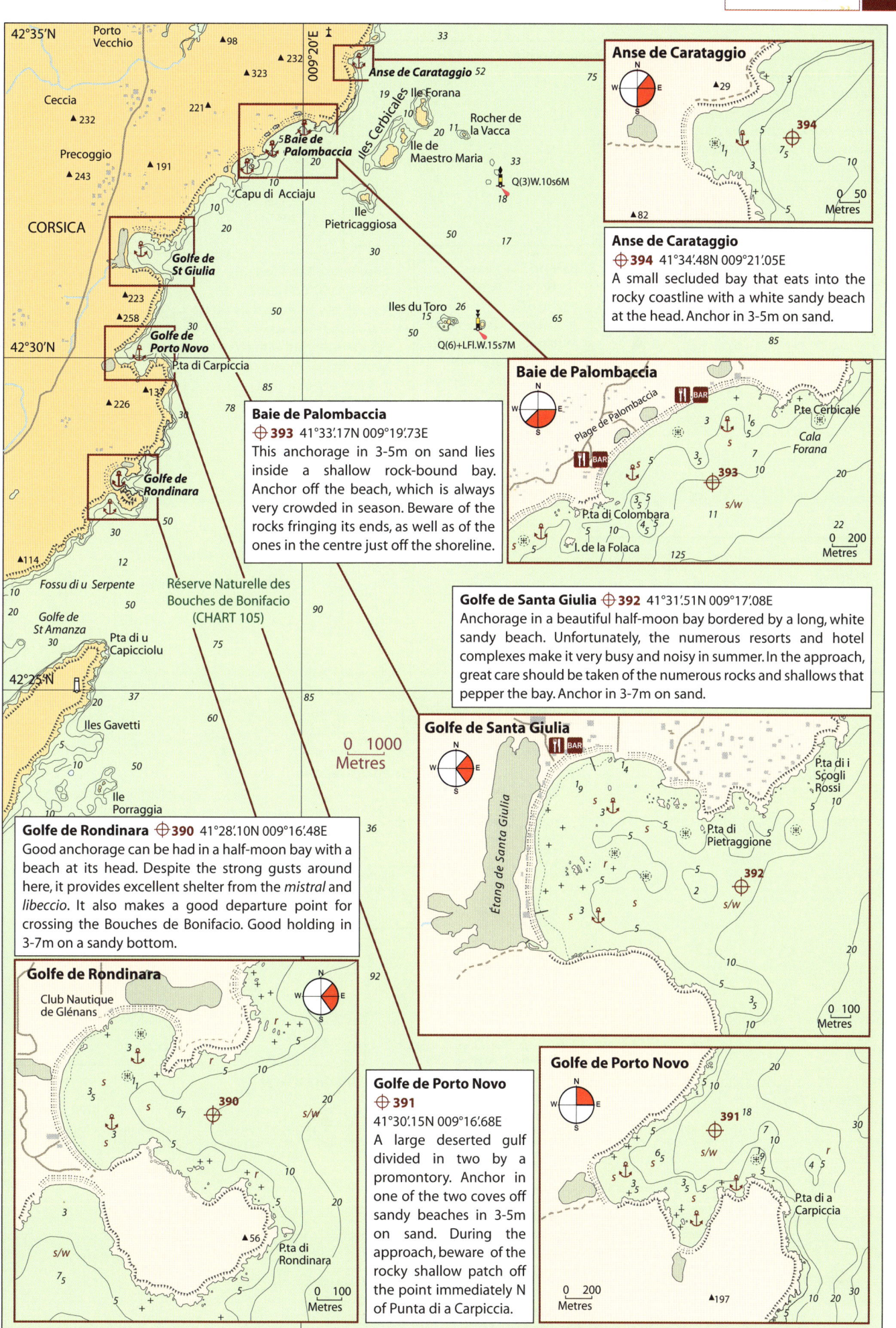

FROM PUNTA DI U CAPICCIOLU TO ANSE DE CARATAGGIO | AREA F | CHART 111

Anse de Carataggio
⊕ **394** 41°34'.48N 009°21'.05E
A small secluded bay that eats into the rocky coastline with a white sandy beach at the head. Anchor in 3-5m on sand.

Baie de Palombaccia
⊕ **393** 41°33'.17N 009°19'.73E
This anchorage in 3-5m on sand lies inside a shallow rock-bound bay. Anchor off the beach, which is always very crowded in season. Beware of the rocks fringing its ends, as well as of the ones in the centre just off the shoreline.

Golfe de Santa Giulia ⊕ **392** 41°31'.51N 009°17'.08E
Anchorage in a beautiful half-moon bay bordered by a long, white sandy beach. Unfortunately, the numerous resorts and hotel complexes make it very busy and noisy in summer. In the approach, great care should be taken of the numerous rocks and shallows that pepper the bay. Anchor in 3-7m on sand.

Golfe de Rondinara ⊕ **390** 41°28'.10N 009°16'.48E
Good anchorage can be had in a half-moon bay with a beach at its head. Despite the strong gusts around here, it provides excellent shelter from the *mistral* and *libeccio*. It also makes a good departure point for crossing the Bouches de Bonifacio. Good holding in 3-7m on a sandy bottom.

Golfe de Porto Novo
⊕ **391**
41°30'.15N 009°16'.68E
A large deserted gulf divided in two by a promontory. Anchor in one of the two coves off sandy beaches in 3-5m on sand. During the approach, beware of the rocky shallow patch off the point immediately N of Punta di a Carpiccia.

159

CHART 112 — AREA F — GOLFE DE PORTO-VECCHIO

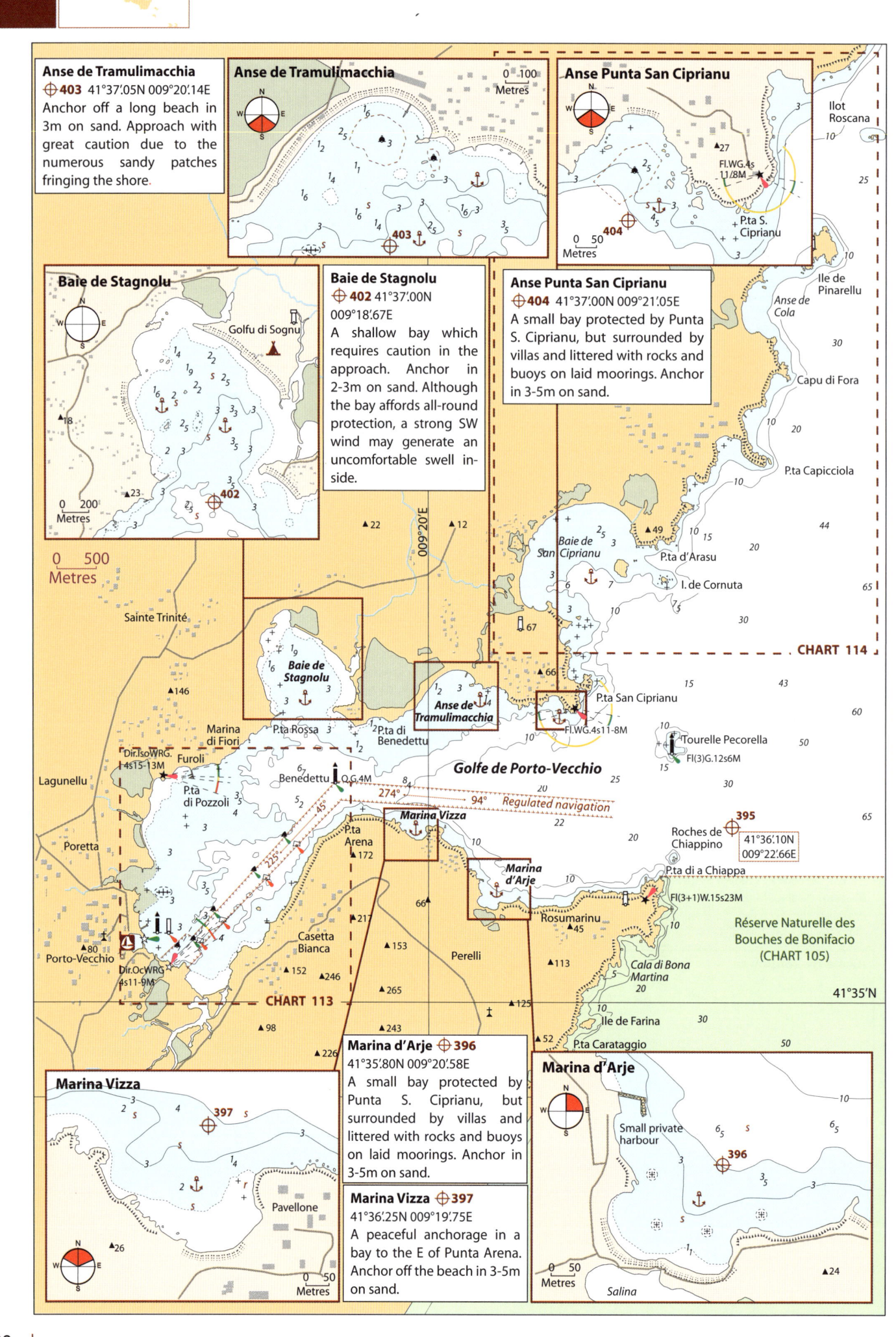

Anse de Tramulimacchia
⊕ 403 41°37'.05N 009°20'.14E
Anchor off a long beach in 3m on sand. Approach with great caution due to the numerous sandy patches fringing the shore.

Anse Punta San Cipriânu
⊕ 404 41°37'.00N 009°21'.05E
A small bay protected by Punta S. Cipriânu, but surrounded by villas and littered with rocks and buoys on laid moorings. Anchor in 3-5m on sand.

Baie de Stagnolu
⊕ 402 41°37'.00N 009°18'.67E
A shallow bay which requires caution in the approach. Anchor in 2-3m on sand. Although the bay affords all-round protection, a strong SW wind may generate an uncomfortable swell inside.

Marina d'Arje
⊕ 396 41°35'.80N 009°20'.58E
A small bay protected by Punta S. Cipriânu, but surrounded by villas and littered with rocks and buoys on laid moorings. Anchor in 3-5m on sand.

Marina Vizza
⊕ 397 41°36'.25N 009°19'.75E
A peaceful anchorage in a bay to the E of Punta Arena. Anchor off the beach in 3-5m on sand.

PORT DE PORTO-VECCHIO | AREA F | CHART 113

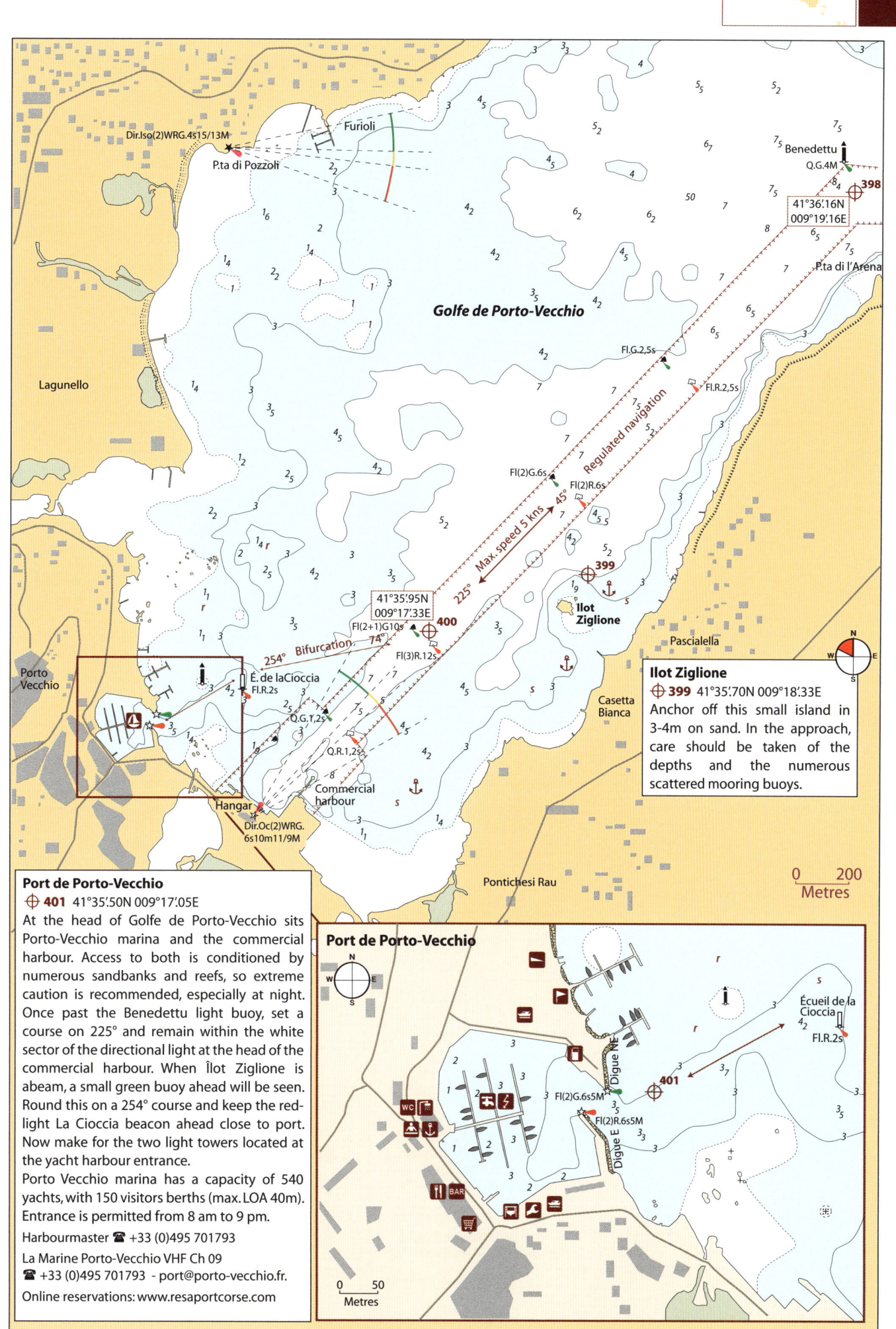

Ilot Ziglione
⊕ 399 41°35'.70N 009°18'.33E
Anchor off this small island in 3-4m on sand. In the approach, care should be taken of the depths and the numerous scattered mooring buoys.

Port de Porto-Vecchio
⊕ 401 41°35'.50N 009°17'.05E
At the head of Golfe de Porto-Vecchio sits Porto-Vecchio marina and the commercial harbour. Access to both is conditioned by numerous sandbanks and reefs, so extreme caution is recommended, especially at night. Once past the Benedettu light buoy, set a course on 225° and remain within the white sector of the directional light at the head of the commercial harbour. When Îlot Ziglione is abeam, a small green buoy ahead will be seen. Round this on a 254° course and keep the red-light La Cioccia beacon ahead close to port. Now make for the two light towers located at the yacht harbour entrance.

Porto Vecchio marina has a capacity of 540 yachts, with 150 visitors berths (max. LOA 40m). Entrance is permitted from 8 am to 9 pm.

Harbourmaster ☎ +33 (0)495 701793

La Marine Porto-Vecchio VHF Ch 09

☎ +33 (0)495 701793 - port@porto-vecchio.fr.

Online reservations: www.resaportcorse.com

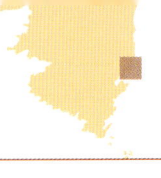

CHART 114 — AREA F — FROM BAIE DE SAN CIPRIANU TO GOLFE DE PINARELLU

Golfe de Pinarellu ⊕ 407 41°40'.73N 009°23'.42E
A large gulf very popular as a stopover with yachts on passage. Together with Baie San Cipriánu, it makes an excellent alternative to the anchorages in Golfe de Porto-Vecchio. The N part is fringed with rocky shallows as far as 500m from the coast. In a night approach, beware of Île Roscana, which lies unlit at the gulf entrance. Care is also needed of the fishfarm off the gulf's S side. The gulf provides some anchorage options on sand, or on sand and weed in 2-7m.

Baie de San Cipriánu ⊕ 405 41°37'.67N 009°21'.75E
A large well-protected bay made busy and noisy by numerous local tourist resorts. A range of anchorages are available on a sandy bottom in the centre of the bay in 3-7m; in the SW corner in 3m; and to the N of Ile San Cipriánu off the beach in 3-4m. Beware of the reefs around the islets and off the S point of the bay. Care is also needed of the numerous moorings that lie scattered off the beach.

Punta Capicciola ⊕ 406 41°38'.50N 009°22'.66E
You can anchor either to the W of the rugged Punta Capicciola, or to the S of the mooring buoys on sand and weed, or on the W side of the bay on sand. Depths are 3-5m in each.

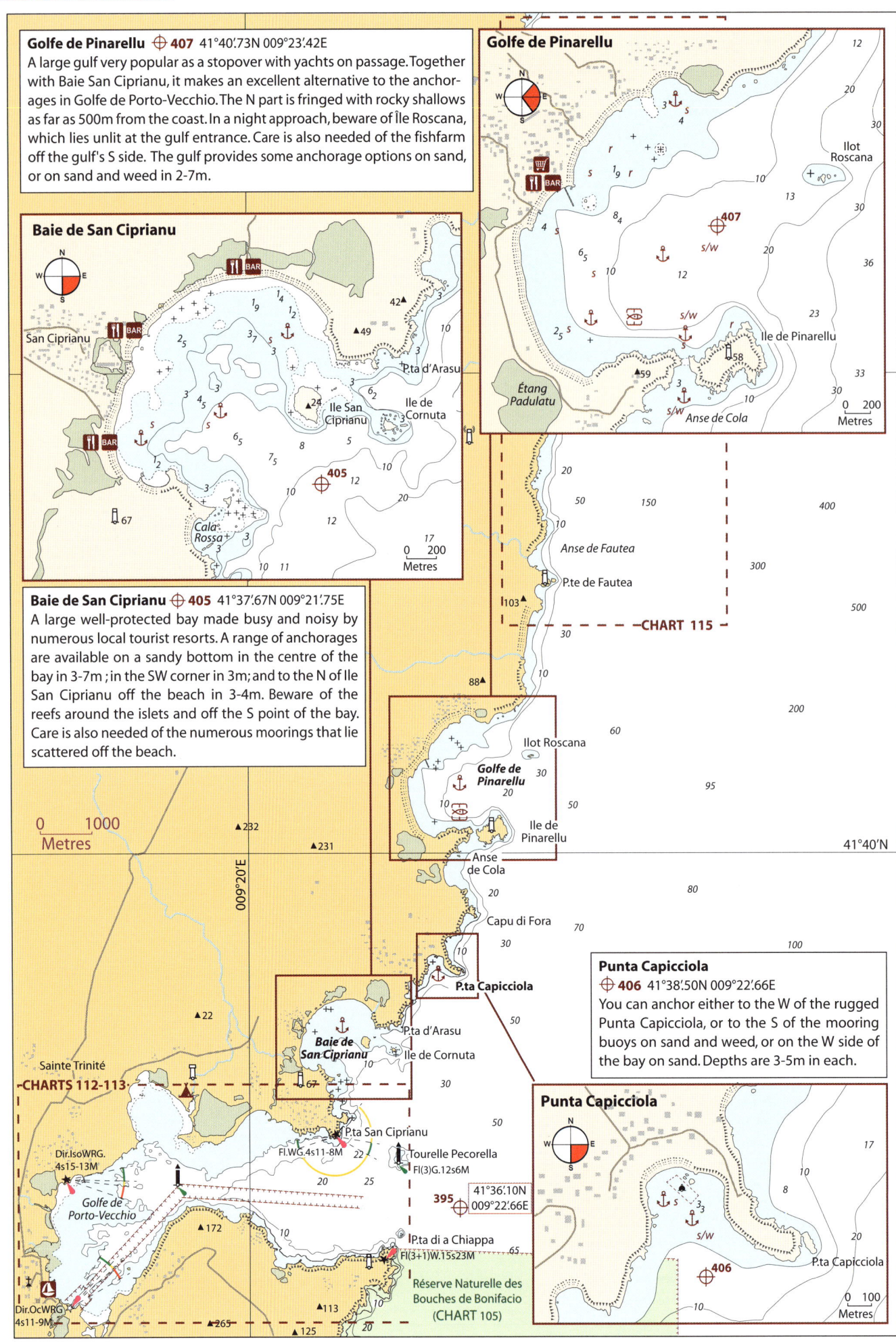

395 41°36'.10N 009°22'.66E

162

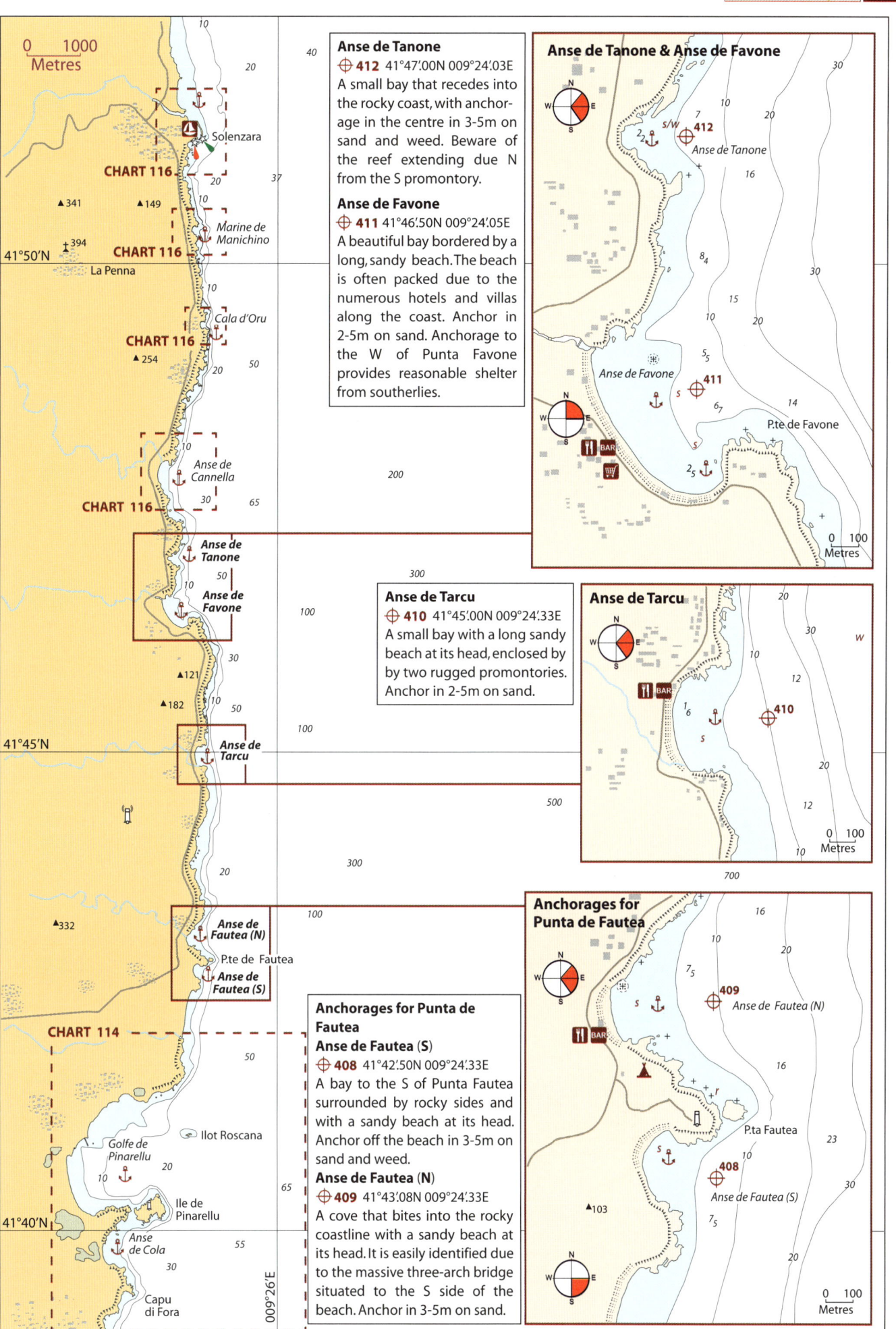

FROM GOLFE DE PINNARELLU TO SOLENZARA | AREA F

CHART 115

Anse de Tanone
⊕ **412** 41°47'.00N 009°24'.03E
A small bay that recedes into the rocky coast, with anchorage in the centre in 3-5m on sand and weed. Beware of the reef extending due N from the S promontory.

Anse de Favone
⊕ **411** 41°46'.50N 009°24'.05E
A beautiful bay bordered by a long, sandy beach. The beach is often packed due to the numerous hotels and villas along the coast. Anchor in 2-5m on sand. Anchorage to the W of Punta Favone provides reasonable shelter from southerlies.

Anse de Tarcu
⊕ **410** 41°45'.00N 009°24'.33E
A small bay with a long sandy beach at its head, enclosed by by two rugged promontories. Anchor in 2-5m on sand.

Anchorages for Punta de Fautea

Anse de Fautea (S)
⊕ **408** 41°42'.50N 009°24'.33E
A bay to the S of Punta Fautea surrounded by rocky sides and with a sandy beach at its head. Anchor off the beach in 3-5m on sand and weed.

Anse de Fautea (N)
⊕ **409** 41°43'.08N 009°24'.33E
A cove that bites into the rocky coastline with a sandy beach at its head. It is easily identified due to the massive three-arch bridge situated to the S side of the beach. Anchor in 3-5m on sand.

163

CHART 116 — AREA F — FROM ANSE DE CANNELLA TO SOLENZARA

NOTE The stretch from Golfe de Pinarellu to Solenzara provides the coast's last few fairweather shelters, after which Taverna is the only harbour until Bastia.

Cala D'Oru ⊕ 414 41°49'.48N 009°24'.35E
A small half-moon cove that bites into the rocky coastline. A sand-and-pebble beach lies at its head. Anchor in the centre of the bay in 3-4m on sand. In the approach, watch out for the underwater reef extending NE and SE from the N point.

Anse de Cannella ⊕ 413 41°47'.85N 009°23'.86E
A semi-deserted bay with a beautiful pebble beach and a coastal road running behind it. Anchor in 3-4m on sand.

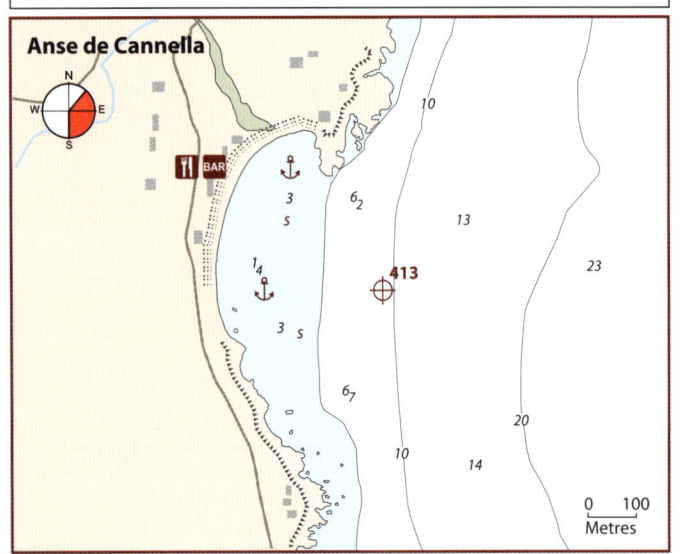

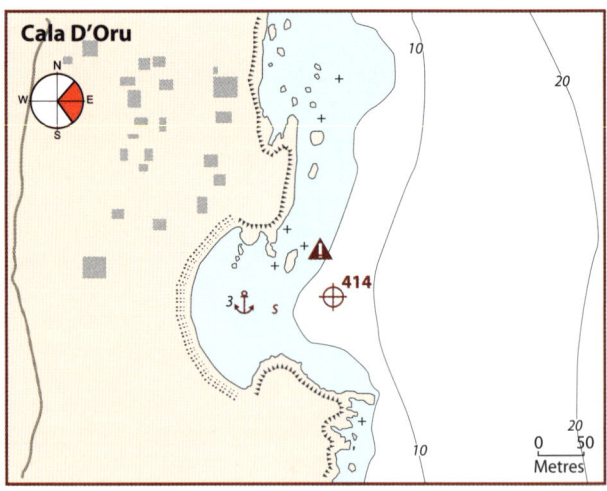

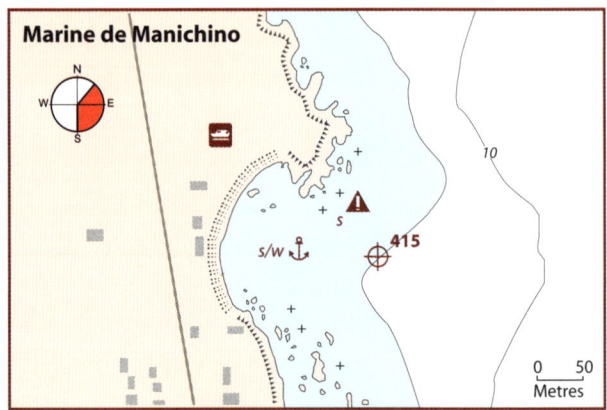

Marine de Manichino
⊕ 415 41°50'.42N 009°24'.24E
A small bay with a beach at its head and partly sheltered to the N by a rocky promontory. The anchorage is best approached on a NW route, as the shore is littered with rocks and shoal water. Anchor in 3-4m on sand and weed. Onshore is a hardstanding area for small motor boats.

Port de Solenzara
⊕ 416 41°51'.34N 009°24'.18E
A lovely harbour, but often packed in summer. It makes a great place to stop-off to break up the journey from N to S, or viceversa. A 26m-high telephone antenna at the root of the inner breakwater makes the harbour easy to identify. The marina accommodates 450 berths, with 150 for visitors (max. LOA 30m). In strong NE to SE winds, entry may become difficult, if not dangerous. Provisions are available from a village which is about ten minutes away. Yachts can anchor to the N of the river mouth off a long sandy beach when conditions are favourable.
Harbourmaster and Mairie di Solenzara:
VHF ch 09 - ☎ +33 (0)495 574642
Entry: 7.00 am - 9.00 pm summer; 8.00 am - 12.00 pm / 2.00 pm - 6.00 pm Monday to Friday for the rest of the year.
capitainerie@mairie-sari-solenzara.fr.
Online reservations:
www.resaportcorse.com
Fuel quay: summer 7.00 am - 12.00 pm / 1.00 pm - 8.00 pm; rest of the year 8.00 am - 12.00 pm / 2.00 pm - 6.00 pm.

FROM SOLENZARA TO BASTIA — AREA F

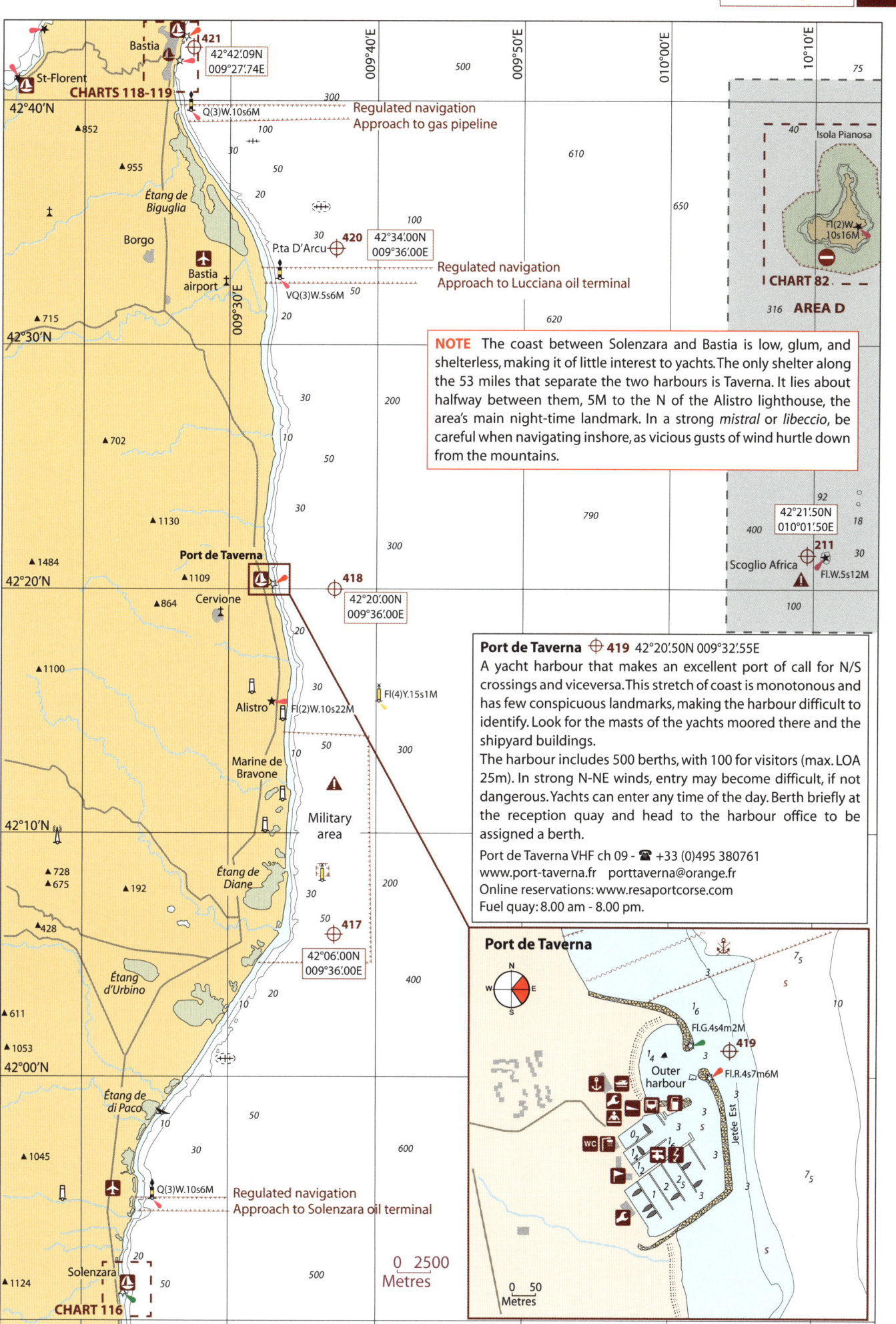

CHART 117

NOTE The coast between Solenzara and Bastia is low, glum, and shelterless, making it of little interest to yachts. The only shelter along the 53 miles that separate the two harbours is Taverna. It lies about halfway between them, 5M to the N of the Alistro lighthouse, the area's main night-time landmark. In a strong *mistral* or *libeccio*, be careful when navigating inshore, as vicious gusts of wind hurtle down from the mountains.

Port de Taverna ⊕ 419 42°20′.50N 009°32′.55E
A yacht harbour that makes an excellent port of call for N/S crossings and viceversa. This stretch of coast is monotonous and has few conspicuous landmarks, making the harbour difficult to identify. Look for the masts of the yachts moored there and the shipyard buildings.

The harbour includes 500 berths, with 100 for visitors (max. LOA 25m). In strong N-NE winds, entry may become difficult, if not dangerous. Yachts can enter any time of the day. Berth briefly at the reception quay and head to the harbour office to be assigned a berth.

Port de Taverna VHF ch 09 - ☎ +33 (0)495 380761
www.port-taverna.fr   porttaverna@orange.fr
Online reservations: www.resaportcorse.com
Fuel quay: 8.00 am - 8.00 pm.

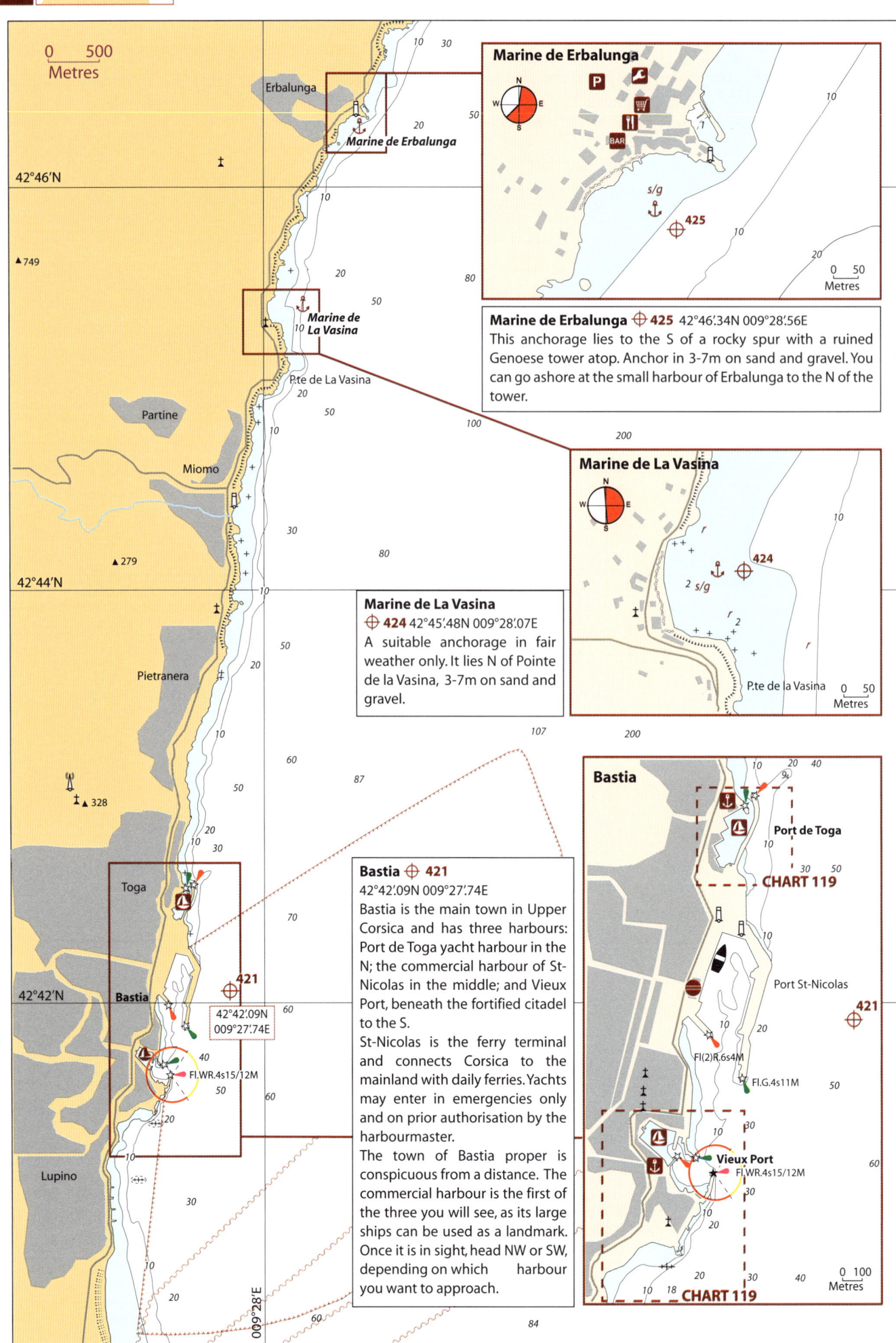

CHART 118 — AREA F — FROM BASTIA TO MARINE DE ERBALUNGA

Marine de Erbalunga ⊕ 425 42°46'.34N 009°28'.56E
This anchorage lies to the S of a rocky spur with a ruined Genoese tower atop. Anchor in 3-7m on sand and gravel. You can go ashore at the small harbour of Erbalunga to the N of the tower.

Marine de La Vasina
⊕ 424 42°45'.48N 009°28'.07E
A suitable anchorage in fair weather only. It lies N of Pointe de la Vasina, 3-7m on sand and gravel.

Bastia ⊕ 421
42°42'.09N 009°27'.74E
Bastia is the main town in Upper Corsica and has three harbours: Port de Toga yacht harbour in the N; the commercial harbour of St-Nicolas in the middle; and Vieux Port, beneath the fortified citadel to the S.
St-Nicolas is the ferry terminal and connects Corsica to the mainland with daily ferries. Yachts may enter in emergencies only and on prior authorisation by the harbourmaster.
The town of Bastia proper is conspicuous from a distance. The commercial harbour is the first of the three you will see, as its large ships can be used as a landmark. Once it is in sight, head NW or SW, depending on which harbour you want to approach.

BASTIA | AREA F

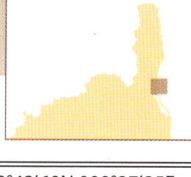

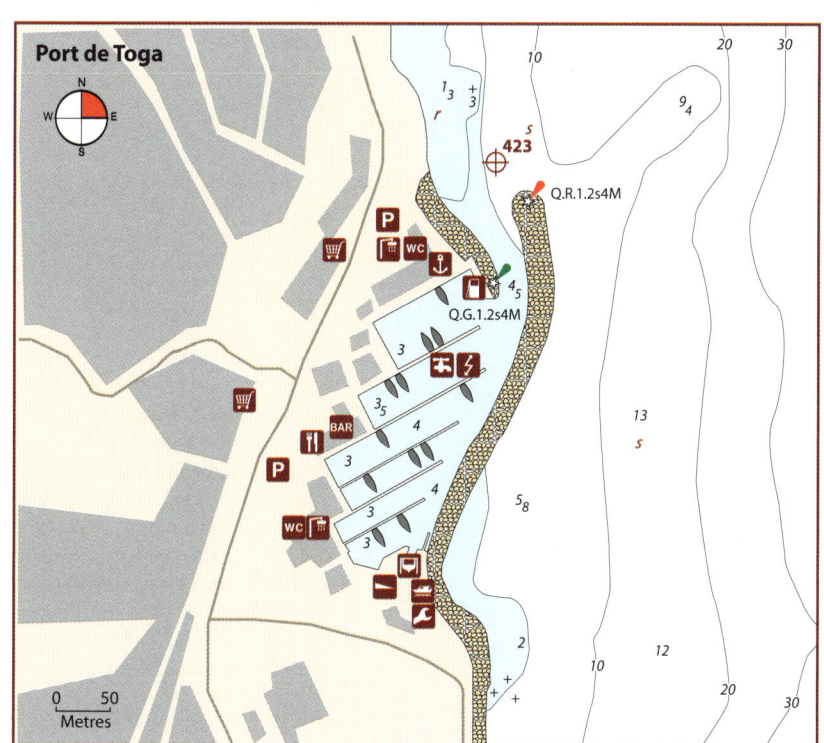

CHART 119

Port de Toga ⊕ 423 42°42'.60N 009°27'.35E

You would struggle to spot the harbour entrance were it not for the tall white tower on the head of the N breakwater bearing the words "Port de Toga". The entrance is hidden behind it. Round the breakwater until the access channel (about 30m wide) comes into sight.
The marina can accommodate 360 yachts (max. LOA 25-30m), with 60 visitors berths. Approach in strong N-NE and SE winds may be difficult. In this case, contact the harbour staff for assistance.
Before entering, contact the marina:
VHF ch 06/11/12 (see times below)
☎ +33 495 349070 (8.00 am - 8.00 pm summer; 8.00 am - 12.00 pm / 2.00 pm - 6.00 pm for the rest of the year).
www.seml-port-toga.fr - port.toga@orange.it
Online reservations: www.resaportcorse.com

Bastia - helpful numbers

Port Authority: harbourmaster on the Madonnetta quay ☎ +33 (0) 495 313110 (8.00 am - 8.00 pm summer; 8.30 am - 12.00 pm / 2.00 pm - 5.00 pm winter)
Harbour services:
Bastia Town Council ☎ +33 (0)495 559510
Customs: ☎ +33 (0)495 348787
Emergency medical services:
Cross Corse VHF ch 16 - ☎ +33 (0)495 201363

Vieux Port ⊕ 422 42°41'.67N 009°27'.22E

This characteristic harbour, which is administered by the local council, has been carved into the coast and sits at the foot of the citadel. It is protected by two long moles (Môle Génois and Jeteé du Dragon), but in strong N-E winds, approach is hazardous and mooring untenable due to the considerable surge inside the harbour. The approach may also be made awkward by the strong SW gusts into the harbour. Should a yacht need to leave its berth, safe emergency shelter can be found in the commercial port of St-Nicolas, but prior authorisation from the harbourmaster is required. Care is needed of manoeuvring ferries, which always have right of way.
The harbour accommodates 270 yachts (max. LOA 35m), with 30 visitors berths. The latter are divided as follows: 20 (max. LOA 12m) on the inner side of Môle Génois on moorings; 10 (max. LOA 30m) on Jeteé du Dragon. The latter mole is reserved for large yachts and you may need to drop your anchor and use a trip line due to the muddy bottom. In the summer, it is prohibited to use an anchor inside the basin.
All the main services and facilities are available nearby and in town.
Porto Vecchio VHF ch 09 (open all day).
Entry: 8.00 am - 8.00 pm summer; 8.30 am - 12.00 pm / 2.00 pm - 5.00 pm for the rest of the year.
☎ +33 (0)495 313110
vieux-port@ville-bastia.fr
Online reservations: www.resaportcorse.com
Fuel quay: 8.00 am - 8.00 pm summer; 8.00 am - 12.00 pm / 2.00 pm - 6.00 pm for the rest of the year.

Anchorage In settled weather, it is possible to anchor SW of the citadel in 5-8m on sand and gravel.

167

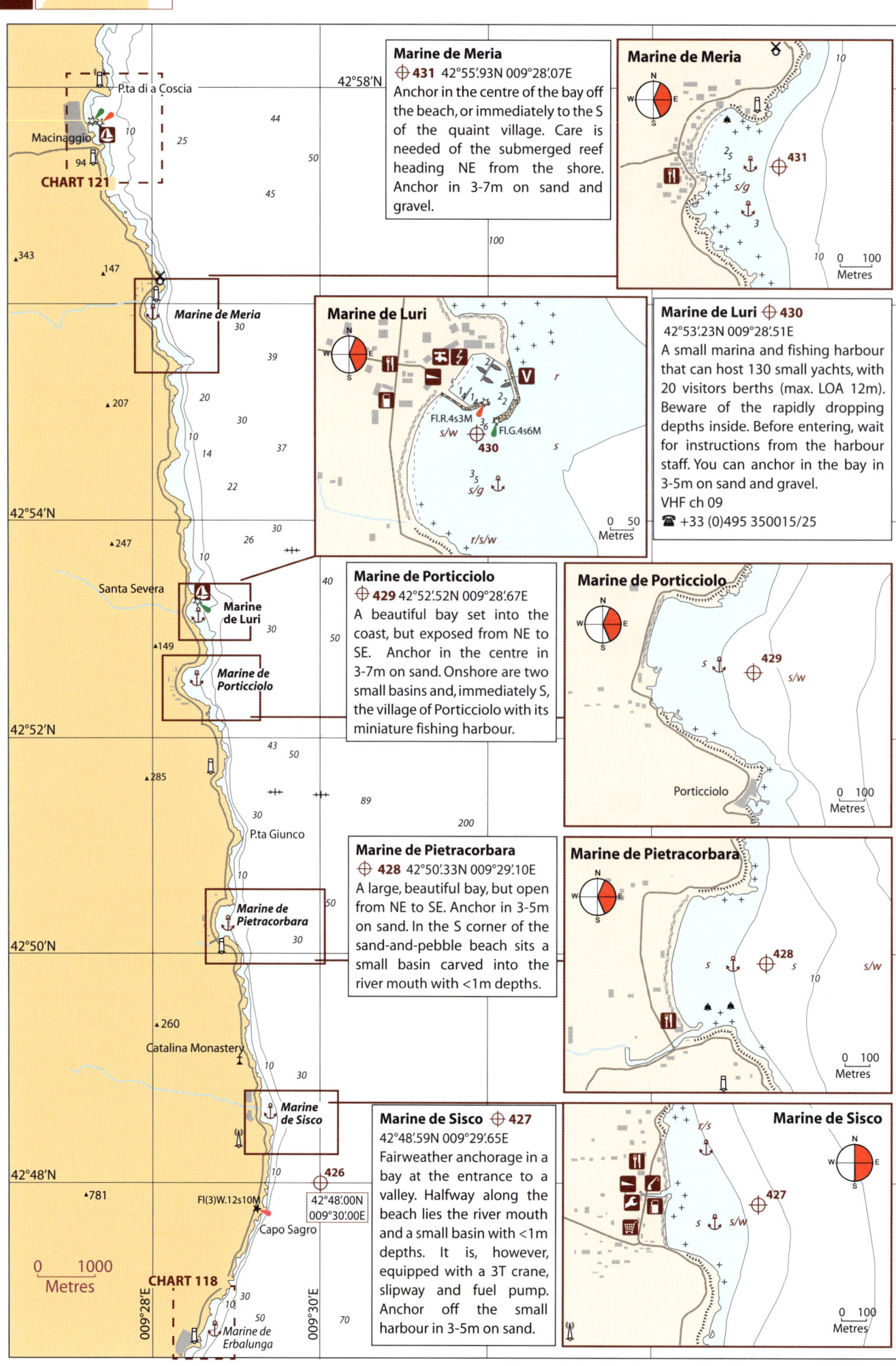

CHART 120 — AREA F — FROM MARINE DE ERBALUNGA TO MACINAGGIO

Marine de Meria
⊕ 431 42°55'.93N 009°28'.07E
Anchor in the centre of the bay off the beach, or immediately to the S of the quaint village. Care is needed of the submerged reef heading NE from the shore. Anchor in 3-7m on sand and gravel.

Marine de Luri ⊕ 430
42°53'.23N 009°28'.51E
A small marina and fishing harbour that can host 130 small yachts, with 20 visitors berths (max. LOA 12m). Beware of the rapidly dropping depths inside. Before entering, wait for instructions from the harbour staff. You can anchor in the bay in 3-5m on sand and gravel.
VHF ch 09
☎ +33 (0)495 350015/25

Marine de Porticciolo
⊕ 429 42°52'.52N 009°28'.67E
A beautiful bay set into the coast, but exposed from NE to SE. Anchor in the centre in 3-7m on sand. Onshore are two small basins and, immediately S, the village of Porticciolo with its miniature fishing harbour.

Marine de Pietracorbara
⊕ 428 42°50'.33N 009°29'.10E
A large, beautiful bay, but open from NE to SE. Anchor in 3-5m on sand. In the S corner of the sand-and-pebble beach sits a small basin carved into the river mouth with <1m depths.

Marine de Sisco ⊕ 427
42°48'.59N 009°29'.65E
Fairweather anchorage in a bay at the entrance to a valley. Halfway along the beach lies the river mouth and a small basin with <1m depths. It is, however, equipped with a 3T crane, slipway and fuel pump. Anchor off the small harbour in 3-5m on sand.

FROM MACINAGGIO TO CENTURI — AREA F

CHART 121

Baie de Macinaggio
⊕ **432** 42°57'.82 N 009°27'.35E

The bay is exposed from NE to SE, but is an excellent alternative to the harbour, even in a strong *mistral* or *libeccio*. Make sure, however, that you have dropped lots of chain and that the anchor has a good grip. Anchor in 3-7m on sand. Good holding in the central part, but further N the bottom is muddy and holding poor.

Port de Macinaggio
⊕ **433** 42°57'.65N 009°27'.25E

Opposite a sleepy fishing village stands the pleasant harbour of Macinaggio. It is very popular as it is Corsica's first or last harbour after the crossing from or for the mainland.

Equipped with comprehensive services and facilities, it has a capacity of 585 berths (max. LOA 40m) with 200 places for visiting yachts. In a *mistral* or *libeccio*, fierce gusts fall down from the surrounding high land and blow within the harbour. However, the hazard is limited to manoeuvring. Strong NE-SE winds may compromise the approach and make it dangerous. When entering, keep close to the outer breakwater, as the inner one is prone to silting.

Harbour services: VHF ch 09
Offices ☎ +33 (0) 495 354257 / (7.00 am - 9.00 pm summer; 8.00 am - 12.00 pm / 2.00 pm - 6.00 pm winter) - port.macinaggio@orange.fr
www.portmacinaggio.com
Online reservations: www.ResaPortCorse.com

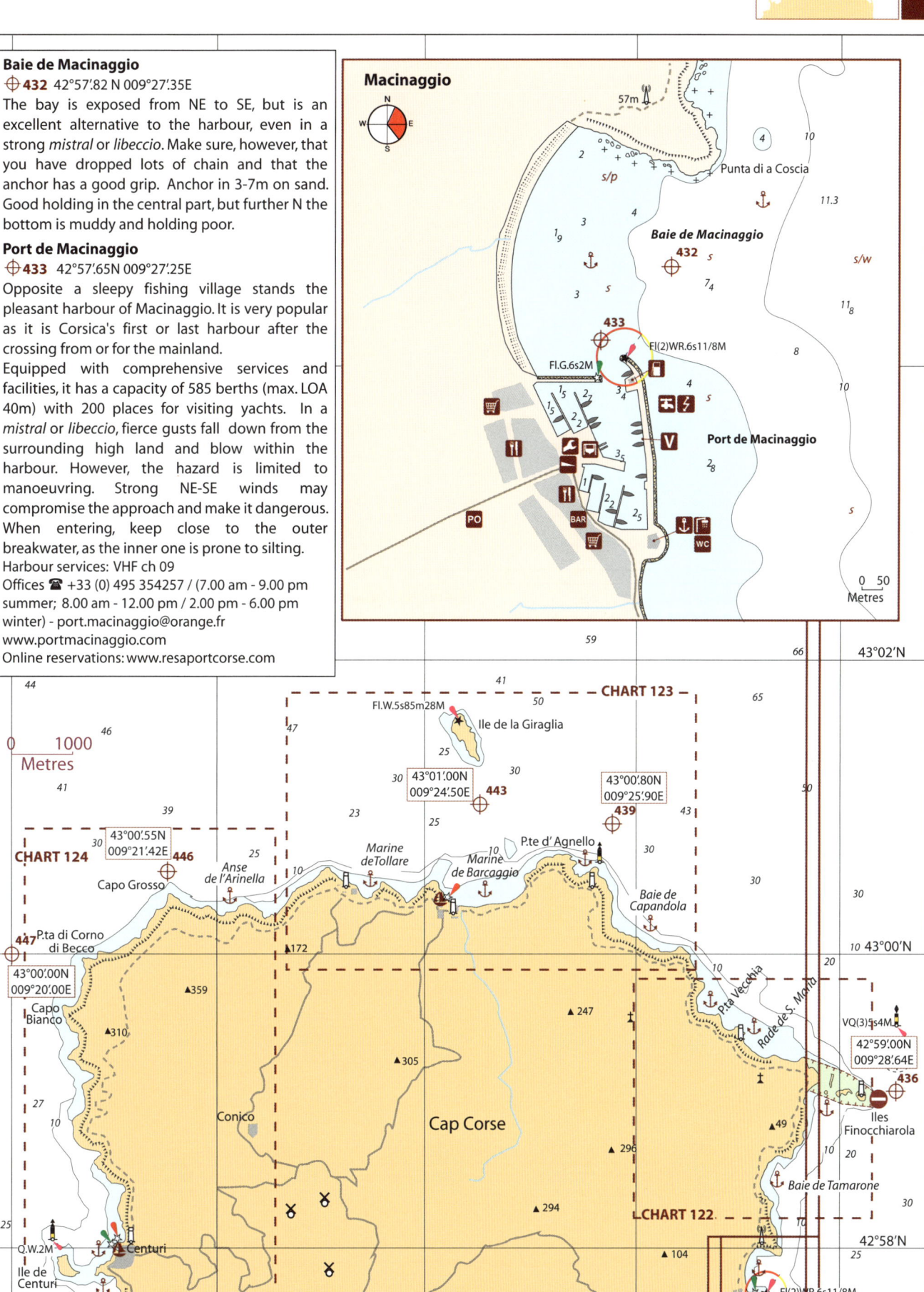

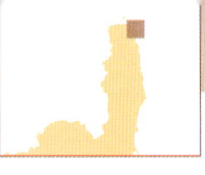

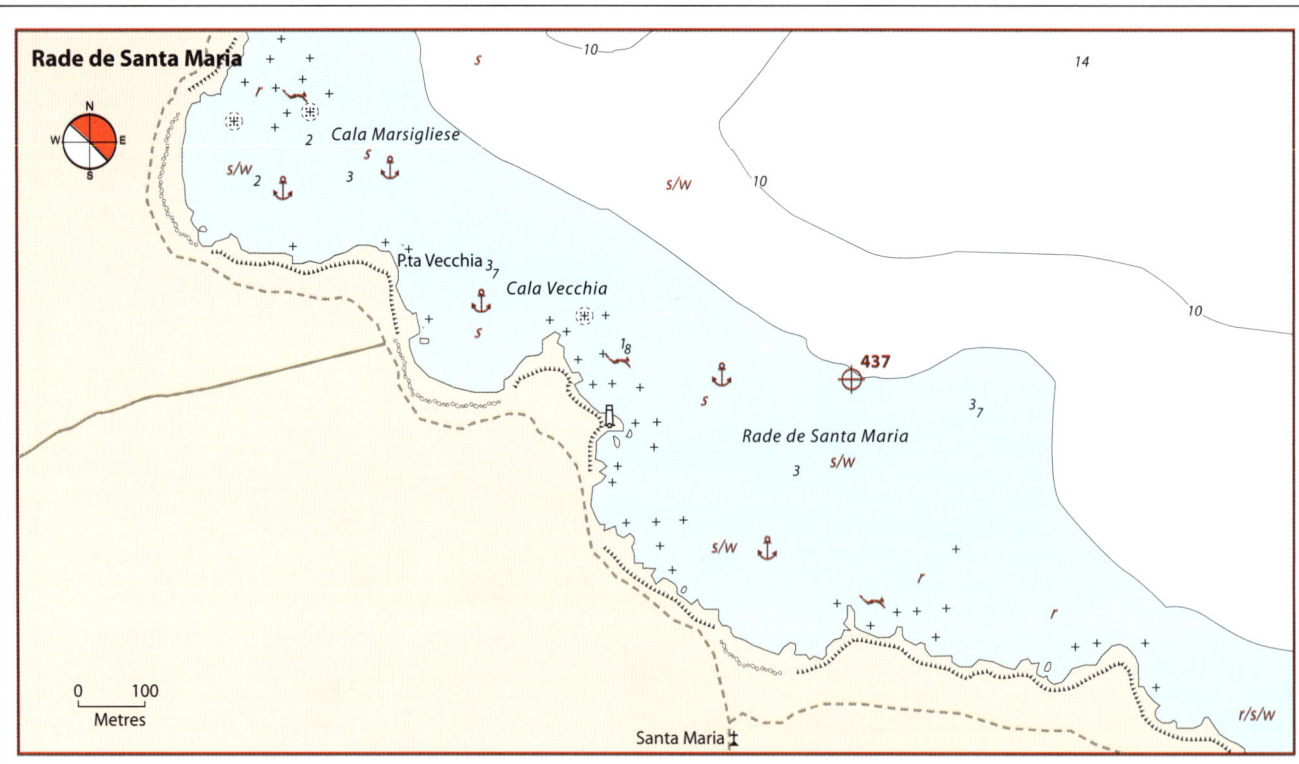

AREA F FROM BAIE DE TAMARONE TO RADE DE SANTA MARIA

CHART 122

Rade de Santa Maria ⊕ 437 42°59'.55N 009°27'.40E
Secluded anchorages, although not quite the case in high season, open from NW to E. The rocky coast is interspersed with bays boasting sand and pebble beaches. A ruined Genoese tower and the chapel of Saint Mary immediately inland are conspicuous. Anchor in one of the coves in 3-7m on sand and weed. Care should be taken of the rocks and reefs off the coast and the points.

Baie de Tamarone ⊕ 434 42°58'.42N 009°27'.48E
A wide bay with a sandy beach that is an alternative anchorage to Baie de Macinaggio. Anchor in the centre in 3-7 m on sand. Keep well clear from the NE promontory as rocky shallows run out from it. Although the bay provides reasonable shelter from strong southerlies and westerlies, gusts fall down from the surrounding mountains.

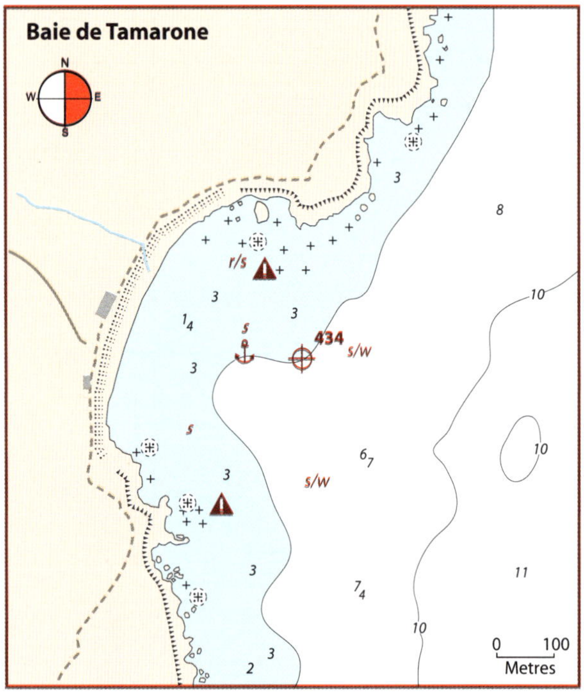

Réserve Naturelle des Îles Finocchiarola
This nature reserve covers 3 hectares and encompasses the three largest islands, plus the islets of the Finocchiarola archipelago, which stretches about 700m seaward. The largest and outermost island is home to an old guardhouse and a dilapidated Genoese tower.
The following are prohibited inside the reserve: anchoring on the mooring buoys that mark the reserve boundary; landing on the islands from 1 March to 31 August; and swimming within 50m of the islets. The reserve is administered by the Finocchiarola Association.

Rade de Finocchiarola ⊕ 435 42°58'.83N 009°28'.08E
A beautiful, peaceful site with anchorage S of Iles Finocchiarola outside the reserve; its boundary is marked by yellow buoys. Anchor in 3-7m on sand, but in certain areas the bottom is muddy and holding poor. Beware also of the below-water rocks bordering the shore. The NW corner of the bay affords the best protection.

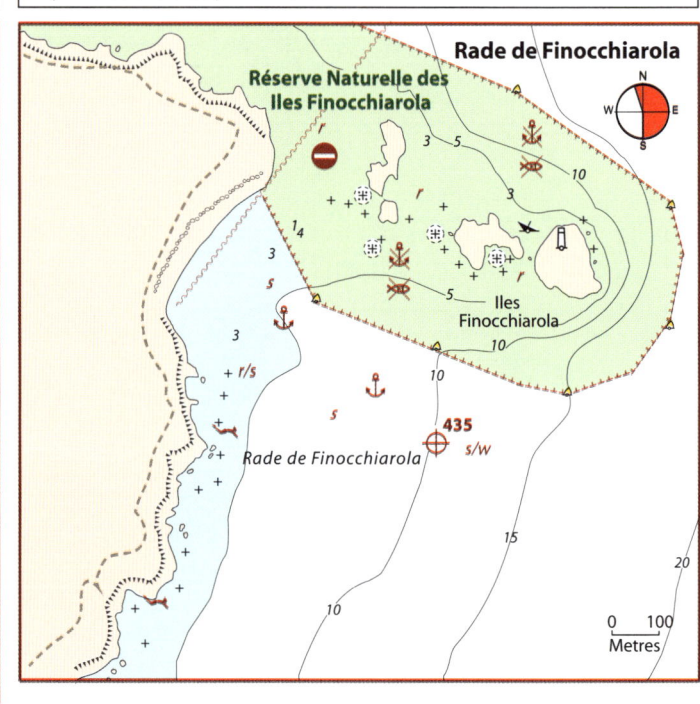

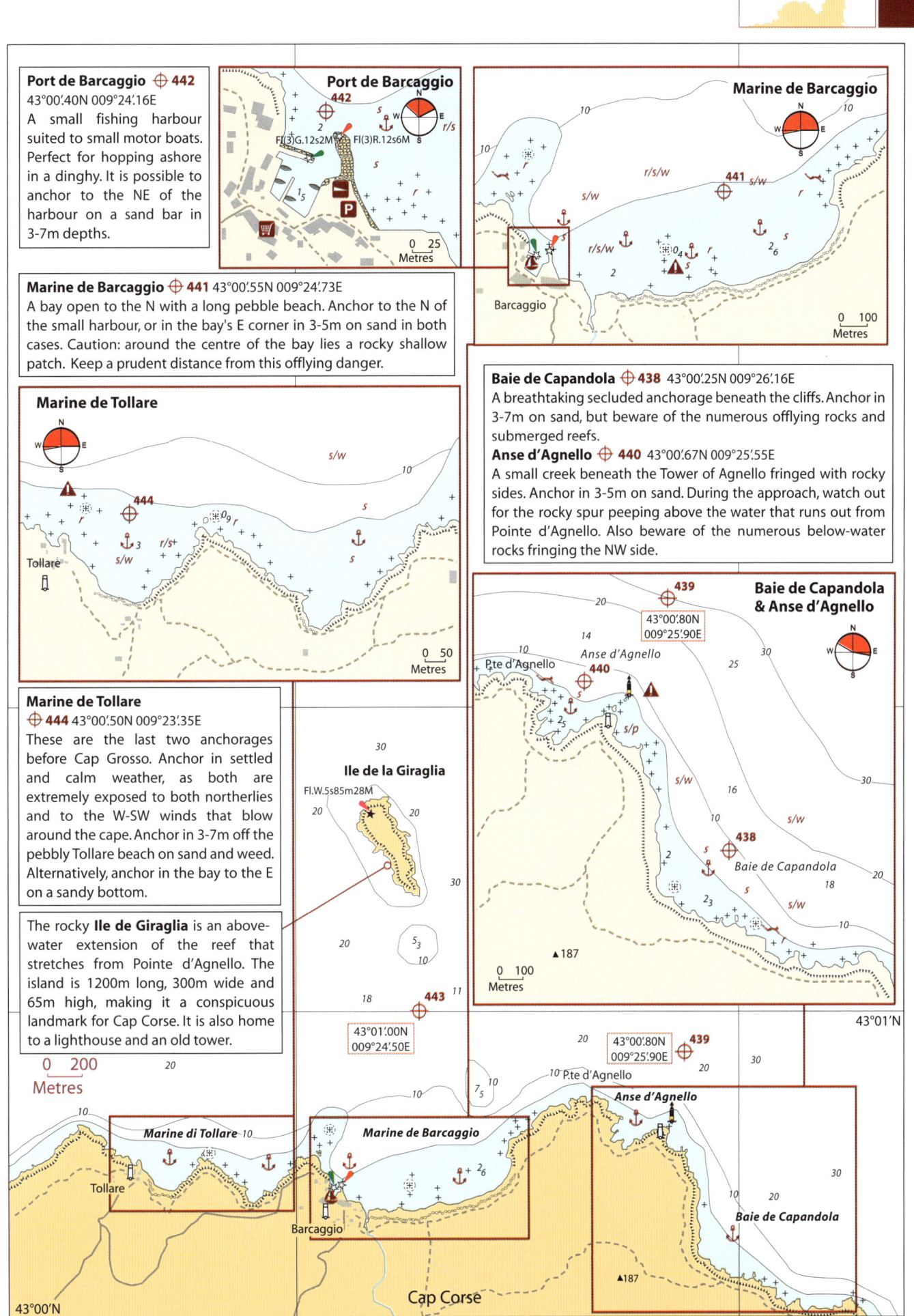

FROM BAIE DE CAPANDOLA TO MARINE DE TOLLARE — AREA F

CHART 123

Port de Barcaggio ⊕ 442
43°00'.40N 009°24'.16E

A small fishing harbour suited to small motor boats. Perfect for hopping ashore in a dinghy. It is possible to anchor to the NE of the harbour on a sand bar in 3-7m depths.

Marine de Barcaggio ⊕ 441 43°00'.55N 009°24'.73E

A bay open to the N with a long pebble beach. Anchor to the N of the small harbour, or in the bay's E corner in 3-5m on sand in both cases. Caution: around the centre of the bay lies a rocky shallow patch. Keep a prudent distance from this offlying danger.

Baie de Capandola ⊕ 438 43°00'.25N 009°26'.16E

A breathtaking secluded anchorage beneath the cliffs. Anchor in 3-7m on sand, but beware of the numerous offlying rocks and submerged reefs.

Anse d'Agnello ⊕ 440 43°00'.67N 009°25'.55E

A small creek beneath the Tower of Agnello fringed with rocky sides. Anchor in 3-5m on sand. During the approach, watch out for the rocky spur peeping above the water that runs out from Pointe d'Agnello. Also beware of the numerous below-water rocks fringing the NW side.

Marine de Tollare
⊕ 444 43°00'.50N 009°23'.35E

These are the last two anchorages before Cap Grosso. Anchor in settled and calm weather, as both are extremely exposed to both northerlies and to the W-SW winds that blow around the cape. Anchor in 3-7m off the pebbly Tollare beach on sand and weed. Alternatively, anchor in the bay to the E on a sandy bottom.

The rocky **Ile de Giraglia** is an above-water extension of the reef that stretches from Pointe d'Agnello. The island is 1200m long, 300m wide and 65m high, making it a conspicuous landmark for Cap Corse. It is also home to a lighthouse and an old tower.

171

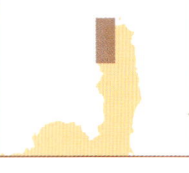

CHART 124 — AREA F — FROM CAPO GROSSO TO CAPU CORVOLI

Port de Centuri ⊕ 449   42°58'.05N 009°20'.94E
This small fishing harbour is wedged deep into the coastline and has a fishing town as a backdrop. Inside, the depths are shallow, so only small motor yachts should attempt access. It can currently host 60 yachts (max. LOA 10m), but is being extended to include another 125. There are 25 visitors berths. Approach is not recommended in strong NW winds, and the *libeccio* creates a considerable surge inside.
Centuri is famed for its lobster and consequently for its restaurants.
Mairie de Centuri ☎ +33 (0)495 356006

Baie de Centuri ⊕ 448   42°57'.91N 009°20'.66E
This anchorage is protected from S-SW winds by Ile de Centuri and by a reef that joins it to the mainland. In strong winds, however, yachts will still be taking their chances, as anchorage is disturbed by an uncomfortable swell that creeps into the bay. This is an open bay, so even night anchorage in windless conditions is disturbed by an uncomfortable tidal wave.
When approaching, watch out for the numerous below-water rocks that run out from the island due 350°. Anchor in 4-7m on sand, or on sand and weed. In some points, holding is poor on the latter.

Anse de l'Arinella ⊕ 445   43°00'.39N 009°22'.48E
Fairweather anchorage, overlooked by the cliffs of Capo Grosso, in 4-7m on sand and weed.

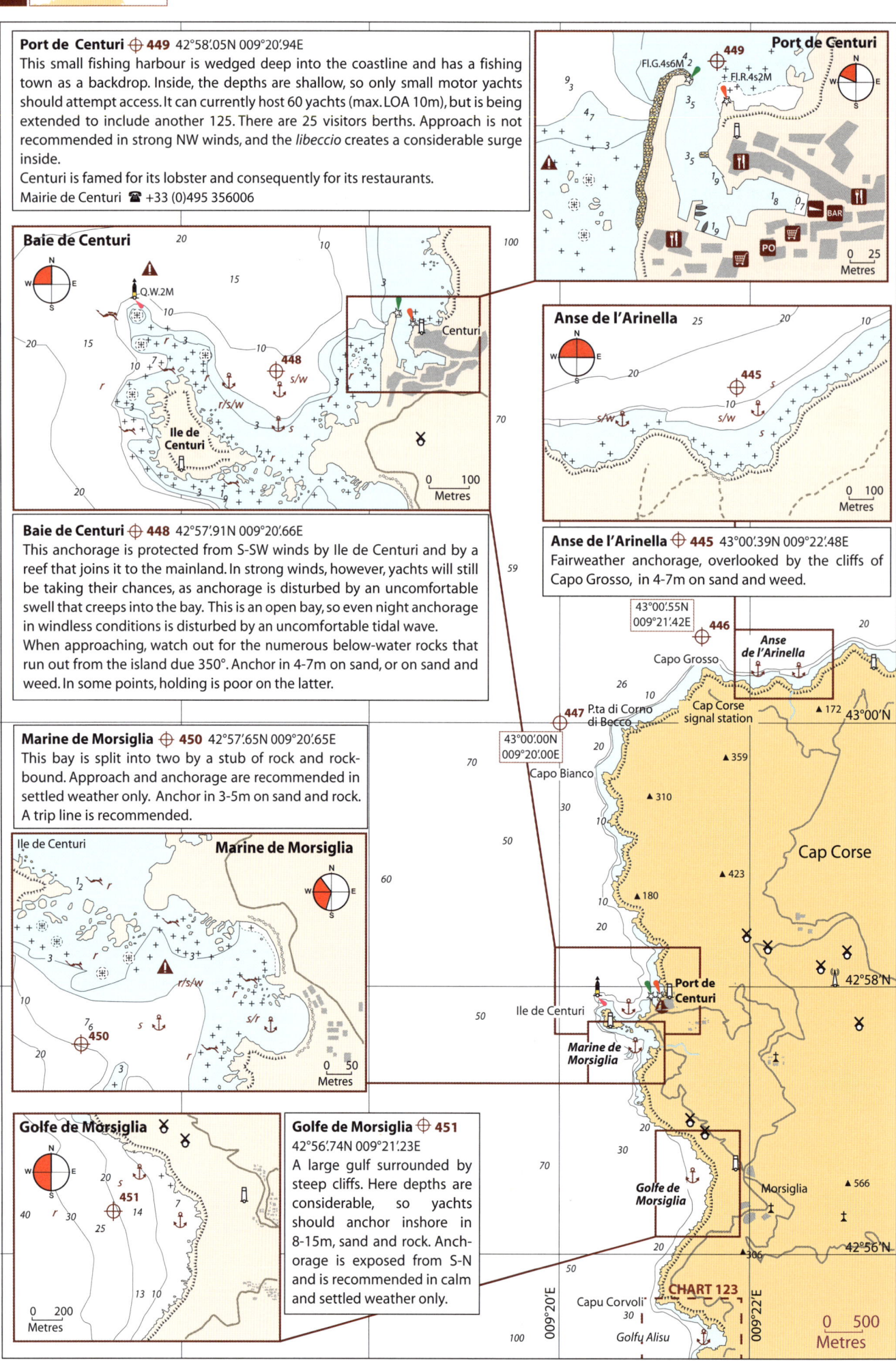

Marine de Morsiglia ⊕ 450   42°57'.65N 009°20'.65E
This bay is split into two by a stub of rock and rock-bound. Approach and anchorage are recommended in settled weather only. Anchor in 3-5m on sand and rock. A trip line is recommended.

Golfe de Morsiglia ⊕ 451   42°56'.74N 009°21'.23E
A large gulf surrounded by steep cliffs. Here depths are considerable, so yachts should anchor inshore in 8-15m, sand and rock. Anchorage is exposed from S-N and is recommended in calm and settled weather only.

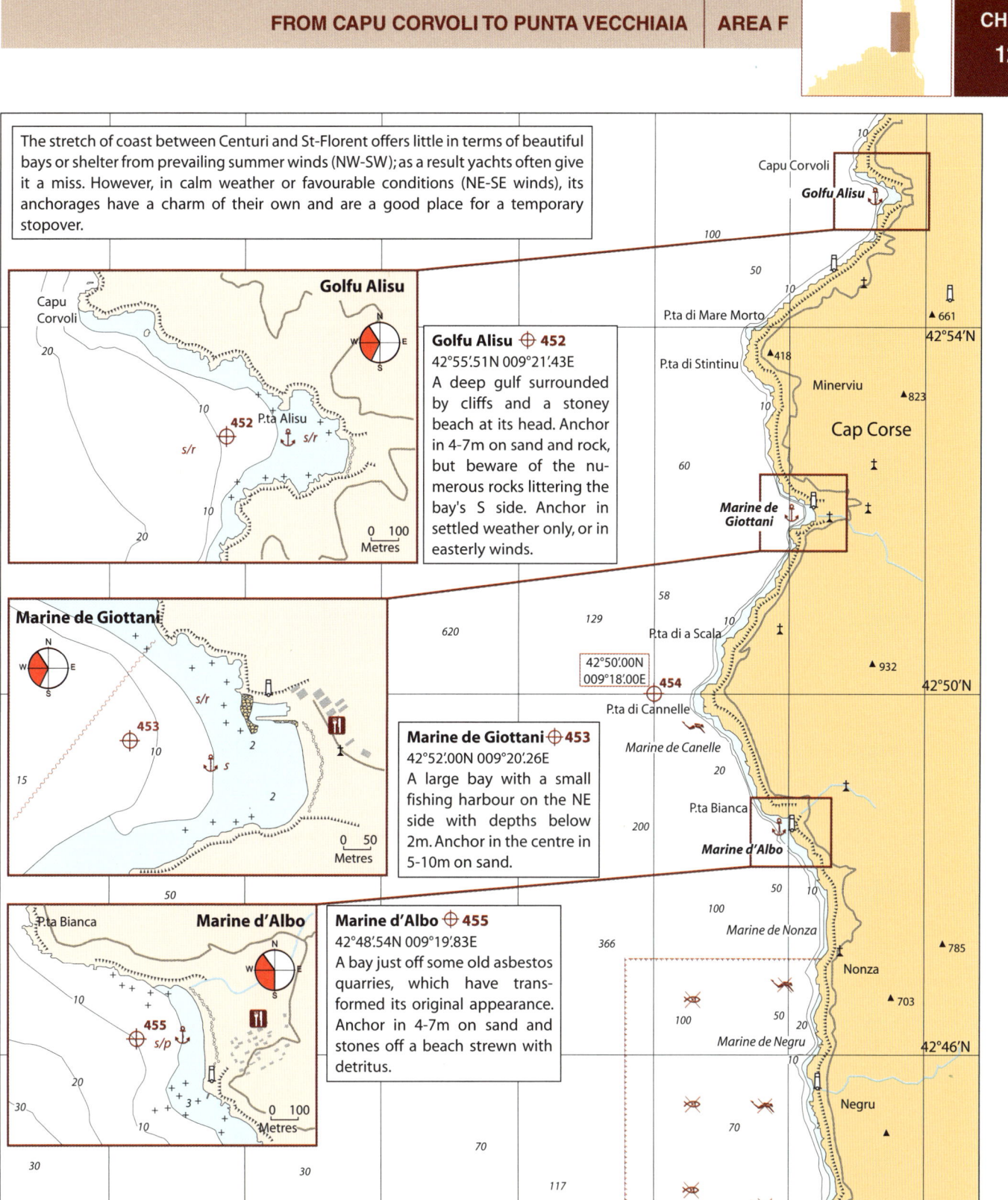

FROM CAPU CORVOLI TO PUNTA VECCHIAIA — AREA F — CHART 125

The stretch of coast between Centuri and St-Florent offers little in terms of beautiful bays or shelter from prevailing summer winds (NW-SW); as a result yachts often give it a miss. However, in calm weather or favourable conditions (NE-SE winds), its anchorages have a charm of their own and are a good place for a temporary stopover.

Golfu Alisu ⊕ 452
42°55'.51N 009°21'.43E
A deep gulf surrounded by cliffs and a stoney beach at its head. Anchor in 4-7m on sand and rock, but beware of the numerous rocks littering the bay's S side. Anchor in settled weather only, or in easterly winds.

Marine de Giottani ⊕ 453
42°52'.00N 009°20'.26E
A large bay with a small fishing harbour on the NE side with depths below 2m. Anchor in the centre in 5-10m on sand.

Marine d'Albo ⊕ 455
42°48'.54N 009°19'.83E
A bay just off some old asbestos quarries, which have transformed its original appearance. Anchor in 4-7m on sand and stones off a beach strewn with detritus.

Cala Farinole ⊕ 456
42°43'.49N 009°19'.85E
Anchor in 4-7m on sand off the pebbly beach to the N in settled weather only.

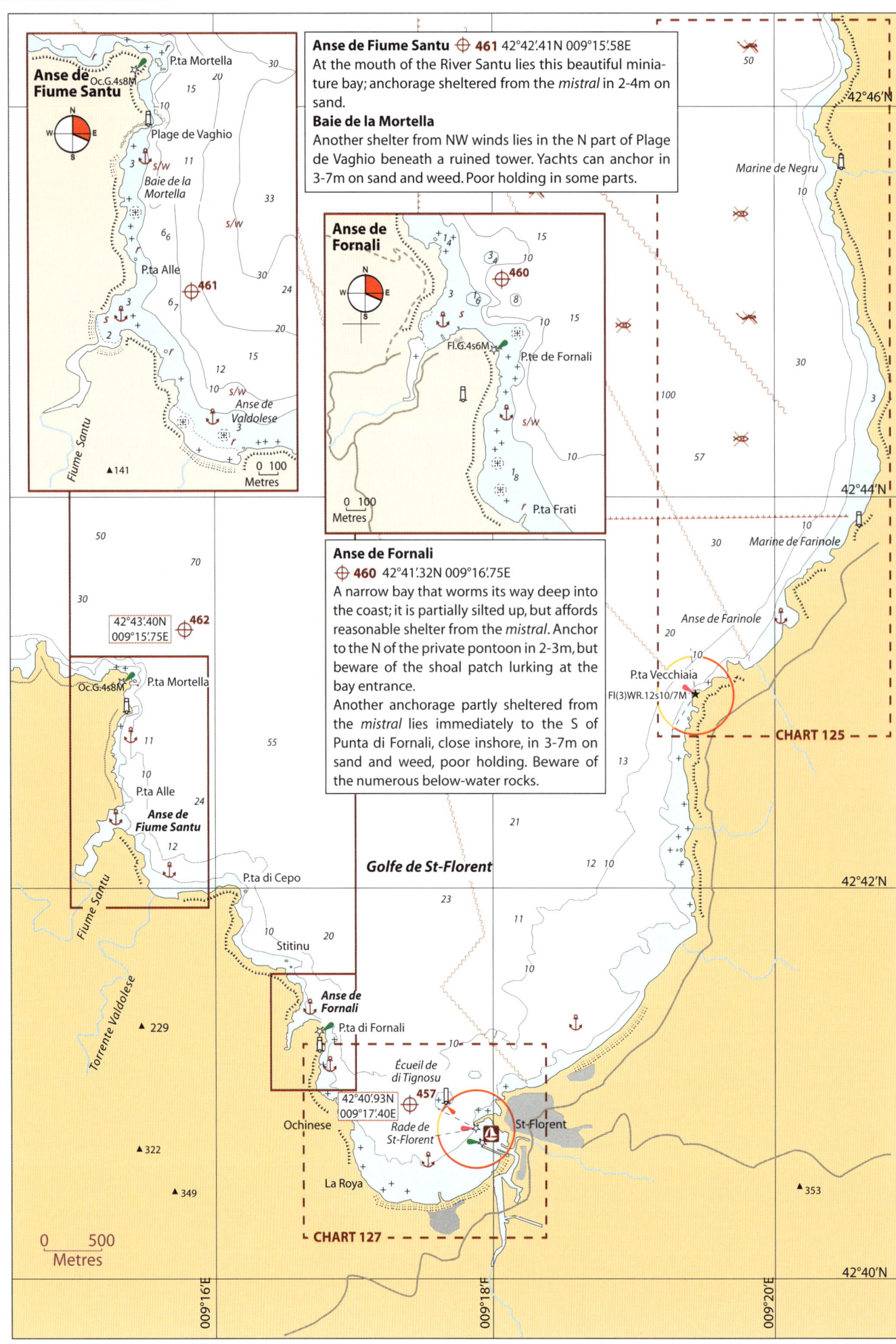

CHART 126 — AREA F — GOLFE DE ST-FLORENT

Anse de Fiume Santu ⊕ 461 42°42′.41N 009°15′.58E
At the mouth of the River Santu lies this beautiful miniature bay; anchorage sheltered from the *mistral* in 2-4m on sand.

Baie de la Mortella
Another shelter from NW winds lies in the N part of Plage de Vaghio beneath a ruined tower. Yachts can anchor in 3-7m on sand and weed. Poor holding in some parts.

Anse de Fornali
⊕ 460 42°41′.32N 009°16′.75E
A narrow bay that worms its way deep into the coast; it is partially silted up, but affords reasonable shelter from the *mistral*. Anchor to the N of the private pontoon in 2-3m, but beware of the shoal patch lurking at the bay entrance.

Another anchorage partly sheltered from the *mistral* lies immediately to the S of Punta di Fornali, close inshore, in 3-7m on sand and weed, poor holding. Beware of the numerous below-water rocks.

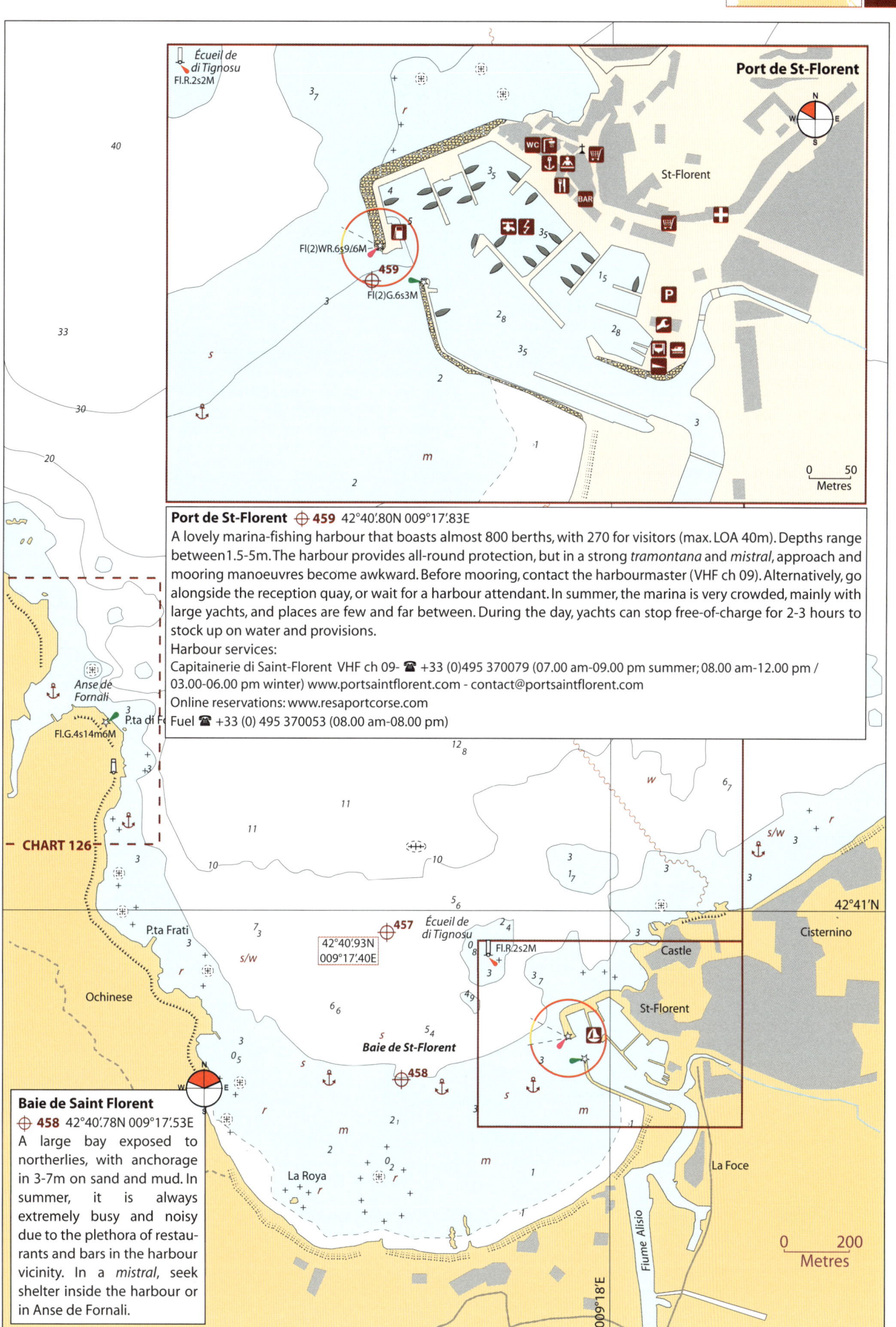

ST-FLORENT | AREA F

CHART 127

Port de St-Florent ⊕ 459 42°40'.80N 009°17'.83E

A lovely marina-fishing harbour that boasts almost 800 berths, with 270 for visitors (max. LOA 40m). Depths range between 1.5-5m. The harbour provides all-round protection, but in a strong *tramontana* and *mistral*, approach and mooring manoeuvres become awkward. Before mooring, contact the harbourmaster (VHF ch 09). Alternatively, go alongside the reception quay, or wait for a harbour attendant. In summer, the marina is very crowded, mainly with large yachts, and places are few and far between. During the day, yachts can stop free-of-charge for 2-3 hours to stock up on water and provisions.

Harbour services:
Capitainerie di Saint-Florent VHF ch 09- ☎ +33 (0)495 370079 (07.00 am-09.00 pm summer; 08.00 am-12.00 pm / 03.00-06.00 pm winter) www.portsaintflorent.com - contact@portsaintflorent.com
Online reservations: www.resaportcorse.com
Fuel ☎ +33 (0) 495 370053 (08.00 am-08.00 pm)

Baie de Saint Florent
⊕ 458 42°40'.78N 009°17'.53E
A large bay exposed to northerlies, with anchorage in 3-7m on sand and mud. In summer, it is always extremely busy and noisy due to the plethora of restaurants and bars in the harbour vicinity. In a *mistral*, seek shelter inside the harbour or in Anse de Fornali.

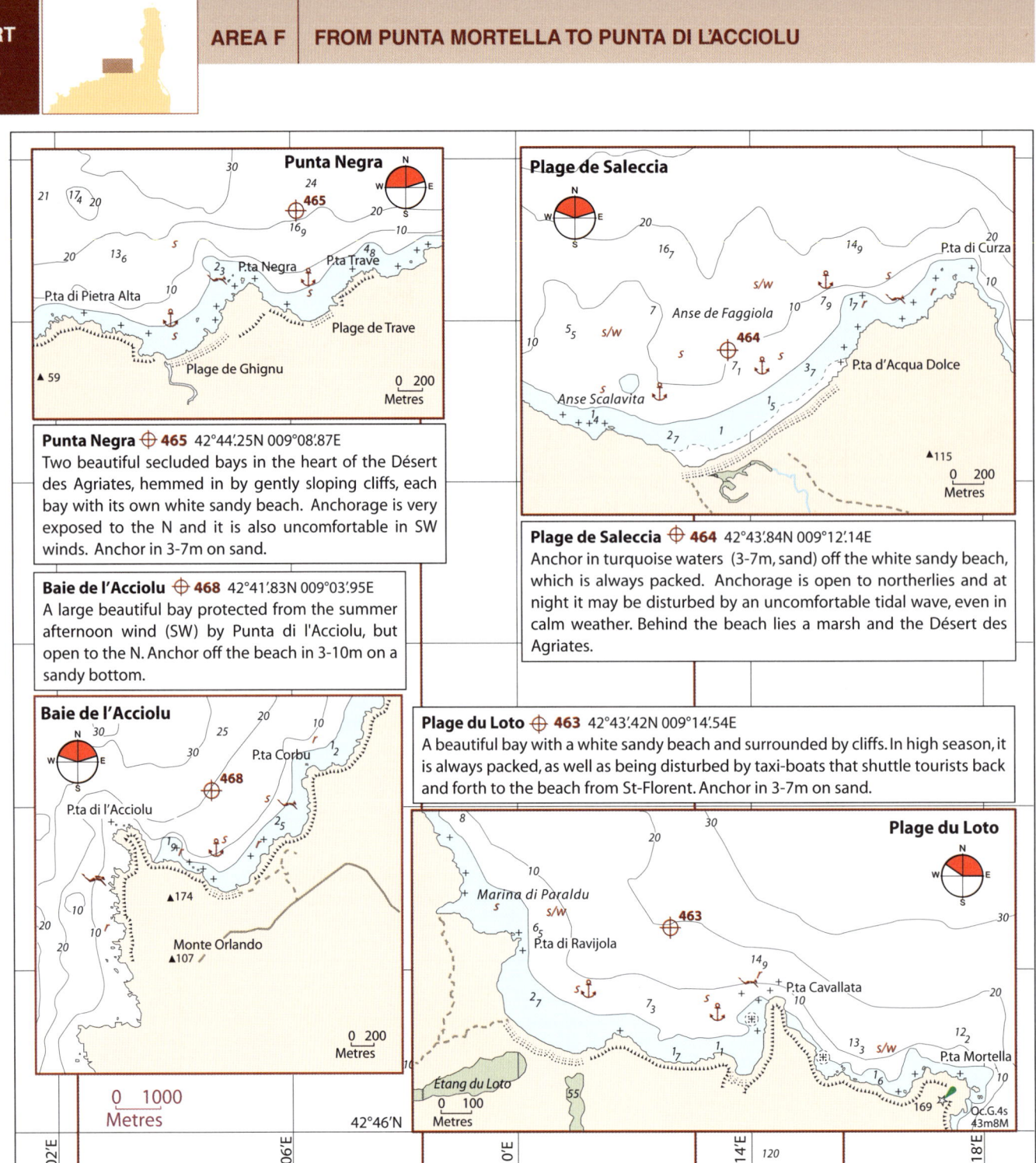

CHART 128 — **AREA F** — **FROM PUNTA MORTELLA TO PUNTA DI L'ACCIOLU**

Punta Negra ⊕ 465 42°44'.25N 009°08'.87E
Two beautiful secluded bays in the heart of the Désert des Agriates, hemmed in by gently sloping cliffs, each bay with its own white sandy beach. Anchorage is very exposed to the N and it is also uncomfortable in SW winds. Anchor in 3-7m on sand.

Baie de l'Acciolu ⊕ 468 42°41'.83N 009°03'.95E
A large beautiful bay protected from the summer afternoon wind (SW) by Punta di l'Acciolu, but open to the N. Anchor off the beach in 3-10m on a sandy bottom.

Plage de Saleccia ⊕ 464 42°43'.84N 009°12'.14E
Anchor in turquoise waters (3-7m, sand) off the white sandy beach, which is always packed. Anchorage is open to northerlies and at night it may be disturbed by an uncomfortable tidal wave, even in calm weather. Behind the beach lies a marsh and the Désert des Agriates.

Plage du Loto ⊕ 463 42°43'.42N 009°14'.54E
A beautiful bay with a white sandy beach and surrounded by cliffs. In high season, it is always packed, as well as being disturbed by taxi-boats that shuttle tourists back and forth to the beach from St-Florent. Anchor in 3-7m on sand.

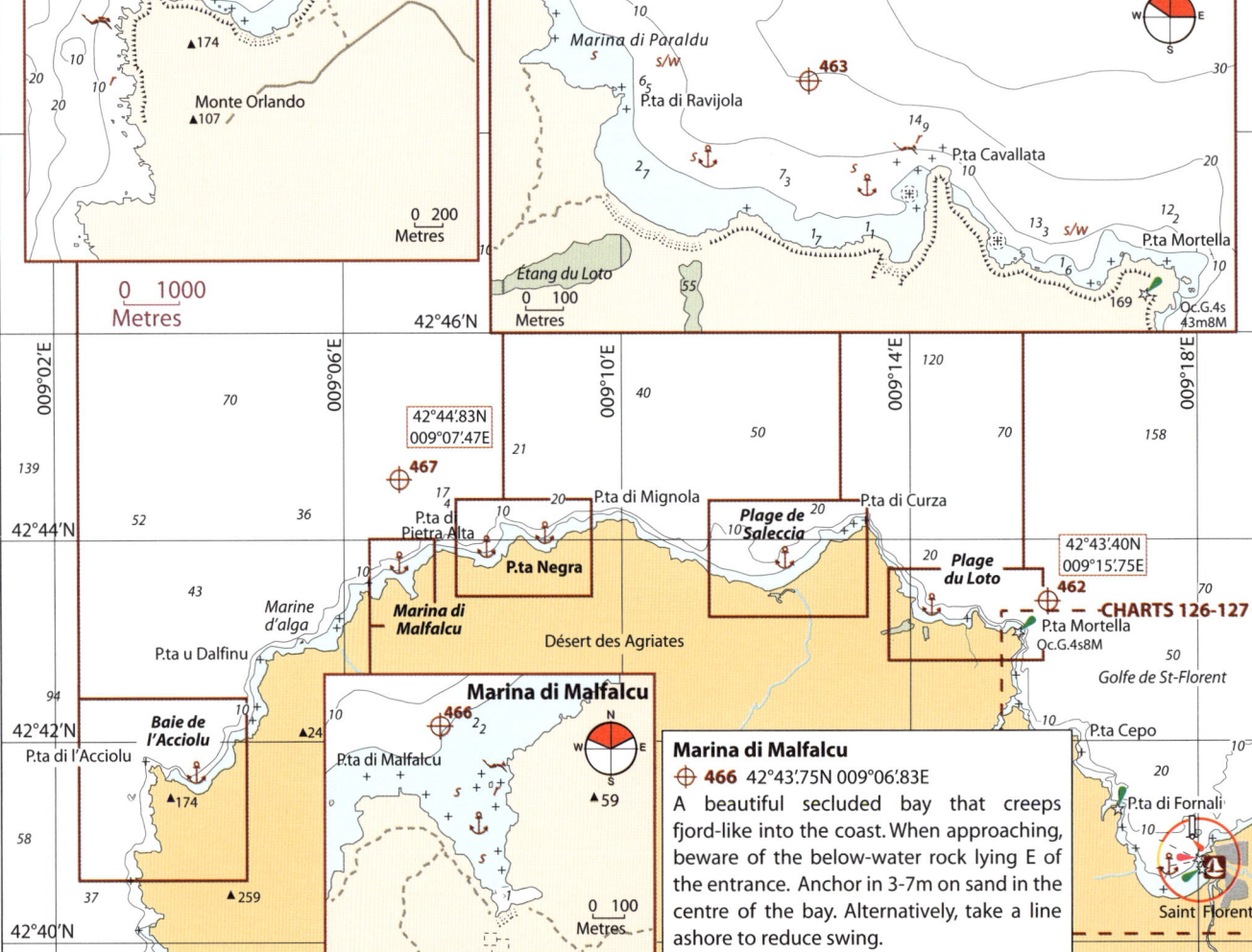

Marina di Malfalcu
⊕ 466 42°43'.75N 009°06'.83E
A beautiful secluded bay that creeps fjord-like into the coast. When approaching, beware of the below-water rock lying E of the entrance. Anchor in 3-7m on sand in the centre of the bay. Alternatively, take a line ashore to reduce swing.

FROM PUNTA DI L'ACCIOLU TO L'ILE ROUSSE | AREA F

CHART 129

Anse de Peraiola ⊕ 469 42°39'.83N 009°03'.50E
A long white, sandy beach with a dune perched behind it makes Anse de Peraiola the last outpost of the Désert des Agriates. Anchorage is in 3-5m on sand, but open from SW to N. The beach is easy to reach by land and is therefore invariably crowded.

To the E of Punta Arco lies a smaller, more secluded cove where yachts can anchor on sand and weed in 5-8m.

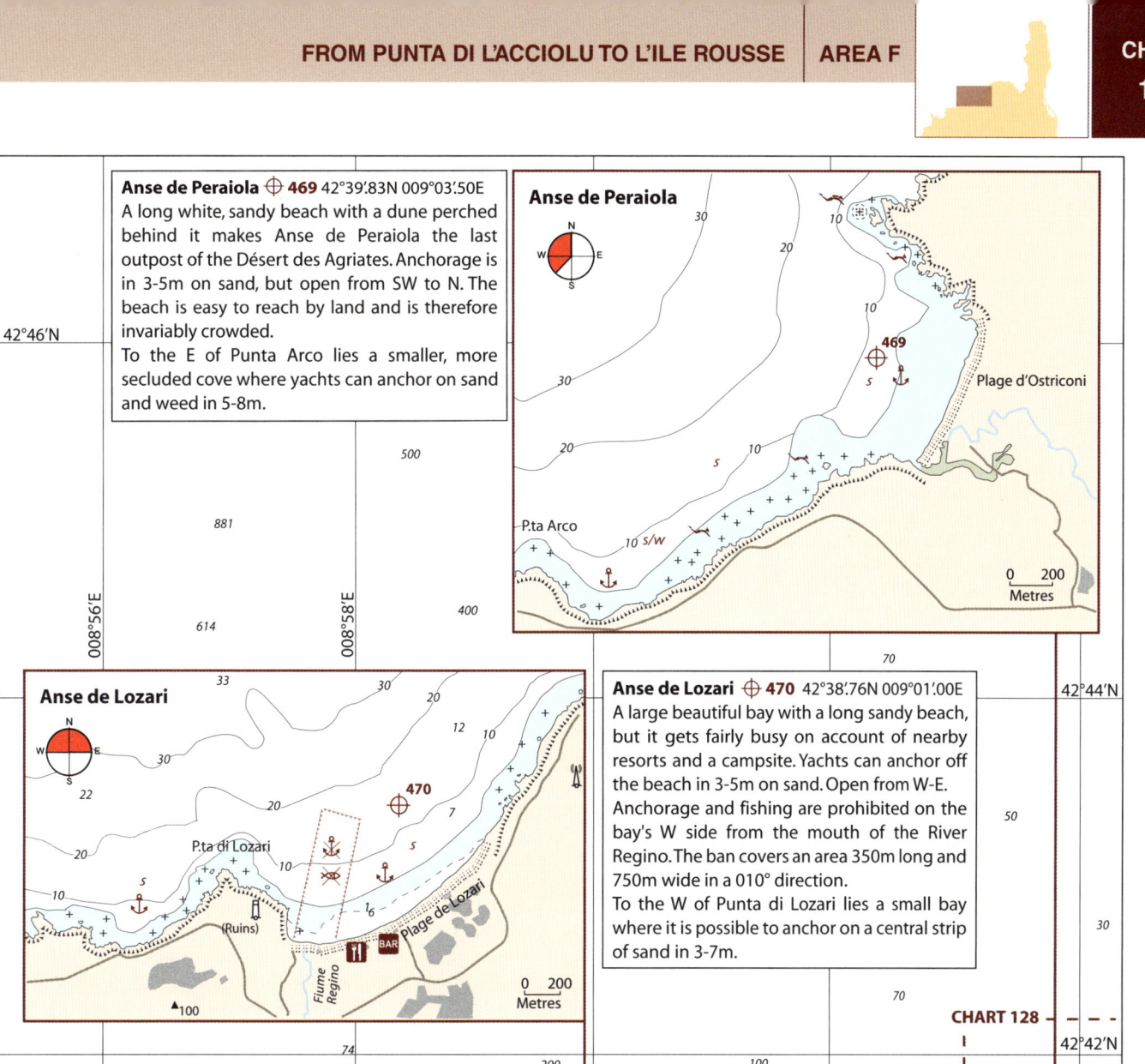

Anse de Lozari ⊕ 470 42°38'.76N 009°01'.00E
A large beautiful bay with a long sandy beach, but it gets fairly busy on account of nearby resorts and a campsite. Yachts can anchor off the beach in 3-5m on sand. Open from W-E. Anchorage and fishing are prohibited on the bay's W side from the mouth of the River Regino. The ban covers an area 350m long and 750m wide in a 010° direction.

To the W of Punta di Lozari lies a small bay where it is possible to anchor on a central strip of sand in 3-7m.

Cala d'Olivu ⊕ 471 42°38'.30N 008°57'.77E
A small cove that bites into the rocky coastline atop of which perches the town of Guardiola. The bay is exposed from W-E and yachts can anchor in 3-8m on sand. Beware of the below-water rock in the centre of the bay entrance.

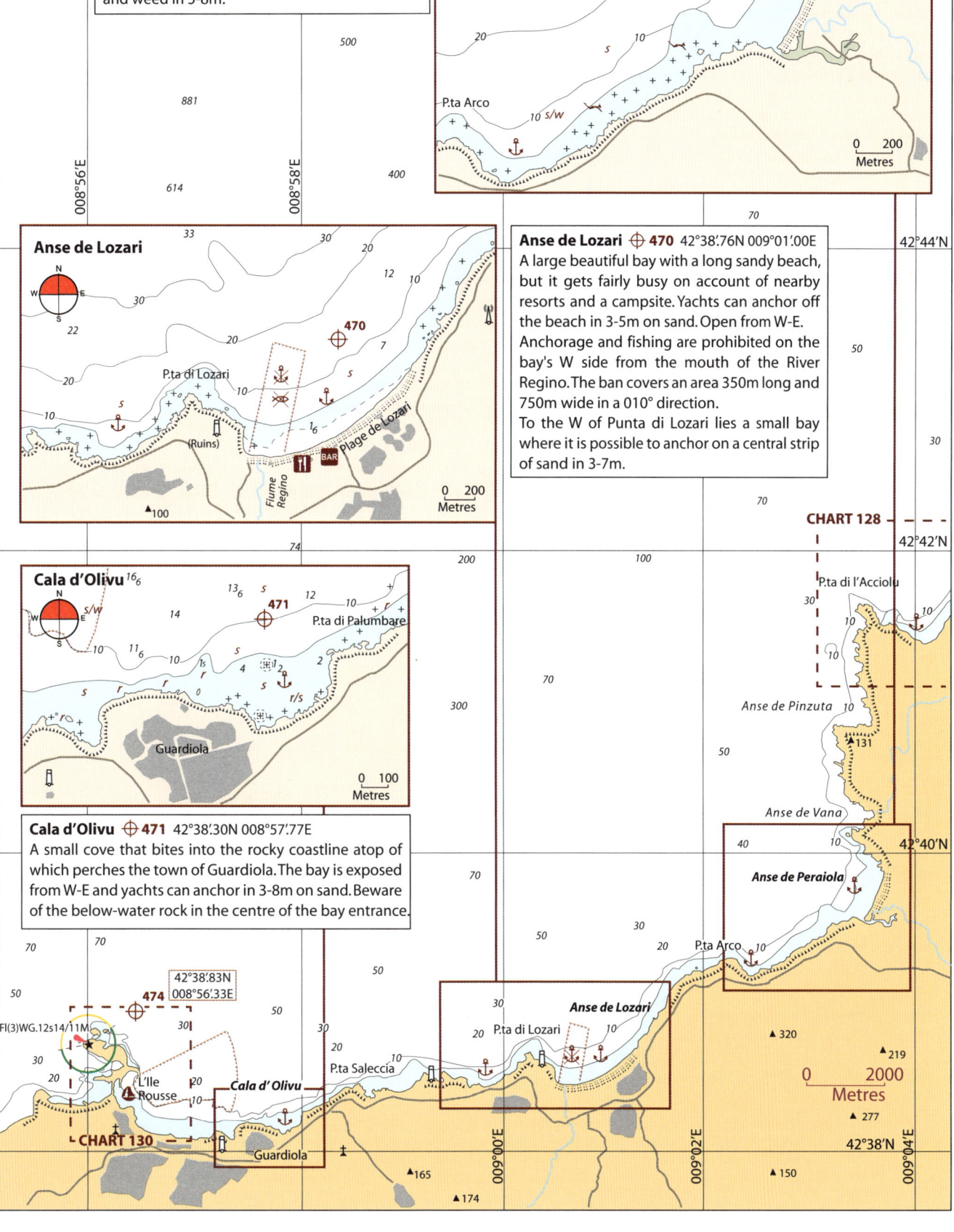

177

CHART 130 — AREA F — L'ILE ROUSSE

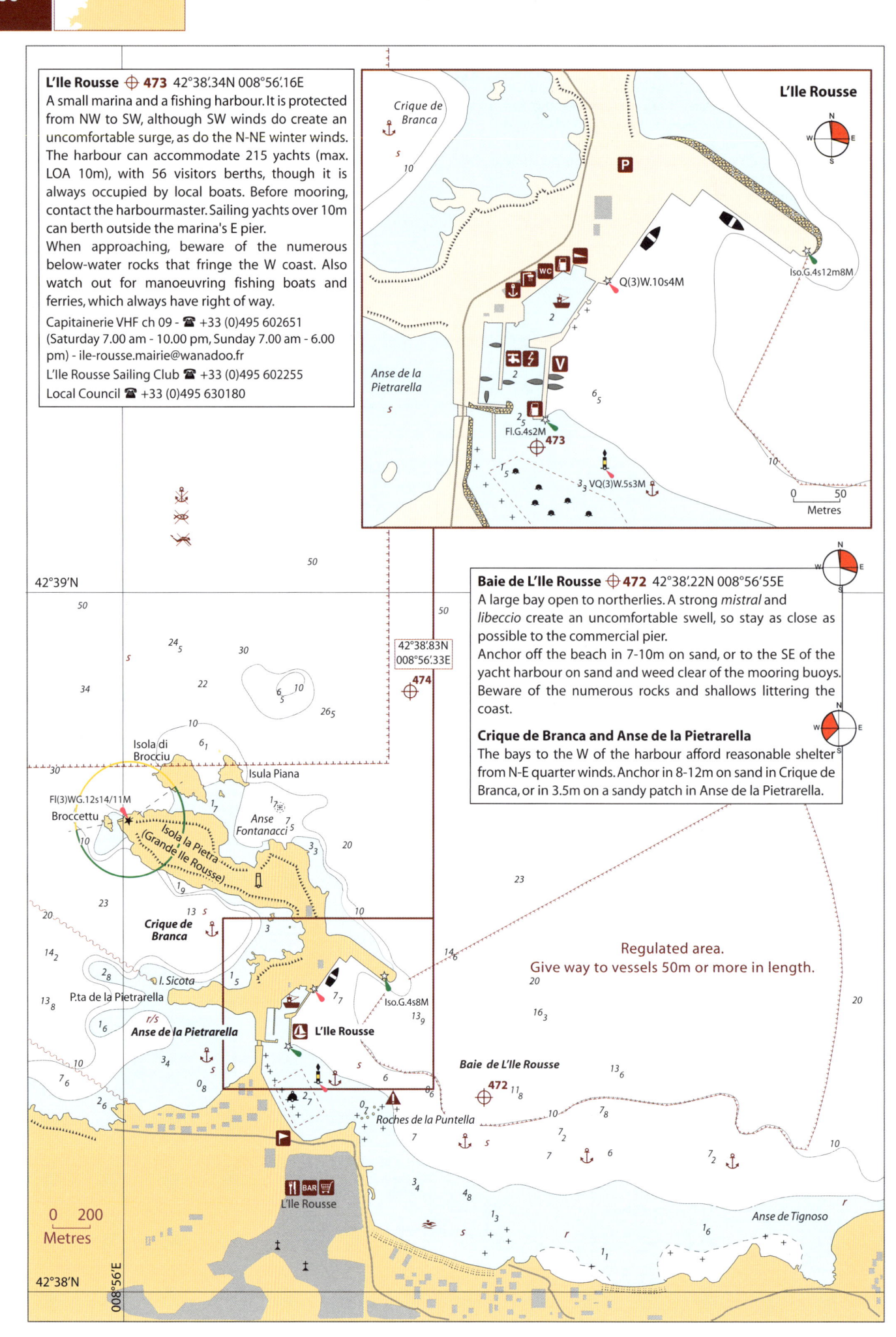

L'Ile Rousse ⊕ 473 42°38'.34N 008°56'.16E
A small marina and a fishing harbour. It is protected from NW to SW, although SW winds do create an uncomfortable surge, as do the N-NE winter winds. The harbour can accommodate 215 yachts (max. LOA 10m), with 56 visitors berths, though it is always occupied by local boats. Before mooring, contact the harbourmaster. Sailing yachts over 10m can berth outside the marina's E pier.
When approaching, beware of the numerous below-water rocks that fringe the W coast. Also watch out for manoeuvring fishing boats and ferries, which always have right of way.
Capitainerie VHF ch 09 - ☎ +33 (0)495 602651 (Saturday 7.00 am - 10.00 pm, Sunday 7.00 am - 6.00 pm) - ile-rousse.mairie@wanadoo.fr
L'Ile Rousse Sailing Club ☎ +33 (0)495 602255
Local Council ☎ +33 (0)495 630180

Baie de L'Ile Rousse ⊕ 472 42°38'.22N 008°56'55E
A large bay open to northerlies. A strong *mistral* and *libeccio* create an uncomfortable swell, so stay as close as possible to the commercial pier.
Anchor off the beach in 7-10m on sand, or to the SE of the yacht harbour on sand and weed clear of the mooring buoys. Beware of the numerous rocks and shallows littering the coast.

Crique de Branca and Anse de la Pietrarella
The bays to the W of the harbour afford reasonable shelter from N-E quarter winds. Anchor in 8-12m on sand in Crique de Branca, or in 3.5m on a sandy patch in Anse de la Pietrarella.

Regulated area. Give way to vessels 50m or more in length.

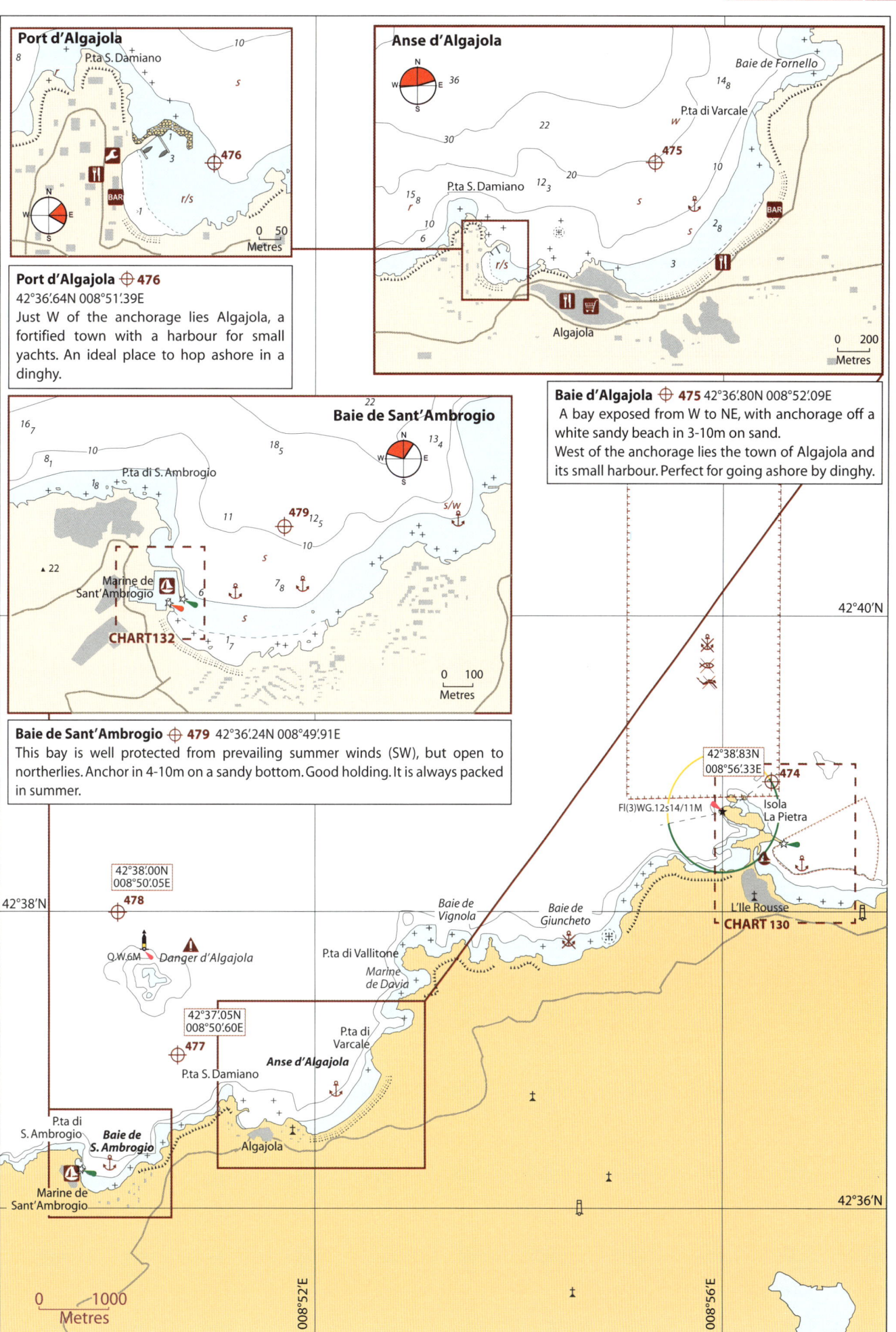

FROM L'ILE ROUSSE TO PUNTA DI SANT'AMBROGIO | AREA F | CHART 131

Port d'Algajola ⊕ 476
42°36'.64N 008°51'.39E
Just W of the anchorage lies Algajola, a fortified town with a harbour for small yachts. An ideal place to hop ashore in a dinghy.

Baie d'Algajola ⊕ 475 42°36'.80N 008°52'.09E
A bay exposed from W to NE, with anchorage off a white sandy beach in 3-10m on sand.
West of the anchorage lies the town of Algajola and its small harbour. Perfect for going ashore by dinghy.

Baie de Sant'Ambrogio ⊕ 479 42°36'.24N 008°49'.91E
This bay is well protected from prevailing summer winds (SW), but open to northerlies. Anchor in 4-10m on a sandy bottom. Good holding. It is always packed in summer.

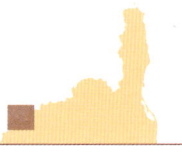

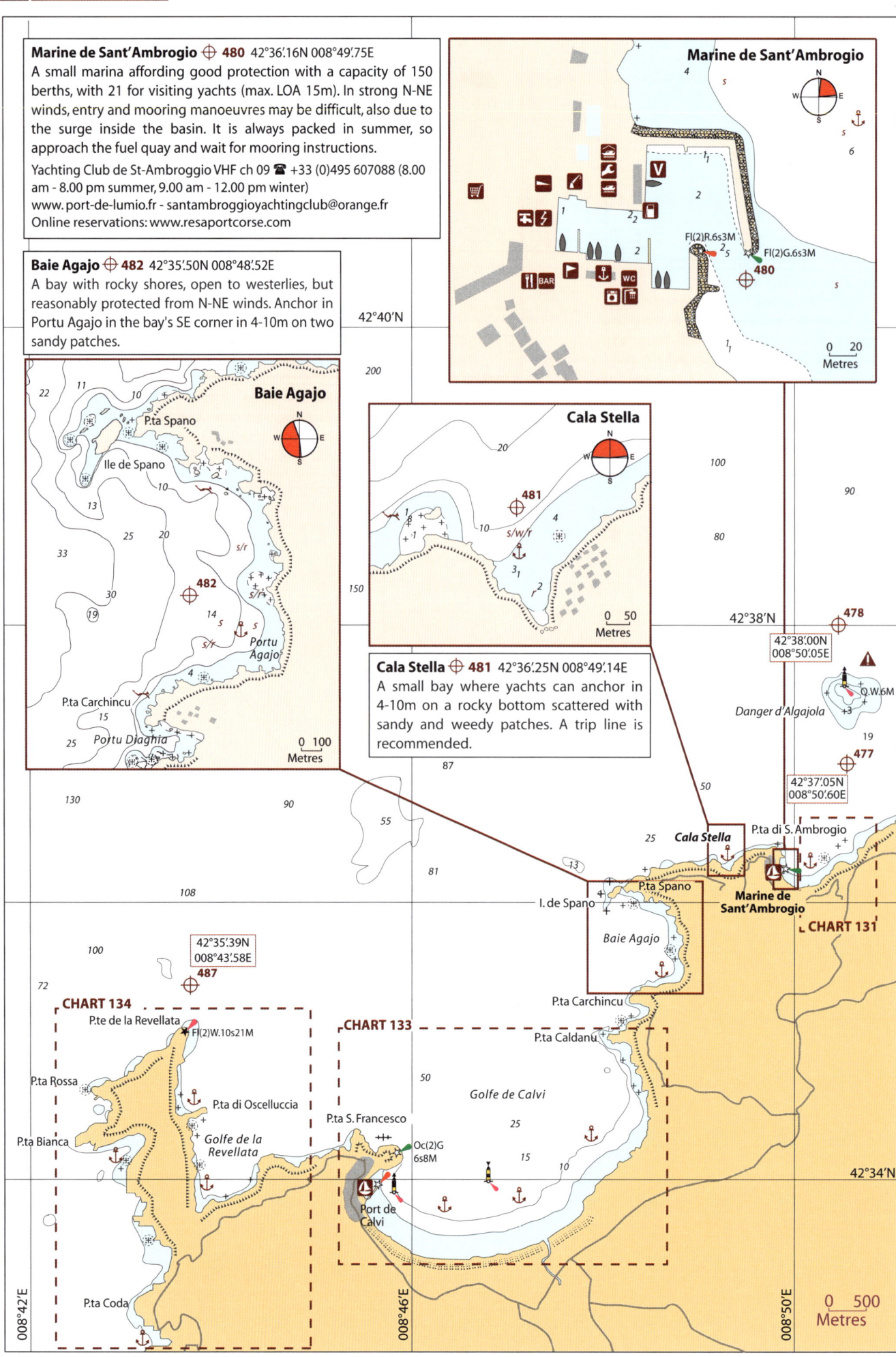

CHART 132

AREA F — FROM PUNTA DI SANT'AMBROGIO TO POINTE DE LA REVELLATA

Marine de Sant'Ambrogio ⊕ 480 42°36'.16N 008°49'.75E
A small marina affording good protection with a capacity of 150 berths, with 21 for visiting yachts (max. LOA 15m). In strong N-NE winds, entry and mooring manoeuvres may be difficult, also due to the surge inside the basin. It is always packed in summer, so approach the fuel quay and wait for mooring instructions.
Yachting Club de St-Ambroggio VHF ch 09 ☎ +33 (0)495 607088 (8.00 am - 8.00 pm summer, 9.00 am - 12.00 pm winter)
www.port-de-lumio.fr - santambroggioyachtingclub@orange.fr
Online reservations: www.resaportcorse.com

Baie Agajo ⊕ 482 42°35'.50N 008°48'.52E
A bay with rocky shores, open to westerlies, but reasonably protected from N-NE winds. Anchor in Portu Agajo in the bay's SE corner in 4-10m on two sandy patches.

Cala Stella ⊕ 481 42°36'.25N 008°49'.14E
A small bay where yachts can anchor in 4-10m on a rocky bottom scattered with sandy and weedy patches. A trip line is recommended.

GOLFE DE CALVI — AREA F — CHART 133

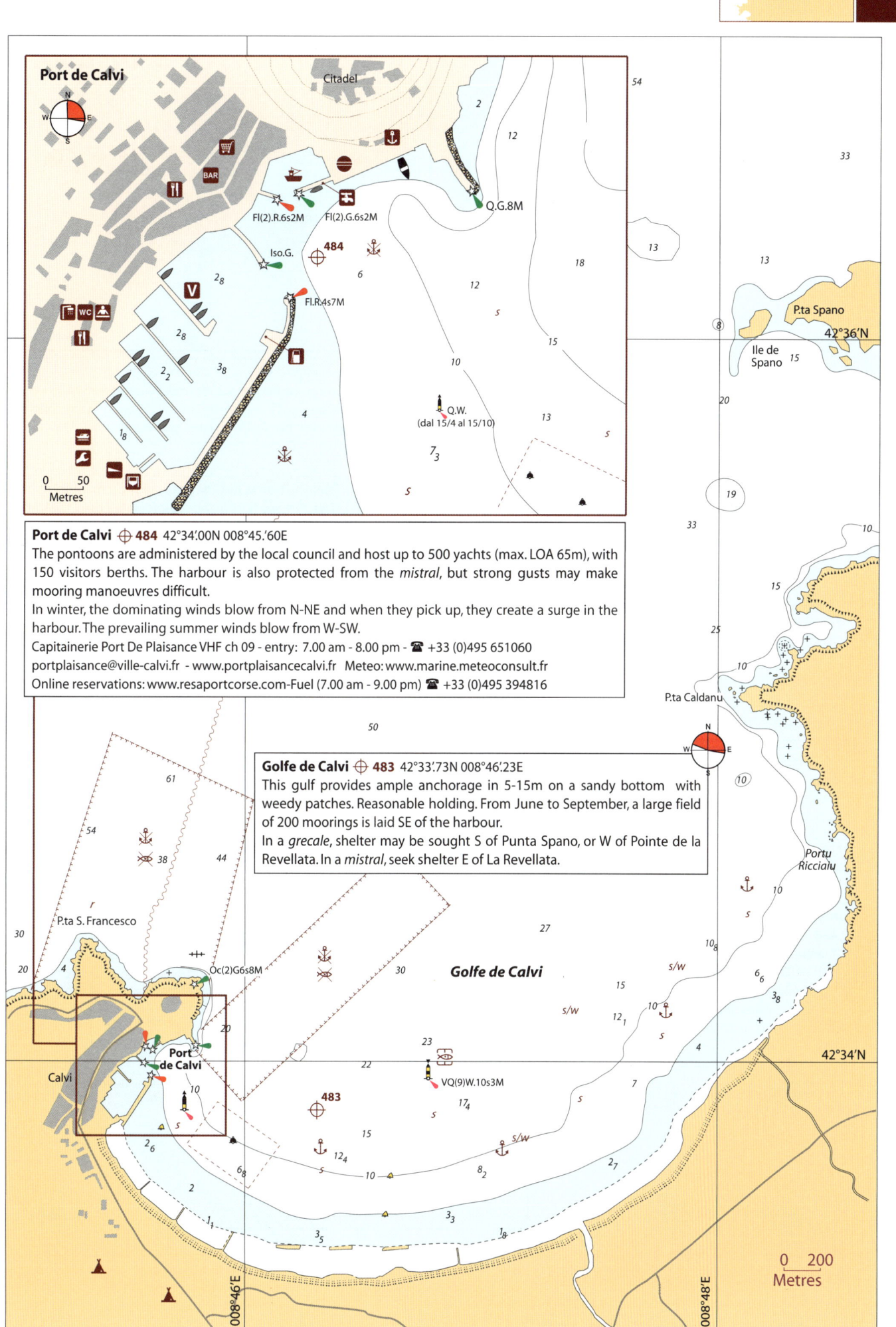

Port de Calvi ⊕ 484 42°34'.00N 008°45'.60E

The pontoons are administered by the local council and host up to 500 yachts (max. LOA 65m), with 150 visitors berths. The harbour is also protected from the *mistral*, but strong gusts may make mooring manoeuvres difficult.

In winter, the dominating winds blow from N-NE and when they pick up, they create a surge in the harbour. The prevailing summer winds blow from W-SW.

Capitainerie Port De Plaisance VHF ch 09 - entry: 7.00 am - 8.00 pm - ☎ +33 (0)495 651060
portplaisance@ville-calvi.fr - www.portplaisancecalvi.fr Meteo: www.marine.meteoconsult.fr
Online reservations: www.resaportcorse.com-Fuel (7.00 am - 9.00 pm) ☎ +33 (0)495 394816

Golfe de Calvi ⊕ 483 42°33'.73N 008°46'.23E

This gulf provides ample anchorage in 5-15m on a sandy bottom with weedy patches. Reasonable holding. From June to September, a large field of 200 moorings is laid SE of the harbour.

In a *grecale*, shelter may be sought S of Punta Spano, or W of Pointe de la Revellata. In a *mistral*, seek shelter E of La Revellata.

CHART 134 — AREA F | PÉNINSULE DE LA REVELLATA

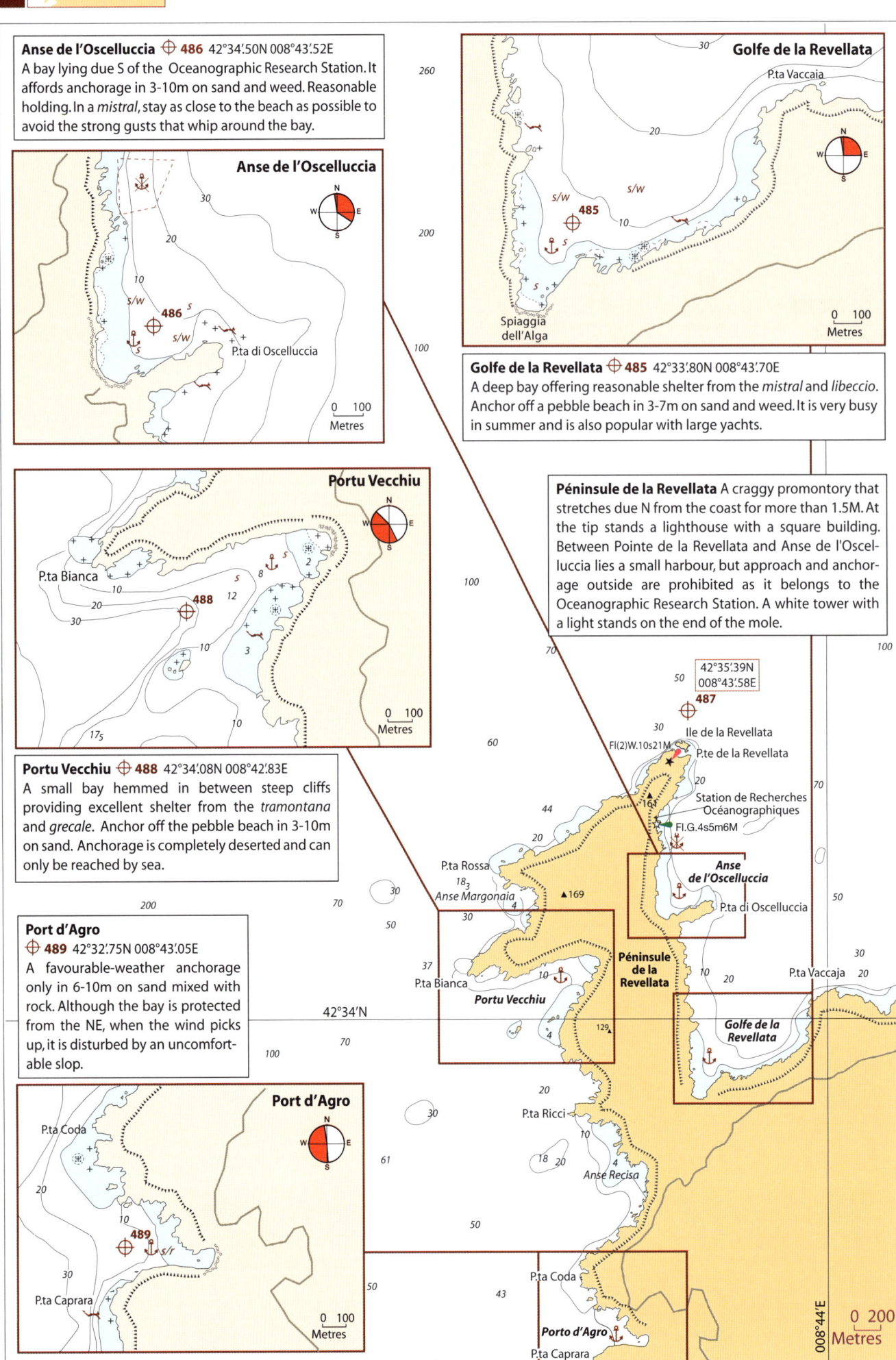

Anse de l'Oscelluccia ⊕ 486 42°34'.50N 008°43'.52E
A bay lying due S of the Oceanographic Research Station. It affords anchorage in 3-10m on sand and weed. Reasonable holding. In a *mistral*, stay as close to the beach as possible to avoid the strong gusts that whip around the bay.

Golfe de la Revellata ⊕ 485 42°33'.80N 008°43'.70E
A deep bay offering reasonable shelter from the *mistral* and *libeccio*. Anchor off a pebble beach in 3-7m on sand and weed. It is very busy in summer and is also popular with large yachts.

Péninsule de la Revellata
A craggy promontory that stretches due N from the coast for more than 1.5M. At the tip stands a lighthouse with a square building. Between Pointe de la Revellata and Anse de l'Oscelluccia lies a small harbour, but approach and anchorage outside are prohibited as it belongs to the Oceanographic Research Station. A white tower with a light stands on the end of the mole.

Portu Vecchiu ⊕ 488 42°34'.08N 008°42'.83E
A small bay hemmed in between steep cliffs providing excellent shelter from the *tramontana* and *grecale*. Anchor off the pebble beach in 3-10m on sand. Anchorage is completely deserted and can only be reached by sea.

Port d'Agro
⊕ 489 42°32'.75N 008°43'.05E
A favourable-weather anchorage only in 6-10m on sand mixed with rock. Although the bay is protected from the NE, when the wind picks up, it is disturbed by an uncomfortable slop.

182

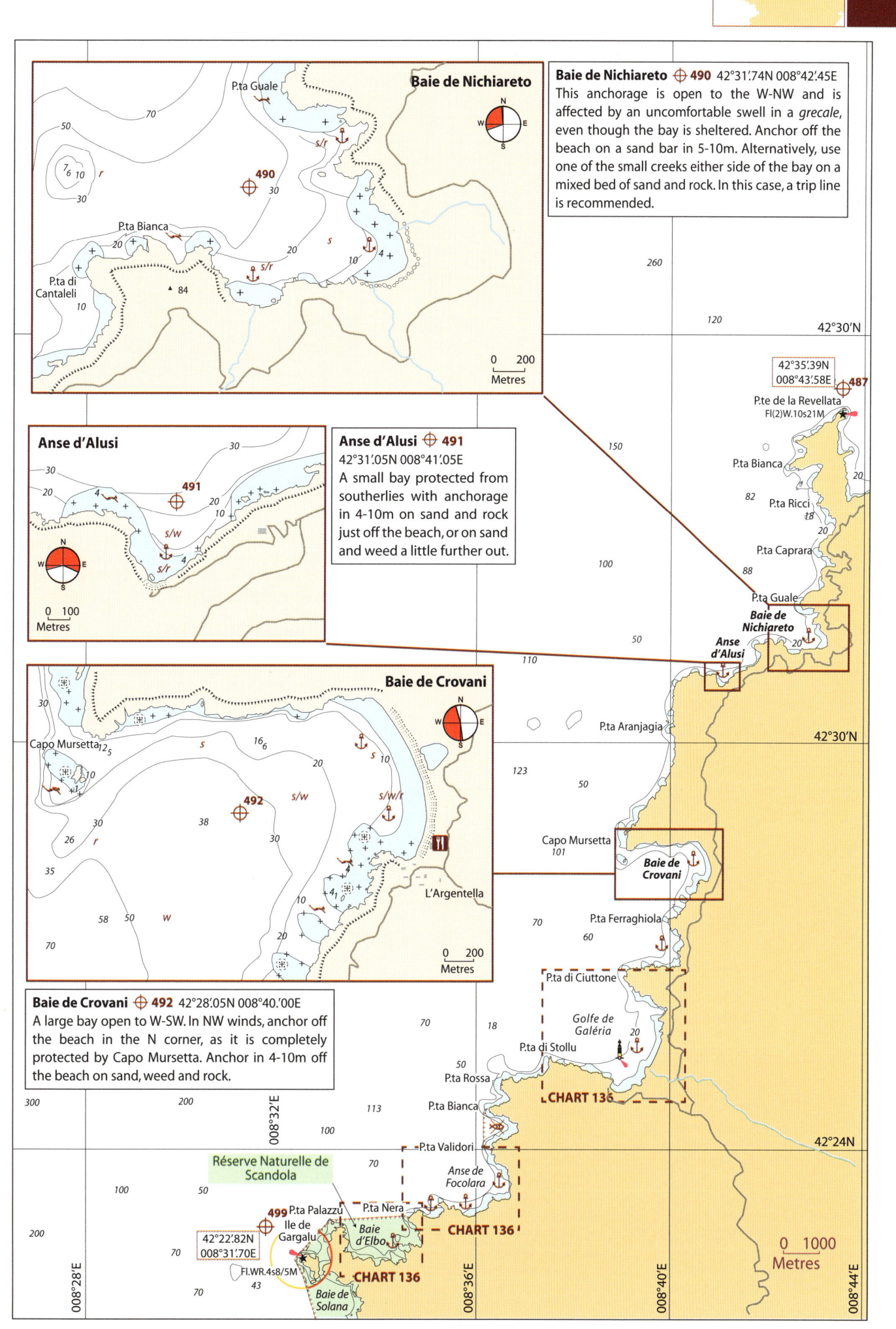

FROM PUNTA GUALE TO PUNTA PALAZZU | **AREA F**

CHART 135

Baie de Nichiareto ⊕ 490 42°31'.74N 008°42'.45E
This anchorage is open to the W-NW and is affected by an uncomfortable swell in a *grecale*, even though the bay is sheltered. Anchor off the beach on a sand bar in 5-10m. Alternatively, use one of the small creeks either side of the bay on a mixed bed of sand and rock. In this case, a trip line is recommended.

Anse d'Alusi ⊕ 491
42°31'.05N 008°41'.05E
A small bay protected from southerlies with anchorage in 4-10m on sand and rock just off the beach, or on sand and weed a little further out.

Baie de Crovani ⊕ 492 42°28'.05N 008°40'.00E
A large bay open to W-SW. In NW winds, anchor off the beach in the N corner, as it is completely protected by Capo Mursetta. Anchor in 4-10m off the beach on sand, weed and rock.

183

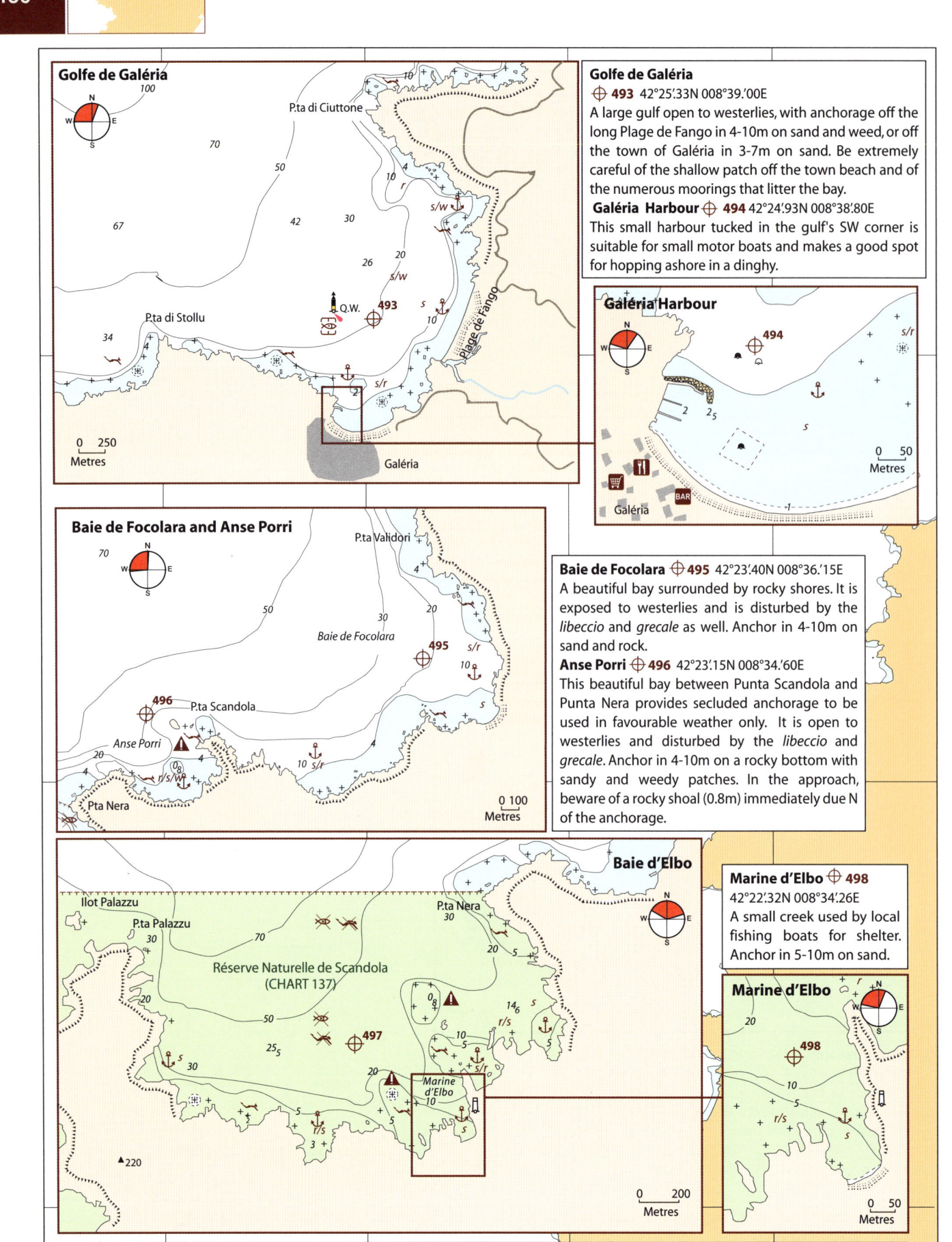

CHART 136 — AREA F — FROM PUNTA DI CIUTTONE TO PUNTA PALAZZU

Golfe de Galéria
⊕ **493** 42°25'.33N 008°39'.00E
A large gulf open to westerlies, with anchorage off the long Plage de Fango in 4-10m on sand and weed, or off the town of Galéria in 3-7m on sand. Be extremely careful of the shallow patch off the town beach and of the numerous moorings that litter the bay.

Galéria Harbour ⊕ **494** 42°24'.93N 008°38'.80E
This small harbour tucked in the gulf's SW corner is suitable for small motor boats and makes a good spot for hopping ashore in a dinghy.

Baie de Focolara
⊕ **495** 42°23'.40N 008°36'.15E
A beautiful bay surrounded by rocky shores. It is exposed to westerlies and is disturbed by the *libeccio* and *grecale* as well. Anchor in 4-10m on sand and rock.

Anse Porri
⊕ **496** 42°23'.15N 008°34'.60E
This beautiful bay between Punta Scandola and Punta Nera provides secluded anchorage to be used in favourable weather only. It is open to westerlies and disturbed by the *libeccio* and *grecale*. Anchor in 4-10m on a rocky bottom with sandy and weedy patches. In the approach, beware of a rocky shoal (0.8m) immediately due N of the anchorage.

Marine d'Elbo
⊕ **498** 42°22'.32N 008°34'.26E
A small creek used by local fishing boats for shelter. Anchor in 5-10m on sand.

Baie d'Elbo
⊕ **497** 42°22'.50N 008°33'.84E
A large bay dwarfed by some of Corsica's most stunning high, sheer red cliffs. The coast is dotted with coves, indentations and grottos. The entire bay from Punta Nera to Punta Palazzu is a nature reserve and the following are prohibited: night anchoring, fishing, diving with breathing equipment, camping and landing ashore and on its islands. Anchorage is allowed from dawn to dusk only in the coves along this stretch of coast on sand with rocky patches. Alternatively, yachts can anchor in 4m on a sandy bottom in Marine d'Elbo, a small creek watched over by a Genoese tower. Approach carefully due to the numerous above- and below-water rocks that litter the bay.

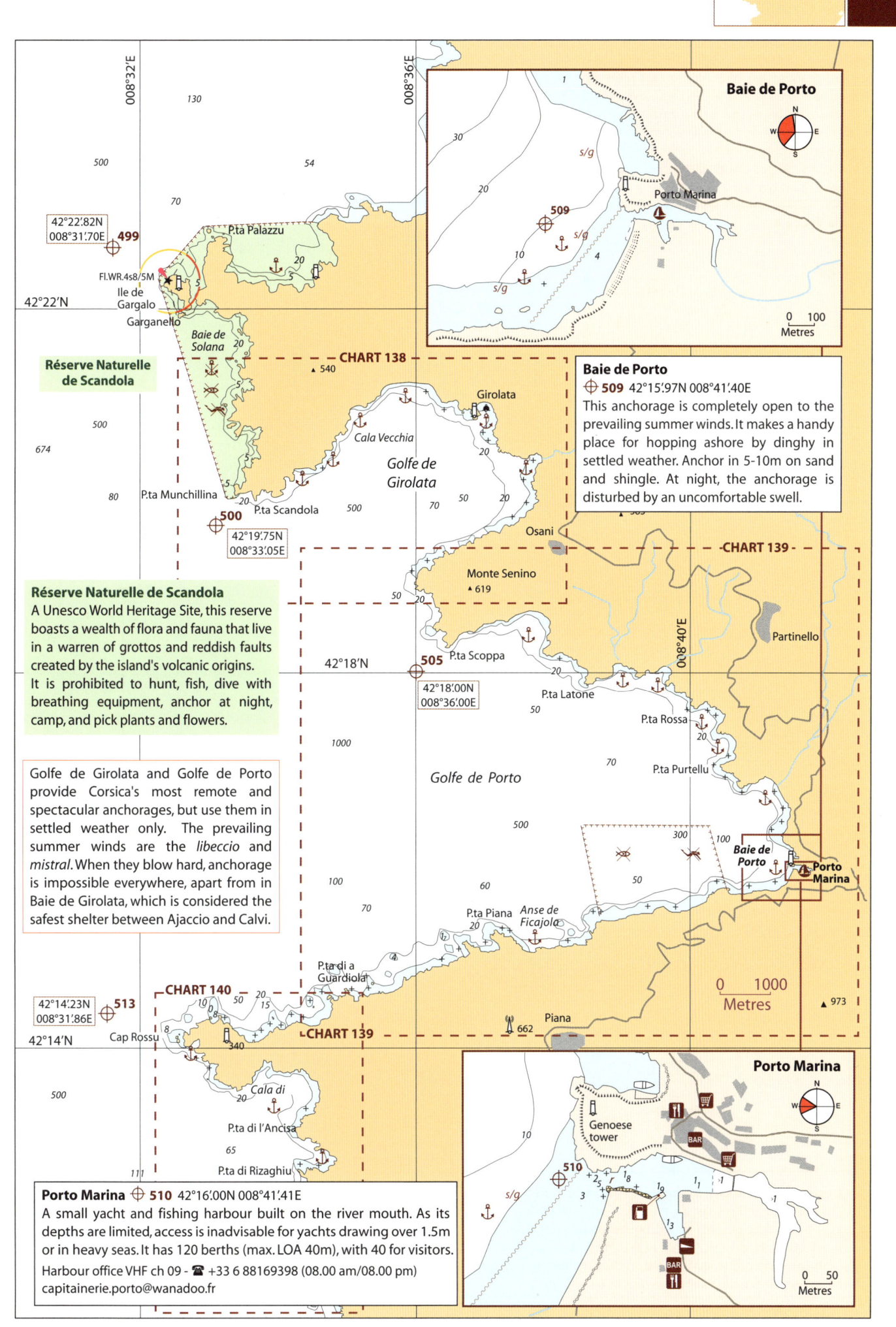

FROM PUNTA SCANDOLA TO CAP ROSSU — AREA F — CHART 137

Baie de Porto

509 42°15'.97N 008°41'.40E

This anchorage is completely open to the prevailing summer winds. It makes a handy place for hopping ashore by dinghy in settled weather. Anchor in 5-10m on sand and shingle. At night, the anchorage is disturbed by an uncomfortable swell.

Réserve Naturelle de Scandola

A Unesco World Heritage Site, this reserve boasts a wealth of flora and fauna that live in a warren of grottos and reddish faults created by the island's volcanic origins. It is prohibited to hunt, fish, dive with breathing equipment, anchor at night, camp, and pick plants and flowers.

Golfe de Girolata and Golfe de Porto provide Corsica's most remote and spectacular anchorages, but use them in settled weather only. The prevailing summer winds are the *libeccio* and *mistral*. When they blow hard, anchorage is impossible everywhere, apart from in Baie de Girolata, which is considered the safest shelter between Ajaccio and Calvi.

Porto Marina

510 42°16'.00N 008°41'.41E

A small yacht and fishing harbour built on the river mouth. As its depths are limited, access is inadvisable for yachts drawing over 1.5m or in heavy seas. It has 120 berths (max. LOA 40m), with 40 for visitors.
Harbour office VHF ch 09 - ☎ +33 6 88169398 (08.00 am/08.00 pm)
capitainerie.porto@wanadoo.fr

185

CHART 138 | AREA F | GOLFE DE GIROLATA

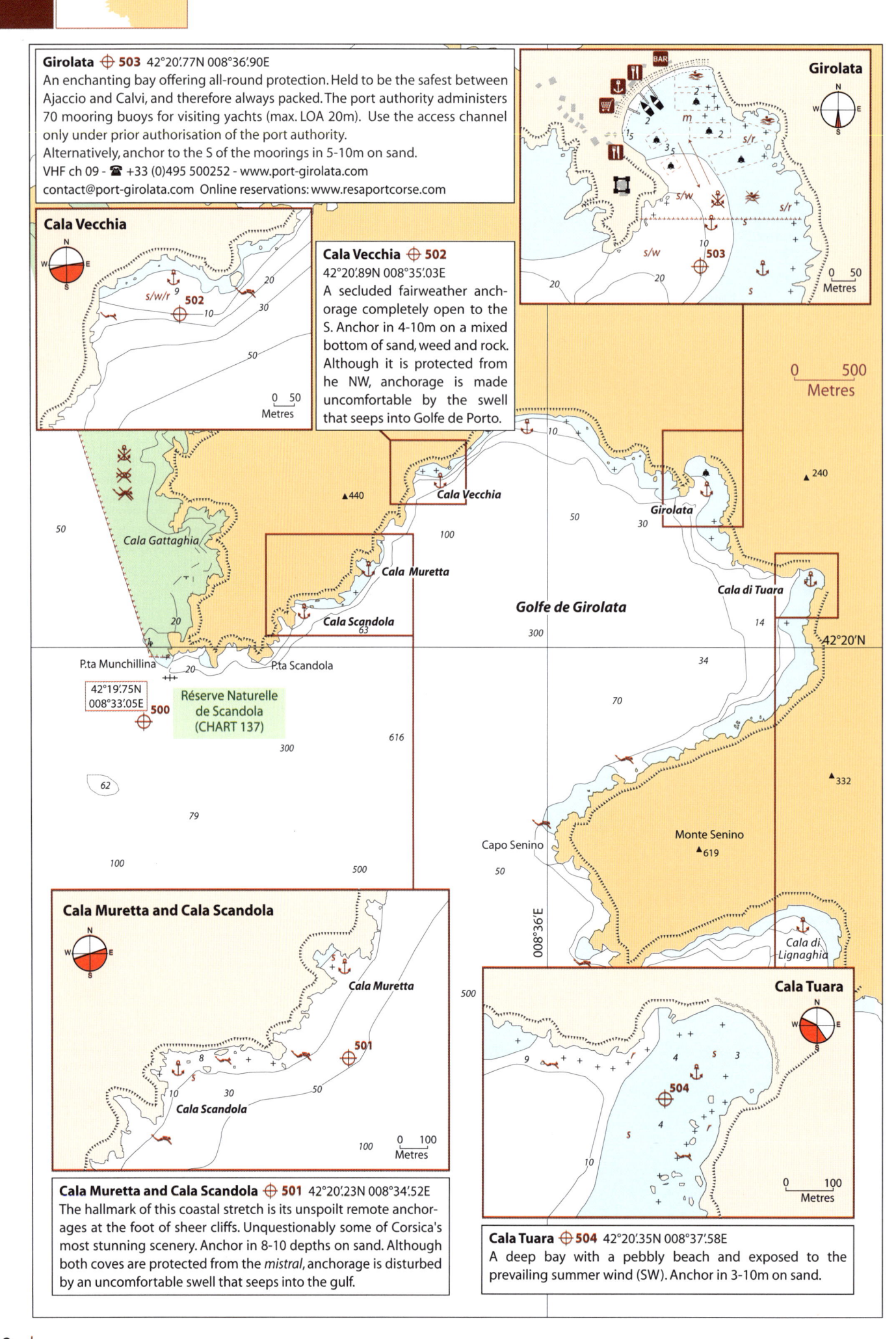

Girolata ⊕ **503** 42°20'.77N 008°36'.90E
An enchanting bay offering all-round protection. Held to be the safest between Ajaccio and Calvi, and therefore always packed. The port authority administers 70 mooring buoys for visiting yachts (max. LOA 20m). Use the access channel only under prior authorisation of the port authority.
Alternatively, anchor to the S of the moorings in 5-10m on sand.
VHF ch 09 - ☎ +33 (0)495 500252 - www.port-girolata.com
contact@port-girolata.com Online reservations: www.ResaportCorse.com

Cala Vecchia ⊕ **502** 42°20'.89N 008°35'.03E
A secluded fairweather anchorage completely open to the S. Anchor in 4-10m on a mixed bottom of sand, weed and rock. Although it is protected from he NW, anchorage is made uncomfortable by the swell that seeps into Golfe de Porto.

Cala Muretta and Cala Scandola ⊕ **501** 42°20'.23N 008°34'.52E
The hallmark of this coastal stretch is its unspoilt remote anchorages at the foot of sheer cliffs. Unquestionably some of Corsica's most stunning scenery. Anchor in 8-10 depths on sand. Although both coves are protected from the *mistral*, anchorage is disturbed by an uncomfortable swell that seeps into the gulf.

Cala Tuara ⊕ **504** 42°20'.35N 008°37'.58E
A deep bay with a pebbly beach and exposed to the prevailing summer wind (SW). Anchor in 3-10m on sand.

186

GOLFE DE PORTO | AREA F

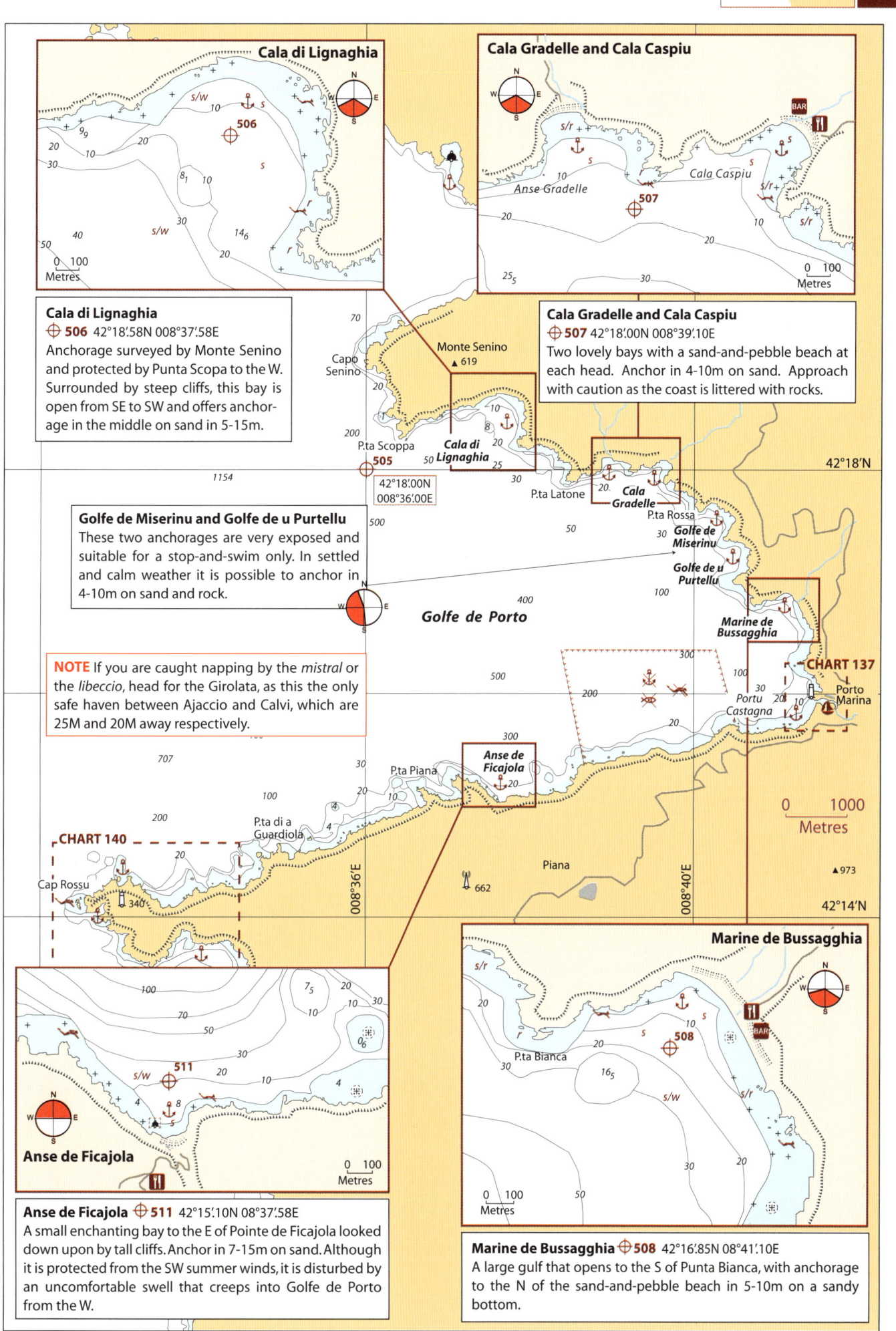

CHART 139

Cala di Lignaghia
⊕ **506** 42°18'.58N 008°37'.58E
Anchorage surveyed by Monte Senino and protected by Punta Scopa to the W. Surrounded by steep cliffs, this bay is open from SE to SW and offers anchorage in the middle on sand in 5-15m.

Cala Gradelle and Cala Caspiu
⊕ **507** 42°18'.00N 008°39'.10E
Two lovely bays with a sand-and-pebble beach at each head. Anchor in 4-10m on sand. Approach with caution as the coast is littered with rocks.

Golfe de Miserinu and Golfe de u Purtellu
These two anchorages are very exposed and suitable for a stop-and-swim only. In settled and calm weather it is possible to anchor in 4-10m on sand and rock.

NOTE If you are caught napping by the *mistral* or the *libeccio*, head for the Girolata, as this the only safe haven between Ajaccio and Calvi, which are 25M and 20M away respectively.

Anse de Ficajola ⊕ 511 42°15'.10N 08°37'.58E
A small enchanting bay to the E of Pointe de Ficajola looked down upon by tall cliffs. Anchor in 7-15m on sand. Although it is protected from the SW summer winds, it is disturbed by an uncomfortable swell that creeps into Golfe de Porto from the W.

Marine de Bussagghia ⊕ 508 42°16'.85N 08°41'.10E
A large gulf that opens to the S of Punta Bianca, with anchorage to the N of the sand-and-pebble beach in 5-10m on a sandy bottom.

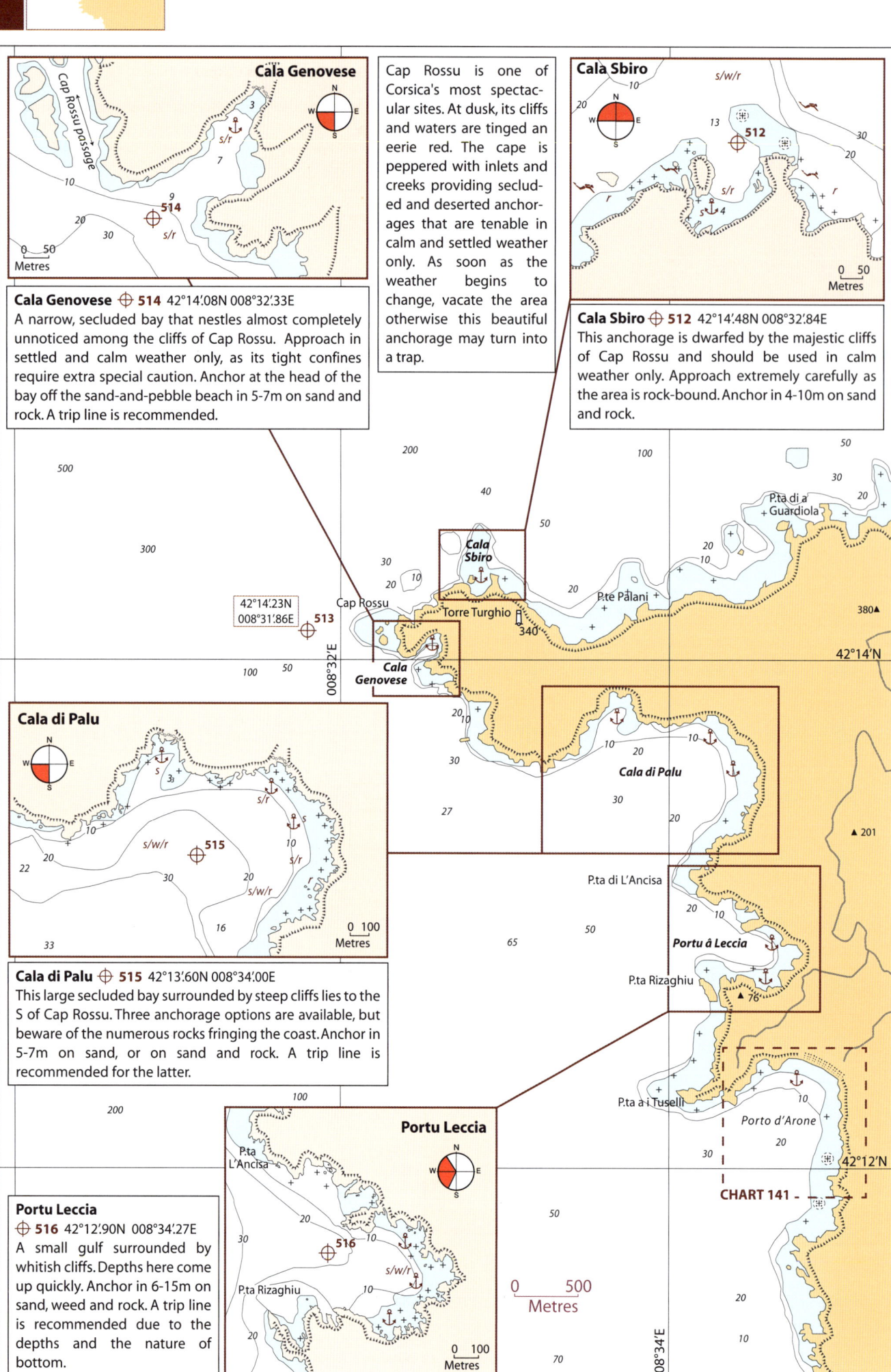

| CHART 140 | AREA F | FROM CAP ROSSU TO PUNTA A I TUSELLI |

Cala Genovese ⊕ 514 42°14'.08N 008°32'.33E
A narrow, secluded bay that nestles almost completely unnoticed among the cliffs of Cap Rossu. Approach in settled and calm weather only, as its tight confines require extra special caution. Anchor at the head of the bay off the sand-and-pebble beach in 5-7m on sand and rock. A trip line is recommended.

Cap Rossu is one of Corsica's most spectacular sites. At dusk, its cliffs and waters are tinged an eerie red. The cape is peppered with inlets and creeks providing secluded and deserted anchorages that are tenable in calm and settled weather only. As soon as the weather begins to change, vacate the area otherwise this beautiful anchorage may turn into a trap.

Cala Sbiro ⊕ 512 42°14'.48N 008°32'.84E
This anchorage is dwarfed by the majestic cliffs of Cap Rossu and should be used in calm weather only. Approach extremely carefully as the area is rock-bound. Anchor in 4-10m on sand and rock.

Cala di Palu ⊕ 515 42°13'.60N 008°34'.00E
This large secluded bay surrounded by steep cliffs lies to the S of Cap Rossu. Three anchorage options are available, but beware of the numerous rocks fringing the coast. Anchor in 5-7m on sand, or on sand and rock. A trip line is recommended for the latter.

Portu Leccia
⊕ 516 42°12'.90N 008°34'.27E
A small gulf surrounded by whitish cliffs. Depths here come up quickly. Anchor in 6-15m on sand, weed and rock. A trip line is recommended due to the depths and the nature of bottom.

188

FROM PUNTA A I TUSELLI TO PUNTA CARGÈSE | AREA F

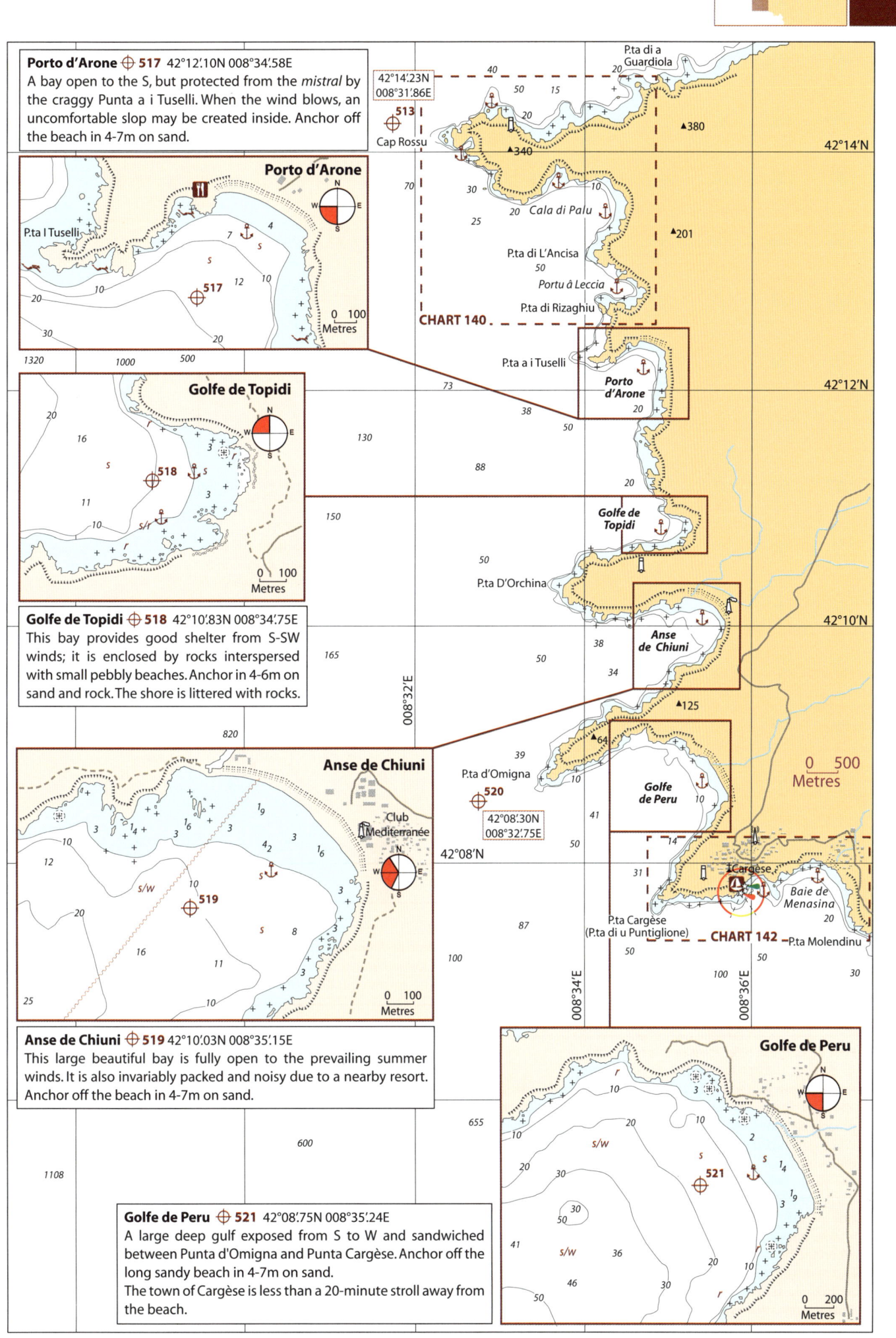

CHART 141

Porto d'Arone ⊕ 517 42°12'.10N 008°34'.58E
A bay open to the S, but protected from the *mistral* by the craggy Punta a i Tuselli. When the wind blows, an uncomfortable slop may be created inside. Anchor off the beach in 4-7m on sand.

Golfe de Topidi ⊕ 518 42°10'.83N 008°34'.75E
This bay provides good shelter from S-SW winds; it is enclosed by rocks interspersed with small pebbly beaches. Anchor in 4-6m on sand and rock. The shore is littered with rocks.

Anse de Chiuni ⊕ 519 42°10'.03N 008°35'.15E
This large beautiful bay is fully open to the prevailing summer winds. It is also invariably packed and noisy due to a nearby resort. Anchor off the beach in 4-7m on sand.

Golfe de Peru ⊕ 521 42°08'.75N 008°35'.24E
A large deep gulf exposed from S to W and sandwiched between Punta d'Omigna and Punta Cargèse. Anchor off the long sandy beach in 4-7m on sand.
The town of Cargèse is less than a 20-minute stroll away from the beach.

189

CHART 142 | AREA F | CARGÈSE

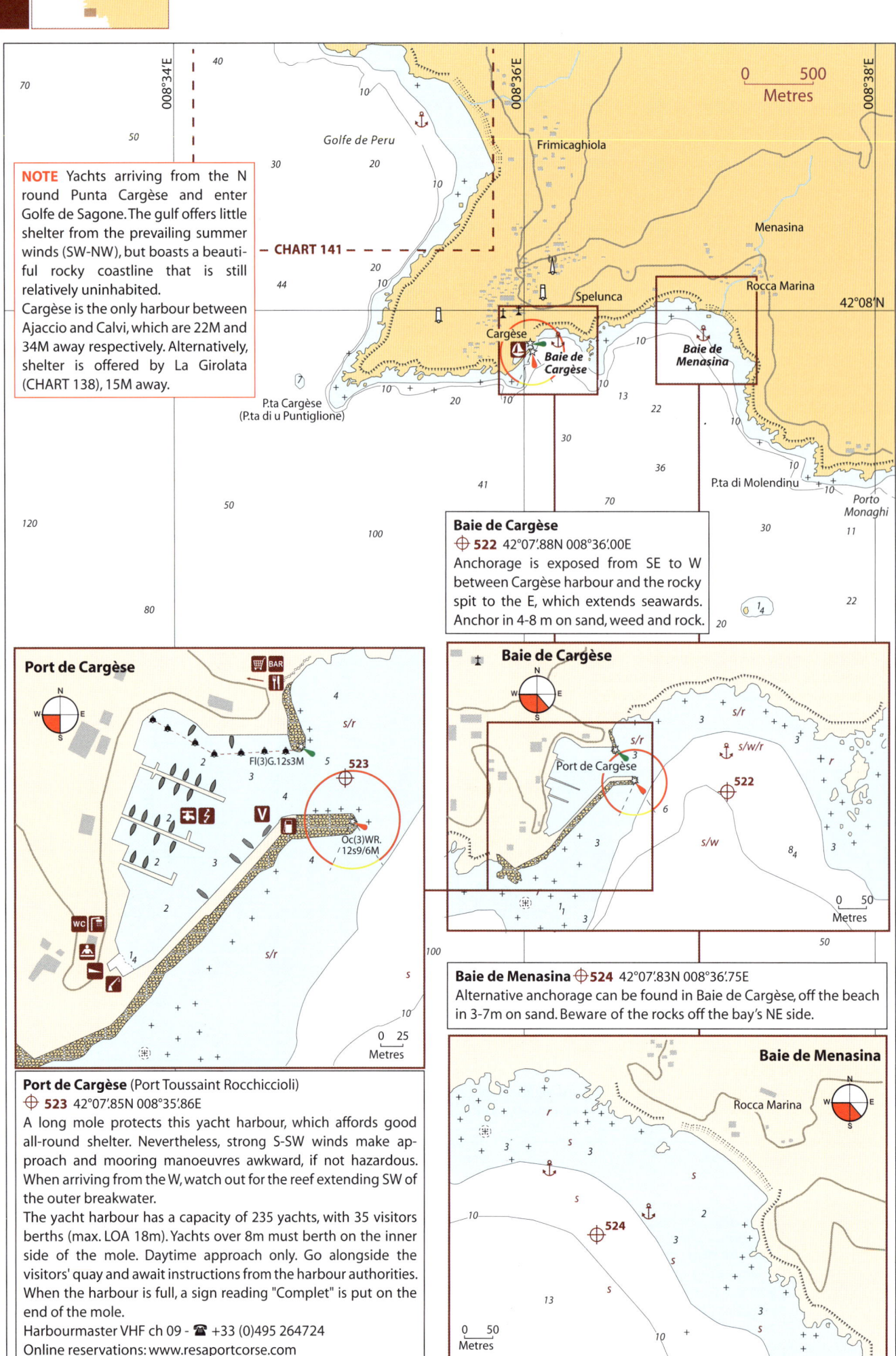

NOTE Yachts arriving from the N round Punta Cargèse and enter Golfe de Sagone. The gulf offers little shelter from the prevailing summer winds (SW-NW), but boasts a beautiful rocky coastline that is still relatively uninhabited.
Cargèse is the only harbour between Ajaccio and Calvi, which are 22M and 34M away respectively. Alternatively, shelter is offered by La Girolata (CHART 138), 15M away.

Baie de Cargèse
⊕ **522** 42°07′.88N 008°36′.00E
Anchorage is exposed from SE to W between Cargèse harbour and the rocky spit to the E, which extends seawards. Anchor in 4-8 m on sand, weed and rock.

Baie de Menasina ⊕ **524** 42°07′.83N 008°36′.75E
Alternative anchorage can be found in Baie de Cargèse, off the beach in 3-7m on sand. Beware of the rocks off the bay's NE side.

Port de Cargèse (Port Toussaint Rocchiccioli)
⊕ **523** 42°07′.85N 008°35′.86E
A long mole protects this yacht harbour, which affords good all-round shelter. Nevertheless, strong S-SW winds make approach and mooring manoeuvres awkward, if not hazardous. When arriving from the W, watch out for the reef extending SW of the outer breakwater.
The yacht harbour has a capacity of 235 yachts, with 35 visitors berths (max. LOA 18m). Yachts over 8m must berth on the inner side of the mole. Daytime approach only. Go alongside the visitors' quay and await instructions from the harbour authorities. When the harbour is full, a sign reading "Complet" is put on the end of the mole.
Harbourmaster VHF ch 09 - ☎ +33 (0)495 264724
Online reservations: www.resaportcorse.com

GOLFE DE SAGONE — AREA F — CHART 143

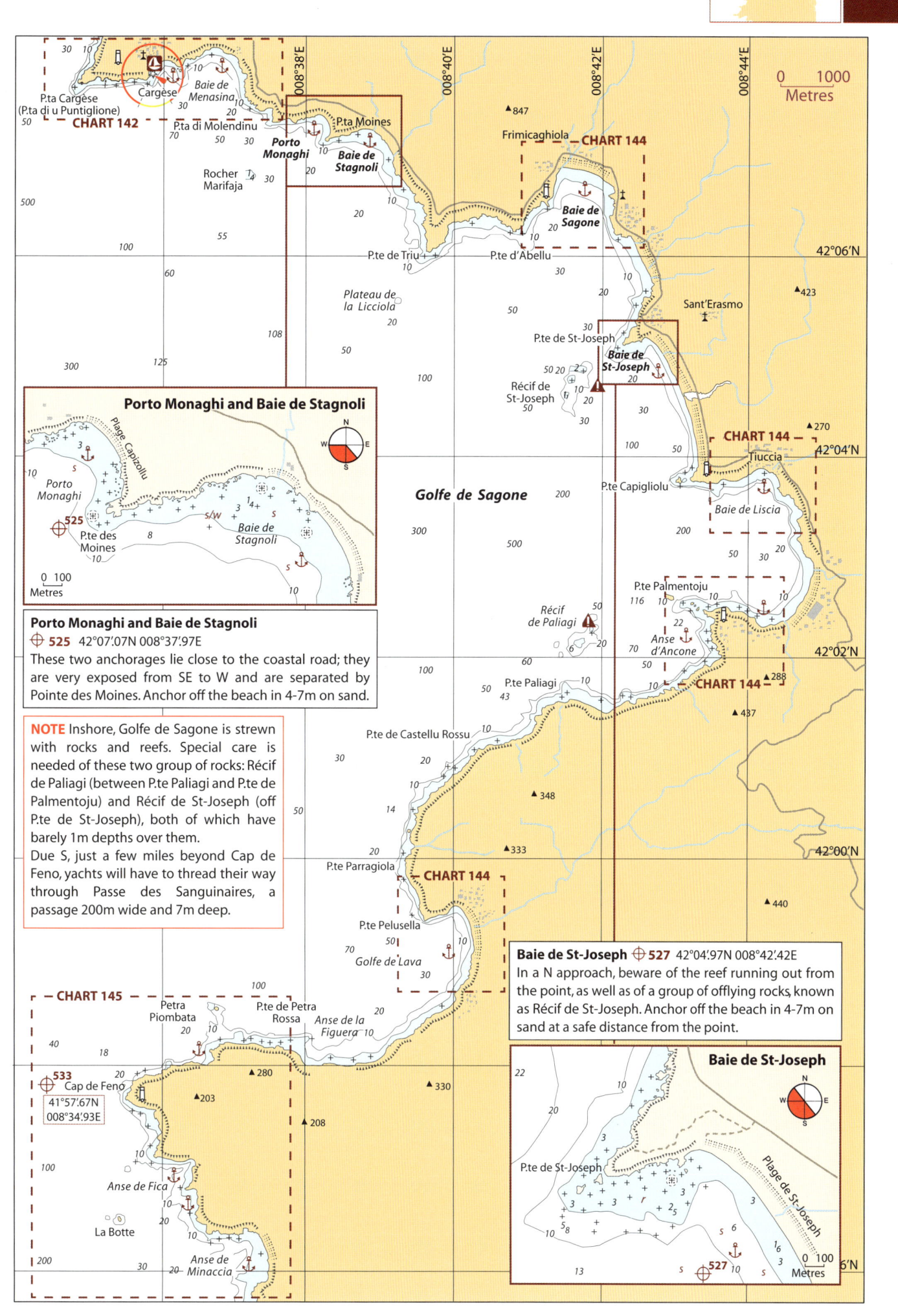

Porto Monaghi and Baie de Stagnoli
⊕ 525 42°07'.07N 008°37'.97E

These two anchorages lie close to the coastal road; they are very exposed from SE to W and are separated by Pointe des Moines. Anchor off the beach in 4-7m on sand.

NOTE Inshore, Golfe de Sagone is strewn with rocks and reefs. Special care is needed of these two group of rocks: Récif de Paliagi (between P.te Paliagi and P.te de Palmentoju) and Récif de St-Joseph (off P.te de St-Joseph), both of which have barely 1m depths over them.
Due S, just a few miles beyond Cap de Feno, yachts will have to thread their way through Passe des Sanguinaires, a passage 200m wide and 7m deep.

Baie de St-Joseph ⊕ 527 42°04'.97N 008°42'.42E
In a N approach, beware of the reef running out from the point, as well as of a group of offlying rocks, known as Récif de St-Joseph. Anchor off the beach in 4-7m on sand at a safe distance from the point.

191

AREA F — GOLFE DE SAGONE AND GOLFE DE LAVA

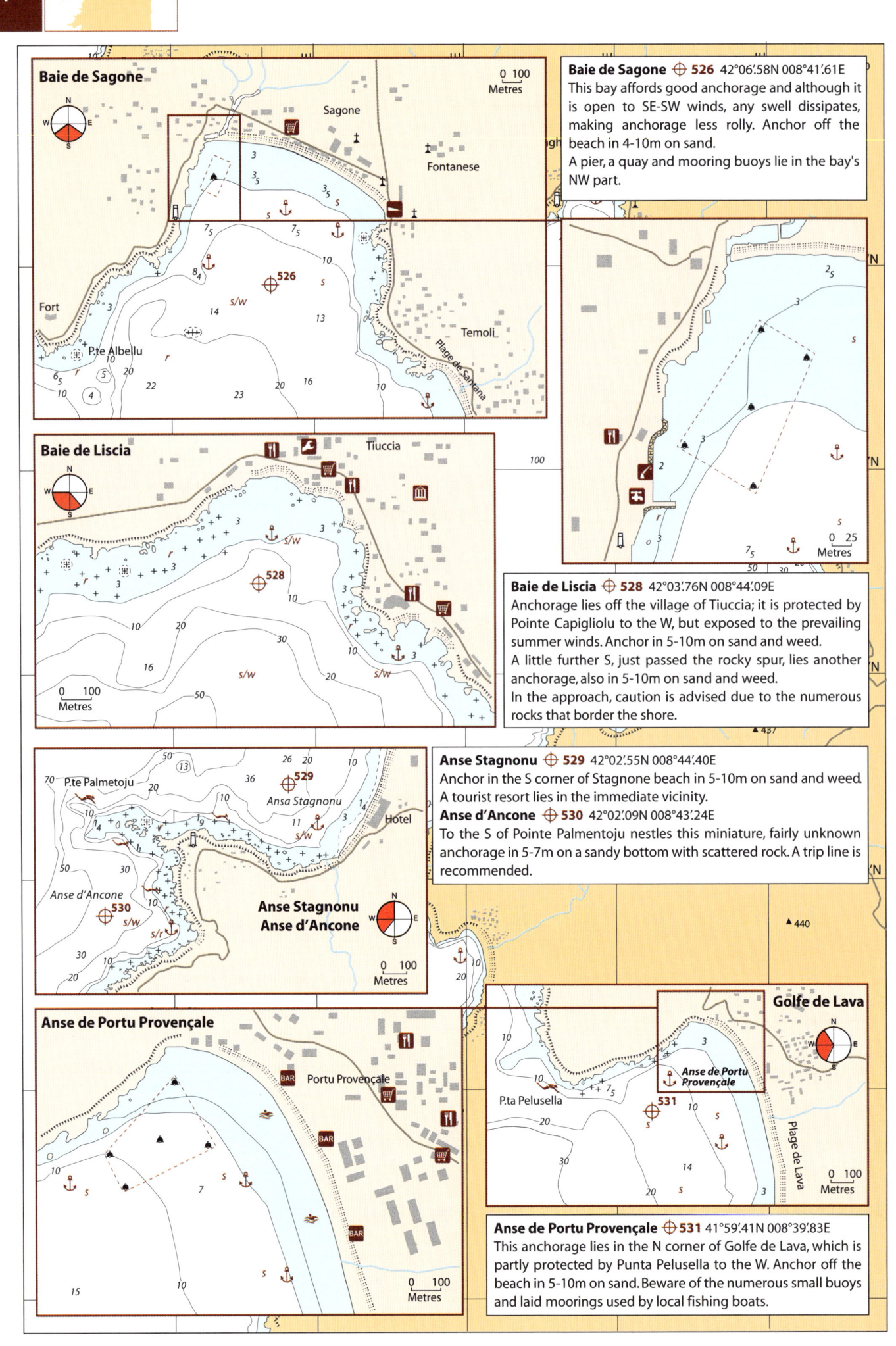

CHART 144

Baie de Sagone ⊕ **526** 42°06'.58N 008°41'.61E
This bay affords good anchorage and although it is open to SE-SW winds, any swell dissipates, making anchorage less rolly. Anchor off the beach in 4-10m on sand.
A pier, a quay and mooring buoys lie in the bay's NW part.

Baie de Liscia ⊕ **528** 42°03'.76N 008°44'.09E
Anchorage lies off the village of Tiuccia; it is protected by Pointe Capigliolu to the W, but exposed to the prevailing summer winds. Anchor in 5-10m on sand and weed.
A little further S, just passed the rocky spur, lies another anchorage, also in 5-10m on sand and weed.
In the approach, caution is advised due to the numerous rocks that border the shore.

Anse Stagnonu ⊕ **529** 42°02'.55N 008°44'.40E
Anchor in the S corner of Stagnone beach in 5-10m on sand and weed. A tourist resort lies in the immediate vicinity.

Anse d'Ancone ⊕ **530** 42°02'.09N 008°43'.24E
To the S of Pointe Palmentoju nestles this miniature, fairly unknown anchorage in 5-7m on a sandy bottom with scattered rock. A trip line is recommended.

Anse de Portu Provençale ⊕ **531** 41°59'.41N 008°39'.83E
This anchorage lies in the N corner of Golfe de Lava, which is partly protected by Punta Pelusella to the W. Anchor off the beach in 5-10m on sand. Beware of the numerous small buoys and laid moorings used by local fishing boats.

FROM CAP DE FENO TO POINTE DE LA PARATA | AREA F

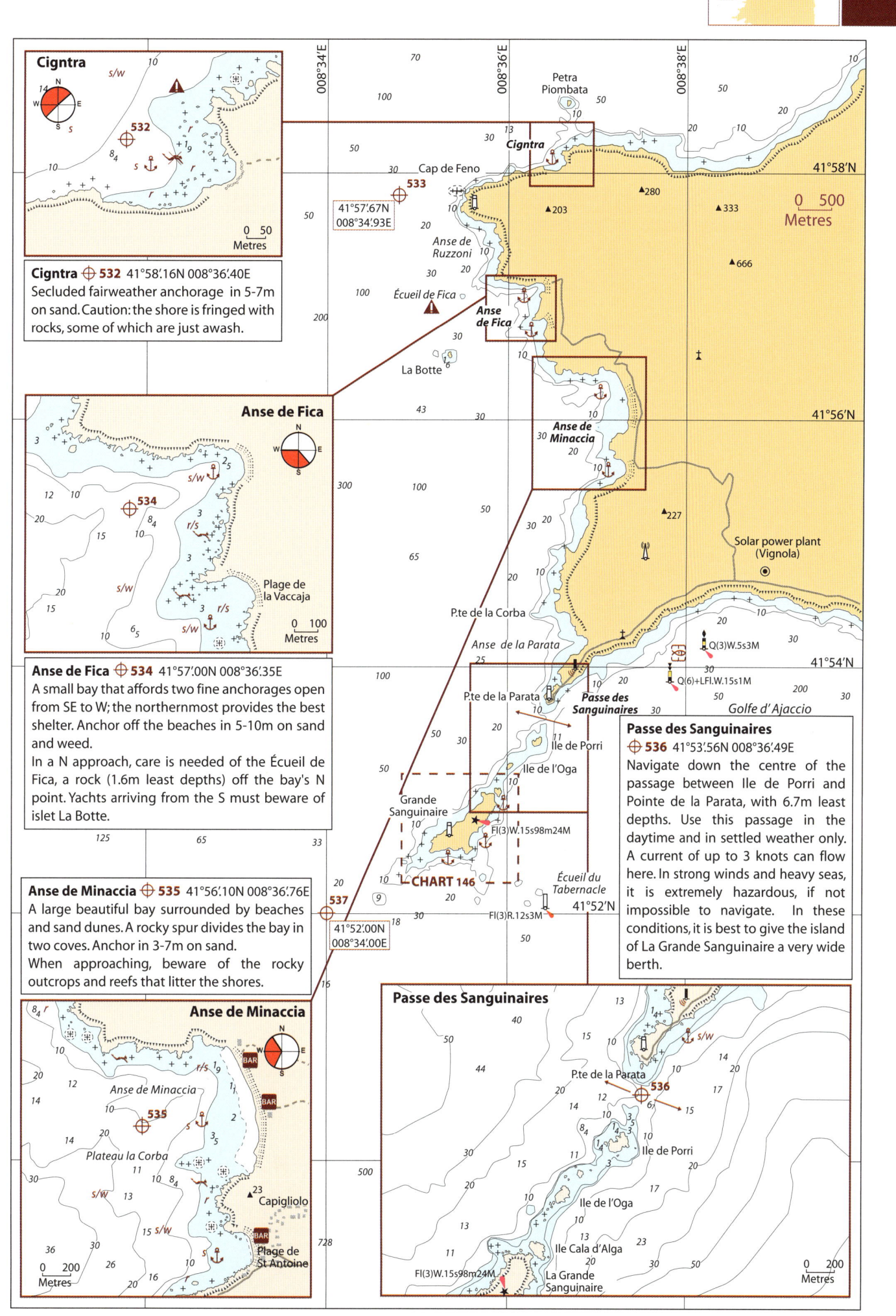

CHART 145

Cigntra

Cigntra ⊕ **532** 41°58'.16N 008°36'.40E
Secluded fairweather anchorage in 5-7m on sand. Caution: the shore is fringed with rocks, some of which are just awash.

Anse de Fica

Anse de Fica ⊕ **534** 41°57'.00N 008°36'.35E
A small bay that affords two fine anchorages open from SE to W; the northernmost provides the best shelter. Anchor off the beaches in 5-10m on sand and weed.
In a N approach, care is needed of the Écueil de Fica, a rock (1.6m least depths) off the bay's N point. Yachts arriving from the S must beware of islet La Botte.

Anse de Minaccia

Anse de Minaccia ⊕ **535** 41°56'.10N 008°36'.76E
A large beautiful bay surrounded by beaches and sand dunes. A rocky spur divides the bay in two coves. Anchor in 3-7m on sand.
When approaching, beware of the rocky outcrops and reefs that litter the shores.

Passe des Sanguinaires

Passe des Sanguinaires ⊕ **536** 41°53'.56N 008°36'.49E
Navigate down the centre of the passage between Ile de Porri and Pointe de la Parata, with 6.7m least depths. Use this passage in the daytime and in settled weather only. A current of up to 3 knots can flow here. In strong winds and heavy seas, it is extremely hazardous, if not impossible to navigate. In these conditions, it is best to give the island of La Grande Sanguinaire a very wide berth.

193

CHART 146 — AREA F — ILES SANGUINAIRES

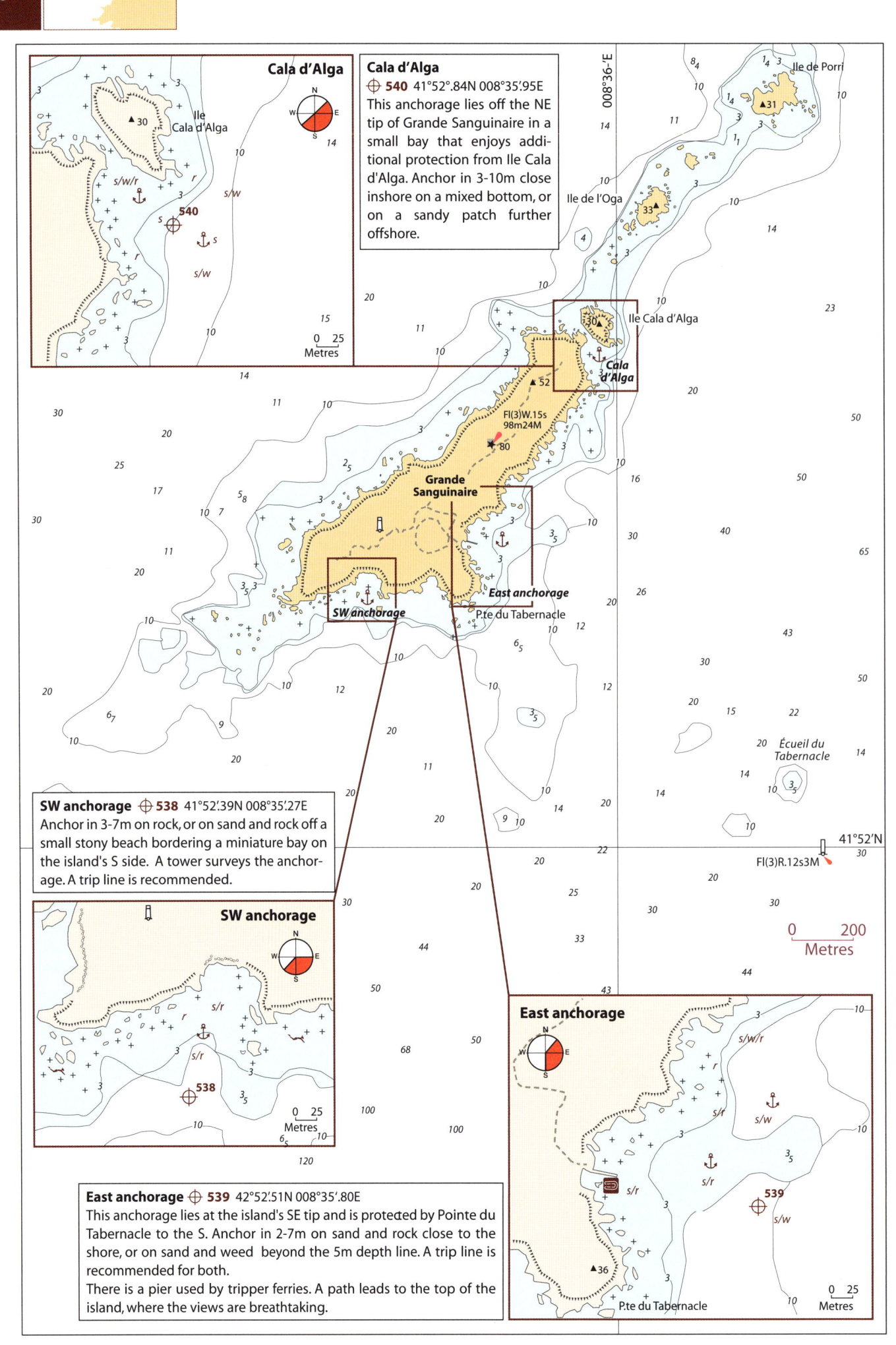

Cala d'Alga
⊕ **540** 41°52'.84N 008°35'.95E
This anchorage lies off the NE tip of Grande Sanguinaire in a small bay that enjoys additional protection from Ile Cala d'Alga. Anchor in 3-10m close inshore on a mixed bottom, or on a sandy patch further offshore.

SW anchorage
⊕ **538** 41°52'.39N 008°35'.27E
Anchor in 3-7m on rock, or on sand and rock off a small stony beach bordering a miniature bay on the island's S side. A tower surveys the anchorage. A trip line is recommended.

East anchorage
⊕ **539** 42°52'.51N 008°35'.80E
This anchorage lies at the island's SE tip and is protected by Pointe du Tabernacle to the S. Anchor in 2-7m on sand and rock close to the shore, or on sand and weed beyond the 5m depth line. A trip line is recommended for both.
There is a pier used by tripper ferries. A path leads to the top of the island, where the views are breathtaking.

GOLFE D'AJACCIO | AREA F | CHART 147

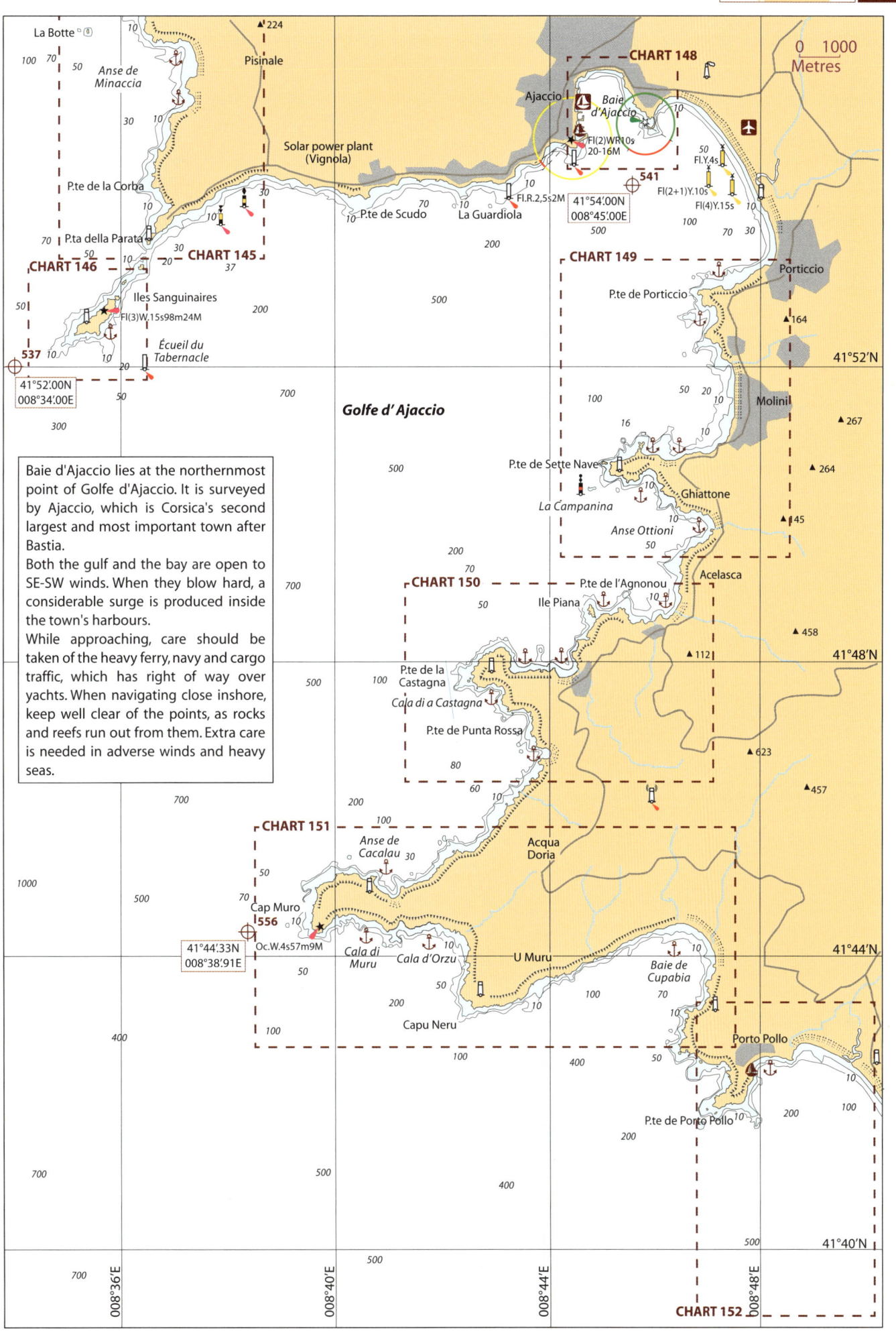

Baie d'Ajaccio lies at the northernmost point of Golfe d'Ajaccio. It is surveyed by Ajaccio, which is Corsica's second largest and most important town after Bastia.

Both the gulf and the bay are open to SE-SW winds. When they blow hard, a considerable surge is produced inside the town's harbours.

While approaching, care should be taken of the heavy ferry, navy and cargo traffic, which has right of way over yachts. When navigating close inshore, keep well clear of the points, as rocks and reefs run out from them. Extra care is needed in adverse winds and heavy seas.

CHART 148 — AREA F — AJACCIO

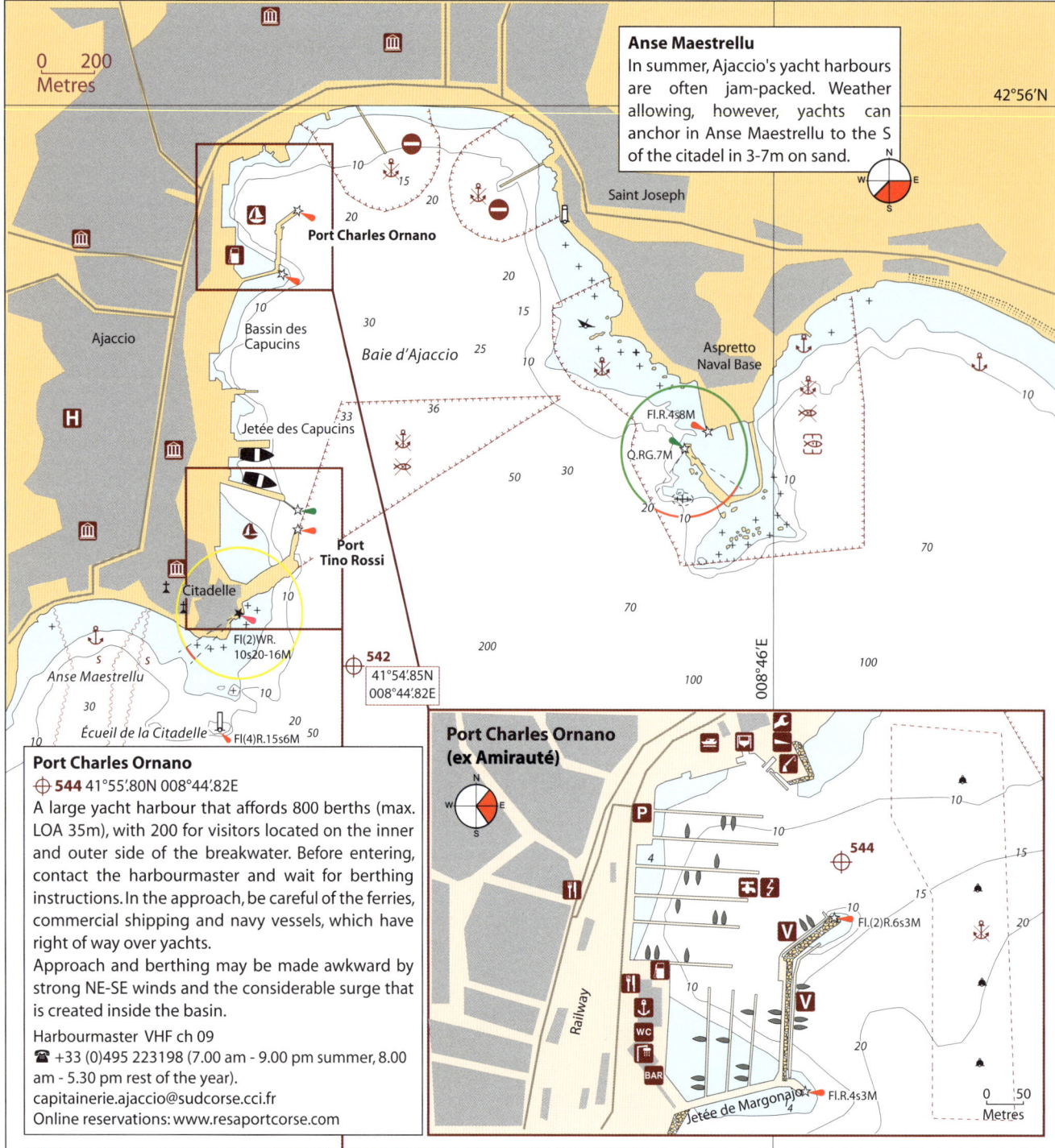

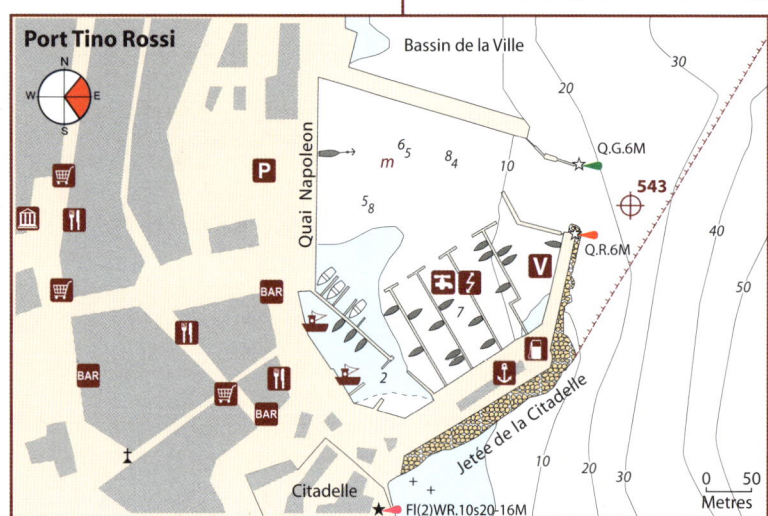

Anse Maestrellu
In summer, Ajaccio's yacht harbours are often jam-packed. Weather allowing, however, yachts can anchor in Anse Maestrellu to the S of the citadel in 3-7m on sand.

Port Charles Ornano
⊕ 544 41°55'.80N 008°44'.82E
A large yacht harbour that affords 800 berths (max. LOA 35m), with 200 for visitors located on the inner and outer side of the breakwater. Before entering, contact the harbourmaster and wait for berthing instructions. In the approach, be careful of the ferries, commercial shipping and navy vessels, which have right of way over yachts.
Approach and berthing may be made awkward by strong NE-SE winds and the considerable surge that is created inside the basin.
Harbourmaster VHF ch 09
☎ +33 (0)495 223198 (7.00 am - 9.00 pm summer, 8.00 am - 5.30 pm rest of the year).
capitainerie.ajaccio@sudcorse.cci.fr
Online reservations: www.ResaportCorse.com

Port Tino Rossi ⊕ 543 41°55'.17N 008°44'.66E
This harbour, also known as Bassin de la Ville, provides 300 berths (max. LOA 100m), with 150 for visitors on the inner and outer side of the outer breakwater. Before entering, contact the harbour authorities and await mooring instructions. The Quai Napoleon is normally set aside for ships and ferries, but the harbourmaster allows yachts to berth there in high season when it is not being used; drop anchor in 8m on mud. A strong surge forms inside the basin in strong E-SE winds. When approaching from the SW, yachts must be careful of Écueil de la Citadelle, a reef that runs out for about 300m. Pass outside this rocky danger.
Port de Plaisance Ajaccio Tino Rossi - VHF ch 09
☎ +33 (0)495 512272 - www.port-ajaccio.com
capitainerie.ajaccio@sudcorse.cci.fr
Online reservations: www.resaportcorse.com
Fuel berth (06:00 am/08:00 pm)

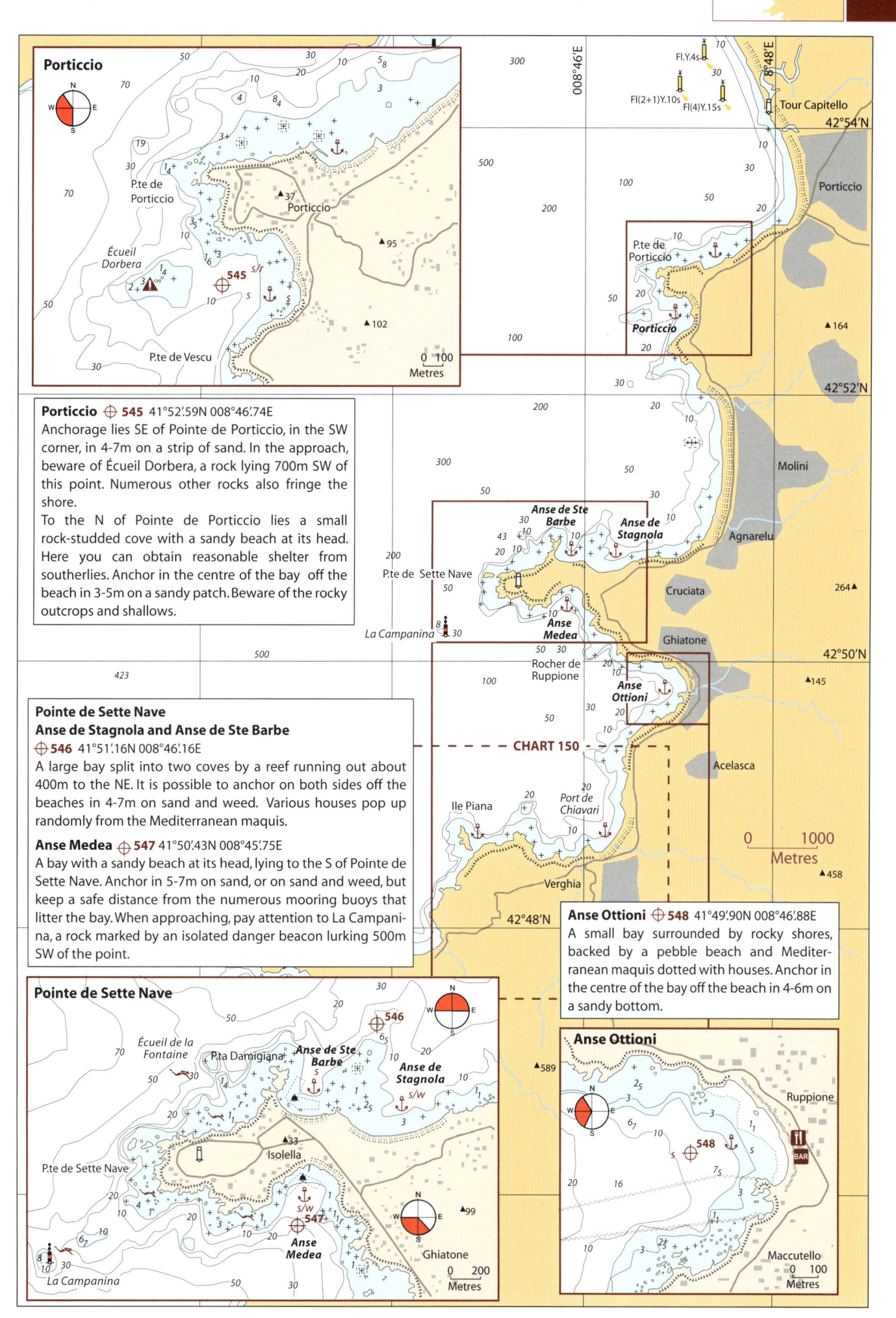

FROM POINTE DE PORTICCIO TO POINTE DE SETTE NAVE — AREA F — CHART 149

Porticcio ⊕ 545 41°52'.59N 008°46'.74E
Anchorage lies SE of Pointe de Porticcio, in the SW corner, in 4-7m on a strip of sand. In the approach, beware of Écueil Dorbera, a rock lying 700m SW of this point. Numerous other rocks also fringe the shore.

To the N of Pointe de Porticcio lies a small rock-studded cove with a sandy beach at its head. Here you can obtain reasonable shelter from southerlies. Anchor in the centre of the bay off the beach in 3-5m on a sandy patch. Beware of the rocky outcrops and shallows.

Pointe de Sette Nave
Anse de Stagnola and Anse de Ste Barbe
⊕ 546 41°51'.16N 008°46'.16E

A large bay split into two coves by a reef running out about 400m to the NE. It is possible to anchor on both sides off the beaches in 4-7m on sand and weed. Various houses pop up randomly from the Mediterranean maquis.

Anse Medea ⊕ 547 41°50'.43N 008°45'.75E
A bay with a sandy beach at its head, lying to the S of Pointe de Sette Nave. Anchor in 5-7m on sand, or on sand and weed, but keep a safe distance from the numerous mooring buoys that litter the bay. When approaching, pay attention to La Campanina, a rock marked by an isolated danger beacon lurking 500m SW of the point.

Anse Ottioni ⊕ 548 41°49'.90N 008°46'.88E
A small bay surrounded by rocky shores, backed by a pebble beach and Mediterranean maquis dotted with houses. Anchor in the centre of the bay off the beach in 4-6m on a sandy bottom.

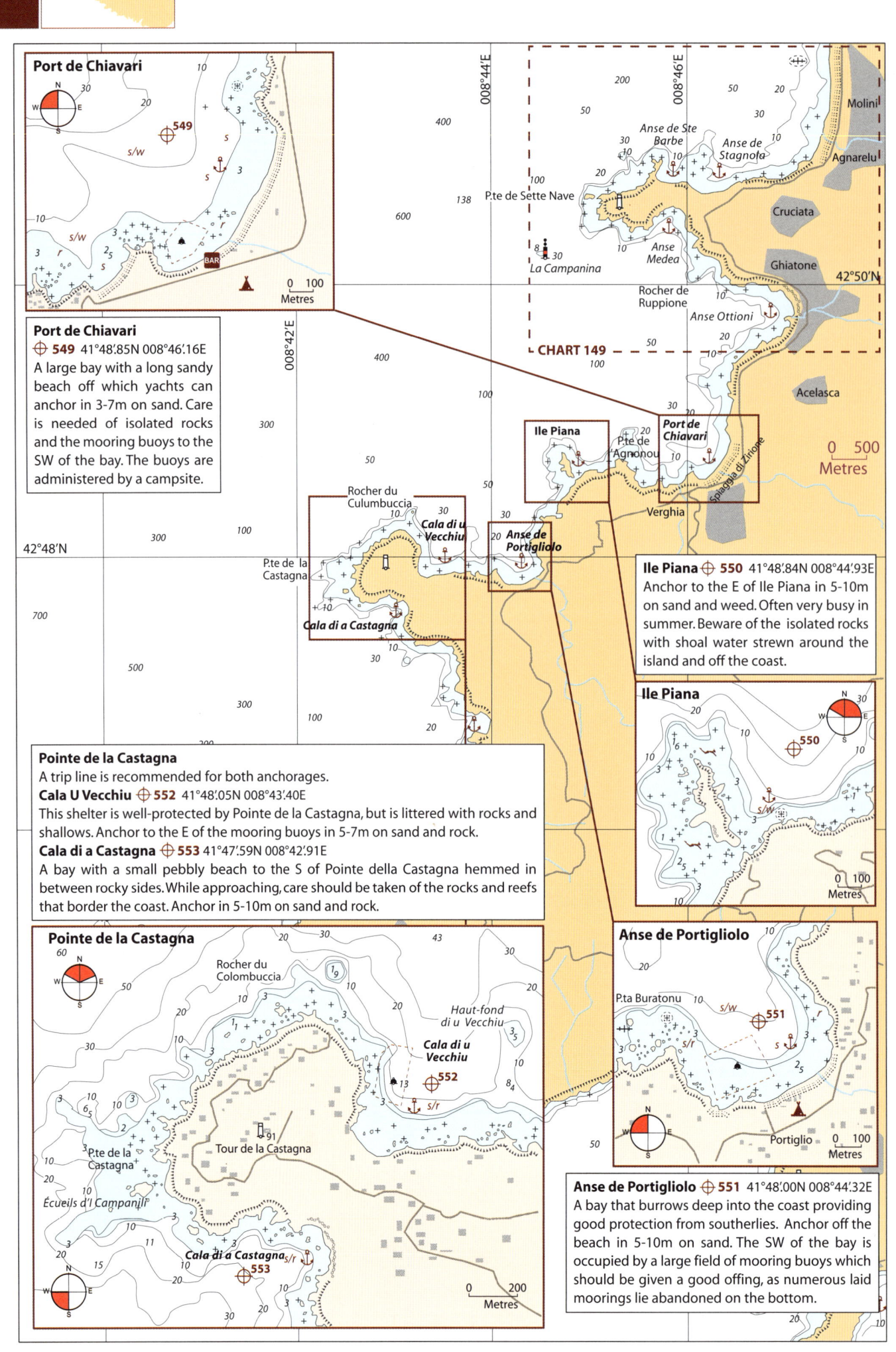

CHART 150 — AREA F — FROM POINTE DE SETTE NAVE TO POINTE DE LA CASTAGNA

Port de Chiavari
⊕ **549** 41°48'.85N 008°46'.16E
A large bay with a long sandy beach off which yachts can anchor in 3-7m on sand. Care is needed of isolated rocks and the mooring buoys to the SW of the bay. The buoys are administered by a campsite.

Ile Piana
⊕ **550** 41°48'.84N 008°44'.93E
Anchor to the E of Ile Piana in 5-10m on sand and weed. Often very busy in summer. Beware of the isolated rocks with shoal water strewn around the island and off the coast.

Pointe de la Castagna
A trip line is recommended for both anchorages.
Cala U Vecchiu ⊕ **552** 41°48'.05N 008°43'.40E
This shelter is well-protected by Pointe de la Castagna, but is littered with rocks and shallows. Anchor to the E of the mooring buoys in 5-7m on sand and rock.
Cala di a Castagna ⊕ **553** 41°47'.59N 008°42'.91E
A bay with a small pebbly beach to the S of Pointe della Castagna hemmed in between rocky sides. While approaching, care should be taken of the rocks and reefs that border the coast. Anchor in 5-10m on sand and rock.

Anse de Portigliolo
⊕ **551** 41°48'.00N 008°44'.32E
A bay that burrows deep into the coast providing good protection from southerlies. Anchor off the beach in 5-10m on sand. The SW of the bay is occupied by a large field of mooring buoys which should be given a good offing, as numerous laid moorings lie abandoned on the bottom.

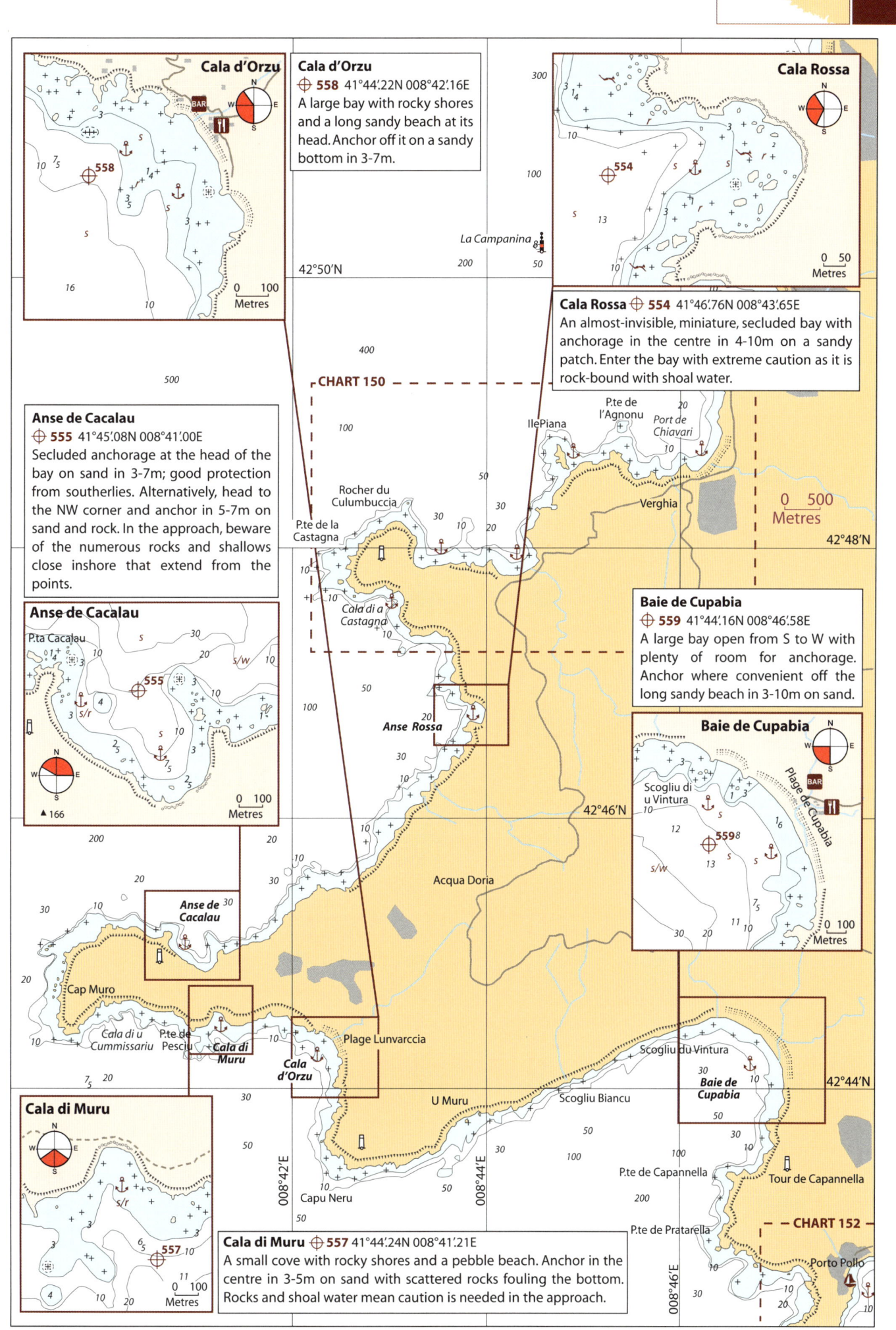

FROM POINTE DE LA CASTAGNA TO BAIE DE CUPABIA | AREA F

CHART 151

Cala d'Orzu
⊕ **558** 41°44′.22N 008°42′.16E
A large bay with rocky shores and a long sandy beach at its head. Anchor off it on a sandy bottom in 3-7m.

Cala Rossa
⊕ **554** 41°46′.76N 008°43′.65E
An almost-invisible, miniature, secluded bay with anchorage in the centre in 4-10m on a sandy patch. Enter the bay with extreme caution as it is rock-bound with shoal water.

Anse de Cacalau
⊕ **555** 41°45′.08N 008°41′.00E
Secluded anchorage at the head of the bay on sand in 3-7m; good protection from southerlies. Alternatively, head to the NW corner and anchor in 5-7m on sand and rock. In the approach, beware of the numerous rocks and shallows close inshore that extend from the points.

Baie de Cupabia
⊕ **559** 41°44′.16N 008°46′.58E
A large bay open from S to W with plenty of room for anchorage. Anchor where convenient off the long sandy beach in 3-10m on sand.

Cala di Muru
⊕ **557** 41°44′.24N 008°41′.21E
A small cove with rocky shores and a pebble beach. Anchor in the centre in 3-5m on sand with scattered rocks fouling the bottom. Rocks and shoal water mean caution is needed in the approach.

199

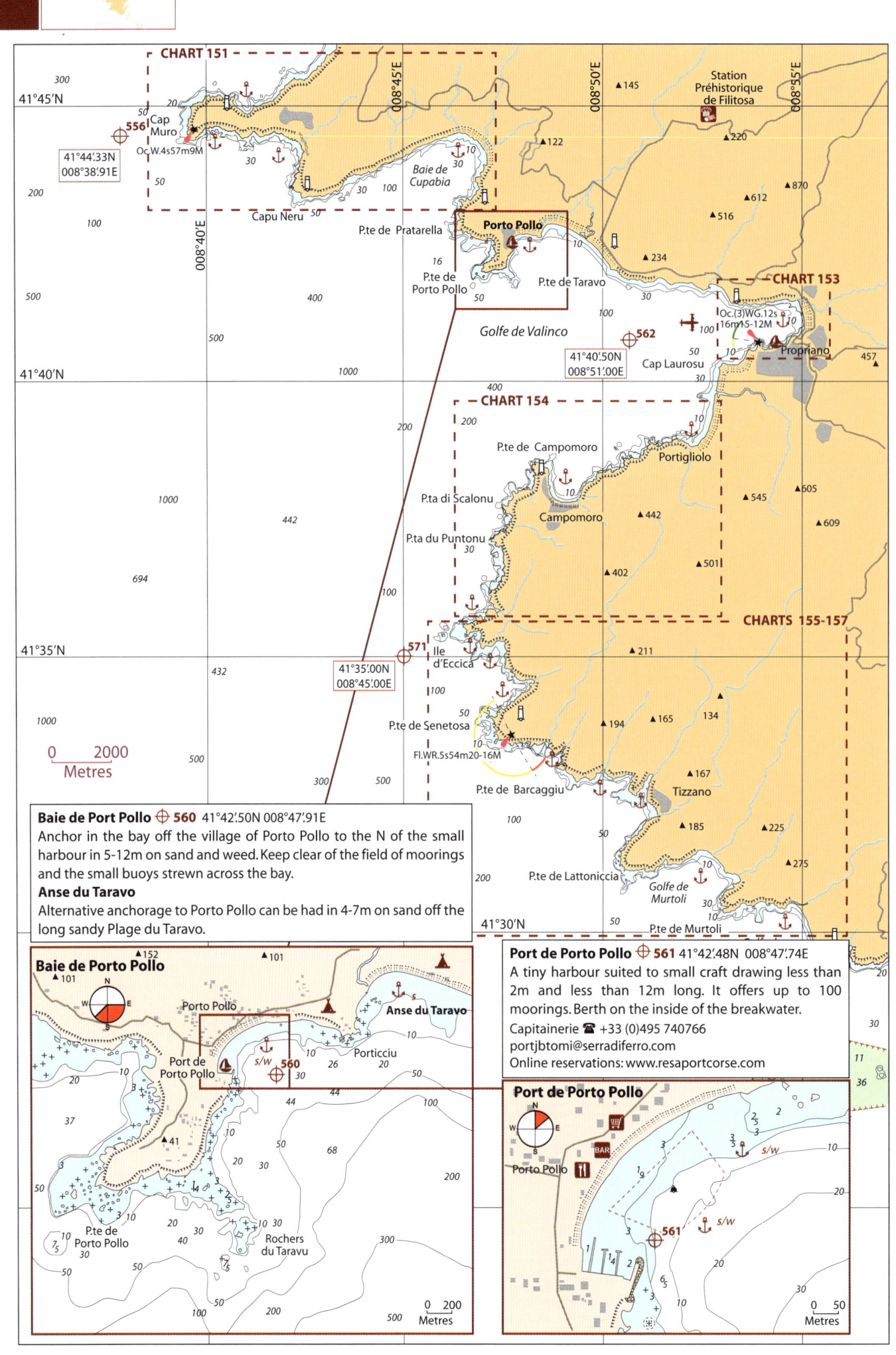

CHART 152 — AREA F — FROM PORTO POLLO TO GOLFE DE MURTOLI

Baie de Port Pollo ⊕ 560 41°42'.50N 008°47'.91E
Anchor in the bay off the village of Porto Pollo to the N of the small harbour in 5-12m on sand and weed. Keep clear of the field of moorings and the small buoys strewn across the bay.

Anse du Taravo
Alternative anchorage to Porto Pollo can be had in 4-7m on sand off the long sandy Plage du Taravo.

Port de Porto Pollo ⊕ 561 41°42'.48N 008°47'.74E
A tiny harbour suited to small craft drawing less than 2m and less than 12m long. It offers up to 100 moorings. Berth on the inside of the breakwater.
Capitainerie ☎ +33 (0)495 740766
portjbtomi@serradiferro.com
Online reservations: www.ResaportCorse.com

GOLFE DE VALINCO AND PORT DE PROPRIANO — AREA F

CHART 153

Golfe de Valinco ⊕ 563 41°41'.07N 008°53'.17E
The town of Propriano overlooks this bay, which opens up at the head of the gulf. It is home to a pleasant yacht, fishing and commercial harbour. In the approach, yachts must give way to the ferries and cargo ships that rumble in and out of the harbour. Care is also needed of Scogliu Longu, a reef lying immediately W of the west mole.

Plage de Baraci ⊕ 564 41°41'.10N 008°54'.58E
A lovely anchorage off the long sandy beach of Baraci, which is often very crowded and noisy in summer. Anchor in 4-8m on sand.

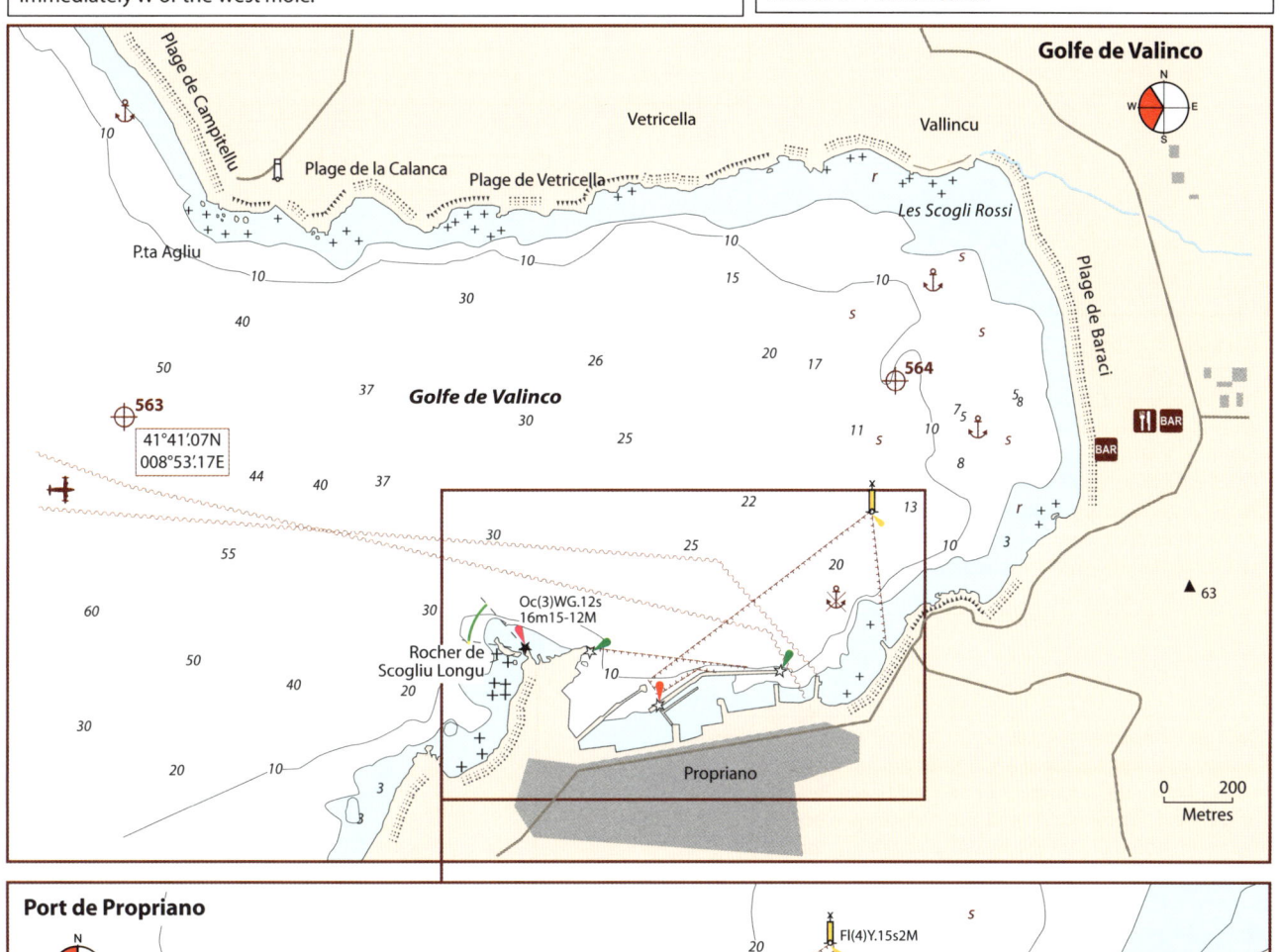

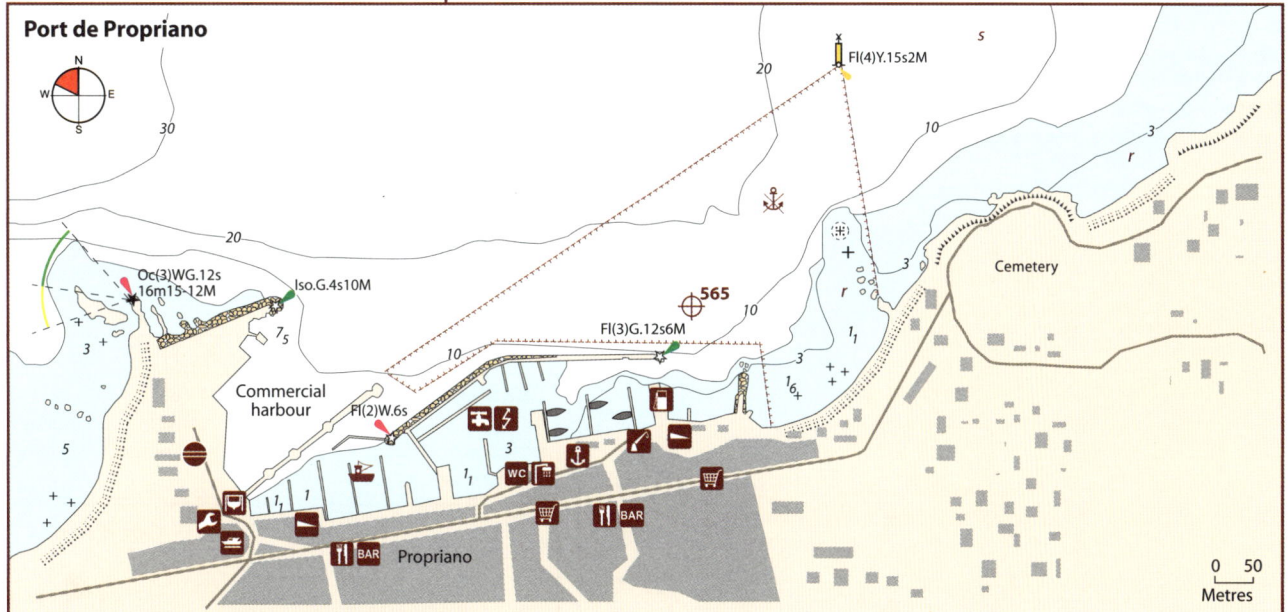

Port de Propriano ⊕ 565 41°40'.70N 008°54'.35E
This large harbour is split into three basins: a commercial harbour to the W; a fishing harbour in the middle, which also offers berths for a large number of yachts; and a yacht harbour (Port de Plaisance) to the E, which affords the best shelter.

Port de Plaisance has 500 berths (max. LOA 70m), with 100 for visitors. The first two hours are free-of-charge, except in high season. In summer, it is always extremely busy, so contact the harbour authority before you arrive and await berthing instructions.

Ships and ferries have right of way. N of Propriano is the prehistoric archaeological site of Filitosa, one of the largest in Europe.

Capitainerie Port de Plaisance VHF ch 09 - ☎ +33 (0)495 761040 - portuvalincu@orange.fr - www.mairie-propriano.com
Online reservations: www.resaportcorse.com - Weather service ☎ +33 (0)836 680820 - Propriano shipyard ☎ +33 (0)495 760470

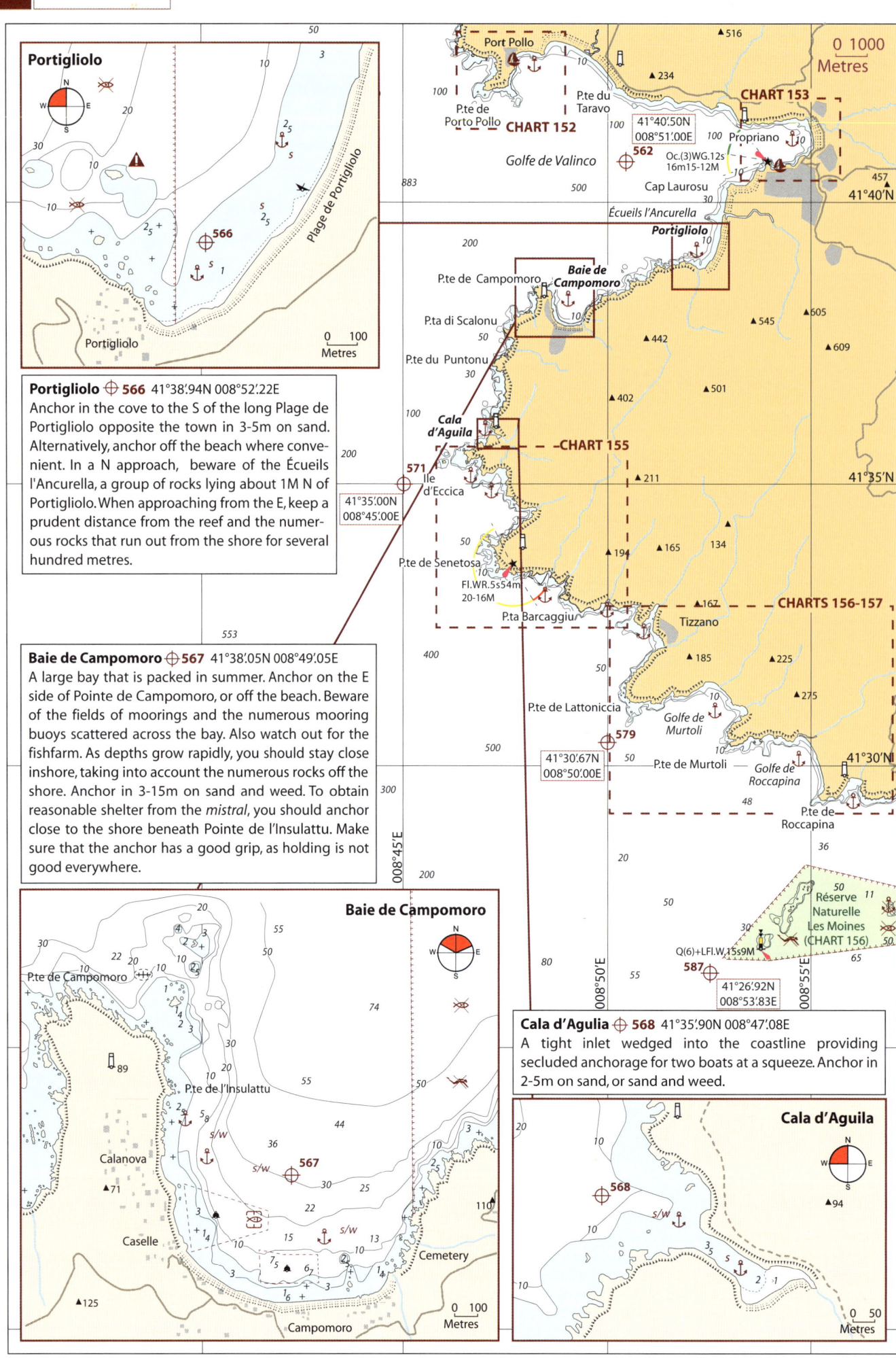

CHART 154 | AREA F | FROM PORTIGLIOLO TO ILE D'ECCICA

Portigliolo ⊕ 566 41°38'.94N 008°52'.22E
Anchor in the cove to the S of the long Plage de Portigliolo opposite the town in 3-5m on sand. Alternatively, anchor off the beach where convenient. In a N approach, beware of the Écueils l'Ancurella, a group of rocks lying about 1M N of Portigliolo. When approaching from the E, keep a prudent distance from the reef and the numerous rocks that run out from the shore for several hundred metres.

Baie de Campomoro ⊕ 567 41°38'.05N 008°49'.05E
A large bay that is packed in summer. Anchor on the E side of Pointe de Campomoro, or off the beach. Beware of the fields of moorings and the numerous mooring buoys scattered across the bay. Also watch out for the fishfarm. As depths grow rapidly, you should stay close inshore, taking into account the numerous rocks off the shore. Anchor in 3-15m on sand and weed. To obtain reasonable shelter from the *mistral*, you should anchor close to the shore beneath Pointe de l'Insulattu. Make sure that the anchor has a good grip, as holding is not good everywhere.

Cala d'Agulia ⊕ 568 41°35'.90N 008°47'.08E
A tight inlet wedged into the coastline providing secluded anchorage for two boats at a squeeze. Anchor in 2-5m on sand, or sand and weed.

FROM ILE D'ECCICA TO ANSE DE PORTU | AREA F

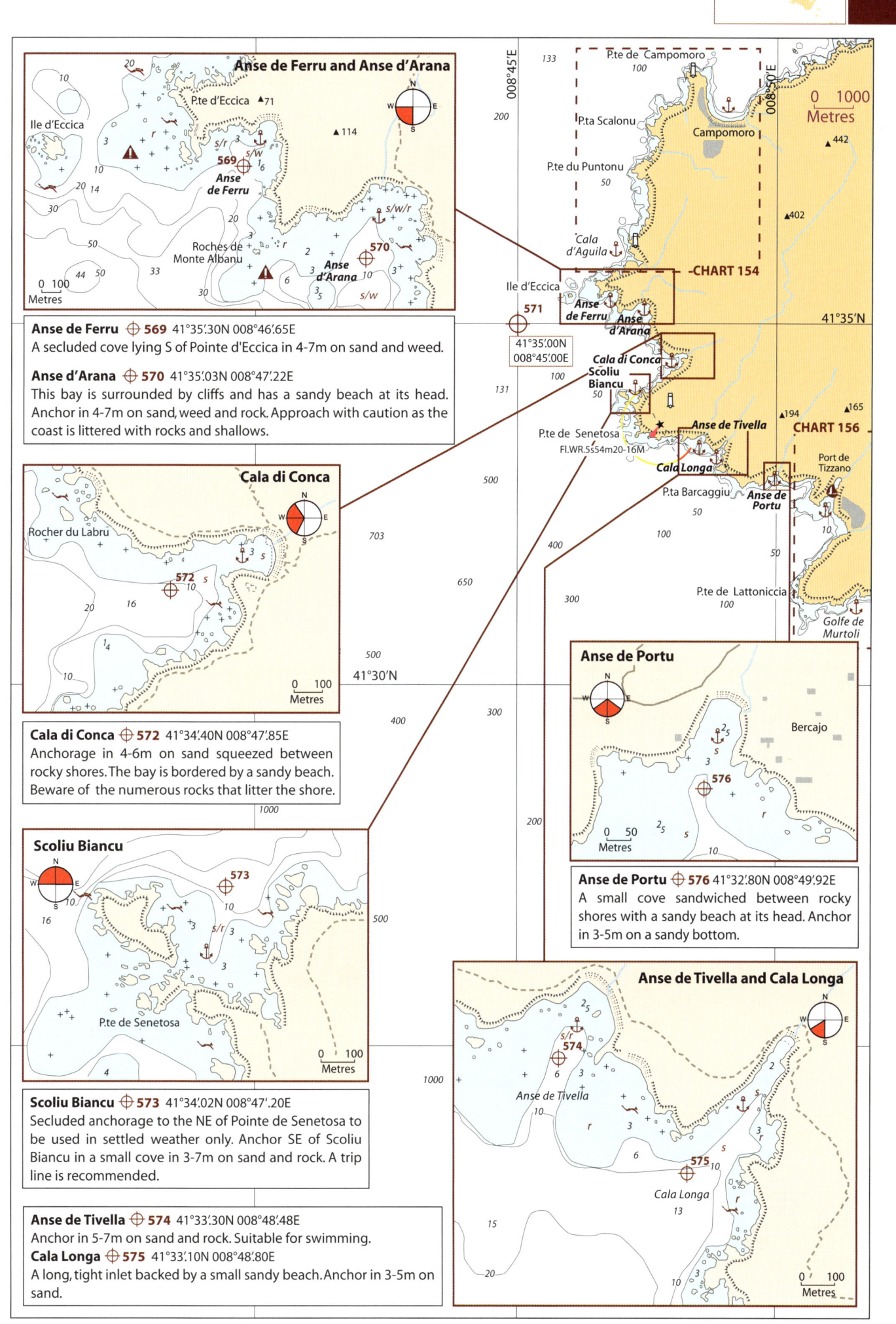

CHART 155

Anse de Ferru ⊕ **569** 41°35'.30N 008°46'.65E
A secluded cove lying S of Pointe d'Eccica in 4-7m on sand and weed.

Anse d'Arana ⊕ **570** 41°35'.03N 008°47'.22E
This bay is surrounded by cliffs and has a sandy beach at its head. Anchor in 4-7m on sand, weed and rock. Approach with caution as the coast is littered with rocks and shallows.

Cala di Conca ⊕ **572** 41°34'.40N 008°47'.85E
Anchorage in 4-6m on sand squeezed between rocky shores. The bay is bordered by a sandy beach. Beware of the numerous rocks that litter the shore.

Scoliu Biancu ⊕ **573** 41°34'.02N 008°47'.20E
Secluded anchorage to the NE of Pointe de Senetosa to be used in settled weather only. Anchor SE of Scoliu Biancu in a small cove in 3-7m on sand and rock. A trip line is recommended.

Anse de Tivella ⊕ **574** 41°33'.30N 008°48'.48E
Anchor in 5-7m on sand and rock. Suitable for swimming.

Cala Longa ⊕ **575** 41°33'.10N 008°48'.80E
A long, tight inlet backed by a small sandy beach. Anchor in 3-5m on sand.

Anse de Portu ⊕ **576** 41°32'.80N 008°49'.92E
A small cove sandwiched between rocky shores with a sandy beach at its head. Anchor in 3-5m on a sandy bottom.

203

CHART 156

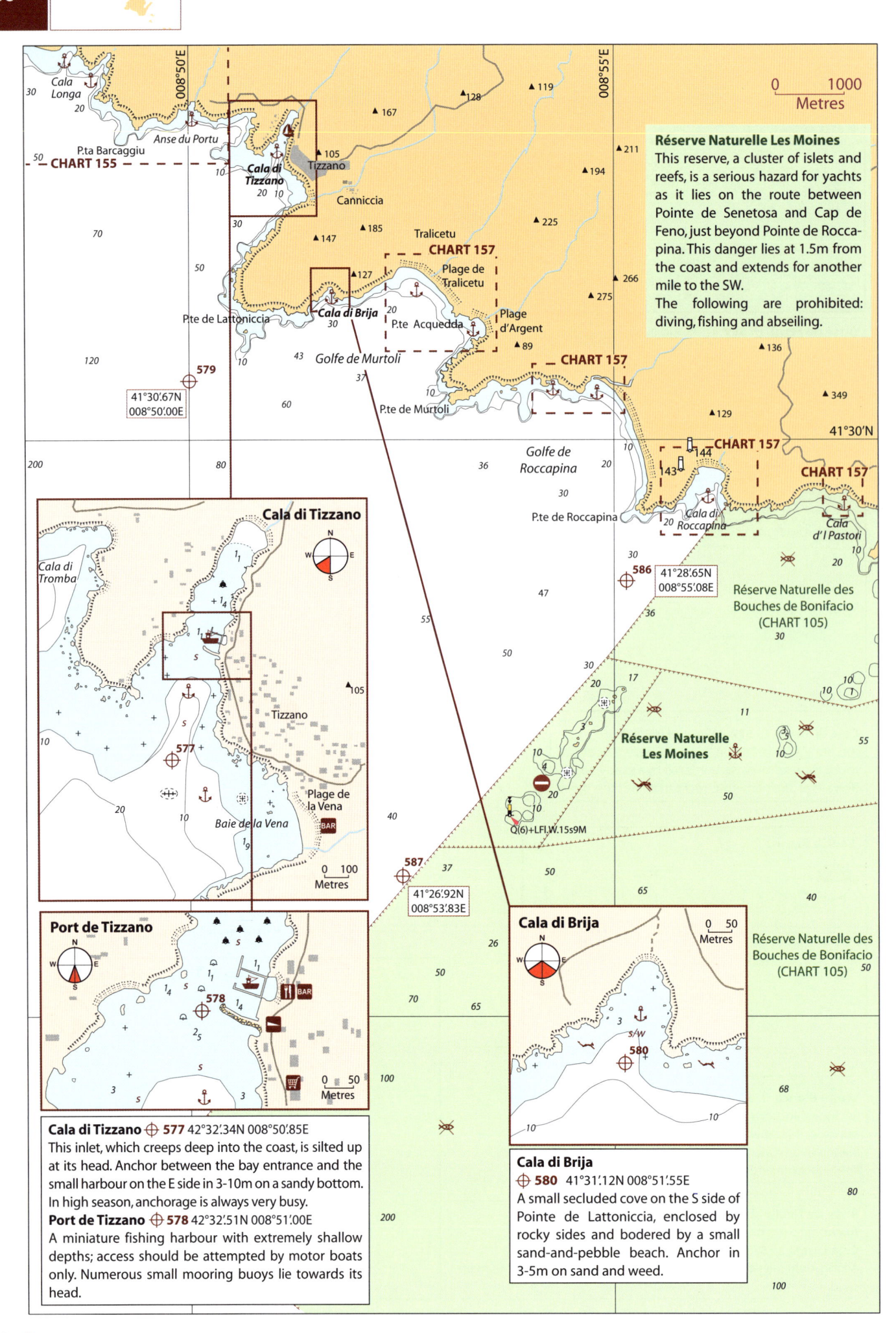

AREA F — FROM CALA DI TIZZANO TO CALA D'I PASTORI

Réserve Naturelle Les Moines
This reserve, a cluster of islets and reefs, is a serious hazard for yachts as it lies on the route between Pointe de Senetosa and Cap de Feno, just beyond Pointe de Roccapina. This danger lies at 1.5m from the coast and extends for another mile to the SW.
The following are prohibited: diving, fishing and abseiling.

Cala di Tizzano ⊕ **577** 42°32'.34N 008°50'.85E
This inlet, which creeps deep into the coast, is silted up at its head. Anchor between the bay entrance and the small harbour on the E side in 3-10m on a sandy bottom. In high season, anchorage is always very busy.

Port de Tizzano ⊕ **578** 42°32'.51N 008°51'.00E
A miniature fishing harbour with extremely shallow depths; access should be attempted by motor boats only. Numerous small mooring buoys lie towards its head.

Cala di Brija ⊕ **580** 41°31'.12N 008°51'.55E
A small secluded cove on the S side of Pointe de Lattoniccia, enclosed by rocky sides and bordered by a small sand-and-pebble beach. Anchor in 3-5m on sand and weed.

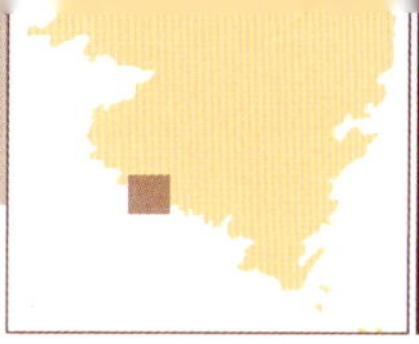

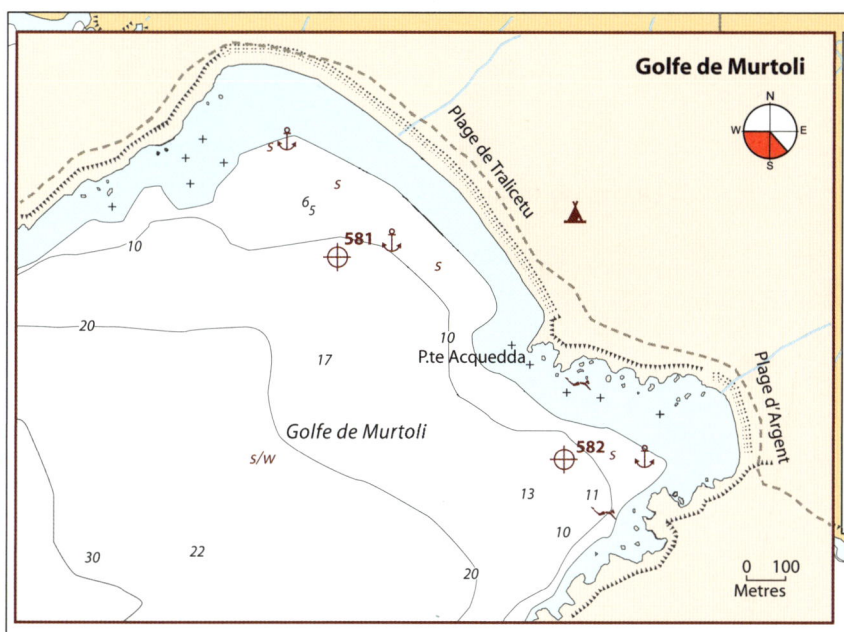

FROM GOLFE DE MURTOLI CALA D'I PASTORI | AREA F | CHART 157

Golfe de Murtoli
This vast gulf is protected by Pointe de Lattoniccia to the W and by Pointe de Murtoli to the E. It is backed by rocky cliffs and two sandy beaches at its head. Anchorages, however, are wide open to southerlies and in the afternoon they are disturbed by the swell produced by the thermal breeze. When approaching, beware of the rocky dangers offlying its points for several hundred metres.

Plage de Tralicetu ⊕ **581** 41°31'.16N 008°52'.58E
Anchor in 3-5m on sand off the long sandy beach, or at the N tip of the bay where you are most protected from northerlies.

Plage d'Argent ⊕ **582** 41°30'.88N 008°53'.04E
A sheltered cove fringed by a small sandy beach. Anchor in 3-7m on sand.

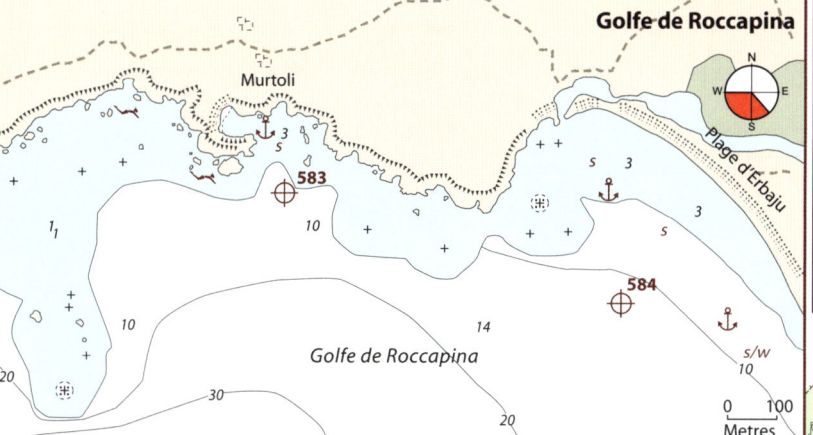

Golfe de Roccapina
A large gulf completely open to SE-W winds, but partly protected to the N by Pointe de Murtoli. A long sandy beach sits at its head.

Murtoli ⊕ **583** 41°30'.41N 008°54'.22E
A miniature anchorage with room for just a few yachts on the inside of a rocky spur in 2-5m on sand.

Plage d'Erbaju ⊕ **584** 41°30'.17N 008°54'.76E
Anchor off the beach, or in the bay to the N in 3-7m on sand, or on sand and weed.

CAUTION When navigating inshore or approaching the bays, beware of the numerous rocks off the coast surrounded by shoal water, but often extending seaward from the points.

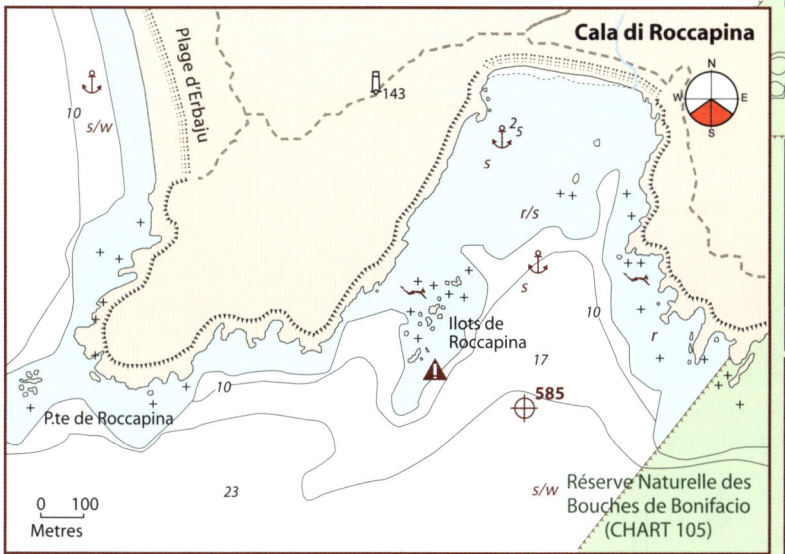

Cala d'I Pastori ⊕ **588** 41°29'.48N 008°57'.58E
A miniature, secluded anchorage in a bay halfway between Cala di Roccapina and Punta di Mucchiu Biancu. In the approach, care is needed of an isolated rock awash (1.2m) lying about 200m to the S.
Anchor in 3-5m on sand in the centre of the bay off the beach.

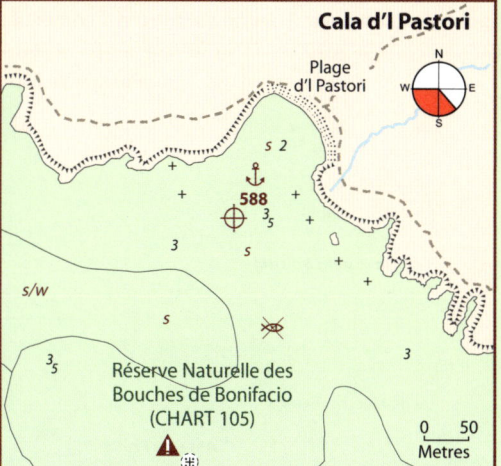

Cala di Roccapina ⊕ **585** 41°29'.25N 008°56'.04E
One of Corsica's best-known anchorages and thus very popular in high season. It is often difficult to find a spot here, but it is well worth stopping to admire its stunning beauty.
In the approach, beware of the rocks projecting from Pointe de Roccapina. Also beware of the Roccapina islets off the E side of the bay.
Anchor in 3-7m in crystal-clear waters on a sandy bottom. The best shelter is obtained in the bay's NW corner in 3m on sand.

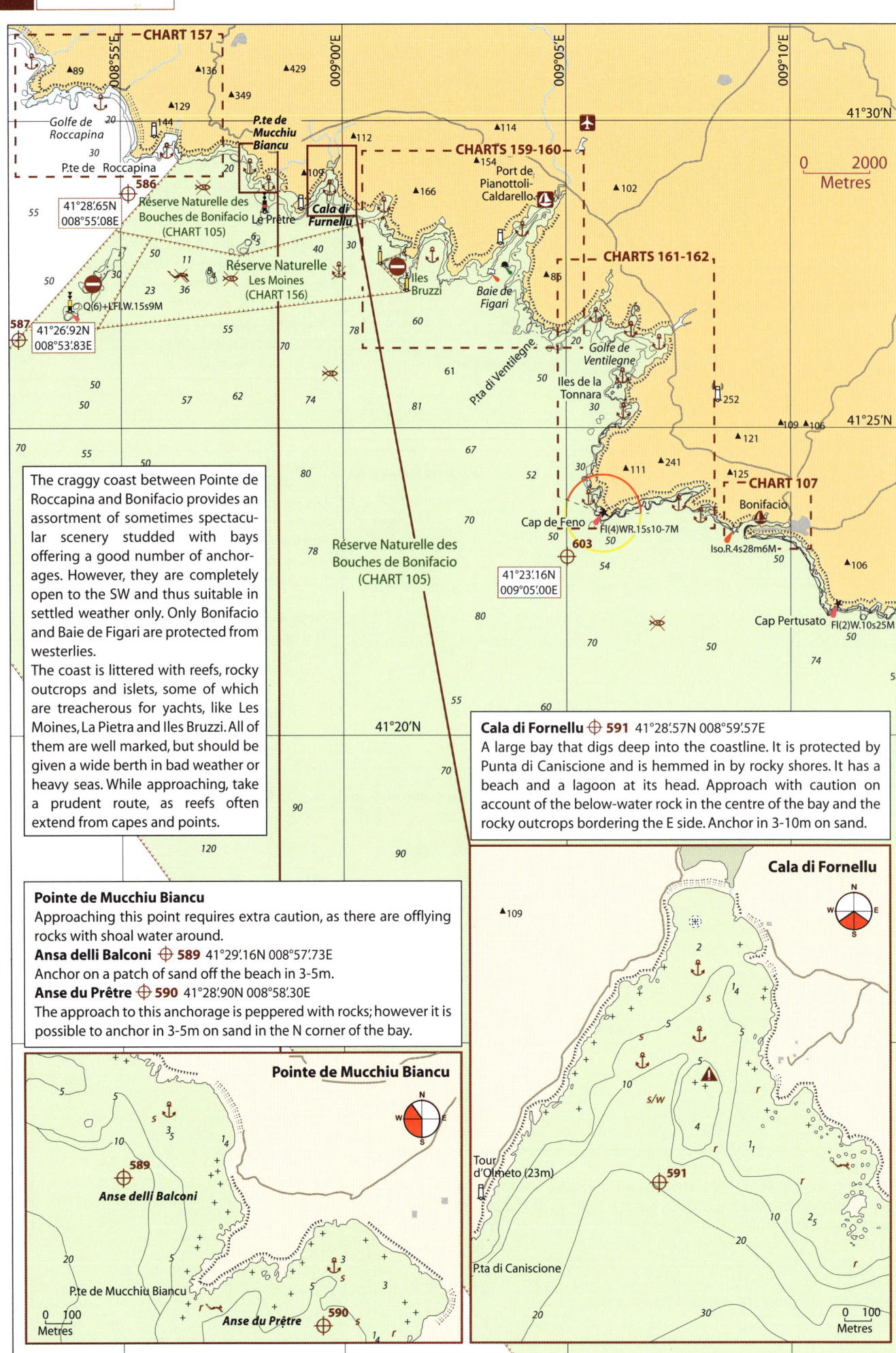

CHART 158 — AREA F — FROM POINTE DE ROCCAPINA TO BONIFACIO

The craggy coast between Pointe de Roccapina and Bonifacio provides an assortment of sometimes spectacular scenery studded with bays offering a good number of anchorages. However, they are completely open to the SW and thus suitable in settled weather only. Only Bonifacio and Baie de Figari are protected from westerlies.

The coast is littered with reefs, rocky outcrops and islets, some of which are treacherous for yachts, like Les Moines, La Pietra and Iles Bruzzi. All of them are well marked, but should be given a wide berth in bad weather or heavy seas. While approaching, take a prudent route, as reefs often extend from capes and points.

Pointe de Mucchiu Biancu
Approaching this point requires extra caution, as there are offlying rocks with shoal water around.

Ansa delli Balconi ⊕ **589** 41°29'.16N 008°57'.73E
Anchor on a patch of sand off the beach in 3-5m.

Anse du Prêtre ⊕ **590** 41°28'.90N 008°58'.30E
The approach to this anchorage is peppered with rocks; however it is possible to anchor in 3-5m on sand in the N corner of the bay.

Cala di Fornellu ⊕ 591 41°28'.57N 008°59'.57E
A large bay that digs deep into the coastline. It is protected by Punta di Caniscione and is hemmed in by rocky shores. It has a beach and a lagoon at its head. Approach with caution on account of the below-water rock in the centre of the bay and the rocky outcrops bordering the E side. Anchor in 3-10m on sand.

RÉSERVE NATURELLE ILES BRUZZI | AREA F | CHART 159

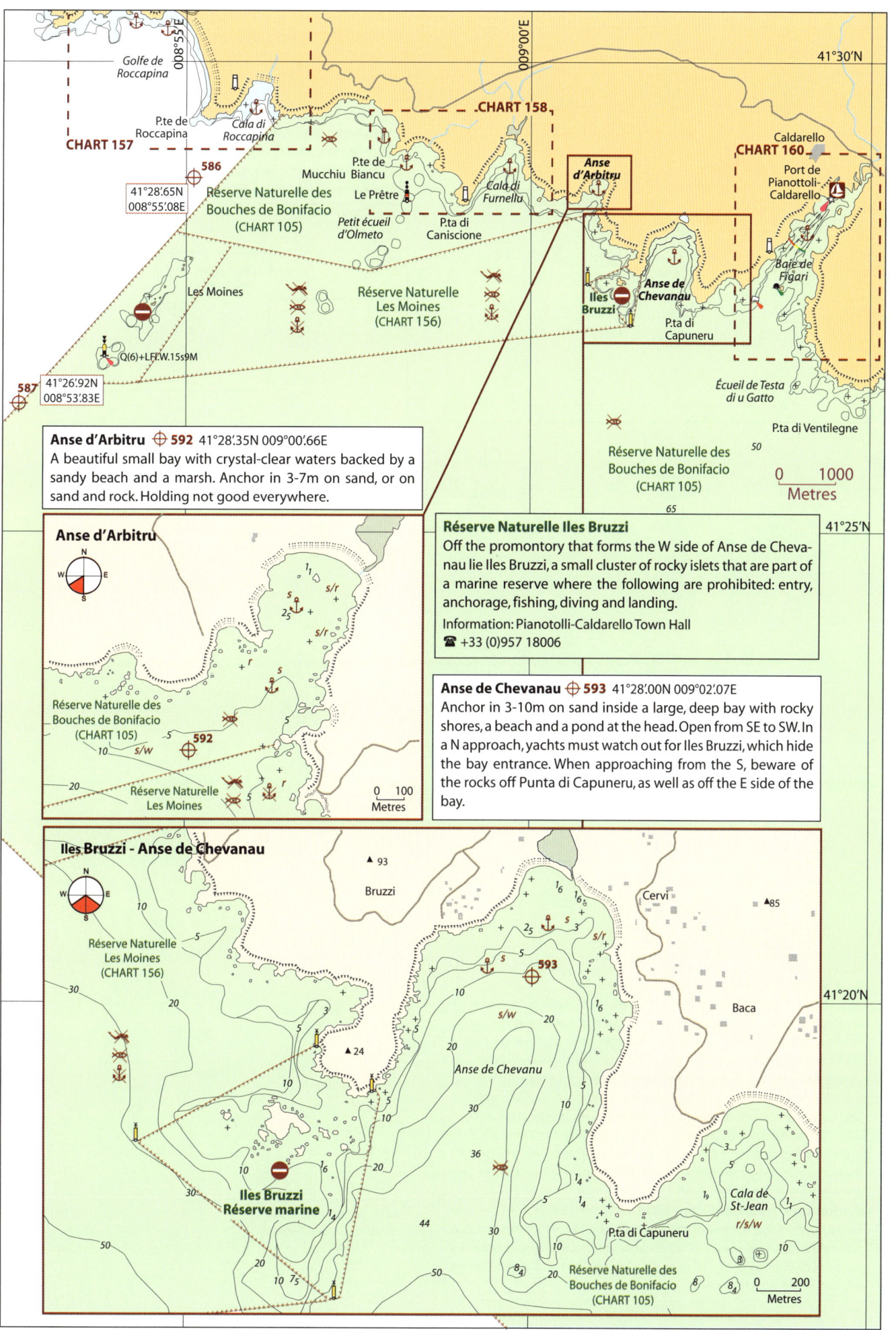

Anse d'Arbitru ⊕ 592 41°28'.35N 009°00'.66E
A beautiful small bay with crystal-clear waters backed by a sandy beach and a marsh. Anchor in 3-7m on sand, or on sand and rock. Holding not good everywhere.

Réserve Naturelle Iles Bruzzi
Off the promontory that forms the W side of Anse de Chevanau lie Iles Bruzzi, a small cluster of rocky islets that are part of a marine reserve where the following are prohibited: entry, anchorage, fishing, diving and landing.

Information: Pianotolli-Caldarello Town Hall
☎ +33 (0)957 18006

Anse de Chevanau ⊕ 593 41°28'.00N 009°02'.07E
Anchor in 3-10m on sand inside a large, deep bay with rocky shores, a beach and a pond at the head. Open from SE to SW. In a N approach, yachts must watch out for Iles Bruzzi, which hide the bay entrance. When approaching from the S, beware of the rocks off Punta di Capuneru, as well as off the E side of the bay.

CHART 160 — AREA F — BAIE DE FIGARI

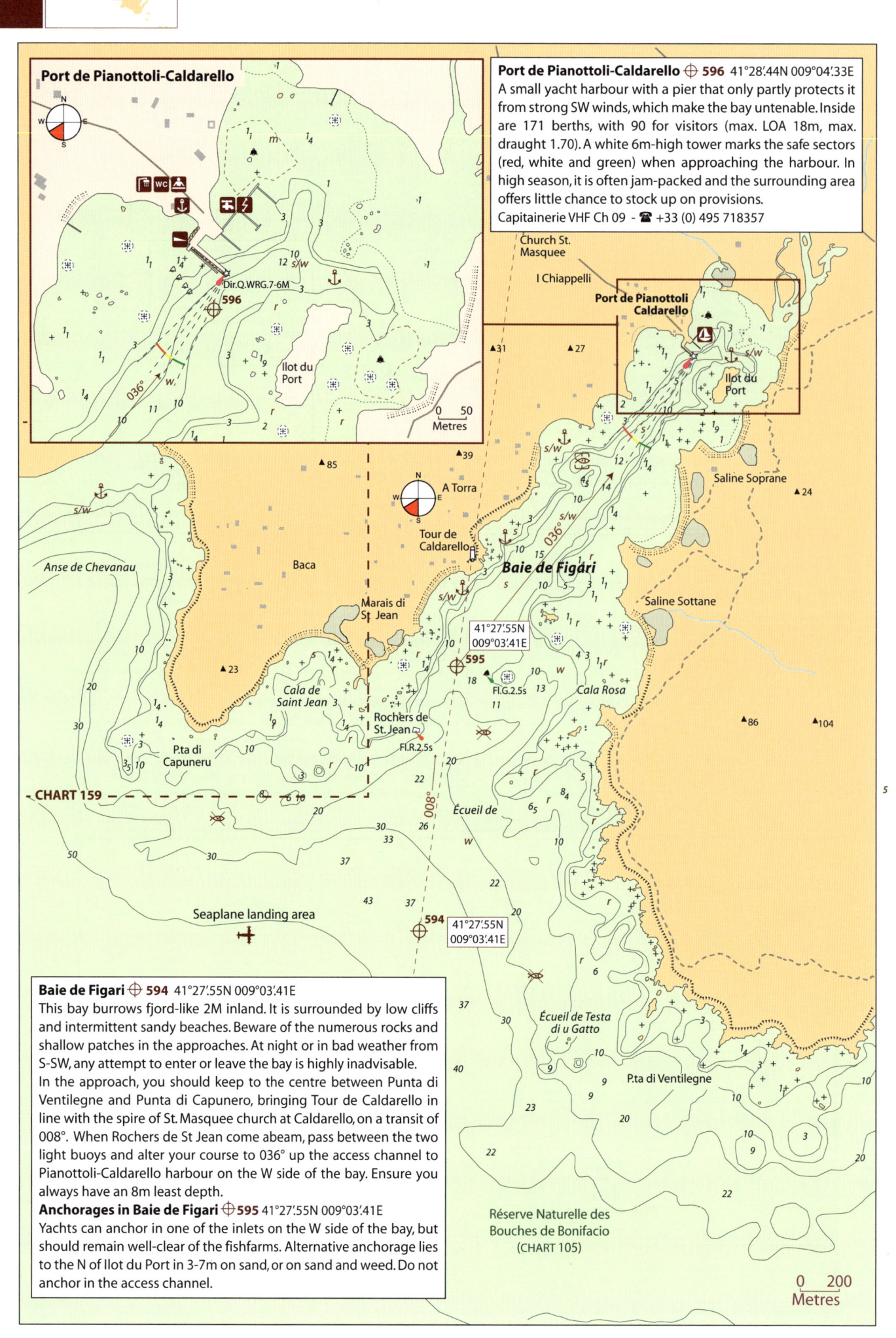

Port de Pianottoli-Caldarello

Port de Pianottoli-Caldarello ⊕ **596** 41°28'.44N 009°04'.33E
A small yacht harbour with a pier that only partly protects it from strong SW winds, which make the bay untenable. Inside are 171 berths, with 90 for visitors (max. LOA 18m, max. draught 1.70). A white 6m-high tower marks the safe sectors (red, white and green) when approaching the harbour. In high season, it is often jam-packed and the surrounding area offers little chance to stock up on provisions.
Capitainerie VHF Ch 09 - ☎ +33 (0) 495 718357

Baie de Figari ⊕ **594** 41°27'.55N 009°03'.41E
This bay burrows fjord-like 2M inland. It is surrounded by low cliffs and intermittent sandy beaches. Beware of the numerous rocks and shallow patches in the approaches. At night or in bad weather from S-SW, any attempt to enter or leave the bay is highly inadvisable.
In the approach, you should keep to the centre between Punta di Ventilegne and Punta di Capunero, bringing Tour de Caldarello in line with the spire of St. Masquee church at Caldarello, on a transit of 008°. When Rochers de St Jean come abeam, pass between the two light buoys and alter your course to 036° up the access channel to Pianottoli-Caldarello harbour on the W side of the bay. Ensure you always have an 8m least depth.

Anchorages in Baie de Figari ⊕ **595** 41°27'.55N 009°03'.41E
Yachts can anchor in one of the inlets on the W side of the bay, but should remain well-clear of the fishfarms. Alternative anchorage lies to the N of Ilot du Port in 3-7m on sand, or on sand and weed. Do not anchor in the access channel.

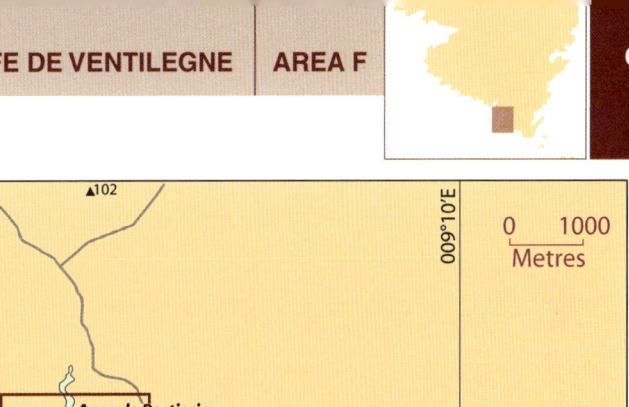

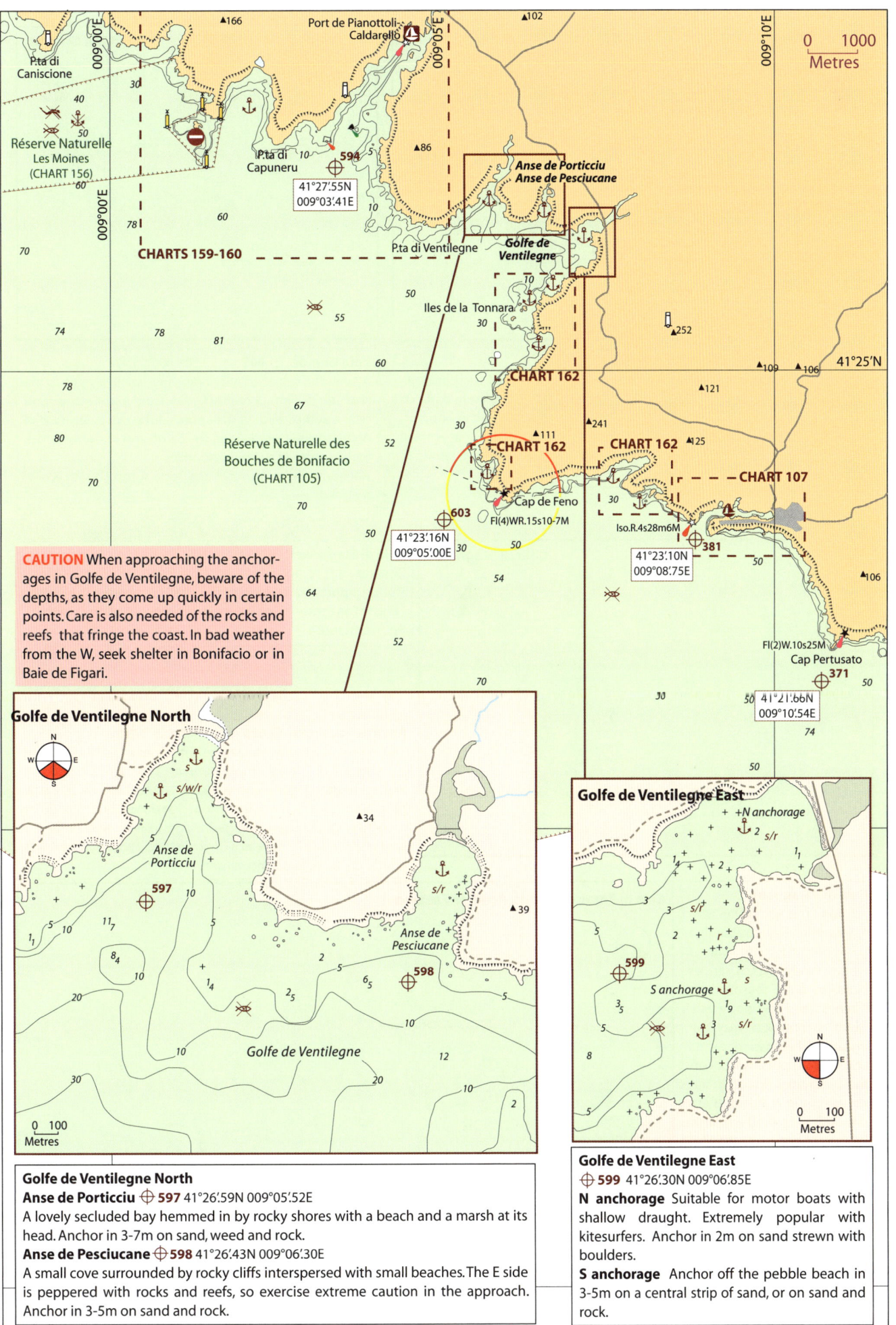

GOLFE DE VENTILEGNE | AREA F | CHART 161

CAUTION When approaching the anchorages in Golfe de Ventilegne, beware of the depths, as they come up quickly in certain points. Care is also needed of the rocks and reefs that fringe the coast. In bad weather from the W, seek shelter in Bonifacio or in Baie de Figari.

Golfe de Ventilegne North
Anse de Porticciu ⊕ **597** 41°26'.59N 009°05'.52E
A lovely secluded bay hemmed in by rocky shores with a beach and a marsh at its head. Anchor in 3-7m on sand, weed and rock.
Anse de Pesciucane ⊕ **598** 41°26'.43N 009°06'.30E
A small cove surrounded by rocky cliffs interspersed with small beaches. The E side is peppered with rocks and reefs, so exercise extreme caution in the approach. Anchor in 3-5m on sand and rock.

Golfe de Ventilegne East
⊕ **599** 41°26'.30N 009°06'.85E
N anchorage Suitable for motor boats with shallow draught. Extremely popular with kitesurfers. Anchor in 2m on sand strewn with boulders.
S anchorage Anchor off the pebble beach in 3-5m on a central strip of sand, or on sand and rock.

209

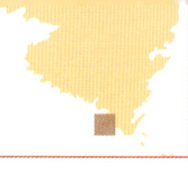

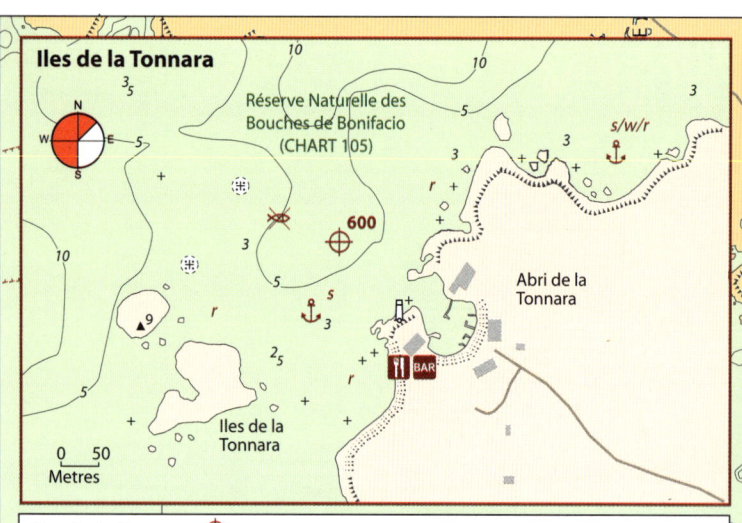

CHART 162 — AREA F — FROM GOLFE DE VENTILEGNE TO BONIFACIO

Iles de la Tonnara ⊕ 600 41°25'.77N 009°06'.16E
A calm-weather anchorage (3-5m on sand) only to the N of the Iles de la Tonnara, a cluster of rocky islets off an old fish-factory. A miniature harbour for small motor boats has been carved into the coastline. Handy for hopping ashore in a dinghy. Another anchorage opens up just further N in a small creek hemmed in by rocky shores. It provides protection from S winds in 3-5m on sand, weed and rock.

Cala Grande ⊕ 602 41°23'.50N 009°05'.47E
A beautiful secluded anchorage in a small bay just to the N of Cap de Feno. It has rocky sides and a stone-and-sand beach at the head. In the approach, be extremely careful of the rocks littered along the E side and of the lone rock in the centre of the bay entrance.
Anchor in 3-5m on sand and rock. A trip line is recommended.

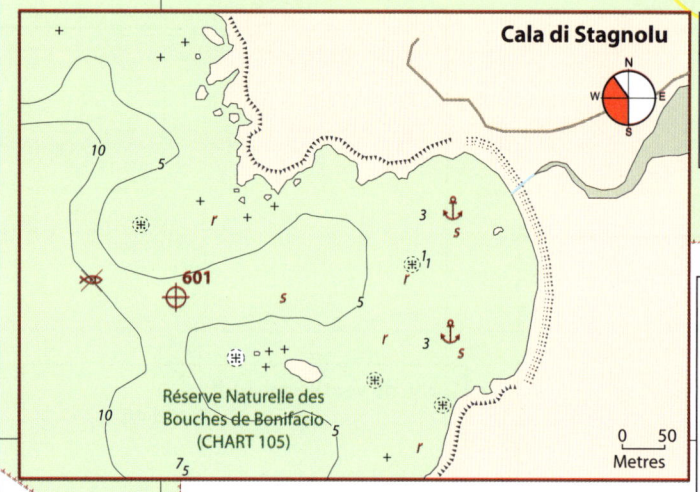

Cala di Stagnolu ⊕ 601 41°25'.16N 009°06'.16E
Deserted anchorage in a bay completely open to southerlies. During approach, beware of an islet surrounded by a reef lying in the centre of the bay entrance. Anchor off the beach in 3-5m on sand.

Anse de Fazziuolu ⊕ 605 41°23'.50N 009°07'.83E
This is not only the west coast's southernmost anchorage, but it is also one of Corsica's most stunning. The bay is enclosed by white limestone cliffs and a beach at its head. It is partly protected by the two islands of Fazziolu. This is another extremely popular anchorage in high season, and finding a spot is laborious. Anchor in 3-5m on a sandy bottom. The bay is home to a Glénans sailing centre.

Cala di Paragnanu
⊕ 604 41°23'.66N 009°07'.50E
A beautiful bay surrounded by limestone cliffs with a white sandy beach at its head. In high season, it is often packed and noisy; as a result anchorage may be disturbed by passing yachts and tripper boats. Anchor off the beach in 3-4m, or in the coves on the N side in 3-5m on sand, or on sand and rock. Beware of the rocks fringing the coast.

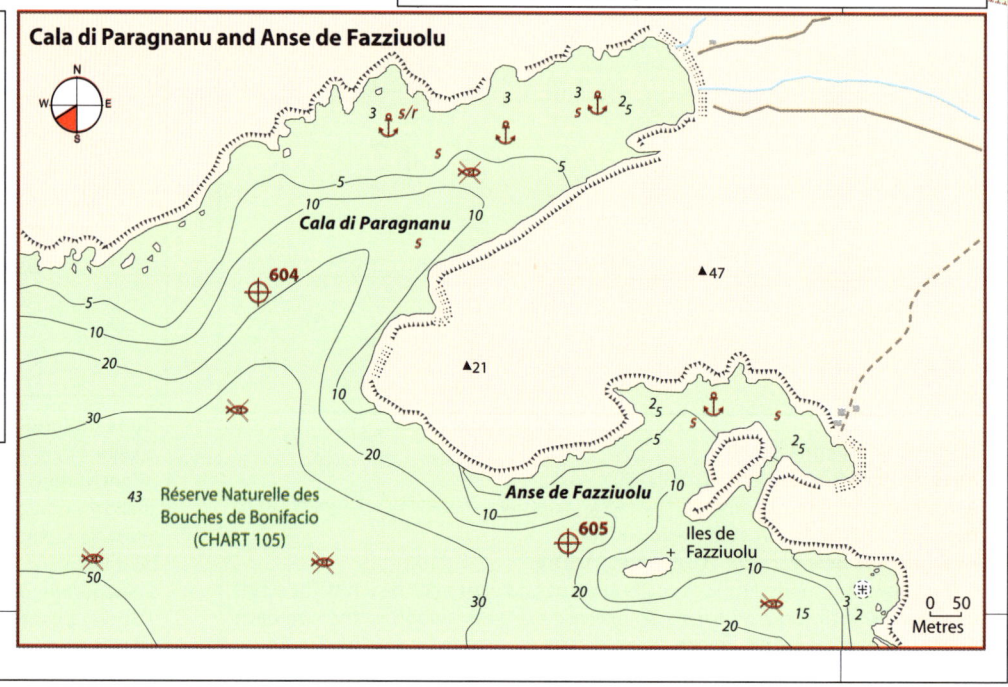

INDEX (the numbers refer to the charts)

A

Ajaccio
    Golfe de, 147
        Port Charles Ornano, 148
        Port Tino Rossi, 148
Albenga Anchorage, 8
Ansa delli Balconi, 158
Ansa Reale, 69
Anse d'Agnello, 123
Anse d'Alusi, 135
Anse d'Ancone, 144
Anse d'Arana, 155
Anse d'Arbitru, 159
Anse de Balistra, 110
Anse de Cacalau, 151
Anse de Cannella, 116
Anse de Carataggio, 111
Anse de Chevanau, 159
Anse de Chiuni, 141
Anse de Fautea, 115
Anse de Favone, 115
Anse de Fazziuolu, 162
Anse de Ferru, 155
Anse de Fica, 145
Anse de Ficajola, 139
Anse de Fiume Santu, 126
Anse de Fornali, 126
Anse de l'Arinella, 124
Anse de l'Oscelluccia, 134
Anse de la Pietrarella, 130
Anse de Lozari, 129
Anse de Minaccia, 145
Anse de Peraiola, 129
Anse de Pesciucane, 161
Anse de Porticciu, 161
Anse de Portigliolo, 150
Anse de Portu, 155
Anse de Portu Provençale, 144
Anse de Stagnola, 149
Anse de Ste Barbe, 149
Anse de Tanone, 115
Anse de Tarcu, 115
Anse de Tivella, 155
Anse de Tramulimacchia, 112
Anse du Portu Provençale, 144
Anse du Prêtre, 158
Anse du Taravo, 152
Anse du Tarcu, 115
Anse Gradelle, 139
Anse Maestrellu, 148
Anse Medea, 149
Anse Ottioni, 149
Anse Porri, 136
Anse Punta San Cipriano, 112
Anse Stagnonu, 144
Antignano, 41
Ardenza, 41
Arenzano, 12
Arma di Taggia, 4
Arno, Fiume, 38
Assonautica De Benedetti
    (La Spezia), 31

B

Baia del Latte, 1
Baia del Quercetano, 42
Baia del Silenzio (Sestri Levante), 23
Baia di Lerici, Anchorage, 33
Baia di Porto Venere, 28
Baia La Colba, 94
Baia Pozzarello, 53
Baia Santa Reparata, 94
Baie Agajo, 132
Baie d'Algajola, 131
Baie d'Elbo, 136
Baie de Campomoro, 154
Baie de Capandola, 123
Baie de Cargèse, 142
Baie de Centuri, 124
Baie de Crovani, 135
Baie de Cupabia, 151
Baie de Figari, 160
    Anchorages, 160
Baie de Focolara, 136
Baie de l'Ile Rousse, 130
Baie de l'Acciolu, 128
Baie de la Mortella, 126
Baie de Liscia, 144
Baie de Macinaggio, 121
Baie de Menasina, 142
Baie de Nichiareto, 135
Baie de Palombaccia, 111
Baie de Port Pollo, 152
Baie de Porto, 137
Baie de Sagone, 144
Baie de San Cipriano, 114
Baie de Sant'Ambrogio, 131
Baie de St-Joseph, 143
Baie de Stagnoli, 143
Baie de Stagnolu (SE Corsica), 112
Baie de Tamarone, 122
Barcaggio, Marine de, 123
    Port de, 123
Bastia, 118-119
    Port de Toga, 119
    Vieux Port, 119
Bergeggi Marine Reserve, 10
Bocca d'Arno (Porto di Pisa), 38
Bocca di Magra, 34
    Anchorage, 34
Bogliasco, 16
Bonassola, 24
Bonifacio, Port de, 107
Bordighera, 1
Borghetto S. Spirito (Poseidon), 8
Bouches de Bonifacio, Réserve
    Naturelle des, 105

C

Cala Arenella, 79
Cala Bagnaia, 66
Cala Balzi Rossi, 1
Cala Barabarca, 72
Cala Barbarossa, 70
Cala Barcaccia, 92
Cala Battistone, 84
Cala Bitta, 86
Cala Bocca d'Inferno, 55
Cala Brigantino, 101

INDEX

Cala Caciarella, 53
Cala Calbugina, 78
Cala Camiciotto, 99
Cala Cannelle (Argentario), 55
Cala Capo Ferrari, 98
Cala Capra, 88
Cala Carbicina, 60
Cala Cardinalino, 88
Cala Caspiu, 139
Cala Cavoli, 73
Cala Ceppo, 61
Cala Chiappara, 32
Cala Civetta (Punta Francese), 49
Cala Connari, 97
Cala Corsara, 97
Cala Cotaccia, 75
Cala Coticcio, 101
Cala Cravieu, 12
Cala d'Agulia, 154
Cala d'Alga (Corsica), 146
    E anchorage, 146
    SW anchorage, 146
Cala d'Alga (I. Spargi), 97
Cala d'I Pastori, 157
Cala d'Olivu, 129
Cala d'Oru, 116
Cala d'Orzu, 151
Cala dei Porcili (Lo Scoglione), 60
Cala del Corvo, 78
Cala del Forte (Ventimiglia), 1
Cala del Gesso, 53
Cala del Lazzaretto, 79
Cala del Moreto, 60
Cala del Pozzale, 29
Cala del Reciso, 62
Cala del Remaiolo, 71
Cala del Vetriolo, 62
Cala dell'Allume, 78
Cala della Chiesa, 108
Cala della Fornace, 29
Cala della Mortola, 60
Cala delle Caldane, 79
Cala delle Cannelle (I. del Giglio), 79
Cala dello Scalo, 58
Cala dello Stagnone, 69
Cala dello Zurletto, 61

Cala di a Castagna, 150
Cala di Brija, 156
Cala di Conca, 155
Cala di Fornellu, 158
Cala di Forno, 50
Cala di Ghiuncu (Ile Lavezzi), 108
Cala di Lignaghia, 139
Cala di Maramozza, 33
Cala di Muru, 151
Cala di Palma, 109
Cala di Palu, 140
Cala di Paragnanu, 162
Cala di Roccapina, 157
Cala di Stagnolu (S Corsica), 162
Cala di Stentinu, 110
Cala di Tizzano, 156
Cala di U Grecu, 108
Cala di U Giunchu (Ile Cavallo), 109
Cala di Zeri, 109
Cala Eco del Mare, 33
Cala Farinole, 125
Cala Ferrigno, 97
Cala Fiascherino, 33
Cala Fico, 91
Cala Fonza, 74
Cala Francese, 98
Cala Galera, 56
    Anchorage, 56
Cala Galenzana, 74
Cala Garibaldi, 101
Cala Gavetta (Porto Mercantile), 99
Cala Genovese, 140
Cala Granara, 97
Cala Grande (Corsica), 162
Cala Grande (Argentario), 53
Cala Granu, 85
Cala Inglese (Marina di Porto Rafael), 89
Cala Innamorata, 71
Cala La Peticchia, 100
Cala Laconia, 86
Cala Lazarina, 108
Cala Le Buche, 75
Cala Le Tombe, 73
Cala Leone, 41
Cala Licciola, 92
Cala Longa (SE Corsica), 106

Cala Longa (SW Corsica), 155
Cala Lunga, 103
Cala Maestra (I. Giannutri), 80
Cala Maestra (I. di Montecristo), 81
Cala Mandriola, 66
Cala Mangiavolpe, 99
Cala Margidore, 72
Cala Marmorata, 92
Cala Martina (Punta Francese), 49
Cala Mezzana, 33
Cala Morcone, 71
Cala Muretta, 138
Cala Muro, 103
Cala Napoletana, 101
Cala Naregno, 70
Cala Nido d'Aquila, 98
Cala Nisportino, 66
Cala Nisporto, 66
Cala Nova, 69
Cala Perla, 69
Cala Piatti, 53
Cala Piscatoio, 66
Cala Piazzoni, 55
Cala Porteddu, 86
Cala Portese, 102
Cala Porto Vecchio (Capraia), 60
Cala Punta Sud (I. Budelli), 104
Cala Rena Bianca, 93
Cala Ripa Barata, 76
Cala Rossa (Corsica), 151
Cala Rossa (I. Capraia), 60
Cala Sambuco, 92
Cala Sansone, 77
Cala Santa Maria, 104
Cala Sbiro, 140
Cala Scandola, 138
Cala Schiavone, 80
Cala Spalmatoi, 80
Cala Spalmatore, 100
Cala Spinosa, 94
Cala Stagnali, 102
Cala Stella (Corsica), 132
Cala Terranera, 69
Cala Trana, 90
Cala Tremonti, 86
Cala Tuara, 138

INDEX

Cala U Vecchiu, 150
Cala Uccellina, 50
Cala Vecchia, 138
Cala Violina (Punta Francese), 49
Cala Villamarina, 96
Cala Volo di Notte, 80
Cala Zuccale, 72
Cala Zupignano, 66
Caldarello (Port de Pianottoli), 160
Calvi, Golfe de,
    Port de, 133
Camogli, 17
Canale di Calma (Genova), 13
Canale di Piombino, 63
Cannigione, 87
Cantiere Navale Golfo di Mola, 70
Cantieri Navali di La Spezia, 32
Capo Bandi, Anchorages, 69
Capo Berta, 6
Capo Castello, 67
Capo d'Uomo, 50
Capo della Vita, 67
Capo Pino, 2
Capraia, Isola, 59-62
    Harbour, 61
    Rada di, 61
Capu Biancu, 110
Carbonifera, 48
Cargèse, Baie de,
    Port de, 142
Castel Sonnino, 41
Castiglioncello, 43
Castiglione della Pescaia, 51
Cavo, 67
Cecina Marina, 44
Centro Velico Caprera (La Spezia), 32
Chioma, Mouth of Fiume, 42
Cigntra, 145
Cinque Terre Marine Reserve, 25-26
Circolo Nautico S. Giovanni, 64
Crique de Branca, 130

D
Darsena Medicea (Portoferraio), 65
Darsena Morosini (Livorno), 40
Diano Marina, 6

E
Edilnautica Marina (Portoferraio), 65
Elba, Isola, 63-77
Elviscot wreck, 73

F
Fetovaia (Golfo di Barbatoia), 73
Finale Ligure, 9
Fiumara del Puntone, 48
Fiume Albenga, Mouth of, 52
Fiume Arno, 38
Fiume Magra, 34
Fiumara del Puntone (Scarlino), 48
Fiume Chioma, Mouth of, 42
Fiume Osa, Mouth of, 52
Formiche di Grosseto, 50
Fortullino, 42
Framura (Porto Pidocchio), 24

G
Galéria harbour, 136
Genova, 13-15
    Genova Porto Vecchio, 15
    Genova Sestri Ponente, 14
Giglio, Isola del,
    Porto, 78-79
Girolata, 138
Golfe de Calvi, 133
Golfe de Galéria, 136
Golfe de la Revellata, 134
Golfe de Lava, 144
Golfe de Miserinu, 139
Golfe de Morsiglia, 124
Golfe de Pinarellu, 114
Golfe de Peru, 141
Golfe de Porto Novo, 111
Golfe de Roccapina, 157
Golfe de Rondinara, 111
Golfe de Santa Giulia, 111
Golfe de St'Amanza, 110
Golfe de Topidi, 141

Golfe de Valinco, 153
Golfe de Ventilegne, 161
Golfo degli Spalmatoi, 80
Golfo della Biodola, 77
Golfo della Lacona, 72
Golfo delle Saline, 88
Golfo di Barbatoia (Fetovaia), 73
Golfo di Mola (Rada di Porto Azzurro), 70
Golfo di Paraggi, 19
Golfo di Ponente (Sestri Levante), 23
Golfo di Procchio, 77
Golfe di U Purtellu, 139
Golfo di Viticcio, 77
Golfo Giorgio Marino (Porto Madonna), 104
Golfo Marconi, Anchorage for, 21
Golfo Stella, Anchorages for, 72
Golfu Alisu, 125
Grande Sanguinaire, 145-146
G.S. Olimpia, 32
Gurgazu, 110

I
Il Grugno (Noli), 10
Ile Cavallo, 109
Ile de la Giraglia, 123
Ile Lavezzi, 106, 108
Ile Piana (S Corsica), 106
Ile Piana (W Corsica), 150
Ile Rousse, 130
Iles Bruzzi, Réserve Naturelle, 159
Iles de la Tonnara, 162
Iles Finocchiarola, Réserve Naturelle 122
Iles Sanguinaires, 146
Ilot Ziglione, 113
Imperia, 5
    Oneglia Harbour, 5
    Porto Maurizio, 5
Isola Bergeggi, 10
Isola Budelli, 95, 103-104
Isola Capraia, 59-62
    Marine Reserve, 59-62
Isola Caprera, 95, 101
Isola d'Elba, 63-77
Isola del Giglio, 78-79

INDEX

Isola del Tino, 29
Isola di Montecristo, 81
Isola Gallinara, 8
Isola Giannutri, 80
Isola Giardinelli, 100
    Anchorages for, 100
Isola Gorgona, 58
Isola La Maddalena, 95, 98-100
Isola Municca, 93
Isola Palmaiola, 68
Isola Palmaria, 29
Isola Pianosa, 82
Isola Razzoli, 95, 103-104
    South anchorages, 104
Isola Santa Maria, 95, 103-104
Isola Santo Stefano, 95, 96
Isola Spargi, 95-97
Isolotti Gemini, 71
Isolotto Cerboli, 63
Isolotto Porco, 102

L

La Maddalena National Park, 95-104
La Spezia, 31
    Rada di, 30-32
Lavagna, 22
Le Cote, 62
Lerici, 33
Les Moines, Réserve Naturelle, 156
Levanto, 24
    Fishing Harbour, 24
L'Ile Rousse, 130
Liscia di Vacca, 85
Livorno, 39-40
Lo Scoglione (Cala dei Porcili), 60

M

Macinaggio, Baie de,
    Port de, 121
Madonna della Ruota, 2
Manarola, 26
Magra, Fiume, 34
Marciana Marina, 76
    Rada di, 76
Maremma Regional Park, 50
Marina Cala de' Medici, 43

Marina Chiavari, 22
Marina d'Arje, 112
Marina degli Aregai, 4
Marina del Fezzano, 31
Marina del Ponte, 99
Marina dell'Orso (Poltu Quatu), 84
Marina di Alassio (Porto Luca Ferrari), 7
Marina di Andora, 7
Marina di Baia Verde (Ospedaletti), 2
Marina di Cala Galera, 56
Marina di Campo, 74
    Rada di, 74
Marina di Carrara, 35
Marina di Castelluccio, 13
Marina di Grosseto (Marina di San
    Rocco), 51
Marina di Loano, 9
Marina di Malfalcu, 128
Marina di Massa, 35
Marina di Porto Rafael (Cala Inglese), 89
Marina di Punta Ala, 49
Marina di Salivoli, 46
Marina di San Lorenzo, 4
Marina di San Rocco (Marina di
    Grosseto), 51
Marina di San Vincenzo, 45
Marina di Scarlino, 48
Marina di Vada, 44
Marina di Varazze, 12
Marina Esaom Cesa (Portoferraio), 65
Marina Fiera di Genova, 14
Marina Genova Aeroporto, 14
Marina Molo Vecchio (Genova),15
Marina Porto Antico (Genova), 15
Marina Portosole (Sanremo), 3
Marina Vizza, 112
Marine d'Albo, 125
Marine d'Elbo, 136
Marine de Barcaggio, 123
Marine de Bussagghia, 139
Marine de Erbalunga, 118
Marine de Giottani, 125
Marine de la Vasina, 118
Marine de Luri, 120
Marine de Manichino, 116
Marine de Meria, 120

Marine de Morsiglia, 124
Marine de Pietracorbara, 120
Marine de Porticciolo, 120
Marine de Sant'Ambrogio, 132
Marine de Sisco, 120
Marine de Tollare, 123
Marine Reserves
    Bergeggi, 10
    Cinque Terre, 25-26
    Isola Capraia, 59-62
    Portofino, 16-19
    Secche della Meloria, 37
Moneglia, 24
Monte Capanne, 63
Monterosso, 25
Mouth of Fiume Albenga, 52
Mouth of Fiume Chioma, 42
Mouth of Fiume Osa, 52
Murtoli, 157

N

National Parks:
    Tuscan Archipelago, 57
    La Maddalena, 95-104
Natural Reserves:
    Bouches de Bonifacio, 105, 156-162
    Iles Finocchiarola, 122
    Les Moines, 156
    Scandola, 137
Navalmare (La Spezia), 32
Nervi, 16
Noli (Il Grugno), 10

O

Oneglia Harbour (Imperia), 5
Osa, Mouth of Fiume, 52
Ospedaletti (Marina di Baia Verde), 2

P

Palau, 89
Passe des Sanguinaires, 145
Passo Cecca di Morto, 104
Passo della Moneta, 100
Péninsule de la Revellata, 134
Pieve Ligure, 17
Piombino, 46-47

INDEX

Porto Antico, 46
Terre Rosse, 47
Porto Vecchio, 47
Plage d'Argent, 157
Plage d'Erbaju, 157
Plage de Baraci, 153
Plage de Saleccia, 128
Plage de Tralicetu, 157
Plage du Lotu, 128
Pointe de la Castagna, 150
Pointe de Mucchiu Biancu, 158
Pointe de Sette Nave, 149
Poltu Quatu (Marina dell'Orso), 84
Pontile Ignazio, 28
Pontili Conca Verde, 91
Pontili Magazzini, 64
Port Charles Ornano, 148
Port d'Agro, 134
Port d'Algajola, 131
Port de Barcaggio, 123
Port de Bonifacio, 107
Port de Calvi, 133
Port de Cargèse, 142
Port de Cavallo, 109
Port de Centuri, 124
Port de Chiavari, 150
Port de Macinaggio, 121
Port de Pianottoli, 160
Port de Porto Pollo (Corsica), 152
Port de Porto-Vecchio (Corsica), 113
Port de Propriano, 153
Port de Solenzara, 116
Port de St-Florent, 127
Port de Taverna, 117
Port de Tizzano, 156
Port de Toga (Bastia), 119
Port Tino Rossi, 148
Porticcio, 149
Porticciolo Nazario Sauro (Livorno), 40
Portigliolo, 154
Porto Antico (Piombino), 46
Porto Azzurro, 70
Porto Baratti, 45
Porto Carlo Riva (Rapallo), 21
Porto Cervo, 85
Porto Cinquale, 36

Porto d'Arone, 141
Porto Del Valle (Porto S. Stefano), 54
Porto della Maremma (Marina di San Rocco), 51
Porto di Pisa (Bocca d'Arno), 38
Porto Duca degli Abruzzi (Genova), 14
Porto Ercole, 56
Porto Lavello, 35
Porto Liscia, 90
Porto Longosardo (Santa Teresa di Gallura), 93
Porto Lotti, 32
Porto Luca Ferrari (Marina di Alassio), 7
Porto Lungo, 100
Porto Madonna (Golfo Giorgio Marino), 104
Porto Marina, 137
Porto Massimo, 100
Porto Maurizio (Imperia), 5
Porto Mediceo (Livorno), 40
Porto Mercantile (Cala Gavetta), 99
Porto Mirabello (La Spezia), 31
Porto Monaghi, 143
Porto Palma, 102
Porto Pidocchio (Framura), 24
Porto Pidocchio (Punta della Chiappa), 18
Porto Pollo (Corsica), 152
Porto Pollo (Porto Puddu) (Sardinia), 90
Porto Pozzo, 91
Porto Puddu (Porto Pollo), 90
Porto Quadro, 93
Porto San Michele, 21
Porto Santo Stefano, 54
   Porto Del Valle, 54
   Porto Vecchio, 54
Porto Vecchio (Castiglioncello), 43
Porto Vecchio (Genova), 15
Porto Vecchio (Piombino), 47
Porto Vecchio (Porto S. Stefano), 54
Porto Vecchio (Porto Pubbico) (Sanremo), 3
Porto Vecchio S. Lorenzo, 4
Porto Venere, 28
   Protected Marine Area of the

   Regional Natural Park, 27-29
   Baia di, 28
Portoferraio, 64
   Rada di, 64
Portofino, 19
   Marine Reserve, 16-19
Portu Leccia, 140
Portu Vecchiu (Péninsule de la Revellata), 134
Poseidon (Borghetto S. Spirito), 8
Propriano, Port de, 153
Protected Marine Area of the Porto Venere Regional Natural Park, 27-29
Punta Ala, 49
Punta Capicciola, 114
Punta Crena anchorages, 9
   N - Spiaggia dei Saraceni, 9
   S - Spiaggia Varigotti, 9
Punta de Fautea anchorages, 115
Punta dell'Acquissucola, 62
Punta della Calamita, 71
Punta della Chiappa (Porto Pidocchio), 18
Punta della Contessa, 72
Punta della Seccatoia, 62
Punta Francese, 49
   Anchorages S of, 49
Punta Lestia, 69
Punta Negra, 128
Punta Nera, 75
Punta Nera (I. d'Elba), 63
Punta Pineda, Anchorages, 26
Punta Polveraia, 75
Punta Rossa (I. La Maddalena), 100

Q

Quercianella, 41

R

Rada di Capraia, 61
Rada di La Spezia, 30-32
Rada di Marciana Marina, 76
Rada di Marina di Campo, 74
Rada di Mezzo Schifo, 89
Rada di Porto Azzurro (Golfo di Mola), 70
Rada di Portoferraio, 64

215

INDEX

Rade de Finocchiarola, 122
Rade de Santa Maria, 122
Rapallo, 21
    Porto pubblico, 21
    Porto Carlo Riva, 21
Recco, 17
Regional Park Maremma, 50
Réserves Naturelles:
    de Scandola, 137
    des Bouches de Bonifacio, 105, 156-162
    des Iles Finocchiarola, 122
    Iles Bruzzi, 159
    Les Moines, 156
Rio Maggiore, 26
Rio Marina, 68
Riva Ligure, 4
Riva Trigoso, 23
Rocce Rosse, 26
Rocchette, 50
Rosignano Solvay, 43
Rossana, 42

S

San Bartolomeo al Mare, 6
San Fruttuoso, 18
San Terenzo, 33
Sanguinaires, Iles, 145-147
    Passe des, 145
Sanremo, 3
    Porto pubblico (Porto Vecchio), 3
    Marina Portosole, 3
Sant'Andrea, 76
Sant'Ilario, 16
Santa Liberata, 54
Santa Margherita Ligure, 20
Santa Teresa di Gallura (Porto Longosardo), 93
Santo Stefano, 54
    Porto Del Valle, 54
    Porto Vecchio, 54
Savona, 11
Scandola, Réserve Naturelle de, 135-138
Scarlino, Marina di, 48
    Fiumara del Puntone, 48

Scogli del Mosè, 62
Scoglio di Ferale, Anchorages, 26
Scoglio Isola Rossa, 55
Scoglio L'Isolotto, 55
Scoliu Biancu, 155
Secche della Meloria Marine Reserve, 37
Seno d'Ortano, 69
Seno dell'Olivo, 28
Seno della Peruccia, 62
Seno delle Grazie, 30
Seno di Cadimare, 31
Seno di Campese, 78
Seno di Canneto, 26
Seno di Pagana, 21
Seno di Paraggi, 19
Seno di Terrizzo, 28
Sestri Levante (Golfo di Ponente), 23
Sestri Ponente (Genova), 14
Sori, 17
Spiagge Bianche, 43
Spiaggia dei Saraceni (Punta Crena), 9
Spiaggia Varigotti (Punta Crena), 9
Stagno Torto, 98
Sturla, 16

T

Talamone, 52
Tellaro, 33
Terre Rosse (Piombino), 47
Tuscan Archipelago National Park, 57

V

Vada, commercial port, 44
Vado Ligure, 10
Varazze, anchorage, 12
Ventimiglia (Cala del Forte), 1
Vernazza, 25
Viareggio, 36
Vieux Port (Bastia), 119
Voltri (Canale di Calma and Marina di Castelluccio), 13